Side By Side Comparision Of The Book of Jasher And The Early Books of The Bible

Jason Hoffman

Side By Side Comparison of The Book of Jasher And The Early Books of The Bible

Fifth Estate
2795 County Hwy 57
Blountsville, AL 35031

First Edition

Cover Designed by An Quigley

Printed on acid-free paper

Library of Congress Control No: 2013937798

ISBN: 9781936533343

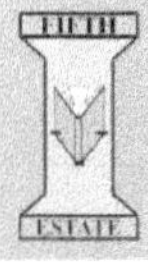

Fifth Estate, 2013

Table of Contents

Introduction

The Bible contains such a richness that you can spend your life in study and never run out of treasure. However after a quarter century in it's tutelage I started to wonder about the texts that were not chosen to be included in the official cannon. Please note that I don't consider any of these to be divinely inspired, just that often, when taken as historical documents, the texts can sometimes fill in a few of the question marks that occasionally surround some events.

Of all that I've read to date, none are as exciting and contain so much "missing" back story as The Book of Jasher. There are as many as five different works going by this title. The one to which I refer was translated from Hebrew in 1613 and is ninety-one chapters long. It covers the period from Creation through Joshua and is considered by many to be the book referenced three times in the Bible (Joshua 10:13, 2 Samuel 1:18 and 2 Timothy 3:8) and by the historian Josephus.

While reading through The Book of Jasher (which by the way is a mistranslation – the Hebrew title is "Sepir Ha Yasher", meaning "The Book of the Upright" or "The Upright or Correct Record") I found myself often flipping through the Pentateuch for cross referencing. Hence the idea for this book. You will find an amazing amount of almost word-for-word parallels which lead one to wonder if perhaps one was a source for the other, or at the very least Moses and the author(s) of this book drew from the same oral traditions.

Initially I thought that Jasher and the Bible disagreed on the age of Moses when he killed the Egyptian but Ken Johnson, in his book *Ancient Post-Flood History* easily explains the supposed contradiction. Otherwise I've yet to find any substantial differences when both cover the same topic. To me this speaks well of the historical accuracy of this text and that it isn't some late authors imaginative "filling in" details in the Biblical record.

And now a couple of technical notes. The text for the Book of Jasher was taken from http://www.sacred-texts.com/chr/apo/jasher/. The text for the Bible is from the World English Bible - http://www.ebible.org/. In almost all cases the two books run parallel. When a verse in Jasher correlates to an out-of-order verse in the Bible that verse appears bracketed and in italics with the appropriate reference. Generally I quote the entire text of both books but starting in Exodus there are large sections that deal with regulations that are not in Jasher and so these chapters are referenced in italicized brackets.

Thank you for purchasing this study. I pray that it will bless your walk and deepen your faith, causing a greater hunger and understanding concerning the time of the patriarchs and the God who created the universe and sent His Son for our salvation.

Sincerely,

Jason Hoffman

Genesis 1

1 In the beginning, God created the heavens and the earth. 2 The earth was formless and empty. Darkness was on the surface of the deep and God's Spirit was hovering over the surface of the waters.

3 God said, "Let there be light," and there was light. 4 God saw the light, and saw that it was good. God divided the light from the darkness. 5 God called the light "day", and the darkness he called "night." There was evening and there was morning, the first day.

6 God said, "Let there be an expanse in the middle of the waters, and let it divide the waters from the waters." 7 God made the expanse, and divided the waters which were under the expanse from the waters which were above the expanse; and it was so. 8 God called the expanse "sky." There was evening and there was morning, a second day.

9 God said, "Let the waters under the sky be gathered together to one place, and let the dry land appear"; and it was so. 10 God called the dry land "earth", and the gathering together of the waters he called "seas." God saw that it was good.

11 God said, "Let the earth yield grass, herbs yielding seeds, and fruit trees bearing fruit after their kind, with their seeds in it, on the earth"; and it was so. 12 The earth yielded grass, herbs yielding seed after their kind, and trees bearing fruit, with their seeds in it, after their kind; and God saw that it was good. 13 There was evening and there was morning, a third day.

14 God said, "Let there be lights in the expanse of sky to divide the day from the night; and let them be for signs to mark seasons, days, and years; 15 and let them be for lights in the expanse of sky to give light on the earth"; and it was so. 16 God made the two great lights: the greater light to rule the day, and the lesser light to rule the night. He also made the stars.

17 God set them in the expanse of sky to give light to the earth, 18 and to rule over the day and over the night, and to divide the light from the darkness. God saw that it was good. 19 There was evening and there was morning, a fourth day.

Genesis 1

20 God said, “Let the waters abound with living
creatures, and let birds fly above the earth in the
open expanse of sky.” 21 God created the large sea
creatures and every living creature that moves, with
which the waters swarmed, after their kind, and
every winged bird after its kind. God saw that it was
good. 22 God blessed them, saying, “Be fruitful, and
multiply, and fill the waters in the seas, and let
birds multiply on the earth.” 23 There was evening
and there was morning, a fifth day.

24 God said, “Let the earth produce living
creatures after their kind, livestock, creeping
things, and animals of the earth after their
kind”; and it was so. 25 God made the animals
of the earth after their kind, and the livestock
after their kind, and everything that creeps on
the ground after its kind. God saw that it was
good.

26 God said, “Let us make man in our image,
after our likeness: and let them have dominion
over the fish of the sea, and over the birds of
the sky, and over the livestock, and over all the
earth, and over every creeping thing that
creeps on the earth.”
27 God created man in his own image. In God’s
image he created him; male and female he
created them.
28 God blessed them. God said to them, “Be
fruitful, multiply, fill the earth, and subdue it. Have
dominion over the fish of the sea, over the birds of
the sky, and over every living thing that moves on
the earth.”

29 God said, “Behold, I have given you every herb
yielding seed, which is on the surface of all the
earth, and every tree, which bears fruit yielding
seed. It will be your food.

30 To every animal of the earth, and to every bird
of the sky, and to everything that creeps on the
earth, in which there is life, I have given every green
herb for food;” and it was so.

31 God saw everything that he had made, and,
behold, it was very good. There was evening and
there was morning, a sixth day.

Jasher 1

Jasher 1

1 And God said, "Let us make man in our image, after our likeness," and God created man in his own image.

Genesis 2
1 The heavens, the earth, and all their vast array
were finished. 2 On the seventh day God finished
his work which he had done; and he rested on the
seventh day from all his work which he had done. 3
God blessed the seventh day, and made it holy,
because he rested in it from all his work of creation
which he had done.

4 This is the history of the generations of the
heavens and of the earth when they were created,
in the day that Yahweh God made the earth and the
heavens. 5 No plant of the field was yet in the
earth, and no herb of the field had yet sprung up;
for Yahweh God had not caused it to rain on the
earth. There was not a man to till the ground, 6 but
a mist went up from the earth, and watered the
whole surface of the ground.

7 Yahweh God formed man from the dust of the
ground, and breathed into his nostrils the breath of
life; and man became a living soul.

2 And God formed man from the ground, and he
blew into his nostrils the breath of life, and man
became a living soul endowed with speech.

8 Yahweh God planted a garden eastward, in Eden,
and there he put the man whom he had formed. 9
Out of the ground Yahweh God made every tree to
grow that is pleasant to the sight, and good for
food, including the tree of life in the middle of the
garden and the tree of the knowledge of good and
evil.

10 A river went out of Eden to water the garden;
and from there it was parted, and became the
source of four rivers. 11 The name of the first is
Pishon: it flows through the whole land of Havilah,
where there is gold; 12 and the gold of that land is
good. Bdellium and onyx stone are also there.

13 The name of the second river is Gihon. It is the
same river that flows through the whole land of
Cush. 14 The name of the third river is Hiddekel.
This is the one which flows in front of Assyria. The
fourth river is the Euphrates.

15 Yahweh God took the man, and put him into the garden of Eden to cultivate and keep it. 16 Yahweh God commanded the man, saying, "You may freely eat of every tree of the garden; 17 but you shall not eat of the tree of the knowledge of good and evil; for in the day that you eat of it, you will surely die."

18 Yahweh God said, "It is not good for the man to be alone. I will make him a helper comparable to him."

3 And the Lord said, "It is not good for man to be alone; I will make unto him a helpmeet."

19 Out of the ground Yahweh God formed every animal of the field, and every bird of the sky, and brought them to the man to see what he would call them. Whatever the man called every living creature became its name. 20 The man gave names to all livestock, and to the birds of the sky, and to every animal of the field; but for man there was not found a helper comparable to him.

21 Yahweh God caused the man to fall into a deep sleep. As the man slept, he took one of his ribs, and closed up the flesh in its place. 22 Yahweh God made a woman from the rib which had taken from the man, and brought her to the man. 23 The man said, "This is now bone of my bones, and flesh of my flesh. She will be called 'woman,' because she was taken out of Man." 24 Therefore a man will leave his father and his mother, and will join with his wife, and they will be one flesh. 25 The man and his wife were both naked, and they were not ashamed.

4 And the Lord caused a deep sleep to fall upon Adam, and he slept, and he took away one of his ribs, and he built flesh upon it, and formed it and brought it to Adam, and Adam awoke from his sleep, and behold a woman was standing before him. 5 And he said, "This is a bone of my bones and it shall be called woman, for this has been taken from man;" and Adam called her name Eve, for she was the mother of all living.

[Genesis 1:28a And God blessed them: and God said unto them, Be fruitful, and multiply, and replenish the earth, and subdue it;]

6 And God blessed them and called their names Adam and Eve in the day that he created them, and the Lord God said, "Be fruitful and multiply and fill the earth."

[Genesis 2:15 Yahweh God took the man, and put him into the garden of Eden to cultivate and keep it. 16 Yahweh God commanded the man, saying, "You may freely eat of every tree of the garden; 17 but you shall not eat of the tree of the knowledge of good and evil; for in the day that you eat of it, you will surely die."]

7 And the Lord God took Adam and his wife, and he placed them in the garden of Eden to dress it and to keep it; and he commanded them and said unto them, "From every tree of the garden you may eat, but from the tree of the knowledge of good and evil you shall not eat, for in the day that you eat thereof you shall surely die."

8 And when God had blessed and commanded them, he went from them, and Adam and his wife dwelt in the garden according to the command which the Lord had commanded them.

Genesis 3

1 Now the serpent was more subtle than any animal of the field which Yahweh God had made. He said to the woman, "Has God really said, 'You shall not eat of any tree of the garden?'"

2 The woman said to the serpent, "We may eat fruit from the trees of the garden, 3 but not the fruit of the tree which is in the middle of the garden. God has said, 'You shall not eat of it. You shall not touch it, lest you die.'" 4 The serpent said to the woman, "You won't surely die, 5 for God knows that in the day you eat it, your eyes will be opened, and you will be like God, knowing good and evil."

6 When the woman saw that the tree was good for food, and that it was a delight to the eyes, and that the tree was to be desired to make one wise, she took some of its fruit, and ate; and she gave some to her husband with her, and he ate it, too. 7 Their eyes were opened, and they both knew that they were naked. They sewed fig leaves together, and made coverings for themselves.

8 They heard the voice of Yahweh God walking in the garden in the cool of the day, and the man and his wife hid themselves from the presence of Yahweh God among the trees of the garden.

9 Yahweh God called to the man, and said to him, "Where are you?" 10 The man said, "I heard your voice in the garden, and I was afraid, because I was naked; and I hid myself."

11 God said, "Who told you that you were naked? Have you eaten from the tree that I commanded you not to eat from?" 12 The man said, "The woman whom you gave to be with me, she gave me fruit from the tree, and I ate it." 13 Yahweh God said to the woman, "What have you done?" The woman said, "The serpent deceived me, and I ate."

14 Yahweh God said to the serpent, "Because you have done this, you are cursed above all livestock, and above every animal of the field. You shall go on your belly and you shall eat dust all the days of your life.

9 And the serpent, which God had created with them in the earth, came to them to incite them to transgress the command of God which he had commanded them.

10 And the serpent enticed and persuaded the woman to eat from the tree of knowledge, and the woman hearkened to the voice of the serpent, and she transgressed the word of God, and took from the tree of the knowledge of good and evil, and she ate, and she took from it and gave also to her husband and he ate.

15 "I will put hostility between you and the woman, and between your offspring and her offspring. He will bruise your head, and you will bruise his heel."

16 To the woman he said, "I will greatly multiply your pain in childbirth. In pain you will bear children. Your desire will be for your husband, and he will rule over you."

11 And Adam and his wife transgressed the command of God which he commanded them, and God knew it, and his anger was kindled against them and he cursed them.

17 To Adam he said, "Because you have listened to your wife's voice, and ate from the tree, about which I commanded you, saying, 'You shall not eat of it,' the ground is cursed for your sake. You will eat from it with much labor all the days of your life.18 It will yield thorns and thistles to you; and you will eat the herb of the field. 19 By the sweat of your face will you eat bread until you return to the ground, for out of it you were taken. For you are dust, and to dust you shall return."

20 The man called his wife Eve because she would be the mother of all the living. 21 Yahweh God made coats of animal skins for Adam and for his wife, and clothed them. 22 Yahweh God said, "Behold, the man has become like one of us, knowing good and evil. Now, lest he reach out his hand, and also take of the tree of life, and eat, and live forever..."

23 Therefore Yahweh God sent him out from the garden of Eden, to till the ground from which he was taken. 24 So he drove out the man; and he placed cherubim at the east of the garden of Eden, and a flaming sword which turned every way, to guard the way to the tree of life.

12 And the Lord God drove them that day from the garden of Eden, to till the ground from which they were taken, and they went and dwelt at the east of the garden of Eden;

Genesis 4

1 The man knew Eve his wife. She conceived, and gave birth to Cain, and said, "I have gotten a man with Yahweh's help." 2 Again she gave birth, to Cain's brother Abel.

and Adam knew his wife Eve and she bore two sons and three daughters. 13 And she called the name of the first born Cain, saying, "I have obtained a man from the Lord," and the name of the other she called Abel, for she said, "In vanity we came into the earth, and in vanity we shall be taken from it."

Abel was a keeper of sheep, but Cain was a tiller of the ground.

14 And the boys grew up and their father gave them a possession in the land; and Cain was a tiller of the ground, and Abel a keeper of sheep.

3 As time passed, Cain brought an offering to
Yahweh from the fruit of the ground. 4 Abel also
brought some of the firstborn of his flock and of its
fat. Yahweh respected Abel and his offering,

15 And it was at the expiration of a few years, that they brought an approximating offering to the Lord, and Cain brought from the fruit of the ground, and Abel brought from the firstlings of his flock from the fat thereof, and God turned and inclined to Abel and his offering, and a fire came down from the Lord from heaven and consumed it.

5 but he didn't respect Cain and his offering. Cain
was very angry, and the expression on his face fell.

16 And unto Cain and his offering the Lord did not turn, and he did not incline to it, for he had brought from the inferior fruit of the ground before the Lord, and Cain was jealous against his brother Abel on account of this, and he sought a pretext to slay him.

6 Yahweh said to Cain, "Why are you angry? Why
has the expression of your face fallen? 7 If you do
well, won't it be lifted up? If you don't do well, sin
crouches at the door. Its desire is for you, but you
are to rule over it."

8 Cain said to Abel, his brother, "Let's go into the field."

17 And in some time after, Cain and Abel his brother, went one day into the field to do their work; and they were both in the field, Cain tilling and ploughing his ground, and Abel feeding his flock; and the flock passed that part which Cain had ploughed in the ground, and it sorely grieved Cain on this account.

18 And Cain approached his brother Abel in anger, and he said unto him, "What is there between me and thee, that thou comest to dwell and bring thy flock to feed in my land?"

19 And Abel answered his brother Cain and said unto him, "What is there between me and thee, that thou shalt eat the flesh of my flock and clothe thyself with their wool?

20 "And now therefore, put off the wool of my sheep with which thou hast clothed thyself, and recompense me for their fruit and flesh which thou hast eaten, and when thou shalt have done this, I will then go from thy land as thou hast said?"

21 And Cain said to his brother Abel, "Surely if I slay thee this day, who will require thy blood from me?"

22 And Abel answered Cain, saying, "Surely God who has made us in the earth, he will avenge my cause, and he will require my blood from thee shouldst thou slay me, for the Lord is the judge and arbiter, and it is he who will requite man according to his evil, and the wicked man according to the wickedness that he may do upon earth. 23 And now, if thou shouldst slay me here, surely God knoweth thy secret views, and will judge thee for the evil which thou didst declare to do unto me this day. "

24 And when Cain heard the words which Abel his brother had spoken, behold the anger of Cain was kindled against his brother Abel for declaring this thing.

While they were in the field, Cain rose up against Abel, his brother, and killed him.

25 And Cain hastened and rose up, and took the iron part of his ploughing instrument, with which he suddenly smote his brother and he slew him, and Cain spilt the blood of his brother Abel upon the earth, and the blood of Abel streamed upon the earth before the flock.

26 And after this Cain repented having slain his brother, and he was sadly grieved, and he wept over him and it vexed him exceedingly. 27 And Cain rose up and dug a hole in the field, wherein he put his brother's body, and he turned the dust over it.

9 Yahweh said to Cain, “Where is Abel, your brother?”

28 And the Lord knew what Cain had done to his brother, and the Lord appeared to Cain and said unto him, "Where is Abel thy brother that was with thee?"

He said, “I don’t know. Am I my brother’s keeper?” 10 Yahweh said, “What have you done? The voice of your brother’s blood cries to me from the ground. 11 Now you are cursed because of the ground, which has opened its mouth to receive your brother’s blood from your hand.

29 And Cain dissembled, and said, "I do not know, am I my brother's keeper?" And the Lord said unto him, "What hast thou done? The voice of thy brother's blood crieth unto me from the ground where thou hast slain him. 30 For thou hast slain thy brother and hast dissembled before me, and didst imagine in thy heart that I saw thee not, nor knew all thy actions. 31 But thou didst this thing and didst slay thy brother for naught and because he spoke rightly to thee, and now, therefore, cursed be thou from the ground which opened its mouth to receive thy brother's blood from thy hand, and wherein thou didst bury him.

12 From now on, when you till the ground, it won't yield its strength to you. You will be a fugitive and a wanderer in the earth."

32 "And it shall be when thou shalt till it, it shall no more give thee its strength as in the beginning, for thorns and thistles shall the ground produce, and thou shalt be moving and wandering in the earth until the day of thy death."

13 Cain said to Yahweh, "My punishment is greater
than I can bear. 14 Behold, you have driven me out
today from the surface of the ground. I will be
hidden from your face, and I will be a fugitive and a
wanderer in the earth. Whoever finds me will kill
me." 15 Yahweh said to him, "Therefore whoever
slays Cain, vengeance will be taken on him
sevenfold." Yahweh appointed a sign for Cain, so
that anyone finding him would not strike him.

16 Cain left Yahweh's presence, and lived in the land of Nod, east of Eden.

33 And at that time Cain went out from the presence of the Lord, from the place where he was, and he went moving and wandering in the land toward the east of Eden, he and all belonging to him.

17 Cain knew his wife. She conceived, and gave birth to Enoch.

34 And Cain knew his wife in those days, and she conceived and bare a son, and he called his name Enoch, saying, "In that time the Lord began to give him rest and quiet in the earth."

He built a city, and called the name of the city, after the name of his son, Enoch.

35 And at that time Cain also began to build a city: and he built the city and he called the name of the city Enoch, according to the name of his son; for in those days the Lord had given him rest upon the earth, and he did not move about and wander as in the beginning.

18 To Enoch was born Irad. Irad became the father of Mehujael. Mehujael became the father of Methushael.

36 And Irad was born to Enoch, and Irad begat Mechuyael and Mechuyael begat Methusael.

Methushael became the father of Lamech. 19
Lamech took two wives: the name of the first one
was Adah, and the name of the second one was
Zillah. 20 Adah gave birth to Jabal, who was the
father of those who dwell in tents and have
livestock. 21 His brother's name was Jubal, who was
the father of all who handle the harp and pipe.

22 Zillah also gave birth to Tubal Cain, the forger of every cutting instrument of brass and iron. Tubal Cain's sister was Naamah.

23 Lamech said to his wives, "Adah and Zillah, hear
my voice. You wives of Lamech, listen to my speech,
for I have slain a man for wounding me, a young
man for bruising me. 24 If Cain will be avenged
seven times, truly Lamech seventy-seven times."

25 Adam knew his wife again. She gave birth to a
son, and named him Seth, "for God has given me
another child instead of Abel, for Cain killed him."

26 A son was also born to Seth, and he named him
Enosh. At that time men began to call on Yahweh's
name.

Genesis 5

1 This is the book of the generations of Adam. In
the day that God created man, he made him in
God's likeness. 2 He created them male and female,
and blessed them. On the day they were created,
he named them "Adam".

3 Adam lived one hundred thirty years, and became
the father of a son in his own likeness, after his
image, and named him Seth. 4 The days of Adam
after he became the father of Seth were eight
hundred years, and he became the father of other
sons and daughters. 5 All the days that Adam lived
were nine hundred thirty years, then he died.

6 Seth lived one hundred five years, then became
the father of Enosh. 7 Seth lived after he became
the father of Enosh eight hundred seven years, and
became the father of other sons and daughters. 8
All of the days of Seth were nine hundred twelve
years, then he died.

Jasher 2

1 And it was in the hundred and thirtieth year of
the life of Adam upon the earth, that he again knew
Eve his wife, and she conceived and bare a son in
his likeness and in his image, and she called his
name Seth, saying, "Because God has appointed me
another seed in the place of Abel, for Cain has slain
him."

2 And Seth lived one hundred and five years, and he
begat a son; and Seth called the name of his son
Enosh, saying, "Because in that time the sons of
men began to multiply, and to afflict their souls and
hearts by transgressing and rebelling against God."

3 And it was in the days of Enosh that the sons of
men continued to rebel and transgress against God,
to increase the anger of the Lord against the sons of
men. 4 And the sons of men went and they served
other gods, and they forgot the Lord who had
created them in the earth: and in those days the
sons of men made images of brass and iron, wood
and stone, and they bowed down and served them.

5 And every man made his god and they bowed down to them, and the sons of men forsook the Lord all the days of Enosh and his children; and the anger of the Lord was kindled on account of their works and abominations which they did in the earth.

6 And the Lord caused the waters of the river Gihon to overwhelm them, and he destroyed and consumed them, and he destroyed the third part of the earth, and notwithstanding this, the sons of men did not turn from their evil ways, and their hands were yet extended to do evil in the sight of the Lord.

7 And in those days there was neither sowing nor reaping in the earth; and there was no food for the sons of men and the famine was very great in those days.

8 And the seed which they sowed in those days in the ground became thorns, thistles and briers; for from the days of Adam was this declaration concerning the earth, of the curse of God, which he cursed the earth, on account of the sin which Adam
sinned before the Lord. 9 And it was when men
continued to rebel and transgress against God, and to corrupt their ways, that the earth also became corrupt.

9 Enosh lived ninety years, and became the father of Kenan.

10 Enosh lived after he became the father of Kenan, eight hundred fifteen years, and became the father
of other sons and daughters. 11 All of the days of
Enosh were nine hundred five years, then he died.

10 And Enosh lived ninety years and he begat Cainan;

11 And Cainan grew up and he was forty years old, and he became wise and had knowledge and skill in all wisdom, and he reigned over all the sons of men, and he led the sons of men to wisdom and knowledge; for Cainan was a very wise man and had understanding in all wisdom, and with his wisdom he ruled over spirits and demons;

12 And Cainan knew by his wisdom that God would destroy the sons of men for having sinned upon earth, and that the Lord would in the latter days bring upon them the waters of the flood.

13 And in those days Cainan wrote upon tablets of stone, what was to take place in time to come, and he put them in his treasures. 14 And Cainan reigned over the whole earth, and he turned some of the sons of men to the service of God. 15 And when Cainan was seventy years old, he begat three sons and two daughters.

12 Kenan lived seventy years, then became the father of Mahalalel. 13 Kenan lived after he became the father of Mahalalel eight hundred forty years, and became the father of other sons and daughters 14 and all of the days of Kenan were nine hundred ten years, then he died.

16 And these are the names of the children of Cainan; the name of the first born Mahlallel, the second Enan, and the third Mered, and their sisters were Adah and Zillah; these are the five children of Cainan that were born to him.

17 And Lamech, the son of Methusael, became related to Cainan by marriage, and he took his two daughters for his wives, and Adah conceived and bare a son to Lamech, and she called his name Jabal. 18 And she again conceived and bare a son, and called his name Jubal; and Zillah, her sister, was barren in those days and had no offspring.

19 For in those days the sons of men began to trespass against God, and to transgress the commandments which he had commanded to Adam, to be fruitful and multiply in the earth. 20 And some of the sons of men caused their wives to drink a draught that would render them barren, in order that they might retain their figures and whereby their beautiful appearance might not fade.

21 And when the sons of men caused some of their wives to drink, Zillah drank with them. 22 And the child-bearing women appeared abominable in the sight of their husbands as widows, whilst their husbands lived, for to the barren ones only they were attached.

23 And in the end of days and years, when Zillah became old, the Lord opened her womb. 24 And she conceived and bare a son and she called his name Tubal Cain, saying, "After I had withered away have I obtained him from the Almighty God."

25 And she conceived again and bare a daughter, and she called her name Naamah, for she said, "After I had withered away have I obtained pleasure and delight."

26 And Lamech was old and advanced in years, and his eyes were dim that he could not see, and Tubal Cain, his son, was leading him and it was one day that Lamech went into the field and Tubal Cain his son was with him, and whilst they were walking in the field, Cain the son of Adam advanced towards them; for Lamech was very old and could not see much, and Tubal Cain his son was very young.

27 And Tubal Cain told his father to draw his bow, and with the arrows he smote Cain, who was yet far off, and he slew him, for he appeared to them to be an animal. 28 And the arrows entered Cain's body although he was distant from them, and he fell to the ground and died. 29 And the Lord requited Cain's evil according to his wickedness, which he had done to his brother Abel, according to the word of the Lord which he had spoken.

30 And it came to pass when Cain had died, that Lamech and Tubal went to see the animal which they had slain, and they saw, and behold Cain their grandfather was fallen dead upon the earth. 31 And Lamech was very much grieved at having done this, and in clapping his hands together he struck his son and caused his death. 32 And the wives of Lamech heard what Lamech had done, and they sought to kill him.

33 And the wives of Lamech hated him from that day, because he slew Cain and Tubal Cain, and the wives of Lamech separated from him, and would not hearken to him in those days. 34 And Lamech came to his wives, and he pressed them to listen to him about this matter.

35 And he said to his wives Adah and Zillah, "Hear my voice O wives of Lamech, attend to my words, for now you have imagined and said that I slew a man with my wounds, and a child with my stripes for their having done no violence, but surely know that I am old and grey-headed, and that my eyes are heavy through age, and I did this thing unknowingly."

36 And the wives of Lamech listened to him in this matter, and they returned to him with the advice of their father Adam, but they bore no children to him from that time, knowing that God's anger was increasing in those days against the sons of men, to destroy them with the waters of the flood for their evil doings.

15 Mahalalel lived sixty-five years, then became the father of Jared. 16 Mahalalel lived after he became the father of Jared eight hundred thirty years, and became the father of other sons and daughters. 17 All of the days of Mahalalel were eight hundred ninety-five years, then he died.

37 And Mahlallel the son of Cainan lived sixty-five years and he begat Jared;

18 Jared lived one hundred sixty-two years, then became the father of Enoch. 19 Jared lived after he became the father of Enoch eight hundred years, and became the father of other sons and daughters. 20 All of the days of Jared were nine hundred sixty-two years, then he died.

and Jared lived sixty-two years and he begat Enoch.

21 Enoch lived sixty-five years, then became the father of Methuselah. 22 After Methuselah's birth, Enoch walked with God for three hundred years, and became the father of more sons and daughters. 23 All the days of Enoch were three hundred sixty-five years.

Jasher 3

1 And Enoch lived sixty-five years and he begat Methuselah; and Enoch walked with God after having begot Methuselah, and he served the Lord, and despised the evil ways of men.

2 And the soul of Enoch was wrapped up in the instruction of the Lord, in knowledge and in understanding; and he wisely retired from the sons of men, and secreted himself from them for many days.

3 And it was at the expiration of many years, whilst he was serving the Lord, and praying before him in his house, that an angel of the Lord called to him from Heaven, and he said, "Here am I."

4 And he said, "Rise, go forth from thy house and from the place where thou dost hide thyself, and appear to the sons of men, in order that thou mayest teach them the way in which they should go and the work which they must accomplish to enter in the ways of God."

5 And Enoch rose up according to the word of the
Lord, and went forth from his house, from his place
and from the chamber in which he was concealed;
and he went to the sons of men and taught them
the ways of the Lord, and at that time assembled
the sons of men and acquainted them with the
instruction of the Lord. 6 And he ordered it to be
proclaimed in all places where the sons of men
dwelt, saying, "Where is the man who wishes to
know the ways of the Lord and good works? Let him
come to Enoch. "

7 And all the sons of men then assembled to him,
for all who desired this thing went to Enoch, and
Enoch reigned over the sons of men according to
the word of the Lord, and they came and bowed to
him and they heard his word.

8 And the spirit of God was upon Enoch, and he
taught all his men the wisdom of God and his ways,
and the sons of men served the Lord all the days of
Enoch, and they came to hear his wisdom. 9 And all
the kings of the sons of men, both first and last,
together with their princes and judges, came to
Enoch when they heard of his wisdom, and they
bowed down to him, and they also required of
Enoch to reign over them, to which he consented.
10 And they assembled in all, one hundred and
thirty kings and princes, and they made Enoch king
over them and they were all under his power and
command.

11 And Enoch taught them wisdom, knowledge,
and the ways of the Lord; and he made peace
amongst them, and peace was throughout the
earth during the life of Enoch. 12 And Enoch
reigned over the sons of men two hundred and
forty-three years, and he did justice and
righteousness with all his people, and he led them
in the ways of the Lord.

[Genesis 5:25 Methuselah lived one hundred eighty-seven years, then became the father of Lamech.]

13 And these are the generations of Enoch,
Methuselah, Elisha, and Elimelech, three sons; and
their sisters were Melca and Nahmah, and
Methuselah lived eighty-seven years and he begat
Lamech.

14 And it was in the fifty-sixth year of the life of Lamech when Adam died; nine hundred and thirty years old was he at his death, and his two sons, with Enoch and Methuselah his son, buried him with great pomp, as at the burial of kings, in the cave which God had told him. 15 And in that place all the sons of men made a great mourning and weeping on account of Adam; it has therefore become a custom among the sons of men to this day. 16 And Adam died because he ate of the tree of knowledge; he and his children after him, as the Lord God had spoken.

17 And it was in the year of Adam's death which was the two hundred and forty-third year of the reign of Enoch, in that time Enoch resolved to separate himself from the sons of men and to secret himself as at first in order to serve the Lord. 18 And Enoch did so, but did not entirely secret himself from them, but kept away from the sons of men three days and then went to them for one day.

19 And during the three days that he was in his chamber, he prayed to, and praised the Lord his God, and the day on which he went and appeared to his subjects he taught them the ways of the Lord, and all they asked him about the Lord he told them.

20 And he did in this manner for many years, and he afterward concealed himself for six days, and appeared to his people one day in seven; and after that once in a month, and then once in a year, until all the kings, princes and sons of men sought for him, and desired again to see the face of Enoch, and to hear his word; but they could not, as all the sons of men were greatly afraid of Enoch, and they feared to approach him on account of the Godlike awe that was seated upon his countenance; therefore no man could look at him, fearing he might be punished and die.

21 And all the kings and princes resolved to assemble the sons of men, and to come to Enoch, thinking that they might all speak to him at the time when he should come forth amongst them, and they did so.

22 And the day came when Enoch went forth and they all assembled and came to him, and Enoch spoke to them the words of the Lord and he taught them wisdom and knowledge, and they bowed down before him and they said, "May the king live! May the king live!"

23 And in some time after, when the kings and princes and the sons of men were speaking to Enoch, and Enoch was teaching them the ways of God, behold an angel of the Lord then called unto Enoch from heaven, and wished to bring him up to heaven to make him reign there over the sons of God, as he had reigned over the sons of men upon earth.

24 When at that time Enoch heard this he went and assembled all the inhabitants of the earth, and taught them wisdom and knowledge and gave them divine instructions, and he said to them, "I have been required to ascend into heaven, I therefore do not know the day of my going. 25 And now therefore I will teach you wisdom and knowledge and will give you instruction before I leave you, how to act upon earth whereby you may live; and he did so."

26 And he taught them wisdom and knowledge, and gave them instruction, and he reproved them, and he placed before them statutes and judgments to do upon earth, and he made peace amongst them, and he taught them everlasting life, and dwelt with them some time teaching them all these things.

27 And at that time the sons of men were with Enoch, and Enoch was speaking to them, and they lifted up their eyes and the likeness of a great horse descended from heaven, and the horse paced in the air;

28 And they told Enoch what they had seen, and Enoch said to them, "On my account does this horse descend upon earth; the time is come when I must go from you and I shall no more be seen by you." 29 And the horse descended at that time and stood before Enoch, and all the sons of men that were with Enoch saw him.

30 And Enoch then again ordered a voice to be proclaimed, saying, "Where is the man who delighteth to know the ways of the Lord his God, let him come this day to Enoch before he is taken from us."

31 And all the sons of men assembled and came to Enoch that day; and all the kings of the earth with their princes and counsellors remained with him that day; and Enoch then taught the sons of men wisdom and knowledge, and gave them divine instruction; and he bade them serve the Lord and walk in his ways all the days of their lives, and he continued to make peace amongst them.

32 And it was after this that he rose up and rode upon the horse; and he went forth and all the sons of men went after him, about eight hundred thousand men; and they went with him one day's journey.

33 And the second day he said to them, "Return home to your tents, why will you go? Perhaps you may die; and some of them went from him, and those that remained went with him six day's journey;" and Enoch said to them every day, "Return to your tents, lest you may die;" but they were not willing to return, and they went with him.

34 And on the sixth day some of the men remained and clung to him, and they said to him, "We will go with thee to the place where thou goest; as the Lord liveth, death only shall separate us." 35 And they urged so much to go with him, that he ceased speaking to them; and they went after him and would not return;

24 Enoch walked with God, and he was not found, for God took him.

36 And when the kings returned they caused a census to be taken, in order to know the number of remaining men that went with Enoch; and it was upon the seventh day that Enoch ascended into heaven in a whirlwind, with horses and chariots of fire.

37 And on the eighth day all the kings that had been with Enoch sent to bring back the number of men that were with Enoch, in that place from which he ascended into heaven. 38 And all those kings went to the place and they found the earth there filled with snow, and upon the snow were large stones of snow, and one said to the other, "Come, let us break through the snow and see, perhaps the men that remained with Enoch are dead, and are now under the stones of snow, and they searched but could not find him, for he had ascended into heaven."

Jasher 4

1 And all the days that Enoch lived upon earth, were three hundred and sixty-five years. 2 And when Enoch had ascended into heaven, all the kings of the earth rose and took Methuselah his son and anointed him, and they caused him to reign over them in the place of his father.

3 And Methuselah acted uprightly in the sight of God, as his father Enoch had taught him, and he likewise during the whole of his life taught the sons of men wisdom, knowledge and the fear of God, and he did not turn from the good way either to the right or to the left.

4 But in the latter days of Methuselah, the sons of men turned from the Lord, they corrupted the earth, they robbed and plundered each other, and they rebelled against God and they transgressed, and they corrupted their ways, and would not hearken to the voice of Methuselah, but rebelled against him.

5 And the Lord was exceedingly wroth against them, and the Lord continued to destroy the seed in those days, so that there was neither sowing nor reaping in the earth. 6 For when they sowed the ground in order that they might obtain food for their support, behold, thorns and thistles were produced which they did not sow. 7 And still the sons of men did not turn from their evil ways, and their hands were still extended to do evil in the sight of God, and they provoked the Lord with their evil ways, and the Lord was very wroth, and repented that he had made man.

8 And he thought to destroy and annihilate them and he did so.

25 Methuselah lived one hundred eighty-seven years, then became the father of Lamech.

[3:13 And these are the generations of Enoch, Methuselah, Elisha, and Elimelech, three sons; and their sisters were Melca and Nahmah, and Methuselah lived eighty-seven years and he begat Lamech.]

26 Methuselah lived after he became the father of Lamech seven hundred eighty-two years, and became the father of other sons and daughters. 27 All the days of Methuselah were nine hundred sixty-nine years, then he died.

9 In those days when Lamech the son of Methuselah was one hundred and sixty years old, Seth the son of Adam died. 10 And all the days that Seth lived, were nine hundred and twelve years, and he died.

11 And Lamech was one hundred and eighty years old when he took Ashmua, the daughter of Elishaa the son of Enoch his uncle, and she conceived.

12 And at that time the sons of men sowed the ground, and a little food was produced, yet the sons of men did not turn from their evil ways, and they trespassed and rebelled against God.

28 Lamech lived one hundred eighty-two years, then became the father of a son. 29 He named him Noah, saying, "This one will comfort us in our work and in the toil of our hands, caused by the ground which Yahweh has cursed."

13 And the wife of Lamech conceived and bare him a son at that time, at the revolution of the year. 14 And Methuselah called his name Noah, saying, "The earth was in his days at rest and free from corruption," and Lamech his father called his name Menachem, saying, "This one shall comfort us in our works and miserable toil in the earth, which God had cursed."

15 And the child grew up and was weaned, and he went in the ways of his father Methuselah, perfect and upright with God. 16 And all the sons of men departed from the ways of the Lord in those days as they multiplied upon the face of the earth with sons and daughters, and they taught one another their evil practices and they continued sinning against the Lord. 17 And every man made unto himself a god, and they robbed and plundered every man his neighbor as well as his relative, and they corrupted the earth, and the earth was filled with violence.

18 And their judges and rulers went to the
daughters of men and took their wives by force
from their husbands according to their choice, and
the sons of men in those days took from the cattle
of the earth, the beasts of the field and the fowls of
the air, and taught the mixture of animals of one
species with the other, in order therewith to
provoke the Lord; and God saw the whole earth and
it was corrupt, for all flesh had corrupted its ways
upon earth, all men and all animals.

19 And the Lord said, "I will blot out man that I
created from the face of the earth, yea from man to
the birds of the air, together with cattle and beasts
that are in the field for I repent that I made them."

20 And all men who walked in the ways of the Lord,
died in those days, before the Lord brought the evil
upon man which he had declared, for this was from
the Lord, that they should not see the evil which
the Lord spoke of concerning the sons of men. 21
And Noah found grace in the sight of the Lord, and
the Lord chose him and his children to raise up seed
from them upon the face of the whole earth.

Jasher 5

1 And it was in the eighty-fourth year of the life of
Noah, that Enoch the son of Seth died, he was nine
hundred and five years old at his death. 2 And in
the one hundred and seventy ninth year of the life
of Noah, Cainan the son of Enosh died, and all the
days of Cainan were nine hundred and ten years,
and he died.

3 And in the two hundred and thirty fourth year of
the life of Noah, Mahlallel the son of Cainan died,
and the days of Mahlallel were eight hundred and
ninety-five years, and he died. 4 And Jared the son
of Mahlallel died in those days, in the three
hundred and thirty-sixth year of the life of Noah;
and all the days of Jared were nine hundred and
sixty-two years, and he died.

5 And all who followed the Lord died in those days,
before they saw the evil which God declared to do
upon earth.

6 And after the lapse of many years, in the four hundred and eightieth year of the life of Noah, when all those men, who followed the Lord had died away from amongst the sons of men, and only Methuselah was then left, God said unto Noah and Methuselah, saying,

7 "Speak ye, and proclaim to the sons of men, saying, 'Thus saith the Lord, return from your evil ways and forsake your works, and the Lord will repent of the evil that he declared to do to you, so that it shall not come to pass.' 8 For thus saith the Lord, 'Behold I give you a period of one hundred and twenty years; if you will turn to me and forsake your evil ways, then will I also turn away from the evil which I told you, and it shall not exist,' saith the Lord."

9 And Noah and Methuselah spoke all the words of the Lord to the sons of men, day after day, constantly speaking to them. 10 But the sons of men would not hearken to them, nor incline their ears to their words, and they were stiffnecked.

11 And the Lord granted them a period of one hundred and twenty years, saying, "If they will return, then will God repent of the evil, so as not to destroy the earth."

12 Noah the son of Lamech refrained from taking a wife in those days, to beget children, for he said, "Surely now God will destroy the earth, wherefore then shall I beget children?"

[Genesis 6:8 But Noah found favor in Yahweh's eyes.]

13 And Noah was a just man, he was perfect in his generation, and the Lord chose him to raise up seed from his seed upon the face of the earth. 14 And the Lord said unto Noah, "Take unto thee a wife, and beget children, for I have seen thee righteous before me in this generation. 15 And thou shalt raise up seed, and thy children with thee, in the midst of the earth;" and Noah went and took a wife, and he chose Naamah the daughter of Enoch, and she was five hundred and eighty years old. 16 And Noah was four hundred and ninety-eight years old, when he took Naamah for a wife.

[Genesis 6:10 Noah became the father of three sons: Shem, Ham, and Japheth.]

17 And Naamah conceived and bare a son, and he called his name Japheth, saying, "God has enlarged me in the earth;" and she conceived again and bare a son, and he called his name Shem, saying, God has made me a remnant, to raise up seed in the midst of the earth.

30 Lamech lived after he became the father of Noah five hundred ninety-five years, and became the father of other sons and daughters. 31 All the days of Lamech were seven hundred seventy-seven years, then he died.

32 Noah was five hundred years old, then Noah became the father of Shem, Ham, and Japheth.

18 And Noah was five hundred and two years old when Naamah bare Shem, and the boys grew up and went in the ways of the Lord, in all that Methuselah and Noah their father taught them.

[Genesis 5:30 Lamech lived after he became the father of Noah five hundred ninety-five years, and became the father of other sons and daughters. 31 All the days of Lamech were seven hundred seventy-seven years, then he died.]

19 And Lamech the father of Noah, died in those days; yet verily he did not go with all his heart in the ways of his father, and he died in the hundred and ninety-fifth year of the life of Noah. 20 And all the days of Lamech were seven hundred and seventy years, and he died.

Genesis 6

1 When men began to multiply on the surface of the ground, and daughters were born to them, 2 God's sons saw that men's daughters were beautiful, and they took any that they wanted for themselves as wives.

3 Yahweh said, "My Spirit will not strive with man forever, because he also is flesh; so his days will be one hundred twenty years." 4 The Nephilim were in the earth in those days, and also after that, when God's sons came in to men's daughters and had children with them. Those were the mighty men who were of old, men of renown.

5 Yahweh saw that the wickedness of man was great in the earth, and that every imagination of the thoughts of man's heart was continually only evil. 6 Yahweh was sorry that he had made man on the earth, and it grieved him in his heart. 7 Yahweh said, "I will destroy man whom I have created from the surface of the ground—man, along with animals, creeping things, and birds of the sky—for I am sorry that I have made them." 8 But Noah found favor in Yahweh's eyes.

9 This is the history of the generations of Noah: Noah was a righteous man, blameless among the people of his time. Noah walked with God. 10 Noah became the father of three sons: Shem, Ham, and Japheth.

21 And all the sons of men who knew the Lord, died in that year before the Lord brought evil upon them; for the Lord willed them to die, so as not to behold the evil that God would bring upon their brothers and relatives, as he had so declared to do.

22 In that time, the Lord said to Noah and Methuselah, "Stand forth and proclaim to the sons of men all the words that I spoke to you in those days, peradventure they may turn from their evil ways, and I will then repent of the evil and will not bring it."

23 And Noah and Methuselah stood forth, and said in the ears of the sons of men, all that God had spoken concerning them. 24 But the sons of men would not hearken, neither would they incline their ears to all their declarations.

11 The earth was corrupt before God, and the earth was filled with violence. 12 God saw the earth, and saw that it was corrupt, for all flesh had corrupted their way on the earth. 13 God said to Noah, "I will bring an end to all flesh, for the earth is filled with violence through them. Behold, I will destroy them and the earth.

25 And it was after this that the Lord said to Noah, "The end of all flesh is come before me, on account of their evil deeds, and behold I will destroy the earth.

14 "Make a ship of gopher wood. You shall make rooms in the ship, and shall seal it inside and outside with pitch. 15 This is how you shall make it. The length of the ship shall be three hundred cubits, its width fifty cubits, and its height thirty cubits.

26 "And do thou take unto thee gopher wood, and go to a certain place and make a large ark, and place it in that spot. 27 And thus shalt thou make it; three hundred cubits its length, fifty cubits broad and thirty cubits high.

16 "You shall make a roof in the ship, and you shall finish it to a cubit upward. You shall set the door of the ship in its side. You shall make it with lower, second, and third levels.

28 "And thou shalt make unto thee a door, open at its side, and to a cubit thou shalt finish above, and cover it within and without with pitch.

17 "I, even I, do bring the flood of waters on this earth, to destroy all flesh having the breath of life from under the sky. Everything that is in the earth will die.

29 "And behold I will bring the flood of waters upon the earth, and all flesh be destroyed, from under the heavens all that is upon earth shall perish.

18 "But I will establish my covenant with you. You shall come into the ship, you, your sons, your wife, and your sons' wives with you.

19 "Of every living thing of all flesh, you shall bring two of every sort into the ship, to keep them alive with you. They shall be male and female.

30 "And thou and thy household shall go and gather two couple of all living things, male and female, and shall bring them to the ark, to raise up seed from them upon earth.

20 "Of the birds after their kind, of the livestock after their kind, of every creeping thing of the ground after its kind, two of every sort will come to you, to keep them alive.

21 "Take with you of all food that is eaten, and gather it to yourself; and it will be for food for you, and for them."

31 "And gather unto thee all food that is eaten by all the animals, that there may be food for thee and for them.

32 "And thou shalt choose for thy sons three maidens, from the daughters of men, and they shall be wives to thy sons."

22 Thus Noah did. He did all that God commanded him.

33 And Noah rose up, and he made the ark, in the place where God had commanded him, and Noah did as God had ordered him.

34 In his five hundred and ninety-fifth year Noah commenced to make the ark, and he made the ark
in five years, as the Lord had commanded. 35 Then
Noah took the three daughters of Eliakim, son of Methuselah, for wives for his sons, as the Lord had
commanded Noah. 36 And it was at that time
Methuselah the son of Enoch died, nine hundred and sixty years old was he, at his death.

Genesis 7

1 Yahweh said to Noah, "Come with all of your household into the ship, for I have seen your righteousness before me in this generation.

Jasher 6

1 At that time, after the death of Methuselah, the Lord said to Noah, "Go thou with thy household into the ark; behold I will gather to thee all the animals of the earth, the beasts of the field and the fowls of the air, and they shall all come and surround the ark.

2 You shall take seven pairs of every clean animal with you, the male and his female. Of the animals that are not clean, take two, the male and his
female. 3 Also of the birds of the sky, seven and seven, male and female, to keep seed alive on the
surface of all the earth. 4 In seven days, I will cause
it to rain on the earth for forty days and forty nights. Every living thing that I have made, I will destroy from the surface of the ground."

2 "And thou shalt go and seat thyself by the doors of the ark, and all the beasts, the animals, and the fowls, shall assemble and place themselves before thee, and such of them as shall come and crouch before thee, shalt thou take and deliver into the hands of thy sons, who shall bring them to the ark, and all that will stand before thee thou shalt leave."

3 And the Lord brought this about on the next day,
and animals, beasts and fowls came in great
multitudes and surrounded the ark. 4 And Noah
went and seated himself by the door of the ark, and of all flesh that crouched before him, he brought into the ark, and all that stood before him he left upon earth.

5 And a lioness came, with her two whelps, male
and female, and the three crouched before Noah, and the two whelps rose up against the lioness and smote her, and made her flee from her place, and she went away, and they returned to their places,
and crouched upon the earth before Noah. 6 And
the lioness ran away, and stood in the place of the lions.

7 And Noah saw this, and wondered greatly, and he rose and took the two whelps, and brought them
into the ark. 8 And Noah brought into the ark from
all living creatures that were upon earth, so that there was none left but which Noah brought into the ark.

5 Noah did everything that Yahweh commanded
him. 6 Noah was six hundred years old when the
flood of waters came on the earth. 7 Noah went
into the ship with his sons, his wife, and his sons' wives, because of the floodwaters.

8 Clean animals, unclean animals, birds, and
everything that creeps on the ground 9 went by
pairs to Noah into the ship, male and female, as God commanded Noah.

9 Two and two came to Noah into the ark, but from the clean animals, and clean fowls, he brought seven couples, as God had commanded him.

10 After the seven days, the floodwaters came on the earth.

10 And all the animals, and beasts, and fowls, were still there, and they surrounded the ark at every place, and the rain had not descended till seven days after.

11 And on that day, the Lord caused the whole earth to shake, and the sun darkened, and the foundations of the world raged, and the whole earth was moved violently, and the lightning flashed, and the thunder roared, and all the fountains in the earth were broken up, such as was not known to the inhabitants before; and God did this mighty act, in order to terrify the sons of men, that there might be no more evil upon earth.

12 And still the sons of men would not return from their evil ways, and they increased the anger of the Lord at that time, and did not even direct their hearts to all this.

11 In the six hundredth year of Noah's life, in the second month, on the seventeenth day of the month, on the same day all the fountains of the great deep were burst open, and the sky's windows were opened. 12 It rained on the earth forty days and forty nights.

13 In the same day Noah, and Shem, Ham, and Japheth—the sons of Noah—and Noah's wife and the three wives of his sons with them, entered into the ship— 14 they, and every animal after its kind, all the livestock after their kind, every creeping thing that creeps on the earth after its kind, and every bird after its kind, every bird of every sort. 15 Pairs from all flesh with the breath of life in them went to Noah into the ship. 16 Those who went in, went in male and female of all flesh, as God commanded him; then Yahweh shut him in.

13 And at the end of seven days, in the six hundredth year of the life of Noah, the waters of the flood were upon the earth. 14 And all the fountains of the deep were broken up, and the windows of heaven were opened, and the rain was upon the earth forty days and forty nights.

15 And Noah and his household, and all the living creatures that were with him, came into the ark on account of the waters of the flood, and the Lord shut him in.

16 And all the sons of men that were left upon the earth, became exhausted through evil on account of the rain, for the waters were coming more violently upon the earth, and the animals and beasts were still surrounding the ark.

17 And the sons of men assembled together, about seven hundred thousand men and women, and they came unto Noah to the ark. 18 And they called to Noah, saying, "Open for us that we may come to thee in the ark--and wherefore shall we die?"

19 And Noah, with a loud voice, answered them
from the ark, saying, "Have you not all rebelled
against the Lord, and said that he does not exist?
And therefore the Lord brought upon you this evil,
to destroy and cut you off from the face of the
earth. 20 Is not this the thing that I spoke to you of
one hundred and twenty years back, and you would
not hearken to the voice of the Lord, and now do
you desire to live upon earth?"

21 And they said to Noah, "We are ready to return to the Lord; Only open for us that we may live and not die."

22 And Noah answered them, saying, "Behold now that you see the trouble of your souls, you wish to return to the Lord; Why did you not return during these hundred and twenty years, which the Lord granted you as the determined period?

23 "But now you come and tell me this on account of the troubles of your souls, now also the Lord will not listen to you, neither will he give ear to you on this day, so that you will not now succeed in your wishes."

24 And the sons of men approached in order to
break into the ark, to come in on account of the
rain, for they could not bear the rain upon them.
25 And the Lord sent all the beasts and animals that
stood round the ark. And the beasts overpowered
them and drove them from that place, and every
man went his way and they again scattered
themselves upon the face of the earth.

17 The flood was forty days on the earth.

26 And the rain was still descending upon the earth, and it descended forty days and forty nights,

and the waters prevailed greatly upon the earth; and all flesh that was upon the earth or in the waters died, whether men, animals, beasts, creeping things or birds of the air, and there only remained Noah and those that were with him in the ark.

The waters increased, and lifted up the ship, and it was lifted up above the earth.

27 And the waters prevailed and they greatly increased upon the earth, and they lifted up the ark and it was raised from the earth.

18 The waters rose, and increased greatly on the earth; and the ship floated on the surface of the waters.

28 And the ark floated upon the face of the waters, and it was tossed upon the waters so that all the living creatures within were turned about like pottage in a cauldron.

29 And great anxiety seized all the living creatures that were in the ark, and the ark was like to be broken.

30 And all the living creatures that were in the ark were terrified, and the lions roared, and the oxen lowed, and the wolves howled, and every living creature in the ark spoke and lamented in its own language, so that their voices reached to a great distance, and Noah and his sons cried and wept in their troubles; they were greatly afraid that they had reached the gates of death.

31 And Noah prayed unto the Lord, and cried unto him on account of this, and he said, "O Lord help us, for we have no strength to bear this evil that has encompassed us, for the waves of the waters have surrounded us, mischievous torrents have terrified us, the snares of death have come before us; answer us, O Lord, answer us, light up thy countenance toward us and be gracious to us, redeem us and deliver us." 32 And the Lord hearkened to the voice of Noah, and the Lord remembered him.

19 The waters rose very high on the earth. All the high mountains that were under the whole sky were covered. 20 The waters rose fifteen cubits higher, and the mountains were covered. 21 All flesh died that moved on the earth, including birds, livestock, animals, every creeping thing that creeps on the earth, and every man.

22 All on the dry land, in whose nostrils was the breath of the spirit of life, died. 23 Every living thing was destroyed that was on the surface of the ground, including man, livestock, creeping things, and birds of the sky. They were destroyed from the earth. Only Noah was left, and those who were with him in the ship.

24 The waters flooded the earth one hundred fifty days.

Genesis 8

1 God remembered Noah, all the animals, and all the livestock that were with him in the ship;

and God made a wind to pass over the earth. The waters subsided. 2 The deep's fountains and the sky's windows were also stopped, and the rain from the sky was restrained.

33 And a wind passed over the earth, and the waters were still and the ark rested. 34 And the fountains of the deep and the windows of heaven were stopped, and the rain from heaven was restrained.

3 The waters continually receded from the earth. After the end of one hundred fifty days the waters decreased. 4 The ship rested in the seventh month, on the seventeenth day of the month, on Ararat's mountains.

35 And the waters decreased in those days, and the ark rested upon the mountains of Ararat.

5 The waters receded continually until the tenth month. In the tenth month, on the first day of the month, the tops of the mountains were visible.

6 At the end of forty days, Noah opened the window of the ship which he had made,

36 And Noah then opened the windows of the ark,

and Noah still called out to the Lord at that time and he said, "O Lord, who didst form the earth and the heavens and all that are therein, bring forth our souls from this confinement, and from the prison wherein thou hast placed us, for I am much wearied with sighing."

37 And the Lord hearkened to the voice of Noah, and said to him, "When though shalt have completed a full year thou shalt then go forth. "

7 and he sent out a raven. It went back and forth, until the waters were dried up from the earth. 8 He himself sent out a dove to see if the waters were abated from the surface of the ground, 9 but the dove found no place to rest her foot, and she returned to him into the ship, for the waters were on the surface of the whole earth. He put out his hand, and took her, and brought her to him into the ship.

10 He waited yet another seven days; and again he sent the dove out of the ship. 11 The dove came back to him at evening and, behold, in her mouth was a freshly plucked olive leaf. So Noah knew that the waters were abated from the earth.

12 He waited yet another seven days, and sent out the dove; and she didn't return to him anymore.

13 In the six hundred first year, in the first month, the first day of the month, the waters were dried up from the earth. Noah removed the covering of the ship, and looked. He saw that the surface of the ground was dried.

38 And at the revolution of the year, when a full year was completed to Noah's dwelling in the ark, the waters were dried from off the earth, and Noah put off the covering of the ark.

14 In the second month, on the twenty-seventh day of the month, the earth was dry.

39 At that time, on the twenty-seventh day of the second month, the earth was dry,

but Noah and his sons, and those that were with him, did not go out from the ark until the Lord told them.

15 God spoke to Noah, saying, 16 "Go out of the
ship, you, and your wife, and your sons, and your
sons' wives with you. 17 Bring out with you every
living thing that is with you of all flesh, including
birds, livestock, and every creeping thing that
creeps on the earth, that they may breed
abundantly in the earth,

40 And the day came that the Lord told them to go out, and they all went out from the ark.

41 And they went and returned every one to his way and to his place, and Noah and his sons dwelt in the land that God had told them, and they served the Lord all their days, and the Lord blessed Noah and his sons on their going out from the ark.

and be fruitful, and multiply on the earth."

42 And he said to them, "Be fruitful and fill all the earth; become strong and increase abundantly in the earth and multiply therein."

18 Noah went out, with his sons, his wife, and his
sons' wives with him. 19 Every animal, every
creeping thing, and every bird, whatever moves on
the earth, after their families, went out of the ship.

20 Noah built an altar to Yahweh, and took of every
clean animal, and of every clean bird, and offered
burnt offerings on the altar. 21 Yahweh smelled the
pleasant aroma. Yahweh said in his heart, "I will not
again curse the ground any more for man's sake
because the imagination of man's heart is evil from
his youth. I will never again strike every living thing,
as I have done.

22 While the earth remains, seed time and harvest, and cold and heat, and summer and winter, and day and night will not cease."

Genesis 9

1 God blessed Noah and his sons, and said to them, "Be fruitful, and multiply, and replenish the earth.

2 "The fear of you and the dread of you will be on every animal of the earth, and on every bird of the sky. Everything that moves along the ground, and all the fish of the sea, are delivered into your hand.

3 "Every moving thing that lives will be food for you. As I gave you the green herb, I have given everything to you.

4 "But flesh with its life, that is, its blood, you shall not eat. 5 I will surely require your blood of your lives; at the hand of every animal I will require it. At the hand of man, even at the hand of every man's brother, I will require the life of man. 6 Whoever sheds man's blood, his blood will be shed by man, for God made man in his own image. 7 Be fruitful and multiply. Increase abundantly in the earth, and multiply in it."

8 God spoke to Noah and to his sons with him, saying, 9 "As for me, behold, I establish my covenant with you, and with your offspring after you, 10 and with every living creature that is with you: the birds, the livestock, and every animal of the earth with you, of all that go out of the ship, even every animal of the earth.

11 "I will establish my covenant with you: All flesh will not be cut off any more by the waters of the flood. There will never again be a flood to destroy the earth." 12 God said, "This is the token of the covenant which I make between me and you and every living creature that is with you, for perpetual generations: 13 I set my rainbow in the cloud, and it will be a sign of a covenant between me and the earth.

14 When I bring a cloud over the earth, that the rainbow will be seen in the cloud, 15 and I will remember my covenant, which is between me and you and every living creature of all flesh, and the waters will no more become a flood to destroy all flesh. 16 The rainbow will be in the cloud. I will look at it, that I may remember the everlasting covenant between God and every living creature of all flesh that is on the earth."

17 God said to Noah, "This is the token of the covenant which I have established between me and all flesh that is on the earth."

18 The sons of Noah who went out from the ship were Shem, Ham, and Japheth. Ham is the father of Canaan. 19 These three were the sons of Noah, and from these, the whole earth was populated.

20 Noah began to be a farmer, and planted a vineyard. 21 He drank of the wine and got drunk. He was uncovered within his tent. 22 Ham, the father of Canaan, saw the nakedness of his father, and told his two brothers outside.

23 Shem and Japheth took a garment, and laid it on
both their shoulders, went in backwards, and
covered the nakedness of their father. Their faces
were backwards, and they didn't see their father's
nakedness. 24 Noah awoke from his wine, and
knew what his youngest son had done to him. 25
He said,"Canaan is cursed. He will be a servant of
servants to his brothers."

26 He said, "Blessed be Yahweh, the God of Shem.
Let Canaan be his servant. 27 May God enlarge
Japheth. Let him dwell in the tents of Shem. Let
Canaan be his servant."

28 Noah lived three hundred fifty years after the
flood. 29 All the days of Noah were nine hundred
fifty years, and then he died.

Genesis 10

1 Now this is the history of the generations of the sons of Noah and of Shem, Ham, and Japheth. Sons were born to them after the flood.

2 The sons of Japheth were: Gomer, Magog, Madai, Javan, Tubal, Meshech, and Tiras.

3 The sons of Gomer were: Ashkenaz, Riphath, and Togarmah.

4 The sons of Javan were: Elishah, Tarshish, Kittim, and Dodanim.

5 Of these were the islands of the nations divided in their lands, everyone after his language, after their families, in their nations.

6 The sons of Ham were: Cush, Mizraim, Put, and
Canaan. 7 The sons of Cush were: Seba, Havilah,
Sabtah, Raamah, and Sabteca. The sons of Raamah
were: Sheba and Dedan.

Jasher 7

1 And these are the names of the sons of Noah: Japheth, Ham and Shem; and children were born to them after the flood, for they had taken wives before the flood.

2 These are the sons of Japheth; Gomer, Magog, Madai, Javan, Tubal, Meshech, and Tiras, seven sons.

3 And the sons of Gomer were Askinaz, Rephath and Tegarmah.

4 And the sons of Magog were Elichanaf and Lubal.
5 And the children of Madai were Achon, Zeelo,
Chazoni and Lot.

6 And the sons of Javan were Elisha, Tarshish, Chittim and Dudonim.

7 And the sons of Tubal were Ariphi, Kesed and
Taari. 8 And the sons of Meshech were Dedon,
Zaron and Shebashni. 9 And the sons of Tiras were
Benib, Gera, Lupirion and Gilak; these are the sons
of Japheth according to their families, and their
numbers in those days were about four hundred
and sixty men.

10 And these are the sons of Ham; Cush, Mitzraim, Phut and Canaan, four sons; and the sons of Cush were Seba, Havilah, Sabta, Raama and Satecha, and the sons of Raama were Sheba and Dedan.

11 And the sons of Mitzraim were Lud, Anom and
Pathros, Chasloth and Chaphtor. 12 And the sons
of Phut were Gebul, Hadan, Benah and Adan.

8 Cush became the father of Nimrod. He began to
be a mighty one in the earth. 9 He was a mighty
hunter before Yahweh. Therefore it is said, "Like
Nimrod, a mighty hunter before Yahweh." 10 The
beginning of his kingdom was Babel, Erech, Accad,
and Calneh, in the land of Shinar. 11 Out of that
land he went into Assyria, and built Nineveh,
Rehoboth Ir, Calah, 12 and Resen between Nineveh
and the great city Calah. 13 Mizraim became the
father of Ludim, Anamim, Lehabim, Naphtuhim, 14
Pathrusim, Casluhim (which the Philistines
descended from), and Caphtorim.

15 Canaan became the father of Sidon (his
firstborn), Heth, 16 the Jebusites, the Amorites, the
Girgashites, 17 the Hivites, the Arkites, the Sinites,
18 the Arvadites, the Zemarites, and the
Hamathites.

13 And the sons of Canaan were Zidon, Heth,
Amori, Gergashi, Hivi, Arkee, Seni, Arodi, Zimodi
and Chamothi.

17b Afterward the families of the Canaanites were
spread abroad. 19 The border of the Canaanites
was from Sidon—as you go toward Gerar—to
Gaza—as you go toward Sodom, Gomorrah,
Admah, and Zeboiim—to Lasha.

20 These are the sons of Ham, after their families,
according to their languages, in their lands and their
nations.

14 These are the sons of Ham, according to their
families, and their numbers in those days were
about seven hundred and thirty men.

21 Children were also born to Shem, the father of
all the children of Eber, the elder brother of
Japheth.

22 The sons of Shem were: Elam, Asshur,
Arpachshad, Lud, and Aram.

15 And these are the sons of Shem; Elam, Ashur,
Arpachshad, Lud and Aram, five sons;

15b and the sons of Elam were Shushan, Machul
and Harmon.

16 And the sons of Ashar were Mirus and Mokil,
and the sons of Arpachshad were Shelach, Anar and
Ashcol.

23 The sons of Aram were: Uz, Hul, Gether, and
Mash.

17 And the sons of Lud were Pethor and Bizayon,
17b and the sons of Aram were Uz, Chul, Gather
and Mash.

24 Arpachshad became the father of Shelah. Shelah became the father of Eber. 25 To Eber were born two sons. The name of the one was Peleg, for in his days the earth was divided. His brother's name was Joktan. 26 Joktan became the father of Almodad, Sheleph, Hazarmaveth, Jerah, 27 Hadoram, Uzal, Diklah, 28 Obal, Abimael, Sheba, 29 Ophir, Havilah, and Jobab. All these were the sons of Joktan. 30 Their dwelling extended from Mesha, as you go toward Sephar, the mountain of the east.

31 These are the sons of Shem, by their families, according to their languages, lands, and nations.

18 These are the sons of Shem, according to their families; and their numbers in those days were about three hundred men.

32 These are the families of the sons of Noah, by their generations, according to their nations. The nations divided from these in the earth after the flood.

Genesis 11

1 The whole earth was of one language and of one speech.

[9:20 And king Nimrod reigned securely, and all the earth was under his control, and all the earth was of one tongue and words of union.]

2 As they traveled east, they found a plain in the land of Shinar, and they lived there. 3 They said to one another, "Come, let's make bricks, and burn them thoroughly." They had brick for stone, and they used tar for mortar.

4 They said, "Come, let's build ourselves a city, and a tower whose top reaches to the sky, and let's make a name for ourselves, lest we be scattered abroad on the surface of the whole earth."

[9:21 And all the princes of Nimrod and his great men took counsel together; Phut, Mitzraim, Cush and Canaan with their families, and they said to each other, "Come let us build ourselves a city and in it a strong tower, and its top reaching heaven, and we will make ourselves famed, so that we may reign upon the whole world, in order that the evil of our enemies may cease from us, that we may reign mightily over them, and that we may not become scattered over the earth on account of their wars."]

5 Yahweh came down to see the city and the tower, which the children of men built. 6 Yahweh said, "Behold, they are one people, and they have all one language, and this is what they begin to do. Now nothing will be withheld from them, which they intend to do.

7 Come, let's go down, and there confuse their language, that they may not understand one another's speech."

[9:32 And God said to the seventy angels who stood foremost before him, to those who were near to him, saying, "Come let us descend and confuse their tongues, that one man shall not understand the language of his neighbor", and they did so unto them.]

8 So Yahweh scattered them abroad from there on the surface of all the earth.

They stopped building the city. 9 Therefore its name was called Babel, because there Yahweh confused the language of all the earth.

[9:37 And they ceased building the city and the tower; therefore he called that place Babel, for there the Lord confounded the Language of the whole earth;]

From there, Yahweh scattered them abroad on the surface of all the earth.

[9:35b and the third division of those who said, "We will ascend to heaven and fight against him, the Lord scattered them throughout the earth."]

10 This is the history of the generations of Shem: Shem was one hundred years old when he became the father of Arpachshad two years after the flood.

19 These are the generations of Shem; Shem begat Arpachshad

11 Shem lived five hundred years after he became the father of Arpachshad, and became the father of more sons and daughters.

12 Arpachshad lived thirty-five years and became the father of Shelah.

and Arpachshad begat Shelach,

13 Arpachshad lived four hundred three years after he became the father of Shelah, and became the father of more sons and daughters.

14 Shelah lived thirty years, and became the father of Eber.

and Shelach begat Eber

15 Shelah lived four hundred three years after he became the father of Eber, and became the father of more sons and daughters.

16 Eber lived thirty-four years, and became the father of Peleg.

and to Eber were born two children, the name of one was Peleg, for in his days the sons of men were divided, and in the latter days, the earth was divided.

17 Eber lived four hundred thirty years after he became the father of Peleg, and became the father of more sons and daughters.

20 And the name of the second was Yoktan, meaning that in his day the lives of the sons of men were diminished and lessened.

21 These are the sons of Yoktan; Almodad, Shelaf, Chazarmoveth, Yerach, Hadurom, Ozel, Diklah, Obal, Abimael, Sheba, Ophir, Havilah and Jobab; all these are the sons of Yoktan.

18 Peleg lived thirty years, and became the father
of Reu. 19 Peleg lived two hundred nine years after
he became the father of Reu, and became the
father of more sons and daughters.

20 Reu lived thirty-two years, and became the father of Serug.

21 Reu lived two hundred seven years after he became the father of Serug, and became the father of more sons and daughters.

22 Serug lived thirty years, and became the father of Nahor.

23 Serug lived two hundred years after he became the father of Nahor, and became the father of more sons and daughters.

24 Nahor lived twenty-nine years, and became the father of Terah.

25 Nahor lived one hundred nineteen years after he became the father of Terah, and became the father of more sons and daughters.

26 Terah lived seventy years, and became the father of Abram, Nahor, and Haran.

22 And Peleg his brother begat Yen,

and Yen begat Serug,

and Serug begat Nahor

and Nahor begat Terah,

and Terah was thirty-eight years old, and he begat Haran and Nahor.

23 And Cush the son of Ham, the son of Noah, took a wife in those days in his old age, and she bare a son, and they called his name Nimrod, saying, "At that time the sons of men again began to rebel and transgress against God," and the child grew up, and his father loved him exceedingly, for he was the son of his old age.

24 And the garments of skin which God made for
Adam and his wife, when they went out of the
garden, were given to Cush. 25 For after the death
of Adam and his wife, the garments were given to
Enoch, the son of Jared, and when Enoch was taken
up to God, he gave them to Methuselah, his son.

26 And at the death of Methuselah, Noah took
them and brought them to the ark, and they were
with him until he went out of the ark. 27 And in
their going out, Ham stole those garments from
Noah his father, and he took them and hid them
from his brothers.

28 And when Ham begat his first born Cush, he gave him the garments in secret, and they were with Cush many days. 29 And Cush also concealed them from his sons and brothers, and when Cush had begotten Nimrod, he gave him those garments through his love for him, and Nimrod grew up, and when he was twenty years old he put on those garments.

30 And Nimrod became strong when he put on the garments, and God gave him might and strength, and he was a mighty hunter in the earth, yea, he was a mighty hunter in the field, and he hunted the animals and he built altars, and he offered upon them the animals before the Lord.

31 And Nimrod strengthened himself, and he rose up from amongst his brethren, and he fought the battles of his brethren against all their enemies round about.

32 And the Lord delivered all the enemies of his brethren in his hands, and God prospered him from time to time in his battles, and he reigned upon earth.

33 Therefore it became current in those days, when a man ushered forth those that he had trained up for battle, he would say to them, "Like God did to Nimrod, who was a mighty hunter in the earth, and who succeeded in the battles that prevailed against his brethren, that he delivered them from the hands of their enemies, so may God strengthen us and deliver us this day."

34 And when Nimrod was forty years old, at that time there was a war between his brethren and the children of Japheth, so that they were in the power of their enemies.

35 And Nimrod went forth at that time, and he assembled all the sons of Cush and their families, about four hundred and sixty men, and he hired also from some of his friends and acquaintances about eighty men, and be gave them their hire, and he went with them to battle, and when he was on the road, Nimrod strengthened the hearts of the people that went with him.

36 And he said to them, "Do not fear, neither be
alarmed, for all our enemies will be delivered into
our hands, and you may do with them as you
please." 37 And all the men that went were about
five hundred, and they fought against their
enemies, and they destroyed them, and subdued
them, and Nimrod placed standing officers over
them in their respective places.

38 And he took some of their children as security,
and they were all servants to Nimrod and to his
brethren, and Nimrod and all the people that were
with him turned homeward.

39 And when Nimrod had joyfully returned from
battle, after having conquered his enemies, all his
brethren, together with those who knew him
before, assembled to make him king over them, and
they placed the regal crown upon his head. 40 And
he set over his subjects and people, princes, judges,
and rulers, as is the custom amongst kings.

41 And he placed Terah the son of Nahor the prince
of his host, and he dignified him and elevated him
above all his princes.

42 And whilst he was reigning according to his
heart's desire, after having conquered all his
enemies around, he advised with his counselors to
build a city for his palace, and they did so. 43 And
they found a large valley opposite to the east, and
they built him a large and extensive city, and
Nimrod called the name of the city that he built
Shinar, for the Lord had vehemently shaken his
enemies and destroyed them.

44 And Nimrod dwelt in Shinar, and he reigned
securely, and he fought with his enemies and he
subdued them, and he prospered in all his battles,
and his kingdom became very great. 45 And all
nations and tongues heard of his fame, and they
gathered themselves to him, and they bowed down
to the earth, and they brought him offerings, and
he became their lord and king, and they all dwelt
with him in the city at Shinar, and Nimrod reigned
in the earth over all the sons of Noah, and they
were all under his power and counsel.

46 And all the earth was of one tongue and words of union, but Nimrod did not go in the ways of the Lord, and he was more wicked than all the men that were before him, from the days of the flood until those days.

47 And he made gods of wood and stone, and he bowed down to them, and he rebelled against the Lord, and taught all his subjects and the people of the earth his wicked ways; and Mardon his son was more wicked than his father.

48 And every one that heard of the acts of Mardon the son of Nimrod would say, concerning him, "From the wicked goeth forth wickedness;" therefore it became a proverb in the whole earth, saying, "From the wicked goeth forth wickedness," and it was current in the words of men from that time to this.

49 And Terah the son of Nahor, prince of Nimrod's host, was in those days very great in the sight of the king and his subjects, and the king and princes loved him, and they elevated him very high.

50 And Terah took a wife and her name was Amthelo the daughter of Cornebo; and the wife of Terah conceived and bare him a son in those days.
51 Terah was seventy years old when he begat him, and Terah called the name of his son that was born to him Abram, because the king had raised him in those days, and dignified him above all his princes that were with him.

Jasher 8

1 And it was in the night that Abram was born, that all the servants of Terah, and all the wise men of Nimrod, and his conjurors came and ate and drank in the house of Terah, and they rejoiced with him on that night.

2 And when all the wise men and conjurors went out from the house of Terah, they lifted up their eyes toward heaven that night to look at the stars, and they saw, and behold one very large star came from the east and ran in the heavens, and he swallowed up the four stars from the four sides of the heavens.

3 And all the wise men of the king and his conjurors were astonished at the sight, and the sages understood this matter, and they knew its import.

4 And they said to each other, "This only betokens
the child that has been born to Terah this night,
who will grow up and be fruitful, and multiply, and
possess all the earth, he and his children for ever,
and he and his seed will slay great kings, and inherit
their lands."

5 And the wise men and conjurors went home that
night, and in the morning all these wise men and
conjurors rose up early, and assembled in an
appointed house.

6 And they spoke and said to each other, "Behold
the sight that we saw last night is hidden from the
king, it has not been made known to him. 7 And
should this thing get known to the king in the latter
days, he will say to us, 'Why have you concealed
this matter from me,' and then we shall all suffer
death; therefore, now let us go and tell the king the
sight which we saw, and the interpretation thereof,
and we shall then remain clear."

8 And they did so, and they all went to the king and
bowed down to him to the ground, and they said,
"May the king live, may the king live. 9 We heard
that a son was born to Terah the son of Nahor, the
prince of thy host, and we yesternight came to his
house, and we ate and drank and rejoiced with him
that night.

10 "And when thy servants went out from the
house of Terah, to go to our respective homes to
abide there for the night, we lifted up our eyes to
heaven, and we saw a great star coming from the
east, and the same star ran with great speed, and
swallowed up four great stars, from the four sides
of the heavens.

11 "And thy servants were astonished at the sight
which we saw, and were greatly terrified, and we
made our judgment upon the sight, and knew by
our wisdom the proper interpretation thereof, that
this thing applies to the child that is born to Terah,
who will grow up and multiply greatly, and become
powerful, and kill all the kings of the earth, and
inherit all their lands, he and his seed forever.

12 "And now our lord and king, behold we have
truly acquainted thee with what we have seen
concerning this child.

13 "If it seemeth good to the king to give his father
value for this child, we will slay him before he shall
grow up and increase in the land, and his evil
increase against us, that we and our children perish
through his evil.

13 "If it seemeth good to the king to give his father
value for this child, we will slay him before he shall
grow up and increase in the land, and his evil
increase against us, that we and our children perish
through his evil."

14 And the king heard their words and they seemed
good in his sight, and he sent and called for Terah,
and Terah came before the king. 15 And the king
said to Terah, "I have been told that a son was
yesternight born to thee, and after this manner was
observed in the heavens at his birth. 16 And now
therefore give me the child, that we may slay him
before his evil springs up against us, and I will give
thee for his value, thy house full of silver and gold."

17 And Terah answered the king and said to him:
"My Lord and king, I have heard thy words, and thy
servant shall do all that his king desireth. 18 But my
lord and king, I will tell thee what happened to me
yesternight, that I may see what advice the king will
give his servant, and then I will answer the king
upon what he has just spoken;" and the king said,
"Speak."

19 And Terah said to the king, "Ayon, son of Mored,
came to me yesternight, saying, 20 'Give unto me
the great and beautiful horse that the king gave
thee, and I will give thee silver and gold, and straw
and provender for its value'; and I said to him, 'Wait
till I see the king concerning thy words, and behold
whatever the king saith, that will I do.' 21 And now
my lord and king, behold I have made this thing
known to thee, and the advice which my king will
give unto his servant, that will I follow."

22 And the king heard the words of Terah, and his
anger was kindled and he considered him in the
light of a fool.

23 And the king answered Terah, and he said to him, "Art thou so silly, ignorant, or deficient in understanding, to do this thing, to give thy beautiful horse for silver and gold or even for straw and provender? 24 Art thou so short of silver and gold, that thou shouldst do this thing, because thou canst not obtain straw and provender to feed thy horse? and what is silver and gold to thee, or straw and provender, that thou shouldst give away that fine horse which I gave thee, like which there is none to be had on the whole earth?"

25 And the king left off speaking, and Terah answered the king, saying, "Like unto this has the king spoken to his servant; 26 I beseech thee, my lord and king, what is this which thou didst say unto me, saying, 'Give thy son that we may slay him, and I will give thee silver and gold for his value; what shall I do with silver and gold after the death of my son?' Who shall inherit me? surely then at my death, the silver and gold will return to my king who gave it."

27 And when the king heard the words of Terah, and the parable which he brought concerning the king, it grieved him greatly and he was vexed at this thing, and his anger burned within him.

28 And Terah saw that the anger of the king was kindled against him, and he answered the king, saying, "All that I have is in the king's power; whatever the king desireth to do to his servant, that let him do, yea, even my son, he is in the king's power, without value in exchange, he and his two brothers that are older than he."

29 And the king said to Terah, "No, but I will purchase thy younger son for a price". 30 And Terah answered the king, saying, "I beseech thee my lord and king to let thy servant speak a word before thee, and let the king hear the word of his servant," and Terah said, "Let my king give me three days' time till I consider this matter within myself, and consult with my family concerning the words of my king;" and he pressed the king greatly to agree to this.

31 And the king hearkened to Terah, and he did so and he gave him three days' time, and Terah went out from the king's presence, and he came home to his family and spoke to them all the words of the king; and the people were greatly afraid.

32 And it was in the third day that the king sent to Terah, saying, "Send me thy son for a price as I spoke to thee; and shouldst thou not do this, I will send and slay all thou hast in thy house, so that thou shalt not even have a dog remaining."

33 And Terah hastened, (as the thing was urgent from the king), and he took a child from one of his servants, which his handmaid had born to him that day, and Terah brought the child to the king and received value for him.

34 And the Lord was with Terah in this matter, that Nimrod might not cause Abram's death, and the king took the child from Terah and with all his might dashed his head to the ground, for he thought it had been Abram; and this was concealed from him from that day, and it was forgotten by the king, as it was the will of Providence not to suffer Abram's death.

35 And Terah took Abram his son secretly, together with his mother and nurse, and he concealed them in a cave, and he brought them their provisions monthly.

36 And the Lord was with Abram in the cave and he grew up, and Abram was in the cave ten years, and the king and his princes, soothsayers and sages, thought that the king had killed Abram.

Jasher 9

1 And Haran, the son of Terah, Abram's oldest brother, took a wife in those days. 2 Haran was thirty-nine years old when he took her;

27 Now this is the history of the generations of Terah. Terah became the father of Abram, Nahor, and Haran.

Haran became the father of Lot.

and the wife of Haran conceived and bare a son, and he called his name Lot.

3 And she conceived again and bare a daughter, and she called her name Milca; and she again conceived and bare a daughter, and she called her name Sarai.
4 Haran was forty-two years old when he begat Sarai, which was in the tenth year of the life of Abram; and in those days Abram and his mother and nurse went out from the cave, as the king and his subjects had forgotten the affair of Abram.

5 And when Abram came out from the cave, he went to Noah and his son Shem, and he remained with them to learn the instruction of the Lord and his ways, and no man knew where Abram was, and Abram served Noah and Shem his son for a long time.

6 And Abram was in Noah's house thirty-nine years, and Abram knew the Lord from three years old, and he went in the ways of the Lord until the day of his death, as Noah and his son Shem had taught him; and all the sons of the earth in those days greatly transgressed against the Lord, and they rebelled against him and they served other gods, and they forgot the Lord who had created them in the earth; and the inhabitants of the earth made unto themselves, at that time, every man his god; gods of wood and stone which could neither speak, hear, nor deliver, and the sons of men served them and they became their gods.

7 And the king and all his servants, and Terah with all his household were then the first of those that
served gods of wood and stone.8 And Terah had twelve gods of large size, made of wood and stone, after the twelve months of the year, and he served each one monthly, and every month Terah would bring his meat offering and drink offering to his gods; thus did Terah all the days.

9 And all that generation were wicked in the sight of the Lord, and they thus made every man his god, but they forsook the Lord who had created them.

10 And there was not a man found in those days in the whole earth, who knew the Lord (for they served each man his own God) except Noah and his household, and all those who were under his counsel knew the Lord in those days.

11 And Abram the son of Terah was waxing great in those days in the house of Noah, and no man knew it, and the Lord was with him. 12 And the Lord gave Abram an understanding heart, and he knew all the works of that generation were vain, and that all their gods were vain and were of no avail.

13 And Abram saw the sun shining upon the earth, and Abram said unto himself "Surely now this sun that shines upon the earth is God, and him will I serve." 14 And Abram served the sun in that day and he prayed to him, and when evening came the sun set as usual, and Abram said within himself, Surely this cannot be God? 15 And Abram still continued to speak within himself, "Who is he who made the heavens and the earth? who created upon earth? where is he?"

16 And night darkened over him, and he lifted up his eyes toward the west, north, south, and east, and he saw that the sun had vanished from the earth, and the day became dark.

17 And Abram saw the stars and moon before him, and he said, "Surely this is the God who created the whole earth as well as man, and behold these his servants are gods around him:" and Abram served the moon and prayed to it all that night. 18 And in the morning when it was light and the sun shone upon the earth as usual, Abram saw all the things that the Lord God had made upon earth.

19 And Abram said unto himself "Surely these are not gods that made the earth and all mankind, but these are the servants of God," and Abram remained in the house of Noah and there knew the Lord and his ways' and he served the Lord all the days of his life, and all that generation forgot the Lord, and served other gods of wood and stone, and rebelled all their days.

[Genesis 11:1 The whole earth was of one language and of one speech.]

20 And king Nimrod reigned securely, and all the earth was under his control, and all the earth was of one tongue and words of union.

[Genesis 11:4 They said, "Come, let's build ourselves a city, and a tower whose top reaches to the sky, and let's make a name for ourselves, lest we be scattered abroad on the surface of the whole earth."]

21 And all the princes of Nimrod and his great men took counsel together; Phut, Mitzraim, Cush and Canaan with their families, and they said to each other, "Come let us build ourselves a city and in it a strong tower, and its top reaching heaven, and we will make ourselves famed, so that we may reign upon the whole world, in order that the evil of our enemies may cease from us, that we may reign mightily over them, and that we may not become scattered over the earth on account of their wars."

22 And they all went before the king, and they told the king these words, and the king agreed with
them in this affair, and he did so. 23 And all the
families assembled consisting of about six hundred thousand men, and they went to seek an extensive piece of ground to build the city and the tower, and they sought in the whole earth and they found none like one valley at the east of the land of Shinar, about two days' walk, and they journeyed there and they dwelt there.

24 And they began to make bricks and burn fires to build the city and the tower that they had imagined
to complete. 25 And the building of the tower was
unto them a transgression and a sin, and they began to build it, and whilst they were building against the Lord God of heaven, they imagined in their hearts to war against him and to ascend into heaven.

26 And all these people and all the families divided themselves in three parts; the first said "We will ascend into heaven and fight against him;" the second said, "We will ascend to heaven and place our own gods there and serve them;" and the third part said, "We will ascend to heaven and smite him with bows and spears;" and God knew all their works and all their evil thoughts, and he saw the city and the tower which they were building.

29 And the Lord knew their thoughts, and it came to pass when they were building they cast the arrows toward the heavens, and all the arrows fell upon them filled with blood, and when they saw them they said to each other, "Surely we have slain all those that are in heaven." 30 For this was from the Lord in order to cause them to err, and in order; to destroy them from off the face of the ground.

[Genesis 11: 5 Yahweh came down to see the city and the tower, which the children of men built. 6 Yahweh said, "Behold, they are one people, and they have all one language, and this is what they begin to do. Now nothing will be withheld from them, which they intend to do.]

32 And God said to the seventy angels who stood foremost before him, to those who were near to him, saying, "Come let us descend and confuse their tongues, that one man shall not understand the language of his neighbor," and they did so unto them. 33 And from that day following, they forgot each man his neighbor's tongue, and they could not understand to speak in one tongue, and when the builder took from the hands of his neighbor lime or stone which he did not order, the builder would cast it away and throw it upon his neighbor, that he would die.

34 And they did so many days, and they killed many of them in this manner.

[Genesis 11:8 So Yahweh scattered them abroad from there on the surface of all the earth.]

35 And the Lord smote the three divisions that were there, and he punished them according to their works and designs; those who said, "We will ascend to heaven and serve our gods, became like apes and elephants; and those who said, We will smite the heaven with arrows," the Lord killed them, one man through the hand of his neighbor; and the third division of those who said, "We will ascend to heaven and fight against him," the Lord scattered them throughout the earth.

36 And those who were left amongst them, when they knew and understood the evil which was coming upon them, they forsook the building, and they also became scattered upon the face of the whole earth.

[Genesis 11:8b They stopped building the city. 9 Therefore its name was called Babel, because there Yahweh confused the language of all the earth.]

37 And they ceased building the city and the tower; therefore he called that place Babel, for there the Lord confounded the Language of the whole earth; behold it was at the east of the land of Shinar.

38 And as to the tower which the sons of men built,
the earth opened its mouth and swallowed up one
third part thereof, and a fire also descended from
heaven and burned another third, and the other
third is left to this day, and it is of that part which
was aloft, and its circumference is three days' walk.
39 And many of the sons of men died in that tower,
a people without number.

Jasher 10

1 And Peleg the son of Eber died in those days, in the forty-eighth year of the life of Abram son of Terah, and all the days of Peleg were two hundred and thirty-nine years.

2 And when the Lord had scattered the sons of men
on account of their sin at the tower, behold they
spread forth into many divisions, and all the sons of
men were dispersed into the four corners of the
earth. 3 And all the families became each according
to its language, its land, or its city.

4 And the sons of men built many cities according
to their families, in all the places where they went,
and throughout the earth where the Lord had
scattered them. 5 And some of them built cities in
places from which they were afterward extirpated,
and they called these cities after their own names,
or the names of their children, or after their
particular occurrences.

6 And the sons of Japheth the son of Noah went and built themselves cities in the places where they were scattered, and they called all their cities after their names, and the sons of Japheth were divided upon the face of the earth into many divisions and languages.

7 And these are the sons of Japheth according to their families, Gomer, Magog, Medai, Javan, Tubal, Meshech and Tiras; these are the children of Japheth according to their generations.

8 And the children of Gomer, according to their cities, were the Francum, who dwell in the land of Franza, by the river Franza, by the river Senah.

9 And the children of Rephath are the Bartonim, who dwell in the land of Bartonia by the river Ledah, which empties its waters in the great sea Gihon, that is, oceanus.

10 And the children of Tugarma are ten families, and these are their names: Buzar, Parzunac, Balgar, Elicanum, Ragbib, Tarki, Bid, Zebuc, Ongal and Tilmaz; all these spread and rested in the north and built themselves cities.

11 And they called their cities after their own names, those are they who abide by the rivers Hithlah and Italac unto this day.

12 But the families of Angoli, Balgar and Parzunac, they dwell by the great river Dubnee; and the names of their cities are also according to their own names.

13 And the children of Javan are the Javanim who dwell in the land of Makdonia, and the children of Medaiare are the Orelum that dwell in the land of Curson, and the children of Tubal are those that dwell in the land of Tuskanah by the river Pashiah.

14 And the children of Meshech are the Shibashni and the children of Tiras are Rushash, Cushni, and Ongolis; all these went and built themselves cities; those are the cities that are situate by the sea Jabus by the river Cura, which empties itself in the river Tragan.

15 And the children of Elishah are the Almanim, and they also went and built themselves cities; those are the cities situate between the mountains of Job and Shibathmo; and of them were the people of Lumbardi who dwell opposite the mountains of Job and Shibathmo, and they conquered the land of Italia and remained there unto this day.

16 And the children of Chittim are the Romim who dwell in the valley of Canopia by the river Tibreu.

17 And the children of Dudonim are those who dwell in the cities of the sea Gihon, in the land of Bordna.

18 These are the families of the children of Japheth according to their cities and languages, when they were scattered after the tower, and they called their cities after their names and occurrences; and these are the names of all their cities according to their families, which they built in those days after the tower.

19 And the children of Ham were Cush, Mitzraim, Phut and Canaan according to their generation and cities.

20 All these went and built themselves cities as they found fit places for them, and they called their cities after the names of their fathers Cush, Mitzraim, Phut and Canaan.

21 And the children of Mitzraim are the Ludim, Anamim, Lehabim, Naphtuchim, Pathrusim, Casluchim and Caphturim, seven families.

22 All these dwell by the river Sihor, that is the brook of Egypt, and they built themselves cities and called them after their own names.

23 And the children of Pathros and Casloch intermarried together, and from them went forth the Pelishtim, the Azathim, and the Gerarim, the Githim and the Ekronim, in all five families; these also built themselves cities, and they called their cities after the names of their fathers unto this day.

24 And the children of Canaan also built themselves cities, and they called their cities after their names, eleven cities and others without number.

25 And four men from the family of Ham went to the land of the plain; these are the names of the four men, Sodom, Gomorrah, Admah and Zeboyim.
26 And these men built themselves four cities in the land of the plain, and they called the names of their cities after their own names.

27 And they and their children and all belonging to them dwelt in those cities, and they were fruitful and multiplied greatly and dwelt peaceably.

28 And Seir the son of Hur, son of Hivi, son of Canaan, went and found a valley opposite to Mount Paran, and he built a city there, and he and his seven sons and his household dwelt there, and he called the city which he built Seir, according to his name; that is the land of Seir unto this day.

29 These are the families of the children of Ham, according to their languages and cities, when they were scattered to their countries after the tower.

30 And some of the children of Shem son of Noah, father of all the children of Eber, also went and built themselves cities in the places wherein they were scattered, and they called their cities after their names.

31 And the sons of Shem were Elam, Ashur, Arpachshad, Lud and Aram, and they built themselves cities and called the names of all their cities after their names.

32 And Ashur son of Shem and his children and household went forth at that time, a very large body of them, and they went to a distant land that they found, and they met with a very extensive valley in the land that they went to, and they built themselves four cities, and they called them after their own names and occurrences.

33 And these are the names of the cities which the children of Ashur built, Ninevah, Resen, Calach and Rehobother; and the children of Ashur dwell there unto this day.

34 And the children of Aram also went and built themselves a city, and they called the name of the city Uz after their eldest brother, and they dwell therein; that is the land of Uz to this day.

35 And in the second year after the tower a man from the house of Ashur, whose name was Bela, went from the land of Ninevah to sojourn with his household wherever he could find a place; and they came until opposite the cities of the plain against Sodom, and they dwelt there.

36 And the man rose up and built there a small city, and called its name Bela, after his name; that is the land of Zoar unto this day.

37 And these are the families of the children of Shem according to their language and cities, after they were scattered upon the earth after the tower.

38 And every kingdom, city, and family of the families of the children of Noah built themselves many cities after this. 39 And they established governments in all their cities, in order to be regulated by their orders; so did all the families of the children of Noah forever.

Jasher 11

1 And Nimrod son of Cush was still in the land of
Shinar, and he reigned over it and dwelt there, and
he built cities in the land of Shinar. 2 And these are
the names of the four cities which he built, and he
called their names after the occurrences that
happened to them in the building of the tower.

3 And he called the first Babel, saying, "Because the Lord there confounded the language of the whole earth; "and the name of the second he called Erech, because from there God dispersed them.

4 And the third he called Eched, saying there was a great battle at that place; and the fourth he called Calnah, because his princes and mighty men were consumed there, and they vexed the Lord, they rebelled and transgressed against him.

5 And when Nimrod had built these cities in the land of Shinar, he placed in them the remainder of his people, his princes and his mighty men that were left in his kingdom.

6 And Nimrod dwelt in Babel, and he there renewed his reign over the rest of his subjects, and he reigned securely, and the subjects and princes of Nimrod called his name Amraphel, saying that at the tower his princes and men fell through his means.

7 And notwithstanding this, Nimrod did not return to the Lord, and he continued in wickedness and teaching wickedness to the sons of men; and Mardon, his son, was worse than his father, and continued to add to the abominations of his father.

8 And he caused the sons of men to sin, therefore it
is said, "From the wicked goeth forth wickedness."
9 At that time there was war between the families
of the children of Ham, as they were dwelling in the
cities which they had built.

10 And Chedorlaomer, king of Elam, went away
from the families of the children of Ham, and he
fought with them and he subdued them, and he
went to the five cities of the plain and he fought
against them and he subdued them, and they were
under his control. 11 And they served him twelve
years, and they gave him a yearly tax.

12 At that time died Nahor, son of Serug, in the
forty-ninth year of the life of Abram son of Terah.
13 And in the fiftieth year of the life of Abram son
of Terah, Abram came forth from the house of
Noah, and went to his father's house. 14 And
Abram knew the Lord, and he went in his ways and
instructions, and the Lord his God was with him.

15 And Terah his father was in those days, still
captain of the host of king Nimrod, and he still
followed strange gods. 16 And Abram came to his
father's house and saw twelve gods standing there
in their temples, and the anger of Abram was
kindled when he saw these images in his father's
house. 17 And Abram said, "As the Lord liveth
these images shall not remain in my father's house;
so shall the Lord who created me do unto me if in
three days' time I do not break them all."

18 And Abram went from them, and his anger burned within him. And Abram hastened and went from the chamber to his father's outer court, and he found his father sitting in the court, and all his servants with him, and Abram came and sat before him.

19 And Abram asked his father, saying, "Father, tell me where is God who created heaven and earth, and all the sons of men upon earth, and who created thee and me." And Terah answered his son Abram and said, "Behold those who created us are all with us in the house."

20 And Abram said to his father, "My lord, shew them to me I pray thee;" and Terah brought Abram into the chamber of the inner court, and Abram saw, and behold the whole room was full of gods of wood and stone, twelve great images and others less than they without number.

21 And Terah said to his son, "Behold these are
they which made all thou seest upon earth, and
which created me and thee, and all mankind." 22
And Terah bowed down to his gods, and he then
went away from them, and Abram, his son, went
away with him.

23 And when Abram had gone from them he went
to his mother and sat before her, and he said to his
mother, "Behold, my father has shown me those
who made heaven and earth, and all the sons of
men. 24 Now, therefore, hasten and fetch a kid
from the flock, and make of it savory meat, that I
may bring it to my father's gods as an offering for
them to eat; perhaps I may thereby become
acceptable to them."

25 And his mother did so, and she fetched a kid, and made savory meat thereof, and brought it to Abram, and Abram took the savory meat from his mother and brought it before his father's gods, and he drew nigh to them that they might eat; and Terah his father, did not know of it.

26 And Abram saw on the day when he was sitting amongst them, that they had no voice, no hearing, no motion, and not one of them could stretch forth his hand to eat.

27 And Abram mocked them, and said, "Surely the savory meat that I prepared has not pleased them, or perhaps it was too little for them, and for that reason they would not eat; therefore tomorrow I will prepare fresh savory meat, better and more plentiful than this, in order that I may see the result."

28 And it was on the next day that Abram directed his mother concerning the savory meat, and his mother rose and fetched three fine kids from the flock, and she made of them some excellent savory meat, such as her son was fond of, and she gave it to her son Abram; and Terah his father did not know of it.

29 And Abram took the savory meat from his mother, and brought it before his father's gods into the chamber; and he came nigh unto them that they might eat, and he placed it before them, and Abram sat before them all day, thinking perhaps they might eat.

30 And Abram viewed them, and behold they had
neither voice nor hearing, nor did one of them
stretch forth his hand to the meat to eat.

31 And in the evening of that day in that house
Abram was clothed with the spirit of God. 32 And
he called out and said, "Wo unto my father and this
wicked generation, whose hearts are all inclined to
vanity, who serve these idols of wood and stone
which can neither eat, smell, hear nor speak, who
have mouths without speech, eyes without sight,
ears without hearing, hands without feeling, and
legs which cannot move; like them are those that
made them and that trust in them."

33 And when Abram saw all these things his anger
was kindled against his father, and he hastened and
took a hatchet in his hand, and came unto the
chamber of the gods, and he broke all his father's
gods.

34 And when he had done breaking the images, he
placed the hatchet in the hand of the great god
which was there before them, and he went out; and
Terah his father came home, for he had heard at
the door the sound of the striking of the hatchet; so
Terah came into the house to know what this was
about.

35 And Terah, having heard the noise of the hatchet
in the room of images, ran to the room to the
images, and he met Abram going out. 36 And Terah
entered the room and found all the idols fallen
down and broken, and the hatchet in the hand of
the largest, which was not broken, and the savory
meat which Abram his son had made was still
before them.

37 And when Terah saw this his anger was greatly
kindled, and he hastened and went from the room
to Abram. 38 And he found Abram his son still
sitting in the house; and he said to him, "What is
this work thou hast done to my gods?"

39 And Abram answered Terah his father and he said, "Not so my lord, for I brought savory meat before them, and when I came nigh to them with the meat that they might eat, they all at once stretched forth their hands to eat before the great one had put forth his hand to eat. 40 And the large one saw their works that they did before him, and his anger was violently kindled against them, and he went and took the hatchet that was in the house and came to them and broke them all, and behold the hatchet is yet in his hand as thou seest."

41 And Terah's anger was kindled against his son Abram, when he spoke this; and Terah said to Abram his son in his anger, "What is this tale that thou hast told? Thou speakest lies to me. 42 Is there in these gods spirit, soul or power to do all thou hast told me? Are they not wood and stone, and have I not myself made them, and canst thou speak such lies, saying that the large god that was with them smote them? It is thou that didst place the hatchet in his hands, and then sayest he smote them all."

43 And Abram answered his father and said to him, "And how canst thou then serve these idols in whom there is no power to do any thing? Can those idols in which thou trustest deliver thee? Can they hear thy prayers when thou callest upon them? Can they deliver thee from the hands of thy enemies, or will they fight thy battles for thee against thy enemies, that thou shouldst serve wood and stone which can neither speak nor hear?

44 "And now surely it is not good for thee nor for the sons of men that are connected with thee, to do these things; are you so silly, so foolish or so short of understanding that you will serve wood and stone, and do after this manner?

45 "And forget the Lord God who made heaven and earth, and who created you in the earth, and thereby bring a great evil upon your souls in this matter by serving stone and wood? 46 Did not our fathers in days of old sin in this matter, and the Lord God of the universe brought the waters of the flood upon them and destroyed the whole earth?

47 "And how can you continue to do this and serve
gods of wood and stone, who cannot hear, or
speak, or deliver you from oppression, thereby
bringing down the anger of the God of the universe
upon you? 48 Now therefore my father refrain
from this, and bring not evil upon thy soul and the
souls of thy household."

49 And Abram hastened and sprang from before his
father, and took the hatchet from his father's
largest idol, with which Abram broke it and ran
away. 50 And Terah, seeing all that Abram had
done, hastened to go from his house, and he went
to the king and he came before Nimrod and stood
before him, and he bowed down to the king; and
the king said, "What dost thou want?"

51 And he said, "I beseech thee my lord, to hear
me--Now fifty years back a child was born to me,
and thus has he done to my gods and thus has he
spoken; and now therefore, my lord and king, send
for him that he may come before thee, and judge
him according to the law, that we may be delivered
from his evil."

52 And the king sent three men of his servants, and
they went and brought Abram before the king. And
Nimrod and all his princes and servants were that
day sitting before him, and Terah sat also before
them. 53 And the king said to Abram, "What is this
that thou hast done to thy father and to his gods?"
And Abram answered the king in the words that he
spoke to his father, and he said, "The large god that
was with them in the house did to them what thou
hast heard."

54 And the king said to Abram, "Had they power to
speak and eat and do as thou hast said?" And
Abram answered the king, saying, "And if there be
no power in them why dost thou serve them and
cause the sons of men to err through thy follies? 55
Dost thou imagine that they can deliver thee or do
anything small or great, that thou shouldst serve
them? And why wilt thou not sense the God of the
whole universe, who created thee and in whose
power it is to kill and keep alive? 56 0 foolish,
simple, and ignorant king, woe unto thee forever.

57 "I thought thou wouldst teach thy servants the upright way, but thou hast not done this, but hast filled the whole earth with thy sins and the sins of thy people who have followed thy ways.

58 "Dost thou not know, or hast thou not heard, that this evil which thou doest, our ancestors sinned therein in days of old, and the eternal God brought the waters of the flood upon them and destroyed them all, and also destroyed the whole earth on their account? And wilt thou and thy people rise up now and do like unto this work, in order to bring down the anger of the Lord God of the universe, and to bring evil upon thee and the whole earth?

59 "Now therefore put away this evil deed which thou doest, and serve the God of the universe, as thy soul is in his hands, and then it will be well with thee.

60 "And if thy wicked heart will not hearken to my words to cause thee to forsake thy evil ways, and to serve the eternal God, then wilt thou die in shame in the latter days, thou, thy people and all who are connected with thee, hearing thy words or walking in thy evil ways."

61 And when Abram had ceased speaking before the king and princes, Abram lifted up his eyes to the heavens, and he said, "The Lord seeth all the wicked, and he will judge them."

Jasher 12

1 And when the king heard the words of Abram he
ordered him to be put into prison; and Abram was
ten days in prison. 2 And at the end of those days
the king ordered that all the kings, princes and
governors of different provinces and the sages
should come before him, and they sat before him,
and Abram was still in the house of confinement.

3 And the king said to the princes and sages, "Have
you heard what Abram, the son of Terah, has done
to his father? Thus has he done to him, and I
ordered him to be brought before me, and thus has
he spoken; his heart did not misgive him, neither
did he stir in my presence, and behold now he is
confined in the prison. 4 And therefore decide
what judgment is due to this man who reviled the
king; who spoke and did all the things that you
heard."

[Compare Daniel 3]

5 And they all answered the king saying, "The man who revileth the king should be hanged upon a tree; but having done all the things that he said, and having despised our gods, he must therefore be burned to death, for this is the law in this matter.

6 "If it pleaseth the king to do this, let him order his servants to kindle a fire both night and day in thy brick furnace, and then we will cast this man into it. And the king did so, and he commanded his servants that they should prepare a fire for three days and three nights in the king's furnace, that is in Casdim; and the king ordered them to take Abram from prison and bring him out to be burned."

7 And all the king's servants, princes, lords, governors, and judges, and all the inhabitants of the land, about nine hundred thousand men, stood opposite the furnace to see Abram.

8 And all the women and little ones crowded upon the roofs and towers to see what was doing with Abram, and they all stood together at a distance; and there was not a man left that did not come on that day to behold the scene.

9 And when Abram was come, the conjurors of the king and the sages saw Abram, and they cried out to the king, saying, "Our sovereign lord, surely this is the man whom we know to have been the child at whose birth the great star swallowed the four stars, which we declared to the king now fifty years since.
10 And behold now his father has also transgressed thy commands, and mocked thee by bringing thee another child, which thou didst kill."
11 And when the king heard their words, he was exceedingly wroth, and he ordered Terah to be brought before him.

12 And the king said, "Hast thou heard what the conjurors have spoken? Now tell me truly, how didst thou; and if thou shalt speak truth thou shalt be acquitted."

13 And seeing that the king's anger was so much kindled, Terah said to the king, "My lord and king, thou hast heard the truth, and what the sages have spoken is right." And the king said, "How couldst thou do this thing, to transgress my orders and to give me a child that thou didst not beget, and to take value for him?"

14 And Terah answered the king, "Because my tender feelings were excited for my son, at that time, and I took a son of my handmaid, and I brought him to the king."

15 And the king said "Who advised thee to this? Tell me, do not hide aught from me, and then thou shalt not die."

16 And Terah was greatly terrified in the king's presence, and he said to the king, "It was Haran my eldest son who advised me to this; and Haran was in those days that Abram was born, two and thirty years old."

17 But Haran did not advise his father to anything,
for Terah said this to the king in order to deliver his
soul from the king, for he feared greatly; and the
king said to Terah, "Haran thy son who advised thee
to this shall die through fire with Abram; for the
sentence of death is upon him for having rebelled
against the king's desire in doing this thing." 18
And Haran at that time felt inclined to follow the
ways of Abram, but he kept it within himself.

19 And Haran said in his heart, "Behold now the king has seized Abram on account of these things which Abram did, and it shall come to pass, that if Abram prevail over the king I will follow him, but if the king prevail I will go after the king."

20 And when Terah had spoken this to the king concerning Haran his son, the king ordered Haran to be seized with Abram.

28 Haran died before his father Terah in the land of his birth, in Ur of the Chaldees.

21 And they brought them both, Abram and Haran
his brother, to cast them into the fire; and all the
inhabitants of the land and the king's servants and
princes and all the women and little ones were
there, standing that day over them. 22 And the
king's servants took Abram and his brother, and
they stripped them of all their clothes excepting
their lower garments which were upon them. 23
And they bound their hands and feet with linen
cords, and the servants of the king lifted them up
and cast them both into the furnace.

24 And the Lord loved Abram and he had
compassion over him, and the Lord came down and
delivered Abram from the fire and he was not
burned. 25 But all the cords with which they bound
him were burned, while Abram remained and
walked about in the fire.

26 And Haran died when they had cast him into the fire, and he was burned to ashes, for his heart was not perfect with the Lord; and those men who cast him into the fire, the flame of the fire spread over them, and they were burned, and twelve men of them died.

27 And Abram walked in the midst of the fire three days and three nights, and all the servants of the king saw him walking in the fire, and they came and told the king, saying, "Behold we have seen Abram walking about in the midst of the fire, and even the lower garments which are upon him are not burned, but the cord with which he was bound is burned."

28 And when the king heard their words his heart
fainted and he would not believe them; so he sent
other faithful princes to see this matter, and they
went and saw it and told it to the king; and the king
rose to go and see it, and he saw Abram walking to
and fro in the midst of the fire, and he saw Haran's
body burned, and the king wondered greatly. 29
And the king ordered Abram to be taken out from
the fire; and his servants approached to take him
out and they could not, for the fire was round
about and the flame ascending toward them from
the furnace.

30 And the king's servants fled from it, and the king rebuked them, saying, "Make haste and bring Abram out of the fire that you shall not die."

31 And the servants of the king again approached to bring Abram out, and the flames came upon them and burned their faces so that eight of them died.

32 And when the king saw that his servants could not approach the fire lest they should be burned, the king called to Abram, "O servant of the God who is in heaven, go forth from amidst the fire and come hither before me;" and Abram hearkened to the voice of the king, and he went forth from the fire and came and stood before the king.

33 And when Abram came out the king and all his servants saw Abram coming before the king, with his lower garments upon him, for they were not burned, but the cord with which he was bound was burned.

34 And the king said to Abram, "How is it that thou wast not burned in the fire?"

35 And Abram said to the king, "The God of heaven and earth in whom I trust and who has all in his power, he delivered me from the fire into which thou didst cast me."

36 And Haran the brother of Abram was burned to
ashes, and they sought for his body, and they found
it consumed. 37 And Haran was eighty-two years
old when he died in the fire of Casdim. And the
king, princes, and inhabitants of the land, seeing
that Abram was delivered from the fire, they came
and bowed down to Abram.

38 And Abram said to them, "Do not bow down to me, but bow down to the God of the world who made you, and serve him, and go in his ways for it is he who delivered me from out of this fire, and it is he who created the souls and spirits of all men, and formed man in his mother's womb, and brought him forth into the world, and it is he who will deliver those who trust in him from all pain."

39 And this thing seemed very wonderful in the eyes of the king and princes, that Abram was saved from the fire and that Haran was burned; and the king gave Abram many presents and he gave him his two head servants from the king's house; the name of one was Oni and the name of the other was Eliezer.

40 And all the kings, princes and servants gave Abram many gifts of silver and gold and pearl, and the king and his princes sent him away, and he went in peace. 41 And Abram went forth from the king in peace, and many of the king's servants followed him, and about three hundred men joined him.

42 And Abram returned on that day and went to his father's house, he and the men that followed him, and Abram served the Lord his God all the days of his life, and he walked in his ways and followed his law. 43 And from that day forward Abram inclined the hearts of the sons of men to serve the Lord.

29 Abram and Nahor married wives. The name of Abram's wife was Sarai, and the name of Nahor's wife was Milcah, the daughter of Haran who was also the father of Iscah. 30 Sarai was barren. She had no child.

44 And at that time Nahor and Abram took unto themselves wives, the daughters of their brother Haran; the wife of Nahor was Milca and the name of Abram's wife was Sarai. And Sarai, wife of Abram, was barren; she had no offspring in those days.

45 And at the expiration of two years from Abram's going out of the fire, that is in the fifty-second year of his life, behold king Nimrod sat in Babel upon the throne, and the king fell asleep and dreamed that he was standing with his troops and hosts in a valley opposite the king's furnace.

46 And he lifted up his eyes and saw a man in the likeness of Abram coming forth from the furnace, and that he came and stood before the king with his drawn sword, and then sprang to the king with his sword, when the king fled from the man, for he was afraid; and while he was running, the man threw an egg upon the king's head, and the egg became a great river.

47 And the king dreamed that all his troops sank in that river and died, and the king took flight with three men who were before him and he escaped.

48 And the king looked at these men and they were clothed in princely dresses as the garments of kings, and had the appearance and majesty of kings.

49 And while they were running, the river again turned to an egg before the king, and there came forth from the egg a young bird which came before the king, and flew at his head and plucked out the king's eye.

50 And the king was grieved at the sight, and he awoke out of his sleep and his spirit was agitated; and he felt a great terror.

51 And in the morning the king rose from his couch in fear, and he ordered all the wise men and magicians to come before him, when the king
related his dream to them. 52 And a wise servant
of the king, whose name was Anuki, answered the king, saying, "This is nothing else but the evil of Abram and his seed which will spring up against my
Lord and king in the latter days. 53 And behold the
day will come when Abram and his seed and the children of his household will war with my king, and they will smite all the king's hosts and his troops.

54 "And as to what thou hast said concerning three men which thou didst see like unto thyself, and which did escape, this means that only thou wilt escape with three kings from the kings of the earth
who will be with thee in battle. 55 And that which
thou sawest of the river which turned to an egg as at first, and the young bird plucking out thine eye, this means nothing else but the seed of Abram
which will slay the king in latter days. 56 This is my
king's dream, and this is its interpretation, and the dream is true, and the interpretation which thy servant has given thee is right.

57 "Now therefore my king, surely thou knowest that it is now fifty-two years since thy sages saw this at the birth of Abram, and if my king will suffer Abram to live in the earth it will be to the injury of my lord and king, for all the days that Abram liveth neither thou nor thy kingdom will be established, for this was known formerly at his birth; and why will not my king slay him, that his evil may be kept from thee in latter days?"

58 And Nimrod hearkened to the voice of Anuki, and he sent some of his servants in secret to go and seize Abram, and bring him before the king to suffer death.

59 And Eliezer, Abram's servant whom the king had given him, was at that time in the presence of the king, and he heard what Anuki had advised the king, and what the king had said to cause Abram's death.
60 And Eliezer said to Abram, "Hasten, rise up and save thy soul, that thou mayest not die through the hands of the king, for thus did he see in a dream concerning thee, and thus did Anuki interpret it, and thus also did Anuki advise the king concerning thee."

61 And Abram hearkened to the voice of Eliezer, and Abram hastened and ran for safety to the house of Noah and his son Shem, and he concealed himself there and found a place of safety; and the king's servants came to Abram's house to seek him, but they could not find him, and they searched through out the country and he was not to be found, and they went and searched in every direction and he was not to be met with.

62 And when the king's servants could not find Abram they returned to the king, but the king's anger against Abram was stilled, as they did not find him, and the king drove from his mind this matter concerning Abram.

63 And Abram was concealed in Noah's house for one month, until the king had forgotten this matter, but Abram was still afraid of the king; and Terah came to see Abram his son secretly in the house of Noah, and Terah was very great in the eyes of the king.

64 And Abram said to his father, "Dost thou not know that the king thinketh to slay me, and to annihilate my name from the earth by the advice of his wicked counsellors?

65 "Now whom hast thou here and what hast thou in this land? Arise, let us go together to the land of Canaan, that we may be delivered from his hand, lest thou perish also through him in the latter days.

66 "Dost thou not know or hast thou not heard, that it is not through love that Nimrod giveth thee all this honor, but it is only for his benefit that he
bestoweth all this good upon thee? 67 And if he do
unto thee greater good than this, surely these are only vanities of the world, for wealth and riches cannot avail in the day of wrath and anger.

68 "Now therefore hearken to my voice, and let us arise and go to the land of Canaan, out of the reach of injury from Nimrod; and serve thou the Lord who created thee in the earth and it will be well with thee; and cast away all the vain things which thou pursuest." 69 And Abram ceased to speak, when Noah and his son Shem answered Terah, saying, "True is the word which Abram hath said unto thee."

70 And Terah hearkened to the voice of his son Abram, and Terah did all that Abram said, for this was from the Lord, that the king should not cause Abram's death.

31 Terah took Abram his son, Lot the son of Haran, his son's son, and Sarai his daughter-in-law, his son Abram's wife. They went from Ur of the Chaldees, to go into the land of Canaan. They came to Haran and lived there.

Jasher 13

1 And Terah took his son Abram and his grandson Lot, the son of Haran, and Sarai his daughter-in-law, the wife of his son Abram, and all the souls of his household and went with them from Ur Casdim to go to the land of Canaan. And when they came as far as the land of Haran they remained there, for it was exceedingly good land for pasture, and of sufficient extent for those who accompanied them.

32 The days of Terah were two hundred five years. Terah died in Haran.

2 And the people of the land of Haran saw that Abram was good and upright with God and men, and that the Lord his God was with him, and some of the people of the land of Haran came and joined Abram, and he taught them the instruction of the Lord and his ways; and these men remained with Abram in his house and they adhered to him.

3 And Abram remained in the land three years, and at the expiration of three years the Lord appeared to Abram and said to him; "I am the Lord who brought thee forth from Ur Casdim, and delivered thee from the hands of all thine enemies.

4 "And now therefore if thou wilt hearken to my voice and keep my commandments, my statutes and my laws, then will I cause thy enemies to fall before thee, and I will multiply thy seed like the stars of heaven, and I will send my blessing upon all the works of thy hands, and thou shalt lack nothing.

5 "Arise now, take thy wife and all belonging to
thee and go to the land of Canaan and remain
there, and I will there be unto thee for a God, and I
will bless thee." And Abram rose and took his wife
and all belonging to him, and he went to the land of
Canaan as the Lord had told him; and Abram was
fifty years old when he went from Haran.

6 And Abram came to the land of Canaan and dwelt
in the midst of the city, and he there pitched his
tent amongst the children of Canaan, inhabitants of
the land.

7 And the Lord appeared to Abram when he came
to the land of Canaan, and said to him, "This is the
land which I gave unto thee and to thy seed after
thee forever, and I will make thy seed like the stars
of heaven, and I will give unto thy seed for an
inheritance all the lands which thou seest. 8 And
Abram built an altar in the place where God had
spoken to him, and Abram there called upon the
name of the Lord."

9 At that time, at the end of three years of Abram's
dwelling in the land of Canaan, in that year Noah
died, which was the fifty-eighth year of the life of
Abram; and all the days that Noah lived were nine
hundred and fifty years and he died.

10 And Abram dwelt in the land of Canaan, he, his
wife, and all belonging to him, and all those that
accompanied him, together with those that joined
him from the people of the land; but Nahor,
Abram's brother, and Terah his father, and Lot the
son of Haran and all belonging to them dwelt in
Haran.

11 In the fifth year of Abram's dwelling in the land
of Canaan the people of Sodom and Gomorrah and
all the cities of the plain revolted from the power of
Chedorlaomer, king of Elam; for all the kings of the
cities of the plain had served Chedorlaomer for
twelve years, and given him a yearly tax, but in
those days in the thirteenth year, they rebelled
against him.

12 And in the tenth year of Abram's dwelling in the land of Canaan there was war between Nimrod king of Shinar and Chedorlaomer king of Elam, and Nimrod came to fight with Chedorlaomer and to subdue him. 13 For Chedorlaomer was at that time one of the princes of the hosts of Nimrod, and when all the people at the tower were dispersed and those that remained were also scattered upon the face of the earth, Chedorlaomer went to the land of Elam and reigned over it and rebelled against his lord.

14 And in those days when Nimrod saw that the cities of the plain had rebelled, he came with pride and anger to war with Chedorlaomer, and Nimrod assembled all his princes and subjects, about seven hundred thousand men, and went against Chedorlaomer, and Chedorlaomer went out to meet him with five thousand men, and they prepared for battle in the valley of Babel which is between Elam and Shinar.

15 And all those kings fought there, and Nimrod and his people were smitten before the people of Chedorlaomer, and there fell from Nimrod's men about six hundred thousand, and Mardon the king's son fell amongst them.

16 And Nimrod fled and returned in shame and disgrace to his land, and he was under subjection to Chedorlaomer for a long time, and Chedorlaomer returned to his land and sent princes of his host to the kings that dwelt around him, to Arioch king of Elasar, and to Tidal king of Goyim, and made a covenant with them, and they were all obedient to his commands.

17 And it was in the fifteenth year of Abram's dwelling in the land of Canaan, which is the seventieth year of the life of Abram, and the Lord appeared to Abram in that year and he said to him, "I am the Lord who brought thee out from Ur Casdim to give thee this land for an inheritance.

18 "Now therefore walk before me and be perfect
and keep my commands, for to thee and to thy
seed I will give this land for an inheritance, from the
river Mitzraim unto the great river Euphrates. 19
And thou shalt come to thy fathers in peace and in
good age, and the fourth generation shall return
here in this land and shall inherit it forever"; and
Abram built an altar, and he called upon the name
of the Lord who appeared to him, and he brought
up sacrifices upon the altar to the Lord.

20 At that time Abram returned and went to Haran to see his father and mother, and his father's household, and Abram and his wife and all belonging to him returned to Haran, and Abram dwelt in Haran five years.

21 And many of the people of Haran, about seventy-two men, followed Abram and Abram taught them the instruction of the Lord and his ways, and he taught them to know the Lord.

22 In those days the Lord appeared to Abram in Haran, and he said to him, "Behold, I spoke unto thee these twenty years back saying,

Genesis 12

1 Now Yahweh said to Abram, “Leave your country,
and your relatives, and your father’s house, and go
to the land that I will show you. 2 I will make of you
a great nation. I will bless you and make your name
great. You will be a blessing. 3 I will bless those who
bless you, and I will curse him who curses you. All
the families of the earth will be blessed through
you.”

23 "Go forth from thy land, from thy birth-place
and from thy father's house, to the land which I
have shown thee to give it to thee and to thy
children, for there in that land will I bless thee, and
make thee a great nation, and make thy name
great, and in thee shall the families of the earth be
blessed. 24 Now therefore arise, go forth from this
place, thou, thy wife, and all belonging to thee, also
every one born in thy house and all the souls thou
hast made in Haran, and bring them out with thee
from here, and rise to return to the land of
Canaan."

4 So Abram went, as Yahweh had told him. Lot went with him.

25 And Abram arose and took his wife Sarai and all
belonging to him and all that were born to him in
his house and the souls which they had made in
Haran, and they came out to go to the land of
Canaan. 26 And Abram went and returned to the
land of Canaan, according to the word of the Lord.
And Lot the son of his brother Haran went with him,

Abram was seventy-five years old when he departed from Haran.

and Abram was seventy-five years old when he went forth from Haran to return to the land of Canaan.

5 Abram took Sarai his wife, Lot his brother's son, all their possessions that they had gathered, and the people whom they had acquired in Haran, and they went to go into the land of Canaan. They entered into the land of Canaan.

27 And he came to the land of Canaan according to the word of the Lord to Abram, and he pitched his tent and he dwelt in the plain of Mamre, and with him was Lot his brother's son, and all belonging to him.

6 Abram passed through the land to the place of Shechem, to the oak of Moreh. The Canaanites were in the land, then.

7 Yahweh appeared to Abram and said, "I will give this land to your offspring." He built an altar there to Yahweh, who had appeared to him.

28 And the Lord again appeared to Abram and said, "To thy seed will I give this land"; and he there built an altar to the Lord who appeared to him, which is still to this day in the plains of Mamre.

8 He left from there to go to the mountain on the east of Bethel and pitched his tent, having Bethel on the west, and Ai on the east. There he built an altar to Yahweh and called on Yahweh's name. 9
Abram traveled, still going on toward the South.

Jasher 14

1 In those days there was in the land of Shinar a wise man who had understanding in all wisdom, and of a beautiful appearance, but he was poor and indigent; his name was Rikayon and he was hard set to support himself. 2 And he resolved to go to Egypt, to Oswiris the son of Anom king of Egypt, to show the king his wisdom; for perhaps he might find grace in his sight, to raise him up and give him maintenance; and Rikayon did so.

3 And when Rikayon came to Egypt he asked the inhabitants of Egypt concerning the king, and the inhabitants of Egypt told him the custom of the king of Egypt, for it was then the custom of the king of Egypt that he went from his royal palace and was seen abroad only one day in the year, and after that the king would return to his palace to remain there.

4 And on the day when the king went forth he passed judgment in the land, and every one having a suit came before the king that day to obtain his request. 5 And when Rikayon heard of the custom in Egypt and that he could not come into the presence of the king, he grieved greatly and was very sorrowful.

6 And in the evening Rikayon went out and found a house in ruins, formerly a bake house in Egypt, and he abode there all night in bitterness of soul and pinched with hunger, and sleep was removed from his eyes.

7 And Rikayon considered within himself what he should do in the town until the king made his appearance, and how he might maintain himself there.

8 And he rose in the morning and walked about, and met in his way those who sold vegetables and various sorts of seed with which they supplied the inhabitants.

9 And Rikayon wished to do the same in order to get a maintenance in the city, but he was unacquainted with the custom of the people, and he was like a blind man among them.

10 And he went and obtained vegetables to sell
them for his support, and the rabble assembled
about him and ridiculed him, and took his
vegetables from him and left him nothing. 11 And
he rose up from there in bitterness of soul, and
went sighing to the bake house in which he had
remained all the night before, and he slept there
the second night.

12 And on that night again he reasoned within
himself how he could save himself from starvation,
and he devised a scheme how to act. 13 And he
rose up in the morning and acted ingeniously, and
went and hired thirty strong men of the rabble,
carrying their war instruments in their hands, and
he led them to the top of the Egyptian sepulchre,
and he placed them there.

14 And he commanded them, saying, "Thus saith the king, Strengthen yourselves and be valiant men, and let no man be buried here until two hundred pieces of silver be given, and then he may be buried;" and those men did according to the order of Rikayon to the people of Egypt the whole of that year.

15 And in eight months time Rikayon and his men gathered great riches of silver and gold, and Rikayon took a great quantity of horses and other animals, and he hired more men, and he gave them horses and they remained with him.

16 And when the year came round, at the time the
king went forth into the town, all the inhabitants of
Egypt assembled together to speak to him
concerning the work of Rikayon and his men. 17
And the king went forth on the appointed day, and
all the Egyptians came before him and cried unto
him, saying,

18 "May the king live forever. What is this thing
thou doest in the town to thy servants, not to suffer
a dead body to be buried until so much silver and
gold be given? Was there ever the like unto this
done in the whole earth, from the days of former
kings yea even from the days of Adam, unto this
day, that the dead should not be buried only for a
set price?

19 "We know it to be the custom of kings to take a
yearly tax from the living, but thou dost not only do
this, but from the dead also thou exactest a tax day
by day. 20 Now, O king, we can no more bear this,
for the whole city is ruined on this account, and
dost thou not know it?"

21 And when the king heard all that they had
spoken he was very wroth, and his anger burned
within him at this affair, for he had known nothing
of it. 22 And the king said, "Who and where is he
that dares to do this wicked thing in my land
without my command? Surely you will tell me." 23
And they told him all the works of Rikayon and his
men, and the king's anger was aroused, and he
ordered Rikayon and his men to be brought before
him.

24 And Rikayon took about a thousand children, sons and daughters, and clothed them in silk and embroidery, and he set them upon horses and sent them to the king by means of his men, and he also took a great quantity of silver and gold and precious stones, and a strong and beautiful horse, as a present for the king, with which he came before the king and bowed down to the earth before him; and the king, his servants and all the inhabitants of Egypt wondered at the work of Rikayon, and they saw his riches and the present that he had brought to the king.

25 And it greatly pleased the king and he wondered at it; and when Rikayon sat before him the king asked him concerning all his works, and Rikayon spoke all his words wisely before the king, his servants and all the inhabitants of Egypt.

26 And when the king heard the words of Rikayon and his wisdom, Rikayon found grace in his sight, and he met with grace and kindness from all the servants of the king and from all the inhabitants of Egypt, on account of his wisdom and excellent speeches, and from that time they loved him exceedingly.

27 And the king answered and said to Rikayon, "Thy
name shall no more be called Rikayon but Pharaoh
shall be thy name, since thou didst exact a tax from
the dead; and he called his name Pharaoh." 28 And
the king and his subjects loved Rikayon for his
wisdom, and they consulted with all the inhabitants
of Egypt to make him prefect under the king. 29
And all the inhabitants of Egypt and its wise men
did so, and it was made a law in Egypt.

30 And they made Rikayon Pharaoh prefect under Oswiris king of Egypt, and Rikayon Pharaoh governed over Egypt, daily administering justice to the whole city, but Oswiris the king would judge the people of the land one day in the year, when he went out to make his appearance.

31 And Rikayon Pharaoh cunningly usurped the government of Egypt, and he exacted a tax from all the inhabitants of Egypt.

32 And all the inhabitants of Egypt greatly loved Rikayon Pharaoh, and they made a decree to call every king that should reign over them and their seed in Egypt, Pharaoh.

33 Therefore all the kings that reigned in Egypt from that time forward were called Pharaoh unto this day.

10 There was a famine in the land. Abram went down into Egypt to live as a foreigner there, for the famine was severe in the land.

11 When he had come near to enter Egypt, he said to Sarai his wife, “See now, I know that you are a beautiful woman to look at. 12 It will happen, when the Egyptians see you, that they will say, ‘This is his wife.’ They will kill me, but they will save you alive. 13 Please say that you are my sister, that it may be well with me for your sake, and that my soul may live because of you.”

Jasher 15

1 And in that year there was a heavy famine throughout the land of Canaan, and the inhabitants of the land could not remain on account of the famine for it was very grievous. 2 And Abram and all belonging to him rose and went down to Egypt on account of the famine, and when they were at the brook Mitzraim they remained there some time to rest from the fatigue of the road.

3 And Abram and Sarai were walking at the border of the brook Mitzraim, and Abram beheld his wife Sarai that she was very beautiful.

4 And Abram said to his wife Sarai, "Since God has created thee with such a beautiful countenance, I am afraid of the Egyptians lest they should slay me and take thee away, for the fear of God is not in these places. 5 Surely then thou shalt do this, Say thou art my sister to all that may ask thee, in order that it may be well with me, and that we may live and not be put to death."

6 And Abram commanded the same to all those that came with him to Egypt on account of the famine; also his nephew Lot he commanded, saying, "If the Egyptians ask thee concerning Sarai say she is the sister of Abram." 7 And yet with all these orders Abram did not put confidence in them, but he took Sarai and placed her in a chest and concealed it amongst their vessels, for Abram was greatly concerned about Sarai on account of the wickedness of the Egyptians.

8 And Abram and all belonging to him rose up from the brook Mitzraim and came to Egypt; and they had scarcely entered the gates of the city when the guards stood up to them saying, "Give tithe to the king from what you have, and then you may come into the town;" and Abram and those that were with him did so.

9 And Abram with the people that were with him came to Egypt, and when they came they brought the chest in which Sarai was concealed and the Egyptians saw the chest. 10 And the king's servants approached Abram, saying, "What hast thou here in this chest which we have not seen? Now open thou the chest and give tithe to the king of all that it contains."

11 And Abram said, "This chest I will not open, but all you demand upon it I will give." And Pharaoh's officers answered Abram, saying, "It is a chest of precious stones, give us the tenth thereof."

12 Abram said, "All that you desire I will give, but you must not open the chest." 13 And the king's officers pressed Abram, and they reached the chest and opened it with force, and they saw, and behold a beautiful woman was in the chest.

14 When Abram had come into Egypt, Egyptians saw that the woman was very beautiful. 15 The princes of Pharaoh saw her, and praised her to Pharaoh; and the woman was taken into Pharaoh's house.

14 And when the officers of the king beheld Sarai they were struck with admiration at her beauty, and all the princes and servants of Pharaoh assembled to see Sarai, for she was very beautiful. And the king's officers ran and told Pharaoh all that they had seen, and they praised Sarai to the king; and Pharaoh ordered her to be brought, and the woman came before the king. 15 And Pharaoh beheld Sarai and she pleased him exceedingly, and he was struck with her beauty, and the king rejoiced greatly on her account, and made presents to those who brought him the tidings concerning her. 16 And the woman was then brought to Pharaoh's house, and Abram grieved on account of his wife, and he prayed to the Lord to deliver her from the hands of Pharaoh.

17 And Sarai also prayed at that time and said, "O Lord God thou didst tell my Lord Abram to go from his land and from his father's house to the land of Canaan, and thou didst promise to do well with him if he would perform thy commands; now behold we have done that which thou didst command us, and we left our land and our families, and we went to a strange land and to a people whom we have not known before.

18 "And we came to this land to avoid the famine, and this evil accident has befallen me; now therefore, O Lord God, deliver us and save us from the hand of this oppressor, and do well with me for the sake of thy mercy."

19 And the Lord hearkened to the voice of Sarai, and the Lord sent an angel to deliver Sarai from the power of Pharaoh.

20 And the king came and sat before Sarai and
behold an angel of the Lord was standing over
them, and he appeared to Sarai and said to her, "Do
not fear, for the Lord has heard thy prayer." 21 And
the king approached Sarai and said to her, "What is
that man to thee who brought thee hither?" and
she said, "He is my brother."

16 He dealt well with Abram for her sake. He had sheep, cattle, male donkeys, male servants, female servants, female donkeys, and camels.

22 And the king said, "It is incumbent upon us to make him great, to elevate him and to do unto him all the good which thou shalt command us"; and at that time the king sent to Abram silver and gold and precious stones in abundance, together with cattle, men servants and maid servants; and the king ordered Abram to be brought, and he sat in the court of the king's house, and the king greatly exalted Abram on that night.

17 Yahweh afflicted Pharaoh and his house with great plagues because of Sarai, Abram's wife.

23 And the king approached to speak to Sarai, and
he reached out his hand to touch her, when the
angel smote him heavily, and he was terrified and
he refrained from reaching to her. 24 And when
the king came near to Sarai, the angel smote him to
the ground, and acted thus to him the whole night,
and the king was terrified. 25 And the angel on that
night smote heavily all the servants of the king, and
his whole household, on account of Sarai, and there
was a great lamentation that night amongst the
people of Pharaoh's house.

26 And Pharaoh, seeing the evil that befell him, said, "Surely on account of this woman has this thing happened to me", and he removed himself at some distance from her and spoke pleasing words to her.

27 And the king said to Sarai, "Tell me I pray thee concerning the man with whom thou camest here"; and Sarai said, "This man is my husband, and I said to thee that he was my brother for I was afraid, lest thou shouldst put him to death through wickedness."

28 And the king kept away from Sarai, and the plagues of the angel of the Lord ceased from him and his household; and Pharaoh knew that he was smitten on account of Sarai, and the king was greatly astonished at this.

18 Pharaoh called Abram and said, "What is this that you have done to me? Why didn't you tell me that she was your wife? 19 Why did you say, 'She is my sister,' so that I took her to be my wife? Now therefore, see your wife, take her, and go your way."

29 And in the morning the king called for Abram and said to him, "What is this thou hast done to me? Why didst thou say, 'She is my sister', owing to which I took her unto me for a wife, and this heavy plague has therefore come upon me and my household. 30 Now therefore here is thy wife, take her and go from our land lest we all die on her account." And Pharaoh took more cattle, men servants and maid servants, and silver and gold, to give to Abram, and he returned unto him Sarai his wife.

31 And the king took a maiden whom he begat by his concubines, and he gave her to Sarai for a handmaid. 32 And the king said to his daughter, "It is better for thee my daughter to be a handmaid in this man's house than to be mistress in my house, after we have beheld the evil that befell us on account of this woman."

20 Pharaoh commanded men concerning him, and they escorted him away with his wife and all that he had.

33 And Abram arose, and he and all belonging to him went away from Egypt; and Pharaoh ordered some of his men to accompany him and all that went with him.

Genesis 13

1 Abram went up out of Egypt—he, his wife, all that he had, and Lot with him—into the South. 2 Abram was very rich in livestock, in silver, and in gold. 3 He went on his journeys from the South even to Bethel, to the place where his tent had been at the beginning, between Bethel and Ai, 4 to the place of the altar, which he had made there at the first. There Abram called on Yahweh's name.

34 And Abram returned to the land of Canaan, to the place where he had made the altar, where he at first had pitched his tent.

5 Lot also, who went with Abram, had flocks, herds, and tents.

35 And Lot the son of Haran, Abram's brother, had a heavy stock of cattle, flocks and herds and tents, for the Lord was bountiful to them on account of Abram.

6 The land was not able to bear them, that they might live together; for their substance was great, so that they could not live together. 7 There was strife between the herdsmen of Abram's livestock and the herdsmen of Lot's livestock. The Canaanites and the Perizzites lived in the land at that time.

36 And when Abram was dwelling in the land the herdsmen of Lot quarrelled with the herdsmen of Abram, for their property was too great for them to remain together in the land, and the land could not bear them on account of their cattle.

37 And when Abram's herdsmen went to feed their flock they would not go into the fields of the people of the land, but the cattle of Lot's herdsmen did otherwise, for they were suffered to feed in the fields of the people of the land. 38 And the people of the land saw this occurrence daily, and they came to Abram and quarrelled with him on account of Lot's herdsmen.

39 And Abram said to Lot, "What is this thou art doing to me, to make me despicable to the inhabitants of the land, that thou orderest thy herdsman to feed thy cattle in the fields of other people? Dost thou not know that I am a stranger in this land amongst the children of Canaan, and why wilt thou do this unto me?"

40 And Abram quarrelled daily with Lot on account of this, but Lot would not listen to Abram, and he continued to do the same and the inhabitants of the land came and told Abram.

8 Abram said to Lot, "Please, let there be no strife between you and me, and between your herdsmen and my herdsmen; for we are relatives. 9 Isn't the whole land before you? Please separate yourself from me. If you go to the left hand, then I will go to the right. Or if you go to the right hand, then I will go to the left."

41 And Abram said unto Lot, "How long wilt thou be to me for a stumbling block with the inhabitants of the land? Now I beseech thee let there be no more quarrelling between us, for we are kinsmen. 42 But I pray thee separate from me, go and choose a place where thou mayest dwell with thy cattle and all belonging to thee, but Keep thyself at a distance from me, thou and thy household. 43 And be not afraid in going from me, for if any one do an injury to thee, let me know and I will avenge thy cause from him, only remove from me."

10 Lot lifted up his eyes, and saw all the plain of the Jordan, that it was well-watered everywhere, before Yahweh destroyed Sodom and Gomorrah, like the garden of Yahweh, like the land of Egypt, as you go to Zoar. 11 So Lot chose the Plain of the Jordan for himself. Lot traveled east, and they separated themselves the one from the other.

44 And when Abram had spoken all these words to Lot, then Lot arose and lifted up his eyes toward the plain of Jordan. 45 And he saw that the whole of this place was well watered, and good for man as well as affording pasture for the cattle. 46 And Lot went from Abram to that place, and he there pitched his tent and he dwelt in Sodom, and they were separated from each other.

12 Abram lived in the land of Canaan, and Lot lived in the cities of the plain, and moved his tent as far as Sodom. 13 Now the men of Sodom were exceedingly wicked and sinners against Yahweh.

14 Yahweh said to Abram, after Lot was separated from him, "Now, lift up your eyes, and look from the place where you are, northward and southward and eastward and westward, 15 for all the land which you see, I will give to you, and to your offspring forever. 16 I will make your offspring as the dust of the earth, so that if a man can number the dust of the earth, then your offspring may also be numbered. 17 Arise, walk through the land in its length and in its width; for I will give it to you."

18 Abram moved his tent, and came and lived by the oaks of Mamre, which are in Hebron, and built an altar there to Yahweh.

47 And Abram dwelt in the plain of Mamre, which is in Hebron, and he pitched his tent there, and Abram remained in that place many years.

Genesis 14

1 In the days of Amraphel, king of Shinar, Arioch, king of Ellasar, Chedorlaomer, king of Elam, and Tidal, king of Goiim,

Jasher 16

1 At that time Chedorlaomer king of Elam sent to all the neighboring kings, to Nimrod, king of Shinar who was then under his power, and to Tidal, king of Goyim, and to Arioch, king of Elasar, with whom he made a covenant, saying, "Come up to me and assist me, that we may smite all the towns of Sodom and its inhabitants, for they have rebelled against me these thirteen years." 2 And these four kings went up with all their camps, about eight hundred thousand men, and they went as they were, and smote every man they found in their road.

2 they made war with Bera, king of Sodom, and with Birsha, king of Gomorrah, Shinab, king of Admah, and Shemeber, king of Zeboiim, and the king of Bela (also called Zoar). 3 All these joined together in the valley of Siddim (also called the Salt Sea).

4 They served Chedorlaomer for twelve years, and in the thirteenth year, they rebelled.

5 In the fourteenth year Chedorlaomer came, and the kings who were with him, and struck the Rephaim in Ashteroth Karnaim, and the Zuzim in Ham, and the Emim in Shaveh Kiriathaim, 6 and the Horites in their Mount Seir, to El Paran, which is by the wilderness. 7 They returned, and came to En Mishpat (also called Kadesh), and struck all the country of the Amalekites, and also the Amorites, that lived in Hazazon Tamar.

3 And the five kings of Sodom and Gomorrah, Shinab king of Admah, Shemeber king of Zeboyim, Bera king of Sodom, Bersha king of Gomorrah, and Bela king of Zoar, went out to meet them, and they all joined together in the valley of Siddim.

8 The king of Sodom, and the king of Gomorrah,
and the king of Admah, and the king of Zeboiim,
and the king of Bela (also called Zoar) went out; and
they set the battle in array against them in the
valley of Siddim; 9 against Chedorlaomer king of
Elam, and Tidal king of Goiim, and Amraphel king of
Shinar, and Arioch king of Ellasar; four kings against
the five.

4 And these nine kings made war in the valley of
Siddim; and the kings of Sodom and Gomorrah
were smitten before the kings of Elam.

10 Now the valley of Siddim was full of tar pits; and
the kings of Sodom and Gomorrah fled, and some
fell there, and those who remained fled to the hills.

5 And the valley of Siddim was full of lime pits and
the kings of Elam pursued the kings of Sodom, and
the kings of Sodom with their camps fled and fell
into the lime pits, and all that remained went to the
mountain for safety, and the five kings of Elam
came after them and pursued them to the gates of
Sodom,

11 They took all the goods of Sodom and
Gomorrah, and all their food, and went their way.
12 They took Lot, Abram's brother's son, who lived
in Sodom, and his goods, and departed. 13 One
who had escaped came and told Abram, the
Hebrew. At that time, he lived by the oaks of
Mamre, the Amorite, brother of Eshcol, and brother
of Aner; and they were allies of Abram.

and they took all that there was in Sodom. 6 And
they plundered all the cities of Sodom and
Gomorrah, and they also took Lot, Abram's
brother's son, and his property, and they seized all
the goods of the cities of Sodom, and they went
away; and Unic, Abram's servant, who was in the
battle, saw this, and told Abram all that the kings
had done to the cities of Sodom, and that Lot was
taken captive by them.

14 When Abram heard that his relative was taken
captive, he led out his trained men, born in his
house, three hundred and eighteen, and pursued as
far as Dan. 15 He divided himself against them by
night, he and his servants, and struck them, and
pursued them to Hobah, which is on the left hand
of Damascus.

7 And Abram heard this, and he rose up with about
three hundred and eighteen men that were with
him, and he that night pursued these kings and
smote them, and they all fell before Abram and his
men, and there was none remaining but the four
kings who fled, and they went each his own road.

16 He brought back all the goods, and also brought
back his relative, Lot, and his goods, and the
women also, and the other people.

8 And Abram recovered all the property of Sodom,
and he also recovered Lot and his property, his
wives and little ones and all belonging to him, so
that Lot lacked nothing.

9 And when he returned from smiting these kings,
he and his men passed the valley of Siddim where
the kings had made war together.

17 The king of Sodom went out to meet him after
his return from the slaughter of Chedorlaomer and
the kings who were with him, at the valley of
Shaveh (that is, the King's Valley).

10 And Bera king of Sodom, and the rest of his men
that were with him, went out from the lime pits
into which they had fallen, to meet Abram and his
men.

Genesis 14

18 Melchizedek king of Salem brought out bread
and wine: and he was priest of God Most High. 19
He blessed him, and said, “Blessed be Abram of God
Most High, possessor of heaven and earth: 20 and
blessed be God Most High, who has delivered your
enemies into your hand.” Abram gave him a tenth
of all.

21 The king of Sodom said to Abram, “Give me the
people, and take the goods for yourself.”

22 Abram said to the king of Sodom, “I have lifted
up my hand to Yahweh, God Most High, possessor
of heaven and earth, 23 that I will not take a thread
nor a sandal strap nor anything that is yours, lest
you should say, ‘I have made Abram rich.’ 24 I will
accept nothing from you except that which the
young men have eaten, and the portion of the men
who went with me: Aner, Eshcol, and Mamre. Let
them take their portion.”

Jasher 16

11 And Adonizedek king of Jerusalem, the same was
Shem, went out with his men to meet Abram and
his people, with bread and wine, and they remained
together in the valley of Melech. 12 And
Adonizedek blessed Abram, and Abram gave him a
tenth from all that he had brought from the spoil of
his enemies, for Adonizedek was a priest before
God.

13 And all the kings of Sodom and Gomorrah who
were there, with their servants, approached Abram
and begged of him to return them their servants
whom he had made captive, and to take unto
himself all the property.

14 And Abram answered the kings of Sodom,
saying, "As the Lord liveth who created heaven and
earth, and who redeemed my soul from all
affliction, and who delivered me this day from my
enemies, and gave them into my hand, I will not
take anything belonging to you, that you may not
boast tomorrow, saying, 'Abram became rich from
our property that he saved.' 15 For the Lord my
God in whom I trust said unto me, Thou shalt lack
nothing, for I will bless thee in all the works of thy
hands.

16 "And now therefore behold, here is all belonging
to you, take it and go; as the Lord liveth I will not
take from you from a living soul down to a shoetie
or thread, excepting the expense of the food of
those who went out with me to battle, as also the
portions of the men who went with me, Anar,
Ashcol, and Mamre, they and their men, as well as
those also who had remained to watch the
baggage, they shall take their portion of the spoil."

17 And the kings of Sodom gave Abram according
to all that he had said, and they pressed him to take
of whatever he chose, but he would not. 18 And he
sent away the kings of Sodom and the remainder of
their men, and he gave them orders about Lot, and
they went to their respective places.

19 And Lot, his brother's son, he also sent away
with his property, and he went with them, and Lot
returned to his home, to Sodom, and Abram and his
people returned to their home to the plains of
Mamre, which is in Hebron.

Genesis 15

1 After these things Yahweh's word came to Abram in a vision, saying, "Don't be afraid, Abram. I am your shield, your exceedingly great reward."

20 At that time the Lord again appeared to Abram in Hebron, and he said to him, "Do not fear, thy reward is very great before me,

2 Abram said, "Lord* Yahweh, what will you give me, since I go childless, and he who will inherit my estate is Eliezer of Damascus?" 3 Abram said, "Behold, to me you have given no children: and, behold, one born in my house is my heir." 4 Behold, Yahweh's word came to him, saying, "This man will not be your heir, but he who will come out of your own body will be your heir."

5 Yahweh brought him outside, and said, "Look now toward the sky, and count the stars, if you are able to count them." He said to Abram, "So will your offspring be." 6 He believed in Yahweh, who credited it to him for righteousness. 7 He said to Abram, "I am Yahweh who brought you out of Ur of the Chaldees, to give you this land to inherit it."

"for I will not leave thee, until I shall have multiplied thee, and blessed thee and made thy seed like the stars in heaven, which cannot be measured nor numbered. 21 And I will give unto thy seed all these lands that thou seest with thine eyes, to them will I give them for an inheritance forever, only be strong and do not fear, walk before me and be perfect."

8 He said, "Lord Yahweh, how will I know that I will inherit it?" 9 He said to him, "Bring me a heifer three years old, a female goat three years old, a ram three years old, a turtledove, and a young pigeon." 10 He brought him all these, and divided them in the middle, and laid each half opposite the other; but he didn't divide the birds. 11 The birds of prey came down on the carcasses, and Abram drove them away.

12 When the sun was going down, a deep sleep fell on Abram. Now terror and great darkness fell on him.

13 He said to Abram, "Know for sure that your offspring will live as foreigners in a land that is not theirs, and will serve them. They will afflict them four hundred years. 14 I will also judge that nation, whom they will serve. Afterward they will come out with great wealth, 15 but you will go to your fathers in peace. You will be buried at a good old age. 16 In the fourth generation they will come here again, for the iniquity of the Amorite is not yet full."

17 It came to pass that, when the sun went down,
and it was dark, behold, a smoking furnace, and a
flaming torch passed between these pieces. 18 In
that day Yahweh made a covenant with Abram,
saying, "I have given this land to your offspring,
from the river of Egypt to the great river, the river
Euphrates:

19 the Kenites, the Kenizzites, the Kadmonites, 20
the Hittites, the Perizzites, the Rephaim, 21 the
Amorites, the Canaanites, the Girgashites, and the
Jebusites."

22 And in the seventy-eighth year of the life of Abram, in that year died Reu, the son of Peleg, and all the days of Reu were two hundred and thirty-nine years, and he died.

Genesis 16

1 Now Sarai, Abram's wife, bore him no children.

23 And Sarai, the daughter of Haran, Abram's wife, was still barren in those days; she did not bear to Abram either son or daughter.

24 And when she saw that she bare no children she took her handmaid Hagar, whom Pharaoh had given her, and she gave her to Abram her husband for a wife.

25 For Hagar learned all the ways of Sarai as Sarai taught her, she was not in any way deficient in following her good ways.

She had a servant, an Egyptian, whose name was
Hagar. 2 Sarai said to Abram, "See now, Yahweh has
restrained me from bearing. Please go in to my
servant. It may be that I will obtain children by her."

26 And Sarai said to Abram, "Behold here is my handmaid Hagar, go to her that she may bring forth upon my knees, that I may also obtain children through her."

Abram listened to the voice of Sarai. 3 Sarai,
Abram's wife, took Hagar the Egyptian, her servant,
after Abram had lived ten years in the land of
Canaan, and gave her to Abram her husband to be
his wife. 4 He went in to Hagar, and she conceived.

27 And at the end of ten years of Abram's dwelling
in the land of Canaan, which is the eighty-fifth year
of Abram's life, Sarai gave Hagar unto him. 28 And
Abram hearkened to the voice of his wife Sarai, and
he took his handmaid Hagar and Abram came to
her and she conceived.

When she saw that she had conceived, her mistress was despised in her eyes.

29 And when Hagar saw that she had conceived she rejoiced greatly, and her mistress was despised in her eyes,

and she said within herself, "This can only be that I
am better before God than Sarai my mistress, for all
the days that my mistress has been with my lord,
she did not conceive, but me the Lord has caused in
so short a time to conceive by him." 30 And when
Sarai saw that Hagar had conceived by Abram, Sarai
was jealous of her handmaid, and Sarai said within
herself, "This is surely nothing else but that she
must be better than I am."

5 Sarai said to Abram, “This wrong is your fault. I gave my servant into your bosom, and when she saw that she had conceived, I was despised in her eyes. Yahweh judge between me and you.”

31 And Sarai said unto Abram, "My wrong be upon
thee, for at the time when thou didst pray before
the Lord for children why didst thou not pray on my
account, that the Lord should give me seed from
thee? 32 And when I speak to Hagar in thy
presence, she despiseth my words, because she has
conceived, and thou wilt say nothing to her; may
the Lord judge between me and thee for what thou
hast done to me."

6 But Abram said to Sarai, “Behold, your maid is in your hand. Do to her whatever is good in your eyes.” Sarai dealt harshly with her, and she fled from her face.

33 And Abram said to Sarai, "Behold thy handmaid is in thy hand, do unto her as it may seem good in thy eyes"; and Sarai afflicted her, and Hagar fled from her to the wilderness.

7 Yahweh’s angel found her by a fountain of water
in the wilderness, by the fountain on the way to
Shur. 8 He said, “Hagar, Sarai’s servant, where did
you come from? Where are you going?” She said, “I
am fleeing from the face of my mistress Sarai.” 9
Yahweh’s angel said to her, “Return to your
mistress, and submit yourself under her hands.” 10
Yahweh’s angel said to her, “I will greatly multiply
your offspring, that they will not be numbered for
multitude.”

34 And an angel of the Lord found her in the place where she had fled, by a well, and he said to her, "Do not fear, for I will multiply thy seed, for thou shalt bear a son and thou shalt call his name Ishmael; now then return to Sarai thy mistress, and submit thyself under her hands."

11 Yahweh’s angel said to her, “Behold, you are
with child, and will bear a son. You shall call his
name Ishmael, because Yahweh has heard your
affliction. 12 He will be like a wild donkey among
men. His hand will be against every man, and every
man’s hand against him. He will live opposite all of
his brothers.”

13 She called the name of Yahweh who spoke to her, “You are a God who sees,” for she said, “Have I even stayed alive after seeing him?”

14 Therefore the well was called Beer Lahai Roi. Behold, it is between Kadesh and Bered.

35 And Hagar called the place of that well Beer-lahai-roi, it is between Kadesh and the wilderness of Bered.

15 Hagar bore a son for Abram. Abram called the
name of his son, whom Hagar bore, Ishmael. 16
Abram was eighty-six years old when Hagar bore
Ishmael to Abram.

36 And Hagar at that time returned to her master's house, and at the end of days Hagar bare a son to Abram, and Abram called his name Ishmael; and Abram was eighty-six years old when he begat him.

Jasher 17

1 And in those days, in the ninety-first year of the life of Abram, the children of Chittim made war with the children of Tubal, for when the Lord had scattered the sons of men upon the face of the earth, the children of Chittim went and embodied themselves in the plain of Canopia, and they built themselves cities there and dwelt by the river Tibreu.

2 And the children of Tubal dwelt in Tuscanah, and their boundaries reached the river Tibreu, and the children of Tubal built a city in Tuscanan, and they called the name Sabinah, after the name of Sabinah son of Tubal their father, and they dwelt there unto this day.

3 And it was at that time the children of Chittim made war with the children of Tubal, and the children of Tubal were smitten before the children of Chittim, and the children of Chittim caused three hundred and seventy men to fall from the children of Tubal.

4 And at that time the children of Tubal swore to
the children of Chittim, saying, "You shall not
intermarry amongst us, and no man shall give his
daughter to any of the sons of Chittim." 5 For all
the daughters of Tubal were in those days fair, for
no women were then found in the whole earth so
fair as the daughters of Tubal.

6 And all who delighted in the beauty of women went to the daughters of Tubal and took wives from them, and the sons of men, kings and princes, who greatly delighted in the beauty of women, took wives in those days from the daughters of Tubal.

7 And at the end of three years after the children of Tubal had sworn to the children of Chittim not to give them their daughters for wives, about twenty men of the children of Chittim went to take some of the daughters of Tubal, but they found none. 8 For the children of Tubal kept their oaths not to intermarry with them, and they would not break their oaths.

9 And in the days of harvest the children of Tubal went into their fields to get in their harvest, when the young men of Chittim assembled and went to the city of Sabinah, and each man took a young woman from the daughters of Tubal, and they came to their cities.

10 And the children of Tubal heard of it and they went to make war with them, and they could not prevail over them, for the mountain was exceedingly high from them, and when they saw they could not prevail over them they returned to their land.

11 And at the revolution of the year the children of Tubal went and hired about ten thousand men from those cities that were near them, and they went to war with the children of Chittim.

12 And the children of Tubal went to war with the children of Chittim, to destroy their land and to distress them, and in this engagement the children of Tubal prevailed over the children of Chittim, and the children of Chittim, seeing that they were greatly distressed, lifted up the children which they had had by the daughters of Tubal, upon the wall which had been built, to be before the eyes of the children of Tubal.

13 And the children of Chittim said to them, "Have you come to make war with your own sons and daughters, and have we not been considered your flesh and bones from that time till now?" 14 And when the children of Tubal heard this they ceased to make war with the children of Chittim, and they went away. 15 And they returned to their cities, and the children of Chittim at that time assembled and built two cities by the sea, and they called one Purtu and the other Ariza.

Genesis 17

1 When Abram was ninety-nine years old, Yahweh appeared to Abram, and said to him, "I am God Almighty. Walk before me, and be blameless. 2 I will make my covenant between me and you, and will multiply you exceedingly."

16 And Abram the son of Terah was then ninety-nine years old. 17 At that time the Lord appeared to him and he said to him, "I will make my covenant between me and thee, and I will greatly multiply thy seed,

3 Abram fell on his face. God talked with him, saying, 4 "As for me, behold, my covenant is with you. You will be the father of a multitude of nations.

5 Your name will no more be called Abram, but your name will be Abraham;

[17:19 And now therefore thy name shall no more be called Abram but Abraham,]

for I have made you the father of a multitude of nations. 6 I will make you exceedingly fruitful, and I will make nations of you. Kings will come out of you.

[17:20 For I will bless you both, and I will multiply your seed after you that you shall become a great nation, and kings shall come forth from you.]

7 I will establish my covenant between me and you and your offspring after you throughout their generations for an everlasting covenant, to be a God to you and to your offspring after you. 8 I will give to you, and to your offspring after you, the land where you are traveling, all the land of Canaan, for an everlasting possession. I will be their God."

9 God said to Abraham, "As for you, you will keep my covenant, you and your offspring after you throughout their generations.

10 This is my covenant, which you shall keep, between me and you and your offspring after you. Every male among you shall be circumcised. 11 You shall be circumcised in the flesh of your foreskin. It will be a token of the covenant between me and you. 12 He who is eight days old will be circumcised among you, every male throughout your generations, he who is born in the house, or bought with money from any foreigner who is not of your offspring. 13 He who is born in your house, and he who is bought with your money, must be circumcised. My covenant will be in your flesh for an everlasting covenant.

and this is the covenant which I make between me and thee, that every male child be circumcised, thou and thy seed after thee. 18 At eight days old shall it be circumcised, and this covenant shall be in your flesh for an everlasting covenant.

14 The uncircumcised male who is not circumcised in the flesh of his foreskin, that soul shall be cut off from his people. He has broken my covenant."

[Genesis 17:5b Your name will no more be called Abram, but your name will be Abraham;]

19 And now therefore thy name shall no more be called Abram but Abraham,

15 God said to Abraham, "As for Sarai your wife, you shall not call her name Sarai, but her name will be Sarah.

and thy wife shall no more be called Sarai but Sarah.

16 I will bless her, and moreover I will give you a son by her. Yes, I will bless her, and she will be a mother of nations. Kings of peoples will come from her."

20 For I will bless you both, and I will multiply your seed after you that you shall become a great nation, and kings shall come forth from you.

17 Then Abraham fell on his face, and laughed, and
said in his heart, "Will a child be born to him who is
one hundred years old? Will Sarah, who is ninety
years old, give birth?" 18 Abraham said to God, "Oh
that Ishmael might live before you!"

19 God said, "No, but Sarah, your wife, will bear
you a son. You shall call his name Isaac. I will
establish my covenant with him for an everlasting
covenant for his offspring after him. 20 As for
Ishmael, I have heard you. Behold, I have blessed
him, and will make him fruitful, and will multiply
him exceedingly. He will become the father of
twelve princes, and I will make him a great nation.
21 But my covenant I establish with Isaac, whom
Sarah will bear to you at this set time next year."

22 When he finished talking with him, God went up from Abraham.

23 Abraham took Ishmael his son, all who were born in his house, and all who were bought with his money; every male among the men of Abraham's house, and circumcised the flesh of their foreskin in the same day, as God had said to him.

Jasher 18

1 And Abraham rose and did all that God had ordered him, and he took the men of his household and those bought with his money, and he circumcised them as the Lord had commanded him.

24 Abraham was ninety-nine years old, when he was circumcised in the flesh of his foreskin.

25 Ishmael, his son, was thirteen years old when he was circumcised in the flesh of his foreskin.

2 And there was not one left whom he did not circumcise, and Abraham and his son Ishmael were circumcised in the flesh of their foreskin; thirteen years old was Ishmael when he was circumcised in the flesh of his foreskin.

26 In the same day both Abraham and Ishmael, his
son, were circumcised. 27 All the men of his house,
those born in the house, and those bought with
money from a foreigner, were circumcised with
him.

Genesis 18

1 Yahweh appeared to him by the oaks of Mamre, as he sat in the tent door in the heat of the day. 2 He lifted up his eyes and looked, and saw that three men stood opposite him. When he saw them, he ran to meet them from the tent door, and bowed himself to the earth,

3 And in the third day Abraham went out of his tent and sat at the door to enjoy the heat of the sun, during the pain of his flesh. 4 And the Lord appeared to him in the plain of Mamre, and sent three of his ministering angels to visit him, and he was sitting at the door of the tent, and he lifted his eyes and saw, and lo three men were coming from a distance, and he rose up and ran to meet them, and he bowed down to them and brought them into his house.

3 and said, "My lord, if now I have found favor in your sight, please don't go away from your servant. 4 Now let a little water be fetched, wash your feet, and rest yourselves under the tree. 5 I will get a morsel of bread so you can refresh your heart. After that you may go your way, now that you have come to your servant." They said, "Very well, do as you have said."

5 And he said to them, "If now I have found favor in your sight, turn in and eat a morsel of bread;" and he pressed them, and they turned in and he gave them water and they washed their feet, and he placed them under a tree at the door of the tent.

6 Abraham hurried into the tent to Sarah, and said, "Quickly prepare three seahs of fine meal, knead it, and make cakes." 7 Abraham ran to the herd, and fetched a tender and good calf, and gave it to the servant. He hurried to dress it. 8 He took butter, milk, and the calf which he had dressed, and set it before them. He stood by them under the tree, and they ate.

6 And Abraham ran and took a calf, tender and good, and he hastened to kill it, and gave it to his servant Eliezer to dress. 7 And Abraham came to Sarah into the tent, and he said to her, "Make ready quickly three measures of fine meal, knead it and make cakes to cover the pot containing the meat," and she did so. 8 And Abraham hastened and brought before them butter and milk, beef and mutton, and gave it before them to eat before the flesh of the calf was sufficiently done, and they did eat.

9 They asked him, "Where is Sarah, your wife?" He said, "See, in the tent."

10 He said, "I will certainly return to you when the season comes round. Behold, Sarah your wife will have a son."

9 And when they had done eating one of them said to him, "I will return to thee according to the time of life, and Sarah thy wife shall have a son."

Sarah heard in the tent door, which was behind him. 11 Now Abraham and Sarah were old, well advanced in age. Sarah had passed the age of childbearing. 12 Sarah laughed within herself, saying, "After I have grown old will I have pleasure, my lord being old also?"

13 Yahweh said to Abraham, "Why did Sarah laugh,
saying, 'Will I really bear a child, yet I am old?' 14 Is
anything too hard for Yahweh? At the set time I will
return to you, when the season comes round, and
Sarah will have a son." 15 Then Sarah denied it,
saying, "I didn't laugh," for she was afraid. He said,
"No, but you did laugh."

10 And the men afterward departed and went their ways, to the places to which they were sent.

11 In those days all the people of Sodom and Gomorrah, and of the whole five cities, were exceedingly wicked and sinful against the Lord and they provoked the Lord with their abominations, and they strengthened in aging abominably and scornfully before the Lord, and their wickedness and crimes were in those days great before the Lord.

12 And they had in their land a very extensive valley, about half a day's walk, and in it there were fountains of water and a great deal of herbage surrounding the water.

13 And all the people of Sodom and Gomorrah went there four times in the year, with their wives and children and all belonging to them, and they rejoiced there with timbrels and dances.

14 And in the time of rejoicing they would all rise and lay hold of their neighbor's wives, and some, the virgin daughters of their neighbors, and they enjoyed them, and each man saw his wife and daughter in the hands of his neighbor and did not say a word.

15 And they did so from morning to night, and they afterward returned home each man to his house and each woman to her tent; so they always did four times in the year.

16 Also when a stranger came into their cities and brought goods which he had purchased with a view to dispose of there, the people of these cities would assemble, men, women and children, young and old, and go to the man and take his goods by force, giving a little to each man until there was an end to all the goods of the owner which he had brought into the land.

17 And if the owner of the goods quarreled with them, saying, "What is this work which you have done to me," then they would approach to him one by one, and each would show him the little which he took and taunt him, saying, "I only took that little which thou didst give me;" and when he heard this from them all, he would arise and go from them in sorrow and bitterness of soul, when they would all arise and go after him, and drive him out of the city with great noise and tumult.

18 And there was a man from the country of Elam who was leisurely going on the road, seated upon his ass, which carried a fine mantle of divers colors, and the mantle was bound with a cord upon the ass.

19 And the man was on his journey passing through
the street of Sodom when the sun set in the
evening, and he remained there in order to abide
during the night, but no one would let him into his
house; and at that time there was in Sodom a
wicked and mischievous man, one skillful to do evil,
and his name was Hedad. 20 And he lifted up his
eyes and saw the traveler in the street of the city,
and he came to him and said, "Whence comest
thou and whither dost thou go?"

21 And the man said to him, "I am traveling from Hebron to Elam where I belong, and as I passed the sun set and no one would suffer me to enter his house, though I had bread and water and also straw and provender for my ass, and am short of nothing."

22 And Hedad answered and said to him, "All that
thou shalt want shall be supplied by me, but in the
street thou shalt not abide all night." 23 And Hedad
brought him to his house, and he took off the
mantle from the ass with the cord, and brought
them to his house, and he gave the ass straw and
provender whilst the traveler ate and drank in
Hedad's house, and he abode there that night.

24 And in the morning the traveler rose up early to continue his journey, when Hedad said to him, "Wait, comfort thy heart with a morsel of bread and then go," and the man did so; and he remained with him, and they both ate and drank together during the day, when the man rose up to go.

25 And Hedad said to him, "Behold now the day is declining, thou hadst better remain all night that thy heart may be comforted;" and he pressed him so that he tarried there all night, and on the second day he rose up early to go away, when Hedad pressed him, saying, "Comfort thy heart with a morsel of bread and then go," and he remained and ate with him also the second day, and then the man rose up to continue his journey.

26 And Hedad said to him, "Behold now the day is declining, remain with me to comfort thy heart and in the morning rise up early and go thy way."

27 And the man would not remain, but rose and saddled his ass, and whilst he was saddling his ass the wife of Hedad said to her husband, "Behold this man has remained with us for two days eating and drinking and he has given us nothing, and now shall he go away from us without giving anything?" and Hedad said to her, "Be silent."

28 And the man saddled his ass to go, and he asked Hedad to give him the cord and mantle to tie it
upon the ass. 29 And Hedad said to him, "What
sayest thou?" And he said to him, "That thou my lord shalt give me the cord and the mantle made with divers colors which thou didst conceal with thee in thy house to take care of it."

30 And Hedad answered the man, saying, "This is the interpretation of thy dream, the cord which thou didst see, means that thy life will be lengthened out like a cord, and having seen the mantle colored with all sorts of colors, means that thou shalt have a vineyard in which thou wilt plant trees of all fruits."

31 And the traveler answered, saying, "Not so my lord, for I was awake when I gave thee the cord and also a mantle woven with different colors, which thou didst take off the ass to put them by for me;" and Hedad answered and said, "Surely I have told thee the interpretation of thy dream and it is a good dream, and this is the interpretation thereof.
32 Now the sons of men give me four pieces of silver, which is my charge for interpreting dreams, and of thee only I require three pieces of silver."

33 And the man was provoked at the words of Hedad, and he cried bitterly, and he brought Hedad to Serak judge of Sodom.

34 And the man laid his cause before Serak the judge, when Hedad replied, saying, "It is not so, but thus the matter stands;" and the judge said to the traveler, "This man Hedad telleth thee truth, for he is famed in the cities for the accurate interpretation of dreams."

35 And the man cried at the word of the judge, and he said, "Not so my Lord, for it was in the day that I gave him the cord and mantle which was upon the ass, in order to put them by in his house;" and they both disputed before the judge, the one saying, "Thus the matter was," and the other declaring otherwise.

36 And Hedad said to the man, "Give me four pieces of silver that I charge for my interpretations of dreams; I will not make any allowance; and give me the expense of the four meals that thou didst eat in my house."

37 And the man said to Hedad, "Truly I will pay thee for what I ate in thy house, only give me the cord and mantle which thou didst conceal in thy house."

38 And Hedad replied before the judge and said to the man, "Did I not tell thee the interpretation of thy dream? the cord means that thy days shall be prolonged like a cord, and the mantle, that thou wilt have a vineyard in which thou wilt plant all kinds of fruit trees.

39 "This is the proper interpretation of thy dream, now give me the four pieces of silver that I require as a compensation, for I will make thee no allowance."

40 And the man cried at the words of Hedad and they both quarreled before the judge, and the judge gave orders to his servants, who drove them rashly from the house.

41 And they went away quarreling from the judge, when the people of Sodom heard them, and they gathered about them and they exclaimed against the stranger, and they drove him rashly from the
city. 42 And the man continued his journey upon his ass with bitterness of soul, lamenting and
weeping. 43 And whilst he was going along he wept at what had happened to him in the corrupt city of Sodom.

Jasher 19

1 And the cities of Sodom had four judges to four cities, and these were their names, Serak in the city of Sodom, Sharkad in Gomorrah, Zabnac in Admah,
and Menon in Zeboyim. 2 And Eliezer Abraham's servant applied to them different names, and he converted Serak to Shakra, Sharkad to Shakrura, Zebnac to Kezobim, and Menon to Matzlodin.

3 And by desire of their four judges the people of Sodom and Gomorrah had beds erected in the streets of the cities, and if a man came to these places they laid hold of him and brought him to one of their beds, and by force made him to lie in them.

4 And as he lay down, three men would stand at his head and three at his feet, and measure him by the length of the bed, and if the man was less than the bed these six men would stretch him at each end, and when he cried out to them they would not
answer him. 5 And if he was longer than the bed they would draw together the two sides of the bed at each end, until the man had reached the gates of
death. 6 And if he continued to cry out to them, they would answer him, saying, "Thus shall it be done to a man that cometh into our land."

7 And when men heard all these things that the people of the cities of Sodom did, they refrained from coming there.

8 And when a poor man came to their land they would give him silver and gold, and cause a proclamation in the whole city not to give him a morsel of bread to eat, and if the stranger should remain there some days, and die from hunger, not having been able to obtain a morsel of bread, then at his death all the people of the city would come and take their silver and gold which they had given to him.

9 And those that could recognize the silver or gold which they had given him took it back, and at his death they also stripped him of his garments, and they would fight about them, and he that prevailed over his neighbor took them.

10 They would after that carry him and bury him under some of the shrubs in the deserts; so they did all the days to any one that came to them and died in their land.

11 And in the course of time Sarah sent Eliezer to
Sodom, to see Lot and inquire after his welfare. 12
And Eliezer went to Sodom, and he met a man of
Sodom fighting with a stranger, and the man of
Sodom stripped the poor man of all his clothes and
went away. 13 And this poor man cried to Eliezer
and supplicated his favor on account of what the
man of Sodom had done to him. 14 And he said to
him, "Why dost thou act thus to the poor man who
came to thy land?"

15 And the man of Sodom answered Eliezer, saying, "Is this man thy brother, or have the people of Sodom made thee a judge this day, that thou speakest about this man?"

16 And Eliezer strove with the man of Sodom on account of the poor man, and when Eliezer approached to recover the poor man's clothes from the man of Sodom, he hastened and with a stone smote Eliezer in the forehead.

17 And the blood flowed copiously from Eliezer's forehead, and when the man saw the blood he caught hold of Eliezer, saying, "Give me my hire for having rid thee of this bad blood that was in thy forehead, for such is the custom and the law in our land."

18 And Eliezer said to him, "Thou hast wounded me and requirest me to pay thee thy hire;" and Eliezer would not hearken to the words of the man of Sodom.

19 And the man laid hold of Eliezer and brought him to Shakra the judge of Sodom for judgment.
20 And the man spoke to the judge, saying, "I beseech thee my lord, thus has this man done, for I smote him with a stone that the blood flowed from his forehead, and he is unwilling to give me my hire."

21 And the judge said to Eliezer, "This man speaketh truth to thee, give him his hire, for this is the custom in our land;" and Eliezer heard the words of the judge, and he lifted up a stone and smote the judge, and the stone struck on his forehead, and the blood flowed copiously from the forehead of the judge, and Eliezer said, "If this then is the custom in your land give thou unto this man what I should have given him, for this has been thy decision, thou didst decree it."
22 And Eliezer left the man of Sodom with the judge, and he went away.

23 And when the kings of Elam had made war with the kings of Sodom, the kings of Elam captured all the property of Sodom, and they took Lot captive, with his property, and when it was told to Abraham he went and made war with the kings of Elam, and he recovered from their hands all the property of Lot as well as the property of Sodom.

24 At that time the wife of Lot bare him a daughter, and he called her name Paltith, saying, "Because God had delivered him and his whole household from the kings of Elam;" and Paltith daughter of Lot grew up, and one of the men of Sodom took her for a wife.

25 And a poor man came into the city to seek a maintenance, and he remained in the city some days, and all the people of Sodom caused a proclamation of their custom not to give this man a morsel of bread to eat, until he dropped dead upon the earth, and they did so.

26 And Paltith the daughter of Lot saw this man lying in the streets starved with hunger, and no one would give him any thing to keep him alive, and he was just upon the point of death. 27 And her soul was filled with pity on account of the man, and she fed him secretly with bread for many days, and the soul of this man was revived.

28 For when she went forth to fetch water she would put the bread in the water pitcher, and when she came to the place where the poor man was, she took the bread from the pitcher and gave it him to eat; so she did many days. 29 And all the people of Sodom and Gomorrah wondered how this man could bear starvation for so many days.

30 And they said to each other, "This can only be that he eats and drinks, for no man can bear starvation for so many days or live as this man has, without even his countenance changing;" and three men concealed themselves in a place where the poor man was stationed, to know who it was that brought him bread to eat.

31 And Paltith daughter of Lot went forth that day to fetch water, and she put bread into her pitcher of water, and she went to draw water by the poor man's place, and she took out the bread from the pitcher and gave it to the poor man and he ate it.

32 And the three men saw what Paltith did to the poor man, and they said to her, "It is thou then who hast supported him, and therefore has he not starved, nor changed in appearance nor died like the rest."

33 And the three men went out of the place in which they were concealed, and they seized Paltith and the bread which was in the poor man's hand. 34 And they took Paltith and brought her before their judges, and they said to them,

"Thus did she do, and it is she who supplied the poor man with bread, therefore did he not die all this time; now therefore declare to us the punishment due to this woman for having transgressed our law." 35 And the people of Sodom and Gomorrah assembled and kindled a fire in the street of the city, and they took the woman and cast her into the fire and she was burned to ashes.

36 And in the city of Admah there was a woman to whom they did the like. 37 For a traveler came into the city of Admah to abide there all night, with the intention of going home in the morning, and he sat opposite the door of the house of the young woman's father, to remain there, as the sun had set when be had reached that place; and the young woman saw him sitting by the door of the house.

38 And he asked her for a drink of water and she said to him, "Who art thou?" and he said to her, "I was this day going on the road, and reached here when the sun set, so I will abide here all night, and in the morning I will arise early and continue my journey." 39 And the young woman went into the house and fetched the man bread and water to eat and drink.

40 And this affair became known to the people of Admah, and they assembled and brought the young woman before the judges, that they should judge her for this act. 41 And the judge said, "The judgment of death must pass upon this woman because she transgressed our law, and this therefore is the decision concerning her."

42 And the people of those cities assembled and brought out the young woman, and anointed her with honey from head to foot, as the judge had decreed, and they placed her before a swarm of bees which were then in their hives, and the bees flew upon her and stung her that her whole body was swelled. 43 And the young woman cried out on account of the bees, but no one took notice of her or pitied her, and her cries ascended to heaven.

44 And the Lord was provoked at this and at all the works of the cities of Sodom, for they had abundance of food, and had tranquility amongst them, and still would not sustain the poor and the needy, and in those days their evil doings and sins became great before the Lord. 45 And the Lord sent for two of the angels that had come to Abraham's house, to destroy Sodom and its cities.

16 The men rose up from there, and looked toward Sodom.

46 And the angels rose up from the door of Abraham's tent, after they had eaten and drunk,

Abraham went with them to see them on their way.
17 Yahweh said, "Will I hide from Abraham what I
do, 18 since Abraham will surely become a great
and mighty nation, and all the nations of the earth
will be blessed in him? 19 For I have known him, to
the end that he may command his children and his
household after him, that they may keep the way of
Yahweh, to do righteousness and justice; to the end
that Yahweh may bring on Abraham that which he
has spoken of him."

20 Yahweh said, "Because the cry of Sodom and
Gomorrah is great, and because their sin is very
grievous, 21 I will go down now, and see whether
their deeds are as bad as the reports which have
come to me. If not, I will know."

22 The men turned from there, and went toward
Sodom, but Abraham stood yet before Yahweh. 23
Abraham came near, and said, "Will you consume
the righteous with the wicked? 24 What if there are
fifty righteous within the city? Will you consume
and not spare the place for the fifty righteous who
are in it? 25 Be it far from you to do things like that,
to kill the righteous with the wicked, so that the
righteous should be like the wicked. May that be far
from you. Shouldn't the Judge of all the earth do
right?"

26 Yahweh said, "If I find in Sodom fifty righteous
within the city, then I will spare the whole place for
their sake."

27 Abraham answered, "See now, I have taken it on
myself to speak to the Lord, although I am dust and
ashes. 28 What if there will lack five of the fifty
righteous? Will you destroy all the city for lack of
five?" He said, "I will not destroy it, if I find forty-
five there."

29 He spoke to him yet again, and said, "What if
there are forty found there?" He said, "I will not do
it for the forty's sake."

30 He said, "Oh don't let the Lord be angry, and I
will speak. What if there are thirty found there?"
He said, "I will not do it, if I find thirty there."

31 He said, "See now, I have taken it on myself to
speak to the Lord. What if there are twenty found
there?" He said, "I will not destroy it for the
twenty's sake."

32 He said, "Oh don't let the Lord be angry, and I will speak just once more. What if ten are found there?" He said, "I will not destroy it for the ten's sake."

33 Yahweh went his way, as soon as he had finished communing with Abraham, and Abraham returned to his place.

Genesis 19

1 The two angels came to Sodom at evening. Lot sat in the gate of Sodom. Lot saw them, and rose up to meet them. He bowed himself with his face to the earth,	and they reached Sodom in the evening, and Lot was then sitting in the gate of Sodom, and when he saw them he rose to meet them, and he bowed down to the ground.
2 and he said, "See now, my lords, please turn aside into your servant's house, stay all night, wash your feet, and you can rise up early, and go on your way." They said, "No, but we will stay in the street all night." 3 He urged them greatly, and they came in with him, and entered into his house. He made them a feast, and baked unleavened bread, and they ate.	47 And he pressed them greatly and brought them into his house, and he gave them victuals which they ate,
4 But before they lay down,	and they abode all night in his house.

the men of the city, the men of Sodom, surrounded the house, both young and old, all the people from every quarter.

5 They called to Lot, and said to him, "Where are the men who came in to you this night? Bring them out to us, that we may have sex with them."

6 Lot went out to them to the door, and shut the door after him. 7 He said, "Please, my brothers, don't act so wickedly. 8 See now, I have two virgin daughters. Please let me bring them out to you, and you may do to them what seems good to you. Only don't do anything to these men, because they have come under the shadow of my roof."

9 They said, "Stand back!" Then they said, "This one fellow came in to live as a foreigner, and he appoints himself a judge. Now will we deal worse with you, than with them!" They pressed hard on the man Lot, and came near to break the door. 10 But the men reached out their hand, and brought Lot into the house to them, and shut the door. 11 They struck the men who were at the door of the house with blindness, both small and great, so that they wearied themselves to find the door.

12 The men said to Lot, "Do you have anybody else here? Sons-in-law, your sons, your daughters, and whoever you have in the city, bring them out of the place: 13 for we will destroy this place, because the outcry against them has grown great before Yahweh that Yahweh has sent us to destroy it."

14 Lot went out, and spoke to his sons-in-law, who were pledged to marry his daughters, and said, "Get up! Get out of this place, for Yahweh will destroy the city." But he seemed to his sons-in-law to be joking.

15 When the morning came, then the angels hurried Lot, saying, "Get up! Take your wife, and your two daughters who are here, lest you be consumed in the iniquity of the city."

48 And the angels said to Lot, "Arise, go forth from this place, thou and all belonging to thee, lest thou be consumed in the iniquity of this city, for the Lord will destroy this place."

16 But he lingered; and the men grabbed his hand, his wife's hand, and his two daughters' hands, Yahweh being merciful to him; and they took him out, and set him outside of the city.

49 And the angels laid hold upon the hand of Lot and upon the hand of his wife, and upon the hands of his children, and all belonging to him, and they brought him forth and set him without the cities.

17 It came to pass, when they had taken them out, that he said, "Escape for your life! Don't look behind you, and don't stay anywhere in the plain. Escape to the mountains, lest you be consumed!"

50 And they said to Lot, "Escape for thy life, and he fled and all belonging to him."

18 Lot said to them, "Oh, not so, my lord. 19 See now, your servant has found favor in your sight, and you have magnified your loving kindness, which you have shown to me in saving my life. I can't escape to the mountain, lest evil overtake me, and I die. 20 See now, this city is near to flee to, and it is a little one. Oh let me escape there (isn't it a little one?), and my soul will live."

21 He said to him, "Behold, I have granted your request concerning this thing also, that I will not overthrow the city of which you have spoken. 22 Hurry, escape there, for I can't do anything until you get there." Therefore the name of the city was called Zoar.

23 The sun had risen on the earth when Lot came to Zoar.

24 Then Yahweh rained on Sodom and on Gomorrah sulfur and fire from Yahweh out of the sky. 25 He overthrew those cities, all the plain, all the inhabitants of the cities, and that which grew on the ground.

51 Then the Lord rained upon Sodom and upon Gomorrah and upon all these cities brimstone and fire from the Lord out of heaven. 52 And he overthrew these cities, all the plain and all the inhabitants of the cities, and that which grew upon the ground;

26 But his wife looked back from behind him, and she became a pillar of salt.

and Ado the wife of Lot looked back to see the destruction of the cities, for her compassion was moved on account of her daughters who remained in Sodom, for they did not go with her. 53 And when she looked back she became a pillar of salt, and it is yet in that place unto this day.

54 And the oxen which stood in that place daily licked up the salt to the extremities of their feet, and in the morning it would spring forth afresh, and they again licked it up unto this day. 55 And Lot and two of his daughters that remained with him fled and escaped to the cave of Adullam, and they remained there for some time.

27 Abraham got up early in the morning to the place where he had stood before Yahweh. 28 He looked toward Sodom and Gomorrah, and toward all the land of the plain, and looked, and saw that the smoke of the land went up as the smoke of a furnace.

56 And Abraham rose up early in the morning to see what had been done to the cities of Sodom; and he looked and beheld the smoke of the cities going up like the smoke of a furnace.

29 When God destroyed the cities of the plain, God remembered Abraham, and sent Lot out of the middle of the overthrow, when he overthrew the cities in which Lot lived.

30 Lot went up out of Zoar, and lived in the mountain, and his two daughters with him; for he was afraid to live in Zoar. He lived in a cave with his two daughters. 31 The firstborn said to the younger, “Our father is old, and there is not a man in the earth to come in to us in the way of all the earth. 32 Come, let’s make our father drink wine, and we will lie with him, that we may preserve our father’s family line.” 33 They made their father drink wine that night: and the firstborn went in, and lay with her father. He didn’t know when she lay down, nor when she arose. 34 It came to pass on the next day, that the firstborn said to the younger, “Behold, I lay last night with my father. Let us make him drink wine again, tonight. You go in, and lie with him, that we may preserve our father’s family line.”

57 And Lot and his two daughters remained in the cave, and they made their father drink wine, and they lay with him, for they said there was no man upon earth that could raise up seed from them, for they thought that the whole earth was destroyed.

35 They made their father drink wine that night
also. The younger went and lay with him. He didn't
know when she lay down, nor when she got up.

36 Thus both of Lot's daughters were with child by
their father. 37 The firstborn bore a son, and
named him Moab. He is the father of the Moabites
to this day. 38 The younger also bore a son, and
called his name Ben Ammi. He is the father of the
children of Ammon to this day.

58 And they both lay with their father, and they conceived and bare sons, and the first born called the name of her son Moab, saying, "From my father did I conceive him;" he is the father of the Moabites unto this day. 59 And the younger also called her son Benami; he is the father of the children of Ammon unto this day.

60 And after this Lot and his two daughters went away from there, and he dwelt on the other side of the Jordan with his two daughters and their sons, and the sons of Lot grew up, and they went and took themselves wives from the land of Canaan, and they begat children and they were fruitful and multiplied.

Genesis 20

1 Abraham traveled from there toward the land of the South, and lived between Kadesh and Shur. He lived as a foreigner in Gerar.

Jasher 20

1 And at that time Abraham journeyed from the plain of Mamre, and he went to the land of the Philistines, and he dwelt in Gerar; it was in the twenty-fifth year of Abraham's being in the land of Canaan, and the hundredth year of the life of Abraham, that he came to Gerar in the land of the Philistines.

2 And when they entered the land he said to Sarah his wife, "Say thou art my sister, to any one that shall ask thee, in order that we may escape the evil of the inhabitants of the land."

2 Abraham said about Sarah his wife, "She is my sister." Abimelech king of Gerar sent, and took Sarah.

3 And as Abraham was dwelling in the land of the Philistines, the servants of Abimelech, king of the Philistines, saw that Sarah was exceedingly beautiful, and they asked Abraham concerning her, and he said, "She is my sister." 4 And the servants
of Abimelech went to Abimelech, saying, "A man from the land of Canaan is come to dwell in the land, and he has a sister that is exceeding fair." 5
And Abimelech heard the words of his servants who praised Sarah to him, and Abimelech sent his officers, and they brought Sarah to the king.

6 And Sarah came to the house of Abimelech, and the king saw that Sarah was beautiful, and she pleased him exceedingly.

7 And he approached her and said to her, "What is that man to thee with whom thou didst come to our land?" and Sarah answered and said "He is my brother, and we came from the land of Canaan to dwell wherever we could find a place."

8 And Abimelech said to Sarah, "Behold my land is before thee, place thy brother in any part of this land that pleases thee, and it will be our duty to exalt and elevate him above all the people of the land since he is thy brother."

9 And Abimelech sent for Abraham, and Abraham came to Abimelech. 10 And Abimelech said to Abraham, "Behold I have given orders that thou shalt be honored as thou desirest on account of thy sister Sarah." 11 And Abraham went forth from the king, and the king's present followed him.

12 As at evening time, before men lie down to rest, the king was sitting upon his throne, and a deep sleep fell upon him, and he lay upon the throne and slept till morning.

13 And he dreamed that an angel of the Lord came to him with a drawn sword in his hand, and the angel stood over Abimelech, and wished to slay him with the sword, and the king was terrified in his dream, and said to the angel, "In what have I sinned against thee that thou comest to slay me with thy sword?"

3 But God came to Abimelech in a dream of the night, and said to him, “Behold, you are a dead man, because of the woman whom you have taken. For she is a man’s wife.”

14 And the angel answered and said to Abimelech, "Behold thou diest on account of the woman which thou didst yesternight bring to thy house, for she is a married woman, the wife of Abraham who came to thy house; now therefore return that man his wife, for she is his wife; and shouldst thou not return her, know that thou wilt surely die, thou and all belonging to thee."

4 Now Abimelech had not come near her. He said, “Lord, will you kill even a righteous nation? 5 Didn’t he tell me, ‘She is my sister?’ She, even she herself, said, ‘He is my brother.’ In the integrity of my heart and the innocence of my hands have I done this.”

6 God said to him in the dream, “Yes, I know that in the integrity of your heart you have done this, and I also withheld you from sinning against me. Therefore I didn’t allow you to touch her.

7 "Now therefore, restore the man's wife. For he is a prophet, and he will pray for you, and you will live. If you don't restore her, know for sure that you will die, you, and all who are yours."

15 And on that night there was a great outcry in the land of the Philistines, and the inhabitants of the land saw the figure of a man standing with a drawn sword in his hand, and he smote the inhabitants of the land with the sword, yea he continued to smite
them. 16 And the angel of the Lord smote the
whole land of the Philistines on that night, and there was a great confusion on that night and on the following morning.

[Genesis 20: 18 For Yahweh had closed up tight all the wombs of the house of Abimelech, because of Sarah, Abraham's wife.]

17 And every womb was closed, and all their issues, and the hand of the Lord was upon them on account of Sarah, wife of Abraham, whom Abimelech had taken.

8 Abimelech rose early in the morning, and called all his servants, and told all these things in their ear. The men were very scared.

18 And in the morning Abimelech rose with terror and confusion and with a great dread, and he sent and had his servants called in, and he related his dream to them, and the people were greatly afraid.

19 And one man standing amongst the servants of the king answered the king, saying, "O sovereign king, restore this woman to her husband, for he is her husband, for the like happened to the king of
Egypt when this man came to Egypt. 20 And he said
concerning his wife, 'She is my sister,' for such is his manner of doing when he cometh to dwell in the land in which he is a stranger.

21 "And Pharaoh sent and took this woman for a wife and the Lord brought upon him grievous plagues until he returned the woman to her
husband. 22 Now therefore, O sovereign king,
know what happened yesternight to the whole land, for there was a very great consternation and great pain and lamentation, and we know that it was on account of the woman which thou didst take."

23 "Now, therefore, restore this woman to her husband, lest it should befall us as it did to Pharaoh king of Egypt and his subjects, and that we may not die;" and Abimelech hastened and called and had Sarah called for, and she came before him,

9 Then Abimelech called Abraham, and said to him, "What have you done to us? How have I sinned against you, that you have brought on me and on my kingdom a great sin? You have done deeds to me that ought not to be done!" 10 Abimelech said to Abraham, "What did you see, that you have done this thing?"

11 Abraham said, "Because I thought, 'Surely the fear of God is not in this place. They will kill me for my wife's sake.'

12 Besides, she is indeed my sister, the daughter of my father, but not the daughter of my mother; and she became my wife. 13 When God caused me to wander from my father's house, I said to her, 'This is your kindness which you shall show to me. Everywhere that we go, say of me, "He is my brother."'"

14 Abimelech took sheep and cattle, male servants and female servants, and gave them to Abraham, and restored Sarah, his wife, to him.

15 Abimelech said, "Behold, my land is before you. Dwell where it pleases you."

16 To Sarah he said, "Behold, I have given your brother a thousand pieces of silver. Behold, it is for you a covering of the eyes to all that are with you. In front of all you are vindicated."

17 Abraham prayed to God. God healed Abimelech, and his wife, and his female servants, and they bore children.

and he had Abraham called for, and he came before him. 24 And Abimelech said to them, "What is this work you have been doing in saying you are brother and sister, and I took this woman for a wife?"

25 And Abraham said, "Because I thought I should suffer death on account of my wife;"

and Abimelech took flocks and herds, and men servants and maid servants, and a thousand pieces of silver, and he gave them to Abraham, and he returned Sarah to him.

26 And Abimelech said to Abraham, "Behold the whole land is before thee, dwell in it wherever thou shalt choose."

27 And Abraham and Sarah, his wife, went forth from the king's presence with honor and respect, and they dwelt in the land, even in Gerar.

28 And all the inhabitants of the land of the Philistines and the king's servants were still in pain, through the plague which the angel had inflicted upon them the whole night on account of Sarah.

29 And Abimelech sent for Abraham, saying, "Pray now for thy servants to the Lord thy God, that he may put away this mortality from amongst us."

30 And Abraham prayed on account of Abimelech and his subjects, and the Lord heard the prayer of Abraham, and he healed Abimelech and all his subjects.

18 For Yahweh had closed up tight all the wombs of the house of Abimelech, because of Sarah, Abraham's wife.

[20:17 And every womb was closed, and all their issues, and the hand of the Lord was upon them on account of Sarah, wife of Abraham, whom Abimelech had taken.]

Genesis 21

1 Yahweh visited Sarah as he had said, and Yahweh did to Sarah as he had spoken. 2 Sarah conceived, and bore Abraham a son in his old age, at the set time of which God had spoken to him.

Jasher 21

1 And it was at that time at the end of a year and four months of Abraham's dwelling in the land of the Philistines in Gerar, that God visited Sarah, and the Lord remembered her, and she conceived and bare a son to Abraham.

3 Abraham called his son who was born to him, whom Sarah bore to him, Isaac. 4 Abraham circumcised his son, Isaac, when he was eight days old, as God had commanded him. 5 Abraham was one hundred years old when his son, Isaac, was born to him.

2 And Abraham called the name of the son which was born to him, which Sarah bare to him, Isaac. 3 And Abraham circumcised his son Isaac at eight days old, as God had commanded Abraham to do unto his seed after him; and Abraham was one hundred, and Sarah ninety years old, when Isaac was born to them.

6 Sarah said, "God has made me laugh. Everyone who hears will laugh with me." 7 She said, "Who would have said to Abraham, that Sarah would nurse children? For I have borne him a son in his old age."

8 The child grew, and was weaned. Abraham made a great feast on the day that Isaac was weaned.

4 And the child grew up and he was weaned, and Abraham made a great feast upon the day that Isaac was weaned.

5 And Shem and Eber and all the great people of the land, and Abimelech king of the Philistines, and his servants, and Phicol, the captain of his host, came to eat and drink and rejoice at the feast which Abraham made upon the day of his son Isaac's being weaned. 6 Also Terah, the father of Abraham, and Nahor his brother, came from Haran, they and all belonging to them, for they greatly rejoiced on hearing that a son had been born to Sarah.

7 And they came to Abraham, and they ate and drank at the feast which Abraham made upon the day of Isaac's being weaned. 8 And Terah and Nahor rejoiced with Abraham, and they remained with him many days in the land of the Philistines.

9 At that time Serug the son of Reu died, in the first year of the birth of Isaac son of Abraham. 10 And all the days of Serug were two hundred and thirty-nine years, and he died.

11 And Ishmael the son of Abraham was grown up in those days; he was fourteen years old when Sarah bare Isaac to Abraham. 12 And God was with Ishmael the son of Abraham, and he grew up, and he learned to use the bow and became an archer. 13 And when Isaac was five years old he was sitting with Ishmael at the door of the tent. 14 And Ishmael came to Isaac and seated himself opposite to him, and he took the bow and drew it and put the arrow in it, and intended to slay Isaac.

9 Sarah saw the son of Hagar the Egyptian, whom she had borne to Abraham, mocking. 10 Therefore she said to Abraham, "Cast out this servant and her son! For the son of this servant will not be heir with my son, Isaac."

15 And Sarah saw the act which Ishmael desired to do to her son Isaac, and it grieved her exceedingly on account of her son, and she sent for Abraham, and said to him, "Cast out this bondwoman and her son, for her son shall not be heir with my son, for thus did he seek to do unto him this day."

11 The thing was very grievous in Abraham's sight on account of his son. 12 God said to Abraham, "Don't let it be grievous in your sight because of the boy, and because of your servant. In all that Sarah says to you, listen to her voice. For your offspring will be accounted as from Isaac. 13 I will also make a nation of the son of the servant, because he is your child."

14 Abraham rose up early in the morning, and took bread and a bottle of water, and gave it to Hagar, putting it on her shoulder; and gave her the child, and sent her away. She departed, and wandered in the wilderness of Beersheba.

16 And Abraham hearkened to the voice of Sarah, and he rose up early in the morning, and he took twelve loaves and a bottle of water which he gave to Hagar, and sent her away with her son, and Hagar went with her son to the wilderness,

15 The water in the bottle was spent, and she cast the child under one of the shrubs. 16 She went and sat down opposite him, a good way off, about a bow shot away. For she said, "Don't let me see the death of the child." She sat over against him, and lifted up her voice, and wept.

17 God heard the voice of the boy. The angel of God called to Hagar out of the sky, and said to her, "What ails you, Hagar? Don't be afraid. For God has heard the voice of the boy where he is. 18 Get up, lift up the boy, and hold him in your hand. For I will make him a great nation."

19 God opened her eyes, and she saw a well of water. She went, filled the bottle with water, and gave the boy drink.

20 God was with the boy, and he grew. He lived in
the wilderness, and became, as he grew up, an
archer. 21 He lived in the wilderness of Paran.

and they dwelt in the wilderness of Paran with the inhabitants of the wilderness, and Ishmael was an archer, and he dwelt in the wilderness a long time.

His mother took a wife for him out of the land of Egypt.

17 And he and his mother afterward went to the land of Egypt, and they dwelt there, and Hagar took a wife for her son from Egypt, and her name was Meribah.

18 And the wife of Ishmael conceived and bare four sons and two daughters, and Ishmael and his mother and his wife and children afterward went
and returned to the wilderness. 19 And they made
themselves tents in the wilderness, in which they dwelt, and they continued to travel and then to rest monthly and yearly.

20 And God gave Ishmael flocks and herds and tents on account of Abraham his father, and the man
increased in cattle. 21 And Ishmael dwelt in deserts
and in tents, traveling and resting for a long time, and he did not see the face of his father.

22 And in some time after, Abraham said to Sarah his wife, "I will go and see my son Ishmael, for I have a desire to see him, for I have not seen him for a long time."

23 And Abraham rode upon one of his camels to the wilderness to seek his son Ishmael, for he heard that he was dwelling in a tent in the wilderness with all belonging to him.

24 And Abraham went to the wilderness, and he reached the tent of Ishmael about noon, and he asked after Ishmael, and he found the wife of Ishmael sitting in the tent with her children, and Ishmael her husband and his mother were not with
them. 25 And Abraham asked the wife of Ishmael,
saying, "Where has Ishmael gone?" and she said, "He has gone to the field to hunt," and Abraham was still mounted upon the camel, for he would not get off to the ground as he had sworn to his wife Sarah that he would not get off from the camel.

26 And Abraham said to Ishmael's wife, "My daughter, give me a little water that I may drink, for I am fatigued from the journey."

27 And Ishmael's wife answered and said to Abraham, "We have neither water nor bread," and she continued sitting in the tent and did not notice Abraham, neither did she ask him who he was.

28 But she was beating her children in the tent, and she was cursing them, and she also cursed her husband Ishmael and reproached him, and Abraham heard the words of Ishmael's wife to her children, and he was very angry and displeased. 29
And Abraham called to the woman to come out to him from the tent, and the woman came and stood opposite to Abraham, for Abraham was still mounted upon the camel.

30 And Abraham said to Ishmael's wife, "When thy husband Ishmael returneth home say these words to him,

31 "'A very old man from the land of the Philistines came hither to seek thee, and thus was his appearance and figure; I did not ask him who he was, and seeing thou wast not here he spoke unto me and said, "When Ishmael thy husband returneth tell him thus did this man say, When thou comest home put away this nail of the tent which thou hast placed here, and place another nail in its stead."'"

32 And Abraham finished his instructions to the woman, and he turned and went off on the camel homeward.

33 And after that Ishmael came from the chase he and his mother, and returned to the tent, and his
wife spoke these words to him, "34 A very old man
from the land of the Philistines came to seek thee, and thus was his appearance and figure; I did not ask him who he was, and seeing thou wast not at home he said to me, 'When thy husband cometh home tell him, thus saith the old man, "Put away the nail of the tent which thou hast placed here and place another nail in its stead."'"

35 And Ishmael heard the words of his wife, and he knew that it was his father, and that his wife did not
honor him. 36 And Ishmael understood his father's
words that he had spoken to his wife, and Ishmael hearkened to the voice of his father, and Ishmael
cast off that woman and she went away. 37 And
Ishmael afterward went to the land of Canaan, and he took another wife and he brought her to his tent to the place where he then dwelt.

38 And at the end of three years Abraham said, "I
will go again and see Ishmael my son, for I have not
seen him for a long time." 39 And he rode upon his
camel and went to the wilderness, and he reached
the tent of Ishmael about noon.

40 And he asked after Ishmael, and his wife came
out of the tent and she said, "He is not here my
lord, for he has gone to hunt in the fields, and to
feed the camels," and the woman said to Abraham,
"Turn in my lord into the tent, and eat a morsel of
bread, for thy soul must be wearied on account of
the journey."

41 And Abraham said to her, "I will not stop for I am
in haste to continue my journey, but give me a little
water to drink, for I have thirst;" and the woman
hastened and ran into the tent and she brought out
water and bread to Abraham, which she placed
before him and she urged him to eat, and he ate
and drank and his heart was comforted and he
blessed his son Ishmael.

42 And he finished his meal and he blessed the
Lord, and he said to Ishmael's wife, "When Ishmael
cometh home say these words to him, '43 A very
old man from the land of the Philistines came hither
and asked after thee, and thou wast not here; and I
brought him out bread and water and he ate and
drank and his heart was comforted. 44 And he
spoke these words to me: "When Ishmael thy
husband cometh home, say unto him, The nail of
the tent which thou hast is very good, do not put it
away from the tent."'"

45 And Abraham finished commanding the woman,
and he rode off to his home to the land of the
Philistines; and when Ishmael came to his tent his
wife went forth to meet him with joy and a cheerful
heart.

46 And she said to him, "An old man came here
from the land of the Philistines and thus was his
appearance, and he asked after thee and thou wast
not here, so I brought out bread and water, and he
ate and drank and his heart was comforted. 47 And
he spoke these words to me, 'When Ishmael thy
husband cometh home say to him, "The nail of the
tent which thou hast is very good, do not put it
away from the tent."'"

48 And Ishmael knew that it was his father, and that his wife had honored him, and the Lord blessed Ishmael.

Jasher 22

1 And Ishmael then rose up and took his wife and
his children and his cattle and all belonging to him,
and he journeyed from there and he went to his
father in the land of the Philistines. 2 And Abraham
related to Ishmael his son the transaction with the
first wife that Ishmael took, according to what she
did. 3 And Ishmael and his children dwelt with
Abraham many days in that land, and Abraham
dwelt in the land of the Philistines a long time.

4 And the days increased and reached twenty six years, and after that Abraham with his servants and all belonging to him went from the land of the Philistines and removed to a great distance, and they came near to Hebron, and they remained there, and the servants of Abraham dug wells of water, and Abraham and all belonging to him dwelt by the water, and the servants of Abimelech king of the Philistines heard the report that Abraham's servants had dug wells of water in the borders of the land.

5 And they came and quarreled with the servants of Abraham, and they robbed them of the great well which they had dug.

22 At that time, Abimelech and Phicol the captain of his army spoke to Abraham, saying

6 And Abimelech king of the Philistines heard of this affair, and he with Phicol the captain of his host and twenty of his men came to Abraham,

"God is with you in all that you do. 23 Now,
therefore, swear to me here by God that you will
not deal falsely with me, nor with my son, nor with
my son's son. But according to the kindness that I
have done to you, you shall do to me, and to the
land in which you have lived as a foreigner." 24
Abraham said, "I will swear."

25 Abraham complained to Abimelech because of a
water well, which Abimelech's servants had
violently taken away. 26 Abimelech said, "I don't
know who has done this thing. You didn't tell me,
and I didn't hear of it until today."

and Abimelech spoke to Abraham concerning his
servants, and Abraham rebuked Abimelech
concerning the well of which his servants had
robbed him. 7 And Abimelech said to Abraham, "As
the Lord liveth who created the whole earth, I did
not hear of the act which my servants did unto thy
servants until this day."

27 Abraham took sheep and cattle, and gave them to Abimelech. Those two made a covenant.

28 Abraham set seven ewe lambs of the flock by themselves. 29 Abimelech said to Abraham, "What do these seven ewe lambs which you have set by themselves mean?" 30 He said, "You shall take these seven ewe lambs from my hand, that it may be a witness to me, that I have dug this well."

8 And Abraham took seven ewe lambs and gave them to Abimelech, saying, "Take these, I pray thee, from my hands that it may be a testimony for me that I dug this well."

9 And Abimelech took the seven ewe lambs which Abraham had given to him, for he had also given him cattle and herds in abundance, and Abimelech swore to Abraham concerning the well, therefore he called that well Beersheba, for there they both swore concerning it.

31 Therefore he called that place Beersheba, because they both swore there. 32 So they made a covenant at Beersheba. Abimelech rose up with Phicol, the captain of his army, and they returned into the land of the Philistines. 33 Abraham planted a tamarisk tree in Beersheba, and called there on the name of Yahweh, the Everlasting God. 34 Abraham lived as a foreigner in the land of the Philistines many days.

10 And they both made a covenant in Beersheba, and Abimelech rose up with Phicol the captain of his host and all his men, and they returned to the land of the Philistines, and Abraham and all belonging to him dwelt in Beersheba and he was in that land a long time.

11 And Abraham planted a large grove in Beersheba, and he made to it four gates facing the four sides of the earth, and he planted a vineyard in it, so that if a traveler came to Abraham he entered any gate which was in his road, and remained there and ate and drank and satisfied himself and then departed.

12 For the house of Abraham was always open to the sons of men that passed and repassed, who came daily to eat and drink in the house of Abraham. 13 And any man who had hunger and came to Abraham's house, Abraham would give him bread that he might eat and drink and be satisfied, and any one that came naked to his house he would clothe with garments as he might choose, and give him silver and gold and make known to him the Lord who had created him in the earth; this did Abraham all his life.

14 And Abraham and his children and all belonging to him dwelt in Beersheba, and he pitched his tent as far as Hebron.

15 And Abraham's brother Nahor and his father and all belonging to them dwelt in Haran, for they did not come with Abraham to the land of Canaan.

16 And children were born to Nahor which Milca
the daughter of Haran, and sister to Sarah,
Abraham's wife, bare to him. 17 And these are the
names of those that were born to him, Uz, Buz,
Kemuel, Kesed, Chazo, Pildash, Tidlaf, and Bethuel,
being eight sons, these are the children of Milca
which she bare to Nahor, Abraham's brother.

18 And Nahor had a concubine and her name was
Reumah, and she also bare to Nahor, Zebach,
Gachash, Tachash and Maacha, being four sons. 19
And the children that were born to Nahor were
twelve sons besides his daughters, and they also
had children born to them in Haran.

20 And the children of Uz the first born of Nahor
were Abi, Cheref, Gadin, Melus, and Deborah their
sister. 21 And the sons of Buz were Berachel,
Naamath, Sheva, and Madonu. 22 And the sons of
Kemuel were Aram and Rechob. 23 And the sons of
Kesed were Anamlech, Meshai, Benon and Yifi; and
the sons of Chazo were Pildash, Mechi and Opher.

24 And the sons of Pildash were Arud, Chamum,
Mered and Moloch. 25 And the sons of Tidlaf were
Mushan, Cushan and Mutzi. 26 And the children of
Bethuel were Sechar, Laban and their sister
Rebecca.

27 These are the families of the children of Nahor, that were born to them in Haran; and Aram the son of Kemuel and Rechob his brother went away from Haran, and they found a valley in the land by the river Euphrates.

28 And they built a city there, and they called the
name of the city after the name of Pethor the son
of Aram, that is Aram Naherayim unto this day. 29
And the children of Kesed also went to dwell where
they could find a place, and they went and they
found a valley opposite to the land of Shinar, and
they dwelt there. 30 And they there built
themselves a city, and they called the name at the
city Kesed after the name of their father, that is the
land Kasdim unto this day, and the Kasdim dwelt in
that land and they were fruitful and multiplied
exceedingly.

31 And Terah, father of Nahor and Abraham, went
and took another wife in his old age, and her name
was Pelilah, and she conceived and bare him a son
and he called his name Zoba. 32 And Terah lived
twenty-five years after he begat Zoba. 33 And
Terah died in that year, that is in the thirty-fifth
year of the birth of Isaac son of Abraham. 34 And
the days of Terah were two hundred and five years,
and he was buried in Haran.

35 And Zoba the son of Terah lived thirty years and
he begat Aram, Achlis and Merik. 36 And Aram son
of Zoba son of Terah, had three wives and he begat
twelve sons and three daughters; and the Lord gave
to Aram the son of Zoba, riches and possessions,
and abundance of cattle, and flocks and herds, and
the man increased greatly.

37 And Aram the son of Zoba and his brother and all his household journeyed from Haran, and they went to dwell where they should find a place, for their property was too great to remain in Haran; for they could not stop in Haran together with their brethren the children of Nahor.

38 And Aram the son of Zoba went with his
brethren, and they found a valley at a distance
toward the eastern country and they dwelt there.
39 And they also built a city there, and they called
the name thereof Aram, after the name of their
eldest brother; that is Aram Zoba to this day.

40 And Isaac the son of Abraham was growing up in those days, and Abraham his father taught him the way of the Lord to know the Lord, and the Lord was with him.

41 And when Isaac was thirty-seven years old, Ishmael his brother was going about with him in the tent. 42 And Ishmael boasted of himself to Isaac, saying, "I was thirteen years old when the Lord spoke to my father to circumcise us, and I did according to the word of the Lord which he spoke to my father, and I gave my soul unto the Lord, and I did not transgress his word which he commanded my father."

43 And Isaac answered Ishmael, saying, "Why dost thou boast to me about this, about a little bit of thy flesh which thou didst take from thy body, concerning which the Lord commanded thee? 44 As the Lord liveth, the God of my father Abraham, if the Lord should say unto my father, 'Take now thy son Isaac and bring him up an offering before me,' I would not refrain but I would joyfully accede to it."

45 And the Lord heard the word that Isaac spoke to Ishmael, and it seemed good in the sight of the Lord, and he thought to try Abraham in this matter.

[Job 1:6 Now on the day when God's sons came to present themselves before Yahweh, Satan also came among them.]

46 And the day arrived when the sons of God came and placed themselves before the Lord, and Satan also came with the sons of God before the Lord.

[Job 1:7 Yahweh said to Satan, "Where have you come from?" Then Satan answered Yahweh, and said, "From going back and forth in the earth, and from walking up and down in it."]

47 And the Lord said unto Satan, "Whence comest thou?" and Satan answered the Lord and said, "From going to and fro in the earth, and from walking up and down in it."

48 And the Lord said to Satan, "What is thy word to me concerning all the children of the earth?" and Satan answered the Lord and said, "I have seen all the children of the earth who serve thee and remember thee when they require anything from thee. 49 And when thou givest them the thing which they require from thee, they sit at their ease, and forsake thee and they remember thee no more.

50 "Hast thou seen Abraham the son of Terah, who at first had no children, and he served thee and erected altars to thee wherever he came, and he brought up offerings upon them, and he proclaimed thy name continually to all the children of the earth. 51 And now that his son Isaac is born to him, he has forsaken thee, he has made a great feast for all the inhabitants of the land, and the Lord he has forgotten.

52 "For amidst all that he has done he brought thee no offering; neither burnt offering nor peace offering, neither ox, lamb nor goat of all that he killed on the day that his son was weaned.

53 "Even from the time of his son's birth till now, being thirty-seven years, he built no altar before thee, nor brought any offering to thee, for he saw that thou didst give what he requested before thee, and he therefore forsook thee."

[Job 1:8 Yahweh said to Satan, "Have you considered my servant, Job? For there is no one like him in the earth, a blameless and an upright man, one who fears God, and turns away from evil."]

54 And the Lord said to Satan, Hast thou thus considered my servant Abraham? for there is none like him upon earth, a perfect and an upright man before me, one that feareth God and avoideth evil; as I live, were I to say unto him, Bring up Isaac thy son before me, he would not withhold him from me, much more if I told him to bring up a burnt offering before me from his flock or herds."

55 And Satan answered the Lord and said, "Speak then now unto Abraham as thou hast said, and thou wilt see whether he will not this day transgress and cast aside thy words."

Genesis 22

1 After these things, God tested Abraham, and said to him, "Abraham!" He said, "Here I am."

2 He said, "Now take your son, your only son, whom you love, even Isaac, and go into the land of Moriah. Offer him there as a burnt offering on one of the mountains which I will tell you of."

Jasher 23

1 At that time the word of the Lord came to Abraham, and he said unto him, "Abraham," and he said, "Here I am."

2 And he said to him, "Take now thy son, thine only son whom thou lovest, even Isaac, and go to the land of Moriah, and offer him there for a burnt offering upon one of the mountains which shall be shown to thee, for there wilt thou see a cloud and the glory of the Lord."

3 And Abraham said within himself, "How shall I separate my son Isaac from Sarah his mother, in order to bring him up for a burnt offering before the Lord?"

4 And Abraham came into the tent, and he sat
before Sarah his wife, and he spoke these words to
her, 5 "My son Isaac is grown up and he has not for
some time studied the service of his God, now
tomorrow I will go and bring him to Shem, and Eber
his son, and there he will learn the ways of the
Lord, for they will teach him to know the Lord as
well as to know that when he prayeth continually
before the Lord, he will answer him, therefore
there he will know the way of serving the Lord his
God."

6 And Sarah said, "Thou hast spoken well, go my
lord and do unto him as thou hast said, but remove
him not at a great distance from me, neither let him
remain there too long, for my soul is bound within
his soul."

7 And Abraham said unto Sarah, "My daughter, let
us pray to the Lord our God that he may do good
with us."

8 And Sarah took her son Isaac and he abode all
that night with her, and she kissed and embraced
him, and gave him instructions till morning. 9 And
she said to him, "O my son, how can my soul
separate itself from thee?" And she still kissed him
and embraced him, and she gave Abraham
instructions concerning him.

10 And Sarah said to Abraham, "O my lord, I pray
thee take heed of thy son, and place thine eyes
over him, for I have no other son nor daughter but
him. 11 O forsake him not. If he be hungry give him
bread, and if he be thirsty give him water to drink;
do not let him go on foot, neither let him sit in the
sun. 12 Neither let him go by himself in the road,
neither force him from whatever he may desire, but
do unto him as he may say to thee." 13 And Sarah
wept bitterly the whole night on account of Isaac,
and she gave him instructions till morning.

14 And in the morning Sarah selected a very fine
and beautiful garment from those garments which
she had in the house, that Abimelech had given to
her. 15 And she dressed Isaac her son therewith,
and she put a turban upon his head, and she
enclosed a precious stone in the top of the turban,
and she gave them provision for the road, and they
went forth, and Isaac went with his father
Abraham, and some of their servants accompanied
them to see them off the road.

16 And Sarah went out with them, and she accompanied them upon the road to see them off, and they said to her, "Return to the tent."

17 And when Sarah heard the words of her son Isaac she wept bitterly, and Abraham her husband wept with her, and their son wept with them a great weeping; also those who went with them wept greatly.

18 And Sarah caught hold of her son Isaac, and she held him in her arms, and she embraced him and continued to weep with him, and Sarah said, "Who knoweth if after this day I shall ever see thee again?"

19 And they still wept together, Abraham, Sarah and Isaac, and all those that accompanied them on the road wept with them, and Sarah afterward turned away from her son, weeping bitterly, and all her men servants and maid servants returned with her to the tent.
20 And Abraham went with Isaac his son to bring him up as an offering before the Lord, as He had commanded him.

3 Abraham rose early in the morning, and saddled his donkey, and took two of his young men with him, and Isaac his son. He split the wood for the burnt offering, and rose up, and went to the place of which God had told him.

21 And Abraham took two of his young men with him,

Ishmael the son of Hagar and Eliezer his servant, and they went together with them, and whilst they were walking in the road the young men spoke these words to themselves,

22 And Ishmael said to Eliezer, "Now my father Abraham is going with Isaac to bring him up for a burnt offering to the Lord, as He commanded him.
23 Now when he returneth he will give unto me all that he possesses, to inherit after him, for I am his first born."

24 And Eliezer answered Ishmael and said, "Surely Abraham did cast thee away with thy mother, and swear that thou shouldst not inherit any thing of all he possesses, and to whom will he give all that he has, with all his treasures, but unto me his servant, who has been faithful in his house, who has served him night and day, and has done all that he desired me? to me will he bequeath at his death all that he possesses."

25 And whilst Abraham was proceeding with his son Isaac along the road, Satan came and appeared to Abraham in the figure of a very aged man, humble and of contrite spirit, and he approached Abraham and said to him, "Art thou silly or brutish, that thou goest to do this thing this day to thine only son?

26 "For God gave thee a son in thy latter days, in thy old age, and wilt thou go and slaughter him this day because he committed no violence, and wilt thou cause the soul of thine only son to perish from the earth? 27 Dost thou not know and understand that this thing cannot be from the Lord? for the Lord cannot do unto man such evil upon earth to say to him, Go slaughter thy child."

28 And Abraham heard this and knew that it was the word of Satan who endeavored to draw him aside from the way of the Lord, but Abraham would not hearken to the voice of Satan, and Abraham rebuked him so that he went away.

29 And Satan returned and came to Isaac; and he appeared unto Isaac in the figure of a young man comely and well favored. 30 And he approached Isaac and said unto him, "Dost thou not know and understand that thy old silly father bringeth thee to the slaughter this day for naught? 31 Now therefore, my son, do not listen nor attend to him, for he is a silly old man, and let not thy precious soul and beautiful figure be lost from the earth."

32 And Isaac heard this, and said unto Abraham, "Hast thou heard, my father, that which this man has spoken? even thus has he spoken."

33 And Abraham answered his son Isaac and said to him, "Take heed of him and do not listen to his words, nor attend to him, for he is Satan, endeavoring to draw us aside this day from the commands of God."

34 And Abraham still rebuked Satan, and Satan
went from them, and seeing he could not prevail
over them he hid himself from them, and he went
and passed before them in the road; and he
transformed himself to a large brook of water in the
road, and Abraham and Isaac and his two young
men reached that place, and they saw a brook large
and powerful as the mighty waters. 35 And they
entered the brook and passed through it, and the
waters at first reached their legs.

36 And they went deeper in the brook and the
waters reached up to their necks, and they were all
terrified on account of the water; and whilst they
were going over the brook Abraham recognized
that place, and he knew that there was no water
there before.

37 And Abraham said to his son Isaac, "I know this
place in which there was no brook nor water, now
therefore it is this Satan who does all this to us, to
draw us aside this day from the commands of God."

38 And Abraham rebuked him and said unto him,
"The Lord rebuke thee, O Satan, begone from us for
we go by the commands of God." 39 And Satan was
terrified at the voice of Abraham, and he went
away from them, and the place again became dry
land as it was at first.

40 And Abraham went with Isaac toward the place
that God had told him.

4 On the third day Abraham lifted up his eyes, and
saw the place far off.

41 And on the third day Abraham lifted up his eyes
and saw the place at a distance which God had told
him of.

42 And a pillar of fire appeared to him that reached
from the earth to heaven, and a cloud of glory upon
the mountain, and the glory of the Lord was seen in
the cloud. 43 And Abraham said to Isaac, "My son,
dost thou see in that mountain, which we perceive
at a distance, that which I see upon it?"

44 And Isaac answered and said unto his father, "I
see and lo a pillar of fire and a cloud, and the glory
of the Lord is seen upon the cloud."

45 And Abraham knew that his son Isaac was
accepted before the Lord for a burnt offering.

46 And Abraham said unto Eliezer and unto Ishmael his son, "Do you also see that which we see upon the mountain which is at a distance?" 47 And they answered and said, "We see nothing more than like the other mountains of the earth." And Abraham knew that they were not accepted before the Lord to go with them,

5 Abraham said to his young men, "Stay here with the donkey. The boy and I will go yonder. We will worship, and come back to you."

and Abraham said to them, "Abide ye here with the ass whilst I and Isaac my son will go to yonder mount and worship there before the Lord and then return to you."

48 And Eliezer and Ishmael remained in that place, as Abraham had commanded.

6 Abraham took the wood of the burnt offering and laid it on Isaac his son. He took in his hand the fire and the knife. They both went together.

49 And Abraham took wood for a burnt offering and placed it upon his son Isaac, and he took the fire and the knife, and they both went to that place.

7 Isaac spoke to Abraham his father, and said, "My father?" He said, "Here I am, my son." He said, "Here is the fire and the wood, but where is the lamb for a burnt offering?"

50 And when they were going along Isaac said to his father, "Behold, I see here the fire and wood, and where then is the lamb that is to be the burnt offering before the Lord?"

8 Abraham said, "God will provide himself the lamb for a burnt offering, my son." So they both went together.

51 And Abraham answered his son Isaac, saying, "The Lord has made choice of thee my son, to be a perfect burnt offering instead of the lamb."

52 And Isaac said unto his father, "I will do all that the Lord spoke to thee with joy and cheerfulness of heart."

53 And Abraham again said unto Isaac his son, "Is there in thy heart any thought or counsel concerning this, which is not proper? tell me my son, I pray thee, O my son conceal it not from me."

54 And Isaac answered his father Abraham and said unto him, "O my father, as the Lord liveth and as thy soul liveth, there is nothing in my heart to cause me to deviate either to the right or to the left from the word that he has spoken to thee.

55 "Neither limb nor muscle has moved or stirred at this, nor is there in my heart any thought or evil counsel concerning this. 56 But I am of joyful and cheerful heart in this matter, and I say, 'Blessed is the Lord who has this day chosen me to be a burnt offering before Him.'"

57 And Abraham greatly rejoiced at the words of Isaac, and they went on and came together to that place that the Lord had spoken of.

9 They came to the place which God had told him of. Abraham built the altar there, and laid the wood in order, bound Isaac his son, and laid him on the altar, on the wood.

58 And Abraham approached to build the altar in that place, and Abraham was weeping, and Isaac took stones and mortar until they had finished building the altar. 59 And Abraham took the wood and placed it in order upon the altar which he had built. 60 And he took his son Isaac and bound him in order to place him upon the wood which was upon the altar, to slay him for a burnt offering before the Lord.

61 And Isaac said to his father, "Bind me securely and then place me upon the altar lest I should turn and move, and break loose from the force of the knife upon my flesh and thereof profane the burnt offering;" and Abraham did so.

62 And Isaac still said to his father, "O my father, when thou shalt have slain me and burnt me for an offering, take with thee that which shall remain of my ashes to bring to Sarah my mother, and say to her, This is the sweet smelling savor of Isaac; but do not tell her this if she should sit near a well or upon any high place, lest she should cast her soul after me and die."

63 And Abraham heard the words of Isaac, and he lifted up his voice and wept when Isaac spake these words; and Abraham's tears gushed down upon Isaac his son, and Isaac wept bitterly, and he said to his father, "Hasten thou, O my father, and do with me the will of the Lord our God as He has commanded thee."

64 And the hearts of Abraham and Isaac rejoiced at this thing which the Lord had commanded them; but the eye wept bitterly whilst the heart rejoiced.

10 Abraham stretched out his hand, and took the knife to kill his son.

65 And Abraham bound his son Isaac, and placed him on the altar upon the wood, and Isaac stretched forth his neck upon the altar before his father, and Abraham stretched forth his hand to take the knife to slay his son as a burnt offering before the Lord.

66 At that time the angels of mercy came before the Lord and spake to him concerning Isaac, saying, "67 O Lord, thou art a merciful and compassionate King over all that thou hast created in heaven and in earth, and thou supportest them all; give therefore ransom and redemption instead of thy servant Isaac, and pity and have compassion upon Abraham and Isaac his son, who are this day performing thy commands. 68 Hast thou seen, O Lord, how Isaac the son of Abraham thy servant is bound down to the slaughter like an animal? now therefore let thy pity be roused for them, O Lord."

11 Yahweh's angel called to him out of the sky, and said, "Abraham, Abraham!" He said, "Here I am."

12 He said, "Don't lay your hand on the boy or do anything to him. For now I know that you fear God, since you have not withheld your son, your only son, from me."

69 At that time the Lord appeared unto Abraham, and called to him, from heaven, and said unto him, "Lay not thine hand upon the lad, neither do thou any thing unto him, for now I know that thou fearest God in performing this act, and in not withholding thy son, thine only son, from me."

13 Abraham lifted up his eyes, and looked, and saw that behind him was a ram caught in the thicket by his horns.

70 And Abraham lifted up his eyes and saw, and behold, a ram was caught in a thicket by his horns;

that was the ram which the Lord God had created in the earth in the day that he made earth and heaven. 71 For the Lord had prepared this ram from that day, to be a burnt offering instead of Isaac.

72 And this ram was advancing to Abraham when Satan caught hold of him and entangled his horns in the thicket, that he might not advance to Abraham, in order that Abraham might slay his son.

Abraham went and took the ram, and offered him up for a burnt offering instead of his son.

73 And Abraham, seeing the ram advancing to him and Satan withholding him, fetched him and brought him before the altar, and he loosened his son Isaac from his binding, and he put the ram in his stead, and Abraham killed the ram upon the altar, and brought it up as an offering in the place of his son Isaac.

74 And Abraham sprinkled some of the blood of the ram upon the altar, and he exclaimed and said, "This is in the place of my son, and may this be considered this day as the blood of my son before the Lord."

14 Abraham called the name of that place Yahweh Will Provide. As it is said to this day, "On Yahweh's mountain, it will be provided."

75 And all that Abraham did on this occasion by the altar, he would exclaim and say, "This is in the room of my son, and may it this day be considered before the Lord in the place of my son;" and Abraham finished the whole of the service by the altar, and the service was accepted before the Lord, and was accounted as if it had been Isaac;

15 Yahweh's angel called to Abraham a second time out of the sky, 16 and said, "I have sworn by myself, says Yahweh, because you have done this thing, and have not withheld your son, your only son, 17 that I will bless you greatly, and I will multiply your offspring greatly like the stars of the heavens, and like the sand which is on the seashore. Your offspring will possess the gate of his enemies. 18 All the nations of the earth will be blessed by your offspring, because you have obeyed my voice."

and the Lord blessed Abraham and his seed on that day.

76 And Satan went to Sarah, and he appeared to her in the figure of an old man very humble and meek, and Abraham was yet engaged in the burnt offering before the Lord.

77 And he said unto her, "Dost thou not know all the work that Abraham has made with thine only son this day? For he took Isaac and built an altar, and killed him, and brought him up as a sacrifice upon the altar, and Isaac cried and wept before his father, but he looked not at him, neither did he have compassion over him."

78 And Satan repeated these words, and he went away from her, and Sarah heard all the words of Satan, and she imagined him to be an old man from amongst the sons of men who had been with her son, and had come and told her these things.

79 And Sarah lifted up her voice and wept and cried
out bitterly on account of her son; and she threw
herself upon the ground and she cast dust upon her
head, and she said, "O my son, Isaac my son, O that
I had this day died instead of thee." And she
continued to weep and said, "It grieves me for thee,
O my son, my son Isaac, O that I had died this day in
thy stead."

80 And she still continued to weep, and said, "It
grieves me for thee after that I have reared thee
and have brought thee up; now my joy is turned
into mourning over thee, I that had a longing for
thee, and cried and prayed to God till I bare thee at
ninety years old; and now hast thou served this day
for the knife and the fire, to be made an offering.
81 But I console myself with thee, my son, in its
being the word of the Lord, for thou didst perform
the command of thy God; for who can transgress
the word of our God, in whose hands is the soul of
every living creature?

82 "Thou art just, O Lord our God, for all thy works
are good and righteous; for I also am rejoiced with
thy word which thou didst command, and whilst
mine eye weepeth bitterly my heart rejoiceth." 83
And Sarah laid her head upon the bosom of one of
her handmaids, and she became as still as a stone.

84 She afterward rose up and went about making
inquiries till she came to Hebron, and she inquired
of all those whom she met walking in the road, and
no one could tell her what had happened to her
son. 85 And she came with her maid servants and
men servants to Kireath-arba, which is Hebron, and
she asked concerning her Son, and she remained
there while she sent some of her servants to seek
where Abraham had gone with Isaac; they went to
seek him in the house of Shem and Eber, and they
could not find him, and they sought throughout the
land and he was not there.

86 And behold, Satan came to Sarah in the shape of an old man, and he came and stood before her, and he said unto her, "I spoke falsely unto thee, for Abraham did not kill his son and he is not dead;" and when she heard the word her joy was so exceedingly violent on account of her son, that her soul went out through joy; she died and was gathered to her people.

19 So Abraham returned to his young men, and they rose up and went together to Beersheba. Abraham lived at Beersheba.

87 And when Abraham had finished his service he returned with his son Isaac to his young men, and they rose up and went together to Beersheba, and they came home.

88 And Abraham sought for Sarah, and could not find her, and he made inquiries concerning her, and they said unto him, "She went as far as Hebron to seek you both where you had gone, for thus was she informed."

89 And Abraham and Isaac went to her to Hebron, and when they found that she was dead they lifted up their voices and wept bitterly over her; and Isaac fell upon his mother's face and wept over her, and he said, "O my mother, my mother, how hast thou left me, and where hast thou gone? O how, how hast thou left me!" 90 And Abraham and Isaac wept greatly and all their servants wept with them on account of Sarah, and they mourned over her a great and heavy mourning.

20 After these things, Abraham was told, "Behold, Milcah, she also has borne children to your brother Nahor: 21 Uz his firstborn, Buz his brother, Kemuel the father of Aram, 22 Chesed, Hazo, Pildash, Jidlaph, and Bethuel." 23 Bethuel became the father of Rebekah. These eight Milcah bore to Nahor, Abraham's brother. 24 His concubine, whose name was Reumah, also bore Tebah, Gaham, Tahash, and Maacah.

Genesis 23

1 Sarah lived one hundred twenty-seven years. This was the length of Sarah's life.

2 Sarah died in Kiriath Arba (also called Hebron), in the land of Canaan. Abraham came to mourn for Sarah, and to weep for her.

Jasher 24

1 And the life of Sarah was one hundred and twenty-seven years, and Sarah died;

3 Abraham rose up from before his dead, and spoke
to the children of Heth, saying, 4 "I am a stranger
and a foreigner living with you. Give me a
possession of a burying-place with you, that I may
bury my dead out of my sight."

5 The children of Heth answered Abraham, saying
to him, 6 "Hear us, my lord. You are a prince of God
among us. Bury your dead in the best of our tombs.
None of us will withhold from you his tomb. Bury
your dead."

7 Abraham rose up, and bowed himself to the
people of the land, even to the children of Heth. 8
He talked with them, saying, "If you agree that I
should bury my dead out of my sight, hear me, and
entreat for me to Ephron the son of Zohar, 9 that
he may give me the cave of Machpelah, which he
has, which is in the end of his field. For the full price
let him give it to me among you for a possession of
a burying-place."

10 Now Ephron was sitting in the middle of the
children of Heth. Ephron the Hittite answered
Abraham in the hearing of the children of Heth,
even of all who went in at the gate of his city,
saying,

11 "No, my lord, hear me. I give you the field, and I
give you the cave that is in it. In the presence of the
children of my people I give it to you. Bury your
dead."

12 Abraham bowed himself down before the
people of the land. 13 He spoke to Ephron in the
audience of the people of the land, saying, "But if
you will, please hear me. I will give the price of the
field. Take it from me, and I will bury my dead
there."

14 Ephron answered Abraham, saying to him, 15
"My lord, listen to me. What is a piece of land
worth four hundred shekels of silver between me
and you? Therefore bury your dead."

and Abraham rose up from before his dead to seek
a burial place to bury his wife Sarah; and he went
and spoke to the children of Heth, the inhabitants
of the land, saying, 2 "I am a stranger and a
sojourner with you in your land; give me a
possession of a burial place in your land, that I may
bury my dead from before me."
3 And the children of Heth said unto Abraham,
"Behold the land is before thee, in the choice of our
sepulchers bury thy dead, for no man shall withhold
thee from burying thy dead."

4 And Abraham said unto them, "If you are
agreeable to this go and entreat for me to Ephron,
the son of Zochar, requesting that he may give me
the cave of Machpelah, which is in the end of his
field, and I will purchase it of him for whatever he
desire for it."

5 And Ephron dwelt among the children of Heth,
and they went and called for him, and he came
before Abraham, and Ephron said unto Abraham,
"Behold all thou requirest thy servant will do;"

and Abraham said, "No, but I will buy the cave and
the field which thou hast for value, In order that it
may be for a possession of a burial place for ever."

6 And Ephron answered and said, "Behold the field
and the cave are before thee, give whatever thou
desirest;"

and Abraham said, "Only at full value will I buy it
from thy hand, and from the hands of those that go
in at the gate of thy city, and from the hand of thy
seed for ever."

16 Abraham listened to Ephron. Abraham weighed
to Ephron the silver which he had named in the
audience of the children of Heth, four hundred
shekels of silver, according to the current
merchants' standard. 17 So the field of Ephron,
which was in Machpelah, which was before Mamre,
the field, the cave which was in it, and all the trees
that were in the field, that were in all of its borders,
were deeded 18 to Abraham for a possession in the
presence of the children of Heth, before all who
went in at the gate of his city.

7 And Ephron and all his brethren heard this, and
Abraham weighed to Ephron four hundred shekels
of silver in the hands of Ephron and in the hands of
all his brethren; and Abraham wrote this
transaction, and he wrote it and testified it with
four witnesses.

8 And these are the names of the witnesses, Amigal
son of Abishna the Hittite, Adichorom son of
Ashunach the Hivite, Abdon son of Achiram the
Gomerite, Bakdil the son of Abudish the Zidonite.

9 And Abraham took the book of the purchase, and
placed it in his treasures, and these are the words
that Abraham wrote in the book, namely:

10 That the cave and the field Abraham bought
from Ephron the Hittite, and from his seed, and
from those that go out of his city, and from their
seed for ever, are to be a purchase to Abraham and
to his seed and to those that go forth from his loins,
for a possession of a burial place for ever; and he
put a signet to it and testified it with witnesses.

11 And the field and the cave that was in it and all
that place were made sure unto Abraham and unto
his seed after him, from the children of Heth;
behold it is before Mamre in Hebron, which is in the
land of Canaan.

19 After this, Abraham buried Sarah his wife in the
cave of the field of Machpelah before Mamre (that
is, Hebron), in the land of Canaan. 20 The field, and
the cave that is in it, were deeded to Abraham for a
possession of a burying place by the children of
Heth.

12 And after this Abraham buried his wife Sarah
there, and that place and all its boundary became
to Abraham and unto his seed for a possession of a
burial place.

13 And Abraham buried Sarah with pomp as
observed at the interment of kings, and she was
buried in very fine and beautiful garments. 14 And
at her bier was Shem, his sons Eber and Abimelech,
together with Anar, Ashcol and Mamre, and all the
grandees of the land followed her bier.

15 And the days of Sarah were one hundred and
twenty-seven years and she died, and Abraham
made a great and heavy mourning, and he
performed the rites of mourning for seven days. 16
And all the inhabitants of the land comforted
Abraham and Isaac his son on account of Sarah.

17 And when the days of their mourning passed by
Abraham sent away his son Isaac, and he went to
the house of Shem and Eber, to learn the ways of
the Lord and his instructions, and Abraham
remained there three years. 18 At that time
Abraham rose up with all his servants, and they
went and returned homeward to Beersheba, and
Abraham and all his servants remained in
Beersheba.

19 And at the revolution of the year Abimelech king of the Philistines died in that year; he was one hundred and ninety-three years old at his death; and Abraham went with his people to the land of the Philistines, and they comforted the whole household and all his servants, and he then turned and went home.

20 And it was after the death of Abimelech that the
people of Gerar took Benmalich his son, and he was
only twelve years old, and they made him lying in
the place of his father. 21 And they called his name
Abimelech after the name of his father, for thus
was it their custom to do in Gerar, and Abimelech
reigned instead of Abimelech his father, and he sat
upon his throne.

22 And Lot the son of Haran also died in those days, in the thirty-ninth year of the life of Isaac, and all the days that Lot lived were one hundred and forty years and he died.

23 And these are the children of Lot, that were born to him by his daughters, the name of the first born was Moab, and the name of the second was Benami.

24 And the two sons of Lot went and took themselves wives from the land of Canaan, and they bare children to them, and the children of Moab were Ed, Mayon, Tarsus, and Kanvil, four sons, these are fathers to the children of Moab unto this day.

25 And all the families of the children of Lot went to dwell wherever they should light upon, for they were fruitful and increased abundantly. 26 And they went and built themselves cities in the land where they dwelt, and they called the names of the cities which they built after their own names.

27 And Nahor the son of Terah, brother to Abraham, died in those days in the fortieth year of the life of Isaac, and all the days of Nahor were one hundred and seventy-two years and he died and was buried in Haran. 28 And when Abraham heard that his brother was dead he grieved sadly, and he mourned over his brother many days.

Genesis 24

1 Abraham was old, and well stricken in age. Yahweh had blessed Abraham in all things.

2 Abraham said to his servant, the elder of his house, who ruled over all that he had, “Please put your hand under my thigh.

3 "I will make you swear by Yahweh, the God of heaven and the God of the earth, that you shall not take a wife for my son of the daughters of the Canaanites, among whom I live.

29 And Abraham called for Eliezer his head servant, to give him orders concerning his house, and he came and stood before him. 30 And Abraham said to him, "Behold I am old, I do not know the day of my death; for I am advanced in days; now therefore rise up, go forth and do not take a wife for my son from this place and from this land, from the daughters of the Canaanites amongst whom we dwell.

4 "But you shall go to my country, and to my relatives, and take a wife for my son Isaac.”

31 "But go to my land and to my birthplace, and take from thence a wife for my son, and the Lord God of Heaven and earth who took me from my father's house and brought me to this place, and said unto me, To thy seed will I give this land for an inheritance for ever, he will send his angel before thee and prosper thy way, that thou mayest obtain a wife for my son from my family and from my father's house."

5 The servant said to him, “What if the woman isn’t willing to follow me to this land? Must I bring your son again to the land you came from?”

32 And the servant answered his master Abraham and said, "Behold I go to thy birthplace and to thy father's house, and take a wife for thy son from there; but if the woman be not willing to follow me to this land, shall I take thy son back to the land of thy birthplace?"

6 Abraham said to him, "Beware that you don't bring my son there again. 7 Yahweh, the God of heaven, who took me from my father's house, and from the land of my birth, who spoke to me, and who swore to me, saying, 'I will give this land to your offspring. He will send his angel before you, and you shall take a wife for my son from there. 8 If the woman isn't willing to follow you, then you shall be clear from this oath to me. Only you shall not bring my son there again."

33 And Abraham said unto him, "Take heed that thou bring not my son hither again, for the Lord before whom I have walked he will send his angel before thee and prosper thy way."

9 The servant put his hand under the thigh of Abraham his master, and swore to him concerning this matter. 10 The servant took ten camels, of his master's camels, and departed, having a variety of good things of his master's with him. He arose, and went to Mesopotamia, to the city of Nahor.

34 And Eliezer did as Abraham ordered him, and Eliezer swore unto Abraham his master upon this matter; and Eliezer rose up and took ten camels of the camels of his master, and ten men from his master's servants with him, and they rose up and went to Haran, the city of Abraham and Nahor, in order to fetch a wife for Isaac the son of Abraham; and whilst they were gone Abraham sent to the house of Shem and Eber, and they brought from thence his son Isaac.

11 He made the camels kneel down outside the city by the well of water at the time of evening, the time that women go out to draw water.

35 And Isaac came home to his father's house to Beersheba, whilst Eliezer and his men came to Haran; and they stopped in the city by the watering place, and he made his camels to kneel down by the water and they remained there.

12 He said, "Yahweh, the God of my master Abraham, please give me success today, and show kindness to my master Abraham.

36 And Eliezer, Abraham's servant, prayed and said, "O God of Abraham my master; send me I pray thee good speed this day and show kindness unto my master, that thou shalt appoint this day a wife for my master's son from his family."

13 Behold, I am standing by the spring of water. The daughters of the men of the city are coming out to draw water. 14 Let it happen, that the young lady to whom I will say, 'Please let down your pitcher, that I may drink,' and she will say, 'Drink, and I will also give your camels a drink,'—let her be the one you have appointed for your servant Isaac. By this I will know that you have shown kindness to my master."

15 Before he had finished speaking, behold, Rebekah came out, who was born to Bethuel the son of Milcah, the wife of Nahor, Abraham's brother, with her pitcher on her shoulder.

37 And the Lord hearkened to the voice of Eliezer, for the sake of his servant Abraham, and he happened to meet with the daughter of Bethuel, the son of Milcah, the wife of Nahor, brother to Abraham, and Eliezer came to her house.

38 And Eliezer related to them all his concerns, and
that he was Abraham's servant, and they greatly
rejoiced at him. 39 And they all blessed the Lord
who brought this thing about, and they gave him
Rebecca, the daughter of Bethuel, for a wife for
Isaac.

16 The young lady was very beautiful to look at, a
virgin. No man had known her.

40 And the young woman was of very comely
appearance, she was a virgin, and Rebecca was ten
years old in those days.

She went down to the spring, filled her pitcher, and
came up. 17 The servant ran to meet her, and said,
"Please give me a drink, a little water from your
pitcher."

18 She said, "Drink, my lord." She hurried, and let
down her pitcher on her hand, and gave him drink.
19 When she had done giving him drink, she said, "I
will also draw for your camels, until they have done
drinking." 20 She hurried, and emptied her pitcher
into the trough, and ran again to the well to draw,
and drew for all his camels.

21 The man looked steadfastly at her, remaining
silent, to know whether Yahweh had made his
journey prosperous or not. 22 As the camels had
done drinking, the man took a golden ring of half a
shekel weight, and two bracelets for her hands of
ten shekels weight of gold, 23 and said, "Whose
daughter are you? Please tell me. Is there room in
your father's house for us to lodge in?"

24 She said to him, "I am the daughter of Bethuel
the son of Milcah, whom she bore to Nahor." 25
She said moreover to him, "We have both straw
and feed enough, and room to lodge in."

26 The man bowed his head, and worshiped
Yahweh. 27 He said, "Blessed be Yahweh, the God
of my master Abraham, who has not forsaken his
loving kindness and his truth toward my master. As
for me, Yahweh has led me on the way to the house
of my master's relatives."

28 The young lady ran, and told her mother's house
about these words. 29 Rebekah had a brother, and
his name was Laban. Laban ran out to the man, to
the spring.

30 When he saw the ring, and the bracelets on his sister's hands, and when he heard the words of Rebekah his sister, saying, "This is what the man said to me," he came to the man. Behold, he was standing by the camels at the spring.

31 He said, "Come in, you blessed of Yahweh. Why do you stand outside? For I have prepared the house, and room for the camels."

32 The man came into the house, and he unloaded the camels. He gave straw and feed for the camels, and water to wash his feet and the feet of the men
who were with him. 33 Food was set before him to
eat, but he said, "I will not eat until I have told my message." He said, "Speak on."

34 He said, "I am Abraham's servant. 35 Yahweh
has blessed my master greatly. He has become great. He has given him flocks and herds, silver and gold, male servants and female servants, and
camels and donkeys. 36 Sarah, my master's wife,
bore a son to my master when she was old. He has
given all that he has to him. 37 My master made me
swear, saying, 'You shall not take a wife for my son from the daughters of the Canaanites, in whose land I live,

38 "but you shall go to my father's house, and to
my relatives, and take a wife for my son.' 39 I asked
my master, 'What if the woman will not follow me?'
40 He said to me, 'Yahweh, before whom I walk, will send his angel with you, and prosper your way. You shall take a wife for my son from my relatives,
and of my father's house. 41 Then will you be clear
from my oath, when you come to my relatives. If they don't give her to you, you shall be clear from my oath.'

42 "I came today to the spring, and said, 'Yahweh, the God of my master Abraham, if now you do
prosper my way which I go— 43 behold, I am
standing by this spring of water. Let it happen, that the maiden who comes out to draw, to whom I will say, "Please give me a little water from your pitcher
to drink," 44 and she will tell me, "Drink, and I will
also draw for your camels,"—let her be the woman whom Yahweh has appointed for my master's son.'

45 "Before I had finished speaking in my heart, behold, Rebekah came out with her pitcher on her shoulder. She went down to the spring, and drew. I said to her, 'Please let me drink.'

46 "She hurried and let down her pitcher from her shoulder, and said, 'Drink, and I will also give your camels a drink.' So I drank, and she also gave the camels a drink. 47 I asked her, and said, 'Whose daughter are you?' She said, 'The daughter of Bethuel, Nahor's son, whom Milcah bore to him.' I put the ring on her nose, and the bracelets on her hands.

48 "I bowed my head, and worshiped Yahweh, and blessed Yahweh, the God of my master Abraham, who had led me in the right way to take my master's brother's daughter for his son. 49 Now if you will deal kindly and truly with my master, tell me. If not, tell me, that I may turn to the right hand, or to the left."

50 Then Laban and Bethuel answered, "The thing proceeds from Yahweh. We can't speak to you bad or good. 51 Behold, Rebekah is before you. Take her, and go, and let her be your master's son's wife, as Yahweh has spoken."

52 When Abraham's servant heard their words, he bowed himself down to the earth to Yahweh.

53 The servant brought out jewels of silver, and jewels of gold, and clothing, and gave them to Rebekah. He also gave precious things to her brother and her mother.

54 They ate and drank, he and the men who were with him, and stayed all night.

41 And Bethuel and Laban and his children made a feast on that night, and Eliezer and his men came and ate and drank and rejoiced there on that night.

They rose up in the morning, and he said, "Send me away to my master."

42 And Eliezer rose up in the morning, he and the men that were with him, and he called to the whole household of Bethuel, saying, "Send me away that I may go to my master;" and they rose up and sent away Rebecca and her nurse Deborah, the daughter of Uz, and they gave her silver and gold, men servants and maid servants, and they blessed her.

55 Her brother and her mother said, "Let the young lady stay with us a few days, at least ten. After that she will go."

56 He said to them, "Don't hinder me, since Yahweh has prospered my way. Send me away that I may go to my master."

57 They said, "We will call the young lady, and ask her." 58 They called Rebekah, and said to her, "Will you go with this man?" She said, "I will go."

59 They sent away Rebekah, their sister, with her nurse, Abraham's servant, and his men.

43 And they sent Eliezer away with his men; and the servants took Rebecca, and he went and returned to his master to the land of Canaan.

60 They blessed Rebekah, and said to her, "Our sister, may you be the mother of thousands of ten thousands, and let your offspring possess the gate of those who hate them."

61 Rebekah arose with her ladies. They rode on the camels, and followed the man. The servant took Rebekah, and went his way. 62 Isaac came from the way of Beer Lahai Roi, for he lived in the land of the South. 63 Isaac went out to meditate in the field at the evening. He lifted up his eyes, and saw, and, behold, there were camels coming.

64 Rebekah lifted up her eyes, and when she saw Isaac, she dismounted from the camel. 65 She said to the servant, "Who is the man who is walking in the field to meet us?" The servant said, "It is my master." She took her veil, and covered herself. 66 The servant told Isaac all the things that he had done.

67 Isaac brought her into his mother Sarah's tent, and took Rebekah, and she became his wife. He loved her. Isaac was comforted after his mother's death.

44 And Isaac took Rebecca and she became his wife, and he brought her into the tent.

[Genesis 25:20 Isaac was forty years old when he took Rebekah, the daughter of Bethuel the Syrian of Paddan Aram, the sister of Laban the Syrian, to be his wife.]

45 And Isaac was forty years old when he took Rebecca, the daughter of his uncle Bethuel, for a wife.

Genesis 25

1 Abraham took another wife, and her name was Keturah.

Jasher 25

1 And it was at that time that Abraham again took a wife in his old age, and her name was Keturah, from the land of Canaan.

2 She bore him Zimran, Jokshan, Medan, Midian, Ishbak, and Shuah.

2 And she bare unto him Zimran, Jokshan, Medan, Midian, Ishbak and Shuach, being six sons.

And the children of Zimran were Abihen, Molich and Narim.

3 Jokshan became the father of Sheba, and Dedan.

3 And the sons of Jokshan were Sheba and Dedan,

The sons of Dedan were Asshurim, Letushim, and Leummim.

and the sons of Medan were Amida, Joab, Gochi, Elisha and Nothach;

4 The sons of Midian were: Ephah, Epher, Hanoch, Abida, and Eldaah.

and the sons of Midian were Ephah, Epher, Chanoch, Abida and Eldaah.

4 And the sons of Ishbak were Makiro, Beyodua and Tator. 5 And the sons of Shuach were Bildad, Mamdad, Munan and Meban;

All these were the children of Keturah.

all these are the families of the children of Keturah the Canaanitish woman which she bare unto Abraham the Hebrew.

5 Abraham gave all that he had to Isaac,
6 but to the sons of Abraham's concubines, Abraham gave gifts. He sent them away from Isaac his son, while he yet lived, eastward, to the east country.

6 And Abraham sent all these away, and he gave them gifts, and they went away from his son Isaac to dwell wherever they should find a place. 7 And all these went to the mountain at the east, and they built themselves six cities in which they dwelt unto this day.

8 But the children of Sheba and Dedan, children of Jokshan, with their children, did not dwell with their brethren in their cities, and they journeyed and encamped in the countries and wildernesses unto this day.

9 And the children of Midian, son of Abraham, went to the east of the land of Cush, and they there found a large valley in the eastern country, and they remained there and built a city, and they dwelt therein, that is the land of Midian unto this day.

10 And Midian dwelt in the city which he built, he and his five sons and all belonging to him. 11 And these are the names of the sons of Midian according to their names in their cities, Ephah, Epher, Chanoch, Abida and Eldaah.

12 And the sons of Ephah were Methach, Meshar, Avi and Tzanua, and the sons of Epher were Ephron, Zur, Alirun and Medin, and the sons of Chanoch were Reuel, Rekem, Azi, Alyoshub and Alad.

13 And the sons of Abida were Chur, Melud, Kerury, Molchi; and the sons of Eldaah were Miker, and Reba, and Malchiyah and Gabol; these are the names of the Midianites according to their families; and afterward the families of Midian spread throughout the land of Midian.

14 And these are the generations of Ishmael the
son Abraham, whom Hagar, Sarah's handmaid, bare
unto Abraham. 15 And Ishmael took a wife from
the land of Egypt, and her name was Ribah, the
same is Meribah. 16 And Ribah bare unto Ishmael
Nebayoth, Kedar, Adbeel, Mibsam and their sister
Bosmath.

17 And Ishmael cast away his wife Ribah, and she went from him and returned to Egypt to the house of her father, and she dwelt there, for she had been very bad in the sight of Ishmael, and in the sight of his father Abraham.

18 And Ishmael afterward took a wife from the land of Canaan, and her name was Malchuth, and she bare unto him Nishma, Dumah, Masa, Chadad, Tema, Yetur, Naphish and Kedma.

19 These are the sons of Ishmael, and these are their names, being twelve princes according to their nations; and the families of Ishmael afterward spread forth, and Ishmael took his children and all the property that he had gained, together with the souls of his household and all belonging to him, and they went to dwell where they should find a place.

20 And they went and dwelt near the wilderness of
Paran, and their dwelling was from Havilah unto
Shur, that is before Egypt as thou comest toward
Assyria. 21 And Ishmael and his sons dwelt in the
land, and they had children born to them, and they
were fruitful and increased abundantly.

22 And these are the names of the sons of Nebayoth the first born of Ishmael; Mend, Send, Mayon; and the sons of Kedar were Alyon, Kezem, Chamad and Eli.

23 And the sons of Adbeel were Chamad and Jabin; and the sons of Mibsam were Obadiah, Ebedmelech and Yeush; these are the families of the children of Ribah the wife of Ishmael.

24 And the sons of Mishma the son of Ishmael were Shamua, Zecaryon and Obed; and the sons of Dumah were Kezed, Eli, Machmad and Amed.

25 And the sons of Masa were Melon, Mula and Ebidadon; and the sons of Chadad were Azur, Minzar and Ebedmelech; and the sons of Tema were Seir, Sadon and Yakol.

7 These are the days of the years of Abraham's life
which he lived: one hundred seventy-five years. 8
Abraham gave up his spirit, and died in a good old
age, an old man, and full of years, and was gathered
to his people. 9 Isaac and Ishmael, his sons, buried
him in the cave of Machpelah, in the field of
Ephron, the son of Zohar the Hittite, which is before
Mamre, 10 the field which Abraham purchased of
the children of Heth. Abraham was buried there
with Sarah, his wife.

11 After the death of Abraham, God blessed Isaac,
his son. Isaac lived by Beer Lahai Roi.

12 Now this is the history of the generations of
Ishmael, Abraham's son, whom Hagar the Egyptian,
Sarah's servant, bore to Abraham. 13 These are the
names of the sons of Ishmael, by their names,
according to the order of their birth: the firstborn of
Ishmael, Nebaioth, then Kedar, Adbeel, Mibsam, 14
Mishma, Dumah, Massa, 15 Hadad, Tema, Jetur,
Naphish, and Kedemah. 16 These are the sons of
Ishmael, and these are their names, by their
villages, and by their encampments: twelve princes,
according to their nations.

17 These are the years of the life of Ishmael: one
hundred thirty-seven years. He gave up his spirit
and died, and was gathered to his people.

26 And the sons of Yetur were Merith, Yaish, Alyo, and Pachoth; and the sons of Naphish were Ebed-Tamed, Abiyasaph and Mir; and the sons of Kedma were Calip, Tachti, and Omir; these were the children of Malchuth the wife of Ishmael according to their families.

27 All these are the families of Ishmael according to their generations, and they dwelt in those lands wherein they had built themselves cities unto this day.

28 And Rebecca the daughter of Bethuel, the wife of Abraham's son Isaac, was barren in those days, she had no offspring; and Isaac dwelt with his father in the land of Canaan; and the Lord was with Isaac; and Arpachshad the son of Shem the son of Noah died in those days, in the forty-eighth year of the life of Isaac, and all the days that Arpachshad lived were four hundred and thirty-eight years, and he died.

[26:29 And it was at that time that Abraham died, in the fifteenth year of the life of Jacob and Esau, the sons of Isaac, and all the days of Abraham were one hundred and seventy-five years, and he died and was gathered to his people in good old age, old and satisfied with days, and Isaac and Ishmael his sons buried him.]

18 They lived from Havilah to Shur that is before Egypt, as you go toward Assyria. He lived opposite all his relatives.

19 This is the history of the generations of Isaac, Abraham's son. Abraham became the father of Isaac.

20 Isaac was forty years old when he took Rebekah, the daughter of Bethuel the Syrian of Paddan Aram, the sister of Laban the Syrian, to be his wife.

[25:45 And Isaac was forty years old when he took Rebecca, the daughter of his uncle Bethuel, for a wife.]

21 Isaac entreated Yahweh for his wife, because she was barren.

Jasher 26

1 And in the fifty-ninth year of the life of Isaac the son of Abraham, Rebecca his wife was still barren in those days.

Yahweh was entreated by him, and Rebekah his wife conceived.

2 And Rebecca said unto Isaac, "Truly I have heard, my lord, that thy mother Sarah was barren in her days until my Lord Abraham, thy father, prayed for
her and she conceived by him. 3 Now therefore
stand up, pray thou also to God and he will hear thy prayer and remember us through his mercies."

4 And Isaac answered his wife Rebecca, saying, "Abraham has already prayed for me to God to multiply his seed, now therefore this barrenness must proceed to us from thee."

5 And Rebecca said unto him, "But arise now thou also and pray, that the Lord may hear thy prayer and grant me children," and Isaac hearkened to the words of his wife, and Isaac and his wife rose up and went to the land of Moriah to pray there and to seek the Lord, and when they had reached that place Isaac stood up and prayed to the Lord on account of his wife because she was barren.

6 And Isaac said, "O Lord God of heaven and earth, whose goodness and mercies fill the earth, thou who didst take my father from his father's house and from his birthplace, and didst bring him unto this land, and didst say unto him, 'To thy seed will I give the land,' and thou didst promise him and didst declare unto him, 'I will multiply thy seed as the stars of heaven and as the sand of the sea,' now may thy words be verified which thou didst speak unto my father.

7 "For thou art the Lord our God, our eyes are toward thee to give us seed of men, as thou didst promise us, for thou art the Lord our God and our eyes are directed toward thee only."

8 And the Lord heard the prayer of Isaac the son of Abraham, and the Lord was entreated of him and Rebecca his wife conceived.

22 The children struggled together within her. She said, "If it is so, why do I live?"

9 And in about seven months after the children struggled together within her, and it pained her greatly that she was wearied on account of them, and she said to all the women who were then in the land, "Did such a thing happen to you as it has to me?" and they said unto her, "No."

10 And she said unto them, "Why am I alone in this amongst all the women that were upon earth?" and she went to the land of Moriah to seek the Lord on account of this; and she went to Shem and Eber his son to make inquiries of them in this matter, and that they should seek the Lord in this thing
respecting her. 11 And she also asked Abraham to
seek and inquire of the Lord about all that had befallen her.

She went to inquire of Yahweh. 23 Yahweh said to
her, "Two nations are in your womb. Two peoples will be separated from your body. The one people will be stronger than the other people. The elder will serve the younger."

12 And they all inquired of the Lord concerning this matter, and they brought her word from the Lord and told her, "Two children are in thy womb, and two nations shall rise from them; and one nation shall be stronger than the other, and the greater shall serve the younger."

24 When her days to be delivered were fulfilled,
behold, there were twins in her womb. 25 The first
came out red all over, like a hairy garment. They named him Esau.

13 And when her days to be delivered were completed, she knelt down, and behold there were twins in her womb, as the Lord had spoken to her.
14 And the first came out red all over like a hairy garment, and all the people of the land called his name Esau, saying, "That this one was made complete from the womb."

26 After that, his brother came out, and his hand had hold on Esau's heel. He was named Jacob. Isaac was sixty years old when she bore them.

15 And after that came his brother, and his hand took hold of Esau's heel, therefore they called his
name Jacob. 16 And Isaac, the son of Abraham,
was sixty years old when he begat them.

27 The boys grew. Esau was a skillful hunter, a man of the field. Jacob was a quiet man, living in tents.

17 And the boys grew up to their fifteenth year, and they came amongst the society of men. Esau was a designing and deceitful man, and an expert hunter in the field, and Jacob was a man perfect and wise, dwelling in tents, feeding flocks and learning the instructions of the Lord and the commands of his father and mother.

18 And Isaac and the children of his household dwelt with his father Abraham in the land of
Canaan, as God had commanded them. 19 And
Ishmael the son of Abraham went with his children and all belonging to them, and they returned there to the land of Havilah, and they dwelt there.

20 And all the children of Abraham's concubines went to dwell in the land of the east, for Abraham had sent them away from his son, and had given them presents, and they went away.

21 And Abraham gave all that he had to his son
Isaac, and he also gave him all his treasures. 22 And
he commanded him saying, "Dost thou not know and understand the Lord is God in heaven and in
earth, and there is no other beside him? 23 And it
was he who took me from my father's house, and from my birth place, and gave me all the delights upon earth; who delivered me from the counsel of the wicked, for in him did I trust.

24 "And he brought me to this place, and he delivered me from Ur Casdim; and he said unto me, 'To thy seed will I give all these lands, and they shall inherit them when they keep my commandments, my statutes and my judgments that I have commanded thee, and which I shall command
them.' 25 Now therefore my son, hearken to my
voice, and keep the commandments of the Lord thy God, which I commanded thee, do not turn from the right way either to the right or to the left, in order that it may be well with thee and thy children after thee forever.

26 "And remember the wonderful works of the Lord, and his kindness that he has shown toward us, in having delivered us from the hands of our enemies, and the Lord our God caused them to fall into our hands; and now therefore keep all that I have commanded thee, and turn not away from the commandments of thy God, and serve none beside him, in order that it may be well with thee and thy seed after thee. 27 And teach thou thy children and thy seed the instructions of the Lord and his commandments, and teach them the upright way in which they should go, in order that it may be well with them forever."

28 And Isaac answered his father and said unto him, "That which my Lord has commanded that will I do, and I will not depart from the commands of the Lord my God, I will keep all that he commanded me; and Abraham blessed his son Isaac, and also his children;" and Abraham taught Jacob the instruction of the Lord and his ways.

[Genesis 25:7 These are the days of the years of Abraham's life which he lived: one hundred seventy-five years. 8 Abraham gave up his spirit, and died in a good old age, an old man, and full of years, and was gathered to his people. 9 Isaac and Ishmael, his sons, buried him in the cave of Machpelah, in the field of Ephron, the son of Zohar the Hittite, which is before Mamre, 10 the field which Abraham purchased of the children of Heth. Abraham was buried there with Sarah, his wife.]

29 And it was at that time that Abraham died, in the fifteenth year of the life of Jacob and Esau, the sons of Isaac, and all the days of Abraham were one hundred and seventy-five years, and he died and was gathered to his people in good old age, old and satisfied with days, and Isaac and Ishmael his sons buried him.

30 And when the inhabitants of Canaan heard that Abraham was dead, they all came with their kings and princes and all their men to bury Abraham. 31 And all the inhabitants of the land of Haran, and all the families of the house of Abraham, and all the princes and grandees, and the sons of Abraham by the concubines, all came when they heard of Abraham's death, and they requited Abraham's kindness, and comforted Isaac his son, and they buried Abraham in the cave which he bought from Ephron the Hittite and his children, for the possession of a burial place.

32 And all the inhabitants of Canaan, and all those who had known Abraham, wept for Abraham a whole year, and men and women mourned over him. 33 And all the little children, and all the inhabitants of the land wept on account of Abraham, for Abraham had been good to them all, and because he had been upright with God and men.

34 And there arose not a man who feared God like unto Abraham, for he had feared his God from his youth, and had served the Lord, and had gone in all his ways during his life, from his childhood to the day of his death. 35 And the Lord was with him and delivered him from the counsel of Nimrod and his people, and when he made war with the four kings of Elam he conquered them.

36 And he brought all the children of the earth to the service of God, and he taught them the ways of the Lord, and caused them to know the Lord. 37 And he formed a grove and he planted a vineyard therein, and he had always prepared in his tent meat and drink to those that passed through the land, that they might satisfy themselves in his house. 38 And the Lord God delivered the whole earth on account of Abraham.

39 And it was after the death of Abraham that God blessed his son Isaac and his children, and the Lord was with Isaac as he had been with his father Abraham, for Isaac kept all the commandments of the Lord as Abraham his father had commanded him; he did not turn to the right or to the left from the right path which his father had commanded him.

Jasher 27

1 And Esau at that time, after the death of Abraham, frequently went in the field to hunt.

2 And Nimrod king of Babel, the same was Amraphel, also frequently went with his mighty men to hunt in the field, and to walk about with his men in the cool of the day. 3 And Nimrod was observing Esau all the days, for a jealousy was formed in the heart of Nimrod against Esau all the days.

4 And on a certain day Esau went in the field to hunt, and he found Nimrod walking in the wilderness with his two men. 5 And all his mighty men and his people were with him in the wilderness, but they removed at a distance from him, and they went from him in different directions to hunt, and Esau concealed himself for Nimrod, and he lurked for him in the wilderness.

6 And Nimrod and his men that were with him did not know him, and Nimrod and his men frequently walked about in the field at the cool of the day, and to know where his men were hunting in the field. 7 And Nimrod and two of his men that were with him came to the place where they were, when Esau started suddenly from his lurking place, and drew his sword, and hastened and ran to Nimrod and cut off his head. 8 And Esau fought a desperate fight with the two men that were with Nimrod, and when they called out to him, Esau turned to them and smote them to death with his sword.

9 And all the mighty men of Nimrod, who had left him to go to the wilderness, heard the cry at a distance, and they knew the voices of those two men, and they ran to know the cause of it, when they found their king and the two men that were with him lying dead in the wilderness. 10 And when Esau saw the mighty men of Nimrod coming at a distance, he fled, and thereby escaped; and Esau took the valuable garments of Nimrod, which Nimrod's father had bequeathed to Nimrod, and with which Nimrod prevailed over the whole land, and he ran and concealed them in his house.

11 And Esau took those garments and ran into the city on account of Nimrod's men, and he came unto his father's house wearied and exhausted from fight, and he was ready to die through grief when he approached his brother Jacob and sat before him.

28 Now Isaac loved Esau, because he ate his venison. Rebekah loved Jacob. 29 Jacob boiled stew. Esau came in from the field, and he was famished.

30 Esau said to Jacob, "Please feed me with that same red stew, for I am famished." Therefore his name was called Edom. 31 Jacob said, "First, sell me your birthright."

32 Esau said, "Behold, I am about to die. What good is the birthright to me?" 33 Jacob said, "Swear to me first." He swore to him. He sold his birthright to Jacob.

12 And he said unto his brother Jacob, "Behold I shall die this day, and wherefore then do I want the birthright?" And Jacob acted wisely with Esau in this matter, and Esau sold his birthright to Jacob, for it was so brought about by the Lord.

34 Jacob gave Esau bread and stew of lentils. He ate and drank, rose up, and went his way. So Esau despised his birthright.

13 And Esau's portion in the cave of the field of Machpelah, which Abraham had bought from the children of Heth for the possession of a burial ground, Esau also sold to Jacob, and Jacob bought all this from his brother Esau for value given. 14 And Jacob wrote the whole of this in a book, and he testified the same with witnesses, and he sealed it, and the book remained in the hands of Jacob.

15 And when Nimrod the son of Cush died, his men lifted him up and brought him in consternation, and buried him in his city, and all the days that Nimrod lived were two hundred and fifteen years and he died.

16 And the days that Nimrod reigned upon the people of the land were one hundred and eighty-five years; and Nimrod died by the sword of Esau in shame and contempt, and the seed of Abraham caused his death as he had seen in his dream.

17 And at the death of Nimrod his kingdom became divided into many divisions, and all those parts that Nimrod reigned over were restored to the respective kings of the land, who recovered them after the death of Nimrod, and all the people of the house of Nimrod were for a long time enslaved to all the other kings of the land.

Genesis 26

1 There was a famine in the land, besides the first famine that was in the days of Abraham. Isaac went to Abimelech king of the Philistines, to Gerar.

Jasher 28

1 And in those days, after the death of Abraham, in that year the Lord brought a heavy famine in the land, and whilst the famine was raging in the land of Canaan, Isaac rose up to go down to Egypt on account of the famine, as his father Abraham had done.

2 Yahweh appeared to him, and said, "Don't go
down into Egypt. Live in the land I will tell you
about. 3 Live in this land, and I will be with you, and
will bless you. For I will give to you, and to your
offspring all these lands, and I will establish the
oath which I swore to Abraham your father. 4 I will
multiply your offspring as the stars of the sky, and
will give all these lands to your offspring. In your
offspring will all the nations of the earth be blessed,
5 because Abraham obeyed my voice, and kept my
requirements, my commandments, my statutes,
and my laws."

2 And the Lord appeared that night to Isaac and he said to him, "Do not go down to Egypt but rise and go to Gerar, to Abimelech king of the Philistines, and remain there till the famine shall cease."

6 Isaac lived in Gerar.

3 And Isaac rose up and went to Gerar, as the Lord commanded him, and he remained there a full year.

7 The men of the place asked him about his wife. He said, "She is my sister," for he was afraid to say, "My wife", lest, he thought, "the men of the place might kill me for Rebekah, because she is beautiful to look at."

4 And when Isaac came to Gerar, the people of the land saw that Rebecca his wife was of a beautiful appearance, and the people of Gerar asked Isaac concerning his wife, and he said, "She is my sister," for he was afraid to say she was his wife lest the people of the land should slay him on account of her.

5 And the princes of Abimelech went and praised the woman to the king, but he answered them not, neither did he attend to their words.

6 But he heard them say that Isaac declared her to be his sister, so the king reserved this within himself.

8 When he had been there a long time, Abimelech king of the Philistines looked out at a window, and saw, and, behold, Isaac was caressing Rebekah, his wife.

7 And when Isaac had remained three months in the land, Abimelech looked out at the window, and he saw, and behold Isaac was sporting with Rebecca his wife, for Isaac dwelt in the outer house belonging to the king, so that the house of Isaac was opposite the house of the king.

9 Abimelech called Isaac, and said, "Behold, surely
she is your wife. Why did you say, 'She is my
sister?'" Isaac said to him, "Because I said, 'Lest I
die because of her.'" 10 Abimelech said, "What is
this you have done to us? One of the people might
easily have lain with your wife, and you would have
brought guilt on us!"

8 And the king said unto Isaac, "What is this thou
hast done to us in saying of thy wife, 'She is my
sister?' How easily might one of the great men of
the people have lain with her, and thou wouldst
then have brought guilt upon us." 9 And Isaac said
unto Abimelech, "Because I was afraid lest I die on
account of my wife, therefore I said, 'She is my
sister.'"

10 At that time Abimelech gave orders to all his princes and great men, and they took Isaac and Rebecca his wife and brought them before the king.

Genesis 26	Jasher 28
11 Abimelech commanded all the people, saying, "He who touches this man or his wife will surely be put to death."	11 And the king commanded that they should dress them in princely garments, and make them ride through the streets of the city, and proclaim before them throughout the land, saying, "This is the man and this is his wife; whoever toucheth this man or his wife shall surely die." And Isaac returned with his wife to the king's house, and the Lord was with Isaac and he continued to wax great and lacked nothing. 12 And the Lord caused Isaac to find favor in the sight of Abimelech, and in the sight of all his subjects, and Abimelech acted well with Isaac, for Abimelech remembered the oath and the covenant that existed between his father and Abraham.
	13 And Abimelech said unto Isaac, "Behold the whole earth is before thee; dwell wherever it may seem good in thy sight until thou shalt return to thy land;" and Abimelech gave Isaac fields and vineyards and the best part of the land of Gerar, to sow and reap and eat the fruits of the ground until the days of the famine should have passed by.
12 Isaac sowed in that land, and reaped in the same year one hundred times what he planted. Yahweh blessed him.	14 And Isaac sowed in that land, and received a hundred-fold in the same year, and the Lord blessed him.
13 The man grew great, and grew more and more until he became very great. 14 He had possessions of flocks, possessions of herds, and a great household. The Philistines envied him.	15 And the man waxed great, and he had possession of flocks and possession of herds and great store of servants.
15 Now all the wells which his father's servants had dug in the days of Abraham his father, the Philistines had stopped, and filled with earth.	
16 Abimelech said to Isaac, "Go from us, for you are much mightier than we." 17 Isaac departed from there, encamped in the valley of Gerar, and lived there.	16 And when the days of the famine had passed away the Lord appeared to Isaac and said unto him, "Rise up, go forth from this place and return to thy land, to the land of Canaan;" and Isaac rose up and returned to Hebron which is in the land of Canaan, he and all belonging to him as the Lord commanded him.

18 Isaac dug again the wells of water, which they
had dug in the days of Abraham his father. For the
Philistines had stopped them after the death of
Abraham. He called their names after the names by
which his father had called them. 19 Isaac's
servants dug in the valley, and found there a well of
springing water. 20 The herdsmen of Gerar argued
with Isaac's herdsmen, saying, "The water is ours."
He called the name of the well Esek, because they
contended with him.

21 They dug another well, and they argued over
that, also. He called its name Sitnah. 22 He left that
place, and dug another well. They didn't argue over
that one. He called it Rehoboth. He said, "For now
Yahweh has made room for us, and we will be
fruitful in the land."
23 He went up from there to Beersheba. 24 Yahweh
appeared to him the same night, and said, "I am the
God of Abraham your father. Don't be afraid, for I
am with you, and will bless you, and multiply your
offspring for my servant Abraham's sake."

25 He built an altar there, and called on Yahweh's
name, and pitched his tent there. There Isaac's
servants dug a well.

26 Then Abimelech went to him from Gerar, and
Ahuzzath his friend, and Phicol the captain of his
army. 27 Isaac said to them, "Why have you come
to me, since you hate me, and have sent me away
from you?"

28 They said, "We saw plainly that Yahweh was
with you. We said, 'Let there now be an oath
between us, even between us and you, and let us
make a covenant with you, 29 that you will do us no
harm, as we have not touched you, and as we have
done to you nothing but good, and have sent you
away in peace.' You are now the blessed of
Yahweh."

30 He made them a feast, and they ate and drank.
31 They rose up some time in the morning, and
swore to one another. Isaac sent them away, and
they departed from him in peace. 32 The same day,
Isaac's servants came, and told him concerning the
well which they had dug, and said to him, "We have
found water." 33 He called it Shibah. Therefore the
name of the city is Beersheba to this day.

34 When Esau was forty years old, he took as wife Judith, the daughter of Beeri the Hittite, and Basemath, the daughter of Elon the Hittite. 35 They grieved Isaac's and Rebekah's spirits.

17 And after this Shelach the son at Arpachshad died in that year, which is the eighteenth year of the lives of Jacob and Esau; and all the days that Shelach lived were four hundred and thirty-three years and he died.

18 At that time Isaac sent his younger son Jacob to the house of Shem and Eber, and he learned the instructions of the Lord, and Jacob remained in the house of Shem and Eber for thirty-two years, and Esau his brother did not go, for he was not willing to go, and he remained in his father's house in the land of Canaan.

19 And Esau was continually hunting in the fields to bring home what he could get, so did Esau all the days. 20 And Esau was a designing and deceitful man, one who hunted after the hearts of men and inveigled them, and Esau was a valiant man in the field, and in the course of time went as usual to hunt; and he came as far as the field of Seir, the same is Edom.

21 And he remained in the land of Seir hunting in the field a year and four months. 22 And Esau there saw in the land of Seir the daughter of a man of Canaan, and her name was Jehudith, the daughter of Beeri, son of Epher, from the families of Heth the son of Canaan. 23 And Esau took her for a wife, and he came unto her; forty years old was Esau when he took her, and he brought her to Hebron, the land of his father's dwelling place, and he dwelt there.

24 And it came to pass in those days, in the hundred and tenth year of the life of Isaac, that is in the fiftieth year of the life of Jacob, in that year died Shem the son of Noah; Shem was six hundred years old at his death. 25 And when Shem died Jacob returned to his father to Hebron which is in the land of Canaan.

26 And in the fifty-sixth year of the life of Jacob, people came from Haran, and Rebecca was told concerning her brother Laban the son of Bethuel. 27 For the wife of Laban was barren in those days, and bare no children, and also all his handmaids bare none to him. 28 And the Lord afterward remembered Adinah the wife of Laban, and she conceived and bare twin daughters, and Laban called the names of his daughters, the name of the elder Leah, and the name of the younger Rachel.

29 And those people came and told these things to Rebecca, and Rebecca rejoiced greatly that the Lord had visited her brother and that he had got children.

Genesis 27

1 When Isaac was old, and his eyes were dim, so that he could not see, he called Esau his elder son, and said to him, "My son?" He said to him, "Here I am."

2 He said, "See now, I am old. I don't know the day of my death. 3 Now therefore, please take your weapons, your quiver and your bow, and go out to the field, and take me venison. 4 Make me savory food, such as I love, and bring it to me, that I may eat, and that my soul may bless you before I die."

5 Rebekah heard when Isaac spoke to Esau his son. Esau went to the field to hunt for venison, and to bring it. 6 Rebekah spoke to Jacob her son, saying, "Behold, I heard your father speak to Esau your brother, saying, 7 'Bring me venison, and make me savory food, that I may eat, and bless you before Yahweh before my death.'

8 "Now therefore, my son, obey my voice according to that which I command you. 9 Go now to the flock, and get me from there two good young goats. I will make them savory food for your father, such as he loves. 10 You shall bring it to your father, that he may eat, so that he may bless you before his death."

Jasher 29

1 And Isaac the son of Abraham became old and advanced in days, and his eyes became heavy through age; they were dim and could not see.

2 At that time Isaac called unto Esau his son, saying, "Get I pray thee thy weapons, thy quiver and thy bow, rise up and go forth into the field and get me some venison, and make me savory meat and bring it to me, that I may eat in order that I may bless thee before my death, as I have now become old and gray-headed."

3 And Esau did so; and he took his weapon and went forth into the field to hunt for venison, as usual, to bring to his father as he had ordered him, so that he might bless him.

4 And Rebecca heard all the words that Isaac had spoken unto Esau, and she hastened and called her son Jacob, saying, "Thus did thy father speak unto thy brother Esau, and thus did I hear, now therefore hasten thou and make that which I shall tell thee.

5 "Rise up and go, I pray thee, to the flock and fetch me two fine kids of the goats, and I will get the savory meat for thy father, and thou shalt bring the savory meat that he may eat before thy brother shall have come from the chase, in order that thy father may bless thee."

11 Jacob said to Rebekah his mother, "Behold, Esau
my brother is a hairy man, and I am a smooth man.
12 What if my father touches me? I will seem to
him as a deceiver, and I would bring a curse on
myself, and not a blessing."

13 His mother said to him, "Let your curse be on
me, my son. Only obey my voice, and go get them
for me."

14 He went, and got them, and brought them to his
mother. His mother made savory food, such as his
father loved.

6 And Jacob hastened and did as his mother had commanded him, and he made the savory meat and brought it before his father before Esau had come from his chase.

15 Rebekah took the good clothes of Esau, her elder
son, which were with her in the house, and put
them on Jacob, her younger son. 16 She put the
skins of the young goats on his hands, and on the
smooth of his neck. 17 She gave the savory food
and the bread, which she had prepared, into the
hand of her son Jacob.

18 He came to his father, and said, "My father?"
He said, "Here I am. Who are you, my son?" 19
Jacob said to his father, "I am Esau your firstborn. I
have done what you asked me to do. Please arise,
sit and eat of my venison, that your soul may bless
me."

7 And Isaac said unto Jacob, "Who art thou, my son?" And he said, "I am thy first born Esau, I have done as thou didst order me, now therefore rise up I pray thee, and eat of my hunt, in order that thy soul may bless me as thou didst speak unto me."

20 Isaac said to his son, "How is it that you have
found it so quickly, my son?" He said, "Because
Yahweh your God gave me success."

21 Isaac said to Jacob, "Please come near, that I
may feel you, my son, whether you are really my
son Esau or not."

22 Jacob went near to Isaac his father. He felt him,
and said, "The voice is Jacob's voice, but the hands
are the hands of Esau." 23 He didn't recognize him,
because his hands were hairy, like his brother,
Esau's hands. So he blessed him. 24 He said, "Are
you really my son Esau?" He said, "I am."

25 He said, "Bring it near to me, and I will eat of my
son's venison, that my soul may bless you."

He brought it near to him, and he ate. He brought
him wine, and he drank. 26 His father Isaac said to
him, “Come near now, and kiss me, my son.” 27 He
came near, and kissed him. He smelled the smell of
his clothing, and blessed him, and said, “Behold, the
smell of my son is as the smell of a field which
Yahweh has blessed. 28 God give you of the dew of
the sky, of the fatness of the earth, and plenty of
grain and new wine. 29 Let peoples serve you, and
nations bow down to you. Be lord over your
brothers. Let your mother’s sons bow down to you.
Cursed be everyone who curses you. Blessed be
everyone who blesses you.”

8 And Isaac rose up and he ate and he drank, and
his heart was comforted, and he blessed Jacob and
Jacob went away from his father;

30 As soon as Isaac had finished blessing Jacob, and
Jacob had just gone out from the presence of Isaac
his father, Esau his brother came in from his
hunting. 31 He also made savory food, and brought
it to his father. He said to his father, “Let my father
arise, and eat of his son’s venison, that your soul
may bless me.” 32 Isaac his father said to him,
“Who are you?” He said, “I am your son, your
firstborn, Esau.”

and as soon as Isaac had blessed Jacob and he had
gone away from him, behold Esau came from his
hunt from the field, and he also made savory meat
and brought it to his father to eat thereof and to
bless him.

33 Isaac trembled violently, and said, “Who, then, is
he who has taken venison, and brought it me, and I
have eaten of all before you came, and have
blessed him? Yes, he will be blessed.”

9 And Isaac said unto Esau, "And who was he that
has taken venison and brought it me before thou
camest and whom I did bless?"

And Esau knew that his brother Jacob had done
this, and the anger of Esau was kindled against his
brother Jacob that he had acted thus toward him.

34 When Esau heard the words of his father, he
cried with an exceeding great and bitter cry, and
said to his father, “Bless me, even me also, my
father.” 35 He said, “Your brother came with
deceit, and has taken away your blessing.”

36 He said, “Isn’t he rightly named Jacob? For he
has supplanted me these two times. He took away
my birthright. See, now he has taken away my
blessing.” He said, “Haven’t you reserved a blessing
for me?”

10 And Esau said, "Is he not rightly called Jacob? for
he has supplanted me twice, he took away my
birthright and now he has taken away my blessing";

37 Isaac answered Esau, “Behold, I have made him
your lord, and all his brothers have I given to him
for servants. With grain and new wine have I
sustained him. What then will I do for you, my
son?”

and Esau wept greatly; and when Isaac heard the
voice of his son Esau weeping, Isaac said unto Esau,
"What can I do, my son, thy brother came with
subtlety and took away thy blessing"; and Esau
hated his brother Jacob on account of the blessing
that his father had given him, and his anger was
greatly roused against him.

38 Esau said to his father, “Have you but one
blessing, my father? Bless me, even me also, my
father.” Esau lifted up his voice, and wept.

39 Isaac his father answered him, “Behold, of the
fatness of the earth will be your dwelling, and of
the dew of the sky from above. 40 By your sword
will you live, and you will serve your brother. It will
happen, when you will break loose, that you shall
shake his yoke from off your neck.”

11 And Jacob was very much afraid of his brother
Esau, and he rose up and fled to the house of Eber
the son of Shem, and he concealed himself there on
account of his brother, and Jacob was sixty-three
years old when he went forth from the land of
Canaan from Hebron, and Jacob was concealed in
Eber's house fourteen years on account of his
brother Esau, and he there continued to learn the
ways of the Lord and his commandments.

12 And when Esau saw that Jacob had fled and
escaped from him, and that Jacob had cunningly
obtained the blessing, then Esau grieved
exceedingly, and he was also vexed at his father
and mother; and he also rose up and took his wife
and went away from his father and mother to the
land of Seir, and he dwelt there; and Esau saw there
a woman from amongst the daughters of Heth
whose name was Bosmath, the daughter of Elon
the Hittite, and he took her for a wife in addition to
his first wife, and Esau called her name Adah, saying
the blessing had in that time passed from him.

13 And Esau dwelt in the land of Seir six months
without seeing his father and mother, and
afterward Esau took his wives and rose up and
returned to the land of Canaan, and Esau placed his
two wives in his father's house in Hebron. 14 And
the wives of Esau vexed and provoked Isaac and
Rebecca with their works, for they walked not in
the ways of the Lord, but served their father's gods
of wood and stone as their father had taught them,
and they were more wicked than their father. 15
And they went according to the evil desires of their
hearts, and they sacrificed and burnt incense to the
Baalim, and Isaac and Rebecca became weary of
them.

[Genesis 27:46 Rebekah said to Isaac, "I am weary of my life because of the daughters of Heth. If Jacob takes a wife of the daughters of Heth, such as these, of the daughters of the land, what good will my life do me?"]

16 And Rebecca said, "I am weary of my life because of the daughters of Heth; if Jacob take a wife of the daughters of Heth, such as these which are of the daughters of the land, what good then is life unto me?"

17 And in those days Adah the wife of Esau conceived and bare him a son, and Esau called the name of the son that was born unto him Eliphaz, and Esau was sixty-five years old when she bare him.

18 And Ishmael the son of Abraham died in those days, in the sixty-forth year of the life of Jacob, and all the days that Ishmael lived were one hundred and thirty-seven years and he died. 19 And when Isaac heard that Ishmael was dead he mourned for him, and Isaac lamented over him many days.

20 And at the end of fourteen years of Jacob's residing in the house of Eber, Jacob desired to see his father and mother, and Jacob came to the house of his father and mother to Hebron, and Esau had in those days forgotten what Jacob had done to him in having taken the blessing from him in those days.

41 Esau hated Jacob because of the blessing with which his father blessed him. Esau said in his heart, "The days of mourning for my father are at hand. Then I will kill my brother Jacob."

21 And when Esau saw Jacob coming to his father and mother he remembered what Jacob had done to him, and he was greatly incensed against him and he sought to slay him. 22 And Isaac the son of Abraham was old and advanced in days, and Esau said, "Now my father's time is drawing nigh that he must die, and when he shall die I will slay my brother Jacob."

42 The words of Esau, her elder son, were told to Rebekah. She sent and called Jacob, her younger son, and said to him, "Behold, your brother Esau comforts himself about you by planning to kill you. 43 Now therefore, my son, obey my voice. Arise, flee to Laban, my brother, in Haran. 44 Stay with him a few days, until your brother's fury turns away; 45 until your brother's anger turn away from you, and he forgets what you have done to him. Then I will send, and get you from there. Why should I be bereaved of you both in one day?"

23 And this was told to Rebecca, and she hastened and sent and called for Jacob her son, and she said unto him, "Arise, go and flee to Haran to my brother Laban, and remain there for some time, until thy brother's anger be turned from thee and then shalt thou come back."

46 Rebekah said to Isaac, "I am weary of my life because of the daughters of Heth. If Jacob takes a wife of the daughters of Heth, such as these, of the daughters of the land, what good will my life do me?"

[29:16 And Rebecca said, "I am weary of my life because of the daughters of Heth; if Jacob take a wife of the daughters of Heth, such as these which are of the daughters of the land, what good then is life unto me?"]

Genesis 28

1 Isaac called Jacob, blessed him, and commanded him, "You shall not take a wife of the daughters of Canaan.

24 And Isaac called unto Jacob and said unto him, "Take not a wife from the daughters of Canaan,

"for thus did our father Abraham command us according to the word of the Lord which he had commanded him, saying, 'Unto thy seed will I give this land;' if thy children keep my covenant that I have made with thee, then will I also perform to thy children that which I have spoken unto thee and I will not forsake them.

25 "Now therefore my son hearken to my voice, to all that I shall command thee, and refrain from taking a wife from amongst the daughters of Canaan;

2 Arise, go to Paddan Aram, to the house of Bethuel your mother's father. Take a wife from there from the daughters of Laban, your mother's brother.

"arise, go to Haran to the house of Bethuel thy mother's father, and take unto thee a wife from there from the daughters of Laban thy mother's brother.

26 "Therefore take heed lest thou shouldst forget the Lord thy God and all his ways in the land to which thou goest, and shouldst get connected with the people of the land and pursue vanity and forsake the Lord thy God.
27 But when thou comest to the land serve there the Lord, do not turn to the right or to the left from the way which I commanded thee and which thou didst learn.
28 And may the Almighty God grant thee favor in the sight of the people of the earth, that thou mayest take there a wife according to thy choice; one who is good and upright in the ways of the Lord.

3 May God Almighty bless you, and make you fruitful, and multiply you, that you may be a company of peoples,
4 and give you the blessing of Abraham, to you, and to your offspring with you, that you may inherit the land where you travel, which God gave to Abraham."

29 "And may God give unto thee and thy seed the blessing of thy father Abraham, and make thee fruitful and multiply thee, and mayest thou become a multitude of people in the land whither thou goest, and may God cause thee to return to this land, the land of thy father's dwelling, with children and with great riches, with joy and with pleasure."

5 Isaac sent Jacob away. He went to Paddan Aram to Laban, son of Bethuel the Syrian, Rebekah's brother, Jacob's and Esau's mother.

30 And Isaac finished commanding Jacob and blessing him, and he gave him many gifts, together with silver and gold, and he sent him away; and Jacob hearkened to his father and mother; he kissed them and arose and went to Padan-aram; and Jacob was seventy-seven years old when he went out from the land of Canaan from Beersheba.

31 And when Jacob went away to go to Haran Esau called unto his son Eliphaz, and secretly spoke unto him, saying, "Now hasten, take thy sword in thy hand and pursue Jacob and pass before him in the road, and lurk for him, and slay him with thy sword in one of the mountains, and take all belonging to him and come back."

32 And Eliphaz the son of Esau was an active man and expert with the bow as his father had taught him, and he was a noted hunter in the field and a valiant man. 33 And Eliphaz did as his father had commanded him, and Eliphaz was at that time thirteen years old, and Eliphaz rose up and went and took ten of his mother's brothers with him and pursued Jacob. 34 And he closely followed Jacob, and he lurked for him in the border of the land of Canaan opposite to the city of Shechem.

35 And Jacob saw Eliphaz and his men pursuing him, and Jacob stood still in the place in which he was going, in order to know what this was, for he did not know the thing; and Eliphaz drew his sword and he went on advancing, he and his men, toward Jacob; and Jacob said unto them, "What is to do with you that you have come hither, and what meaneth it that you pursue with your swords."

36 And Eliphaz came near to Jacob and he answered and said unto him, "Thus did my father command me, and now therefore I will not deviate from the orders which my father gave me;" and when Jacob saw that Esau had spoken to Eliphaz to employ force, Jacob then approached and supplicated Eliphaz and his men, saying to him, "37 Behold all that I have and which my father and mother gave unto me, that take unto thee and go from me, and do not slay me, and may this thing be accounted unto thee a righteousness."

38 And the Lord caused Jacob to find favor in the sight of Eliphaz the son of Esau, and his men, and they hearkened to the voice of Jacob, and they did not put him to death, and Eliphaz and his men took all belonging to Jacob together with the silver and gold that he had brought with him from Beersheba; they left him nothing.

39 And Eliphaz and his men went away from him and they returned to Esau to Beersheba, and they told him all that had occurred to them with Jacob, and they gave him all that they had taken from Jacob.

40 And Esau was indignant at Eliphaz his son, and at his men that were with him, because they had not put Jacob to death.

41 And they answered and said unto Esau, "Because Jacob supplicated us in this matter not to slay him, our pity was excited toward him, and we took all belonging to him and brought it unto thee;" and Esau took all the silver and gold which Eliphaz had taken from Jacob and he put them by in his house.

6 Now Esau saw that Isaac had blessed Jacob and
sent him away to Paddan Aram, to take him a wife
from there, and that as he blessed him he gave him
a command, saying, "You shall not take a wife of
the daughters of Canaan," 7 and that Jacob obeyed
his father and his mother, and was gone to Paddan
Aram. 8 Esau saw that the daughters of Canaan
didn't please Isaac, his father. 9 Esau went to
Ishmael, and took, besides the wives that he had,
Mahalath the daughter of Ishmael, Abraham's son,
the sister of Nebaioth, to be his wife.

42 At that time when Esau saw that Isaac had
blessed Jacob, and had commanded him, saying,
"Thou shalt not take a wife from amongst the
daughters of Canaan, and that the daughters of
Canaan were bad in the sight of Isaac and Rebecca,"
43 Then he went to the house of Ishmael his uncle,
and in addition to his older wives he took Machlath
the daughter of Ishmael, the sister of Nebayoth, for
a wife.

10 Jacob went out from Beersheba, and went toward Haran.

11 He came to a certain place, and stayed there all
night, because the sun had set. He took one of the
stones of the place, and put it under his head, and
lay down in that place to sleep. 12 He dreamed.
Behold, a stairway set upon the earth, and its top
reached to heaven. Behold, the angels of God
ascending and descending on it.

Jasher 30

1 And Jacob went forth continuing his road to Haran,

and he came as far as mount Moriah, and he tarried there all night near the city of Luz;

13 Behold, Yahweh stood above it, and said, "I am
Yahweh, the God of Abraham your father, and the
God of Isaac. The land whereon you lie, to you will I
give it, and to your offspring.

and the Lord appeared there unto Jacob on that night, and he said unto him, "I am the Lord God of Abraham and the God of Isaac thy father; the land upon which thou liest I will give unto thee and thy seed.

14 Your offspring will be as the dust of the earth,
and you will spread abroad to the west, and to the
east, and to the north, and to the south. In you and
in your offspring will all the families of the earth be
blessed. 15 Behold, I am with you, and will keep
you, wherever you go, and will bring you again into
this land. For I will not leave you, until I have done
that which I have spoken of to you."

2 And behold I am with thee and will keep thee wherever thou goest, and I will multiply thy seed as the stars of Heaven, and I will cause all thine enemies to fall before thee; and when they shall make war with thee they shall not prevail over thee, and I will bring thee again unto this land with joy, with children, and with great riches."

16 Jacob awakened out of his sleep, and he said,
"Surely Yahweh is in this place, and I didn't know
it." 17 He was afraid, and said, "How dreadful is this
place! This is none other than God's house, and this
is the gate of heaven." 18 Jacob rose up early in the
morning, and took the stone that he had put under
his head, and set it up for a pillar, and poured oil on
its top. 19 He called the name of that place Bethel,
but the name of the city was Luz at the first.

3 And Jacob awoke from his sleep and he rejoiced greatly at the vision which he had seen; and he called the name of that place Bethel.

20 Jacob vowed a vow, saying, "If God will be with
me, and will keep me in this way that I go, and will
give me bread to eat, and clothing to put on, 21 so
that I come again to my father's house in peace,
and Yahweh will be my God, 22 then this stone,
which I have set up for a pillar, will be God's house.
Of all that you will give me I will surely give a tenth
to you."

Genesis 29

1 Then Jacob went on his journey, and came to the
land of the children of the east. 2 He looked, and
behold, a well in the field, and, behold, three flocks
of sheep lying there by it. For out of that well they
watered the flocks. The stone on the well's mouth
was large.

4 And Jacob rose up from that place quite rejoiced, and when he walked his feet felt light to him for joy, and he went from there to the land of the children of the East, and he returned to Haran and he set by the shepherd's well.

3 There all the flocks were gathered. They rolled the
stone from the well's mouth, and watered the
sheep, and put the stone again on the well's mouth
in its place. 4 Jacob said to them, "My relatives,
where are you from?" They said, "We are from
Haran."

5 And he there found some men; going from Haran to feed their flocks, and Jacob made inquiries of them, and they said, "We are from Haran."

5 He said to them, "Do you know Laban, the son of Nahor?" They said, "We know him." 6 He said to them, "Is it well with him?" They said, "It is well. See, Rachel, his daughter, is coming with the sheep."

6 And he said unto them, "Do you know Laban, the son of Nahor?" and they said, "We know him, and behold his daughter Rachel is coming along to feed her father's flock."

7 He said, "Behold, it is still the middle of the day, not time to gather the livestock together. Water the sheep, and go and feed them." 8 They said, "We can't, until all the flocks are gathered together, and they roll the stone from the well's mouth. Then we water the sheep."

9 While he was yet speaking with them, Rachel came with her father's sheep, for she kept them.

7 Whilst he was yet speaking with them, Rachel the daughter of Laban came to feed her father's sheep, for she was a shepherdess.

10 When Jacob saw Rachel the daughter of Laban, his mother's brother, and the sheep of Laban, his mother's brother, Jacob went near, and rolled the stone from the well's mouth, and watered the flock of Laban his mother's brother. 11 Jacob kissed Rachel, and lifted up his voice, and wept.

8 And when Jacob saw Rachel, the daughter of Laban, his mother's brother, he ran and kissed her, and lifted up his voice and wept.

12 Jacob told Rachel that he was her father's brother, and that he was Rebekah's son. She ran and told her father.

9 And Jacob told Rachel that he was the son of Rebecca, her father's sister, and Rachel ran and told her father,

and Jacob continued to cry because he had nothing with him to bring to the house of Laban.

13 When Laban heard the news of Jacob, his sister's son, he ran to meet Jacob, and embraced him, and kissed him, and brought him to his house. Jacob told Laban all these things.

10 And when Laban heard that his sister's son Jacob had come, he ran and kissed him and embraced him and brought him into the house and gave him bread, and he ate. 11 And Jacob related to Laban what his brother Esau had done to him, and what his son Eliphaz had done to him in the road.

14 Laban said to him, "Surely you are my bone and my flesh." He lived with him for a month. 15 Laban said to Jacob, "Because you are my brother, should you therefore serve me for nothing? Tell me, what will your wages be?"

12 And Jacob resided in Laban's house for one month, and Jacob ate and drank in the house of Laban, and afterward Laban said unto Jacob, "Tell me what shall be thy wages, for how canst thou serve me for nought?"

16 Laban had two daughters. The name of the elder was Leah, and the name of the younger was Rachel. 17 Leah's eyes were weak, but Rachel was beautiful in form and attractive. 18 Jacob loved Rachel.

13 And Laban had no sons but only daughters, and his other wives and handmaids were still barren in those days; and these are the names of Laban's daughters which his wife Adinah had borne unto him; the name of the elder was Leah and the name of the younger was Rachel; and Leah was tender-eyed, but Rachel was beautiful and well favored, and Jacob loved her.

He said, "I will serve you seven years for Rachel, your younger daughter." 19 Laban said, "It is better that I give her to you, than that I should give her to another man. Stay with me."

14 And Jacob said unto Laban, "I will serve thee seven years for Rachel thy younger daughter;" and Laban consented to this and Jacob served Laban seven years for his daughter Rachel.

15 And in the second year of Jacob's dwelling in Haran, that is in the seventy ninth year of the life of Jacob, in that year died Eber the son of Shem, he was four hundred and sixty-four years old at his death. 16 And when Jacob heard that Eber was dead he grieved exceedingly, and he lamented and mourned over him many days.

17 And in the third year of Jacob's dwelling in Haran, Bosmath, the daughter of Ishmael, the wife of Esau, bare unto him a son, and Esau called his name Reuel.

18 And in the fourth year of Jacob's residence in the house of Laban, the Lord visited Laban and remembered him on account of Jacob, and sons were born unto him, and his first born was Beor, his second was Alib, and the third was Chorash.

19 And the Lord gave Laban riches and honor, sons and daughters, and the man increased greatly on account of Jacob. 20 And Jacob in those days served Laban in all manner of work, in the house and in the field, and the blessing of the Lord was in all that belonged to Laban in the house and in the field.

21 And in the fifth year died Jehudith, the daughter of Beeri, the wife of Esau, in the land of Canaan, and she had no sons but daughters only.

22 And these are the names of her daughters which she bare to Esau, the name of the elder was Marzith, and the name of the younger was Puith.

23 And when Jehudith died, Esau rose up and went to Seir to hunt in the field, as usual, and Esau dwelt in the land of Seir for a long time.

24 And in the sixth year Esau took for a wife, in addition to his other wives, Ahlibamah, the daughter of Zebeon the Hivite, and Esau brought her to the land of Canaan. 25 And Ahlibamah conceived and bare unto Esau three sons, Yeush, Yaalan, and Korah.

26 And in those days, in the land of Canaan, there was a quarrel between the herdsmen of Esau and the herdsmen of the inhabitants of the land of Canaan, for Esau's cattle and goods were too abundant for him to remain in the land of Canaan, in his father's house, and the land of Canaan could not bear him on account of his cattle.

27 And when Esau saw that his quarreling increased
with the inhabitants of the land of Canaan, he rose
up and took his wives and his sons and his
daughters, and all belonging to him, and the cattle
which he possessed, and all his property that he
had acquired in the land of Canaan, and he went
away from the inhabitants of the land to the land of
Seir, and Esau and all belonging to him dwelt in the
land of Seir. 28 But from time to time Esau would
go and see his father and mother in the land of
Canaan, and Esau intermarried with the Horites,
and he gave his daughters to the sons of Seir, the
Horite.

29 And he gave his elder daughter Marzith to Anah, the son of Zebeon, his wife's brother, and Puith he gave to Azar, the son of Bilhan the Horite; and Esau dwelt in the mountain, he and his children, and they were fruitful and multiplied.

Jasher 31

20 Jacob served seven years for Rachel. They
seemed to him but a few days, for the love he had
for her. 21 Jacob said to Laban, “Give me my wife,
for my days are fulfilled, that I may go in to her.”
22 Laban gathered together all the men of the
place, and made a feast.

1 And in the seventh year, Jacob's service which he served Laban was completed, and Jacob said unto Laban, "Give me my wife, for the days of my service are fulfilled;" and Laban did so, and Laban and Jacob assembled all the people of that place and they made a feast.

2 And in the evening Laban came to the house, and afterward Jacob came there with the people of the feast, and Laban extinguished all the lights that were there in the house.

3 And Jacob said unto Laban, "Wherefore dost thou do this thing unto us?" and Laban answered, "Such is our custom to act in this land."

23 In the evening, he took Leah his daughter, and brought her to him. He went in to her.

4 And afterward Laban took his daughter Leah, and he brought her to Jacob, and he came to her and Jacob did not know that she was Leah.

24 Laban gave Zilpah his servant to his daughter Leah for a servant.

5 And Laban gave his daughter Leah his maid Zilpah for a handmaid.

6 And all the people at the feast knew what Laban had done to Jacob, but they did not tell the thing to Jacob. 7 And all the neighbors came that night to Jacob's house, and they ate and drank and rejoiced, and played before Leah upon timbrels, and with dances, and they responded before Jacob, "Heleah, Heleah." 8 And Jacob heard their words but did not understand their meaning, but he thought such might be their custom in this land. 9 And the neighbors spoke these words before Jacob during the night, and all the lights that were in the house Laban had that night extinguished.

25 In the morning, behold, it was Leah. He said to Laban, "What is this you have done to me? Didn't I serve with you for Rachel? Why then have you deceived me?"

10 And in the morning, when daylight appeared, Jacob turned to his wife and he saw, and behold it was Leah that had been lying in his bosom, and Jacob said, "Behold now I know what the neighbors said last night, 'Heleah,' they said, and I knew it not." 11 And Jacob called unto Laban, and said unto him, "What is this that thou didst unto me? Surely I served thee for Rachel, and why didst thou deceive me and didst give me Leah?"

26 Laban said, "It is not done so in our place, to give the younger before the firstborn. 27 Fulfill the week of this one, and we will give you the other also for the service which you will serve with me yet seven other years."

12 And Laban answered Jacob, saying, "Not so is it done in our place to give the younger before the elder now therefore if thou desirest to take her sister likewise, take her unto thee for the service which thou wilt serve me for another seven years."

28 Jacob did so, and fulfilled her week. He gave him Rachel his daughter as wife. 29 Laban gave to Rachel his daughter Bilhah, his servant, to be her servant.

13 And Jacob did so, and he also took Rachel for a wife, and he served Laban seven years more, and Jacob also came to Rachel, and he loved Rachel more than Leah, and Laban gave her his maid Bilhah for a handmaid.

30 He went in also to Rachel, and he loved also Rachel more than Leah, and served with him yet seven other years.

31 Yahweh saw that Leah was hated, and he opened her womb, but Rachel was barren. 32 Leah conceived, and bore a son, and she named him Reuben. For she said, "Because Yahweh has looked at my affliction. For now my husband will love me." 33 She conceived again, and bore a son, and said, "Because Yahweh has heard that I am hated, he has therefore given me this son also." She named him Simeon. 34 She conceived again, and bore a son. Said, "Now this time will my husband be joined to me, because I have borne him three sons." Therefore his name was called Levi. 35 She conceived again, and bore a son. She said, "This time will I praise Yahweh." Therefore she named him Judah. Then she stopped bearing.

14 And when the Lord saw that Leah was hated, the Lord opened her womb, and she conceived and bare Jacob four sons in those days. 15 And these are their names, Reuben Simeon, Levi, and Judah, and she afterward left bearing.

Genesis 30

1 When Rachel saw that she bore Jacob no children, Rachel envied her sister.

16 And at that time Rachel was barren, and she had no offspring, and Rachel envied her sister Leah,

She said to Jacob, "Give me children, or else I will die." 2 Jacob's anger burned against Rachel, and he said, "Am I in God's place, who has withheld from you the fruit of the womb?"

3 She said, "Behold, my maid Bilhah. Go in to her, that she may bear on my knees, and I also may obtain children by her." 4 She gave him Bilhah her servant as wife, and Jacob went in to her.

and when Rachel saw that she bare no children to Jacob, she took her handmaid Bilhah,

5 Bilhah conceived, and bore Jacob a son. 6 Rachel said, "God has judged me, and has also heard my voice, and has given me a son." Therefore called she his name Dan. 7 Bilhah, Rachel's servant, conceived again, and bore Jacob a second son. 8 Rachel said, "With mighty wrestlings have I wrestled with my sister, and have prevailed." She named him Naphtali.

and she bare Jacob two sons, Dan and Naphtali.

9 When Leah saw that she had finished bearing, she took Zilpah, her servant, and gave her to Jacob as a wife. 10 Zilpah, Leah's servant, bore Jacob a son. 11 Leah said, "How fortunate!" She named him Gad. 12 Zilpah, Leah's servant, bore Jacob a second son. 13 Leah said, "Happy am I, for the daughters will call me happy." She named him Asher.

17 And when Leah saw that she had left bearing, she also took her handmaid Zilpah, and she gave her to Jacob for a wife, and Jacob also came to Zilpah, and she also bare Jacob two sons, Gad and Asher.

14 Reuben went in the days of wheat harvest, and found mandrakes in the field, and brought them to his mother, Leah. Then Rachel said to Leah, "Please give me some of your son's mandrakes." 15 She said to her, "Is it a small matter that you have taken away my husband? Would you take away my son's mandrakes, also?" Rachel said, "Therefore he will lie with you tonight for your son's mandrakes."

16 Jacob came from the field in the evening, and Leah went out to meet him, and said, "You must come in to me; for I have surely hired you with my son's mandrakes." He lay with her that night.

17 God listened to Leah, and she conceived, and bore Jacob a fifth son. 18 Leah said, "God has given me my hire, because I gave my servant to my husband." She named him Issachar. 19 Leah conceived again, and bore a sixth son to Jacob. 20 Leah said, "God has endowed me with a good dowry. Now my husband will live with me, because I have borne him six sons." She named him Zebulun. 21 Afterwards, she bore a daughter, and named her Dinah.

18 And Leah again conceived and bare Jacob in those days two sons and one daughter, and these are their names, Issachar, Zebulon, and their sister Dinah.

19 And Rachel was still barren in those days, and Rachel prayed unto the Lord at that time, and she said, "O Lord God remember me and visit me, I beseech thee, for now my husband will cast me off, for I have borne him no children. 20 Now O Lord God, hear my supplication before thee, and see my affliction, and give me children like one of the handmaids, that I may no more bear my reproach."

22 God remembered Rachel, and God listened to her, and opened her womb. 23 She conceived, bore a son, and said, "God has taken away my reproach." 24 She named him Joseph, saying, "May Yahweh add another son to me."

21 And God heard her and opened her womb, and Rachel conceived and bare a son, and she said, "The Lord has taken away my reproach," and she called his name Joseph, saying, "May the Lord add to me another son;" and Jacob was ninety-one years old when she bare him.

22 At that time Jacob's mother, Rebecca, sent her nurse Deborah the daughter of Uz, and two of Isaac's servants unto Jacob. 23 And they came to Jacob to Haran and they said unto him, "Rebecca has sent us to thee that thou shalt return to thy father's house to the land of Canaan;" and Jacob hearkened unto them in this which his mother had spoken.

25 When Rachel had borne Joseph, Jacob said to Laban, “Send me away, that I may go to my own place, and to my country. 26 Give me my wives and my children for whom I have served you, and let me go; for you know my service with which I have served you.”

27 Laban said to him, “If now I have found favor in your eyes, stay here, for I have divined that Yahweh has blessed me for your sake.” 28 He said, “Appoint me your wages, and I will give it.”

29 He said to him, “You know how I have served you, and how your livestock have fared with me. 30 For it was little which you had before I came, and it has increased to a multitude. Yahweh has blessed you wherever I turned. Now when will I provide for my own house also?”

31 He said, “What shall I give you?” Jacob said, “You shall not give me anything. If you will do this thing for me, I will again feed your flock and keep it. 32 I will pass through all your flock today, removing from there every speckled and spotted one, and every black one among the sheep, and the spotted and speckled among the goats. This will be my hire. 33 So my righteousness will answer for me hereafter, when you come concerning my hire that is before you. Every one that is not speckled and spotted among the goats, and black among the sheep, that might be with me, will be counted stolen.”

34 Laban said, “Behold, let it be according to your word.” 35 That day, he removed the male goats that were streaked and spotted, and all the female goats that were speckled and spotted, every one that had white in it, and all the black ones among the sheep, and gave them into the hand of his sons.

36 He set three days’ journey between himself and Jacob, and Jacob fed the rest of Laban’s flocks.

24 At that time, the other seven years which Jacob served Laban for Rachel were completed, and it was at the end of fourteen years that he had dwelt in Haran that Jacob said unto Laban, "Give me my wives and send me away, that I may go to my land, for behold my mother did send unto me from the land at Canaan that I should return to my father's house."

25 And Laban said unto him, "Not so I pray thee; if I have found favor in thy sight do not leave me; appoint me thy wages and I will give them, and remain with me."

26 And Jacob said unto him, "This is what thou shalt give me for wages, that I shall this day pass through all thy flock and take away from them every lamb that is speckled and spotted and such as are brown amongst the sheep, and amongst the goats, and if thou wilt do this thing for me I will return and feed thy flock and keep them as at first."

27 And Laban did so, and Laban removed from his flock all that Jacob had said and gave them to him. 28 And Jacob placed all that he had removed from Laban's flock in the hands of his sons, and Jacob was feeding the remainder of Laban's flock.

29 And when the servants of Isaac which he had sent unto Jacob saw that Jacob would not then return with them to the land of Canaan to his father, they then went away from him, and they returned home to the land of Canaan.

30 And Deborah remained with Jacob in Haran, and she did not return with the servants of Isaac to the land of Canaan, and Deborah resided with Jacob's wives and children in Haran.

37 Jacob took to himself rods of fresh poplar, almond, plane tree, peeled white streaks in them, and made the white appear which was in the rods.
38 He set the rods which he had peeled opposite the flocks in the gutters in the watering-troughs where the flocks came to drink. They conceived
when they came to drink. 39 The flocks conceived before the rods, and the flocks produced streaked, speckled, and spotted.

31 And Jacob served Laban six years longer, and when the sheep brought forth, Jacob removed from them such as were speckled and spotted, as he had determined with Laban, and Jacob did so at Laban's for six years, and the man increased abundantly and he had cattle and maid servants and men servants, camels, and asses.

40 Jacob separated the lambs, and set the faces of the flocks toward the streaked and all the black in the flock of Laban: and he put his own droves apart, and didn't put them into Laban's flock.

41 Whenever the stronger of the flock conceived, Jacob laid the rods in front of the eyes of the flock in the gutters, that they might conceive among the
rods; 42 but when the flock were feeble, he didn't
put them in. So the feebler were Laban's, and the stronger Jacob's.

43 The man increased exceedingly, and had large flocks, female servants and male servants, and camels and donkeys.

32 And Jacob had two hundred drove of cattle, and his cattle were of large size and of beautiful appearance and were very productive, and all the families of the sons of men desired to get some of the cattle of Jacob, for they were exceedingly prosperous.

33 And many of the sons of men came to procure some of Jacob's flock, and Jacob gave them a sheep for a man servant or a maid servant or for an ass or a camel, or whatever Jacob desired from them they
gave him. 34 And Jacob obtained riches and honor
and possessions by means of these transactions with the sons of men, and the children of Laban envied him of this honor.

Genesis 31

1 He heard the words of Laban's sons, saying, "Jacob has taken away all that was our father's. From that which was our father's, has he gotten all this wealth."

2 Jacob saw the expression on Laban's face, and, behold, it was not toward him as before.

35 And in the course of time he heard the words of Laban's sons, saying, "Jacob has taken away all that was our father's, and of that which was our father's has he acquired all this glory."

36 And Jacob beheld the countenance of Laban and of his children, and behold it was not toward him in those days as it had been before.

3 Yahweh said to Jacob, "Return to the land of your fathers, and to your relatives, and I will be with you."

37 And the Lord appeared to Jacob at the expiration of the six years, and said unto him, "Arise, go forth out of this land, and return to the land of thy birthplace and I will be with thee."

4 Jacob sent and called Rachel and Leah to the field to his flock, 5 and said to them, "I see the expression on your father's face, that it is not toward me as before; but the God of my father has been with me. 6 You know that I have served your father with all of my strength.

7 "Your father has deceived me, and changed my wages ten times, but God didn't allow him to hurt me. 8 If he said this, 'The speckled will be your wages,' then all the flock bore speckled. If he said this, 'The streaked will be your wages,' then all the flock bore streaked.

9 Thus God has taken away your father's livestock, and given them to me. 10 During mating season, I lifted up my eyes, and saw in a dream, and behold, the male goats which leaped on the flock were streaked, speckled, and grizzled. 11 The angel of God said to me in the dream, 'Jacob,' and I said, 'Here I am.' 12 He said, 'Now lift up your eyes, and behold, all the male goats which leap on the flock are streaked, speckled, and grizzled, for I have seen all that Laban does to you. 13 I am the God of Bethel, where you anointed a pillar, where you vowed a vow to me. Now arise, get out from this land, and return to the land of your birth.'"

14 Rachel and Leah answered him, "Is there yet any portion or inheritance for us in our father's house? 15 Aren't we accounted by him as foreigners? For he has sold us, and has also quite devoured our money. 16 For all the riches which God has taken away from our father, that is ours and our children's. Now then, whatever God has said to you, do."

17 Then Jacob rose up, and set his sons and his wives on the camels, 18 and he took away all his livestock, and all his possessions which he had gathered, including the livestock which he had gained in Paddan Aram, to go to Isaac his father, to the land of Canaan.

38 And Jacob rose up at that time and he mounted his children and wives and all belonging to him upon camels, and he went forth to go to the land of Canaan to his father Isaac.

19 Now Laban had gone to shear his sheep: and
Rachel stole the teraphim that were her father's.

38 And Jacob rose up at that time and he mounted
his children and wives and all belonging to him
upon camels, and he went forth to go to the land of
Canaan to his father Isaac. 40 And Rachel stole her
father's images, and she took them and she
concealed them upon the camel upon which she
sat, and she went on.

20 Jacob deceived Laban the Syrian, in that he
didn't tell him that he was running away. 21 So he
fled with all that he had. He rose up, passed over
the River, and set his face toward the mountain of
Gilead.

41 And this is the manner of the images; in taking a man who is the first born and slaying him and taking the hair off his head, and taking salt and salting the head and anointing it in oil, then taking a small tablet of copper or a tablet of gold and writing the name upon it, and placing the tablet under his tongue, and taking the head with the tablet under the tongue and putting it in the house, and lighting up lights before it and bowing down to it.

42 And at the time when they bow down to it, it
speaketh to them in all matters that they ask of it,
through the power of the name which is written in
it. 43 And some make them in the figures of men,
of gold and silver, and go to them in times known to
them, and the figures receive the influence of the
stars, and tell them future things, and in this
manner were the images which Rachel stole from
her father.

44 And Rachel stole these images which were her father's, in order that Laban might not know through them where Jacob had gone.

22 Laban was told on the third day that Jacob had fled.

45 And Laban came home and he asked concerning Jacob and his household, and he was not to be found, and Laban sought his images to know where Jacob had gone, and could not find them, and he went to some other images, and he inquired of them and they told him that Jacob had fled from him to his father's, to the land of Canaan.

23 He took his relatives with him, and pursued him seven days' journey. He overtook him in the mountain of Gilead.

46 And Laban then rose up and he took his brothers and all his servants, and he went forth and pursued Jacob, and he overtook him in mount Gilead.

24 God came to Laban, the Syrian, in a dream of the night, and said to him, "Be careful that you don't speak to Jacob either good or bad."

25 Laban caught up with Jacob. Now Jacob had pitched his tent in the mountain, and Laban with his relatives encamped in the mountain of Gilead.

26 Laban said to Jacob, "What have you done, that you have deceived me, and carried away my daughters like captives of the sword? 27 Why did you flee secretly, and deceive me, and didn't tell me, that I might have sent you away with mirth and with songs, with tambourine and with harp; 28 and didn't allow me to kiss my sons and my daughters? Now have you done foolishly.

47 And Laban said unto Jacob, "What is this thou hast done to me to flee and deceive me, and lead my daughters and their children as captives taken by the sword? 48 And thou didst not suffer me to kiss them and send them away with joy, and thou didst steal my gods and didst go away."

29 It is in the power of my hand to hurt you, but the God of your father spoke to me last night, saying, 'Be careful that you don't speak to Jacob either good or bad.' 30 Now, you want to be gone, because you greatly longed for your father's house, but why have you stolen my gods?"

31 Jacob answered Laban, "Because I was afraid, for I said, 'Lest you should take your daughters from me by force.' 32 Anyone you find your gods with shall not live. Before our relatives, discern what is yours with me, and take it." For Jacob didn't know that Rachel had stolen them.

49 And Jacob answered Laban, saying, "Because I was afraid lest thou wouldst take thy daughters by force from me; and now with whomsoever thou findest thy gods he shall die."

33 Laban went into Jacob's tent, into Leah's tent, and into the tent of the two female servants; but he didn't find them. He went out of Leah's tent, and entered into Rachel's tent. 34 Now Rachel had taken the teraphim, put them in the camel's saddle, and sat on them. Laban felt around all the tent, but didn't find them. 35 She said to her father, "Don't let my lord be angry that I can't rise up before you; for I'm having my period." He searched, but didn't find the teraphim.

50 And Laban searched for the images and he examined in all Jacob's tents and furniture, but could not find them.

36 Jacob was angry, and argued with Laban. Jacob answered Laban, "What is my trespass? What is my sin, that you have hotly pursued me? 37 Now that you have felt around in all my stuff, what have you found of all your household stuff? Set it here before my relatives and your relatives, that they may judge between us two.

38 “These twenty years I have been with you. Your
ewes and your female goats have not cast their
young, and I haven’t eaten the rams of your flocks.
39 That which was torn of animals, I didn’t bring to
you. I bore its loss. Of my hand you required it,
whether stolen by day or stolen by night. 40 This
was my situation: in the day the drought consumed
me, and the frost by night; and my sleep fled from
my eyes.

41 These twenty years I have been in your house. I
served you fourteen years for your two daughters,
and six years for your flock, and you have changed
my wages ten times. 42 Unless the God of my
father, the God of Abraham, and the fear of Isaac,
had been with me, surely now you would have sent
me away empty. God has seen my affliction and the
labor of my hands, and rebuked you last night.”

43 Laban answered Jacob, “The daughters are my daughters, the children are my children, the flocks are my flocks, and all that you see is mine: and what can I do today to these my daughters, or to their children whom they have borne?

44 Now come, let us make a covenant, you and I; and let it be for a witness between me and you.”

45 Jacob took a stone, and set it up for a pillar. 46
Jacob said to his relatives, “Gather stones.” They
took stones, and made a heap. They ate there by
the heap. 47 Laban called it Jegar Sahadutha, but
Jacob called it Galeed.

48 Laban said, “This heap is witness between me
and you today.” Therefore it was named Galeed 49
and Mizpah, for he said, “Yahweh watch between
me and you, when we are absent one from another.
50 If you afflict my daughters, or if you take wives
besides my daughters, no man is with us; behold,
God is witness between me and you.”

51 And Laban said unto Jacob, "We will make a covenant together and it shall be a testimony between me and thee; if thou shalt afflict my daughters, or shalt take other wives besides my daughters, even God shall be a witness between me and thee in this matter."

52 And they took stones and made a heap, and Laban said, "This heap is a witness between me and thee," therefore he called the name thereof Gilead.

51 Laban said to Jacob, "See this heap, and see the
pillar, which I have set between me and you. 52
May this heap be a witness, and the pillar be a
witness, that I will not pass over this heap to you,
and that you will not pass over this heap and this
pillar to me, for harm. 53 The God of Abraham, and
the God of Nahor, the God of their father, judge
between us." Then Jacob swore by the fear of his
father, Isaac.

54 Jacob offered a sacrifice in the mountain, and
called his relatives to eat bread. They ate bread,
and stayed all night in the mountain. 55 Early in the
morning, Laban rose up, and kissed his sons and his
daughters, and blessed them. Laban departed and
returned to his place.

53 And Jacob and Laban offered sacrifice upon the mount, and they ate there by the heap, and they tarried in the mount all night, and Laban rose up early in the morning, and he wept with his daughters and he kissed them, and he returned unto his place.

Genesis 32

1 Jacob went on his way, and the angels of God met
him. 2 When he saw them, Jacob said, "This is God's
army." He called the name of that place Mahanaim.

54 And he hastened and sent off his son Beor, who was seventeen years old, with Abichorof the son of Uz, the son of Nahor, and with them were ten men.
55 And they hastened and went and passed on the road before Jacob, and they came by another road to the land of Seir.

56 And they came unto Esau and said unto him, "Thus saith thy brother and relative, thy mother's brother Laban, the son of Bethuel, saying, 57 'Hast thou heard what Jacob thy brother has done unto me, who first came to me naked and bare, and I went to meet him, and brought him to my house with honor, and I made him great, and I gave him my two daughters for wives and also two of my maids.

58 "And God blessed him on my account, and he increased abundantly, and had sons, daughters and maid servants. 59 He has also an immense stock of flocks and herds, camels and asses, also silver and gold in abundance; and when he saw that his wealth increased, he left me whilst I went to shear my sheep, and he rose up and fled in secrecy.

60 "And he lifted his wives and children upon
camels, and he led away all his cattle and property
which he acquired in my land, and he lifted up his
countenance to go to his father Isaac, to the land of
Canaan. 61 And he did not suffer me to kiss my
daughters and their children, and he led my
daughters as captives taken by the sword, and he
also stole my gods and he fled.

62 And now I have left him in the mountain of the
brook of Jabuk, him and all belonging to him; he
lacketh nothing. 63 If it be thy wish to go to him, go
then and there wilt thou find him, and thou canst
do unto him as thy soul desireth; and Laban's
messengers came and told Esau all these things."

64 And Esau heard all the words of Laban's messengers, and his anger was greatly kindled against Jacob, and he remembered his hatred, and his anger burned within him.

65 And Esau hastened and took his children and servants and the souls of his household, being sixty men, and he went and assembled all the children of Seir the Horite and their people, being three hundred and forty men, and took all this number of four hundred men with drawn swords, and he went unto Jacob to smite him.

66 And Esau divided this number into several parts,
and he took the sixty men of his children and
servants and the souls of his household as one
head, and gave them in care of Eliphaz his eldest
son. 67 And the remaining heads he gave to the
care of the six sons of Seir the Horite, and he placed
every man over his generations and children. 68
And the whole of this camp went as it was, and
Esau went amongst them toward Jacob, and he
conducted them with speed.

69 And Laban's messengers departed from Esau and went to the land of Canaan, and they came to the house of Rebecca the mother of Jacob and Esau.

70 And they told her saying, "Behold thy son Esau has gone against his brother Jacob with four hundred men, for he heard that he was coming, and he is gone to make war with him, and to smite him and to take all that he has."

71 And Rebecca hastened and sent seventy two men from the servants of Isaac to meet Jacob on the road; for she said, "Peradventure, Esau may make war in the road when he meets him."

72 And these messengers went on the road to meet Jacob, and they met him in the road of the brook on the opposite side of the brook Jabuk, and Jacob said when he saw them, This camp is destined to me from God, and Jacob called the name of that place Machnayim."

73 And Jacob knew all his father's people, and he kissed them and embraced them and came with them, and Jacob asked them concerning his father and mother, and they said, "They were well."

74 And these messengers said unto Jacob, "Rebecca thy mother has sent us to thee, saying, 'I have heard, my son, that thy brother Esau has gone forth against thee on the road with men from the children of Seir the Horite. 75 And therefore, my son, hearken to my voice and see with thy counsel what thou wilt do, and when he cometh up to thee, supplicate him, and do not speak rashly to him, and give him a present from what thou possessest, and from what God has favored thee with.

76 "And when he asketh thee concerning thy affairs, conceal nothing from him, perhaps he may turn from his anger against thee and thou wilt thereby save thy soul, thou and all belonging to thee, for it is thy duty to honor him, for he is thy elder brother."

77 And when Jacob heard the words of his mother which the messengers had spoken to him, Jacob lifted up his voice and wept bitterly, and did as his mother then commanded him.

3 Jacob sent messengers in front of him to Esau, his brother, to the land of Seir, the field of Edom.

Jasher 32

1 And at that time Jacob sent messengers to his brother Esau toward the land of Seir, and he spoke to him words of supplication.

4 He commanded them, saying, "This is what you shall tell my lord, Esau: 'This is what your servant, Jacob, says. I have lived as a foreigner with Laban, and stayed until now.

2 And he commanded them, saying, "Thus shall ye say to my lord, to Esau, 'Thus saith thy servant Jacob, "Let not my lord imagine that my father's blessing with which he did bless me has proved beneficial to me. 3 For I have been these twenty years with Laban, and he deceived me and changed my wages ten times, as it has all been already told unto my lord. 4 And I served him in his house very laboriously, and God afterward saw my affliction, my labor and the work of my hands, and he caused me to find grace and favor in his sight.

5 I have cattle, donkeys, flocks, male servants, and female servants. I have sent to tell my lord, that I may find favor in your sight.'"

5 "And I afterward through God's great mercy and kindness acquired oxen and asses and cattle, and men servants and maid servants. 6 And now I am coming to my land and my home to my father and mother, who are in the land of Canaan; and I have sent to let my lord know all this in order to find favor in the sight of my lord, so that he may not imagine that I have of myself obtained wealth, or that the blessing with which my father blessed me has benefited me."'"

7 And those messengers went to Esau, and found him on the borders of the land of Edom going toward Jacob, and four hundred men of the children of Seir the Horite were standing with drawn swords. 8 And the messengers of Jacob told Esau all the words that Jacob had spoken to them concerning Esau.

9 And Esau answered them with pride and contempt, and said unto them, "Surely I have heard and truly it has been told unto me what Jacob has done to Laban, who exalted him in his house and gave him his daughters for wives, and he begat sons and daughters, and abundantly increased in wealth and riches in Laban's house through his means.

10 And when he saw that his wealth was abundant and his riches great he fled with all belonging to him, from Laban's house, and he led Laban's daughters away from the face of their father, as captives taken by the sword without telling him of it.

11 "And not only to Laban has Jacob done thus but
also unto me has he done so and has twice
supplanted me, and shall I be silent? 12 Now
therefore I have this day come with my camps to
meet him, and I will do unto him according to the
desire of my heart."

6 The messengers returned to Jacob, saying, "We came to your brother Esau. Not only that, but he comes to meet you, and four hundred men with him."

13 And the messengers returned and came to Jacob and said unto him, "We came to thy brother, to Esau, and we told him all thy words, and thus has he answered us, and behold he cometh to meet thee with four hundred men.

14 "Now then know and see what thou shalt do, and pray before God to deliver thee from him."

7 Then Jacob was greatly afraid and was distressed.

15 And when he heard the words of his brother which he had spoken to the messengers of Jacob, Jacob was greatly afraid and he was distressed.

16 And Jacob prayed to the Lord his God, and he
said, "O Lord God of my fathers, Abraham and
Isaac, thou didst say unto me when I went away
from my father's house, saying, 17 'I am the Lord
God of thy father Abraham and the God of Isaac,
unto thee do I give this land and thy seed after
thee, and I will make thy seed as the stars of
heaven, and thou shalt spread forth to the four
sides of heaven, and in thee and in thy seed shall all
the families of the earth be blessed.'

18 "And thou didst establish thy words, and didst
give unto me riches and children and cattle, as the
utmost wishes of my heart didst thou give unto thy
servant; thou didst give unto me all that I asked
from thee, so that I lacked nothing. 19 And thou
didst afterward say unto me, Return to thy parents
and to thy birth place and I will still do well with
thee.

20 "And now that I have come, and thou didst
deliver me from Laban, I shall fall in the hands of
Esau who will slay me, yea, together with the
mothers of my children. 21 Now therefore, O Lord
God, deliver me, I pray thee, also from the hands of
my brother Esau, for I am greatly afraid of him. 22
And if there is no righteousness in me, do it for the
sake of Abraham and my father Isaac. 23 For I
know that through kindness and mercy have I
acquired this wealth; now therefore I beseech thee
to deliver me this day with thy kindness and to
answer me."

He divided the people who were with him, and the flocks, and the herds, and the camels, into two companies;

24 And Jacob ceased praying to the Lord, and he divided the people that were with him with the flocks and cattle into two camps, and he gave the half to the care of Damesek, the son of Eliezer, Abraham's servant, for a camp, with his children, and the other half he gave to the care of his brother Elianus the son of Eliezer, to be for a camp with his children.

8 and he said, "If Esau comes to the one company, and strikes it, then the company which is left will escape."

25 And he commanded them, saying, "Keep yourselves at a distance with your camps, and do not come too near each other, and if Esau come to one camp and slay it, the other camp at a distance from it will escape him."

9 Jacob said, "God of my father Abraham, and God of my father Isaac, Yahweh, who said to me, 'Return to your country, and to your relatives, and I will do you good,' 10 I am not worthy of the least of all the loving kindnesses, and of all the truth, which you have shown to your servant; for with just my staff I crossed over this Jordan; and now I have become two companies.

11 "Please deliver me from the hand of my brother, from the hand of Esau: for I fear him, lest he come and strike me, and the mothers with the children. 12 You said, 'I will surely do you good, and make your offspring as the sand of the sea, which can't be numbered because there are so many.'"

26 And Jacob tarried there that night, and during the whole night he gave his servants instructions concerning the forces and his children.

27 And the Lord heard the prayer of Jacob on that day, and the Lord then delivered Jacob from the hands of his brother Esau.

28 And the Lord sent three angels of the angels of heaven, and they went before Esau and came to him.

29 And these angels appeared unto Esau and his people as two thousand men, riding upon horses furnished with all sorts of war instruments, and they appeared in the sight of Esau and all his men to be divided into four camps, with four chiefs to them.

30 And one camp went on and they found Esau coming with four hundred men toward his brother Jacob, and this camp ran toward Esau and his people and terrified them, and Esau fell off the horse in alarm, and all his men separated from him in that place, for they were greatly afraid.

31 And the whole of the camp shouted after them when they fled from Esau, and all the warlike men
answered, saying, 32 "Surely we are the servants of
Jacob, who is the servant of God, and who then can stand against us? And Esau said unto them, O then, my lord and brother Jacob is your lord, whom I have not seen for these twenty years, and now that I have this day come to see him, do you treat me in this manner?"

33 And the angels answered him saying, "As the Lord liveth, were not Jacob of whom thou speaketh thy brother, we had not let one remaining from thee and thy people, but only on account of Jacob we will do nothing to them."

34 And this camp passed from Esau and his men and it went away, and Esau and his men had gone from them about a league when the second camp came toward him with all sorts of weapons, and they also did unto Esau and his men as the first camp had done to them.

35 And when they had left it to go on, behold the third camp came toward him and they were all terrified, and Esau fell off the horse, and the whole camp cried out, and said, "Surely we are the servants of Jacob, who is the servant of God, and who can stand against us?"

36 And Esau again answered them saying, "O then, Jacob my lord and your lord is my brother, and for twenty years I have not seen his countenance and hearing this day that he was coming, I went this day to meet him, and do you treat me in this manner?"

37 And they answered him, and said unto him, "As the Lord liveth, were not Jacob thy brother as thou didst say, we had not left a remnant from thee and thy men, but on account of Jacob of whom thou speakest being thy brother, we will not meddle with thee or thy men."

38 And the third camp also passed from them, and he still continued his road with his men toward Jacob, when the fourth camp came toward him, and they also did unto him and his men as the others had done. 39 And when Esau beheld the evil which the four angels had done to him and to his men, he became greatly afraid of his brother Jacob, and he went to meet him in peace. 40 And Esau concealed his hatred against Jacob, because he was afraid of his life on account of his brother Jacob, and because he imagined that the four camps that he had lighted upon were Jacob's servants.

13 He stayed there that night, and took from that which he had with him, a present for Esau, his brother: 14 two hundred female goats and twenty male goats, two hundred ewes and twenty rams, 15 thirty milk camels and their colts, forty cows, ten bulls, twenty female donkeys and ten foals.

41 And Jacob tarried that night with his servants in their camps, and he resolved with his servants to give unto Esau a present from all that he had with him, and from all his property; and Jacob rose up in the morning, he and his men, and they chose from amongst the cattle a present for Esau. 42 And this is the amount of the present which Jacob chose from his flock to give unto his brother Esau: and he selected two hundred and forty head from the flocks, and he selected from the camels and asses thirty each, and of the herds he chose fifty kine.

16 He delivered them into the hands of his servants, every herd by itself, and said to his servants, "Pass over before me, and put a space between herd and herd."

43 And he put them all in ten droves, and he placed each sort by itself, and he delivered them into the hands of ten of his servants, each drove by itself.

17 He commanded the foremost, saying, "When Esau, my brother, meets you, and asks you, saying, 'Whose are you? Where are you going? Whose are these before you?' 18 Then you shall say, 'They are your servant, Jacob's. It is a present sent to my lord, Esau. Behold, he also is behind us.'"

44 And he commanded them, and said unto them, "Keep yourselves at a distance from each other, and put a space between the droves, and when Esau and those who are with him shall meet you and ask you, saying, 'Whose are you, and whither do you go, and to whom belongeth all this before you,' you shall say unto them, 'We are the servants of Jacob, and we come to meet Esau in peace, and behold Jacob cometh behind us. 45 And that which is before us is a present sent from Jacob to his brother Esau.'

19 He commanded also the second, and the third, and all that followed the herds, saying, "This is how you shall speak to Esau, when you find him. 20 You shall say, 'Not only that, but behold, your servant, Jacob, is behind us.'" For, he said, "I will appease him with the present that goes before me, and afterward I will see his face. Perhaps he will accept me."

46 "And if they shall say unto you, 'Why doth he delay behind you, from coming to meet his brother and to see his face,' then you shall say unto them, 'Surely he cometh joyfully behind us to meet his brother, for he said, "I will appease him with the present that goeth to him, and after this I will see his face, peradventure he will accept of me."'"

21 So the present passed over before him, and he himself stayed that night in the camp. 22 He rose up that night, and took his two wives, and his two servants, and his eleven sons, and crossed over the ford of the Jabbok.

47 So the whole present passed on in the hands of his servants, and went before him on that day, and he lodged that night with his camps by the border of the brook of Jabuk, and he rose up in the midst of the night, and he took his wives and his maid servants, and all belonging to him, and he that night passed them over the ford Jabuk.

23 He took them, and sent them over the stream, and sent over that which he had. 24 Jacob was left alone, and wrestled with a man there until the breaking of the day. 25 When he saw that he didn't prevail against him, he touched the hollow of his thigh, and the hollow of Jacob's thigh was strained, as he wrestled.

48 And when he passed all belonging to him over the brook, Jacob was left by himself, and a man met him, and he wrestled with him that night until the breaking of the day, and the hollow of Jacob's thigh was out of joint through wrestling with him.

26 The man said, "Let me go, for the day breaks." Jacob said, "I won't let you go, unless you bless me." 27 He said to him, "What is your name?" He said, "Jacob". 28 He said, "Your name will no longer be called Jacob, but Israel; for you have fought with God and with men, and have prevailed." 29 Jacob asked him, "Please tell me your name." He said, "Why is it that you ask what my name is?" He blessed him there.

30 Jacob called the name of the place Peniel for, he said, "I have seen God face to face, and my life is preserved."

31 The sun rose on him as he passed over Peniel, and he limped because of his thigh.

49 And at the break of day the man left Jacob there, and he blessed him and went away, and Jacob passed the brook at the break of day, and he halted upon his thigh.

32 Therefore the children of Israel don't eat the sinew of the hip, which is on the hollow of the thigh, to this day, because he touched the hollow of Jacob's thigh in the sinew of the hip.

50 And the sun rose upon him when he had passed the brook, and he came up to the place of his cattle and children. 51 And they went on till midday, and whilst they were going the present was passing on before them.

Genesis 33

1 Jacob lifted up his eyes, and looked, and, behold, Esau was coming, and with him four hundred men. He divided the children between Leah, Rachel, and the two servants. 2 He put the servants and their children in front, Leah and her children after, and Rachel and Joseph at the rear.

52 And Jacob lifted up his eyes and looked, and behold Esau was at a distance, coming along with many men, about four hundred, and Jacob was greatly afraid of his brother. 53 And Jacob hastened and divided his children unto his wives and his handmaids, and his daughter Dinah he put in a chest, and delivered her into the hands of his servants.

3 He himself passed over in front of them, and bowed himself to the ground seven times, until he came near to his brother.

54 And he passed before his children and wives to meet his brother, and he bowed down to the ground, yea he bowed down seven times until he approached his brother, and God caused Jacob to find grace and favor in the sight of Esau and his men, for God had heard the prayer of Jacob.

55 And the fear of Jacob and his terror fell upon his brother Esau, for Esau was greatly afraid of Jacob for what the angels of God had done to Esau, and Esau's anger against Jacob was turned into kindness.

4 Esau ran to meet him, embraced him, fell on his neck, kissed him, and they wept.

56 And when Esau saw Jacob running toward him, he also ran toward him and he embraced him, and he fell upon his neck, and they kissed and they wept.

57 And God put fear and kindness toward Jacob in the hearts of the men that came with Esau, and they also kissed Jacob and embraced him. 58 And also Eliphaz, the son of Esau, with his four brothers, sons of Esau, wept with Jacob, and they kissed him and embraced him, for the fear of Jacob had fallen upon them all.

5 He lifted up his eyes, and saw the women and the children; and said, "Who are these with you?" He said, "The children whom God has graciously given your servant."

59 And Esau lifted up his eyes and saw the women with their offspring, the children of Jacob, walking behind Jacob and bowing along the road to Esau.
60 And Esau said unto Jacob, "Who are these with thee, my brother? Are they thy children or thy servants?" and Jacob answered Esau and said, "They are my children which God hath graciously given to thy servant."

6 Then the servants came near with their children, and they bowed themselves. 7 Leah also and her children came near, and bowed themselves. After them, Joseph came near with Rachel, and they bowed themselves.

8 Esau said, "What do you mean by all this company which I met?" Jacob said, "To find favor in the sight of my lord."

61 And whilst Jacob was speaking to Esau and his men, Esau beheld the whole camp, and he said unto Jacob, "Whence didst thou get the whole of the camp that I met yesternight?" and Jacob said, "To find favor in the sight of my lord, it is that which God graciously gave to thy servant."

9 Esau said, "I have enough, my brother; let that which you have be yours."

62 And the present came before Esau, and Jacob pressed Esau, saying, "Take I pray thee the present that I have brought to my lord," and Esau said, "Wherefore is this my purpose? Keep that which thou hast unto thyself."

63 And Jacob said, "It is incumbent upon me to give all this, since I have seen thy face, that thou still livest in peace."

10 Jacob said, "Please, no, if I have now found favor in your sight, then receive my present at my hand, because I have seen your face, as one sees the face of God, and you were pleased with me. 11 Please take the gift that I brought to you, because God has dealt graciously with me, and because I have enough." He urged him, and he took it.

64 And Esau refused to take the present, and Jacob said unto him, "I beseech thee my lord, if now I have found favor in thy sight, then receive my present at my hand, for I have therefore seen thy face, as though I had seen a god-like face, because thou wast pleased with me." 65 And Esau took the present, and Jacob also gave unto Esau silver and gold and bdellium, for he pressed him so much that he took them.

66 And Esau divided the cattle that were in the camp, and he gave the half to the men who had come with him, for they had come on hire, and the other half he delivered unto the hands of his children. 67 And the silver and gold and bdellium he gave in the hands of Eliphaz his eldest son,

12 Esau said, "Let us take our journey, and let us go, and I will go before you."

and Esau said unto Jacob, "Let us remain with thee, and we will go slowly along with thee until thou comest to my place with me, that we may dwell there together."

13 Jacob said to him, "My lord knows that the children are tender, and that the flocks and herds with me have their young, and if they overdrive them one day, all the flocks will die. 14 Please let my lord pass over before his servant, and I will lead on gently, according to the pace of the livestock that are before me and according to the pace of the children, until I come to my lord to Seir."

68 And Jacob answered his brother and said, "I would do as my lord speaketh unto me, but my lord knoweth that the children are tender, and the flocks and herds with their young who are with me, go but slowly, for if they went swiftly they would all die, for thou knowest their burdens and their fatigue. 69 Therefore let my lord pass on before his servant, and I will go on slowly for the sake of the children and the flock, until I come to my lord's place to Seir."

15 Esau said, "Let me now leave with you some of the folk who are with me." He said, "Why? Let me find favor in the sight of my lord."

70 And Esau said unto Jacob, "I will place with thee some of the people that are with me to take care of thee in the road, and to bear thy fatigue and burden," and he said, "What needeth it my lord, if I may find grace in thy sight? 71 Behold I will come unto thee to Seir to dwell there together as thou hast spoken, go thou then with thy people for I will follow thee."

72 And Jacob said this to Esau in order to remove Esau and his men from him, so that Jacob might afterward go to his father's house to the land of Canaan.

16 So Esau returned that day on his way to Seir. 17 Jacob traveled to Succoth, built himself a house, and made shelters for his livestock. Therefore the name of the place is called Succoth.

73 And Esau hearkened to the voice of Jacob, and Esau returned with the four hundred men that were with him on their road to Seir, and Jacob and all belonging to him went that day as far as the extremity of the land of Canaan in its borders, and he remained there some time.

18 Jacob came in peace to the city of Shechem, which is in the land of Canaan, when he came from Paddan Aram; and encamped before the city.

Jasher 33

1 And in some time after Jacob went away from the borders of the land, and he came to the land of Shalem, that is the city of Shechem, which is in the land of Canaan, and he rested in front of the city.

19 He bought the parcel of ground where he had spread his tent, at the hand of the children of Hamor, Shechem's father, for one hundred pieces of money.

20 He erected an altar there, and called it El Elohe Israel.

2 And he bought a parcel of the field which was there, from the children of Hamor the people of the land, for five shekels.

3 And Jacob there built himself a house, and he pitched his tent there, and he made booths for his cattle, therefore he called the name of that place Succoth. 4 And Jacob remained in Succoth a year and six months.

5 At that time some of the women of the inhabitants of the land went to the city of Shechem to dance and rejoice with the daughters of the people of the city, and when they went forth then Rachel and Leah the wives of Jacob with their families also went to behold the rejoicing of the daughters of the city.

Genesis 34

1 Dinah, the daughter of Leah, whom she bore to Jacob, went out to see the daughters of the land.

6 And Dinah the daughter of Jacob also went along with them and saw the daughters of the city, and they remained there before these daughters whilst all the people of the city were standing by them to behold their rejoicings, and all the great people of the city were there.

2 Shechem the son of Hamor the Hivite, the prince of the land, saw her.

7 And Shechem the son of Hamor, the prince of the land was also standing there to see them. 8 And Shechem beheld Dinah the daughter of Jacob sitting with her mother before the daughters of the city, and the damsel pleased him greatly, and he there asked his friends and his people, saying, "Whose daughter is that sitting amongst the women, whom I do not know in this city?"

9 And they said unto him, "Surely this is the daughter of Jacob the son of Isaac the Hebrew, who has dwelt in this city for some time," and when it was reported that the daughters of the land were going forth to rejoice she went with her mother and maid servants to sit amongst them as thou seest.

He took her, lay with her, and humbled her. 3 His soul joined to Dinah, the daughter of Jacob, and he loved the young lady, and spoke kindly to the young lady. 4 Shechem spoke to his father, Hamor, saying, “Get me this young lady as a wife.”

10 And Shechem beheld Dinah the daughter of Jacob, and when he looked at her his soul became fixed upon Dinah. 11 And he sent and had her taken by force, and Dinah came to the house of Shechem and he seized her forcibly and lay with her and humbled her, and he loved her exceedingly and placed her in his house.

5 Now Jacob heard that he had defiled Dinah, his daughter;

12 And they came and told the thing unto Jacob,

and his sons were with his livestock in the field. Jacob held his peace until they came.

6 Hamor the father of Shechem went out to Jacob to talk with him.

7 The sons of Jacob came in from the field when they heard it. The men were grieved, and they were very angry, because he had done folly in Israel in lying with Jacob's daughter; a thing ought not to be done.

and when Jacob heard that Shechem had defiled his
daughter Dinah, Jacob sent twelve of his servants to
fetch Dinah from the house of Shechem, and they
went and came to the house of Shechem to take
away Dinah from there. 13 And when they came
Shechem went out to them with his men and drove
them from his house, and he would not suffer them
to come before Dinah, but Shechem was sitting
with Dinah kissing and embracing her before their
eyes.

14 And the servants of Jacob came back and told him, saying, "When we came, he and his men drove us away, and thus did Shechem do unto Dinah before our eyes."

15 And Jacob knew moreover that Shechem had defiled his daughter, but he said nothing, and his sons were feeding his cattle in the field, and Jacob remained silent till their return.

16 And before his sons came home Jacob sent two maidens from his servants' daughters to take care of Dinah in the house of Shechem, and to remain with her, and Shechem sent three of his friends to his father Hamor the son of Chiddekem, the son of Pered, saying, "Get me this damsel for a wife."

17 And Hamor the son of Chiddekem the Hivite came to the house of Shechem his son, and he sat before him, and Hamor said unto his son, Shechem, "Is there then no woman amongst the daughters of thy people that thou wilt take an Hebrew woman who is not of thy people?"

18 And Shechem said to him, "Her only must thou get for me, for she is delightful in my sight; and Hamor did according to the word of his son, for he was greatly beloved by him."

19 And Hamor went forth to Jacob to commune with him concerning this matter,

and when he had gone from the house of his son Shechem, before he came to Jacob to speak unto him, behold the sons of Jacob had come from the field, as soon as they heard the thing that Shechem the son of Hamor had done.

20 And the men were very much grieved concerning their sister, and they all came home fired with anger, before the time of gathering in their cattle.

21 And they came and sat before their father and they spoke unto him kindled with wrath, saying, "Surely death is due to this man and to his household, because the Lord God of the whole earth commanded Noah and his children that man shall never rob, nor commit adultery; now behold Shechem has both ravaged and committed fornication with our sister, and not one of all the people of the city spoke a word to him. 22 Surely thou knowest and understandest that the judgment of death is due to Shechem, and to his father, and to the whole city on account of the thing which he has done."

23 And whilst they were speaking before their father in this matter, behold Hamor the father of Shechem came to speak to Jacob the words of his son concerning Dinah, and he sat before Jacob and before his sons.

8 Hamor talked with them, saying, "The soul of my son, Shechem, longs for your daughter. Please give her to him as a wife. 9 Make marriages with us. Give your daughters to us, and take our daughters for yourselves. 10 You shall dwell with us, and the land will be before you. Live and trade in it, and get possessions in it."

24 And Hamor spoke unto them, saying, "The soul of my son Shechem longeth for your daughter; I pray you give her unto him for a wife and intermarry with us; give us your daughters and we will give you our daughters, and you shall dwell with us in our land and we will be as one people in the land. 25 For our land is very extensive, so dwell ye and trade therein and get possessions in it, and do therein as you desire, and no one shall prevent you by saying a word to you."

26 And Hamor ceased speaking unto Jacob and his sons, and behold Shechem his son had come after him, and he sat before them.

11 Shechem said to her father and to her brothers, "Let me find favor in your eyes, and whatever you will tell me I will give. 12 Ask me a great amount for a dowry, and I will give whatever you ask of me, but give me the young lady as a wife."

27 And Shechem spoke before Jacob and his sons, saying, "May I find favor in your sight that you will give me your daughter, and whatever you say unto me that will I do for her. 28 Ask me for abundance of dowry and gift, and I will give it, and whatever you shall say unto me that will I do, and whoever he be that will rebel against your orders, he shall die; only give me the damsel for a wife."

29 "And Simeon and Levi answered Hamor and Shechem his son deceitfully, saying, "All you have spoken unto us we will do for you.

30 And behold our sister is in your house, but keep away from her until we send to our father Isaac concerning this matter, for we can do nothing without his consent. 31 For he knoweth the ways of our father Abraham, and whatever he sayeth unto us we will tell you, we will conceal nothing from you."

32 And Simeon and Levi spoke this unto Shechem and his father in order to find a pretext, and to seek counsel what was to be done to Shechem and to his city in this matter. 33 And when Shechem and his father heard the words of Simeon and Levi, it seemed good in their sight, and Shechem and his father came forth to go home.

34 And when they had gone, the sons of Jacob said unto their father, saying, "Behold, we know that death is due to these wicked ones and to their city, because they transgressed that which God had commanded unto Noah and his children and his seed after them.

35 "And also because Shechem did this thing to our sister Dinah in defiling her, for such vileness shall never be done amongst us. 36 Now therefore know and see what you will do, and seek counsel and pretext what is to be done to them, in order to kill all the inhabitants of this city."

37 And Simeon said to them, "Here is a proper advice for you: tell them to circumcise every male amongst them as we are circumcised, and if they do not wish to do this, we shall take our daughter from them and go away. 38 And if they consent to do this and will do it, then when they are sunk down with pain, we will attack them with our swords, as upon one who is quiet and peaceable, and we will slay every male person amongst them."

39 And Simeon's advice pleased them, and Simeon and Levi resolved to do unto them as it was proposed.

40 And on the next morning Shechem and Hamor his father came again unto Jacob and his sons, to speak concerning Dinah, and to hear what answer the sons of Jacob would give to their words.

13 The sons of Jacob answered Shechem and Hamor his father with deceit, and spoke, because he had defiled Dinah their sister,

41 And the sons of Jacob spoke deceitfully to them, saying, "We told our father Isaac all your words, and your words pleased him. 42 But he spoke unto us, saying, 'Thus did Abraham his father command him from God the Lord of the whole earth, that any man who is not of his descendants that should wish to take one of his daughters, shall cause every male belonging to him to be circumcised, as we are circumcised, and then we may give him our daughter for a wife.'

14 and said to them, "We can't do this thing, to give our sister to one who is uncircumcised; for that is a reproach to us. 15 Only on this condition will we consent to you. If you will be as we are, that every male of you be circumcised; 16 then will we give our daughters to you, and we will take your daughters to us, and we will dwell with you, and we will become one people. 17 But if you will not listen to us, to be circumcised, then we will take our sister and we will be gone."

43 "Now we have made known to you all our ways that our father spoke unto us, for we cannot do this of which you spoke unto us, to give our daughter to an uncircumcised man, for it is a disgrace to us. 44 But herein will we consent to you, to give you our daughter, and we will also take unto ourselves your daughters, and will dwell amongst you and be one people as you have spoken, if you will hearken to us, and consent to be like us, to circumcise every male belonging to you, as we are circumcised. 45 And if you will not hearken unto us, to have every male circumcised as we are circumcised, as we have commanded, then we will come to you, and take our daughter from you and go away."

18 Their words pleased Hamor and Shechem, Hamor's son. 19 The young man didn't wait to do this thing, because he had delight in Jacob's daughter, and he was honored above all the house of his father.

46 And Shechem and his father Hamor heard the words of the sons of Jacob, and the thing pleased them exceedingly, and Shechem and his father Hamor hastened to do the wishes of the sons of Jacob, for Shechem was very fond of Dinah, and his soul was riveted to her.

20 Hamor and Shechem, his son, came to the gate of their city, and talked with the men of their city, saying, 21 "These men are peaceful with us. Therefore let them live in the land and trade in it. For behold, the land is large enough for them. Let us take their daughters to us for wives, and let us give them our daughters.

47 And Shechem and his father Hamor hastened to the gate of the city, and they assembled all the men of their city and spoke unto them the words of the sons of Jacob, saying, 48 "We came to these men, the sons of Jacob, and we spoke unto them concerning their daughter, and these men will consent to do according to our wishes, and behold our land is of great extent for them, and they will dwell in it, and trade in it, and we shall be one people; we will take their daughters, and our daughters we will give unto them for wives.

22 Only on this condition will the men consent to us to live with us, to become one people, if every male among us is circumcised, as they are circumcised.
23 Won't their livestock and their possessions and all their animals be ours? Only let us give our consent to them, and they will dwell with us."

49 "But only on this condition will these men consent to do this thing, that every male amongst us be circumcised as they are circumcised, as their God commanded them, and when we shall have done according to their instructions to be circumcised, then will they dwell amongst us, together with their cattle and possessions, and we shall be as one people with them."

24 All who went out of the gate of his city listened to Hamor, and to Shechem his son;

50 And when all the men of the city heard the words of Shechem and his father Hamor, then all the men of their city were agreeable to this proposal, and they obeyed to be circumcised, for Shechem and his father Hamor were greatly esteemed by them, being the princes of the land.

and every male was circumcised, all who went out of the gate of his city.

51 And on the next day, Shechem and Hamor his father rose up early in the morning, and they assembled all the men of their city into the middle of the city, and they called for the sons of Jacob, who circumcised every male belonging to them on that day and the next.

52 And they circumcised Shechem and Hamor his father, and the five brothers of Shechem, and then every one rose up and went home, for this thing was from the Lord against the city of Shechem, and from the Lord was Simeon's counsel in this matter, in order that the Lord might deliver the city of Shechem into the hands of Jacob's two sons.

Jasher 34

1 And the number of all the males that were circumcised, were six hundred and forty-five men, and two hundred and forty-six children.

2 But Chiddekem, son of Pered, the father of Hamor, and his six brothers, would not listen unto Shechem and his father Hamor, and they would not be circumcised, for the proposal of the sons of Jacob was loathsome in their sight, and their anger was greatly roused at this, that the people of the city had not hearkened to them.

3 And in the evening of the second day, they found
eight small children who had not been circumcised,
for their mothers had concealed them from
Shechem and his father Hamor, and from the men
of the city. 4 And Shechem and his father Hamor
sent to have them brought before them to be
circumcised, when Chiddekem and his six brothers
sprang at them with their swords, and sought to
slay them. 5 And they sought to slay also Shechem
and his father Hamor and they sought to slay Dinah
with them on account of this matter.

6 And they said unto them, "What is this thing that
you have done? Are there no women amongst the
daughters of your brethren the Canaanites, that
you wish to take unto yourselves daughters of the
Hebrews, whom ye knew not before, and will do
this act which your fathers never commanded you?
7 Do you imagine that you will succeed through this
act which you have done? And what will you
answer in this affair to your brethren the
Canaanites, who will come tomorrow and ask you
concerning this thing?

8 "And if your act shall not appear just and good in
their sight, what will you do for your lives, and me
for our lives, in your not having hearkened to our
voices? 9 And if the inhabitants of the land and all
your brethren the children of Ham, shall hear of
your act, saying,

10 "'On account of a Hebrew woman did Shechem
and Hamor his father, and all the inhabitants of
their city, do that with which they had been
unacquainted and which their ancestors never
commanded them, where then will you fly or where
conceal your shame, all your days before your
brethren, the inhabitants of the land of Canaan?'

11 "Now therefore we cannot bear up against this
thing which you have done, neither can we be
burdened with this yoke upon us, which our
ancestors did not command us. 12 Behold
tomorrow we will go and assemble all our brethren,
the Canaanitish brethren who dwell in the land, and
we will all come and smite you and all those who
trust in you, that there shall not be a remnant left
from you or them."

13 And when Hamor and his son Shechem and all the people of the city heard the words of Chiddekem and his brothers, they were terribly afraid of their lives at their words, and they repented of what they had done.

14 And Shechem and his father Hamor answered their father Chiddekem and his brethren, and they said unto them, "All the words which you spoke unto us are true. 15 Now do not say, nor imagine in your hearts that on account of the love of the Hebrews we did this thing that our ancestors did not command us.

16 "But because we saw that it was not their intention and desire to accede to our wishes concerning their daughter as to our taking her, except on this condition, so we hearkened to their voices and did this act which you saw, in order to obtain our desire from them.

17 "And when we shall have obtained our request from them, we will then return to them and do unto them that which you say unto us. 18 We beseech you then to wait and tarry until our flesh shall be healed and we again become strong, and we will then go together against them, and do unto them that which is in your hearts and in ours."

19 And Dinah the daughter of Jacob heard all these words which Chiddekem and his brothers had spoken, and what Hamor and his son Shechem and the people of their city had answered them.

20 And she hastened and sent one of her maidens, that her father had sent to take care of her in the house of Shechem, to Jacob her father and to her brethren, saying: 21 "Thus did Chiddekem and his brothers advise concerning you, and thus did Hamor and Shechem and the people of the city answer them."

22 And when Jacob heard these words he was filled with wrath, and he was indignant at them, and his anger was kindled against them.

23 And Simeon and Levi swore and said, "As the Lord liveth, the God of the whole earth, by this time tomorrow, there shall not be a remnant left in the whole city."

24 And twenty young men had concealed themselves who were not circumcised, and these young men fought against Simeon and Levi, and Simeon and Levi killed eighteen of them, and two fled from them and escaped to some lime pits that were in the city, and Simeon and Levi sought for them, but could not find them.

25 On the third day, when they were sore, two of Jacob's sons, Simeon and Levi, Dinah's brothers, each took his sword, came upon the unsuspecting city, and killed all the males.

25 And Simeon and Levi continued to go about in
the city, and they killed all the people of the city at
the edge of the sword, and they left none
remaining. 26 And there was a great consternation
in the midst of the city, and the cry of the people of
the city ascended to heaven, and all the women
and children cried aloud. 27 And Simeon and Levi
slew all the city; they left not a male remaining in
the whole city.

26 They killed Hamor and Shechem, his son, with the edge of the sword, and took Dinah out of Shechem's house, and went away.

28 And they slew Hamor and Shechem his son at the edge of the sword, and they brought away Dinah from the house of Shechem and they went from there.

27 Jacob's sons came on the dead, and plundered the city, because they had defiled their sister.

29 And the sons of Jacob went and returned, and came upon the slain, and spoiled all their property which was in the city and the field.

30 And whilst they were taking the spoil, three hundred men stood up and threw dust at them and struck them with stones, when Simeon turned to them and he slew them all with the edge of the sword, and Simeon turned before Levi, and came into the city.

28 They took their flocks, their herds, their donkeys,
that which was in the city, that which was in the
field, 29 and all their wealth. They took captive all
their little ones and their wives, and took as plunder
everything that was in the house.

31 And they took away their sheep and their oxen and their cattle, and also the remainder of the women and little ones, and they led all these away, and they opened a gate and went out and came unto their father Jacob with vigor.

30 Jacob said to Simeon and Levi, "You have troubled me, to make me odious to the inhabitants of the land, among the Canaanites and the Perizzites. I am few in number. They will gather themselves together against me and strike me, and I will be destroyed, I and my house."

32 And when Jacob saw all that they had done to
the city, and saw the spoil that they took from
them, Jacob was very angry at them, and Jacob said
unto them, "What is this that you have done to me?
Behold I obtained rest amongst the Canaanitish
inhabitants of the land, and none of them meddled
with me. 33 And now you have done to make me
obnoxious to the inhabitants of the land, amongst
the Canaanites and the Perizzites, and I am but of a
small number, and they will all assemble against me
and slay me when they hear of your work with their
brethren, and I and my household will be
destroyed."

31 They said, “Should he deal with our sister as with a prostitute?”

34 And Simeon and Levi and all their brothers with them answered their father Jacob and said unto him, "Behold we live in the land, and shall Shechem do this to our sister? Why art thou silent at all that Shechem has done? And shall he deal with our sister as with a harlot in the streets?"

35 And the number of women whom Simeon and Levi took captives from the city of Shechem, whom they did not slay, was eighty-five who had not known man.

36 And amongst them was a young damsel of beautiful appearance and well favored, whose name was Bunah, and Simeon took her for a wife, and the number of the males which they took captives and did not slay, was forty-seven men, and the rest they slew.

37 And all the young men and women that Simeon and Levi had taken captives from the city of Shechem, were servants to the sons of Jacob and to their children after them, until the day of the sons of Jacob going forth from the land of Egypt.

38 And when Simeon and Levi had gone forth from the city, the two young men that were left, who had concealed themselves in the city, and did not die amongst the people of the city, rose up, and these young men went into the city and walked about in it, and found the city desolate without man, and only women weeping, and these young men cried out and said, "Behold, this is the evil which the sons of Jacob the Hebrew did to this city in their having this day destroyed one of the Canaanitish cities, and were not afraid of their lives of all the land of Canaan."

39 And these men left the city and went to the city of Tapnach, and they came there and told the inhabitants of Tapnach all that had befallen them, and all that the sons of Jacob had done to the city of Shechem.

40 And the information reached Jashub king of
Tapnach, and he sent men to the city of Shechem to
see those young men, for the king did not believe
them in this account, saying, "How could two men
lay waste such a large town as Shechem?" 41 And
the messengers of Jashub came back and told him,
saying, "We came unto the city, and it is destroyed,
there is not a man there; only weeping women;
neither is any flock or cattle there, for all that was
in the city the sons of Jacob took away."

42 And Jashub wondered at this, saying, "How could two men do this thing, to destroy so large a city, and not one man able to stand against them?"

43 For the like has not been from the days of Nimrod, and not even from the remotest time, has the like taken place; and Jashub, king of Tapnach, said to his people, "Be courageous and we will go and fight against these Hebrews, and do unto them as they did unto the city, and we will avenge the cause of the people of the city."

44 And Jashub, king of Tapnach, consulted with his
counsellors about this matter, and his advisers said
unto him, "Alone thou wilt not prevail over the
Hebrews, for they must be powerful to do this work
to the whole city. 45 If two of them laid waste the
whole city, and no one stood against them, surely if
thou wilt go against them, they will all rise against
us and destroy us likewise. 46 But if thou wilt send
to all the kings that surround us, and let them come
together, then we will go with them and fight
against the sons of Jacob; then wilt thou prevail
against them."

47 And Jashub heard the words of his counsellors, and their words pleased him and his people, and he did so; and Jashub king of Tapnach sent to all the kings of the Amorites that surrounded Shechem and Tapnach, saying,

48 "Go up with me and assist me, and we will smite Jacob the Hebrew and all his sons, and destroy them from the earth, for thus did he do to the city of Shechem, and do you not know of it?"

49 And all the kings of the Amorites heard the evil
that the sons of Jacob had done to the city of
Shechem, and they were greatly astonished at
them. 50 And the seven kings of the Amorites
assembled with all their armies, about ten thousand
men with drawn swords, and they came to fight
against the sons of Jacob; and Jacob heard that the
kings of the Amorites had assembled to fight
against his sons, and Jacob was greatly afraid, and it
distressed him.

51 And Jacob exclaimed against Simeon and Levi,
saying, "What is this act that you did? Why have
you injured me, to bring against me all the children
of Canaan to destroy me and my household? for I
was at rest, even I and my household, and you have
done this thing to me, and provoked the inhabitants
of the land against me by your proceedings."

52 And Judah answered his father, saying, "Was it
for naught my brothers Simeon and Levi killed all
the inhabitants of Shechem? Surely it was because
Shechem had humbled our sister, and transgressed
the command of our God to Noah and his children,
for Shechem took our sister away by force, and
committed adultery with her."

53 And Shechem did all this evil and not one of the
inhabitants of his city interfered with him, to say,
"Why wilt thou do this? surely for this my brothers
went and smote the city, and the Lord delivered it
into their hands, because its inhabitants had
transgressed the commands of our God. Is it then
for naught that they have done all this? 54 And now
why art thou afraid or distressed, and why art thou
displeased at my brothers, and why is thine anger
kindled against them?

55 "Surely our God who delivered into their hand
the city of Shechem and its people, he will also
deliver into our hands all the Canaanitish kings who
are coming against us, and we will do unto them as
my brothers did unto Shechem. 56 Now be tranquil
about them and cast away thy fears, but trust in the
Lord our God, and pray unto him to assist us and
deliver us, and deliver our enemies into our hands."

57 And Judah called to one of his father's servants, "Go now and see where those kings, who are coming against us, are situated with their armies." 58 And the servant went and looked far off, and went up opposite Mount Sihon, and saw all the camps of the kings standing in the fields, and he returned to Judah and said, "Behold the kings are situated in the field with all their camps, a people exceedingly numerous, like unto the sand upon the sea shore."

59 And Judah said unto Simeon and Levi, and unto all his brothers, "Strengthen yourselves and be sons of valor, for the Lord our God is with us, do not fear them. 60 Stand forth each man, girt with his weapons of war, his bow and his sword, and we will go and fight against these uncircumcised men; the Lord is our God, He will save us."

61 And they rose up, and each girt on his weapons of war, great and small, eleven sons of Jacob, and all the servants of Jacob with them. 62 And all the servants of Isaac who were with Isaac in Hebron, all came to them equipped in all sorts of war instruments, and the sons of Jacob and their servants, being one hundred and twelve men, went towards these kings, and Jacob also went with them.

63 And the sons of Jacob sent unto their father Isaac the son of Abraham to Hebron, the same is Kireath-arba, saying, 64 "Pray we beseech thee for us unto the Lord our God, to protect us from the hands of the Canaanites who are coming against us, and to deliver them into our hands."

65 And Isaac the son of Abraham prayed unto the Lord for his sons, and he said, "O Lord God, thou didst promise my father, saying, 'I will multiply thy seed as the stars of heaven, and thou didst also promise me, and establish thou thy word, now that the kings of Canaan are coming together, to make war with my children because they committed no violence.' 66 Now therefore, O Lord God, God of the whole earth, pervert, I pray thee, the counsel of these kings that they may not fight against my sons.

67 "And impress the hearts of these kings and their people with the terror of my sons and bring down their pride, and that they may turn away from my sons. 68 And with thy strong hand and outstretched arm deliver my sons and their servants from them, for power and might are in thy hands to do all this."

69 And the sons of Jacob and their servants went toward these kings, and they trusted in the Lord their God, and whilst they were going, Jacob their father also prayed unto the Lord and said, "O Lord God, powerful and exalted God, who has reigned from days of old, from thence till now and forever;

70 "Thou art He who stirreth up wars and causeth them to cease, in thy hand are power and might to exalt and to bring down; O may my prayer be acceptable before thee that thou mayest turn to me with thy mercies, to impress the hearts of these kings and their people with the terror of my sons, and terrify them and their camps, and with thy great kindness deliver all those that trust in thee, for it is thou who canst bring people under us and reduce nations under our power."

Jasher 35

1 And all the kings of the Amorites came and took their stand in the field to consult with their counsellors what was to be done with the sons of Jacob, for they were still afraid of them, saying, "Behold, two of them slew the whole of the city of Shechem."

2 And the Lord heard the prayers of Isaac and Jacob, and he filled the hearts of all these kings' advisers with great fear and terror that they unanimously exclaimed, "3 Are you silly this day, or is there no understanding in you, that you will fight with the Hebrews, and why will you take a delight in your own destruction this day? 4 Behold two of them came to the city of Shechem without fear or terror, and they killed all the inhabitants of the city, that no man stood up against them, and how will you be able to fight with them all?

5 "Surely you know that their God is exceedingly fond of them, and has done mighty things for them, such as have not been done from days of old, and amongst all the gods of nations, there is none can do like unto his mighty deeds.

6 "Surely he delivered their father Abraham, the Hebrew, from the hand of Nimrod, and from the hand of all his people who had many times sought
to slay him. 7 He delivered him also from the fire in
which king Nimrod had cast him, and his God delivered him from it.

8 "And who else can do the like? Surely it was Abraham who slew the five kings of Elam, when they had touched his brother's son who in those days dwelt in Sodom.

9 "And took his servant that was faithful in his house and a few of his men, and they pursued the kings of Elam in one night and killed them, and restored to his brother's son all his property which they had taken from him.

10 "And surely you know the God of these Hebrews is much delighted with them, and they are also delighted with him, for they know that he delivered them from all their enemies.

11 "And behold through his love toward his God, Abraham took his only and precious son and intended to bring him up as a burnt offering to his God, and had it not been for God who prevented him from doing this, he would then have done it
through his love to his God. 12 And God saw all his
works, and swore unto him, and promised him that he would deliver his sons and all his seed from every trouble that would befall them, because he had done this thing, and through his love to his God stifled his compassion for his child.

13 "And have you not heard what their God did to Pharaoh king of Egypt, and to Abimelech king of Gerar, through taking Abraham's wife, who said of her, She is my sister, lest they might slay him on account of her, and think of taking her for a wife? and God did unto them and their people all that
you heard of. 14 And behold, we ourselves saw with
our eyes that Esau, the brother of Jacob, came to him with four hundred men, with the intention of slaying him, for he called to mind that he had taken away from him his father's blessing.

15 "And he went to meet him when he came from
Syria, to smite the mother with the children, and
who delivered him from his hands but his God in
whom he trusted? he delivered him from the hand
of his brother and also from the hands of his
enemies, and surely he again will protect them.

16 "Who does not know that it was their God who
inspired them with strength to do to the town of
Shechem the evil which you heard of? 17 Could it
then be with their own strength that two men could
destroy such a large city as Shechem had it not
been for their God in whom they trusted? he said
and did unto them all this to slay the inhabitants of
the city in their city.

18 "And can you then prevail over them who have
come forth together from your city to fight with the
whole of them, even if a thousand times as many
more should come to your assistance? 19 Surely
you know and understand that you do not come to
fight with them, but you come to war with their
God who made choice of them, and you have
therefore all come this day to be destroyed. 20
Now therefore refrain from this evil which you are
endeavoring to bring upon yourselves, and it will be
better for you not to go to battle with them,
although they are but few in numbers, because
their God is with them."

21 And when the kings of the Amorites heard all the
words of their advisers, their hearts were filled with
terror, and they were afraid of the sons of Jacob
and would not fight against them. 22 And they
inclined their ears to the words of their advisers,
and they listened to all their words, and the words
of the counsellors greatly pleased the kings, and
they did so.

23 And the kings turned and refrained from the
sons of Jacob, for they durst not approach them to
make war with them, for they were greatly afraid of
them, and their hearts melted within them from
their fear of them.

24 For this proceeded from the Lord to them, for he
heard the prayers of his servants Isaac and Jacob,
for they trusted in him; and all these kings returned
with their camps on that day, each to his own city,
and they did not at that time fight with the sons of
Jacob.

25 And the sons of Jacob kept their station that day till evening opposite mount Sihon, and seeing that these kings did not come to fight against them, the sons of Jacob returned home.

Genesis 35

1 God said to Jacob, "Arise, go up to Bethel, and live there. Make there an altar to God, who appeared to you when you fled from the face of Esau your brother."

Jasher 36

1 At that time the Lord appeared unto Jacob saying, "Arise, go to Bethel and remain there, and make there an altar to the Lord who appeareth unto thee, who delivered thee and thy sons from affliction."

2 Then Jacob said to his household, and to all who were with him, "Put away the foreign gods that are among you, purify yourselves, change your
garments. 3 Let us arise, and go up to Bethel. I will make there an altar to God, who answered me in the day of my distress, and was with me on the way which I went."

2 And Jacob rose up with his sons and all belonging to him, and they went and came to Bethel according to the word of the Lord.

4 They gave to Jacob all the foreign gods which were in their hands, and the rings which were in their ears; and Jacob hid them under the oak which
was by Shechem. 5 They traveled, and a terror of God was on the cities that were around them, and they didn't pursue the sons of Jacob.

6 So Jacob came to Luz (that is, Bethel), which is in the land of Canaan, he and all the people who were
with him. 7 He built an altar there, and called the place El Beth El; because there God was revealed to him, when he fled from the face of his brother.

3 And Jacob was ninety-nine years old when he went up to Bethel, and Jacob and his sons and all the people that were with him, remained in Bethel in Luz, and he there built an altar to the Lord who appeared unto him, and Jacob and his sons remained in Bethel six months.

8 Deborah, Rebekah's nurse, died, and she was buried below Bethel under the oak; and its name
was called Allon Bacuth. 9 God appeared to Jacob again, when he came from Paddan Aram, and blessed him.

10 God said to him, "Your name is Jacob. Your name shall not be Jacob any more, but your name will be
Israel." He named him Israel. 11 God said to him, "I am God Almighty. Be fruitful and multiply. A nation and a company of nations will be from you, and
kings will come out of your body. 12 The land which I gave to Abraham and Isaac, I will give it to you, and to your offspring after you will I give the land."

13 God went up from him in the place where he spoke with him. 14 Jacob set up a pillar in the place where he spoke with him, a pillar of stone. He poured out a drink offering on it, and poured oil on it. 15 Jacob called the name of the place where God spoke with him "Bethel".

4 At that time died Deborah the daughter of Uz, the nurse of Rebecca, who had been with Jacob; and Jacob buried her beneath Bethel under an oak that was there.

5 And Rebecca the daughter of Bethuel, the mother of Jacob, also died at that time in Hebron, the same is Kireath-arba, and she was buried in the cave of Machpelah which Abraham had bought from the children of Heth.

6 And the life of Rebecca was one hundred and thirty-three years, and she died and when Jacob heard that his mother Rebecca was dead he wept bitterly for his mother, and made a great mourning for her, and for Deborah her nurse beneath the oak, and he called the name of that place Allon-bachuth.

7 And Laban the Syrian died in those days, for God smote him because he transgressed the covenant that existed between him and Jacob. 8 And Jacob was a hundred years old when the Lord appeared unto him, and blessed him and called his name Israel, and Rachel the wife of Jacob conceived in those days.

16 They traveled from Bethel. There was still some distance to come to Ephrath, and Rachel travailed. She had hard labor. 17 When she was in hard labor, the midwife said to her, "Don't be afraid, for now you will have another son." 18 As her soul was departing (for she died), she named him Benoni but his father named him Benjamin. 19 Rachel died, and was buried on the way to Ephrath (also called Bethlehem).

9 And at that time Jacob and all belonging to him journeyed from Bethel to go to his father's house, to Hebron. 10 And whilst they were going on the road, and there was yet but a little way to come to Ephrath, Rachel bare a son and she had hard labor and she died.

20 Jacob set up a pillar on her grave. The same is the Pillar of Rachel's grave to this day. 21 Israel traveled, and spread his tent beyond the tower of Eder.

11 And Jacob buried her in the way to Ephrath, which is Bethlehem, and he set a pillar upon her grave, which is there unto this day; and the days of Rachel were forty-five years and she died.

12 And Jacob called the name of his son that was born to him, which Rachel bare unto him, Benjamin, for he was born to him in the land on the right hand.

22 While Israel lived in that land, Reuben went and lay with Bilhah, his father's concubine, and Israel heard of it.

13 And it was after the death of Rachel, that Jacob pitched his tent in the tent of her handmaid Bilhah.

14 And Reuben was jealous for his mother Leah on account of this, and he was filled with anger, and he rose up in his anger and went and entered the tent of Bilhah and he thence removed his father's bed.
15 At that time the portion of birthright, together with the kingly and priestly offices, was removed from the sons of Reuben, for he had profaned his father's bed, and the birthright was given unto Joseph, the kingly office to Judah, and the priesthood unto Levi, because Reuben had defiled his father's bed.

Now the sons of Jacob were twelve.

16 And these are the generations of Jacob who were born to him in Padan-aram, and the sons of Jacob were twelve.

23 The sons of Leah: Reuben (Jacob's firstborn), Simeon, Levi, Judah, Issachar, and Zebulun.
24 The sons of Rachel: Joseph and Benjamin.

17 The sons of Leah were Reuben the first born, and Simeon, Levi, Judah, Issachar, Zebulun, and their sister Dinah; and the sons of Rachel were Joseph and Benjamin.

25 The sons of Bilhah (Rachel's servant): Dan and Naphtali.
26 The sons of Zilpah (Leah's servant): Gad and Asher. These are the sons of Jacob, who were born to him in Paddan Aram.

18 The sons of Zilpah, Leah's handmaid, were Gad and Asher, and the sons of Bilhah, Rachel's handmaid, were Dan and Naphtali; these are the sons of Jacob which were born to him in Padan-aram.

27 Jacob came to Isaac his father, to Mamre, to Kiriath Arba (which is Hebron), where Abraham and Isaac lived as foreigners.

19 And Jacob and his sons and all belonging to him journeyed and came to Mamre, which is Kireath-arba, that is in Hebron, where Abraham and Isaac sojourned, and Jacob with his sons and all belonging to him, dwelt with his father in Hebron.

28 The days of Isaac were one hundred eighty years.
29 Isaac gave up the spirit, and died, and was gathered to his people, old and full of days. Esau and Jacob, his sons, buried him.

Genesis 36

1 Now this is the history of the generations of Esau (that is, Edom).

2 Esau took his wives from the daughters of Canaan: Adah the daughter of Elon, the Hittite; and Oholibamah the daughter of Anah, the daughter of Zibeon, the Hivite;
3 and Basemath, Ishmael's daughter, sister of Nebaioth.

20 And his brother Esau and his sons, and all
belonging to him went to the land of Seir and dwelt
there, and had possessions in the land of Seir, and
the children of Esau were fruitful and multiplied
exceedingly in the land of Seir. 21 And these are
the generations of Esau that were born to him in
the land of Canaan, and the sons of Esau were five.

4 Adah bore to Esau Eliphaz.
Basemath bore Reuel.
5 Oholibamah bore Jeush, Jalam, and Korah. These
are the sons of Esau, who were born to him in the
land of Canaan.

22 And Adah bare to Esau his first born Eliphaz,
and she also bare to him Reuel,
and Ahlibamah bare to him Jeush, Yaalam and
Korah.

6 Esau took his wives, his sons, his daughters, and
all the members of his household, with his
livestock, all his animals, and all his possessions,
which he had gathered in the land of Canaan, and
went into a land away from his brother Jacob.

7 For their substance was too great for them to
dwell together, and the land of their travels
couldn't bear them because of their livestock. 8
Esau lived in the hill country of Seir. Esau is Edom.

9 This is the history of the generations of Esau the
father of the Edomites in the hill country of Seir:

23 These are the children of Esau who were born to
him in the land of Canaan;

10 these are the names of Esau's sons: Eliphaz, the
son of Adah, the wife of Esau; and Reuel, the son of
Basemath, the wife of Esau. 11 The sons of Eliphaz
were Teman, Omar, Zepho, and Gatam, and Kenaz.

12 Timna was concubine to Eliphaz, Esau's son; and
she bore to Eliphaz Amalek. These are the sons of
Adah, Esau's wife. 13 These are the sons of Reuel:
Nahath, Zerah, Shammah, and Mizzah. These were
the sons of Basemath, Esau's wife. 14 These were
the sons of Oholibamah, the daughter of Anah, the
daughter of Zibeon, Esau's wife: she bore to Esau
Jeush, Jalam, and Korah.

15 These are the chiefs of the sons of Esau: the sons
of Eliphaz the firstborn of Esau: chief Teman, chief
Omar, chief Zepho, chief Kenaz, 16 chief Korah,
chief Gatam, chief Amalek: these are the chiefs who
came of Eliphaz in the land of Edom; these are the
sons of Adah.

and the sons of Eliphaz the son of Esau were
Teman, Omar, Zepho, Gatam, Kenaz and Amalex,

17 These are the sons of Reuel, Esau's son: chief
Nahath, chief Zerah, chief Shammah, chief Mizzah:
these are the chiefs who came of Reuel in the land
of Edom; these are the sons of Basemath, Esau's
wife.

and the sons of Reuel were Nachath, Zerach, Shamah and Mizzah.

18 These are the sons of Oholibamah, Esau's wife:
chief Jeush, chief Jalam, chief Korah: these are the
chiefs who came of Oholibamah the daughter of
Anah, Esau's wife. 19 These are the sons of Esau
(that is, Edom), and these are their chiefs.

20 These are the sons of Seir the Horite, the
inhabitants of the land: Lotan, Shobal, Zibeon,
Anah, 21 Dishon, Ezer, and Dishan. These are the
chiefs who came of the Horites, the children of Seir
in the land of Edom.

[36:26 And these are the names of the sons of Seir the Horite, inhabitants of the land of Seir, Lotan, Shobal, Zibeon, Anah, Dishan, Ezer and Dishon, being seven sons.]

22 The children of Lotan were Hori and Heman.
Lotan's sister was Timna.

[36:27 And the children of Lotan were Hori, Heman and their sister Timna, that is Timna who came to Jacob and his sons, and they would not give ear to her, and she went and became a concubine to Eliphaz the son of Esau, and she bare to him Amalek.]

23 These are the children of Shobal: Alvan,
Manahath, Ebal, Shepho, and Onam. 24 These are
the children of Zibeon: Aiah and Anah. This is Anah
who found the hot springs in the wilderness, as he
fed the donkeys of Zibeon his father.

[36:28 And the sons of Shobal were Alvan, Manahath, Ebal, Shepho, and Onam, and the sons of Zibeon were Ajah, and Anah, this was that Anah who found the Yemim in the wilderness when he fed the asses of Zibeon his father.]

25 These are the children of Anah: Dishon and
Oholibamah, the daughter of Anah. 26 These are
the children of Dishon: Hemdan, Eshban, Ithran,
and Cheran. 27 These are the children of Ezer:
Bilhan, Zaavan, and Akan. 28 These are the children
of Dishan: Uz and Aran. 29 These are the chiefs who
came of the Horites: chief Lotan, chief Shobal, chief
Zibeon, chief Anah, 30 chief Dishon, chief Ezer, and
chief Dishan: these are the chiefs who came of the
Horites, according to their chiefs in the land of Seir.

31 These are the kings who reigned in the land of
Edom, before any king reigned over the children of
Israel. 32 Bela, the son of Beor, reigned in Edom.
The name of his city was Dinhabah. 33 Bela died,
and Jobab, the son of Zerah of Bozrah, reigned in
his place. 34 Jobab died, and Husham of the land of
the Temanites reigned in his place. 35 Husham died,
and Hadad, the son of Bedad, who struck Midian in
the field of Moab, reigned in his place. The name of
his city was Avith. 36 Hadad died, and Samlah of
Masrekah reigned in his place.

37 Samlah died, and Shaul of Rehoboth by the river,
reigned in his place. 38 Shaul died, and Baal Hanan,
the son of Achbor reigned in his place. 39 Baal
Hanan the son of Achbor died, and Hadar reigned in
his place. The name of his city was Pau. His wife's
name was Mehetabel, the daughter of Matred, the
daughter of Mezahab.

40 These are the names of the chiefs who came
from Esau, according to their families, after their
places, and by their names: chief Timna, chief
Alvah, chief Jetheth,

24 And the sons of Jeush were Timnah, Alvah,
Jetheth;

41 chief Oholibamah, chief Elah, chief Pinon, 42
chief Kenaz,

and the sons of Yaalam were Alah, Phinor and
Kenaz.

chief Teman, chief Mibzar, 43 chief Magdiel, and
chief Iram. These are the chiefs of Edom, according
to their habitations in the land of their possession.
This is Esau, the father of the Edomites.

25 And the sons of Korah were Teman, Mibzar,
Magdiel and Eram; these are the families of the
sons of Esau according to their dukedoms in the
land of Seir.

*[Genesis 36:20 These are the sons of Seir the Horite,
the inhabitants of the land: Lotan, Shobal, Zibeon,
Anah, 21 Dishon, Ezer, and Dishan. These are the
chiefs who came of the Horites, the children of Seir
in the land of Edom.]*

26 And these are the names of the sons of Seir the
Horite, inhabitants of the land of Seir, Lotan,
Shobal, Zibeon, Anah, Dishan, Ezer and Dishon,
being seven sons.

*[Genesis 36:22 The children of Lotan were Hori and
Heman. Lotan's sister was Timna.]*

27 And the children of Lotan were Hori, Heman and
their sister Timna, that is Timna who came to Jacob
and his sons, and they would not give ear to her,
and she went and became a concubine to Eliphaz
the son of Esau, and she bare to him Amalek.

*[Genesis 36:23 These are the children of Shobal:
Alvan, Manahath, Ebal, Shepho, and Onam. 24
These are the children of Zibeon: Aiah and Anah.
This is Anah who found the hot springs in the
wilderness, as he fed the donkeys of Zibeon his
father.]*

28 And the sons of Shobal were Alvan, Manahath,
Ebal, Shepho, and Onam, and the sons of Zibeon
were Ajah, and Anah, this was that Anah who found
the Yemim in the wilderness when he fed the asses
of Zibeon his father.

29 And whilst he was feeding his father's asses he
led them to the wilderness at different times to
feed them. 30 And there was a day that he brought
them to one of the deserts on the sea shore,
opposite the wilderness of the people, and whilst
he was feeding them, behold a very heavy storm
came from the other side of the sea and rested
upon the asses that were feeding there, and they all
stood still.

31 And afterward about one hundred and twenty great and terrible animals came out from the wilderness at the other side of the sea, and they all came to the place where the asses were, and they placed themselves there.

32 And those animals, from their middle downward, were in the shape of the children of men, and from their middle upward, some had the likeness of bears, and some the likeness of the keephas, with tails behind them from between their shoulders reaching down to the earth, like the tails of the ducheephath, and these animals came and mounted and rode upon these asses, and led them away, and they went away unto this day.

33 And one of these animals approached Anah and
smote him with his tail, and then fled from that
place. 34 And when he saw this work he was
exceedingly afraid of his life, and he fled and
escaped to the city. 35 And he related to his sons
and brothers all that had happened to him, and
many men went to seek the asses but could not
find them, and Anah and his brothers went no more
to that place from that day following, for they were
greatly afraid of their lives.

36 And the children of Anah the son of Seir, were Dishon and his sister Ahlibamah, and the children of Dishon were Hemdan, Eshban, Ithran and Cheran, and the children of Ezer were Bilhan, Zaavan and Akan, and the children of Dishon were Uz and Aran.

37 These are the families of the children of Seir the
Horite, according to their dukedoms in the land of
Seir. 38 And Esau and his children dwelt in the land
of Seir the Horite, the inhabitant of the land, and
they had possessions in it and were fruitful and
multiplied exceedingly, and Jacob and his children
and all belonging to them, dwelt with their father
Isaac in the land of Canaan, as the Lord had
commanded Abraham their father.

Jasher 37

1 And in the one hundred and fifth year of the life of Jacob, that is the ninth year of Jacob's dwelling with his children in the land of Canaan, he came from Padan-aram.

2 And in those days Jacob journeyed with his children from Hebron, and they went and returned to the city of Shechem, they and all belonging to them, and they dwelt there, for the children of Jacob obtained good and fat pasture land for their cattle in the city of Shechem, the city of Shechem having then been rebuilt, and there were in it about three hundred men and women.

3 And Jacob and his children and all belonging to him dwelt in the part of the field which Jacob had bought from Hamor the father of Shechem, when he came from Padan-aram before Simeon and Levi had smitten the city.

4 And all those kings of the Canaanites and
Amorites that surrounded the city of Shechem,
heard that the sons of Jacob had again come to
Shechem and dwelt there. 5 And they said, "Shall
the sons of Jacob the Hebrew again come to the
city and dwell therein, after that they have smitten
its inhabitants and driven them out? shall they now
return and also drive out those who are dwelling in
the city or slay them?"

6 And all the kings of Canaan again assembled, and
they came together to make war with Jacob and his
sons. 7 And Jashub king of Tapnach sent also to all
his neighboring kings, to Elan king of Gaash, and to
Ihuri king of Shiloh, and to Parathon king of Chazar,
and to Susi king of Sarton, and to Laban king of
Bethchoran, and to Shabir king of Othnay-mah,
saying, 8 "Come up to me and assist me, and let us
smite Jacob the Hebrew and his sons, and all
belonging to him, for they are again come to
Shechem to possess it and to slay its inhabitants as
before."

9 And all these kings assembled together and came with all their camps, a people exceedingly plentiful like the sand upon the sea shore, and they were all opposite to Tapnach.

10 And Jashub king of Tapnach went forth to them with all his army, and he encamped with them opposite to Tapnach without the city, and all these kings they divided into seven divisions, being seven camps against the sons of Jacob.

11 And they sent a declaration to Jacob and his son, saying, "Come you all forth to us that we may have an interview together in the plain, and revenge the cause of the men of Shechem whom you slew in their city, and you will now again return to the city of Shechem and dwell therein, and slay its inhabitants as before."

12 And the sons of Jacob heard this and their anger was kindled exceedingly at the words of the kings of Canaan, and ten of the sons of Jacob hastened and rose up, and each of them girt on his weapons of war; and there were one hundred and two of their servants with them equipped in battle array.

13 And all these men, the sons of Jacob with their servants, went toward these kings, and Jacob their father was with them, and they all stood upon the heap of Shechem.

14 And Jacob prayed to the Lord for his sons, and he spread forth his hands to the Lord, and he said, "O God, thou art an Almighty God, thou art our father, thou didst form us and we are the works of thine hands; I pray thee deliver my sons through thy mercy from the hand of their enemies, who are this day coming to fight with them and save them from their hand, for in thy hand is power and might, to save the few from the many.

15 "And give unto my sons, thy servants, strength of heart and might to fight with their enemies, to subdue them, and make their enemies fall before them, and let not my sons and their servants die through the hands of the children of Canaan.

16 "But if it seemeth good in thine eyes to take away the lives of my sons and their servants, take them in thy great mercy through the hands of thy ministers, that they may not perish this day by the hands of the kings of the Amorites."

17 And when Jacob ceased praying to the Lord the
earth shook from its place, and the sun darkened,
and all these kings were terrified and a great
consternation seized them. 18 And the Lord
hearkened to the prayer of Jacob, and the Lord
impressed the hearts of all the kings and their hosts
with the terror and awe of the sons of Jacob. 19
For the Lord caused them to hear the voice of
chariots, and the voice of mighty horses from the
sons of Jacob, and the voice of a great army
accompanying them.

20 And these kings were seized with great terror at
the sons of Jacob, and whilst they were standing in
their quarters, behold the sons of Jacob advanced
upon them, with one hundred and twelve men,
with a great and tremendous shouting. 21 And
when the kings saw the sons of Jacob advancing
toward them, they were still more panic struck, and
they were inclined to retreat from before the sons
of Jacob as at first, and not to fight with them. 22
But they did not retreat, saying, "It would be a
disgrace to us thus twice to retreat from before the
Hebrews."

23 And the sons of Jacob came near and advanced
against all these kings and their armies, and they
saw, and behold it was a very mighty people,
numerous as the sand of the sea. 24 And the sons
of Jacob called unto the Lord and said, "Help us O
Lord, help us and answer us, for we trust in thee,
and let us not die by the hands of these
uncircumcised men, who this day have come
against us."

25 And the sons of Jacob girt on their weapons of
war, and they took in their hands each man his
shield and his javelin, and they approached to
battle.

26 And Judah, the son of Jacob, ran first before his
brethren, and ten of his servants with him, and he
went toward these kings.

27 And Jashub, king of Tapnach, also came forth
first with his army before Judah, and Judah saw
Jashub and his army coming toward him, and
Judah's wrath was kindled, and his anger burned
within him, and he approached to battle in which
Judah ventured his life.

28 And Jashub and all his army were advancing
toward Judah, and he was riding upon a very strong
and powerful horse, and Jashub was a very valiant
man, and covered with iron and brass from head to
foot. 29 And whilst he was upon the horse, he shot
arrows with both hands from before and behind, as
was his manner in all his battles, and he never
missed the place to which he aimed his arrows.

30 And when Jashub came to fight with Judah, and
was darting many arrows against Judah, the Lord
bound the hand of Jashub, and all the arrows that
he shot rebounded upon his own men. 31 And
notwithstanding this, Jashub kept advancing toward
Judah, to challenge him with the arrows, but the
distance between them was about thirty cubits, and
when Judah saw Jashub darting forth his arrows
against him, he ran to him with his wrath-excited
might.

32 And Judah took up a large stone from the
ground, and its weight was sixty shekels, and Judah
ran toward Jashub, and with the stone struck him
on his shield, that Jashub was stunned with the
blow, and fell off from his horse to the ground. 33
And the shield burst asunder out of the hand of
Jashub, and through the force of the blow sprang to
the distance of about fifteen cubits, and the shield
fell before the second camp.

34 And the kings that came with Jashub saw at a
distance the strength of Judah, the son of Jacob,
and what he had done to Jashub, and they were
terribly afraid of Judah.

35 And they assembled near Jashub's camp, seeing
his confusion, and Judah drew his sword and smote
forty-two men of the camp of Jashub, and the
whole of Jashub's camp fled before Judah, and no
man stood against him, and they left Jashub and
fled from him, and Jashub was still prostrate upon
the ground.

36 And Jashub seeing that all the men of his camp
had fled from him, hastened and rose up with
terror against Judah, and stood upon his legs
opposite Judah.

37 And Jashub had a single combat with Judah,
placing shield toward shield, and Jashub's men all
fled, for they were greatly afraid of Judah. 38 And
Jashub took his spear in his hand to strike Judah
upon his head, but Judah had quickly placed his
shield to his head against Jashub's spear, so that the
shield of Judah received the blow from Jashub's
spear, and the shield was split in too. 39 And when
Judah saw that his shield was split, he hastily drew
his sword and smote Jashub at his ankles, and cut
off his feet that Jashub fell upon the ground, and
the spear fell from his hand.

40 And Judah hastily picked up Jashub's spear, with
which he severed his head and cast it next to his
feet. 41 And when the sons of Jacob saw what
Judah had done to Jashub, they all ran into the
ranks of the other kings, and the sons of Jacob
fought with the army of Jashub, and the armies of
all the kings that were there.

42 And the sons of Jacob caused fifteen thousand of
their men to fall, and they smote them as if smiting
at gourds, and the rest fled for their lives. 43 And
Judah was still standing by the body of Jashub, and
stripped Jashub of his coat of mail. 44 And Judah
also took off the iron and brass that was about
Jashub, and behold nine men of the captains of
Jashub came along to fight against Judah.

45 And Judah hastened and took up a stone from
the ground, and with it smote one of them upon
the head, and his skull was fractured, and the body
also fell from the horse to the ground.

46 And the eight captains that remained, seeing the
strength of Judah, were greatly afraid and they fled,
and Judah with his ten men pursued them, and they
overtook them and slew them. 47 And the sons of
Jacob were still smiting the armies of the kings, and
they slew many of them, but those kings daringly
kept their stand with their captains, and did not
retreat from their places, and they exclaimed
against those of their armies that fled from before
the sons of Jacob, but none would listen to them,
for they were afraid of their lives lest they should
die.

48 And all the sons of Jacob, after having smitten
the armies of the kings, returned and came before
Judah, and Judah was still slaying the eight captains
of Jashub, and stripping off their garments.

49 And Levi saw Elon, king of Gaash, advancing
toward him, with his fourteen captains to smite
him, but Levi did not know it for certain. 50 And
Elon with his captains approached nearer, and Levi
looked back and saw that battle was given him in
the rear, and Levi ran with twelve of his servants,
and they went and slew Elon and his captains with
the edge of the sword.

Jasher 38

1 And Ihuri king of Shiloh came up to assist Elon,
and he approached Jacob, when Jacob drew his
bow that was in his hand and with an arrow struck
Ihuri which caused his death. 2 And when Ihuri king
of Shiloh was dead, the four remaining kings fled
from their station with the rest of the captains, and
they endeavored to retreat, saying, "We have no
more strength with the Hebrews after their having
killed the three kings and their captains who were
more powerful than we are."

3 And when the sons of Jacob saw that the
remaining kings had removed from their station,
they pursued them, and Jacob also came from the
heap of Shechem from the place where he was
standing, and they went after the kings and they
approached them with their servants. 4 And the
kings and the captains with the rest of their armies,
seeing that the sons of Jacob approached them,
were afraid of their lives and fled till they reached
the city of Chazar.

5 And the sons of Jacob pursued them to the gate
of the city of Chazar, and they smote a great
smiting amongst the kings and their armies, about
four thousand men, and whilst they were smiting
the army of the kings, Jacob was occupied with his
bow confining himself to smiting the kings, and he
slew them all. 6 And he slew Parathon king of
Chazar at the gate of the city of Chazar, and he
afterward smote Susi king of Sarton, and Laban king
of Bethchorin, and Shabir king of Machnaymah, and
he slew them all with arrows, an arrow to each of
them, and they died.

7 And the sons of Jacob seeing that all the kings
were dead and that they were broken up and
retreating, continued to carry on the battle with the
armies of the kings opposite the gate of Chazar, and
they still smote about four hundred of their men. 8
And three men of the servants of Jacob fell in that
battle, and when Judah saw that three of his
servants had died, it grieved him greatly, and his
anger burned within him against the Amorites.

9 And all the men that remained of the armies of
the kings were greatly afraid of their lives, and they
ran and broke the gate of the walls of the city of
Chazar, and they all entered the city for safety. 10
And they concealed themselves in the midst of the
city of Chazar, for the city of Chazar was very large
and extensive, and when all these armies had
entered the city, the sons of Jacob ran after them to
the city.

11 And four mighty men, experienced in battle,
went forth from the city and stood against the
entrance of the city, with drawn swords and spears
in their hands, and they placed themselves opposite
the sons of Jacob, and would not suffer them to
enter the city. 12 And Naphtali ran and came
between them and with his sword smote two of
them, and cut off their heads at one stroke. 13 And
he turned to the other two, and behold they had
fled, and he pursued them, overtook them, smote
them and slew them.

14 And the sons of Jacob came to the city and saw,
and behold there was another wall to the city, and
they sought for the gate of the wall and could not
find it, and Judah sprang upon the top of the wall,
and Simeon and Levi followed him, and they all
three descended from the wall into the city. 15 And
Simeon and Levi slew all the men who ran for safety
into the city, and also the inhabitants of the city
with their wives and little ones, they slew with the
edge of the sword, and the cries of the city
ascended up to heaven.

16 And Dan and Naphtali sprang upon the wall to
see what caused the noise of lamentation, for the
sons of Jacob felt anxious about their brothers, and
they heard the inhabitants of the city speaking with
weeping and supplications, saying, "Take all that we
possess in the city and go away, only do not put us
to death."

17 And when Judah, Simeon, and Levi had ceased
smiting the inhabitants of the city, they ascended
the wall and called to Dan and Naphtali, who were
upon the wall, and to the rest of their brothers, and
Simeon and Levi informed them of the entrance
into the city, and all the sons of Jacob came to fetch
the spoil. 18 And the sons of Jacob took the spoil of
the city of Chazar, the flocks and herds, and the
property, and they took all that could be captured,
and went away that day from the city.

19 And on the next day the sons of Jacob went to
Sarton, for they heard that the men of Sarton who
had remained in the city were assembling to fight
with them for having slain their king, and Sarton
was a very high and fortified city, and it had a deep
rampart surrounding the city.

20 And the pillar of the rampart was about fifty
cubits and its breadth forty cubits, and there was
no place for a man to enter the city on account of
the rampart, and the sons of Jacob saw the rampart
of the city, and they sought an entrance in it but
could not find it. 21 For the entrance to the city
was at the rear, and every man that wished to come
into the city came by that road and went around
the whole city, and he afterwards entered the city.

22 And the sons of Jacob seeing they could not find
the way into the city, their anger was kindled
greatly, and the inhabitants of the city seeing that
the sons of Jacob were coming to them were
greatly afraid of them, for they had heard of their
strength and what they had done to Chazar. 23
And the inhabitants of the city of Sarton could not
go out toward the sons of Jacob after having
assembled in the city to fight against them, lest
they might thereby get into the city, but when they
saw that they were coming toward them, they were
greatly afraid of them, for they had heard of their
strength and what they had done to Chazar.

24 So the inhabitants of Sarton speedily took away
the bridge of the road of the city, from its place,
before the sons of Jacob came, and they brought it
into the city. 25 And the sons of Jacob came and
sought the way into the city, and could not find it
and the inhabitants of the city went up to the top of
the wall, and saw, and behold the sons of Jacob
were seeking an entrance into the city.

26 And the inhabitants of the city reproached the
sons of Jacob from the top of the wall, and they
cursed them, and the sons of Jacob heard the
reproaches, and they were greatly incensed, and
their anger burned within them. 27 And the sons of
Jacob were provoked at them, and they all rose and
sprang over the rampart with the force of their
strength, and through their might passed the forty
cubits' breadth of the rampart.

28 And when they had passed the rampart they
stood under the wall of the city, and they found all
the gates of the city enclosed with iron doors. 29
And the sons of Jacob came near to break open the
doors of the gates of the city, and the inhabitants
did not let them, for from the top of the wall they
were casting stones and arrows upon them.

30 And the number of the people that were upon
the wall was about four hundred men, and when
the sons of Jacob saw that the men of the city
would not let them open the gates of the city, they
sprang and ascended the top of the wall, and Judah
went up first to the east part of the city. 31 And
Gad and Asher went up after him to the west
corner of the city, and Simeon and Levi to the
north, and Dan and Reuben to the south.

32 And the men who were on the top of the wall,
the inhabitants of the city, seeing that the sons of
Jacob were coming up to them, they all fled from
the wall, descended into the city, and concealed
themselves in the midst of the city. 33 And Issachar
and Naphtali that remained under the wall
approached and broke the gates of the city, and
kindled a fire at the gates of the city, that the iron
melted, and all the sons of Jacob came into the city,
they and all their men, and they fought with the
inhabitants of the city of Sarton, and smote them
with the edge of the sword, and no man stood up
before them.

34 And about two hundred men fled from the city, and they all went and hid themselves in a certain tower in the city, and Judah pursued them to the tower and he broke down the tower, which fell upon the men, and they all died. 35 And the sons of Jacob went up the road of the roof of that tower, and they saw, and behold there was another strong and high tower at a distance in the city, and the top of it reached to heaven, and the sons of Jacob hastened and descended, and went with all their men to that tower, and found it filled with about three hundred men, women and little ones.

36 And the sons of Jacob smote a great smiting amongst those men in the tower and they ran away and fled from them. 37 And Simeon and Levi pursued them, when twelve mighty and valiant men came out to them from the place where they had concealed themselves.

38 And those twelve men maintained a strong battle against Simeon and Levi, and Simeon and Levi could not prevail over them, and those valiant men broke the shields of Simeon and Levi, and one of them struck at Levi's head with his sword, when Levi hastily placed his hand to his head, for he was afraid of the sword, and the sword struck Levi's hand, and it wanted but little to the hand of Levi being cut off.

39 And Levi seized the sword of the valiant man in his hand, and took it forcibly from the man, and with it he struck at the head of the powerful man, and he severed his head.

40 And eleven men approached to fight with Levi, for they saw that one of them was killed, and the sons of Jacob fought, but the sons of Jacob could not prevail over them, for those men were very powerful. 41 And the sons of Jacob seeing that they could not prevail over them, Simeon gave a loud and tremendous shriek, and the eleven powerful men were stunned at the voice of Simeon's shrieking.

42 And Judah at a distance knew the voice of Simeon's shouting, and Naphtali and Judah ran with their shields to Simeon and Levi, and found them fighting with those powerful men, unable to prevail
over them as their shields were broken. 43 And
Naphtali saw that the shields of Simeon and Levi were broken, and he took two shields from his servants and brought them to Simeon and Levi.

44 And Simeon, Levi and Judah on that day fought all three against the eleven mighty men until the time of sunset, but they could not prevail over them.

45 And this was told unto Jacob, and he was sorely grieved, and he prayed unto the Lord, and he and Naphtali his son went against these mighty men.

46 And Jacob approached and drew his bow, and came nigh unto the mighty men, and slew three of their men with the bow, and the remaining eight turned back, and behold, the war waged against them in the front and rear, and they were greatly afraid of their lives, and could not stand before the sons of Jacob, and they fled from before them.

47 And in their flight they met Dan and Asher coming toward them, and they suddenly fell upon them, and fought with them, and slew two of them, and Judah and his brothers pursued them, and smote the remainder of them, and slew them.

48 And all the sons of Jacob returned and walked about the city, searching if they could find any men, and they found about twenty young men in a cave in the city, and Gad and Asher smote them all, and Dan and Naphtali lighted upon the rest of the men who had fled and escaped from the second tower,
and they smote them all. 49 And the sons of Jacob
smote all the inhabitants of the city of Sarton, but the women and little ones they left in the city and did not slay them.

50 And all the inhabitants of the city of Sarton were
powerful men, one of them would pursue a
thousand, and two of them would not flee from ten
thousand of the rest of men. 51 And the sons of
Jacob slew all the inhabitants of the city of Sarton
with the edge of the sword, that no man stood up
against them, and they left the women in the city.
52 And the sons of Jacob took all the spoil of the
city, and captured what they desired, and they took
flocks and herds and property from the city, and the
sons of Jacob did unto Sarton and its inhabitants as
they had done to Chazar and its inhabitants, and
they turned and went away.

Jasher 39

1 And when the sons of Jacob went from the city of Sarton, they had gone about two hundred cubits when they met the inhabitants of Tapnach coming toward them, for they went out to fight with them, because they had smitten the king of Tapnach and all his men.

2 So all that remained in the city of Tapnach came out to fight with the sons of Jacob, and they thought to retake from them the booty and the spoil which they had captured from Chazar and Sarton.

3 And the rest of the men of Tapnach fought with
the sons of Jacob in that place, and the sons of
Jacob smote them, and they fled before them, and
they pursued them to the city of Arbelan, and they
all fell before the sons of Jacob. 4 And the sons of
Jacob returned and came to Tapnach, to take away
the spoil of Tapnach, and when they came to
Tapnach they heard that the people of Arbelan had
gone out to meet them to save the spoil of their
brethren, and the sons of Jacob left ten of their
men in Tapnach to plunder the city, and they went
out toward the people of Arbelan.

5 And the men of Arbelan went out with their wives
to fight with the sons of Jacob, for their wives were
experienced in battle, and they went out, about
four hundred men and women. 6 And all the sons
of Jacob shouted with a loud voice, and they all ran
toward the inhabitants of Arbelan, and with a great
and tremendous voice. 7 And the inhabitants of
Arbelan heard the noise of the shouting of the sons
of Jacob, and their roaring like the noise of lions
and like the roaring of the sea and its waves.

8 And fear and terror possessed their hearts on account of the sons of Jacob, and they were terribly afraid of them, and they retreated and fled before them into the city, and the sons of Jacob pursued them to the gate of the city, and they came upon them in the city.

9 And the sons of Jacob fought with them in the city, and all their women were engaged in slinging against the sons of Jacob, and the combat was very severe amongst them the whole of that day till evening.

10 And the sons of Jacob could not prevail over them, and the sons of Jacob had almost perished in that battle, and the sons of Jacob cried unto the Lord and greatly gained strength toward evening, and the sons of Jacob smote all the inhabitants of Arbelan by the edge of the sword, men, women and little ones.

11 And also the remainder of the people who had fled from Sarton, the sons of Jacob smote them in Arbelan, and the sons of Jacob did unto Arbelan and Tapnach as they had done to Chazar and Sarton, and when the women saw that all the men were dead, they went upon the roofs of the city and smote the sons of Jacob by showering down stones like rain.

12 And the sons of Jacob hastened and came into the city and seized all the women and smote them with the edge of the sword, and the sons of Jacob captured all the spoil and booty, flocks and herds and cattle.

13 And the sons of Jacob did unto Machnaymah as they had done to Tapnach, to Chazar and to Shiloh, and they turned from there and went away.

14 And on the fifth day the sons of Jacob heard that the people of Gaash had gathered against them to battle, because they had slain their king and their captains, for there had been fourteen captains in the city of Gaash, and the sons of Jacob had slain them all in the first battle.

15 And the sons of Jacob that day girt on their
weapons of war, and they marched to battle
against the inhabitants of Gaash, and in Gaash
there was a strong and mighty people of the people
of the Amorites, and Gaash was the strongest and
best fortified city of all the cities of the Amorites,
and it had three walls.

16 And the sons of Jacob came to Gaash and they
found the gates of the city locked, and about five
hundred men standing at the top of the outer-most
wall, and a people numerous as the sand upon the
sea shore were in ambush for the sons of Jacob
from without the city at the rear thereof. 17 And
the sons of Jacob approached to open the gates of
the city, and whilst they were drawing nigh, behold
those who were in ambush at the rear of the city
came forth from their places and surrounded the
sons of Jacob.

18 And the sons of Jacob were enclosed between
the people of Gaash, and the battle was both to
their front and rear, and all the men that were upon
the wall, were casting from the wall upon them,
arrows and stones. 19 And Judah, seeing that the
men of Gaash were getting too heavy for them,
gave a most piercing and tremendous shriek and all
the men of Gaash were terrified at the voice of
Judah's cry, and men fell from the wall at his
powerful shriek, and all those that were from
without and within the city were greatly afraid of
their lives.

20 And the sons of Jacob still came nigh to break
the doors of the city, when the men of Gaash threw
stones and arrows upon them from the top of the
wall, and made them flee from the gate. 21 And
the sons of Jacob returned against the men of
Gaash who were with them from without the city,
and they smote them terribly, as striking against
gourds, and they could not stand against the sons
of Jacob, for fright and terror had seized them at
the shriek of Judah.

22 And the sons of Jacob slew all those men who
were without the city, and the sons of Jacob still
drew nigh to effect an entrance into the city, and to
fight under the city walls, but they could not for all
the inhabitants of Gaash who remained in the city
had surrounded the walls of Gaash in every
direction, so that the sons of Jacob were unable to
approach the city to fight with them.

23 And the sons of Jacob came nigh to one corner
to fight under the wall, the inhabitants of Gaash
threw arrows and stones upon them like showers of
rain, and they fled from under the wall. 24 And the
people of Gaash who were upon the wall, seeing
that the sons of Jacob could not prevail over them
from under the wall, reproached the sons of Jacob
in these words, saying,

25 "What is the matter with you in the battle that
you cannot prevail? can you then do unto the
mighty city of Gaash and its inhabitants as you did
to the cities of the Amorites that were not so
powerful? Surely to those weak ones amongst us
you did those things, and slew them in the entrance
of the city, for they had no strength when they
were terrified at the sound of your shouting. 26
And will you now then be able to fight in this place?
Surely here you will all die, and we will avenge the
cause of those cities that you have laid waste."

27 And the inhabitants of Gaash greatly reproached
the sons of Jacob and reviled them with their gods,
and continued to cast arrows and stones upon
them from the wall.

28 And Judah and his brothers heard the words of
the inhabitants of Gaash and their anger was
greatly roused, and Judah was jealous of his God in
this matter, and he called out and said, "O Lord,
help, send help to us and our brothers." 29 And he
ran at a distance with all his might, with his drawn
sword in his hand, and he sprang from the earth
and by dint of his strength, mounted the wall, and
his sword fell from his hand.

30 And Judah shouted upon the wall, and all the men that were upon the wall were terrified, and some of them fell from the wall into the city and died, and those who were yet upon the wall, when they saw Judah's strength, they were greatly afraid and fled for their lives into the city for safety.

31 And some were emboldened to fight with Judah upon the wall, and they came nigh to slay him when they saw there was no sword in Judah's hand, and they thought of casting him from the wall to his brothers, and twenty men of the city came up to assist them, and they surrounded Judah and they all shouted over him, and approached him with drawn swords, and they terrified Judah, and Judah cried out to his brothers from the wall.

32 And Jacob and his sons drew the bow from under the wall, and smote three of the men that were upon the top of the wall, and Judah continued to cry and he exclaimed, "O Lord help us, O Lord deliver us," and he cried out with a loud voice upon the wall, and the cry was heard at a great distance.

33 And after this cry he again repeated to shout, and all the men who surrounded Judah on the top of the wall were terrified, and they each threw his sword from his hand at the sound of Judah's shouting and his tremor, and fled.

34 And Judah took the swords which had fallen from their hands, and Judah fought with them and slew twenty of their men upon the wall.

35 And about eighty men and women still ascended
the wall from the city and they all surrounded
Judah, and the Lord impressed the fear of Judah in
their hearts, that they were unable to approach
him. 36 And Jacob and all who were with him drew
the bow from under the wall, and they slew ten
men upon the wall, and they fell below the wall,
before Jacob and his sons. 37 And the people upon
the wall seeing that twenty of their men had fallen,
they still ran toward Judah with drawn swords, but
they could not approach him for they were greatly
terrified at Judah's strength.

38 And one of their mighty men whose name was Arud approached to strike Judah upon the head with his sword, when Judah hastily put his shield to his head, and the sword hit the shield, and it was split in two.

39 And this mighty man after he had struck Judah ran for his life, at the fear of Judah, and his feet slipped upon the wall and he fell amongst the sons of Jacob who were below the wall, and the sons of Jacob smote him and slew him.

40 And Judah's head pained him from the blow of the powerful man, and Judah had nearly died from it. 41 And Judah cried out upon the wall owing to the pain produced by the blow, when Dan heard him, and his anger burned within him, and he also rose up and went at a distance and ran and sprang from the earth and mounted the wall with his wrath-excited strength.

42 And when Dan came upon the wall near unto Judah all the men upon the wall fled, who had stood against Judah, and they went up to the second wall, and they threw arrows and stones upon Dan and Judah from the second wall, and endeavored to drive them from the wall. 43 And the arrows and stones struck Dan and Judah, and they had nearly been killed upon the wall, and wherever Dan and Judah fled from the wall, they were attacked with arrows and stones from the second wall.

44 And Jacob and his sons were still at the entrance of the city below the first wall, and they were not able to draw their bow against the inhabitants of the city, as they could not be seen by them, being upon the second wall. 45 And Dan and Judah when they could no longer bear the stones and arrows that fell upon them from the second wall, they both sprang upon the second wall near the people of the city, and when the people of the city who were upon the second wall saw that Dan and Judah had come to them upon the second wall, they all cried out and descended below between the walls.

46 And Jacob and his sons heard the noise of the shouting from the people of the city, and they were still at the entrance of the city, and they were anxious about Dan and Judah who were not seen by them, they being upon the second wall.

47 And Naphtali went up with his wrath-excited might and sprang upon the first wall to see what caused the noise of shouting which they had heard in the city, and Issachar and Zebulun drew nigh to break the doors of the city, and they opened the gates of the city and came into the city.

48 And Naphtali leaped from the first wall to the second, and came to assist his brothers, and the inhabitants of Gaash who were upon the wall, seeing that Naphtali was the third who had come up to assist his brothers, they all fled and descended into the city, and Jacob and all his sons and all their young men came into the city to them.

49 And Judah and Dan and Naphtali descended from the wall into the city and pursued the inhabitants of the city, and Simeon and Levi were from without the city and knew not that the gate was opened, and they went up from there to the wall and came down to their brothers into the city.

50 And the inhabitants of the city had all descended into the city, and the sons of Jacob came to them in different directions, and the battle waged against them from the front and the rear, and the sons of Jacob smote them terribly, and slew about twenty thousand of them men and women, not one of them could stand up against the sons of Jacob.

51 And the blood flowed plentifully in the city, and
it was like a brook of water, and the blood flowed
like a brook to the outer part of the city, and
reached the desert of Bethchorin. 52 And the
people of Bethchorin saw at a distance the blood
flowing from the city of Gaash, and about seventy
men from amongst them ran to see the blood, and
they came to the place where the blood was.

53 And they followed the track of the blood and came to the wall of the city of Gaash, and they saw the blood issue from the city, and they heard the voice of crying from the inhabitants of Gaash, for it ascended unto heaven, and the blood was continuing to flow abundantly like a brook of water.

54 And all the sons of Jacob were still smiting the
inhabitants of Gaash, and were engaged in slaying
them till evening, about twenty thousand men and
women, and the people of Chorin said, "Surely this
is the work of the Hebrews, for they are still
carrying on war in all the cities of the Amorites." 55
And those people hastened and ran to Bethchorin,
and each took his weapons of war, and they cried
out to all the inhabitants of Bethchorin, who also
girt on their weapons of war to go and fight with
the sons of Jacob.

56 And when the sons of Jacob had done smiting the inhabitants of Gaash, they walked about the city to strip all the slain, and coming in the innermost part of the city and farther on they met three very powerful men, and there was no sword in their hand.

57 And the sons of Jacob came up to the place
where they were, and the powerful men ran away,
and one of them had taken Zebulun, who he saw
was a young lad and of short stature, and with his
might dashed him to the ground. 58 And Jacob ran
to him with his sword and Jacob smote him below
his loins with the sword, and cut him in two, and
the body fell upon Zebulun.

59 And the second one approached and seized
Jacob to fell him to the ground, and Jacob turned to
him and shouted to him, whilst Simeon and Levi ran
and smote him on the hips with the sword and
felled him to the ground. 60 And the powerful man
rose up from the ground with wrath-excited might,
and Judah came to him before he had gained his
footing, and struck him upon the head with the
sword, and his head was split and he died.

61 And the third powerful man, seeing that his companions were killed, ran from before the sons of Jacob, and the sons of Jacob pursued him in the city; and whilst the powerful man was fleeing he found one of the swords of the inhabitants of the city, and he picked it up and turned to the sons of Jacob and fought them with that sword.

62 And the powerful man ran to Judah to strike him upon the head with the sword, and there was no shield in the hand of Judah; and whilst he was aiming to strike him, Naphtali hastily took his shield and put it to Judah's head, and the sword of the powerful man hit the shield of Naphtali and Judah escaped the sword.

63 And Simeon and Levi ran upon the powerful man with their swords and struck at him forcibly with their swords, and the two swords entered the body of the powerful man and divided it in two, length-wise. 64 And the sons of Jacob smote the three mighty men at that time, together with all the inhabitants of Gaash, and the day was about to decline.

65 And the sons of Jacob walked about Gaash and took all the spoil of the city, even the little ones and women they did not suffer to live, and the sons of Jacob did unto Gaash as they had done to Sarton and Shiloh.

Jasher 40

1 And the sons of Jacob led away all the spoil of Gaash, and went out of the city by night. 2 They were going out marching toward the castle of Bethchorin, and the inhabitants of Bethchorin were going to the castle to meet them, and on that night the sons of Jacob fought with the inhabitants of Bethchorin, in the castle of Bethchorin.

3 And all the inhabitants of Bethchorin were mighty men, one of them would not flee from before a thousand men, and they fought on that night upon the castle, and their shouts were heard on that night from afar, and the earth quaked at their shouting.

4 And all the sons of Jacob were afraid of those men, as they were not accustomed to fight in the dark, and they were greatly confounded, and the sons of Jacob cried unto the Lord, saying, "Give help to us O Lord, deliver us that we may not die by the hands of these uncircumcised men."

5 And the Lord hearkened to the voice of the sons of Jacob, and the Lord caused great terror and confusion to seize the people of Bethchorin, and they fought amongst themselves the one with the other in the darkness of night, and smote each other in great numbers.

6 And the sons of Jacob, knowing that the Lord had brought a spirit of perverseness amongst those men, and that they fought each man with his neighbor, went forth from among the bands of the people of Bethchorin and went as far as the descent of the castle of Bethchorin, and farther, and they tarried there securely with their young men on that night.

7 And the people of Bethchorin fought the whole night, one man with his brother, and the other with his neighbor, and they cried out in every direction upon the castle, and their cry was heard at a distance, and the whole earth shook at their voice, for they were powerful above all the people of the
earth. 8 And all the inhabitants of the cities of the
Canaanites, the Hittites, the Amorites, the Hivites and all the kings of Canaan, and also those who were on the other side of the Jordan, heard the noise of the shouting on that night.

9 And they said, "Surely these are the battles of the Hebrews who are fighting against the seven cities, who came nigh unto them; and who can stand against those Hebrews?"

10 And all the inhabitants of the cities of the Canaanites, and all those who were on the other side of the Jordan, were greatly afraid of the sons of Jacob, for they said, "Behold the same will be done to us as was done to those cities, for who can stand against their mighty strength?"

11 And the cries of the Chorinites were very great on that night, and continued to increase; and they smote each other till morning, and numbers of them were killed.

12 And the morning appeared, and all the sons of Jacob rose up at daybreak and went up to the castle, and they smote those who remained of the Chorinites in a terrible manner, and they were all killed in the castle.

13 And the sixth day appeared, and all the
inhabitants of Canaan saw at a distance all the
people of Bethchorin lying dead in the castle of
Bethchorin, and strewed about as the carcasses of
lambs and goats. 14 And the sons of Jacob led all
the spoil which they had captured from Gaash and
went to Bethchorin, and they found the city full of
people like the sand of the sea, and they fought
with them, and the sons of Jacob smote them there
till evening time.

15 And the sons of Jacob did unto Bethchorin as
they had done to Gaash and Tapnach, and as they
had done to Chazar, to Sarton and to Shiloh. 16
And the sons of Jacob took with them the spoil of
Bethchorin and all the spoil of the cities, and on
that day they went home to Shechem. 17 And the
sons of Jacob came home to the city of Shechem,
and they remained without the city, and they then
rested there from the war, and tarried there all
night.

18 And all their servants together with all the spoil that they had taken from the cities, they left without the city, and they did not enter the city, for they said, "Peradventure there may be yet more fighting against us, and they may come to besiege us in Shechem."

19 And Jacob and his sons and their servants remained on that night and the next day in the portion of the field which Jacob had purchased from Hamor for five shekels, and all that they had captured was with them.

20 And all the booty which the sons of Jacob had captured, was in the portion of the field, immense as the sand upon the sea shore.

21 And the inhabitants of the land observed them from afar, and all the inhabitants of the land were afraid of the sons of Jacob who had done this thing, for no king from the days of old had ever done the like.

22 And the seven kings of the Canaanites resolved to make peace with the sons of Jacob, for they were greatly afraid of their lives, on account of the sons of Jacob.

23 And on that day, being the seventh day, Japhia king of Hebron sent secretly to the king of Ai, and to the king of Gibeon, and to the king of Shalem, and to the king of Adulam, and to the king of Lachish, and to the king of Chazar, and to all the Canaanitish kings who were under their subjection, saying,

24 "Go up with me, and come to me that we may go to the sons of Jacob, and I will make peace with them, and form a treaty with them, lest all your lands be destroyed by the swords of the sons of Jacob, as they did to Shechem and the cities around it, as you have heard and seen.
25 And when you come to me, do not come with many men, but let every king bring his three head captains, and every captain bring three of his officers.
26 And come all of you to Hebron, and we will go together to the sons of Jacob, and supplicate them that they shall form a treaty of peace with us."
27 And all those kings did as the king of Hebron had sent to them, for they were all under his counsel and command, and all the kings of Canaan assembled to go to the sons of Jacob, to make peace with them; and the sons of Jacob returned and went to the portion of the field that was in Shechem, for they did not put confidence in the kings of the land.

28 And the sons of Jacob returned and remained in the portion of the field ten days, and no one came to make war with them.
29 And when the sons of Jacob saw that there was no appearance of war, they all assembled and went to the city of Shechem, and the sons of Jacob remained in Shechem.

30 And at the expiration of forty days, all the kings of the Amorites assembled from all their places and came to Hebron, to Japhia, king of Hebron.
31 And the number of kings that came to Hebron, to make peace with the sons of Jacob, was twenty-one kings, and the number of captains that came with them was sixty-nine, and their men were one hundred and eighty-nine, and all these kings and their men rested by Mount Hebron.

32 And the king of Hebron went out with his three
captains and nine men, and these kings resolved to
go to the sons of Jacob to make peace. 33 And they
said unto the king of Hebron, "Go thou before us
with thy men, and speak for us unto the sons of
Jacob, and we will come after thee and confirm thy
words," and the king of Hebron did so.

34 And the sons of Jacob heard that all the kings of
Canaan had gathered together and rested in
Hebron, and the sons of Jacob sent four of their
servants as spies, saying, "Go and spy these kings,
and search and examine their men whether they
are few or many, and if they are but few in number,
number them all and come back."

35 And the servants of Jacob went secretly to these
kings, and did as the sons of Jacob had commanded
them, and on that day they came back to the sons
of Jacob, and said unto them, "We came unto those
kings, and they are but few in number, and we
numbered them all, and behold, they were two
hundred and eighty-eight, kings and men."

36 And the sons of Jacob said, "They are but few in
number, therefore we will not all go out to them;"
and in the morning the sons of Jacob rose up and
chose sixty two of their men, and ten of the sons of
Jacob went with them; and they girt on their
weapons of war, for they said, "They are coming to
make war with us, for they knew not that they were
coming to make peace with them." 37 And the
sons of Jacob went with their servants to the gate
of Shechem, toward those kings, and their father
Jacob was with them.

38 And when they had come forth, behold, the king
of Hebron and his three captains and nine men with
him were coming along the road against the sons of
Jacob, and the sons of Jacob lifted up their eyes,
and saw at a distance Japhia, king of Hebron, with
his captains, coming toward them, and the sons of
Jacob took their stand at the place of the gate of
Shechem, and did not proceed. 39 And the king of
Hebron continued to advance, he and his captains,
until he came nigh to the sons of Jacob, and he and
his captains bowed down to them to the ground,
and the king of Hebron sat with his captains before
Jacob and his sons.

40 And the sons of Jacob said unto him, "What has befallen thee, O king of Hebron? why hast thou come to us this day? what dost thou require from us? and the king of Hebron said unto Jacob, I beseech thee my lord, all the kings of the Canaanites have this day come to make peace with you."

41 And the sons of Jacob heard the words of the king of Hebron, and they would not consent to his proposals, for the sons of Jacob had no faith in him, for they imagined that the king of Hebron had spoken deceitfully to them.

42 And the king of Hebron knew from the words of the sons of Jacob, that they did not believe his words, and the king of Hebron approached nearer to Jacob, and said unto him, "I beseech thee, my lord, to be assured that all these kings have come to you on peaceable terms, for they have not come with all their men, neither did they bring their weapons of war with them, for they have come to seek peace from my lord and his sons."

43 And the sons of Jacob answered the king of Hebron, saying, "Send thou to all these kings, and if thou speakest truth unto us, let them each come singly before us, and if they come unto us unarmed, we shall then know that they seek peace from us."

44 And Japhia, king of Hebron, sent one of his men to the kings, and they all came before the sons of Jacob, and bowed down to them to the ground, and these kings sat before Jacob and his sons, and they spoke unto them, saying,

45 "We have heard all that you did unto the kings of the Amorites with your sword and exceedingly mighty arm, so that no man could stand up before you, and we were afraid of you for the sake of our lives, lest it should befall us as it did to them.
46 So we have come unto you to form a treaty of peace between us, and now therefore contract with us a covenant of peace and truth, that you will not meddle with us, inasmuch as we have not meddled with you."

47 And the sons of Jacob knew that they had really come to seek peace from them, and the sons of Jacob listened to them, and formed a covenant with them.

48 And the sons of Jacob swore unto them that they would not meddle with them, and all the kings of the Canaanites swore also to them, and the sons of Jacob made them tributary from that day forward.

49 And after this all the captains of these kings
came with their men before Jacob, with presents in
their hands for Jacob and his sons, and they bowed
down to him to the ground. 50 And these kings
then urged the sons of Jacob and begged of them to
return all the spoil they had captured from the
seven cities of the Amorites, and the sons of Jacob
did so, and they returned all that they had
captured, the women, the little ones, the cattle and
all the spoil which they had taken, and they sent
them off, and they went away each to his city.

51 And all these kings again bowed down to the sons of Jacob, and they sent or brought them many gifts in those days, and the sons of Jacob sent off these kings and their men, and they went peaceably away from them to their cities, and the sons of Jacob also returned to their home, to Shechem.

52 And there was peace from that day forward between the sons of Jacob and the kings of the Canaanites, until the children of Israel came to inherit the land of Canaan.

Jasher 41

1 And at the revolution of the year the sons of Jacob journeyed from Shechem, and they came to Hebron, to their father Isaac, and they dwelt there, but their flocks and herds they fed daily in Shechem, for there was there in those days good and fat pasture, and Jacob and his sons and all their household dwelt in the valley of Hebron.

2 And it was in those days, in that year, being the hundred and sixth year of the life of Jacob, in the tenth year of Jacob's coming from Padan-aram, that Leah the wife of Jacob died; she was fifty-one years old when she died in Hebron.

3 And Jacob and his sons buried her in the cave of the field of Machpelah, which is in Hebron, which Abraham had bought from the children of Heth, for the possession of a burial place. 4 And the sons of Jacob dwelt with their father in the valley of Hebron, and all the inhabitants of the land knew their strength and their fame went throughout the land.

5 And Joseph the son of Jacob, and his brother Benjamin, the sons of Rachel, the wife of Jacob, were yet young in those days, and did not go out with their brethren during their battles in all the cities of the Amorites.

Genesis 37

1 Jacob lived in the land of his father's travels, in the land of Canaan. 2 This is the history of the generations of Jacob. Joseph, being seventeen years old, was feeding the flock with his brothers. He was a boy with the sons of Bilhah and Zilpah, his father's wives. Joseph brought an evil report of them to their father.

5 And Joseph the son of Jacob, and his brother Benjamin, the sons of Rachel, the wife of Jacob, were yet young in those days, and did not go out with their brethren during their battles in all the cities of the Amorites.

6 And when Joseph saw the strength of his brethren, and their greatness, he praised them and extolled them, but he ranked himself greater than them, and extolled himself above them;

3 Now Israel loved Joseph more than all his children, because he was the son of his old age, and he made him a coat of many colors.

and Jacob, his father, also loved him more than any of his sons, for he was a son of his old age, and through his love toward him, he made him a coat of many colors.

7 And when Joseph saw that his father loved him more than his brethren, he continued to exalt himself above his brethren, and he brought unto his father evil reports concerning them.

4 His brothers saw that their father loved him more than all his brothers, and they hated him, and couldn't speak peaceably to him.

8 And the sons of Jacob seeing the whole of Joseph's conduct toward them, and that their father loved him more than any of them, they hated him and could not speak peaceably to him all the days.

9 And Joseph was seventeen years old, and he was still magnifying himself above his brethren, and thought of raising himself above them.

5 Joseph dreamed a dream, and he told it to his brothers, and they hated him all the more. 6 He said to them, “Please hear this dream which I have dreamed: 7 for behold, we were binding sheaves in the field, and behold, my sheaf arose and also stood upright; and behold, your sheaves came around, and bowed down to my sheaf.”

10 At that time he dreamed a dream, and he came unto his brothers and told them his dream, and he said unto them, "I dreamed a dream, and behold we were all binding sheaves in the field, and my sheaf rose and placed itself upon the ground and your sheaves surrounded it and bowed down to it."

8 His brothers said to him, “Will you indeed reign over us? Or will you indeed have dominion over us?”

11 And his brethren answered him and said unto him, "What meaneth this dream that thou didst dream? dost thou imagine in thy heart to reign or rule over us?"

12 And he still came, and told the thing to his father Jacob, and Jacob kissed Joseph when he heard these words from his mouth, and Jacob blessed Joseph.

They hated him all the more for his dreams and for his words.

13 And when the sons of Jacob saw that their father had blessed Joseph and had kissed him, and that he loved him exceedingly, they became jealous of him and hated him the more.

9 He dreamed yet another dream, and told it to his brothers, and said, “Behold, I have dreamed yet another dream: and behold, the sun and the moon and eleven stars bowed down to me.”

14 And after this Joseph dreamed another dream and related the dream to his father in the presence of his brethren, and Joseph said unto his father and brethren, "Behold I have again dreamed a dream, and behold the sun and the moon and the eleven stars bowed down to me."

10 He told it to his father and to his brothers. His father rebuked him, and said to him, “What is this dream that you have dreamed? Will I and your mother and your brothers indeed come to bow ourselves down to you to the earth?”

15 And his father heard the words of Joseph and his dream, and seeing that his brethren hated Joseph on account of this matter, Jacob therefore rebuked Joseph before his brethren on account of this thing, saying, "What meaneth this dream which thou hast dreamed, and this magnifying thyself before thy brethren who are older than thou art? 16 Dost thou imagine in thy heart that I and thy mother and thy eleven brethren will come and bow down to thee, that thou speakest these things?"

11 His brothers envied him, but his father kept this saying in mind.

17 And his brethren were jealous of him on account of his words and dreams, and they continued to hate him, and Jacob reserved the dreams in his heart.

12 His brothers went to feed their father’s flock in
Shechem. 13 Israel said to Joseph, “Aren’t your
brothers feeding the flock in Shechem? Come, and I
will send you to them.” He said to him, “Here I am.”

18 And the sons of Jacob went one day to feed their
father's flock in Shechem, for they were still
herdsmen in those days; and whilst the sons of
Jacob were that day feeding in Shechem they
delayed, and the time of gathering in the cattle was
passed, and they had not arrived. 19 And Jacob
saw that his sons were delayed in Shechem, and
Jacob said within himself, "Peradventure the people
of Shechem have risen up to fight against them,
therefore they have delayed coming this day."

14 He said to him, “Go now, see whether it is well
with your brothers, and well with the flock; and
bring me word again.”

20 And Jacob called Joseph his son and commanded
him, saying, "Behold thy brethren are feeding in
Shechem this day, and behold they have not yet
come back; go now therefore and see where they
are, and bring me word back concerning the
welfare of thy brethren and the welfare of the flock.

So he sent him out of the valley of Hebron, and he
came to Shechem.

21 And Jacob sent his son Joseph to the valley of
Hebron, and Joseph came for his brothers to
Shechem, and could not find them, and Joseph
went about the field which was near Shechem, to
see where his brothers had turned, and he missed
his road in the wilderness, and knew not which way
he should go.

15 A certain man found him, and behold, he was
wandering in the field. The man asked him, “What
are you looking for?” 16 He said, “I am looking for
my brothers. Tell me, please, where they are
feeding the flock.” 17 The man said, “They have left
here, for I heard them say, ‘Let us go to Dothan.’”
Joseph went after his brothers, and found them in
Dothan.

22 And an angel of the Lord found him wandering in
the road toward the field, and Joseph said unto the
angel of the Lord, "I seek my brethren; hast thou
not heard where they are feeding?" and the angel
of the Lord said unto Joseph, "I saw thy brethren
feeding here, and I heard them say they would go
to feed in Dothan." 23 And Joseph hearkened to
the voice of the angel of the Lord, and he went to
his brethren in Dothan and he found them in
Dothan feeding the flock.

18 They saw him afar off, and before he came near
to them, they conspired against him to kill him.

24 And Joseph advanced to his brethren, and
before he had come nigh unto them, they had
resolved to slay him.

19 They said to one another, “Behold, this dreamer
comes. 20 Come now therefore, and let’s kill him,
and cast him into one of the pits, and we will say,
‘An evil animal has devoured him.’ We will see what
will become of his dreams.”

25 And Simeon said to his brethren, "Behold the
man of dreams is coming unto us this day, and now
therefore come and let us kill him and cast him in
one of the pits that are in the wilderness, and when
his father shall seek him from us, we will say an evil
beast has devoured him."

21 Reuben heard it, and delivered him out of their hand, and said, “Let’s not take his life.” 22 Reuben said to them, “Shed no blood. Throw him into this pit that is in the wilderness, but lay no hand on him”—that he might deliver him out of their hand, to restore him to his father.

26 And Reuben heard the words of his brethren concerning Joseph, and he said unto them, "You should not do this thing, for how can we look up to our father Jacob? Cast him into this pit to die there, but stretch not forth a hand upon him to spill his blood"; and Reuben said this in order to deliver him from their hand, to bring him back to his father.

23 When Joseph came to his brothers, they stripped Joseph of his coat, the coat of many colors that was on him;

27 And when Joseph came to his brethren he sat before them, and they rose upon him and seized him and smote him to the earth, and stripped the coat of many colors which he had on.

24 and they took him, and threw him into the pit. The pit was empty. There was no water in it.

28 And they took him and cast him into a pit, and in the pit there was no water, but serpents and scorpions. And Joseph was afraid of the serpents and scorpions that were in the pit. And Joseph cried out with a loud voice, and the Lord hid the serpents and scorpions in the sides of the pit, and they did no harm unto Joseph.

29 And Joseph called out from the pit to his brethren, and said unto them, "What have I done unto you, and in what have I sinned? why do you not fear the Lord concerning me? am I not of your bones and flesh, and is not Jacob your father, my father? why do you do this thing unto me this day, and how will you be able to look up to our father Jacob?"

30 And he continued to cry out and call unto his brethren from the pit, and he said, "O Judah, Simeon, and Levi, my brethren, lift me up from the place of darkness in which you have placed me, and come this day to have compassion on me, ye children of the Lord, and sons of Jacob my father. And if I have sinned unto you, are you not the sons of Abraham, Isaac, and Jacob? if they saw an orphan they had compassion over him, or one that was hungry, they gave him bread to eat, or one that was thirsty, they gave him water to drink, or one that was naked, they covered him with garments!

31 "And how then will you withhold your pity from your brother, for I am of your flesh and bones, and if I have sinned unto you, surely you will do this on account of my father!"

32 And Joseph spoke these words from the pit, and
his brethren could not listen to him, nor incline
their ears to the words of Joseph, and Joseph was
crying and weeping in the pit.

33 And Joseph said, "O that my father knew, this
day, the act which my brothers have done unto me,
and the words which they have this day spoken
unto me."

34 And all his brethren heard his cries and weeping
in the pit, and his brethren went and removed
themselves from the pit, so that they might not
hear the cries of Joseph and his weeping in the pit.

25 They sat down to eat bread, and they lifted up
their eyes and looked, and saw a caravan of
Ishmaelites was coming from Gilead, with their
camels bearing spices and balm and myrrh, going to
carry it down to Egypt.

Jasher 42

1 And they went and sat on the opposite side,
about the distance of a bow-shot, and they sat
there to eat bread, and whilst they were eating,
they held counsel together what was to be done
with him, whether to slay him or to bring him back
to his father. 2 They were holding the counsel,
when they lifted up their eyes, and saw, and behold
there was a company of Ishmaelites coming at a
distance by the road of Gilead, going down to
Egypt.

26 Judah said to his brothers, "What profit is it if we
kill our brother and conceal his blood? 27 Come,
and let's sell him to the Ishmaelites, and not let our
hand be on him; for he is our brother, our flesh."
His brothers listened to him.

3 And Judah said unto them, "What gain will it be to
us if we slay our brother? peradventure God will
require him from us; this then is the counsel
proposed concerning him, which you shall do unto
him: Behold this company of Ishmaelites going
down to Egypt, 4 Now therefore, come let us
dispose of him to them, and let not our hand be
upon him, and they will lead him along with them,
and he will be lost amongst the people of the land,
and we will not put him to death with our own
hands." And the proposal pleased his brethren and
they did according to the word of Judah.

28 Midianites who were merchants passed by,

5 And whilst they were discoursing about this
matter, and before the company of Ishmaelites had
come up to them, seven trading men of Midian
passed by them, and as they passed they were
thirsty, and they lifted up their eyes and saw the pit
in which Joseph was immured, and they looked,
and behold every species of bird was upon him.

6 And these Midianites ran to the pit to drink water, for they thought that it contained water, and on coming before the pit they heard the voice of Joseph crying and weeping in the pit, and they looked down into the pit, and they saw and behold there was a youth of comely appearance and well favored.

and they drew and lifted up Joseph out of the pit,

7 And they called unto him and said, "Who art thou and who brought thee hither, and who placed thee in this pit, in the wilderness?" and they all assisted to raise up Joseph and they drew him out, and brought him up from the pit, and took him and went away on their journey and passed by his brethren.

8 And these said unto them, "Why do you do this, to take our servant from us and to go away? surely we placed this youth in the pit because he rebelled against us, and you come and bring him up and lead him away; now then give us back our servant."

9 And the Midianites answered and said unto the sons of Jacob, "Is this your servant, or does this man attend you? peradventure you are all his servants, for he is more comely and well favored than any of you, and why do you all speak falsely unto us? 10 Now therefore we will not listen to your words, nor attend to you, for we found the youth in the pit in the wilderness, and we took him; we will therefore go on."

11 And all the sons of Jacob approached them and rose up to them and said unto them, "Give us back our servant, and why will you all die by the edge of the sword?" And the Midianites cried out against them, and they drew their swords, and approached to fight with the sons of Jacob.

12 And behold Simeon rose up from his seat against them, and sprang upon the ground and drew his sword and approached the Midianites and he gave a terrible shout before them, so that his shouting was heard at a distance, and the earth shook at Simeon's shouting.

13 And the Midianites were terrified on account of Simeon and the noise of his shouting, and they fell upon their faces, and were excessively alarmed.

14 And Simeon said unto them, "Verily I am Simeon, the son of Jacob the Hebrew, who have, only with my brother, destroyed the city of Shechem and the cities of the Amorites; so shall God moreover do unto me, that if all your brethren the people of Midian, and also the kings of Canaan, were to come with you, they could not fight against me.
15 Now therefore give us back the youth whom you have taken, lest I give your flesh to the birds of the skies and the beasts of the earth."

16 And the Midianites were more afraid of Simeon, and they approached the sons of Jacob with terror and fright, and with pathetic words, saying, "
17 Surely you have said that the young man is your servant, and that he rebelled against you, and therefore you placed him in the pit; what then will you do with a servant who rebels against his master? Now therefore sell him unto us, and we will give you all that you require for him;" and the Lord was pleased to do this in order that the sons of Jacob should not slay their brother.

18 And the Midianites saw that Joseph was of a comely appearance and well-favored; they desired him in their hearts and were urgent to purchase him from his brethren.

19 And the sons of Jacob hearkened to the Midianites and they sold their brother Joseph to them for twenty pieces of silver, and Reuben their brother was not with them, and the Midianites took Joseph and continued their journey to Gilead.

20 They were going along the road, and the Midianites repented of what they had done, in having purchased the young man, and one said to the other, "What is this thing that we have done, in taking this youth from the Hebrews, who is of comely appearance and well favored.

21 "Perhaps this youth is stolen from the land of the Hebrews, and why then have we done this thing? and if he should be sought for and found in our hands we shall die through him.

22 "Now surely hardy and powerful men have sold him to us, the strength of one of whom you saw this day; perhaps they stole him from his land with their might and with their powerful arm, and have therefore sold him to us for the small value which we gave unto them."

23 And whilst they were thus discoursing together, they looked, and behold the company of Ishmaelites which was coming at first, and which the sons of Jacob saw, was advancing toward the Midianites, and the Midianites said to each other, "Come let us sell this youth to the company of Ishmaelites who are coming toward us, and we will take for him the little that we gave for him, and we will be delivered from his evil."

and sold Joseph to the Ishmaelites for twenty pieces of silver.

24 And they did so, and they reached the Ishmaelites, and the Midianites sold Joseph to the Ishmaelites for twenty pieces of silver which they had given for him to his brethren.

25 And the Midianites went on their road to Gilead, and the Ishmaelites took Joseph and they let him ride upon one of the camels, and they were leading him to Egypt.

26 And Joseph heard that the Ishmaelites were proceeding to Egypt, and Joseph lamented and wept at this thing that he was to be so far removed from the land of Canaan, from his father, and he wept bitterly whilst he was riding upon the camel, and one of their men observed him, and made him go down from the camel and walk on foot, and notwithstanding this Joseph continued to cry and weep, and he said, "O my father, my father."

27 And one of the Ishmaelites rose up and smote Joseph upon the cheek, and still he continued to weep; and Joseph was fatigued in the road, and was unable to proceed on account of the bitterness of his soul, and they all smote him and afflicted him in the road, and they terrified him in order that he might cease from weeping.

28 And the Lord saw the ambition of Joseph and his trouble, and the Lord brought down upon those men darkness and confusion, and the hand of every one that smote him became withered.

29 And they said to each other, "What is this thing
that God has done to us in the road?" and they
knew not that this befell them on account of
Joseph. And the men proceeded on the road, and
they passed along the road of Ephrath where
Rachel was buried. 30 And Joseph reached his
mother's grave, and Joseph hastened and ran to his
mother's grave, and fell upon the grave and wept.
31 And Joseph cried aloud upon his mother's grave,
and he said, "O my mother, my mother, O thou who
didst give me birth, awake now, and rise and see
thy son, how he has been sold for a slave, and no
one to pity him. 32 O rise and see thy son, weep
with me on account of my troubles, and see the
heart of my brethren.

33 "Arouse my mother, arouse, awake from thy
sleep for me, and direct thy battles against my
brethren. O how have they stripped me of my coat,
and sold me already twice for a slave, and
separated me from my father, and there is no one
to pity me. 34 Arouse and lay thy cause against
them before God, and see whom God will justify in
the judgment, and whom he will condemn. 35 Rise,
O my mother, rise, awake from thy sleep and see
my father how his soul is with me this day, and
comfort him and ease his heart."
36 And Joseph continued to speak these words, and
Joseph cried aloud and wept bitterly upon his
mother's grave; and he ceased speaking, and from
bitterness of heart he became still as a stone upon
the grave.

37 And Joseph heard a voice speaking to him from
beneath the ground, which answered him with
bitterness of heart, and with a voice of weeping and
praying in these words:

38 "My son, my son Joseph, I have heard the voice
of thy weeping and the voice of thy lamentation; I
have seen thy tears; I know thy troubles, my son,
and it grieves me for thy sake, and abundant grief is
added to my grief. 39 Now therefore my son,
Joseph my son, hope to the Lord, and wait for him
and do not fear, for the Lord is with thee, he will
deliver thee from all trouble. 40 Rise my son, go
down unto Egypt with thy masters, and do not fear,
for the Lord is with thee, my son." And she
continued to speak like unto these words unto
Joseph, and she was still.

41 And Joseph heard this, and he wondered greatly at this, and he continued to weep; and after this one of the Ishmaelites observed him crying and weeping upon the grave, and his anger was kindled against him, and he drove him from there, and he smote him and cursed him.

42 And Joseph said unto the men, "May I find grace in your sight to take me back to my father's house, and he will give you abundance of riches."

43 And they answered him, saying, "Art thou not a slave, and where is thy father? and if thou hadst a father thou wouldst not already twice have been sold for a slave for so little value; and their anger was still roused against him," and they continued to smite him and to chastise him, and Joseph wept bitterly.

44 And the Lord saw Joseph's affliction, and Lord again smote these men, and chastised them, and the Lord caused darkness to envelope them upon the earth, and the lightning flashed and the thunder roared, and the earth shook at the voice of the thunder and of the mighty wind, and the men were terrified and knew not where they should go.

45 And the beasts and camels stood still, and they led them, but they would not go, they smote them, and they crouched upon the ground; and the men said to each other, "What is this that God has done to us? what are our transgressions, and what are our sins that this thing has thus befallen us?"

46 And one of them answered and said unto them, "Perhaps on account of the sin of afflicting this slave has this thing happened this day to us; now therefore implore him strongly to forgive us, and then we shall know on whose account this evil befalleth us, and if God shall have compassion over us, then we shall know that all this cometh to us on account of the sin of afflicting this slave."

47 And the men did so, and they supplicated Joseph and pressed him to forgive them; and they said, "We have sinned to the Lord and to thee, now therefore vouchsafe to request of thy God that he shall put away this death from amongst us, for we have sinned to him."

48 And Joseph did according to their words, and the Lord hearkened to Joseph, and the Lord put away the plague which he had inflicted upon those men on account of Joseph, and the beasts rose up from the ground and they conducted them, and they went on, and the raging storm abated and the earth became tranquilized, and the men proceeded on their journey to go down to Egypt, and the men knew that this evil had befallen them on account of Joseph.

49 And they said to each other, "Behold we know that it was on account of his affliction that this evil befell us; now therefore why shall we bring this death upon our souls? Let us hold counsel what to do to this slave."

50 And one answered and said, "Surely he told us to bring him back to his father; now therefore come, let us take him back and we will go to the place that he will tell us, and take from his family the price that we gave for him and we will then go away."

51 And one answered again and said, "Behold this counsel is very good, but we cannot do so for the way is very far from us, and we cannot go out of our road."

52 And one more answered and said unto them, "This is the counsel to be adopted, we will not swerve from it; behold we are this day going to Egypt, and when we shall have come to Egypt, we will sell him there at a high price, and we will be delivered from his evil."

They brought Joseph into Egypt.

53 And this thing pleased the men and they did so, and they continued their journey to Egypt with Joseph.

Jasher 43

1 And when the sons of Jacob had sold their brother Joseph to the Midianites, their hearts were smitten on account of him, and they repented of their acts, and they sought for him to bring him back, but could not find him.

29 Reuben returned to the pit;

2 And Reuben returned to the pit in which Joseph had been put, in order to lift him out, and restore him to his father, and Reuben stood by the pit, and he heard not a word, and he called out "Joseph! Joseph!" and no one answered or uttered a word.

3 And Reuben said, "Joseph has died through fright, or some serpent has caused his death;" and Reuben descended into the pit, and he searched for Joseph and could not find him in the pit, and he came out again.

and saw that Joseph wasn't in the pit; and he tore his clothes. 30 He returned to his brothers, and said, "The child is no more; and I, where will I go?"

4 And Reuben tore his garments and he said, "The child is not there, and how shall I reconcile my father about him if he be dead?" and he went to his brethren and found them grieving on account of Joseph, and counseling together how to reconcile their father about him, and Reuben said unto his brethren, "I came to the pit and behold Joseph was not there, what then shall we say unto our father, for my father will only seek the lad from me."

5 And his brethren answered him saying, "Thus and thus we did, and our hearts afterward smote us on account of this act, and we now sit to seek a pretext how we shall reconcile our father to it."

6 And Reuben said unto them, "What is this you have done to bring down the grey hairs of our father in sorrow to the grave? the thing is not good, that you have done."

7 And Reuben sat with them, and they all rose up
and swore to each other not to tell this thing unto
Jacob, and they all said, "The man who will tell this
to our father or his household, or who will report
this to any of the children of the land, we will all
rise up against him and slay him with the sword." 8
And the sons of Jacob feared each other in this
matter, from the youngest to the oldest, and no
one spoke a word, and they concealed the thing in
their hearts.

9 And they afterward sat down to determine and invent something to say unto their father Jacob concerning all these things.

10 And Issachar said unto them, "Here is an advice
for you if it seem good in your eyes to do this thing,
take the coat which belongeth to Joseph and tear it,
and kill a kid of the goats and dip it in its blood. 11
And send it to our father and when he seeth it he
will say an evil beast has devoured him, therefore
tear ye his coat and behold his blood will be upon
his coat, and by your doing this we shall be free of
our father's murmurings."

12 And Issachar's advice pleased them, and they hearkened unto him and they did according to the word of Issachar which he had counselled them.

31 They took Joseph's coat, and killed a male goat,
and dipped the coat in the blood. 32 They took the
coat of many colors, and they brought it to their father, and said, "We have found this. Examine it, now, whether it is your son's coat or not."

13 And they hastened and took Joseph's coat and tore it, and they killed a kid of the goats and dipped the coat in the blood of the kid, and then trampled it in the dust, and they sent the coat to their father Jacob by the hand of Naphtali, and they
commanded him to say these words: 14 "We had
gathered in the cattle and had come as far as the road to Shechem and farther, when we found this coat upon the road in the wilderness dipped in blood and in dust; now therefore know whether it be thy son's coat or not."

15 And Naphtali went and he came unto his father and he gave him the coat, and he spoke unto him all the words which his brethren had commanded him.

16 And Jacob saw Joseph's coat and he knew it and he fell upon his face to the ground, and became as still as a stone, and he afterward rose up and cried out with a loud and weeping voice and he said, "It is the coat of my son Joseph!"

17 And Jacob hastened and sent one of his servants to his sons, who went to them and found them
coming along the road with the flock. 18 And the
sons of Jacob came to their father about evening, and behold their garments were torn and dust was upon their heads, and they found their father crying out and weeping with a loud voice.

19 And Jacob said unto his sons, "Tell me truly what evil have you this day suddenly brought upon me?" and they answered their father Jacob, saying, "We were coming along this day after the flock had been gathered in, and we came as far as the city of Shechem by the road in the wilderness, and we found this coat filled with blood upon the ground, and we knew it and we sent unto thee if thou couldst know it."

33 He recognized it, and said, “It is my son’s coat. An evil animal has devoured him. Joseph is without doubt torn in pieces.”

20 And Jacob heard the words of his sons and he cried out with a loud voice, and he said, "It is the coat of my son, an evil beast has devoured him; Joseph is rent in pieces, for I sent him this day to see whether it was well with you and well with the flocks and to bring me word again from you, and he went as I commanded him, and this has happened to him this day whilst I thought my son was with you."

21 And the sons of Jacob answered and said, "He did not come to us, neither have we seen him from the time of our going out from thee until now."

34 Jacob tore his clothes, and put sackcloth on his waist, and mourned for his son many days.

22 And when Jacob heard their words he again cried out aloud, and he rose up and tore his garments, and he put sackcloth upon his loins, and he wept bitterly and he mourned and lifted up his voice in weeping and exclaimed and said these words,

23 "Joseph my son, O my son Joseph, I sent thee this day after the welfare of thy brethren, and behold thou hast been torn in pieces; through my hand has this happened to my son.

24 "It grieves me for thee Joseph my son, it grieves me for thee; how sweet wast thou to me during life, and now how exceedingly bitter is thy death to me.

25 "O that I had died in thy stead Joseph my son, for it grieves me sadly for thee my son, O my son, my son. Joseph my son, where art thou, and where hast thou been drawn? arouse, arouse from thy place, and come and see my grief for thee, O my son Joseph. 26 Come now and number the tears gushing from my eyes down my cheeks, and bring them up before the Lord, that his anger may turn from me.

27 "O Joseph my son, how didst thou fall, by the hand of one by whom no one had fallen from the beginning of the world unto this day; for thou hast been put to death by the smiting of an enemy, inflicted with cruelty, but surely I know that this has happened to thee, on account of the multitude of my sins.

28 Arouse now and see how bitter is my trouble for thee my son, although I did not rear thee, nor fashion thee, nor give thee breath and soul, but it was God who formed thee and built thy bones and covered them with flesh, and breathed in thy nostrils the breath of life, and then he gave thee unto me. 29 Now truly God who gave thee unto me, he has taken thee from me, and such then has befallen thee."

35 All his sons and all his daughters rose up to comfort him, but he refused to be comforted.

[43:34 And all his sons and his servants and his servant's children rose up and stood round him to comfort him, and he refused to be comforted.]

He said, "For I will go down to Sheol to my son mourning." His father wept for him.

30 And Jacob continued to speak like unto these words concerning Joseph, and he wept bitterly; he fell to the ground and became still.

31 And all the sons of Jacob seeing their father's trouble, they repented of what they had done, and they also wept bitterly.

32 And Judah rose up and lifted his father's head from the ground, and placed it upon his lap, and he wiped his father's tears from his cheeks, and Judah wept an exceeding great weeping, whilst his father's head was reclining upon his lap, still as a stone.

[Genesis 37:35 All his sons and all his daughters rose up to comfort him, but he refused to be comforted.]

33 And the sons of Jacob saw their father's trouble, and they lifted up their voices and continued to weep, and Jacob was yet lying upon the ground still as a stone. 34 And all his sons and his servants and his servant's children rose up and stood round him to comfort him, and he refused to be comforted.

35 And the whole household of Jacob rose up and mourned a great mourning on account of Joseph and their father's trouble, and the intelligence reached Isaac, the son of Abraham, the father of Jacob, and he wept bitterly on account of Joseph, he and all his household, and he went from the place where he dwelt in Hebron, and his men with him, and he comforted Jacob his son, and he refused to be comforted.

36 And after this, Jacob rose up from the ground,
and his tears were running down his cheeks, and he
said unto his sons, "Rise up and take your swords
and your bows, and go forth into the field, and seek
whether you can find my son's body and bring it
unto me that I may bury it. 37 Seek also, I pray you,
among the beasts and hunt them, and that which
shall come the first before you seize and bring it
unto me, perhaps the Lord will this day pity my
affliction, and prepare before you that which did
tear my son in pieces, and bring it unto me, and I
will avenge the cause of my son."

38 And his sons did as their father had commanded
them, and they rose up early in the morning, and
each took his sword and his bow in his hand, and
they went forth into the field to hunt the beasts.

39 And Jacob was still crying aloud and weeping
and walking to and fro in the house, and smiting his
hands together, saying, "Joseph my son, Joseph my
son."

40 And the sons of Jacob went into the wilderness
to seize the beasts, and behold a wolf came toward
them, and they seized him, and brought him unto
their father, and they said unto him, "This is the
first we have found, and we have brought him unto
thee as thou didst command us, and thy son's body
we could not find."

41 And Jacob took the beast from the hands of his
sons, and he cried out with a loud and weeping
voice, holding the beast in his hand, and he spoke
with a bitter heart unto the beast, "Why didst thou
devour my son Joseph, and how didst thou have no
fear of the God of the earth, or of my trouble for
my son Joseph? 42 And thou didst devour my son
for naught, because he committed no violence, and
didst thereby render me culpable on his account,
therefore God will require him that is persecuted."

43 And the Lord opened the mouth of the beast in
order to comfort Jacob with its words, and it
answered Jacob and spoke these words unto him,
44 "As God liveth who created us in the earth, and
as thy soul liveth, my lord, I did not see thy son,
neither did I tear him to pieces, but from a distant
land I also came to seek my son who went from me
this day, and I know not whether he be living or
dead.

45 "And I came this day into the field to seek my
son, and your sons found me, and seized me and
increased my grief, and have this day brought me
before thee, and I have now spoken all my words to
thee. 46 And now therefore, O son of man, I am in
thy hands, and do unto me this day as it may seem
good in thy sight, but by the life of God who created
me, I did not see thy son, nor did I tear him to
pieces, neither has the flesh of man entered my
mouth all the days of my life."

47 And when Jacob heard the words of the beast he
was greatly astonished, and sent forth the beast
from his hand, and she went her way.

48 And Jacob was still crying aloud and weeping for
Joseph day after day, and he mourned for his son
many days.

36 The Midianites sold him into Egypt to Potiphar, an officer of Pharaoh's, the captain of the guard.

Jasher 44

1 And the sons of Ishmael who had bought Joseph
from the Midianites, who had bought him from his
brethren, went to Egypt with Joseph, and they
came upon the borders of Egypt, and when they
came near unto Egypt, they met four men of the
sons of Medan the son of Abraham, who had gone
forth from the land of Egypt on their journey.

2 And the Ishmaelites said unto them, "Do you
desire to purchase this slave from us?" and they
said, "Deliver him over to us," and they delivered
Joseph over to them, and they beheld him, that he
was a very comely youth and they purchased him
for twenty shekels.

3 And the Ishmaelites continued their journey to
Egypt and the Medanim also returned that day to
Egypt, and the Medanim said to each other,
"Behold we have heard that Potiphar, an officer of
Pharaoh, captain of the guard, seeketh a good
servant who shall stand before him to attend him,
and to make him overseer over his house and all
belonging to him. 4 Now therefore come let us sell
him to him for what we may desire, if he be able to
give unto us that which we shall require for him."

5 And these Medanim went and came to the house of Potiphar, and said unto him, "We have heard that thou seekest a good servant to attend thee, behold we have a servant that will please thee, if thou canst give unto us that which we may desire, and we will sell him unto thee."

6 And Potiphar said, "Bring him before me, and I will see him, and if he please me I will give unto you that which you may require for him."

7 And the Medanim went and brought Joseph and placed him before Potiphar, and he saw him, and he pleased him exceedingly, and Potiphar said unto them, "Tell me what you require for this youth?"

8 And they said, "Four hundred pieces of silver we desire for him," and Potiphar said, "I will give it you if you bring me the record of his sale to you, and will tell me his history, for perhaps he may be stolen, for this youth is neither a slave, nor the son of a slave, but I observe in him the appearance of a goodly and handsome person."

9 And the Medanim went and brought unto him the Ishmaelites who had sold him to them, and they told him, saying, "He is a slave and we sold him to them."

10 And Potiphar heard the words of the Ishmaelites in his giving the silver unto the Medanim, and the Medanim took the silver and went on their journey, and the Ishmaelites also returned home.

Genesis 38

1 At that time, Judah went down from his brothers, and visited a certain Adullamite, whose name was Hirah. 2 Judah saw there a daughter of a certain Canaanite whose name was Shua. He took her, and went in to her. 3 She conceived, and bore a son; and he named him Er. 4 She conceived again, and bore a son; and she named him Onan. 5 She yet again bore a son, and named him Shelah: and he was at Chezib, when she bore him.

[45:4 And Judah went at that time to Adulam, and he came to a man of Adulam, and his name was Hirah, and Judah saw there the daughter of a man from Canaan, and her name was Aliyath, the daughter of Shua, and he took her, and came to her, and Aliyath bare unto Judah, Er, Onan and Shiloh; three sons.]

6 Judah took a wife for Er, his firstborn, and her name was Tamar.

[45:23 And in those days Judah went to the house of Shem and took Tamar the daughter of Elam, the son of Shem, for a wife for his first born Er.]

7 Er, Judah's firstborn, was wicked in Yahweh's sight. Yahweh killed him.

[45:24 And Er came to his wife Tamar, and she became his wife, and when he came to her he outwardly destroyed his seed, and his work was evil in the sight of the Lord, and the Lord slew him.]

8 Judah said to Onan, "Go in to your brother's wife, and perform the duty of a husband's brother to her, and raise up offspring for your brother."

[45:25 And it was after the death of Er, Judah's first born, that Judah said unto Onan, "Go to thy brother's wife and marry her as the next of kin, and raise up seed to thy brother."]

9 Onan knew that the offspring wouldn't be his; and when he went in to his brother's wife, he spilled it on the ground, lest he should give offspring to his brother. 10 The thing which he did was evil in Yahweh's sight, and he killed him also.

[45:26 And Onan took Tamar for a wife and he came to her, and Onan also did like unto the work of his brother, and his work was evil in the sight of the Lord, and he slew him also.]

11 Then Judah said to Tamar, his daughter-in-law, "Remain a widow in your father's house, until Shelah, my son, is grown up"; for he said, "Lest he also die, like his brothers." Tamar went and lived in her father's house.

[45:27 And when Onan died, Judah said unto Tamar, "Remain in thy father's house until my son Shiloh shall have grown up", and Judah did no more delight in Tamar, to give her unto Shiloh, for he said," Peradventure he will also die like his brothers." 28 And Tamar rose up and went and remained in her father's house, and Tamar was in her father's house for some time.]

12 After many days, Shua's daughter, the wife of Judah, died. Judah was comforted, and went up to his sheep shearers to Timnah, he and his friend Hirah, the Adullamite.

[45:29 And at the revolution of the year, Aliyath the wife of Judah died; and Judah was comforted for his wife, and after the death of Aliyath, Judah went up with his friend Hirah to Timnah to shear their sheep.]

13 Tamar was told, "Behold, your father-in-law is going up to Timnah to shear his sheep."

[45:30 And Tamar heard that Judah had gone up to Timnah to shear the sheep, and that Shiloh was grown up, and Judah did not delight in her.]

14 She took off of her the garments of her widowhood, and covered herself with her veil, and wrapped herself, and sat in the gate of Enaim, which is by the way to Timnah; for she saw that Shelah was grown up, and she wasn't given to him as a wife.

[45:31 And Tamar rose up and put off the garments of her widowhood, and she put a veil upon her, and she entirely covered herself, and she went and sat in the public thoroughfare, which is upon the road to Timnah.]

15 When Judah saw her, he thought that she was a prostitute, for she had covered her face.

16 He turned to her by the way, and said, "Please come, let me come in to you," for he didn't know that she was his daughter-in-law. She said, "What will you give me, that you may come in to me?"

17 He said, "I will send you a young goat from the flock." She said, "Will you give me a pledge, until you send it?"

18 He said, "What pledge will I give you?" She said, "Your signet and your cord, and your staff that is in your hand."

He gave them to her, and came in to her, and she conceived by him.

[45:32 And Judah passed and saw her and took her and he came to her, and she conceived by him,]

19 She arose, and went away, and put off her veil from her, and put on the garments of her widowhood. 20 Judah sent the young goat by the hand of his friend, the Adullamite, to receive the pledge from the woman's hand, but he didn't find her. 21 Then he asked the men of her place, saying, "Where is the prostitute, that was at Enaim by the road?" They said, "There has been no prostitute here."

22 He returned to Judah, and said, "I haven't found her; and also the men of the place said, 'There has been no prostitute here.'" 23 Judah said, "Let her keep it, lest we be shamed. Behold, I sent this young goat, and you haven't found her."

24 About three months later, Judah was told, "Tamar, your daughter-in-law, has played the prostitute. Judah said, "Bring her out, and let her be burned."Moreover, behold, she is with child by prostitution."

25 When she was brought out, she sent to her father-in-law, saying, "By the man, whose these are, I am with child." She also said, "Please discern whose are these—the signet, and the cords, and the staff."

26 Judah acknowledged them, and said, "She is more righteous than I, because I didn't give her to Shelah, my son." He knew her again no more.

27 In the time of her travail, behold, twins were in her womb. 28 When she travailed, one put out a hand, and the midwife took and tied a scarlet thread on his hand, saying, "This came out first." 29 As he drew back his hand, behold, his brother came out, and she said, "Why have you made a breach for yourself?" Therefore his name was called Perez. 30 Afterward his brother came out, that had the scarlet thread on his hand, and his name was called Zerah.

[45:32b and at the time of being delivered, behold, there were twins in her womb, and he called the name of the first Perez, and the name of the second Zarah.]

Genesis 39

1 Joseph was brought down to Egypt. Potiphar, an officer of Pharaoh's, the captain of the guard, an Egyptian, bought him from the hand of the Ishmaelites that had brought him down there.

11 And Potiphar took Joseph and brought him to his house that he might serve him, and Joseph found favor in the sight of Potiphar, and he placed confidence in him, and made him overseer over his house, and all that belonged to him he delivered over into his hand.

2 Yahweh was with Joseph, and he was a prosperous man. He was in the house of his master the Egyptian. 3 His master saw that Yahweh was with him, and that Yahweh made all that he did prosper in his hand.

12 And the Lord was with Joseph and he became a prosperous man, and the Lord blessed the house of Potiphar for the sake of Joseph.

4 Joseph found favor in his sight. He ministered to him, and he made him overseer over his house, and all that he had he put into his hand. 5 From the time that he made him overseer in his house, and over all that he had, Yahweh blessed the Egyptian's house for Joseph's sake. Yahweh's blessing was on all that he had, in the house and in the field.

13 And Potiphar left all that he had in the hand of Joseph, and Joseph was one that caused things to come in and go out, and everything was regulated by his wish in the house of Potiphar.

6 He left all that he had in Joseph's hand. He didn't concern himself with anything, except for the food which he ate.

Joseph was well-built and handsome.

14 And Joseph was eighteen years old, a youth with beautiful eyes and of comely appearance, and like unto him was not in the whole land of Egypt.

15 At that time whilst he was in his master's house, going in and out of the house and attending his master, Zelicah, his master's wife, lifted up her eyes toward Joseph and she looked at him, and behold he was a youth comely and well favored. 16 And she coveted his beauty in her heart, and her soul was fixed upon Joseph, and she enticed him day after day, and Zelicah persuaded Joseph daily, but Joseph did not lift up his eyes to behold his master's wife.

17 And Zelicah said unto him, "How goodly are thy appearance and form, truly I have looked at all the slaves, and have not seen so beautiful a slave as thou art; and Joseph said unto her, Surely he who created me in my mother's womb created all mankind."

18 And she said unto him, "How beautiful are thine eyes, with which thou hast dazzled all the inhabitants of Egypt, men and women;" and he said unto her, "How beautiful they are whilst we are alive, but shouldst thou behold them in the grave, surely thou wouldst move away from them."

19 And she said unto him, "How beautiful and pleasing are all thy words; take now, I pray thee, the harp which is in the house, and play with thy hands and let us hear thy words."

20 And he said unto her," How beautiful and pleasing are my words when I speak the praise of my God and his glory;" and she said unto him, "How very beautiful is the hair of thy head, behold the golden comb which is in the house, take it I pray thee, and curl the hair of thy head."

21 And he said unto her, "How long wilt thou speak these words? cease to utter these words to me, and rise and attend to thy domestic affairs."

22 And she said unto him, "There is no one in my house, and there is nothing to attend to but to thy words and to thy wish;" yet notwithstanding all this, she could not bring Joseph unto her, neither did he place his eye upon her, but directed his eyes below to the ground.

7 After these things, his master's wife set her eyes on Joseph; and she said, "Lie with me." 8 But he refused,

23 And Zelicah desired Joseph in her heart, that he should lie with her, and at the time that Joseph was sitting in the house doing his work, Zelicah came and sat before him, and she enticed him daily with her discourse to lie with her, or ever to look at her, but Joseph would not hearken to her.

24 And she said unto him, "If thou wilt not do according to my words, I will chastise thee with the punishment of death, and put an iron yoke upon thee."

25 And Joseph said unto her, "Surely God who created man looseth the fetters of prisoners, and it is he who will deliver me from thy prison and from thy judgment."

26 And when she could not prevail over him, to persuade him, and her soul being still fixed upon him, her desire threw her into a grievous sickness.

27 And all the women of Egypt came to visit her, and they said unto her, "Why art thou in this declining state? thou that lackest nothing; surely thy husband is a great and esteemed prince in the sight of the king, shouldst thou lack anything of what thy heart desireth?"

28 And Zelicah answered them, saying, "This day it shall be made known to you, whence this disorder springs in which you see me", and she commanded her maid servants to prepare food for all the women, and she made a banquet for them, and all the women ate in the house of Zelicah.

29 And she gave them knives to peel the citrons to eat them, and she commanded that they should dress Joseph in costly garments, and that he should appear before them, and Joseph came before their eyes and all the women looked on Joseph, and could not take their eyes from off him, and they all cut their hands with the knives that they had in their hands, and all the citrons that were in their
hands were filled with blood. 30 And they knew
not what they had done but they continued to look at the beauty of Joseph, and did not turn their eyelids from him.

31 And Zelicah saw what they had done, and she
said unto them, "What is this work that you have
done? behold I gave you citrons to eat and you
have all cut your hands." 32 And all the women
saw their hands, and behold they were full of blood,
and their blood flowed down upon their garments,
and they said unto her, "This slave in your house
has overcome us, and we could not turn our eyelids
from him on account of his beauty."

33 And she said unto them, "Surely this happened
to you in the moment that you looked at him, and
you could not contain yourselves from him; how
then can I refrain when he is constantly in my
house, and I see him day after day going in and out
of my house? how then can I keep from declining or
even from perishing on account of this?"

34 And they said unto her, "The words are true, for
who can see this beautiful form in the house and
refrain from him, and is he not thy slave and
attendant in thy house, and why dost thou not tell
him that which is in thy heart, and sufferest thy soul
to perish through this matter?"

35 And she said unto them, "I am daily endeavoring
to persuade him, and he will not consent to my
wishes, and I promised him everything that is good,
and yet I could meet with no return from him; I am
therefore in a declining state as you see." 36 And
Zelicah became very ill on account of her desire
toward Joseph, and she was desperately lovesick on
account of him, and all the people of the house of
Zelicah and her husband knew nothing of this
matter, that Zelicah was ill on account of her love to
Joseph.

37 And all the people of her house asked her,
saying, "Why art thou ill and declining, and lackest
nothing? and she said unto them, I know not this
thing which is daily increasing upon me." 38 And all
the women and her friends came daily to see her,
and they spoke with her, and she said unto them,
"This can only be through the love of Joseph;" and
they said unto her, "Entice him and seize him
secretly, perhaps he may hearken to thee, and put
off this death from thee."

39 And Zelicah became worse from her love to Joseph, and she continued to decline, till she had scarce strength to stand.

40 And on a certain day Joseph was doing his master's work in the house, and Zelicah came secretly and fell suddenly upon him, and Joseph rose up against her, and he was more powerful than she, and he brought her down to the ground.

41 And Zelicah wept on account of the desire of her heart toward him, and she supplicated him with weeping, and her tears flowed down her cheeks, and she spoke unto him in a voice of supplication and in bitterness of soul, saying,

42 "Hast thou ever heard, seen or known of so beautiful a woman as I am, or better than myself, who speak daily unto thee, fall into a decline through love for thee, confer all this honor upon thee, and still thou wilt not hearken to my voice?

43 "And if it be through fear of thy master lest he punish thee, as the king liveth no harm shall come to thee from thy master through this thing; now, therefore pray listen to me, and consent for the sake of the honor which I have conferred upon thee, and put off this death from me, and why should I die for thy sake? and she ceased to speak."

and said to his master's wife, "Behold, my master doesn't know what is with me in the house, and he has put all that he has into my hand. 9 No one is greater in this house than I am, and he has not kept back anything from me but you, because you are his wife. How then can I do this great wickedness, and sin against God?"

44 And Joseph answered her, saying, "Refrain from me, and leave this matter to my master; behold my master knoweth not what there is with me in the house, for all that belongeth to him he has delivered into my hand, and how shall I do these things in my master's house? 45 For he hath also greatly honored me in his house, and he hath also made me overseer over his house, and he hath exalted me, and there is no one greater in this house than I am, and my master hath refrained nothing from me, excepting thee who art his wife, how then canst thou speak these words unto me, and how can I do this great evil and sin to God and to thy husband?

10 As she spoke to Joseph day by day, he didn't listen to her, to lie by her, or to be with her.

46 "Now therefore refrain from me, and speak no more such words as these, for I will not hearken to thy words." But Zelicah would not hearken to Joseph when he spoke these words unto her, but she daily enticed him to listen to her.

11 About this time, he went into the house to do his work, and there were none of the men of the house inside.

47 And it was after this that the brook of Egypt was filled above all its sides, and all the inhabitants of Egypt went forth, and also the king and princes went forth with timbrels and dances, for it was a great rejoicing in Egypt, and a holiday at the time of the inundation of the sea Sihor, and they went there to rejoice all the day.

48 And when the Egyptians went out to the river to rejoice, as was their custom, all the people of the house of Potiphar went with them, but Zelicah would not go with them, for she said, "I am indisposed," and she remained alone in the house, and no other person was with her in the house.

49 And she rose up and ascended to her temple in the house, and dressed herself in princely garments, and she placed upon her head precious stones of onyx stones, inlaid with silver and gold, and she beautified her face and skin with all sorts of women's purifying liquids, and she perfumed the temple and the house with cassia and frankincense, and she spread myrrh and aloes, and she afterward sat in the entrance of the temple, in the passage of the house, through which Joseph passed to do his work, and behold Joseph came from the field, and entered the house to do his master's work.

50 And he came to the place through which he had
to pass, and he saw all the work of Zelicah, and he
turned back. 51 And Zelicah saw Joseph turning
back from her, and she called out to him, saying
"What aileth thee Joseph? come to thy work, and
behold I will make room for thee until thou shalt
have passed to thy seat."

52 And Joseph returned and came to the house, and passed from thence to the place of his seat, and he sat down to do his master's work as usual and behold Zelicah came to him and stood before him in princely garments, and the scent from her clothes was spread to a distance.

12 She caught him by his garment, saying, "Lie with me!"

53 And she hastened and caught hold of Joseph and his garments, and she said unto him, "As the king liveth if thou wilt not perform my request thou shalt die this day," and she hastened and stretched forth her other hand and drew a sword from beneath her garments, and she placed it upon Joseph's neck, and she said, "Rise and perform my request, and if not thou diest this day."

He left his garment in her hand, and ran outside.

54 And Joseph was afraid of her at her doing this thing, and he rose up to flee from her, and she seized the front of his garments, and in the terror of his flight the garment which Zelicah seized was torn, and Joseph left the garment in the hand of Zelicah, and he fled and got out, for he was in fear.

13 When she saw that he had left his garment in her hand, and had run outside,

55 And when Zelicah saw that Joseph's garment was torn, and that he had left it in her hand, and had fled, she was afraid of her life, lest the report should spread concerning her, and she rose up and acted with cunning, and put off the garments in which she was dressed, and she put on her other garments.

56 And she took Joseph's garment, and she laid it beside her, and she went and seated herself in the place where she had sat in her illness, before the people of her house had gone out to the river, and she called a young lad who was then in the house, and she ordered him to call the people of the house to her.

14 she called to the men of her house, and spoke to them, saying, "Behold, he has brought in a Hebrew to us to mock us. He came in to me to lie with me, and I cried with a loud voice. 15 When he heard that I lifted up my voice and cried, he left his garment by me, and ran outside."

57 And when she saw them she said unto them with a loud voice and lamentation, "See what a Hebrew your master has brought to me in the house, for he came this day to lie with me. 58 For when you had gone out he came to the house, and seeing that there was no person in the house, he came unto me, and caught hold of me, with intent to lie with me. 59 And I seized his garments and tore them and called out against him with a loud voice, and when I had lifted up my voice he was afraid of his life and left his garment before me, and fled."

16 She laid up his garment by her, until his master came home.

60 And the people of her house spoke nothing, but their wrath was very much kindled against Joseph, and they went to his master and told him the words of his wile.

17 She spoke to him according to these words, saying, "The Hebrew servant, whom you have brought to us, came in to me to mock me, 18 and as I lifted up my voice and cried, he left his garment by me, and ran outside."

61 And Potiphar came home enraged, and his wife cried out to him, saying, "What is this thing that thou hast done unto me in bringing a Hebrew servant into my house, for he came unto me this day to sport with me; thus did he do unto me this day."

19 When his master heard the words of his wife, which she spoke to him, saying, "This is what your servant did to me," his wrath was kindled.

62 And Potiphar heard the words of his wife, and he ordered Joseph to be punished with severe stripes, and they did so to him.

63 And whilst they were smiting him, Joseph called out with a loud voice, and he lifted up his eyes to heaven, and he said, "O Lord God, thou knowest that I am innocent of all these things, and why shall I die this day through falsehood, by the hand of these uncircumcised wicked men, whom thou knowest?"

64 And whilst Potiphar's men were beating Joseph, he continued to cry out and weep, and there was a child there eleven months old, and the Lord opened the mouth of the child, and he spake these words before Potiphar's men, who were smiting Joseph, saying, 65 "What do you want of this man, and why do you do this evil unto him? my mother speaketh falsely and uttereth lies; thus was the transaction."

66 And the child told them accurately all that happened, and all the words of Zelicah to Joseph day after day did he declare unto them. 67 And all the men heard the words of the child and they wondered greatly at the child's words, and the child ceased to speak and became still.

68 And Potiphar was very much ashamed at the words of his son, and he commanded his men not to beat Joseph any more, and the men ceased beating Joseph.

69 And Potiphar took Joseph and ordered him to be brought to justice before the priests, who were judges belonging to the king, in order to judge him concerning this affair.

70 And Potiphar and Joseph came before the priests who were the king's judges, and he said unto them, "Decide I pray you, what judgment is due to a servant, for thus has he done."

71 And the priests said unto Joseph, "Why didst thou do this thing to thy master?" and Joseph answered them, saying, "Not so my lords, thus was the matter;" and Potiphar said unto Joseph, "Surely I entrusted in thy hands all that belonged to me, and I withheld nothing from thee but my wife, and how couldst thou do this evil?"

72 And Joseph answered saying, "Not so my lord, as
the Lord liveth, and as thy soul liveth, my lord, the
word which thou didst hear from thy wife is untrue,
for thus was the affair this day. 73 A year has
elapsed to me since I have been in thy house; hast
thou seen any iniquity in me, or any thing which
might cause thee to demand my life?"

74 And the priests said unto Potiphar, "Send, we pray thee, and let them bring before us Joseph's torn garment, and let us see the tear in it, and if it shall be that the tear is in front of the garment, then his face must have been opposite to her and she must have caught hold of him, to come to her, and with deceit did thy wife do all that she has spoken."

75 And they brought Joseph's garment before the priests who were judges, and they saw and behold the tear was in front of Joseph, and all the judging priests knew that she had pressed him, and they said, "The judgment of death is not due to this slave for he has done nothing, but his judgment is, that he be placed in the prison house on account of the report, which through him has gone forth against thy wife."

20 Joseph’s master took him, and put him into the prison, the place where the king’s prisoners were bound, and he was there in custody.

76 And Potiphar heard their words, and he placed him in the prison house, the place where the king's prisoners are confined, and Joseph was in the house of confinement twelve years.

77 And notwithstanding this, his master's wife did not turn from him, and she did not cease from speaking to him day after day to hearken to her, and at the end of three months Zelicah continued going to Joseph to the house of confinement day by day, and she enticed him to hearken to her, and Zelicah said unto Joseph, "How long wilt thou remain in this house? but hearken now to my voice, and I will bring thee out of this house."

78 And Joseph answered her, saying, "It is better for me to remain in this house than to hearken to thy words, to sin against God;" and she said unto him, "If thou wilt not perform my wish, I will pluck out thine eyes, add fetters to thy feet, and will deliver thee into the hands of them whom thou didst not know before."

79 And Joseph answered her and said, "Behold the God of the whole earth is able to deliver me from all that thou canst do unto me, for he openeth the eyes of the blind, and looseth those that are bound, and preserveth all strangers who are unacquainted with the land."

80 And when Zelicah was unable to persuade Joseph to hearken to her, she left off going to entice him; and Joseph was still confined in the house of confinement. And Jacob the father of Joseph, and all his brethren who were in the land of Canaan still mourned and wept in those days on account of Joseph, for Jacob refused to be comforted for his son Joseph, and Jacob cried aloud, and wept and mourned all those days.

21 But Yahweh was with Joseph, and showed kindness to him, and gave him favor in the sight of the keeper of the prison. 22 The keeper of the prison committed to Joseph's hand all the prisoners who were in the prison. Whatever they did there, he was responsible for it. 23 The keeper of the prison didn't look after anything that was under his hand, because Yahweh was with him; and that which he did, Yahweh made it prosper.

Jasher 45

1 And it was at that time in that year, which is the year of Joseph's going down to Egypt after his brothers had sold him, that Reuben the son of Jacob went to Timnah and took unto him for a wife Eliuram, the daughter of Avi the Canaanite, and he came to her.

2 And Eliuram the wife of Reuben conceived and bare him Hanoch, Palu, Chetzron and Carmi, four sons; and Simeon his brother took his sister Dinah for a wife, and she bare unto him Memuel, Yamin, Ohad, Jachin and Zochar, five sons.

3 And he afterward came to Bunah the Canaanitish woman, the same is Bunah whom Simeon took captive from the city of Shechem, and Bunah was before Dinah and attended upon her, and Simeon came to her, and she bare unto him Saul.

[Genesis 38: 1 At that time, Judah went down from his brothers, and visited a certain Adullamite, whose name was Hirah. 2 Judah saw there a daughter of a certain Canaanite whose name was Shua. He took her, and went in to her. 3 She conceived, and bore a son; and he named him Er. 4 She conceived again, and bore a son; and she named him Onan. 5 She yet again bore a son, and named him Shelah: and he was at Chezib, when she bore him.]

4 And Judah went at that time to Adulam, and he came to a man of Adulam, and his name was Hirah, and Judah saw there the daughter of a man from Canaan, and her name was Aliyath, the daughter of Shua, and he took her, and came to her, and Aliyath bare unto Judah, Er, Onan and Shiloh; three sons.

[Genesis 46:12 The sons of Judah: Er, Onan, Shelah, Perez, and Zerah; but Er and Onan died in the land of Canaan. The sons of Perez were Hezron and Hamul.]

5 And Levi and Issachar went to the land of the east, and they took unto themselves for wives the daughters of Jobab the son of Yoktan, the son of Eber; and Jobab the son of Yoktan had two daughters; the name of the elder was Adinah, and the name of the younger was Aridah. 6 And Levi took Adinah, and Issachar took Aridah, and they came to the land of Canaan, to their father's house, and Adinah bare unto Levi, Gershon, Kehath and Merari; three sons.

[Genesis 46:13 The sons of Issachar: Tola, Puvah, Iob, and Shimron. Genesis 46:23 The son of Dan: Hushim.]

7 And Aridah bare unto Issachar Tola, Puvah, Job and Shomron, four sons; and Dan went to the land of Moab and took for a wife Aphlaleth, the daughter of Chamudan the Moabite, and he brought her to the land of Canaan.
8 And Aphlaleth was barren, she had no offspring, and God afterward remembered Aphlaleth the wife of Dan, and she conceived and bare a son, and she called his name Chushim.

9 And Gad and Naphtali went to Haran and took from thence the daughters of Amuram the son of Uz, the son of Nahor, for wives.

10 And these are the names of the daughters of Amuram; the name of the elder was Merimah, and the name of the younger Uzith; and Naphtali took Merimah, and Gad took Uzith; and brought them to the land of Canaan, to their father's house.

[Genesis 46:24 The sons of Naphtali: Jahzeel, Guni, Jezer, and Shillem.]

[Genesis 46:16 The sons of Gad: Ziphion, Haggi, Shuni, Ezbon, Eri, Arodi, and Areli.]

11 And Merimah bare unto Naphtali Yachzeel, Guni, Jazer and Shalem, four sons;

and Uzith bare unto Gad Zephion, Chagi, Shuni, Ezbon, Eri, Arodi and Arali, seven sons.

12 And Asher went forth and took Adon the daughter of Aphlal, the son of Hadad, the son of Ishmael, for a wife, and he brought her to the land of Canaan.

13 And Adon the wife of Asher died in those days: she had no offspring; and it was after the death of Adon that Asher went to the other side of the river and took for a wife Hadurah the daughter of Abimael, the son of Eber, the son of Shem.

14 And the young woman was of a comely appearance, and a woman of sense, and she had been the wife of Malkiel the son of Elam, the son of Shem.
15 And Hadurah bare a daughter unto Malkiel, and he called her name Serach, and Malkiel died after this, and Hadurah went and remained in her father's house.

16 And after the death of the wife at Asher he went and took Hadurah for a wife, and brought her to the land of Canaan, and Serach her daughter he also brought with them, and she was three years old, and the damsel was brought up in Jacob's house.

17 And the damsel was of a comely appearance, and she went in the sanctified ways of the children of Jacob; she lacked nothing, and the Lord gave her wisdom and understanding.

[Genesis 46:17 The sons of Asher: Imnah, Ishvah, Ishvi, Beriah, and Serah their sister. The sons of Beriah: Heber and Malchiel.]

18 And Hadurah the wife of Asher conceived and bare unto him Yimnah, Yishvah, Yishvi and Beriah; four sons.

[Genesis 46:14 The sons of Zebulun: Sered, Elon, and Jahleel. 15 These are the sons of Leah, whom she bore to Jacob in Paddan Aram, with his daughter Dinah. All the souls of his sons and his daughters were thirty-three.]

19 And Zebulun went to Midian, and took for a wife Merishah the daughter of Molad, the son of Abida, the son of Midian, and brought her to the land of Canaan. 20 And Merushah bare unto Zebulun Sered, Elon and Yachleel; three sons.

[Genesis 46:21 The sons of Benjamin: Bela, Becher, Ashbel, Gera, Naaman, Ehi, Rosh, Muppim, Huppim, and Ard. 22 These are the sons of Rachel, who were born to Jacob: all the souls were fourteen.]

21 And Jacob sent to Aram, the son of Zoba, the son of Terah, and he took for his son Benjamin Mechalia the daughter of Aram, and she came to the land of Canaan to the house of Jacob; and Benjamin was ten years old when he took Mechalia the daughter of Aram for a wife. 22 And Mechalia conceived and bare unto Benjamin Bela, Becher, Ashbel, Gera and Naaman, five sons; and Benjamin went afterward and took for a wife Aribath, the daughter of Shomron, the son of Abraham, in addition to his first wife, and he was eighteen years old; and Aribath bare unto Benjamin Achi, Vosh, Mupim, Chupim, and Ord; five sons.

[Genesis 38:6 Judah took a wife for Er, his firstborn, and her name was Tamar.]

23 And in those days Judah went to the house of Shem and took Tamar the daughter of Elam, the son of Shem, for a wife for his first born Er.

[Genesis 38:7 Er, Judah's firstborn, was wicked in Yahweh's sight. Yahweh killed him.]

24 And Er came to his wife Tamar, and she became his wife, and when he came to her he outwardly destroyed his seed, and his work was evil in the sight of the Lord, and the Lord slew him.

[Genesis 38:8 Judah said to Onan, "Go in to your brother's wife, and perform the duty of a husband's brother to her, and raise up offspring for your brother."]

25 And it was after the death of Er, Judah's first born, that Judah said unto Onan, "Go to thy brother's wife and marry her as the next of kin, and raise up seed to thy brother."

[Genesis 38:9 Onan knew that the offspring wouldn't be his; and when he went in to his brother's wife, he spilled it on the ground, lest he should give offspring to his brother. 10 The thing which he did was evil in Yahweh's sight, and he killed him also.]

26 And Onan took Tamar for a wife and he came to her, and Onan also did like unto the work of his brother, and his work was evil in the sight of the Lord, and he slew him also.

[Genesis 38:11 Then Judah said to Tamar, his daughter-in-law, "Remain a widow in your father's house, until Shelah, my son, is grown up"; for he said, "Lest he also die, like his brothers." Tamar went and lived in her father's house.]

27 And when Onan died, Judah said unto Tamar, "Remain in thy father's house until my son Shiloh shall have grown up", and Judah did no more delight in Tamar, to give her unto Shiloh, for he said," Peradventure he will also die like his brothers." 28 And Tamar rose up and went and remained in her father's house, and Tamar was in her father's house for some time.

[Genesis 38:12 After many days, Shua's daughter, the wife of Judah, died. Judah was comforted, and went up to his sheep shearers to Timnah, he and his friend Hirah, the Adullamite.]

29 And at the revolution of the year, Aliyath the wife of Judah died; and Judah was comforted for his wife, and after the death of Aliyath, Judah went up with his friend Hirah to Timnah to shear their sheep.

[Genesis 38:13 Tamar was told, "Behold, your father-in-law is going up to Timnah to shear his sheep."]

30 And Tamar heard that Judah had gone up to Timnah to shear the sheep, and that Shiloh was grown up, and Judah did not delight in her.

[Genesis 38:14 She took off of her the garments of her widowhood, and covered herself with her veil, and wrapped herself, and sat in the gate of Enaim, which is by the way to Timnah; for she saw that Shelah was grown up, and she wasn't given to him as a wife.]

31 And Tamar rose up and put off the garments of her widowhood, and she put a veil upon her, and she entirely covered herself, and she went and sat in the public thoroughfare, which is upon the road to Timnah.

[Genesis 38:18 He gave them to her, and came in to her, and she conceived by him.]

32 And Judah passed and saw her and took her and he came to her, and she conceived by him,

[Genesis 38:27 In the time of her travail, behold, twins were in her womb. 28 When she travailed, one put out a hand, and the midwife took and tied a scarlet thread on his hand, saying, "This came out first." 29 As he drew back his hand, behold, his brother came out, and she said, "Why have you made a breach for yourself?" Therefore his name was called Perez. 30 Afterward his brother came out, that had the scarlet thread on his hand, and his name was called Zerah.]

and at the time of being delivered, behold, there were twins in her womb, and he called the name of the first Perez, and the name of the second Zarah.

Jasher 46

1 In those days Joseph was still confined in the prison house in the land of Egypt.

2 At that time the attendants of Pharaoh were standing before him, the chief of the butlers and the chief of the bakers which belonged to the king of Egypt.

3 And the butler took wine and placed it before the king to drink, and the baker placed bread before the king to eat, and the king drank of the wine and ate of the bread, he and his servants and ministers that ate at the king's table.

Genesis 40

1 After these things, the butler of the king of Egypt and his baker offended their lord, the king of Egypt.

4 And whilst they were eating and drinking, the butler and the baker remained there, and Pharaoh's ministers found many flies in the wine, which the butler had brought, and stones of nitre were found in the baker's bread.

2 Pharaoh was angry with his two officers, the chief cup bearer and the chief baker. 3 He put them in custody in the house of the captain of the guard, into the prison, the place where Joseph was bound.

4 The captain of the guard assigned them to Joseph, and he took care of them. They stayed in prison many days.

5 And the captain of the guard placed Joseph as an attendant on Pharaoh's officers, and Pharaoh's officers were in confinement one year.

5 They both dreamed a dream, each man his dream, in one night, each man according to the interpretation of his dream, the cup bearer and the baker of the king of Egypt, who were bound in the prison. 6 Joseph came in to them in the morning, and saw them, and saw that they were sad.

6 And at the end of the year, they both dreamed dreams in one night, in the place of confinement where they were, and in the morning Joseph came to them to attend upon them as usual, and he saw them, and behold their countenances were dejected and sad.

7 He asked Pharaoh's officers who were with him in custody in his master's house, saying, "Why do you look so sad today?" 8 They said to him, "We have dreamed a dream, and there is no one who can interpret it." Joseph said to them, "Don't interpretations belong to God? Please tell it to me."

7 And Joseph asked them, "Why are your countenances sad and dejected this day?" and they said unto him, "We dreamed a dream, and there is no one to interpret it"; and Joseph said unto them, "Relate, I pray you, your dream unto me, and God shall give you an answer of peace as you desire."

9 The chief cup bearer told his dream to Joseph, and said to him, "In my dream, behold, a vine was in front of me, 10 and in the vine were three branches. It was as though it budded, it blossomed, and its clusters produced ripe grapes. 11 Pharaoh's cup was in my hand; and I took the grapes, and pressed them into Pharaoh's cup, and I gave the cup into Pharaoh's hand."

8 And the butler related his dream unto Joseph, and he said, "I saw in my dream, and behold a large vine was before me, and upon that vine I saw three branches, and the vine speedily blossomed and reached a great height, and its clusters were ripened and became grapes. 9 And I took the grapes and pressed them in a cup, and placed it in Pharaoh's hand and he drank;"

12 Joseph said to him, "This is its interpretation: the three branches are three days. 13 Within three more days, Pharaoh will lift up your head, and restore you to your office. You will give Pharaoh's cup into his hand, the way you did when you were his cup bearer. 14 But remember me when it will be well with you, and please show kindness to me, and make mention of me to Pharaoh, and bring me out of this house. 15 For indeed, I was stolen away out of the land of the Hebrews, and here also have I done nothing that they should put me into the dungeon."

and Joseph said unto him, "The three branches that were upon the vine are three days. 10 Yet within three days, the king will order thee to be brought out and he will restore thee to thy office, and thou shalt give the king his wine to drink as at first when thou wast his butler; but let me find favor in thy sight, that thou shalt remember me to Pharaoh when it will be well with thee, and do kindness unto me, and get me brought forth from this prison, for I was stolen away from the land of Canaan and was sold for a slave in this place.

11 "And also that which was told thee concerning my master's wife is false, for they placed me in this dungeon for naught;" and the butler answered Joseph, saying, "If the king deal well with me as at first, as thou last interpreted to me, I will do all that thou desirest, and get thee brought out of this dungeon."

16 When the chief baker saw that the interpretation was good, he said to Joseph, "I also was in my dream, and behold, three baskets of white bread were on my head. 17 In the uppermost basket there were all kinds of baked food for Pharaoh, and the birds ate them out of the basket on my head."

12 And the baker, seeing that Joseph had accurately interpreted the butler's dream, also approached, and related the whole of his dream to Joseph. 13 And he said unto him, "In my dream I saw and behold three white baskets upon my head, and I looked, and behold there were in the upper-most basket all manner of baked meats for Pharaoh, and behold the birds were eating them from off my head."

18 Joseph answered, "This is its interpretation. The three baskets are three days. 19 Within three more days, Pharaoh will lift up your head from off you, and will hang you on a tree; and the birds will eat your flesh from off you."

14 And Joseph said unto him, "The three baskets which thou didst see are three days, yet within three days Pharaoh will take off thy head, and hang thee upon a tree, and the birds will eat thy flesh from off thee, as thou sawest in thy dream."

15 In those days the queen was about to be delivered, and upon that day she bare a son unto the king of Egypt, and they proclaimed that the king had gotten his first born son and all the people of Egypt together with the officers and servants of Pharaoh rejoiced greatly.

20 On the third day, which was Pharaoh's birthday, he made a feast for all his servants, and he lifted up the head of the chief cup bearer and the head of the chief baker among his servants.

21 He restored the chief cup bearer to his position again, and he gave the cup into Pharaoh's hand; 22 but he hanged the chief baker, as Joseph had interpreted to them.

16 And upon the third day of his birth Pharaoh made a feast for his officers and servants, for the hosts of the land of Zoar and of the land of Egypt.

17 And all the people of Egypt and the servants of Pharaoh came to eat and drink with the king at the feast of his son, and to rejoice at the king's rejoicing.

18 And all the officers of the king and his servants were rejoicing at that time for eight days at the feast, and they made merry with all sorts of musical instruments, with timbrels and with dances in the king's house for eight days.

23 Yet the chief cup bearer didn't remember Joseph, but forgot him.

19 And the butler, to whom Joseph had interpreted his dream, forgot Joseph, and he did not mention him to the king as he had promised, for this thing was from the Lord in order to punish Joseph because he had trusted in man.

20 And Joseph remained after this in the prison house two years, until he had completed twelve years.

Jasher 47

1 And Isaac the son of Abraham was still living in those days in the land of Canaan; he was very aged, one hundred and eighty years old, and Esau his son, the brother of Jacob, was in the land of Edom, and he and his sons had possessions in it amongst the children of Seir.

2 And Esau heard that his father's time was drawing nigh to die, and he and his sons and household came unto the land of Canaan, unto his father's house, and Jacob and his sons went forth from the place where they dwelt in Hebron, and they all came to their father Isaac, and they found Esau and his sons in the tent.

3 And Jacob and his sons sat before his father Isaac, and Jacob was still mourning for his son Joseph.

4 And Isaac said unto Jacob, "Bring me hither thy sons and I will bless them;" and Jacob brought his eleven children before his father Isaac. 5 And Isaac placed his hands upon all the sons of Jacob, and he took hold of them and embraced them, and kissed them one by one, and Isaac blessed them on that day, and he said unto them, "May the God of your fathers bless you and increase your seed like the stars of heaven for number."

6 And Isaac also blessed the sons of Esau, saying, "May God cause you to be a dread and a terror to all that will behold you, and to all your enemies."

7 And Isaac called Jacob and his sons, and they all came and sat before Isaac, and Isaac said unto Jacob, "The Lord God of the whole earth said unto me, 'Unto thy seed will I give this land for an inheritance if thy children keep my statutes and my ways, and I will perform unto them the oath which I swore unto thy father Abraham.'

8 "Now therefore my son, teach thy children and thy children's children to fear the Lord, and to go in the good way which will please the Lord thy God, for if you keep the ways of the Lord and his statutes the Lord will also keep unto you his covenant with Abraham, and will do well with you and your seed all the days."

9 And when Isaac had finished commanding Jacob and his children, he gave up the ghost and died, and was gathered unto his people.

10 And Jacob and Esau fell upon the face of their father Isaac, and they wept, and Isaac was one hundred and eighty years old when he died in the land of Canaan, in Hebron, and his sons carried him to the cave of Machpelah, which Abraham had bought from the children of Heth for a possession of a burial place.

11 And all the kings of the land of Canaan went with
Jacob and Esau to bury Isaac, and all the kings of
Canaan showed Isaac great honor at his death. 12
And the sons of Jacob and the sons of Esau went
barefooted round about, walking and lamenting
until they reached Kireath-arba.

13 And Jacob and Esau buried their father Isaac in
the cave of Machpelah, which is in Kireath-arba in
Hebron, and they buried him with very great honor,
as at the funeral of kings. 14 And Jacob and his
sons, and Esau and his sons, and all the kings of
Canaan made a great and heavy mourning, and
they buried him and mourned for him many days.

15 And at the death of Isaac, he left his cattle and
his possessions and all belonging to him to his sons;
and Esau said unto Jacob, "Behold I pray thee, all
that our father has left we will divide it in two parts,
and I will have the choice," and Jacob said, "We will
do so." 16 And Jacob took all that Isaac had left in
the land of Canaan, the cattle and the property, and
he placed them in two parts before Esau and his
sons, and he said unto Esau, "Behold all this is
before thee, choose thou unto thyself the half
which thou wilt take."

17 And Jacob said unto Esau, "Hear thou I pray thee
what I will speak unto thee, saying, 'The Lord God
of heaven and earth spoke unto our fathers
Abraham and Isaac, saying, "Unto thy seed will I
give this land for an inheritance forever."' 18 Now
therefore all that our father has left is before thee,
and behold all the land is before thee; choose thou
from them what thou desirest.

19 "If thou desirest the whole land take it for thee
and thy children forever, and I will take this riches,
and it thou desirest the riches take it unto thee, and
I will take this land for me and for my children to
inherit it forever."

20 And Nebayoth, the son of Ishmael, was then in
the land with his children, and Esau went on that
day and consulted with him, saying. 21 "Thus has
Jacob spoken unto me, and thus has he answered
me, now give thy advice and we will hear."

22 And Nebayoth said, "What is this that Jacob hath
spoken unto thee? behold all the children of
Canaan are dwelling securely in their land, and
Jacob sayeth he will inherit it with his seed all the
days. 23 Go now therefore and take all thy father's
riches and leave Jacob thy brother in the land, as he
has spoken."

24 And Esau rose up and returned to Jacob, and did
all that Nebayoth the son of Ishmael had advised;
and Esau took all the riches that Isaac had left, the
souls, the beasts, the cattle and the property, and
all the riches; he gave nothing to his brother Jacob;
and Jacob took all the land of Canaan, from the
brook of Egypt unto the river Euphrates, and he
took it for an everlasting possession, and for his
children and for his seed after him forever. 25
Jacob also took from his brother Esau the cave of
Machpelah, which is in Hebron, which Abraham had
bought from Ephron for a possession of a burial
place for him and his seed forever.

26 And Jacob wrote all these things in the book of
purchase, and he signed it, and he testified all this
with four faithful witnesses. 27 And these are the
words which Jacob wrote in the book, saying: The
land of Canaan and all the cities of the Hittites, the
Hivites, the Jebusites, the Amorites, the Perizzites,
and the Gergashites, all the seven nations from the
river of Egypt unto the river Euphrates.

28 And the city of Hebron Kireath-arba, and the cave which is in it, the whole did Jacob buy from his brother Esau for value, for a possession and for an inheritance for his seed after him forever.

29 And Jacob took the book of purchase and the signature, the command and the statutes and the revealed book, and he placed them in an earthen vessel in order that they should remain for a long time, and he delivered them into the hands of his children.

30 Esau took all that his father had left him after his
death from his brother Jacob, and he took all the
property, from man and beast, camel and ass, ox
and lamb, silver and gold, stones and bdellium, and
all the riches which had belonged to Isaac the son
of Abraham; there was nothing left which Esau did
not take unto himself, from all that Isaac had left
after his death. 31 And Esau took all this, and he
and his children went home to the land of Seir the
Horite, away from his brother Jacob and his
children.

32 And Esau had possessions amongst the children of Seir, and Esau returned not to the land of Canaan from that day forward. 33 And the whole land of Canaan became an inheritance to the children of Israel for an everlasting inheritance, and Esau with all his children inherited the mountain of Seir.

Jasher 48

1 In those days, after the death of Isaac, the Lord commanded and caused a famine upon the whole earth.

Genesis 41

1 At the end of two full years, Pharaoh dreamed: and behold, he stood by the river.

2 At that time Pharaoh king of Egypt was sitting upon his throne in the land of Egypt, and lay in his bed and dreamed dreams, and Pharaoh saw in his dream that he was standing by the side of the river of Egypt.

2 Behold, there came up out of the river seven cattle, sleek and fat, and they fed in the marsh grass.

3 And whilst he was standing he saw and behold seven fat fleshed and well favored kine came up out of the river.

3 Behold, seven other cattle came up after them out of the river, ugly and thin, and stood by the other cattle on the brink of the river. 4 The ugly and thin cattle ate up the seven sleek and fat cattle. So Pharaoh awoke.

4 And seven other kine, lean fleshed and ill favored, came up after them, and the seven ill favored ones swallowed up the well favored ones, and still their appearance was ill as at first.

5 He slept and dreamed a second time: and behold, seven heads of grain came up on one stalk, healthy and good. 6 Behold, seven heads of grain, thin and blasted with the east wind, sprung up after them. 7 The thin heads of grain swallowed up the seven healthy and full ears. Pharaoh awoke, and behold, it was a dream.

5 And he awoke, and he slept again and he dreamed a second time, and he saw and behold seven ears of corn came up upon one stalk, rank and good, and seven thin ears blasted with the east wind sprang, up after them, and the thin ears swallowed up the full ones, and Pharaoh awoke out of his dream.

8 In the morning, his spirit was troubled, and he sent and called for all of Egypt's magicians and wise men.

6 And in the morning the king remembered his dreams, and his spirit was sadly troubled on account of his dreams, and the king hastened and sent and called for all the magicians of Egypt, and the wise men, and they came and stood before Pharaoh.

7 And the king said unto them, "I have dreamed dreams, and there is none to interpret them;" and they said unto the king, "Relate thy dreams to thy servants and let us hear them."

Pharaoh told them his dreams,

8 And the king related his dreams to them,

and they all answered and said with one voice to the king, "May the king live forever;" and this is the interpretation of thy dreams.

9 "The seven good kine which thou didst see denote seven daughters that will be born unto thee in the latter days, and the seven kine which thou sawest come up after them, and swallowed them up, are for a sign that the daughters which will be born unto thee will all die in the life-time of the king.

10 "And that which thou didst see in the second dream of seven full good ears of corn coming up upon one stalk, this is their interpretation, that thou wilt build unto thyself in the latter days seven cities throughout the land of Egypt; and that which thou sawest of the seven blasted ears of corn springing up after them and swallowing them up whilst thou didst behold them with thine eyes, is for a sign that the cities which thou wilt build will all be destroyed in the latter days, in the life-time of the king."

11 And when they spoke these words the king did not incline his ear to their words, neither did he fix his heart upon them, for the king knew in his wisdom that they did not give a proper interpretation of the dreams; and when they had finished speaking before the king, the king answered them, saying, "What is this thing that you have spoken unto me? Surely you have uttered falsehood and spoken lies; therefore now give the proper interpretation of my dreams, that you may not die."

12 And the king commanded after this, and he sent and called again for other wise men, and they came and stood before the king, and the king related his dreams to them, and they all answered him according to the first interpretation, and the king's anger was kindled and he was very wroth, and the king said unto them, "Surely you speak lies and utter falsehood in what you have said."

13 And the king commanded that a proclamation
should be issued throughout the land of Egypt,
saying, "It is resolved by the king and his great men,
that any wise man who knoweth and
understandeth the interpretation of dreams, and
will not come this day before the king, shall die. 14
And the man that will declare unto the king the
proper interpretation of his dreams, there shall be
given unto him all that he will require from the
king."

And all the wise men of the land of Egypt came
before the king, together with all the magicians and
sorcerers that were in Egypt and in Goshen, in
Rameses, in Tachpanches, in Zoar, and in all the
places on the borders of Egypt, and they all stood
before the king. 15 And all the nobles and the
princes, and the attendants belonging to the king,
came together from all the cities of Egypt, and they
all sat before the king, and the king related his
dreams before the wise men, and the princes, and
all that sat before the king were astonished at the
vision.

16 And all the wise men who were before the king
were greatly divided in their interpretation of his
dreams; some of them interpreted them to the
king, saying, "The seven good kine are seven kings,
who from the king's issue will be raised over Egypt.
17 And the seven bad kine are seven princes, who
will stand up against them in the latter days and
destroy them; and the seven ears of corn are the
seven great princes belonging to Egypt, who will fall
in the hands of the seven less powerful princes of
their enemies, in the wars of our lord the king."
18 And some of them interpreted to the king in this
manner, saying, "The seven good kine are the
strong cities of Egypt, and the seven bad kine are
the seven nations of the land of Canaan, who will
come against the seven cities of Egypt in the latter
days and destroy them.

19 "And that which thou sawest in the second
dream, of seven good and bad ears of corn, is a sign
that the government of Egypt will again return to
thy seed as at first. 20 And in his reign the people
of the cities of Egypt will turn against the seven
cities of Canaan who are stronger than they are,
and will destroy them, and the government of Egypt
will return to thy seed."

21 And some of them said unto the king, "This is the interpretation of thy dreams; the seven good kine are seven queens, whom thou wilt take for wives in the latter days, and the seven bad kine denote that those women will all die in the lifetime of the king.

22 And the seven good and bad ears of corn which thou didst see in the second dream are fourteen children, and it will be in the latter days that they will stand up and fight amongst themselves, and seven of them will smite the seven that are more powerful."

23 And some of them said these words unto the king, saying, "The seven good kine denote that seven children will be born to thee, and they will slay seven of thy children's children in the latter days; and the seven good ears of corn which thou didst see in the second dream, are those princes against whom seven other less powerful princes will fight and destroy them in the latter days, and avenge thy children's cause, and the government will again return to thy seed."

but there was no one who could interpret them to Pharaoh.

24 And the king heard all the words of the wise men of Egypt and their interpretation of his dreams, and none of them pleased the king.

25 And the king knew in his wisdom that they did not altogether speak correctly in all these words, for this was from the Lord to frustrate the words of the wise men of Egypt, in order that Joseph might go forth from the house of confinement, and in order that he should become great in Egypt. 26
And the king saw that none amongst all the wise men and magicians of Egypt spoke correctly to him, and the king's wrath was kindled, and his anger burned within him.

27 And the king commanded that all the wise men and magicians should go out from before him, and they all went out from before the king with shame and disgrace. 28 And the king commanded that a proclamation be sent throughout Egypt to slay all the magicians that were in Egypt, and not one of them should be suffered to live. 29 And the captains of the guards belonging to the king rose up, and each man drew his sword, and they began to smite the magicians of Egypt, and the wise men.

9 Then the chief cup bearer spoke to Pharaoh, saying, “I remember my faults today. 10 Pharaoh was angry with his servants, and put me in custody in the house of the captain of the guard, me and the chief baker.

11 We dreamed a dream in one night, I and he. We dreamed each man according to the interpretation of his dream. 12 There was with us there a young man, a Hebrew, servant to the captain of the guard, and we told him, and he interpreted to us our dreams. To each man according to his dream he interpreted. 13 As he interpreted to us, so it was. He restored me to my office, and he hanged him.”

14 Then Pharaoh sent and called Joseph, and they brought him hastily out of the dungeon. He shaved himself, changed his clothing, and came in to Pharaoh.

30 And after this Merod, chief butler to the king, came and bowed down before the king and sat before him. 31 And the butler said unto the king, "May the king live forever, and his government be exalted in the land. 32 Thou wast angry with thy servant in those days, now two years past, and didst place me in the ward, and I was for some time in the ward, I and the chief of the bakers.

33 "And there was with us a Hebrew servant belonging to the captain of the guard, his name was Joseph, for his master had been angry with him and placed him in the house of confinement, and he attended us there.

34 "And in some time after when we were in the ward, we dreamed dreams in one night, I and the chief of the bakers; we dreamed, each man according to the interpretation of his dream. 35 And we came in the morning and told them to that servant, and he interpreted to us our dreams, to each man according to his dream, did he correctly interpret. 36 And it came to pass as he interpreted to us, so was the event; there fell not to the ground any of his words.

37 "And now therefore my lord and king do not slay the people of Egypt for naught; behold that slave is still confined in the house by the captain of the guard his master, in the house of confinement.

38 If it pleaseth the king let him send for him that he may come before thee and he will make known to thee, the correct interpretation of the dream which thou didst dream."

39 And the king heard the words of the chief butler, and the king ordered that the wise men of Egypt should not be slain.

40 And the king ordered his servants to bring Joseph before him, and the king said unto them, "Go to him and do not terrify him lest he be confused and will not know to speak properly."

41 And the servants of the king went to Joseph, and they brought him hastily out of the dungeon, and the king's servants shaved him, and he changed his prison garment and he came before the king.

42 And the king was sitting upon his royal throne in a princely dress girt around with a golden ephod, and the fine gold which was upon it sparkled, and the carbuncle and the ruby and the emerald, together with all the precious stones that were upon the king's head, dazzled the eye, and Joseph wondered greatly at the king.

43 And the throne upon which the king sat was covered with gold and silver, and with onyx stones, and it had seventy steps.

44 And it was their custom throughout the land of Egypt, that every man who came to speak to the king, if he was a prince or one that was estimable in the sight of the king, he ascended to the king's throne as far as the thirty-first step, and the king would descend to the thirty-sixth step, and speak with him.

45 If he was one of the common people, he ascended to the third step, and the king would descend to the fourth and speak to him, and their custom was, moreover, that any man who understood to speak in all the seventy languages, he ascended the seventy steps, and went up and spoke till he reached the king.

46 And any man who could not complete the seventy, he ascended as many steps as the languages which he knew to speak in.

47 And it was customary in those days in Egypt that no one should reign over them, but who understood to speak in the seventy languages.

48 And when Joseph came before the king he bowed down to the ground before the king, and he ascended to the third step, and the king sat upon the fourth step and spoke with Joseph.

15 Pharaoh said to Joseph, "I have dreamed a dream, and there is no one who can interpret it. I have heard it said of you, that when you hear a dream you can interpret it."

49 And the king said unto Joseph, "I dreamed a dream, and there is no interpreter to interpret it properly, and I commanded this day that all the magicians of Egypt and the wise men thereof, should come before me, and I related my dreams to them, and no one has properly interpreted them to me. 50 And after this I this day heard concerning thee, that thou art a wise man, and canst correctly interpret every dream that thou hearest."

16 Joseph answered Pharaoh, saying, “It isn’t in me. God will give Pharaoh an answer of peace.”

51 And Joseph answered Pharaoh, saying, "Let Pharaoh relate his dreams that he dreamed; surely the interpretations belong to God;"

17 Pharaoh spoke to Joseph, “In my dream, behold,
I stood on the brink of the river: 18 and behold,
there came up out of the river seven cattle, fat and
sleek. They fed in the marsh grass, 19 and behold,
seven other cattle came up after them, poor and
very ugly and thin, such as I never saw in all the
land of Egypt for ugliness. 20 The thin and ugly
cattle ate up the first seven fat cattle, 21 and when
they had eaten them up, it couldn’t be known that
they had eaten them, but they were still ugly, as at
the beginning. So I awoke.

and Pharaoh related his dreams to Joseph, the dream of the kine, and the dream of the ears of corn, and the king left off speaking.

22 I saw in my dream, and behold, seven heads of
grain came up on one stalk, full and good: 23 and
behold, seven heads of grain, withered, thin, and
blasted with the east wind, sprung up after them.
24 The thin heads of grain swallowed up the seven
good heads of grain. I told it to the magicians, but
there was no one who could explain it to me.”

52 And Joseph was then clothed with the spirit of God before the king, and he knew all the things that would befall the king from that day forward, and he knew the proper interpretation of the king's dream, and he spoke before the king.

25 Joseph said to Pharaoh, “The dream of Pharaoh is one. What God is about to do he has declared to Pharaoh.

53 And Joseph found favor in the sight of the king, and the king inclined his ears and his heart, and he heard all the words of Joseph. And Joseph said unto the king, "Do not imagine that they are two dreams, for it is only one dream, for that which God has chosen to do throughout the land he has shown to the king in his dream, and this is the proper interpretation of thy dream:

26 "The seven good cattle are seven years; and the
seven good heads of grain are seven years. The
dream is one. 27 The seven thin and ugly cattle that
came up after them are seven years, and also the
seven empty heads of grain blasted with the east
wind; they will be seven years of famine.

54 "The seven good kine and ears of corn are seven
years, and the seven bad kine and ears of corn are
also seven years; it is one dream. 55 Behold the
seven years that are coming there will be a great
plenty throughout the land, and after that the
seven years of famine will follow them, a very
grievous famine; and all the plenty will be forgotten
from the land, and the famine will consume the
inhabitants of the land.

28 "That is the thing which I spoke to Pharaoh.
What God is about to do he has shown to Pharaoh.
29 Behold, there come seven years of great plenty
throughout all the land of Egypt. 30 There will arise
after them seven years of famine, and all the plenty
will be forgotten in the land of Egypt. The famine
will consume the land, 31 and the plenty will not be
known in the land by reason of that famine which
follows; for it will be very grievous.

32 "The dream was doubled to Pharaoh, because the thing is established by God, and God will shortly bring it to pass.

56 "The king dreamed one dream, and the dream was therefore repeated unto Pharaoh because the thing is established by God, and God will shortly bring it to pass.

33 "Now therefore let Pharaoh look for a discreet and wise man, and set him over the land of Egypt.

57 "Now therefore I will give thee counsel and deliver thy soul and the souls of the inhabitants of the land from the evil of the famine, that thou seek throughout thy kingdom for a man very discreet and wise, who knoweth all the affairs of government, and appoint him to superintend over the land of Egypt.

34 "Let Pharaoh do this, and let him appoint
overseers over the land, and take up the fifth part
of the land of Egypt's produce in the seven
plenteous years. 35 Let them gather all the food of
these good years that come, and lay up grain under
the hand of Pharaoh for food in the cities, and let
them keep it. 36 The food will be for a store to the
land against the seven years of famine, which will
be in the land of Egypt; that the land not perish
through the famine."

58 And let the man whom thou placest over Egypt
appoint officers under him, that they gather in all
the food of the good years that are coming, and let
them lay up corn and deposit it in thy appointed
stores. 59 And let them keep that food for the
seven years of famine, that it may be found for thee
and thy people and thy whole land, and that thou
and thy land be not cut off by the famine.

60 "Let all the inhabitants of the land be also ordered that they gather in, every man the produce of his field, of all sorts of food, during the seven good years, and that they place it in their stores, that it may be found for them in the days of the famine and that they may live upon it.

61 "This is the proper interpretation of thy dream, and this is the counsel given to save thy soul and the souls of all thy subjects."

62 And the king answered and said unto Joseph, "Who sayeth and who knoweth that thy words are correct?" And he said unto the king, "This shall be a sign for thee respecting all my words, that they are true and that my advice is good for thee. 63 Behold thy wife sitteth this day upon the stool of delivery, and she will bear thee a son and thou wilt rejoice with him; when thy child shall have gone forth from his mother's womb, thy first born son that has been born these two years back shall die, and thou wilt be comforted in the child that will be born unto thee this day."

64 And Joseph finished speaking these words to the king, and he bowed down to the king and he went out, and when Joseph had gone out from the king's presence, those signs which Joseph had spoken unto the king came to pass on that day.

65 And the queen bare a son on that day and the king heard the glad tidings about his son, and he rejoiced, and when the reporter had gone forth from the king's presence, the king's servants found the first born son of the king fallen dead upon the ground.

66 And there was great lamentation and noise in the king's house, and the king heard it, and he said, "What is the noise and lamentation that I have heard in the house?" and they told the king that his first born son had died; then the king knew that all Joseph's words that he had spoken were correct, and the king was consoled for his son by the child that was born to him on that day as Joseph had spoken.

37 The thing was good in the eyes of Pharaoh, and in the eyes of all his servants.

Jasher 49

1 After these things the king sent and assembled all his officers and servants, and all the princes and nobles belonging to the king, and they all came before the king.

2 And the king said unto them, "Behold you have seen and heard all the words of this Hebrew man, and all the signs which he declared would come to pass, and not any of his words have fallen to the ground. 3 You know that he has given a proper interpretation of the dream, and it will surely come to pass, now therefore take counsel, and know what you will do and how the land will be delivered from the famine.

38 Pharaoh said to his servants, "Can we find such a one as this, a man in whom is the Spirit of God?"

4 Seek now and see whether the like can be found, in whose heart there is wisdom and knowledge, and I will appoint him over the land.

5 "For you have heard what the Hebrew man has advised concerning this to save the land therewith from the famine, and I know that the land will not be delivered from the famine but with the advice of the Hebrew man, him that advised me."

6 And they all answered the king and said, "The counsel which the Hebrew has given concerning this is good; now therefore, our lord and king, behold the whole land is in thy hand, do that which seemeth good in thy sight. 7 Him whom thou chooses, and whom thou in thy wisdom knowest to be wise and capable of delivering the land with his wisdom, him shall the king appoint to be under him over the land."

8 And the king said to all the officers: "I have thought that since God has made known to the Hebrew man all that he has spoken, there is none so discreet and wise in the whole land as he is; if it seem good in your sight I will place him over the land, for he will save the land with his wisdom."

9 And all the officers answered the king and said, "But surely it is written in the laws of Egypt, and it should not be violated, that no man shall reign over Egypt, nor be the second to the king, but one who has knowledge in all the languages of the sons of men.

10 "Now therefore our lord and king, behold this Hebrew man can only speak the Hebrew language, and how then can he be over us the second under government, a man who not even knoweth our language?

11 "Now we pray thee send for him, and let him
come before thee, and prove him in all things, and
do as thou see fit." 12 And the king said, "It shall be
done tomorrow, and the thing that you have
spoken is good;" and all the officers came on that
day before the king.

13 And on that night the Lord sent one of his ministering angels, and he came into the land of Egypt unto Joseph, and the angel of the Lord stood over Joseph, and behold Joseph was lying in the bed at night in his master's house in the dungeon, for his master had put him back into the dungeon on account of his wife.

14 And the angel roused him from his sleep, and Joseph rose up and stood upon his legs, and behold the angel of the Lord was standing opposite to him; and the angel of the Lord spoke with Joseph, and he taught him all the languages of man in that night, and he called his name Jehoseph.

15 And the angel of the Lord went from him, and Joseph returned and lay upon his bed, and Joseph was astonished at the vision which he saw.

16 And it came to pass in the morning that the king
sent for all his officers and servants, and they all
came and sat before the king, and the king ordered
Joseph to be brought, and the king's servants went
and brought Joseph before Pharaoh. 17 And the
king came forth and ascended the steps of the
throne, and Joseph spoke unto the king in all
languages, and Joseph went up to him and spoke
unto the king until he arrived before the king in the
seventieth step, and he sat before the king.

18 And the king greatly rejoiced on account of Joseph, and all the king's officers rejoiced greatly with the king when they heard all the words of Joseph.

19 And the thing seemed good in the sight of the king and the officers, to appoint Joseph to be second to the king over the whole land of Egypt, and the king spoke to Joseph, saying,

39 Pharaoh said to Joseph, "Because God has shown you all of this, there is no one so discreet and wise as you. 40 You shall be over my house, and according to your word will all my people be ruled.

20 "Now thou didst give me counsel to appoint a wise man over the land of Egypt, in order with his wisdom to save the land from the famine; now therefore, since God has made all this known to thee, and all the words which thou hast spoken, there is not throughout the land a discreet and wise man like unto thee.

[Genesis 41:45 Pharaoh called Joseph's name Zaphenath-Paneah;]

21 And thy name no more shall be called Joseph, but Zaphnath Paaneah shall be thy name; thou shalt be second to me, and according to thy word shall be all the affairs of my government, and at thy word shall my people go out and come in.

"Only in the throne I will be greater than you."

22 "Also from under thy hand shall my servants and officers receive their salary which is given to them monthly, and to thee shall all the people of the land bow down; only in my throne will I be greater than thou."

41 Pharaoh said to Joseph, "Behold, I have set you over all the land of Egypt." 42 Pharaoh took off his signet ring from his hand, and put it on Joseph's hand, and arrayed him in robes of fine linen, and put a gold chain about his neck,

23 And the king took off his ring from his hand and put it upon the hand of Joseph, and the king dressed Joseph in a princely garment, and he put a golden crown upon his head, and he put a golden chain upon his neck.

43 and he made him to ride in the second chariot which he had. They cried before him, "Bow the knee!" He set him over all the land of Egypt.

24 And the king commanded his servants, and they made him ride in the second chariot belonging to the king, that went opposite to the king's chariot, and he caused him to ride upon a great and strong horse from the king's horses, and to be conducted through the streets of the land of Egypt. 25 And the king commanded that all those that played upon timbrels, harps and other musical instruments should go forth with Joseph; one thousand timbrels, one thousand mecholoth, and one thousand nebalim went after him.

26 And five thousand men, with drawn swords glittering in their hands, and they went marching and playing before Joseph, and twenty thousand of the great men of the king girt with girdles of skin covered with gold, marched at the right hand of Joseph, and twenty thousand at his left, and all the women and damsels went upon the roofs or stood in the streets playing and rejoicing at Joseph, and gazed at the appearance of Joseph and at his beauty.

27 And the king's people went before him and behind him, perfuming the road with frankincense and with cassia, and with all sorts of fine perfume, and scattered myrrh and aloes along the road, and twenty men proclaimed these words before him throughout the land in a loud voice:

28 "Do you see this man whom the king has chosen to be his second? all the affairs of government shall be regulated by him, and he that transgresses his orders, or that does not bow down before him to the ground, shall die, for he rebels against the king and his second."

29 And when the heralds had ceased proclaiming, all the people of Egypt bowed down to the ground before Joseph and said, "May the king live, also may his second live;" and all the inhabitants of Egypt bowed down along the road, and when the heralds approached them, they bowed down, and they rejoiced with all sorts of timbrels, mechol and nebal before Joseph.

30 And Joseph upon his horse lifted up his eyes to heaven, and called out and said, "He raiseth the poor man from the dust, He lifteth up the needy from the dunghill. O Lord of Hosts, happy is the man who trusteth in thee."

31 And Joseph passed throughout the land of Egypt with Pharaoh's servants and officers, and they showed him the whole land of Egypt and all the king's treasures.

32 And Joseph returned and came on that day before Pharaoh, and the king gave unto Joseph a possession in the land of Egypt, a possession of fields and vineyards, and the king gave unto Joseph three thousand talents of silver and one thousand talents of gold, and onyx stones and bdellium and many gifts.

33 And on the next day the king commanded all the people of Egypt to bring unto Joseph offerings and gifts, and that he that violated the command of the king should die; and they made a high place in the street of the city, and they spread out garments there, and whoever brought anything to Joseph put it into the high place. 34 And all the people of Egypt cast something into the high place, one man a golden ear-ring, and the other rings and ear-rings, and different vessels of gold and silver work, and onyx stones and bdellium did he cast upon the high place; every one gave something of what he possessed.

35 And Joseph took all these and placed them in his treasuries, and all the officers and nobles belonging to the king exalted Joseph, and they gave him many gifts, seeing that the king had chosen him to be his second.

44 Pharaoh said to Joseph, "I am Pharaoh, and without you shall no man lift up his hand or his foot in all the land of Egypt."

[49:37 "I am Pharaoh, and beside thee none shall dare to lift up his hand or his foot to regulate my people throughout the land of Egypt."]

45 Pharaoh called Joseph's name Zaphenath-Paneah;

[49: 21 And thy name no more shall be called Joseph, but Zaphnath Paaneah shall be thy name;]

and he gave him Asenath, the daughter of Potiphera priest of On as a wife. Joseph went out over the land of Egypt.

36 And the king sent to Potiphera, the son of Ahiram priest of On, and he took his young daughter Osnath and gave her unto Joseph for a wife.

[Genesis 41:44 Pharaoh said to Joseph, "I am Pharaoh, and without you shall no man lift up his hand or his foot in all the land of Egypt."]

37 And the damsel was very comely, a virgin, one whom man had not known, and Joseph took her for a wife; and the king said unto Joseph, "I am Pharaoh, and beside thee none shall dare to lift up his hand or his foot to regulate my people throughout the land of Egypt."

46 Joseph was thirty years old when he stood before Pharaoh king of Egypt. Joseph went out from the presence of Pharaoh, and went throughout all the land of Egypt.

38 And Joseph was thirty years old when he stood before Pharaoh, and Joseph went out from before the king, and he became the king's second in Egypt.

39 And the king gave Joseph a hundred servants to attend him in his house, and Joseph also sent and purchased many servants and they remained in the house of Joseph. 40 Joseph then built for himself a very magnificent house like unto the houses of kings, before the court of the king's palace, and he made in the house a large temple, very elegant in appearance and convenient for his residence; three years was Joseph in erecting his house.

41 And Joseph made unto himself a very elegant throne of abundance of gold and silver, and he covered it with onyx stones and bdellium, and he made upon it the likeness of the whole land of Egypt, and the likeness of the river of Egypt that watereth the whole land of Egypt; and Joseph sat securely upon his throne in his house and the Lord increased Joseph's wisdom. 42 And all the inhabitants of Egypt and Pharaoh's servants and his princes loved Joseph exceedingly, for this thing was from the Lord to Joseph.

43 And Joseph had an army that made war, going out in hosts and troops to the number of forty thousand six hundred men, capable of bearing arms to assist the king and Joseph against the enemy, besides the king's officers and his servants and inhabitants of Egypt without number. 44 And Joseph gave unto his mighty men, and to all his host, shields and javelins, and caps and coats of mail and stones for slinging.

Jasher 50

1 At that time the children of Tarshish came against the sons of Ishmael, and made war with them, and the children of Tarshish spoiled the Ishmaelites for a long time. 2 And the children of Ishmael were small in number in those days, and they could not prevail over the children of Tarshish, and they were sorely oppressed.

3 And the old men of the Ishmaelites sent a record to the king of Egypt, saying, "Send I pray thee unto thy servants officers and hosts to help us to fight against the children of Tarshish, for we have been consuming away for a long time."

4 And Pharaoh sent Joseph with the mighty men and host which were with him, and also his mighty men from the king's house. 5 And they went to the land of Havilah to the children of Ishmael, to assist them against the children of Tarshish, and the children of Ishmael fought with the children of Tarshish, and Joseph smote the Tarshishites and he subdued all their land, and the children of Ishmael dwell therein unto this day.

6 And when the land of Tarshish was subdued, all the Tarshishites ran away, and came on the border of their brethren the children of Javan, and Joseph with all his mighty men and host returned to Egypt, not one man of them missing.

47 In the seven plenteous years the earth produced abundantly.

7 And at the revolution of the year, in the second year of Joseph's reigning over Egypt, the Lord gave great plenty throughout the land for seven years as Joseph had spoken, for the Lord blessed all the produce of the earth in those days for seven years, and they ate and were greatly satisfied.

48 He gathered up all the food of the seven years which were in the land of Egypt, and laid up the food in the cities: the food of the field, which was around every city, he laid up in the same.

8 And Joseph at that time had officers under him, and they collected all the food of the good years, and heaped corn year by year, and they placed it in the treasuries of Joseph.

49 Joseph laid up grain as the sand of the sea, very much, until he stopped counting, for it was without number.

9 And at any time when they gathered the food Joseph commanded that they should bring the corn in the ears, and also bring with it some of the soil of the field, that it should not spoil. 10 And Joseph did according to this year by year, and he heaped up corn like the sand of the sea for abundance, for his stores were immense and could not be numbered for abundance.

11 And also all the inhabitants of Egypt gathered all sorts of food in their stores in great abundance during the seven good years, but they did not do unto it as Joseph did.

12 And all the food which Joseph and the Egyptians had gathered during the seven years of plenty, was secured for the land in stores for the seven years of famine, for the support of the whole land. 13 And the inhabitants of Egypt filled each man his store and his concealed place with corn, to be for support during the famine.

50 To Joseph were born two sons before the year of
famine came, whom Asenath, the daughter of
Potiphera priest of On, bore to him. 51 Joseph
called the name of the firstborn Manasseh, "For",
he said, "God has made me forget all my toil, and all
my father's house." 52 The name of the second, he
called Ephraim: "For God has made me fruitful in
the land of my affliction."

53 The seven years of plenty, that were in the land
of Egypt, came to an end. 54 The seven years of
famine began to come, just as Joseph had said.
There was famine in all lands, but in all the land of
Egypt there was bread.

55 When all the land of Egypt was famished, the
people cried to Pharaoh for bread,

14 And Joseph placed all the food that he had gathered in all the cities of Egypt, and he closed all the stores and placed sentinels over them.

15 And Joseph's wife Osnath the daughter of Potiphera bare him two sons, Manasseh and Ephraim, and Joseph was thirty-four years old when he begat them.

16 And the lads grew up and they went in his ways
and in his instructions, they did not deviate from
the way which their father taught them, either to
the right or left. 17 And the Lord was with the lads,
and they grew up and had understanding and skill
in all wisdom and in all the affairs of government,
and all the king's officers and his great men of the
inhabitants of Egypt exalted the lads, and they were
brought up amongst the king's children.

18 And the seven years of plenty that were throughout the land were at an end, and the seven years of famine came after them as Joseph had spoken, and the famine was throughout the land.

19 And all the people of Egypt saw that the famine had commenced in the land of Egypt, and all the people of Egypt opened their stores of corn for the famine prevailed over them.

20 And they found all the food that was in their stores, full of vermin and not fit to eat, and the famine prevailed throughout the land, and all the inhabitants of Egypt came and cried before Pharaoh, for the famine was heavy upon them.

21 And they said unto Pharaoh, "Give food unto thy servants, and wherefore shall we die through hunger before thy eyes, even we and our little ones?"

22 And Pharaoh answered them, saying, "And wherefore do you cry unto me? did not Joseph command that the corn should be laid up during the seven years of plenty for the years of famine? and wherefore did you not hearken to his voice?"

23 And the people of Egypt answered the king, saying, "As thy soul liveth, our lord, thy servants have done all that Joseph ordered, for thy servants also gathered in all the produce of their fields during the seven years of plenty and laid it in the stores unto this day. 24 And when the famine prevailed over thy servants we opened our stores, and behold all our produce was filled with vermin and was not fit for food."

and Pharaoh said to all the Egyptians, "Go to Joseph. What he says to you, do."

25 And when the king heard all that had befallen the inhabitants of Egypt, the king was greatly afraid on account of the famine, and he was much terrified; and the king answered the people of Egypt, saying, "Since all this has happened unto you, go unto Joseph, do whatever he shall say unto you, transgress not his commands."

26 And all the people of Egypt went forth and came unto Joseph, and said unto him, "Give unto us food, and wherefore shall we die before thee through hunger? For we gathered in our produce during the seven years as thou didst command, and we put it in store, and thus has it befallen us."

56 The famine was over all the surface of the earth.

Joseph opened all the store houses, and sold to the Egyptians. The famine was severe in the land of Egypt.

27 And when Joseph heard all the words of the people of Egypt and what had befallen them, Joseph opened all his stores of the produce and he sold it unto the people of Egypt.

28 And the famine prevailed throughout the land, and the famine was in all countries, but in the land of Egypt there was produce for sale.

29 And all the inhabitants of Egypt came unto Joseph to buy corn, for the famine prevailed over them, and all their corn was spoiled, and Joseph daily sold it to all the people of Egypt.

57 All countries came into Egypt, to Joseph, to buy grain, because the famine was severe in all the earth.

30 And all the inhabitants of the land of Canaan and the Philistines, and those beyond the Jordan, and the children of the east and all the cities of the lands far and nigh heard that there was corn in Egypt, and they all came to Egypt to buy corn, for the famine prevailed over them.

31 And Joseph opened the stores of corn and placed officers over them, and they daily stood and sold to all that came.

32 And Joseph knew that his brethren also would come to Egypt to buy corn, for the famine prevailed throughout the earth. And Joseph commanded all his people that they should cause it to be proclaimed throughout the land of Egypt, saying,

33 "It is the pleasure of the king, of his second and of their great men, that any person who wishes to buy corn in Egypt shall not send his servants to Egypt to purchase, but his sons, and also any Egyptian or Canaanite, who shall come from any of the stores from buying corn in Egypt, and shall go and sell it throughout the land, he shall die, for no one shall buy but for the support of his household.
34 And any man leading two or three beasts shall die, for a man shall only lead his own beast."

35 And Joseph placed sentinels at the gates of Egypt, and commanded them, saying, "Any person who may come to buy corn, suffer him not to enter until his name, and the name of his father, and the name of his father's father be written down, and whatever is written by day, send their names unto me in the evening that I may know their names."
36 And Joseph placed officers throughout the land of Egypt, and he commanded them to do all these things.

37 And Joseph did all these things, and made these statutes, in order that he might know when his brethren should come to Egypt to buy corn; and Joseph's people caused it daily to be proclaimed in Egypt according to these words and statutes which Joseph had commanded.

38 And all the inhabitants of the east and west country, and of all the earth, heard of the statutes and regulations which Joseph had enacted in Egypt, and the inhabitants of the extreme parts of the earth came and they bought corn in Egypt day after day, and then went away.

39 And all the officers of Egypt did as Joseph had commanded, and all that came to Egypt to buy corn, the gate keepers would write their names, and their fathers' names, and daily bring them in the evening before Joseph.

Genesis 42

1 Now Jacob saw that there was grain in Egypt, and Jacob said to his sons, "Why do you look at one another?" 2 He said, "Behold, I have heard that there is grain in Egypt. Go down there, and buy for us from there, so that we may live, and not die."

3 Joseph's ten brothers went down to buy grain from Egypt.

4 But Jacob didn't send Benjamin, Joseph's brother, with his brothers; for he said, "Lest perhaps harm happen to him."

Jasher 51

1 And Jacob afterward heard that there was corn in Egypt, and he called unto his sons to go to Egypt to buy corn, for upon them also did the famine prevail, and he called unto his sons, saying, 2 "Behold I hear that there is corn in Egypt, and all the people of the earth go there to purchase, now therefore why will you show yourselves satisfied before the whole earth? go you also down to Egypt and buy us a little corn amongst those that come there, that we may not die."

3 And the sons of Jacob hearkened to the voice of their father, and they rose up to go down to Egypt in order to buy corn amongst the rest that came there.

4 And Jacob their father commanded them, saying, "When you come into the city do not enter together in one gate, on account of the inhabitants of the land."

5 And the sons of Jacob went forth and they went to Egypt, and the sons of Jacob did all as their father had commanded them, and Jacob did not send Benjamin, for he said, "Lest an accident might befall him on the road like his brother;" and ten of Jacob's sons went forth.

6 And whilst the sons of Jacob were going on the road, they repented of what they had done to Joseph, and they spoke to each other, saying, "We know that our brother Joseph went down to Egypt, and now we will seek him where we go, and if we find him we will take him from his master for a ransom, and if not, by force, and we will die for him."

7 And the sons of Jacob agreed to this thing and strengthened themselves on account of Joseph, to deliver him from the hand of his master, and the sons of Jacob went to Egypt; and when they came near to Egypt they separated from each other, and they came through ten gates of Egypt, and the gate keepers wrote their names on that day, and brought them to Joseph in the evening.

8 And Joseph read the names from the hand of the gate-keepers of the city, and he found that his brethren had entered at the ten gates of the city, and Joseph at that time commanded that it should be proclaimed throughout the land of Egypt, saying,
9 "Go forth all ye store guards, close all the corn stores and let only one remain open, that those who come may purchase from it." 10 And all the officers of Joseph did so at that time, and they closed all the stores and left only one open.

11 And Joseph gave the written names of his brethren to him that was set over the open store, and he said unto him, "Whosoever shall come to thee to buy corn, ask his name, and when men of these names shall come before thee, seize them and send them, and they did so."

5 The sons of Israel came to buy among those who came, for the famine was in the land of Canaan.

12 And when the sons of Jacob came into the city, they joined together in the city to seek Joseph before they bought themselves corn.

13 And they went to the walls of the harlots, and they sought Joseph in the walls of the harlots for three days, for they thought that Joseph would come in the walls of the harlots, for Joseph was very comely and well favored, and the sons of Jacob sought Joseph for three days, and they could not find him.

14 And the man who was set over the open store sought for those names which Joseph had given him, and he did not find them. 15 And he sent to Joseph, saying, "These three days have passed, and those men whose names thou didst give unto me have not come;" and Joseph sent servants to seek the men in all Egypt, and to bring them before Joseph.

16 And Joseph's servants went and came into Egypt and could not find them, and went to Goshen and they were not there, and then went to the city of Rameses and could not find them.

17 And Joseph continued to send sixteen servants to seek his brothers, and they went and spread themselves in the four corners of the city, and four of the servants went into the house of the harlots, and they found the ten men there seeking their brother.

18 And those four men took them and brought them before him, and they bowed down to him to the ground, and Joseph was sitting upon his throne in his temple, clothed with princely garments, and upon his head was a large crown of gold, and all the mighty men were sitting around him.

6 Joseph was the governor over the land. It was he who sold to all the people of the land. Joseph's brothers came, and bowed themselves down to him with their faces to the earth.

19 And the sons of Jacob saw Joseph, and his figure and comeliness and dignity of countenance seemed wonderful in their eyes, and they again bowed down to him to the ground.

7 Joseph saw his brothers, and he recognized them, but acted like a stranger to them, and spoke roughly with them. He said to them, "Where did you come from?" They said, "From the land of Canaan to buy food."

20 And Joseph saw his brethren, and he knew them, but they knew him not, for Joseph was very great in their eyes, therefore they knew him not. 21 And Joseph spoke to them, saying, "From whence come ye?" and they all answered and said, "Thy servants have come from the land of Canaan to buy corn, for the famine prevails throughout the earth, and thy servants heard that there was corn in Egypt, so they have come amongst the other comers to buy corn for their support."

8 Joseph recognized his brothers, but they didn't recognize him.

9 Joseph remembered the dreams which he dreamed about them, and said to them, "You are spies! You have come to see the nakedness of the land."

22 And Joseph answered them, saying, "If you have come to purchase as you say, why do you come through ten gates of the city? It can only be that you have come to spy through the land."

10 They said to him, "No, my lord, but your servants have come to buy food. 11 We are all one man's sons; we are honest men. Your servants are not spies."

3 And they all together answered Joseph, and said, "Not so my lord, we are right, thy servants are not spies, but we have come to buy corn, for thy servants are all brothers, the sons of one man in the land of Canaan, and our father commanded us, saying, When you come to the city do not enter together at one gate on account of the inhabitants of the land."

12 He said to them, "No, but you have come to see the nakedness of the land!"

24 And Joseph again answered them and said, "That is the thing which I spoke unto you, you have come to spy through the land, therefore you all came through ten gates of the city; you have come to see the nakedness of the land.

25 "Surely every one that cometh to buy corn goeth his way, and you are already three days in the land, and what do you do in the walls of harlots in which you have been for these three days? Surely spies do like unto these things."

13 They said, “We, your servants, are twelve brothers, the sons of one man in the land of Canaan; and behold, the youngest is today with our father, and one is no more.”

26 And they said unto Joseph, "Far be it from our lord to speak thus, for we are twelve brothers, the sons of our father Jacob, in the land of Canaan, the son of Isaac, the son of Abraham, the Hebrew, and behold the youngest is with our father this day in the land of Canaan, and one is not, for he was lost from us, and we thought perhaps he might be in this land, so we are seeking him throughout the land, and have come even to the houses of harlots to seek him there."

27 And Joseph said unto them, "And have you then sought him throughout the earth, that there only remained Egypt for you to seek him in? And what also should your brother do in the houses of harlots, although he were in Egypt? have you not said, That you are from the sons of Isaac, the son of Abraham, and what shall the sons of Jacob do then in the houses of harlots?"

28 And they said unto him, "Because we heard that Ishmaelites stole him from us, and it was told unto us that they sold him in Egypt, and thy servant, our brother, is very comely and well favored, so we thought he would surely be in the houses of harlots, therefore thy servants went there to seek him and give ransom for him."

29 And Joseph still answered them, saying, "Surely you speak falsely and utter lies, to say of yourselves that you are the sons of Abraham; as Pharaoh liveth you are spies, therefore have you come to the houses of harlots that you should not be known."

30 And Joseph said unto them, "And now if you find him, and his master requireth of you a great price, will you give it for him?" and they said, "It shall be given."

31 And he said unto them, "And if his master will not consent to part with him for a great price, what will you do unto him on his account?" and they answered him, saying, "If he will not give him unto us we will slay him, and take our brother and go away."

14 Joseph said to them, "It is like I told you, saying,
'You are spies!'

32 And Joseph said unto them, "That is the thing
which I have spoken to you; you are spies, for you
are come to slay the inhabitants of the land, for we
heard that two of your brethren smote all the
inhabitants of Shechem, in the land of Canaan, on
account of your sister, and you now come to do the
like in Egypt on account of your brother.

15 "By this you shall be tested. By the life of
Pharaoh, you shall not go out from here, unless
your youngest brother comes here. 16 Send one of
you, and let him get your brother, and you shall be
bound, that your words may be tested, whether
there is truth in you, or else by the life of Pharaoh
surely you are spies."

33 "Only hereby shall I know that you are true men;
if you will send home one from amongst you to
fetch your youngest brother from your father, and
to bring him here unto me, and by doing this thing I
will know that you are right."

17 He put them all together into custody for three
days.

34 And Joseph called to seventy of his mighty men,
and he said unto them, "Take these men and bring
them into the ward." 35 And the mighty men took
the ten men, they laid hold of them and put them
into the ward, and they were in the ward three
days.

18 Joseph said to them the third day, "Do this, and
live, for I fear God. 19 If you are honest men, then
let one of your brothers be bound in your prison;
but you go, carry grain for the famine of your
houses. 20 Bring your youngest brother to me; so
will your words be verified, and you won't die."
They did so.

36 And on the third day Joseph had them brought
out of the ward, and he said unto them, "Do this for
yourselves if you be true men, so that you may live,
one of your brethren shall be confined in the ward
whilst you go and take home the corn for your
household to the land of Canaan, and fetch your
youngest brother, and bring him here unto me, that
I may know that you are true men when you do this
thing."

21 They said to one another, "We are certainly
guilty concerning our brother, in that we saw the
distress of his soul, when he begged us, and we
wouldn't listen. Therefore this distress has come
upon us."

22 Reuben answered them, saying, "Didn't I tell
you, saying, 'Don't sin against the child,' and you
wouldn't listen? Therefore also, behold, his blood is
required." 23 They didn't know that Joseph
understood them; for there was an interpreter
between them.

24 He turned himself away from them, and wept. Then he returned to them, and spoke to them,

37 And Joseph went out from them and came into the chamber, and wept a great weeping, for his pity was excited for them, and he washed his face, and returned to them again, and he took Simeon from them and ordered him to be bound, but Simeon was not willing to be done so, for he was a very powerful man and they could not bind him.

38 And Joseph called unto his mighty men and seventy valiant men came before him with drawn swords in their hands, and the sons of Jacob were terrified at them.

39 And Joseph said unto them, "Seize this man and confine him in prison until his brethren come to him," and Joseph's valiant men hastened and they all laid hold of Simeon to bind him, and Simeon gave a loud and terrible shriek and the cry was
heard at a distance. 40 And all the valiant men of
Joseph were terrified at the sound of the shriek, that they fell upon their faces, and they were greatly afraid and fled.

41 And all the men that were with Joseph fled, for they were greatly afraid of their lives, and only Joseph and Manasseh his son remained there, and Manassah the son of Joseph saw the strength of
Simeon, and he was exceedingly wroth. 42 And
Manassah the son of Joseph rose up to Simeon, and Manassah smote Simeon a heavy blow with his fist against the back of his neck, and Simeon was stilled of his rage.

and took Simeon from among them, and bound him before their eyes.

43 And Manassah laid hold of Simeon and he seized him violently and he bound him and brought him into the house of confinement, and all the sons of Jacob were astonished at the act of the youth.

44 And Simeon said unto his brethren, "None of you must say that this is the smiting of an Egyptian, but it is the smiting of the house of my father."

25 Then Joseph gave a command to fill their bags with grain, and to restore each man's money into his sack, and to give them food for the way. So it was done to them.

45 And after this Joseph ordered him to be called who was set over the storehouse, to fill their sacks with corn as much as they could carry, and to restore every man's money into his sack, and to give them provision for the road, and thus did he unto them.

46 And Joseph commanded them, saying, "Take heed lest you transgress my orders to bring your brother as I have told you, and it shall be when you bring your brother hither unto me, then will I know that you are true men, and you shall traffic in the land, and I will restore unto you your brother, and you shall return in peace to your father." 47 And they all answered and said, "According as our lord speaketh so will we do," and they bowed down to him to the ground.

26 They loaded their donkeys with their grain, and departed from there. 27 As one of them opened his sack to give his donkey food in the lodging place, he saw his money. Behold, it was in the mouth of his sack.

48 And every man lifted his corn upon his ass, and they went out to go to the land of Canaan to their father; and they came to the inn and Levi spread his sack to give provender to his ass, when he saw and behold his money in full weight was still in his sack.

28 He said to his brothers, “My money is restored! Behold, it is in my sack!” Their hearts failed them, and they turned trembling to one another, saying, “What is this that God has done to us?”

49 And the man was greatly afraid, and he said unto his brethren, "My money is restored, and lo, it is even in my sack," and the men were greatly afraid, and they said, "What is this that God hath done unto us?"

50 And they all said, "And where is the Lord's kindness with our fathers, with Abraham, Isaac, end Jacob, that the Lord has this day delivered us into the hands of the king of Egypt to contrive against us?"

51 And Judah said unto them, "Surely we are guilty sinners before the Lord our God in having sold our brother, our own flesh, and wherefore do you say, 'Where is the Lord's kindness with our fathers?'"

52 And Reuben said unto them, "Said I not unto you, 'Do not sin against the lad,' and you would not listen to me? Now God requireth him from us, and how dare you say, 'Where is the Lord's kindness with our fathers,' whilst you have sinned unto the Lord?"

29 They came to Jacob their father, to the land of Canaan,

53 And they tarried over night in that place, and they rose up early in the morning and laded their asses with their corn, and they led them and went on and came to their father's house in the land of Canaan.

and told him all that had happened to them, saying, 30 "The man, the lord of the land, spoke roughly with us, and took us for spies of the country. 31 We said to him, 'We are honest men. We are no spies. 32 We are twelve brothers, sons of our father; one is no more, and the youngest is today with our father in the land of Canaan.' 33 The man, the lord of the land, said to us, 'By this I will know that you are honest men: leave one of your brothers with me, and take grain for the famine of your houses, and go your way. 34 Bring your youngest brother to me. Then I will know that you are not spies, but that you are honest men. So I will deliver your brother to you, and you shall trade in the land.'"

54 And Jacob and his household went out to meet his sons, and Jacob saw and behold their brother Simeon was not with them, and Jacob said unto his sons, "Where is your brother Simeon, whom I do not see?" and his sons told him all that had befallen them in Egypt.

35 As they emptied their sacks, behold, each man's bundle of money was in his sack. When they and their father saw their bundles of money, they were afraid.

36 Jacob, their father, said to them, "You have bereaved me of my children! Joseph is no more, Simeon is no more, and you want to take Benjamin away. All these things are against me."

Jasher 52

1 And they entered their house, and every man opened his sack and they saw and behold every man's bundle of money was there, at which they and their father were greatly terrified.

2 And Jacob said unto them, "What is this that you have done to me? I sent your brother Joseph to inquire after your welfare and you said unto me. A wild beast did devour him. 3 And Simeon went with you to buy food and you say the king of Egypt hath confined him in prison, and you wish to take Benjamin to cause his death also, and bring down my grey hairs with sorrow to the grave on account of Benjamin and his brother Joseph. 4 Now therefore my son shall not go down with you, for his brother is dead and he is left alone, and mischief may befall him by the way in which you go, as it befell his brother."

37 Reuben spoke to his father, saying, "Kill my two sons, if I don't bring him to you. Entrust him to my care, and I will bring him to you again." 38 He said, "My son shall not go down with you; for his brother is dead, and he only is left. If harm happens to him along the way in which you go, then you will bring down my gray hairs with sorrow to Sheol."

5 And Reuben said unto his father, "Thou shalt slay my two sons if I do not bring thy son and place him before thee;" and Jacob said unto his sons, "Abide ye here and do not go down to Egypt, for my son shall not go down with you to Egypt, nor die like his brother."

6 And Judah said unto them, "Refrain ye from him until the corn is finished, and he will then say, 'Take down your brother,' when he will find his own life and the life of his household in danger from the famine."

Genesis 43

1 The famine was severe in the land. 2 When they had eaten up the grain which they had brought out of Egypt, their father said to them, "Go again, buy us a little more food."

7 And in those days the famine was sore throughout the land, and all the people of the earth went and came to Egypt to buy food, for the famine prevailed greatly amongst them, and the sons of Jacob remained in Canaan a year and two months until their corn was finished.

8 And it came to pass after their corn was finished, the whole household of Jacob was pinched with hunger, and all the infants of the sons of Jacob came together and they approached Jacob, and they all surrounded him, and they said unto him, "Give unto us bread, and wherefore shall we all perish through hunger in thy presence?"

9 Jacob heard the words of his son's children, and he wept a great weeping, and his pity was roused for them, and Jacob called unto his sons and they all came and sat before him.

10 And Jacob said unto them, "And have you not seen how your children have been weeping over me this day, saying, 'Give unto us bread, and there is none?' now therefore return and buy for us a little food."

3 Judah spoke to him, saying, "The man solemnly warned us, saying, 'You shall not see my face, unless your brother is with you.' 4 If you'll send our brother with us, we'll go down and buy you food, 5 but if you'll not send him, we'll not go down, for the man said to us, 'You shall not see my face, unless your brother is with you.'"

11 And Judah answered and said unto his father, "If thou wilt send our brother with us we will go down and buy corn for thee, and if thou wilt not send him then we will not go down, for surely the king of Egypt particularly enjoined us, saying, 'You shall not see my face unless your brother be with you,' for the king of Egypt is a strong and mighty king, and behold if we shall go to him without our brother we shall all be put to death.

12 "Dost thou not know and hast thou not heard that this king is very powerful and wise, and there is not like unto him in all the earth? Behold we have seen all the kings of the earth and we have not seen one like that king, the king of Egypt; surely amongst all the kings of the earth there is none greater than Abimelech king of the Philistines, yet the king of Egypt is greater and mightier than he, and Abimelech can only be compared to one of his officers.

13 "Father, thou hast not seen his palace and his throne, and all his servants standing before him; thou hast not seen that king upon his throne in his pomp and royal appearance, dressed in his kingly robes with a large golden crown upon his head; thou hast not seen the honor and glory which God has given unto him, for there is not like unto him in all the earth. 14 Father, thou hast not seen the wisdom, the understanding and the knowledge which God has given in his heart, nor heard his sweet voice when he spake unto us.

15 "We know not, father, who made him acquainted with our names and all that befell us, yet he asked also after thee, saying, 'Is your father still living, and is it well with him?' 16 Thou hast not seen the affairs of the government of Egypt regulated by him, without inquiring of Pharaoh his lord; thou hast not seen the awe and fear which he impressed upon all the Egyptians.

17 "And also when we went from him, we threatened to do unto Egypt like unto the rest of the cities of the Amorites, and we were exceedingly wroth against all his words which he spoke concerning us as spies, and now when we shall again come before him his terror will fall upon us all, and not one of us will be able to speak to him either a little or a great thing. 18 Now therefore father, send we pray thee the lad with us, and we will go down and buy thee food for our support, and not die through hunger?"

6 Israel said, "Why did you treat me so badly, telling the man that you had another brother?"

And Jacob said, "Why have you dealt so ill with me to tell the king you had a brother? What is this thing that you have done unto me?"

7 They said, "The man asked directly concerning ourselves, and concerning our relatives, saying, 'Is your father still alive? Have you another brother?' We just answered his questions. Is there any way we could know that he would say, 'Bring your brother down?'"

8 Judah said to Israel, his father, "Send the boy with me, and we'll get up and go, so that we may live, and not die, both we, and you, and also our little ones. 9 I'll be collateral for him. From my hand will you require him. If I don't bring him to you, and set him before you, then let me bear the blame forever,

19 And Judah said unto Jacob his father, "Give the lad into my care and we will rise up and go down to Egypt and buy corn, and then return, and it shall be when we return if the lad be not with us, then let me bear thy blame forever.

Genesis 43

10 "for if we hadn't delayed, surely we would have returned a second time by now."

11 Their father, Israel, said to them, "If it must be
so, then do this. Take from the choice fruits of the
land in your bags, and carry down a present for the
man, a little balm, a little honey, spices and myrrh,
nuts, and almonds; 12 and take double money in
your hand, and take back the money that was
returned in the mouth of your sacks. Perhaps it was
an oversight. 13 Take your brother also, get up, and
return to the man. 14 May God Almighty give you
mercy before the man, that he may release to you
your other brother and Benjamin. If I am bereaved
of my children, I am bereaved."

Jasher 52

20 "Hast thou seen all our infants weeping over thee through hunger and there is no power in thy hand to satisfy them? now let thy pity be roused for them and send our brother with us and we will go.

21 "For how will the Lord's kindness to our ancestors be manifested to thee when thou sayest that the king of Egypt will take away thy son? as the Lord liveth I will not leave him until I bring him and place him before thee; but pray for us unto the Lord, that he may deal kindly with us, to cause us to be received favorably and kindly before the king of Egypt and his men, for had we not delayed surely now we had returned a second time with thy son."

22 And Jacob said unto his sons, "I trust in the Lord God that he may deliver you and give you favor in the sight of the king of Egypt, and in the sight of all his men.

23 "Now therefore rise up and go to the man, and take for him in your hands a present from what can be obtained in the land and bring it before him, and may the Almighty God give you mercy before him that he may send Benjamin and Simeon your brethren with you."

24 And all the men rose up, and they took their brother Benjamin, and they took in their hands a large present of the best of the land, and they also took a double portion of silver.

25 And Jacob strictly commanded his sons concerning Benjamin, Saying, "Take heed of him in the way in which you are going, and do not separate yourselves from him in the road, neither in Egypt."

26 And Jacob rose up from his sons and spread forth his hands and he prayed unto the Lord on account of his sons, saying, "O Lord God of heaven and earth, remember thy covenant with our father Abraham, remember it with my father Isaac and deal kindly with my sons and deliver them not into the hands of the king of Egypt; do it I pray thee O God for the sake of thy mercies and redeem all my children and rescue them from Egyptian power, and send them their two brothers."

27 And all the wives of the sons of Jacob and their children lifted up their eyes to heaven and they all wept before the Lord, and cried unto him to deliver their fathers from the hand of the king of Egypt.

28 And Jacob wrote a record to the king of Egypt and gave it into the hand of Judah and into the hands of his sons for the king of Egypt, saying, 29 "From thy servant Jacob, son of Isaac, son of Abraham the Hebrew, the prince of God, to the powerful and wise king, the revealer of secrets, king of Egypt, greeting.

30 "Be it known to my lord the king of Egypt, the famine was sore upon us in the land of Canaan, and I sent my sons to thee to buy us a little food from thee for our support. 31 For my sons surrounded me and I being very old cannot see with my eyes, for my eyes have become very heavy through age, as well as with daily weeping for my son, for Joseph who was lost from before me, and I commanded my sons that they should not enter the gates of the city when they came to Egypt, on account of the inhabitants of the land.

32 "And I also commanded them to go about Egypt
to seek for my son Joseph, perhaps they might find
him there, and they did so, and thou didst consider
them as spies of the land. 33 Have we not heard
concerning thee that thou didst interpret Pharaoh's
dream and didst speak truly unto him? how then
dost thou not know in thy wisdom whether my sons
are spies or not?

34 "Now therefore, my lord and king, behold I have
sent my son before thee, as thou didst speak unto
my sons; I beseech thee to put thy eyes upon him
until he is returned to me in peace with his
brethren. 35 For dost thou not know, or hast thou
not heard that which our God did unto Pharaoh
when he took my mother Sarah, and what he did
unto Abimelech king of the Philistines on account of
her, and also what our father Abraham did unto the
nine kings of Elam, how he smote them all with a
few men that were with him?

36 "And also what my two sons Simeon and Levi did
unto the eight cities of the Amorites, how they
destroyed them on account of their sister Dinah?
37 And also on account of their brother Benjamin
they consoled themselves for the loss of his brother
Joseph; what will they then do for him when they
see the hand of any people prevailing over them,
for his sake?

38 "Dost thou not know, O king of Egypt, that the
power of God is with us, and that also God ever
heareth our prayers and forsaketh us not all the
days? 39 And when my sons told me of thy dealings
with them, I called not unto the Lord on account of
thee, for then thou wouldst have perished with thy
men before my son Benjamin came before thee,
but I thought that as Simeon my son was in thy
house, perhaps thou mightest deal kindly with him,
therefore I did not this thing unto thee.

40 "Now therefore behold Benjamin my son cometh unto thee with my sons, take heed of him and put thy eyes upon him, and then will God place
his eyes over thee and throughout thy kingdom. 41
Now I have told thee all that is in my heart, and behold my sons are coming to thee with their brother, examine the face of the whole earth for their sake and send them back in peace with their brethren."

42 And Jacob gave the record to his sons into the care of Judah to give it unto the king of Egypt.

15 The men took that present, and they took double money in their hand, and Benjamin; and got up, went down to Egypt, and stood before Joseph.

Jasher 53

1 And the sons of Jacob rose up and took Benjamin and the whole of the presents, and they went and came to Egypt and they stood before Joseph.

16 When Joseph saw Benjamin with them,

2 And Joseph beheld his brother Benjamin with them and he saluted them, and these men came to Joseph's house.

he said to the steward of his house, "Bring the men into the house, and butcher an animal, and prepare; for the men will dine with me at noon."

3 And Joseph commanded the superintendent of his house to give to his brethren to eat, and he did so unto them.

17 The man did as Joseph commanded, and the man brought the men to Joseph's house.

18 The men were afraid, because they were brought to Joseph's house; and they said, "Because of the money that was returned in our sacks at the first time, we're brought in; that he may seek occasion against us, attack us, and seize us as slaves, along with our donkeys."

19 They came near to the steward of Joseph's house, and they spoke to him at the door of the
house, 20 and said, "Oh, my lord, we indeed came
down the first time to buy food. 21 When we came
to the lodging place, we opened our sacks, and behold, each man's money was in the mouth of his sack, our money in full weight. We have brought it
back in our hand. 22 We have brought down other
money in our hand to buy food. We don't know who put our money in our sacks."

4 And at noon time Joseph sent for the men to come before him with Benjamin, and the men told the superintendent of Joseph's house concerning the silver that was returned in their sacks,

23 He said, "Peace be to you. Don't be afraid. Your God, and the God of your father, has given you treasure in your sacks. I received your money." He brought Simeon out to them.

and he said unto them, "It will be well with you, fear not," and he brought their brother Simeon unto them.

5 And Simeon said unto his brethren, "The lord of the Egyptians has acted very kindly unto me, he did not keep me bound, as you saw with your eyes, for when you went out from the city he let me free and dealt kindly with me in his house."

6 And Judah took Benjamin by the hand, and they came before Joseph, and they bowed down to him to the ground.

24 The man brought the men into Joseph's house, and gave them water, and they washed their feet. He gave their donkeys fodder.

25 They prepared the present for Joseph's coming at noon, for they heard that they should eat bread there.

26 When Joseph came home, they brought him the present which was in their hand into the house, and bowed themselves down to him to the earth. 27 He asked them of their welfare, and said, "Is your father well, the old man of whom you spoke? Is he yet alive?" 28 They said, "Your servant, our father, is well. He is still alive." They bowed down humbly.

7 And the men gave the present unto Joseph and they all sat before him, and Joseph said unto them, "Is it well with you, is it well with your children, is it well with your aged father?" and they said, "It is well," and Judah took the record which Jacob had sent and gave it into the hand of Joseph.

8 And Joseph read the letter and knew his father's writing, and he wished to weep and he went into an inner room and he wept a great weeping; and he went out.

29 He lifted up his eyes, and saw Benjamin, his brother, his mother's son, and said, "Is this your youngest brother, of whom you spoke to me?" He said, "God be gracious to you, my son."

9 And he lifted up his eyes and beheld his brother Benjamin, and he said, "Is this your brother of whom you spoke unto me?" And Benjamin approached Joseph, and Joseph placed his hand upon his head and he said unto him, "May God be gracious unto thee my son."

30 Joseph hurried, for his heart yearned over his brother; and he sought a place to weep. He entered into his room, and wept there. 31 He washed his face, and came out. He controlled himself, and said, "Serve the meal."

10 And when Joseph saw his brother, the son of his mother, he again wished to weep, and he entered the chamber, and he wept there, and he washed his face, and went out and refrained from weeping, and he said, "Prepare food."

11 And Joseph had a cup from which he drank, and it was of silver beautifully inlaid with onyx stones and bdellium, and Joseph struck the cup in the sight of his brethren whilst they were sitting to eat with him.

32 They served him by himself, and them by themselves, and the Egyptians, that ate with him, by themselves, because the Egyptians don't eat bread with the Hebrews, for that is an abomination to the Egyptians.

12 And Joseph said unto the men, "I know by this cup that Reuben the first born, Simeon and Levi and Judah, Issachar and Zebulun are children from one mother, seat yourselves to eat according to your births."

33 They sat before him, the firstborn according to his birthright, and the youngest according to his youth, and the men marveled one with another.

13 And he also placed the others according to their births, and he said, "I know that this your youngest brother has no brother, and I, like him, have no brother, he shall therefore sit down to eat with
me." 14 And Benjamin went up before Joseph and
sat upon the throne, and the men beheld the acts of Joseph, and they were astonished at them;

34 He sent portions to them from before him, but Benjamin's portion was five times as much as any of theirs.

and the men ate and drank at that time with Joseph, and he then gave presents unto them, and Joseph gave one gift unto Benjamin, and Manasseh and Ephraim saw the acts of their father, and they also gave presents unto him, and Osnath gave him one present, and they were five presents in the hand of Benjamin.

15 And Joseph brought them out wine to drink, and they would not drink, and they said, "From the day on which Joseph was lost we have not drunk wine, nor eaten any delicacies."

They drank, and were merry with him.

16 And Joseph swore unto them, and he pressed them hard, and they drank plentifully with him on that day, and Joseph afterward turned to his brother Benjamin to speak with him, and Benjamin was still sitting upon the throne before Joseph.

17 And Joseph said unto him, "Hast thou begotten any children?" and he said, "Thy servant has ten sons, and these are their names, Bela, Becher, Ashbal, Gera, Naaman, Achi, Rosh, Mupim, Chupim, and Ord, and I called their names after my brother whom I have not seen."

18 And he ordered them to bring before him his map of the stars, whereby Joseph knew all the times, and Joseph said unto Benjamin, "I have heard that the Hebrews are acquainted with all wisdom, dost thou know anything of this?"

19 And Benjamin said, "Thy servant is knowing also in all the wisdom which my father taught me," and Joseph said unto Benjamin, "Look now at this instrument and understand where thy brother Joseph is in Egypt, who you said went down to Egypt."

20 And Benjamin beheld that instrument with the map of the stars of heaven, and he was wise and looked therein to know where his brother was, and Benjamin divided the whole land of Egypt into four divisions, and he found that he who was sitting upon the throne before him was his brother Joseph, and Benjamin wondered greatly, and when Joseph saw that his brother Benjamin was so much astonished, he said unto Benjamin, "What hast thou seen, and why art thou astonished?"

21 And Benjamin said unto Joseph, "I can see by this that Joseph my brother sitteth here with me upon the throne," and Joseph said unto him, "I am Joseph thy brother, reveal not this thing unto thy brethren; behold I will send thee with them when they go away, and I will command them to be brought back again into the city, and I will take thee away from them.

22 "And if they dare their lives and fight for thee, then shall I know that they have repented of what they did unto me, and I will make myself known to them, and if they forsake thee when I take thee, then shalt thou remain with me, and I will wrangle with them, and they shall go away, and I will not become known to them."

Genesis 44

1 He commanded the steward of his house, saying, "Fill the men's sacks with food, as much as they can carry, and put each man's money in his sack's mouth. 2 Put my cup, the silver cup, in the sack's mouth of the youngest, with his grain money." He did according to the word that Joseph had spoken.

23 At that time Joseph commanded his officer to fill their sacks with food, and to put each man's money into his sack, and to put the cup in the sack of Benjamin, and to give them provision for the road, and they did so unto them.

3 As soon as the morning was light, the men were sent away, they and their donkeys. 4 When they had gone out of the city, and were not yet far off, Joseph said to his steward, "Up, follow after the men. When you overtake them, ask them, 'Why have you rewarded evil for good? 5 Isn't this that from which my lord drinks, and by which he indeed divines? You have done evil in so doing.'"

24 And on the next day the men rose up early in the morning, and they loaded their asses with their corn, and they went forth with Benjamin, and they went to the land of Canaan with their brother Benjamin. 25 They had not gone far from Egypt when Joseph commanded him that was set over his house, saying, "Rise, pursue these men before they get too far from Egypt, and say unto them, 'Why have you stolen my master's cup?'"

6 He overtook them, and he spoke these words to them. 7 They said to him, "Why does my lord speak such words as these? Far be it from your servants that they should do such a thing! 8 Behold, the money, which we found in our sacks' mouths, we brought again to you out of the land of Canaan. How then should we steal silver or gold out of your lord's house? 9 With whomever of your servants it is found, let him die, and we also will be my lord's slaves."

26 And Joseph's officer rose up and he reached them, and he spoke unto them all the words of Joseph; and when they heard this thing they became exceedingly wroth, and they said, "He with whom thy master's cup shall be found shall die, and we will also become slaves."

10 He said, "Now also let it be according to your words: He with whom it is found will be my slave; and you will be blameless."

11 Then they hurried, and each man took his sack down to the ground, and each man opened his sack. 12 He searched, beginning with the oldest, and ending at the youngest. The cup was found in Benjamin's sack. 13 Then they tore their clothes, and each man loaded his donkey, and returned to the city.

27 And they hastened and each man brought down his sack from his ass, and they looked in their bags and the cup was found in Benjamin's bag, and they all tore their garments and they returned to the city, and they smote Benjamin in the road, continually smiting him until he came into the city, and they stood before Joseph.

28 And Judah's anger was kindled, and he said, "This man has only brought me back to destroy Egypt this day."

14 Judah and his brothers came to Joseph's house, and he was still there. They fell on the ground before him.

29 And the men came to Joseph's house, and they found Joseph sitting upon his throne, and all the mighty men standing at his right and left.

15 Joseph said to them, "What deed is this that you have done? Don't you know that such a man as I can indeed divine?"

30 And Joseph said unto them, "What is this act that you have done, that you took away my silver cup and went away? But I know that you took my cup in order to know thereby in what part of the land your brother was."

16 Judah said, "What will we tell my lord? What will we speak? Or how will we clear ourselves? God has found out the iniquity of your servants. Behold, we are my lord's slaves, both we, and he also in whose hand the cup is found."

31 And Judah said, "What shall we say to our lord, what shall we speak and how shall we justify ourselves, God has this day found the iniquity of all thy servants, therefore has he done this thing to us this day."

17 He said, "Far be it from me that I should do so. The man in whose hand the cup is found, he will be my slave; but as for you, go up in peace to your father."

32 And Joseph rose up and caught hold of Benjamin and took him from his brethren with violence, and he came to the house and locked the door at them, and Joseph commanded him that was set over his house that he should say unto them, "Thus saith the king, 'Go in peace to your father,' behold I have taken the man in whose hand my cup was found."

Jasher 54

1 And when Judah saw the dealings of Joseph with them, Judah approached him and broke open the door, and came with his brethren before Joseph.

18 Then Judah came near to him, and said, "Oh, my lord, please let your servant speak a word in my lord's ears, and don't let your anger burn against your servant; for you are even as Pharaoh.

2 And Judah said unto Joseph, "Let it not seem grievous in the sight of my lord, may thy servant I pray thee speak a word before thee?" and Joseph said unto him, "Speak."

3 And Judah spoke before Joseph, and his brethren were there standing before them; and Judah said unto Joseph, "Surely when we first came to our lord to buy food, thou didst consider us as spies of the land, and we brought Benjamin before thee, and thou still makest sport of us this day. 4 Now therefore let the king hear my words, and send I pray thee our brother that he may go along with us to our father, lest thy soul perish this day with all the souls of the inhabitants of Egypt.

5 "Dost thou not know what two of my brethren, Simeon and Levi, did unto the city of Shechem, and unto seven cities of the Amorites, on account of our sister Dinah, and also what they would do for the sake of their brother Benjamin?

6 "And I with my strength, who am greater and mightier than both of them, come this day upon thee and thy land if thou art unwilling to send our brother.

7 "Hast thou not heard what our God who made choice of us did unto Pharaoh on account of Sarah our mother, whom he took away from our father, that he smote him and his household with heavy plagues, that even unto this day the Egyptians relate this wonder to each other? So will our God do unto thee on account of Benjamin whom thou hast this day taken from his father, and on account of the evils which thou this day heapest over us in thy land; for our God will remember his covenant with our father Abraham and bring evil upon thee, because thou hast grieved the soul of our father this day.

8 "Now therefore hear my words that I have this day spoken unto thee, and send our brother that he may go away lest thou and the people of thy land die by the sword, for you cannot all prevail over me."

9 And Joseph answered Judah, saying, "Why hast thou opened wide thy mouth and why dost thou boast over us, saying, 'Strength is with thee?' as Pharaoh liveth, if I command all my valiant men to fight with you, surely thou and these thy brethren would sink in the mire."

10 And Judah said unto Joseph, "Surely it becometh thee and thy people to fear me; as the Lord liveth if I once draw my sword I shall not sheathe it again until I shall this day have slain all Egypt, and I will commence with thee and finish with Pharaoh thy master."

11 And Joseph answered and said unto him, "Surely strength belongeth not alone to thee; I am stronger and mightier than thou, surely if thou drawest thy sword I will put it to thy neck and the necks of all thy brethren."

12 And Judah said unto him, "Surely if I this day open my mouth against thee I would swallow thee up that thou be destroyed from off the earth and perish this day from thy kingdom."

And Joseph said, "Surely if thou openest thy mouth I have power and might to close thy mouth with a stone until thou shalt not be able to utter a word; see how many stones are before us, truly I can take a stone, and force it into thy mouth and break thy jaws."

13 And Judah said, "God is witness between us, that we have not hitherto desired to battle with thee, only give us our brother and we will go from thee; and Joseph answered and said, 'As Pharaoh liveth, if all the kings of Canaan came together with you, you should not take him from my hand.'

14 "Now therefore go your way to your father, and your brother shall be unto me for a slave, for he has robbed the king's house." And Judah said, "What is it to thee or to the character of the king, surely the king sendeth forth from his house, throughout the land, silver and gold either in gifts or expenses, and thou still talkest about thy cup which thou didst place in our brother's bag and sayest that he has
stolen it from thee? 15 God forbid that our brother
Benjamin or any of the seed of Abraham should do this thing to steal from thee, or from any one else, whether king, prince, or any man.

16 "Now therefore cease this accusation lest the whole earth hear thy words, saying, 'For a little silver the king of Egypt wrangled with the men, and he accused them and took their brother for a slave.'"

17 And Joseph answered and said, "Take unto you this cup and go from me and leave your brother for a slave, for it is the judgment of a thief to be a slave."

18 And Judah said, "Why art thou not ashamed of thy words, to leave our brother and to take thy cup? Surely if thou givest us thy cup, or a thousand times as much, we will not leave our brother for the silver which is found in the hand of any man, that we will not die over him."

19 And Joseph answered, "And why did you forsake your brother and sell him for twenty pieces of silver unto this day, and why then will you not do the same to this your brother?"

20 And Judah said, "The Lord is witness between me and thee that we desire not thy battles; now therefore give us our brother and we will go from thee without quarreling."

21 And Joseph answered and said, "If all the kings of the land should assemble they will not be able to take your brother from my hand;" and Judah said, "What shall we say unto our father, when he seeth that our brother cometh not with us, and will grieve over him?"

22 And Joseph answered and said, "This is the thing which you shall tell unto your father, saying, 'The rope has gone after the bucket.'"

23 And Judah said, "Surely thou art a king, and why speakest thou these things, giving a false judgment? Woe unto the king who is like unto thee."

24 And Joseph answered and said, "There is no false judgment in the word that I spoke on account of your brother Joseph, for all of you sold him to the Midianites for twenty pieces of silver, and you all denied it to your father and said unto him, 'An evil beast has devoured him, Joseph has been torn to pieces.'"

25 And Judah said, "Behold the fire of Shem burneth in my heart, now I will burn all your land with fire;" and Joseph answered and said, "Surely thy sister-in-law Tamar, who killed your sons, extinguished the fire of Shechem."

26 And Judah said, "If I pluck out a single hair from my flesh, I will fill all Egypt with its blood."

27 And Joseph answered and said, "Such is your custom to do as you did to your brother whom you sold, and you dipped his coat in blood and brought it to your father in order that he might say an evil beast devoured him and here is his blood."

28 And when Judah heard this thing he was exceedingly wroth and his anger burned within him, and there was before him in that place a stone, the weight of which was about four hundred shekels, and Judah's anger was kindled and he took the stone in one hand and cast it to the heavens and caught it with his left hand.

29 And he placed it afterward under his legs, and he sat upon it with all his strength and the stone was turned into dust from the force of Judah.

30 And Joseph saw the act of Judah and he was very much afraid, but he commanded Manassah his son and he also did with another stone like unto the act of Judah, and Judah said unto his brethren, "Let not any of you say, 'This man is an Egyptian, but by his doing this thing he is of our father's family.'"

31 And Joseph said, "Not to you only is strength given, for we are also powerful men, and why will you boast over us all?" and Judah said unto Joseph, "Send I pray thee our brother and ruin not thy country this day."

32 And Joseph answered and said unto them, "Go and tell your father, an evil beast hath devoured him as you said concerning your brother Joseph."

33 And Judah spoke to his brother Naphtali, and he said unto him, "Make haste, go now and number all the streets of Egypt and come and tell me;" and Simeon said unto him, "Let not this thing be a trouble to thee; now I will go to the mount and take up one large stone from the mount and level it at every one in Egypt, and kill all that are in it."

34 And Joseph heard all these words that his brethren spoke before him, and they did not know that Joseph understood them, for they imagined that he knew not to speak Hebrew.

35 And Joseph was greatly afraid at the words of his brethren lest they should destroy Egypt, and he commanded his son Manasseh, saying, "Go now make haste and gather unto me all the inhabitants of Egypt, and all the valiant men together, and let them come to me now upon horseback and on foot and with all sorts of musical instruments," and Manasseh went and did so.

36 And Naphtali went as Judah had commanded him, for Naphtali was lightfooted as one of the swift stags, and he would go upon the ears of corn and they would not break under him.

37 And he went and numbered all the streets of Egypt, and found them to be twelve, and he came hastily and told Judah, and Judah said unto his brethren, "Hasten you and put on every man his sword upon his loins and we will come over Egypt, and smite them all, and let not a remnant remain."

38 And Judah said, "Behold, I will destroy three of the streets with my strength, and you shall each destroy one street;" and when Judah was speaking this thing, behold the inhabitants of Egypt and all the mighty men came toward them with all sorts of musical instruments and with loud shouting.

39 And their number was five hundred cavalry and ten thousand infantry, and four hundred men who could fight without sword or spear, only with their hands and strength.

40 And all the mighty men came with great storming and shouting, and they all surrounded the sons of Jacob and terrified them, and the ground quaked at the sound of their shouting.

41 And when the sons of Jacob saw these troops they were greatly afraid of their lives, and Joseph did so in order to terrify the sons of Jacob to become tranquilized.

42 And Judah, seeing some of his brethren terrified, said unto them, "Why are you afraid whilst the grace of God is with us?" and when Judah saw all the people of Egypt surrounding them at the command of Joseph to terrify them, only Joseph commanded them, saying, "Do not touch any of them."

43 Then Judah hastened and drew his sword, and uttered a loud and bitter scream, and he smote with his sword, and he sprang upon the ground and he still continued to shout against all the people.

44 And when he did this thing the Lord caused the terror of Judah and his brethren to fall upon the valiant men and all the people that surrounded
them. 45 And they all fled at the sound of the
shouting, and they were terrified and fell one upon the other, and many of them died as they fell, and they all fled from before Judah and his brethren and from before Joseph.

46 And whilst they were fleeing, Judah and his brethren pursued them unto the house of Pharaoh, and they all escaped, and Judah again sat before Joseph and roared at him like a lion, and gave a great and tremendous shriek at him.

47 And the shriek was heard at a distance, and all the inhabitants of Succoth heard it, and all Egypt quaked at the sound of the shriek, and also the walls of Egypt and of the land of Goshen fell in from the shaking of the earth, and Pharaoh also fell from his throne upon the ground, and also all the pregnant women of Egypt and Goshen miscarried when they heard the noise of the shaking, for they were terribly afraid.

48 And Pharaoh sent word, saying, "What is this thing that has this day happened in the land of Egypt?" And they came and told him all the things from beginning to end, and Pharaoh was alarmed and he wondered and was greatly afraid.

49 And his fright increased when he heard all these things, and he sent unto Joseph, saying, "Thou hast brought unto me the Hebrews to destroy all Egypt; what wilt thou do with that thievish slave? Send him away and let him go with his brethren, and let us not perish through their evil, even we, you and all Egypt.

50 "And if thou desirest not to do this thing, cast off from thee all my valuable things, and go with them to their land, if thou delightest in it, for they will this day destroy my whole country and slay all my people; even all the women of Egypt have miscarried through their screams; see what they have done merely by their shouting and speaking, moreover if they fight with the sword, they will destroy the land; now therefore choose that which thou desirest, whether me or the Hebrews, whether Egypt or the land of the Hebrews."

19 My lord asked his servants, saying, ‘Have you a
father, or a brother?’ 20 We said to my lord, ‘We
have a father, an old man, and a child of his old age,
a little one; and his brother is dead, and he alone is
left of his mother; and his father loves him.’ 21 You
said to your servants, ‘Bring him down to me, that I
may set my eyes on him.’ 22 We said to my lord,
‘The boy can’t leave his father: for if he should
leave his father, his father would die.’ 23 You said
to your servants, ‘Unless your youngest brother
comes down with you, you will see my face no
more.’

51 And they came and told Joseph all the words of
Pharaoh that he had said concerning him, and
Joseph was greatly afraid at the words of Pharaoh
and Judah and his brethren were still standing
before Joseph indignant and enraged, and all the
sons of Jacob roared at Joseph, like the roaring of
the sea and its waves. 52 And Joseph was greatly
afraid of his brethren and on account of Pharaoh,
and Joseph sought a pretext to make himself known
unto his brethren, lest they should destroy all
Egypt.

53 And Joseph commanded his son Manasseh, and
Manasseh went and approached Judah, and placed
his hand upon his shoulder, and the anger of Judah
was stilled. 54 And Judah said unto his brethren,
"Let no one of you say that this is the act of an
Egyptian youth for this is the work of my father's
house."

55 And Joseph seeing and knowing that Judah's
anger was stilled, he approached to speak unto
Judah in the language of mildness.

56 And Joseph said unto Judah, "Surely you speak
truth and have this day verified your assertions
concerning your strength, and may your God who
delighteth in you, increase your welfare; but tell me
truly why from amongst all thy brethren dost thou
wrangle with me on account of the lad, as none of
them have spoken one word to me concerning
him."

24 When we came up to your servant my father, we told him the words of my lord. 25 Our father said, 'Go again, buy us a little food.' 26 We said, 'We can't go down. If our youngest brother is with us, then we will go down: for we may not see the man's face, unless our youngest brother is with us.' 27 Your servant, my father, said to us, 'You know that my wife bore me two sons: 28 and the one went out from me, and I said, "Surely he is torn in pieces"; and I haven't seen him since. 29 If you take this one also from me, and harm happens to him, you will bring down my gray hairs with sorrow to Sheol.'

30 "Now therefore when I come to your servant my father, and the boy is not with us; since his life is bound up in the boy's life; 31 it will happen, when he sees that the boy is no more, that he will die. Your servants will bring down the gray hairs of your servant, our father, with sorrow to Sheol.

32 "For your servant became collateral for the boy to my father, saying, 'If I don't bring him to you, then I will bear the blame to my father forever.'

57 And Judah answered Joseph, saying, "Surely thou must know that I was security for the lad to his father, saying, 'If I brought him not unto him I should bear his blame forever.'

33 "Now therefore, please let your servant stay instead of the boy, my lord's slave; and let the boy go up with his brothers. 34 For how will I go up to my father, if the boy isn't with me?—lest I see the evil that will come on my father."

58 "Therefore have I approached thee from amongst all my brethren, for I saw that thou wast unwilling to suffer him to go from thee; now therefore may I find grace in thy sight that thou shalt send him to go with us, and behold I will remain as a substitute for him, to serve thee in whatever thou desirest, for wheresoever thou shalt send me I will go to serve thee with great energy.

59 "Send me now to a mighty king who has rebelled against thee, and thou shalt know what I will do unto him and unto his land; although he may have cavalry and infantry or an exceeding mighty people, I will slay them all and bring the king's head before thee. 60 Dost thou not know or hast thou not heard that our father Abraham with his servant Eliezer smote all the kings of Elam with their hosts in one night, they left not one remaining? and ever since that day our father's strength was given unto us for an inheritance, for us and our seed forever."

61 And Joseph answered and said, "You speak truth, and falsehood is not in your mouth, for it was also told unto us that the Hebrews have power and that the Lord their God delighteth much in them, and who then can stand before them?

62 "However, on this condition will I send your brother, if you will bring before me his brother the son of his mother, of whom you said that he had gone from you down to Egypt; and it shall come to pass when you bring unto me his brother I will take him in his stead, because not one of you was security for him to your father, and when he shall come unto me, I will then send with you his brother for whom you have been security."

63 And Judah's anger was kindled against Joseph when he spoke this thing, and his eyes dropped blood with anger, and he said unto his brethren, "How doth this man this day seek his own destruction and that of all Egypt!"

64 And Simeon answered Joseph, saying, "Did we not tell thee at first that we knew not the particular spot to which he went, and whether he be dead or alive, and wherefore speaketh my lord like unto these things?"

65 And Joseph observing the countenance of Judah discerned that his anger began to kindle when he spoke unto him, saying, "Bring unto me your other brother instead of this brother."

66 And Joseph said unto his brethren, "Surely you said that your brother was either dead or lost, now if I should call him this day and he should come before you, would you give him unto me instead of his brother?" 67 And Joseph began to speak and call out, "Joseph, Joseph, come this day before me, and appear to thy brethren and sit before them."

68 And when Joseph spoke this thing before them, they looked each a different way to see from whence Joseph would come before them.

Genesis 45

1 Then Joseph couldn't control himself before all those who stood before him, and he cried, "Cause everyone to go out from me!" No one else stood with him, while Joseph made himself known to his brothers. 2 He wept aloud. The Egyptians heard, and the house of Pharaoh heard.

[54:73 And the voice was heard in the house of Joseph that they were Joseph's brethren, and it pleased Pharaoh exceedingly, for he was afraid of them lest they should destroy Egypt.]

3 Joseph said to his brothers, "I am Joseph! Does my father still live?" His brothers couldn't answer him; for they were terrified at his presence.

69 And Joseph observed all their acts, and said unto them, "Why do you look here and there? I am Joseph whom you sold to Egypt, now therefore let it not grieve you that you sold me, for as a support during the famine did God send me before you." 70 And his brethren were terrified at him when they heard the words of Joseph, and Judah was exceedingly terrified at him.

4 Joseph said to his brothers, "Come near to me, please." They came near. "He said, I am Joseph, your brother, whom you sold into Egypt. 5 Now don't be grieved, nor angry with yourselves, that you sold me here, for God sent me before you to preserve life.

6 "For these two years the famine has been in the land, and there are yet five years, in which there will be no plowing and no harvest. 7 God sent me before you to preserve for you a remnant in the earth, and to save you alive by a great deliverance. 8 So now it wasn't you who sent me here, but God, and he has made me a father to Pharaoh, lord of all his house, and ruler over all the land of Egypt.

9 Hurry, and go up to my father, and tell him, 'This is what your son Joseph says, "God has made me lord of all Egypt. Come down to me. Don't wait. 10 You shall dwell in the land of Goshen, and you will be near to me, you, your children, your children's children, your flocks, your herds, and all that you have. 11 There I will nourish you; for there are yet five years of famine; lest you come to poverty, you, and your household, and all that you have."'

12 Behold, your eyes see, and the eyes of my
brother Benjamin, that it is my mouth that speaks
to you. 13 You shall tell my father of all my glory in
Egypt, and of all that you have seen. You shall hurry
and bring my father down here."

71 And when Benjamin heard the words of Joseph he was before them in the inner part of the house, and Benjamin ran unto Joseph his brother, and embraced him and fell upon his neck, and they wept.

14 He fell on his brother Benjamin's neck, and
wept, and Benjamin wept on his neck. 15 He kissed
all his brothers, and wept on them. After that his
brothers talked with him.

72 And when Joseph's brethren saw that Benjamin had fallen upon his brother's neck and wept with him, they also fell upon Joseph and embraced him, and they wept a great weeping with Joseph.

16 The report of it was heard in Pharaoh's house, saying, "Joseph's brothers have come." It pleased Pharaoh well, and his servants.

73 And the voice was heard in the house of Joseph that they were Joseph's brethren, and it pleased Pharaoh exceedingly, for he was afraid of them lest they should destroy Egypt.

74 And Pharaoh sent his servants unto Joseph to congratulate him concerning his brethren who had come to him, and all the captains of the armies and troops that were in Egypt came to rejoice with Joseph, and all Egypt rejoiced greatly about Joseph's brethren.

17 Pharaoh said to Joseph, "Tell your brothers, 'Do
this. Load your animals, and go, travel to the land of
Canaan. 18 Take your father and your households,
and come to me, and I will give you the good of the
land of Egypt, and you will eat the fat of the land.'
19 Now you are commanded: do this. Take wagons
out of the land of Egypt for your little ones, and for
your wives, and bring your father, and come. 20
Also, don't concern yourselves about your
belongings, for the good of all the land of Egypt is
yours." 21 The sons of Israel did so.

75 And Pharaoh sent his servants to Joseph, saying, "Tell thy brethren to fetch all belonging to them and let them come unto me, and I will place them in the best part of the land of Egypt," and they did so.

Joseph gave them wagons, according to the commandment of Pharaoh, and gave them provision for the way.

22 He gave each one of them changes of clothing, but to Benjamin he gave three hundred pieces of silver and five changes of clothing.

76 And Joseph commanded him that was set over his house to bring out to his brethren gifts and garments, and he brought out to them many garments being robes of royalty and many gifts, and Joseph divided them amongst his brethren. 77 And he gave unto each of his brethren a change of garments of gold and silver, and three hundred pieces of silver, and Joseph commanded them all to be dressed in these garments, and to be brought before Pharaoh.

78 And Pharaoh seeing that all Joseph's brethren were valiant men, and of beautiful appearance, he greatly rejoiced.

23 He sent the following to his father: ten donkeys loaded with the good things of Egypt, and ten female donkeys loaded with grain and bread and provision for his father by the way. 24 So he sent his brothers away, and they departed. He said to them, “See that you don’t quarrel on the way.”

[54:88 And he said unto them, "Do not quarrel on the road, for this thing was from the Lord to keep a great people from starvation, for there will be yet five years of famine in the land."]

25 They went up out of Egypt, and came into the land of Canaan, to Jacob their father.

79 And they afterward went out from the presence of Pharaoh to go to the land of Canaan, to their father, and their brother Benjamin was with them.

80 And Joseph rose up and gave unto them eleven chariots from Pharaoh, and Joseph gave unto them his chariot, upon which he rode on the day of his being crowned in Egypt, to fetch his father to Egypt; and Joseph sent to all his brothers' children, garments according to their numbers, and a hundred pieces of silver to each of them, and he also sent garments to the wives of his brethren from the garments of the king's wives, and he sent them.

81 And he gave unto each of his brethren ten men to go with them to the land of Canaan to serve them, to serve their children and all belonging to them in coming to Egypt. 82 And Joseph sent by the hand of his brother Benjamin ten suits of garments for his ten sons, a portion above the rest of the children of the sons of Jacob.

83 And he sent to each fifty pieces of silver, and ten chariots on the account of Pharaoh, and he sent to his father ten asses laden with all the luxuries of Egypt, and ten she asses laden with corn and bread and nourishment for his father, and to all that were with him as provisions for the road.

84 And he sent to his sister Dinah garments of silver and gold, and frankincense and myrrh, and aloes and women's ornaments in great plenty, and he sent the same from the wives of Pharaoh to the wives of Benjamin.

85 And he gave unto all his brethren, also to their wives, all sorts of onyx stones and bdellium, and from all the valuable things amongst the great people of Egypt, nothing of all the costly things was left but what Joseph sent of to his father's
household. 86 And he sent his brethren away, and they went, and he sent his brother Benjamin with them.

87 And Joseph went out with them to accompany them on the road unto the borders of Egypt, and he commanded them concerning his father and his household, to come to Egypt.

88 And he said unto them, "Do not quarrel on the road, for this thing was from the Lord to keep a great people from starvation, for there will be yet five years of famine in the land."

89 And he commanded them, saying, "When you come unto the land of Canaan, do not come suddenly before my father in this affair, but act in
your wisdom." 90 And Joseph ceased to command them, and he turned and went back to Egypt, and the sons of Jacob went to the land of Canaan with joy and cheerfulness to their father Jacob.

91 And they came unto the borders of the land, and they said to each other, "What shall we do in this matter before our father, for if we come suddenly to him and tell him the matter, he will be greatly alarmed at our words and will not believe us."

92 And they went along until they came nigh unto
their houses, and they found Serach, the daughter
of Asher, going forth to meet them, and the damsel
was very good and subtle, and knew how to play
upon the harp. 93 And they called unto her and she
came before them, and she kissed them, and they
took her and gave unto her a harp, saying, "Go now
before our father, and sit before him, and strike
upon the harp, and speak these words."

94 And they commanded her to go to their house,
and she took the harp and hastened before them,
and she came and sat near Jacob. 95 And she
played well and sang, and uttered in the sweetness
of her words, Joseph my uncle is living, and he
ruleth throughout the land of Egypt, and is not
dead. 96 And she continued to repeat and utter
these words, and Jacob heard her words and they
were agreeable to him.

97 He listened whilst she repeated them twice and thrice, and joy entered the heart of Jacob at the sweetness of her words, and the spirit of God was upon him, and he knew all her words to be true.

98 And Jacob blessed Serach when she spoke these words before him, and he said unto her, "My daughter, may death never prevail over thee, for thou hast revived my spirit; only speak yet before me as thou hast spoken, for thou hast gladdened me with all thy words."

99 And she continued to sing these words, and Jacob listened and it pleased him, and he rejoiced, and the spirit of God was upon him.

100 Whilst he was yet speaking with her, behold his
sons came to him with horses and chariots and
royal garments and servants running before them.
101 And Jacob rose up to meet them, and saw his
sons dressed in royal garments and he saw all the
treasures that Joseph had sent to them.

26 They told him, saying, “Joseph is still alive, and he is ruler over all the land of Egypt.” His heart fainted, for he didn’t believe them. 27 They told him all the words of Joseph, which he had said to them. When he saw the wagons which Joseph had sent to carry him, the spirit of Jacob, their father, revived.

102 And they said unto him, "Be informed that our brother Joseph is living, and it is he who ruleth throughout the land of Egypt, and it is he who spoke unto us as we told thee." 103 And Jacob heard all the words of his sons, and his heart palpitated at their words, for he could not believe them until he saw all that Joseph had given them and what he had sent him, and all the signs which Joseph had spoken unto them. 104 And they opened out before him, and showed him all that Joseph had sent, they gave unto each what Joseph had sent him, and he knew that they had spoken the truth, and he rejoiced exceedingly an account of his son.

28 Israel said, “It is enough. Joseph my son is still alive. I will go and see him before I die.”

105 And Jacob said, "It is enough for me that my son Joseph is still living, I will go and see him before I die."

106 And his sons told him all that had befallen them, and Jacob said, "I will go down to Egypt to see my son and his offspring."

107 And Jacob rose up and put on the garments which Joseph had sent him, and after he had washed, and shaved his hair, he put upon his head the turban which Joseph had sent him.

108 And all the people of Jacob's house and their wives put on the garments which Joseph had sent to them, and they greatly rejoiced at Joseph that he was still living and that he was ruling in Egypt, 109 And all the inhabitants of Canaan heard of this thing, and they came and rejoiced much with Jacob that he was still living. 110 And Jacob made a feast for them for three days, and all the kings of Canaan and nobles of the land ate and drank and rejoiced in the house of Jacob.

Jasher 55

1 And it came to pass after this that Jacob said, "I will go and see my son in Egypt and will then come back to the land of Canaan of which God had spoken unto Abraham, for I cannot leave the land of my birth-place."

[Genesis 46:3 He said, “I am God, the God of your father. Don’t be afraid to go down into Egypt, for there I will make of you a great nation."]

2 Behold the word of the Lord came unto him, saying, "Go down to Egypt with all thy household and remain there, fear not to go down to Egypt for I will there make thee a great nation."

3 And Jacob said within himself, "I will go and see my son whether the fear of his God is yet in his heart amidst all the inhabitants of Egypt."

4 And the Lord said unto Jacob, "Fear not about Joseph, for he still retaineth his integrity to serve me, as will seem good in thy sight," and Jacob rejoiced exceedingly concerning his son.

Genesis 46

1 Israel traveled with all that he had, and came to Beersheba,

5 At that time Jacob commanded his sons and household to go to Egypt according to the word of the Lord unto him, and Jacob rose up with his sons and all his household, and he went out from the land of Canaan from Beersheba, with joy and gladness of heart, and they went to the land of Egypt.

and offered sacrifices to the God of his father, Isaac.
2 God spoke to Israel in the visions of the night, and said, "Jacob, Jacob!" He said, "Here I am."

3 He said, "I am God, the God of your father. Don't be afraid to go down into Egypt, for there I will make of you a great nation. 4 I will go down with you into Egypt. I will also surely bring you up again. Joseph will close your eyes."

[55:2 Behold the word of the Lord came unto him, saying, "Go down to Egypt with all thy household and remain there, fear not to go down to Egypt for I will there make thee a great nation."]

5 Jacob rose up from Beersheba, and the sons of Israel carried Jacob, their father, their little ones, and their wives, in the wagons which Pharaoh had sent to carry him. 6 They took their livestock, and their goods, which they had gotten in the land of Canaan, and came into Egypt—Jacob, and all his offspring with him, 7 his sons, and his sons' sons with him, his daughters, and his sons' daughters, and he brought all his offspring with him into Egypt.

8 These are the names of the children of Israel, who came into Egypt, Jacob and his sons: Reuben, Jacob's firstborn. 9 The sons of Reuben: Hanoch, Pallu, Hezron, and Carmi. 10 The sons of Simeon: Jemuel, Jamin, Ohad, Jachin, Zohar, and Shaul the son of a Canaanite woman.

11 The sons of Levi: Gershon, Kohath, and Merari.
12 The sons of Judah: Er, Onan, Shelah, Perez, and Zerah; but Er and Onan died in the land of Canaan. The sons of Perez were Hezron and Hamul.

[45:6b and Adinah bare unto Levi, Gershon, Kehath and Merari; three sons.]

13 The sons of Issachar: Tola, Puvah, Iob, and Shimron.

[45:7 And Aridah bare unto Issachar Tola, Puvah, Job and Shomron, four sons;]

14 The sons of Zebulun: Sered, Elon, and Jahleel. 15
These are the sons of Leah, whom she bore to Jacob
in Paddan Aram, with his daughter Dinah. All the
souls of his sons and his daughters were thirty-
three.

[45:20 And Merushah bare unto Zebulun Sered, Elon and Yachleel; three sons.]

16 The sons of Gad: Ziphion, Haggi, Shuni, Ezbon, Eri, Arodi, and Areli.

[45:11b and Uzith bare unto Gad Zephion, Chagi, Shuni, Ezbon, Eri, Arodi and Arali, seven sons.]

17 The sons of Asher: Imnah, Ishvah, Ishvi, Beriah, and Serah their sister. The sons of Beriah: Heber and Malchiel.

[45:18 And Hadurah the wife of Asher conceived and bare unto him Yimnah, Yishvah, Yishvi and Beriah; four sons.]

18 These are the sons of Zilpah, whom Laban gave to Leah, his daughter, and these she bore to Jacob, even sixteen souls.

19 The sons of Rachel, Jacob's wife: Joseph and
Benjamin. 20 To Joseph in the land of Egypt were
born Manasseh and Ephraim, whom Asenath, the
daughter of Potiphera, priest of On, bore to him.

21 The sons of Benjamin: Bela, Becher, Ashbel,
Gera, Naaman, Ehi, Rosh, Muppim, Huppim, and
Ard. 22 These are the sons of Rachel, who were
born to Jacob: all the souls were fourteen.

[45:22 And Mechalia conceived and bare unto Benjamin Bela, Becher, Ashbel, Gera and Naaman, five sons; and Benjamin went afterward and took for a wife Aribath, the daughter of Shomron, the son of Abraham, in addition to his first wife, and he was eighteen years old; and Aribath bare unto Benjamin Achi, Vosh, Mupim, Chupim, and Ord; five sons.]

23 The son of Dan: Hushim.

[45:8 And Aphlaleth was barren, she had no offspring, and God afterward remembered Aphlaleth the wife of Dan, and she conceived and bare a son, and she called his name Chushim.]

24 The sons of Naphtali: Jahzeel, Guni, Jezer, and Shillem.

[45:11 And Merimah bare unto Naphtali Yachzeel, Guni, Jazer and Shalem, four sons;]

25 These are the sons of Bilhah, whom Laban gave to Rachel, his daughter, and these she bore to Jacob: all the souls were seven.

26 All the souls who came with Jacob into Egypt,
who were his direct offspring, besides Jacob's sons'
wives, all the souls were sixty-six. 27 The sons of
Joseph, who were born to him in Egypt, were two
souls. All the souls of the house of Jacob, who came
into Egypt, were seventy.

[59:19 And all the souls that went forth from the loins of Jacob, were seventy souls; these are they who came with Jacob their father unto Egypt to dwell there: and Joseph and all his brethren dwelt securely in Egypt, and they ate of the best of Egypt all the days of the life of Joseph.]

28 He sent Judah before him to Joseph, to show the way before him to Goshen, and they came into the land of Goshen.

6 And it came to pass when they came near Egypt, Jacob sent Judah before him to Joseph that he might show him a situation in Egypt, and Judah did according to the word of his father, and he hastened and ran and came to Joseph, and they assigned for them a place in the land of Goshen for all his household, and Judah returned and came along the road to his father.

29 Joseph prepared his chariot,

7 And Joseph harnessed the chariot, and he assembled all his mighty men and his servants and all the officers of Egypt in order to go and meet his father Jacob, and Joseph's mandate was proclaimed in Egypt, saying, "All that do not go to meet Jacob shall die."

8 And on the next day Joseph went forth with all Egypt a great and mighty host, all dressed in garments of fine linen and purple and with instruments of silver and gold and with their instruments of war with them.

9 And they all went to meet Jacob with all sorts of musical instruments, with drums and timbrels, strewing myrrh and aloes all along the road, and they all went after this fashion, and the earth shook at their shouting.

10 And all the women of Egypt went upon the roofs of Egypt and upon the walls to meet Jacob, and upon the head of Joseph was Pharaoh's regal crown, for Pharaoh had sent it unto him to put on at the time of his going to meet his father.

11 And when Joseph came within fifty cubits of his father, he alighted from the chariot and he walked toward his father, and when all the officers of Egypt and her nobles saw that Joseph had gone on foot toward his father, they also alighted and walked on
foot toward Jacob. 12 And when Jacob approached
the camp of Joseph, Jacob observed the camp that was coming toward him with Joseph, and it gratified him and Jacob was astonished at it.

13 And Jacob said unto Judah, "Who is that man whom I see in the camp of Egypt dressed in kingly robes with a very red garment upon him and a royal crown upon his head, who has alighted from his chariot and is coming toward us?" and Judah answered his father, saying, "He is thy son Joseph the king; and Jacob rejoiced in seeing the glory of his son."

14 And Joseph came nigh unto his father and he bowed to his father, and all the men of the camp bowed to the ground with him before Jacob.

and went up to meet Israel, his father, in Goshen. He presented himself to him, and fell on his neck, and wept on his neck a good while.

15 And behold Jacob ran and hastened to his son Joseph and fell upon his neck and kissed him, and they wept, and Joseph also embraced his father and kissed him, and they wept and all the people of Egypt wept with them.

30 Israel said to Joseph, "Now let me die, since I have seen your face, that you are still alive."

16 And Jacob said unto Joseph, "Now I will die cheerfully after I have seen thy face, that thou art still living and with glory."

17 And the sons of Jacob and their wives and their children and their servants, and all the household of Jacob wept exceedingly with Joseph, and they kissed him and wept greatly with him. 18 And
Joseph and all his people returned afterward home to Egypt, and Jacob and his sons and all the children of his household came with Joseph to Egypt, and Joseph placed them in the best part of Egypt, in the land of Goshen.

31 Joseph said to his brothers, and to his father's house, "I will go up, and speak with Pharaoh, and will tell him, 'My brothers, and my father's house, who were in the land of Canaan, have come to me.
32 These men are shepherds, for they have been keepers of livestock, and they have brought their flocks, and their herds, and all that they have.' 33 It
will happen, when Pharaoh summons you, and will say, 'What is your occupation?' 34 that you shall
say, 'Your servants have been keepers of livestock from our youth even until now, both we, and our fathers:' that you may dwell in the land of Goshen; for every shepherd is an abomination to the Egyptians."

19 And Joseph said unto his father and unto his brethren, "I will go up and tell Pharaoh, saying, 'My brethren and my father's household and all belonging to them have come unto me, and behold they are in the land of Goshen.'" 20 And Joseph did
so and took from his brethren Reuben, Issachar Zebulun and his brother Benjamin and he placed them before Pharaoh.

Genesis 47

1 Then Joseph went in and told Pharaoh, and said, "My father and my brothers, with their flocks, their herds, and all that they own, have come out of the land of Canaan; and behold, they are in the land of Goshen."

21 And Joseph spoke unto Pharaoh, saying, "My brethren and my father's household and all belonging to them, together with their flocks and cattle have come unto me from the land of Canaan, to sojourn in Egypt; for the famine was sore upon them."

2 From among his brothers he took five men, and
presented them to Pharaoh. 3 Pharaoh said to his
brothers, "What is your occupation?" They said to Pharaoh, "Your servants are shepherds, both we, and our fathers."

4 They said to Pharaoh, "We have come to live as foreigners in the land, for there is no pasture for your servants' flocks. For the famine is severe in the land of Canaan. Now therefore, please let your servants dwell in the land of Goshen."

5 Pharaoh spoke to Joseph, saying, "Your father and
your brothers have come to you. 6 The land of
Egypt is before you. Make your father and your brothers dwell in the best of the land. Let them dwell in the land of Goshen. If you know any able men among them, then put them in charge of my livestock."

22 And Pharaoh said unto Joseph, "Place thy father and brethren in the best part of the land, withhold not from them all that is good, and cause them to eat of the fat of the land."

23 And Joseph answered, saying, "Behold I have stationed them in the land of Goshen, for they are shepherds, therefore let them remain in Goshen to feed their flocks apart from the Egyptians."

24 And Pharaoh said unto Joseph, "Do with thy brethren all that they shall say unto thee;" and the sons of Jacob bowed down to Pharaoh, and they went forth from him in peace,

7 Joseph brought in Jacob, his father, and set him before Pharaoh, and Jacob blessed Pharaoh.

and Joseph afterward brought his father before Pharaoh.

8 Pharaoh said to Jacob, "How many are the days of
the years of your life?" 9 Jacob said to Pharaoh,
"The days of the years of my pilgrimage are one hundred thirty years. Few and evil have been the days of the years of my life, and they have not attained to the days of the years of the life of my fathers in the days of their pilgrimage."

10 Jacob blessed Pharaoh, and went out from the presence of Pharaoh.

25 And Jacob came and bowed down to Pharaoh, and Jacob blessed Pharaoh, and he then went out; and Jacob and all his sons, and all his household dwelt in the land of Goshen.

26 In the second year, that is in the hundred and thirtieth year of the life of Jacob, Joseph maintained his father and his brethren, and all his father's household, with bread according to their little ones, all the days of the famine; they lacked nothing.

11 Joseph placed his father and his brothers, and gave them a possession in the land of Egypt, in the best of the land, in the land of Rameses, as Pharaoh had commanded.

27 And Joseph gave unto them the best part of the whole land; the best of Egypt had they all the days of Joseph; and Joseph also gave unto them and unto the whole of his father's household, clothes and garments year by year; and the sons of Jacob remained securely in Egypt all the days of their brother.

28 And Jacob always ate at Joseph's table, Jacob and his sons did not leave Joseph's table day or night, besides what Jacob's children consumed in their houses.

12 Joseph nourished his father, his brothers, and all of his father's household, with bread, according to their families.

29 And all Egypt ate bread during the days of the famine from the house of Joseph, for all the Egyptians sold all belonging to them on account of the famine.

13 There was no bread in all the land; for the famine was very severe, so that the land of Egypt and the land of Canaan fainted by reason of the
famine. 14 Joseph gathered up all the money that
was found in the land of Egypt, and in the land of Canaan, for the grain which they bought: and Joseph brought the money into Pharaoh's house.

30 And Joseph purchased all the lands and fields of Egypt for bread on the account of Pharaoh, and Joseph supplied all Egypt with bread all the days of the famine, and Joseph collected all the silver and gold that came unto him for the corn which they bought throughout the land, and he accumulated much gold and silver, besides an immense quantity of onyx stones, bdellium and valuable garments which they brought unto Joseph from every part of the land when their money was spent.

15 When the money was all spent in the land of
Egypt, and in the land of Canaan, all the Egyptians
came to Joseph, and said, “Give us bread, for why
should we die in your presence? For our money
fails.” 16 Joseph said, “Give me your livestock; and
I will give you food for your livestock, if your money
is gone.”

17 They brought their livestock to Joseph, and
Joseph gave them bread in exchange for the horses,
and for the flocks, and for the herds, and for the
donkeys: and he fed them with bread in exchange
for all their livestock for that year. 18 When that
year was ended, they came to him the second year,
and said to him, “We will not hide from my lord
how our money is all spent, and the herds of
livestock are my lord’s. There is nothing left in the
sight of my lord, but our bodies, and our lands.

19 "Why should we die before your eyes, both we
and our land? Buy us and our land for bread, and
we and our land will be servants to Pharaoh. Give
us seed, that we may live, and not die, and that the
land won’t be desolate.”

31 And Joseph took all the silver and gold that came
into his hand, about seventy two talents of gold and
silver, and also onyx stones and bdellium in great
abundance, and Joseph went and concealed them
in four parts, and he concealed one part in the
wilderness near the Red sea, and one part by the
river Perath, and the third and fourth part he
concealed in the desert opposite to the wilderness
of Persia and Media.
32 And he took part of the gold and silver that was
left, and gave it unto all his brothers and unto all his
father's household, and unto all the women of his
father's household, and the rest he brought to the
house of Pharaoh, about twenty talents of gold and
silver.

33 And Joseph gave all the gold and silver that was
left unto Pharaoh, and Pharaoh placed it in the
treasury, and the days of the famine ceased after
that in the land, and they sowed and reaped in the
whole land, and they obtained their usual quantity
year by year; they lacked nothing.

20 So Joseph bought all the land of Egypt for Pharaoh, for every man of the Egyptians sold his field, because the famine was severe on them, and the land became Pharaoh's.

21 As for the people, he moved them to the cities from one end of the border of Egypt even to the other end of it.

22 Only he didn't buy the land of the priests, for the priests had a portion from Pharaoh, and ate their portion which Pharaoh gave them. That is why they didn't sell their land.

23 Then Joseph said to the people, "Behold, I have bought you and your land today for Pharaoh. Behold, here is seed for you, and you shall sow the
land. 24 It will happen at the harvests, that you shall give a fifth to Pharaoh, and four parts will be your own, for seed of the field, for your food, for them of your households, and for food for your
little ones." 25 They said, "You have saved our lives! Let us find favor in the sight of my lord, and we will be Pharaoh's servants."

26 Joseph made it a statute concerning the land of Egypt to this day, that Pharaoh should have the fifth. Only the land of the priests alone didn't become Pharaoh's.

34 And Joseph dwelt securely in Egypt, and the whole land was under his advice, and his father and all his brethren dwelt in the land of Goshen and
took possession of it. 35 And Joseph was very aged, advanced in days, and his two sons, Ephraim and Manasseh, remained constantly in the house of Jacob, together with the children of the sons of Jacob their brethren, to learn the ways of the Lord and his law.

27 Israel lived in the land of Egypt, in the land of Goshen; and they got themselves possessions therein, and were fruitful, and multiplied exceedingly.

36 And Jacob and his sons dwelt in the land of Egypt in the land of Goshen, and they took possession in it, and they were fruitful and multiplied in it.

28 Jacob lived in the land of Egypt seventeen years. So the days of Jacob, the years of his life, were one hundred forty-seven years.

Jasher 56

1 And Jacob lived in the land of Egypt seventeen years, and the days of Jacob, and the years of his life were a hundred and forty seven years.

29 The time came near that Israel must die, and he called his son Joseph, and said to him, "If now I have found favor in your sight, please put your hand under my thigh, and deal kindly and truly with me. Please don't bury me in Egypt, 30 but when I sleep with my fathers, you shall carry me out of Egypt, and bury me in their burying place." He said, "I will do as you have said."

2 At that time Jacob was attacked with that illness of which he died and he sent and called for his son Joseph from Egypt, and Joseph his son came from Egypt and Joseph came unto his father. 3 And Jacob said unto Joseph and unto his sons, "Behold I die, and the God of your ancestors will visit you, and bring you back to the land, which the Lord sware to give unto you and unto your children after you, now therefore when I am dead, bury me in the cave which is in Machpelah in Hebron in the land of Canaan, near my ancestors."

31 He said, "Swear to me," and he swore to him. Israel bowed himself on the bed's head.

4 And Jacob made his sons swear to bury him in Machpelah, in Hebron, and his sons swore unto him concerning this thing.

5 And he commanded them, saying, "Serve the Lord your God, for he who delivered your fathers will also deliver you from all trouble."

6 And Jacob said, "Call all your children unto me," and all the children of Jacob's sons came and sat before him, and Jacob blessed them, and he said unto them, "The Lord God of your fathers shall grant you a thousand times as much and bless you, and may he give you the blessing of your father Abraham;" and all the children of Jacob's sons went forth on that day after he had blessed them.

7 And on the next day Jacob again called for his sons, and they all assembled and came to him and sat before him, and Jacob on that day blessed his sons before his death, each man did he bless according to his blessing; behold it is written in the book of the law of the Lord appertaining to Israel.

8 And Jacob said unto Judah, "I know my son that thou art a mighty man for thy brethren; reign over them, and thy sons shall reign over their sons forever.

9 "Only teach thy sons the bow and all the weapons of war, in order that they may fight the battles of their brother who will rule over his enemies."

Genesis 48

1 After these things, someone said to Joseph, "Behold, your father is sick." He took with him his two sons, Manasseh and Ephraim. 2 Someone told Jacob, and said, "Behold, your son Joseph comes to you," and Israel strengthened himself, and sat on the bed.

3 Jacob said to Joseph, "God Almighty appeared to me at Luz in the land of Canaan, and blessed me, 4 and said to me, 'Behold, I will make you fruitful, and multiply you, and I will make of you a company of peoples, and will give this land to your offspring after you for an everlasting possession.'

5 "Now your two sons, who were born to you in the land of Egypt before I came to you into Egypt, are mine; Ephraim and Manasseh, even as Reuben and Simeon, will be mine. 6 Your issue, whom you become the father of after them, will be yours. They will be called after the name of their brothers in their inheritance. 7 As for me, when I came from Paddan, Rachel died by me in the land of Canaan on the way, when there was still some distance to come to Ephrath, and I buried her there on the way to Ephrath (also called Bethlehem)."

8 Israel saw Joseph's sons, and said, "Who are these?" 9 Joseph said to his father, "They are my sons, whom God has given me here." He said, "Please bring them to me, and I will bless them."

10 Now the eyes of Israel were dim for age, so that he couldn't see. He brought them near to him; and he kissed them, and embraced them. 11 Israel said to Joseph, "I didn't think I would see your face, and behold, God has let me see your offspring also."

12 Joseph brought them out from between his knees, and he bowed himself with his face to the earth.

13 Joseph took them both, Ephraim in his right hand toward Israel's left hand, and Manasseh in his left hand toward Israel's right hand, and brought them near to him.

14 Israel stretched out his right hand, and laid it on
Ephraim's head, who was the younger, and his left
hand on Manasseh's head, guiding his hands
knowingly, for Manasseh was the firstborn.

15 He blessed Joseph, and said, "The God before
whom my fathers Abraham and Isaac walked, the
God who has fed me all my life long to this day, 16
the angel who has redeemed me from all evil, bless
the lads, and let my name be named on them, and
the name of my fathers Abraham and Isaac. Let
them grow into a multitude upon the earth."

17 When Joseph saw that his father laid his right
hand on the head of Ephraim, it displeased him. He
held up his father's hand, to remove it from
Ephraim's head to Manasseh's head. 18 Joseph said
to his father, "Not so, my father; for this is the
firstborn; put your right hand on his head."

19 His father refused, and said, "I know, my son, I
know. He also will become a people, and he also
will be great. However, his younger brother will be
greater than he, and his offspring will become a
multitude of nations." 20 He blessed them that day,
saying, "In you will Israel bless, saying, 'God make
you as Ephraim and as Manasseh'" He set Ephraim
before Manasseh.

21 Israel said to Joseph, "Behold, I am dying, but
God will be with you, and bring you again to the
land of your fathers. 22 Moreover I have given to
you one portion above your brothers, which I took
out of the hand of the Amorite with my sword and
with my bow."

Genesis 49

1 Jacob called to his sons, and said: "Gather
yourselves together, that I may tell you that which
will happen to you in the days to come. 2 Assemble
yourselves, and hear, you sons of Jacob. Listen to
Israel, your father.

3 "Reuben, you are my firstborn, my might, and the
beginning of my strength; excelling in dignity, and
excelling in power. 4 Boiling over like water, you
shall not excel; because you went up to your
father's bed, then defiled it. He went up to my
couch.

5 "Simeon and Levi are brothers. Their swords are
weapons of violence. 6 My soul, don't come into
their council. My glory, don't be united to their
assembly; for in their anger they killed men. In their
self-will they hamstrung cattle.

7 "Cursed be their anger, for it was fierce; and their
wrath, for it was cruel. I will divide them in Jacob,
and scatter them in Israel.

8 "Judah, your brothers will praise you. Your hand
will be on the neck of your enemies. Your father's
sons will bow down before you. 9 Judah is a lion's
cub. From the prey, my son, you have gone up. He
stooped down, he crouched as a lion, as a lioness.
Who will rouse him up? 10 The scepter will not
depart from Judah, nor the ruler's staff from
between his feet, until he comes to whom it
belongs. To him will the obedience of the peoples
be.

11 "Binding his foal to the vine, his donkey's colt to
the choice vine; he has washed his garments in
wine, his robes in the blood of grapes. 12 His eyes
will be red with wine, his teeth white with milk.

13 "Zebulun will dwell at the haven of the sea. He
will be for a haven of ships. His border will be on
Sidon.

14 "Issachar is a strong donkey, lying down
between the saddlebags. 15 He saw a resting place,
that it was good, the land, that it was pleasant. He
bows his shoulder to the burden, and becomes a
servant doing forced labor.

16 "Dan will judge his people, as one of the tribes of
Israel. 17 Dan will be a serpent on the trail, an
adder in the path, That bites the horse's heels, so
that his rider falls backward. 18 I have waited for
your salvation, Yahweh.

19 "A troop will press on Gad, but he will press on
their heel.

20 "Asher's food will be rich. He will produce royal
dainties.

21 "Naphtali is a doe set free, who bears beautiful
fawns.

22 "Joseph is a fruitful vine, a fruitful vine by a
spring. His branches run over the wall. 23 The
archers have severely grieved him, shot at him, and
persecute him: 24 But his bow remained strong.
The arms of his hands were made strong, by the
hands of the Mighty One of Jacob, (from there is
the shepherd, the stone of Israel),

25 "even by the God of your father, who will help
you; by the Almighty, who will bless you, with
blessings of heaven above, blessings of the deep
that lies below, blessings of the breasts, and of the
womb. 26 The blessings of your father have
prevailed above the blessings of your ancestors,
above the boundaries of the ancient hills. They will
be on the head of Joseph, on the crown of the head
of him who is separated from his brothers.

27 "Benjamin is a ravenous wolf. In the morning he
will devour the prey. At evening he will divide the
plunder."

28 All these are the twelve tribes of Israel, and this
is what their father spoke to them and blessed
them. He blessed everyone according to his
blessing.

29 He instructed them, and said to them, "I am to
be gathered to my people. Bury me with my fathers
in the cave that is in the field of Ephron the Hittite,
30 in the cave that is in the field of Machpelah,
which is before Mamre, in the land of Canaan,
which Abraham bought with the field from Ephron
the Hittite as a burial place. 31 There they buried
Abraham and Sarah, his wife. There they buried
Isaac and Rebekah, his wife, and there I buried
Leah: 32 the field and the cave that is therein,
which was purchased from the children of Heth."

10 And Jacob again commanded his sons on that
day, saying, "Behold I shall be this day gathered
unto my people; carry me up from Egypt, and bury
me in the cave of Machpelah as I have commanded
you.

11 "Howbeit take heed I pray you that none of your sons carry me, only yourselves, and this is the manner you shall do unto me, when you carry my body to go with it to the land of Canaan to bury me,
12 Judah, Issachar and Zebulun shall carry my bier at the eastern side; Reuben, Simeon and Gad at the south, Ephraim, Manasseh and Benjamin at the west, Dan, Asher and Naphtali at the north.

13 "Let not Levi carry with you, for he and his sons will carry the ark of the covenant of the Lord with the Israelites in the camp, neither let Joseph my son carry, for as a king so let his glory be; howbeit, Ephraim and Manasseh shall be in their stead.

14 "Thus shall you do unto me when you carry me away; do not neglect any thing of all that I command you; and it shall come to pass when you do this unto me, that the Lord will remember you favorably and your children after you forever.

15 "And you my sons, honor each his brother and his relative, and command your children and your children's children after you to serve the Lord God of your ancestors all the days.

16 "In order that you may prolong your days in the land, you and your children and your children's children for ever, when you do what is good and upright in the sight of the Lord your God, to go in all his ways.

17 "And thou, Joseph my son, forgive I pray thee the prongs of thy brethren and all their misdeeds in the injury that they heaped upon thee, for God intended it for thine and thy children's benefit.

18 "And O my son leave not thy brethren to the inhabitants of Egypt, neither hurt their feelings, for behold I consign them to the hand of God and in thy hand to guard them from the Egyptians; and the sons of Jacob answered their father saying, 'O, our father, all that thou hast commanded us, so will we do; may God only be with us.'"

19 And Jacob said unto his sons, "So may God be with you when you keep all his ways; turn not from his ways either to the right or the left in performing
what is good and upright in his sight. 20 For I know
that many and grievous troubles will befall you in the latter days in the land, yea your children and children's children, only serve the Lord and he will save you from all trouble.

21 "And it shall come to pass when you shall go after God to serve him and will teach your children after you, and your children's children, to know the Lord, then will the Lord raise up unto you and your children a servant from amongst your children, and the Lord will deliver you through his hand from all affliction, and bring you out of Egypt and bring you back to the land of your fathers to inherit it securely."

33 When Jacob finished charging his sons, he gathered up his feet into the bed, and yielded up the spirit, and was gathered to his people.

22 And Jacob ceased commanding his sons, and he drew his feet into the bed, he died and was gathered to his people.

Genesis 50

1 Joseph fell on his father's face, wept on him, and kissed him.

23 And Joseph fell upon his father and he cried out and wept over him and he kissed him, and he called out in a bitter voice, and he said, "O my father, my father."

24 And his son's wives and all his household came and fell upon Jacob, and they wept over him, and cried in a very loud voice concerning Jacob. 25 And all the sons of Jacob rose up together, and they tore their garments, and they all put sackcloth upon their loins, and they fell upon their faces, and they cast dust upon their heads toward the heavens.

26 And the thing was told unto Osnath Joseph's wife, and she rose up and put on a sack and she with all the Egyptian women with her came and mourned and wept for Jacob. 27 And also all the people of Egypt who knew Jacob came all on that day when they heard this thing, and all Egypt wept for many days. 28 And also from the land of Canaan did the women come unto Egypt when they heard that Jacob was dead, and they wept for him in Egypt for seventy days.

2 Joseph commanded his servants, the physicians, to embalm his father; and the physicians embalmed Israel.

29 And it came to pass after this that Joseph commanded his servants the doctors to embalm his father with myrrh and frankincense and all manner of incense and perfume, and the doctors embalmed Jacob as Joseph had commanded them.

30 And all the people of Egypt and the elders and all the inhabitants of the land of Goshen wept and mourned over Jacob, and all his sons and the children of his household lamented and mourned over their father Jacob many days.

3 Forty days were fulfilled for him, for that is how many the days it takes to embalm. The Egyptians wept for him for seventy days. 4 When the days of weeping for him were past, Joseph spoke to the house of Pharaoh, saying, "If now I have found favor in your eyes, please speak in the ears of Pharaoh, saying, 5 'My father made me swear, saying, "Behold, I am dying. Bury me in my grave which I have dug for myself in the land of Canaan." Now therefore, please let me go up and bury my father, and I will come again.'"

31 And after the days of his weeping had passed away, at the end of seventy days, Joseph said unto Pharaoh, "I will go up and bury my father in the land of Canaan as he made me swear, and then I will return."

6 Pharaoh said, "Go up, and bury your father, just like he made you swear." 7 Joseph went up to bury his father; and with him went up all the servants of Pharaoh, the elders of his house, all the elders of the land of Egypt,

32 And Pharaoh sent Joseph, saying, "Go up and bury thy father as he said, and as he made thee swear;" and Joseph rose up with all his brethren to go to the land of Canaan to bury their father Jacob as he had commanded them.

33 And Pharaoh commanded that it should be proclaimed throughout Egypt, saying, "Whoever goeth not up with Joseph and his brethren to the land of Canaan to bury Jacob, shall die."

34 And all Egypt heard of Pharaoh's proclamation, and they all rose up together, and all the servants of Pharaoh, and the elders of his house, and all the elders of the land of Egypt went up with Joseph, and all the officers and nobles of Pharaoh went up as the servants of Joseph, and they went to bury Jacob in the land of Canaan.

35 And the sons of Jacob carried the bier upon which he lay; according to all that their father commanded them, so did his sons unto him. 36
And the bier was of pure gold, and it was inlaid round about with onyx stones and bdellium; and the covering of the bier was gold woven work, joined with threads, and over them were hooks of onyx stones and bdellium.

37 And Joseph placed upon the head of his father Jacob a large golden crown, and he put a golden scepter in his hand, and they surrounded the bier as was the custom of kings during their lives.

8 All the house of Joseph, his brothers, and his father's house. Only their little ones, their flocks, and their herds, they left in the land of Goshen.

9 There went up with him both chariots and horsemen. It was a very great company.

38 And all the troops of Egypt went before him in this array, at first all the mighty men of Pharaoh, and the mighty men of Joseph, and after them the rest of the inhabitants of Egypt, and they were all girded with swords and equipped with coats of mail, and the trappings of war were upon them.

39 And all the weepers and mourners went at a distance opposite to the bier, going and weeping and lamenting, and the rest of the people went after the bier. 40 And Joseph and his household went together near the bier barefooted and weeping, and the rest of Joseph's servants went around him; each man had his ornaments upon him, and they were all armed with their weapons of war.

41 And fifty of Jacob's servants went in front of the bier, and they strewed along the road myrrh and aloes, and all manner of perfume, and all the sons of Jacob that carried the bier walked upon the perfumery, and the servants of Jacob went before them strewing the perfume along the road.

10 They came to the threshing floor of Atad, which is beyond the Jordan, and there they lamented with a very great and severe lamentation.

42 And Joseph went up with a heavy camp, and they did after this manner every day until they reached the land of Canaan, and they came to the threshing floor of Atad, which was on the other side of Jordan, and they mourned an exceeding great and heavy mourning in that place.

He mourned for his father seven days. 11 When the inhabitants of the land, the Canaanites, saw the mourning in the floor of Atad, they said, "This is a grievous mourning by the Egyptians." Therefore its name was called Abel Mizraim, which is beyond the Jordan.

[56:68 And Joseph and his brethren made a mourning of seven days for their father.]

43 And all the kings of Canaan heard of this thing and they all went forth, each man from his house, thirty-one kings of Canaan, and they all came with their men to mourn and weep over Jacob. 44 And all these kings beheld Jacob's bier, and behold Joseph's crown was upon it, and they also put their crowns upon the bier, and encircled it with crowns.

45 And all these kings made in that place a great and heavy mourning with the sons of Jacob and Egypt over Jacob, for all the kings of Canaan knew the valor of Jacob and his sons.

46 And the report reached Esau, saying, "Jacob died in Egypt, and his sons and all Egypt are conveying him to the land of Canaan to bury him."

47 And Esau heard this thing, and he was dwelling in mount Seir, and he rose up with his sons and all his people and all his household, a people exceedingly great, and they came to mourn and weep over Jacob.

48 And it came to pass, when Esau came he mourned for his brother Jacob, and all Egypt and all Canaan again rose up and mourned a great mourning with Esau over Jacob in that place.

49 And Joseph and his brethren brought their father Jacob from that place, and they went to Hebron to bury Jacob in the cave by his fathers.

50 And they came unto Kireath-arba, to the cave, and as they came Esau stood with his sons against Joseph and his brethren as a hindrance in the cave, saying, "Jacob shall not be buried therein, for it belongeth to us and to our father."

51 And Joseph and his brethren heard the words of
Esau's sons, and they were exceedingly wroth, and
Joseph approached unto Esau, saying, "What is this
thing which they have spoken? Surely my father
Jacob bought it from thee for great riches after the
death of Isaac, now five and twenty years ago, and
also all the land of Canaan he bought from thee and
from thy sons, and thy seed after thee. 52 And
Jacob bought it for his sons and his seed after him
for an inheritance for ever, and why speakest thou
these things this day?"

53 And Esau answered, saying, "Thou speakest
falsely and utterest lies, for I sold not anything
belonging to me in all this land, as thou sayest,
neither did my brother Jacob buy aught belonging
to me in this land." 54 And Esau spoke these things
in order to deceive Joseph with his words, for Esau
knew that Joseph was not present in those days
when Esau sold all belonging to him in the land of
Canaan to Jacob.

55 And Joseph said unto Esau, "Surely my father inserted these things with thee in the record of purchase, and testified the record with witnesses, and behold it is with us in Egypt." 56 And Esau answered, saying unto him, "Bring the record, all that thou wilt find in the record, so will we do."

57 And Joseph called unto Naphtali his brother, and he said, "Hasten quickly, stay not, and run I pray thee to Egypt and bring all the records; the record of the purchase, the sealed record and the open record, and also all the first records in which all the transactions of the birth-right are written, fetch thou. 58 And thou shalt bring them unto us hither, that we may know from them all the words of Esau and his sons which they spoke this day."

59 And Naphtali hearkened to the voice of Joseph and he hastened and ran to go down to Egypt, and Naphtali was lighter on foot than any of the stags that were upon the wilderness, for he would go upon ears of corn without crushing them.

60 And when Esau saw that Naphtali had gone to fetch the records, he and his sons increased their resistance against the cave, and Esau and all his people rose up against Joseph and his brethren to battle. 61 And all the sons of Jacob and the people of Egypt fought with Esau and his men, and the sons of Esau and his people were smitten before the sons of Jacob, and the sons of Jacob slew of Esau's people forty men.

62 And Chushim the son of Dan, the son of Jacob, was at that time with Jacob's sons, but he was about a hundred cubits distant from the place of battle, for he remained with the children of Jacob's sons by Jacob's bier to guard it.

63 And Chushim was dumb and deaf, still he understood the voice of consternation amongst men. 64 And he asked, saying, "Why do you not bury the dead, and what is this great consternation?" and they answered him the words of Esau and his sons; and he ran to Esau in the midst of the battle, and he slew Esau with a sword, and he cut off his head, and it sprang to a distance, and Esau fell amongst the people of the battle.

65 And when Chushim did this thing the sons of Jacob prevailed over the sons of Esau, and the sons of Jacob buried their father Jacob by force in the cave, and the sons of Esau beheld it.

12 His sons did to him just as he commanded them,
13 for his sons carried him into the land of Canaan, and buried him in the cave of the field of Machpelah, which Abraham bought with the field, for a possession of a burial site, from Ephron the Hittite, before Mamre.

66 And Jacob was buried in Hebron, in the cave of Machpelah which Abraham had bought from the sons of Heth for the possession of a burial place, and he was buried in very costly garments.

67 And no king had such honor paid him as Joseph paid unto his father at his death, for he buried him with great honor like unto the burial of kings.

[Genesis 50:10b He mourned for his father seven days.]

68 And Joseph and his brethren made a mourning of seven days for their father.

14 Joseph returned into Egypt—he, and his brothers, and all that went up with him to bury his father, after he had buried his father.

15 When Joseph's brothers saw that their father was dead, they said, "It may be that Joseph will hate us, and will fully pay us back for all the evil
which we did to him." 16 They sent a message to
Joseph, saying, "Your father commanded before he
died, saying, 17 'You shall tell Joseph, "Now please
forgive the disobedience of your brothers, and their sin, because they did evil to you."' Now, please forgive the disobedience of the servants of the God of your father." Joseph wept when they spoke to him.

18 His brothers also went and fell down before his face; and they said, "Behold, we are your servants."
19 Joseph said to them, "Don't be afraid, for am I in
the place of God? 20 As for you, you meant evil
against me, but God meant it for good, to bring to pass, as it is today, to save many people alive. 21
Now therefore don't be afraid. I will nourish you and your little ones." He comforted them, and spoke kindly to them.

Jasher 57

1 And it was after this that the sons of Esau waged war with the sons of Jacob, and the sons of Esau fought with the sons of Jacob in Hebron, and Esau was still lying dead, and not buried.

2 And the battle was heavy between them, and the sons of Esau were smitten before the sons of Jacob, and the sons of Jacob slew of the sons of Esau eighty men, and not one died of the people of the sons of Jacob; and the hand of Joseph prevailed over all the people of the sons of Esau, and he took Zepho, the son of Eliphaz, the son of Esau, and fifty of his men captive, and he bound them with chains of iron, and gave them into the hand of his servants to bring them to Egypt.

3 And it came to pass when the sons of Jacob had taken Zepho and his people captive, all those that remained were greatly afraid of their lives from the house of Esau, lest they should also be taken captive, and they all fled with Eliphaz the son of Esau and his people, with Esau's body, and they went on their road to Mount Seir.

4 And they came unto Mount Seir and they buried Esau in Seir, but they had not brought his head with them to Seir, for it was buried in that place where the battle had been in Hebron.

5 And it came to pass when the sons of Esau had fled from before the sons of Jacob, the sons of Jacob pursued them unto the borders of Seir, but they did not slay a single man from amongst them when they pursued them, for Esau's body which they carried with them excited their confusion, so they fled and the sons of Jacob turned back from them and came up to the place where their brethren were in Hebron, and they remained there on that day, and on the next day until they rested from the battle.

6 And it came to pass on the third day they assembled all the sons of Seir the Horite, and they assembled all the children of the east, a multitude of people like the sand of the sea, and they went and came down to Egypt to fight with Joseph and his brethren, in order to deliver their brethren.

7 And Joseph and all the sons of Jacob heard that
the sons of Esau and the children of the east had
come upon them to battle in order to deliver their
brethren. 8 And Joseph and his brethren and the
strong men of Egypt went forth and fought in the
city of Rameses, and Joseph and his brethren dealt
out a tremendous blow amongst the sons of Esau
and the children of the east.

9 And they slew of them six hundred thousand
men, and they slew amongst them all the mighty
men of the children of Seir the Horite; there were
only a few of them left, and they slew also a great
many of the children of the east, and of the children
of Esau; and Eliphaz the son of Esau, and the
children of the east all fled before Joseph and his
brethren.

10 And Joseph and his brethren pursued them until
they came unto Succoth, and they yet slew of them
in Succoth thirty men, and the rest escaped and
they fled each to his city. 11 And Joseph and his
brethren and the mighty men of Egypt turned back
from them with joy and cheerfulness of heart, for
they had smitten all their enemies.

12 And Zepho the son of Eliphaz and his men were
still slaves in Egypt to the sons of Jacob, and their
pains increased. 13 And when the sons of Esau and
the sons of Seir returned to their land, the sons of
Seir saw that they had all fallen into the hands of
the sons of Jacob, and the people of Egypt, on
account of the battle of the sons of Esau.

14 And the sons of Seir said unto the sons of Esau,
"You have seen andtherefore you know that this
camp was on your account, and not one mighty
man or an adept in war remaineth. 15 Now
therefore go forth from our land, go from us to the
land of Canaan to the land of the dwelling of your
fathers; wherefore shall your children inherit the
effects of our children in latter days?"

16 And the children of Esau would not listen to the
children of Seir, and the children of Seir considered
to make war with them.

17 And the children of Esau sent secretly to Angeas
king of Africa, the same is Dinhabah, saying,

18 "Send unto us some of thy men and let them
come unto us, and we will fight together with the
children of Seir the Horite, for they have resolved to
fight with us to drive us away from the land."

19 And Angeas king of Dinhabah did so, for he was
in those days friendly to the children of Esau, and
Angeas sent five hundred valiant infantry to the
children of Esau, and eight hundred cavalry.

20 And the children of Seir sent unto the children of
the east and unto the children of Midian, saying,
"You have seen what the children of Esau have
done unto us, upon whose account we are almost
all destroyed, in their battle with the sons of Jacob.
21 Now therefore come unto us and assist us, and
we will fight them together, and we will drive them
from the land and be avenged of the cause of our
brethren who died for their sakes in their battle
with their brethren the sons of Jacob."

22 And all the children of the east listened to the
children of Seir, and they came unto them about
eight hundred men with drawn swords, and the
children of Esau fought with the children of Seir at
that time in the wilderness of Paran. 23 And the
children of Seir prevailed then over the sons of
Esau, and the children of Seir slew on that day of
the children of Esau in that battle about two
hundred men of the people of Angeas king of
Dinhabah.

24 And on the second day the children of Esau
came again to fight a second time with the children
of Seir, and the battle was sore upon the children of
Esau this second time, and it troubled them greatly
on account of the children of Seir. 25 And when the
children of Esau saw that the children of Seir were
more powerful than they were, some men of the
children of Esau turned and assisted the children of
Seir their enemies.

26 And there fell yet of the people of the children
of Esau in the second battle fifty-eight men of the
people at Angeas king of Dinhabah.

27 And on the third day the children of Esau heard
that some of their brethren had turned from them
to fight against them in the second battle; and the
children of Esau mourned when they heard this
thing.

28 And they said, "What shall we do unto our
brethren who turned from us to assist the children
of Seir our enemies?" and the children of Esau again
sent to Angeas king of Dinhabah, saying, 29 "Send
unto us again other men that with them we may
fight with the children of Seir, for they have already
twice been heavier than we were." 30 And Angeas
again sent to the children of Esau about six hundred
valiant men, and they came to assist the children of
Esau.

31 And in ten days' time the children of Esau again
waged war with the children of Seir in the
wilderness of Paran, and the battle was very severe
upon the children of Seir, and the children of Esau
prevailed at this time over the children of Seir, and
the children of Seir were smitten before the
children of Esau, and the children of Esau slew from
them about two thousand men.

32 And all the mighty men of the children of Seir
died in this battle, and there only remained their
young children that were left in their cities. 33 And
all Midian and the children of the east betook
themselves to flight from the battle, and they left
the children of Seir and fled when they saw that the
battle was severe upon them, and the children of
Esau pursued all the children of the east until they
reached their land.

34 And the children of Esau slew yet of them about two hundred and fifty men and from the people of the children of Esau there fell in that battle about thirty men, but this evil came upon them through their brethren turning from them to assist the children of Seir the Horite, and the children of Esau again heard of the evil doings of their brethren, and they again mourned on account of this thing.

35 And it came to pass after the battle, the children of Esau turned back and came home unto Seir, and the children of Esau slew those who had remained in the land of the children of Seir; they slew also their wives and little ones, they left not a soul alive except fifty young lads and damsels whom they suffered to live, and the children of Esau did not put them to death, and the lads became their slaves, and the damsels they took for wives.

36 And the children of Esau dwelt in Seir in the place of the children of Seir, and they inherited their land and took possession of it. 37 And the children of Esau took all belonging in the land to the children of Seir, also their flocks, their bullocks and their goods, and all belonging to the children of Seir, did the children of Esau take, and the children of Esau dwelt in Seir in the place of the children of Seir unto this day, and the children of Esau divided the land into divisions to the five sons of Esau, according to their families.

38 And it came to pass in those days, that the children of Esau resolved to crown a king over them in the land of which they became possessed. And they said to each other, "Not so, for he shall reign over us in our land, and we shall be under his counsel and he shall fight our battles, against our enemies," and they did so.

39 And all the children of Esau swore, saying, "That none of their brethren should ever reign over them, but a strange man who is not of their brethren, for the souls of all the children of Esau were embittered every man against his son, brother and friend, on account of the evil they sustained from their brethren when they fought with the children of Seir."

40 Therefore the sons of Esau swore, saying, "From that day forward they would not choose a king from their brethren, but one from a strange land unto this day." 41 And there was a man there from the people of Angeas king of Dinhabah; his name was Bela the son of Beor, who was a very valiant man, beautiful and comely and wise in all wisdom, and a man of sense and counsel; and there was none of the people of Angeas like unto him.

42 And all the children of Esau took him and
anointed him and they crowned him for a king, and
they bowed down to him, and they said unto him,
"May the king live, may the king live." 43 And they
spread out the sheet, and they brought him each
man earrings of gold and silver or rings or bracelets,
and they made him very rich in silver and in gold, in
onyx stones and bdellium, and they made him a
royal throne, and they placed a regal crown upon
his head, and they built a palace for him and he
dwelt therein, and he became king over all the
children of Esau.

44 And the people of Angeas took their hire for
their battle from the children of Esau, and they
went and returned at that time to their master in
Dinhabah. 45 And Bela reigned over the children of
Esau thirty years, and the children of Esau dwelt in
the land instead of the children of Seir, and they
dwelt securely in their stead unto this day.

Jasher 58

1 And it came to pass in the thirty-second year of
the Israelites going down to Egypt, that is in the
seventy-first year of the life of Joseph, in that year
died Pharaoh king of Egypt, and Magron his son
reigned in his stead. 2 And Pharaoh commanded
Joseph before his death to be a father to his son,
Magron, and that Magron should be under the care
of Joseph and under his counsel.

3 And all Egypt consented to this thing that Joseph
should be king over them, for all the Egyptians
loved Joseph as of heretofore, only Magron the son
of Pharaoh sat upon, his father's throne, and he
became king in those days in his father's stead. 4
Magron was forty-one years old when he began to
reign, and forty years he reigned in Egypt, and all
Egypt called his name Pharaoh after the name of his
father, as it was their custom to do in Egypt to
every king that reigned over them.

5 And it came to pass when Pharaoh reigned in his father's stead, he placed the laws of Egypt and all the affairs of government in the hand of Joseph, as his father had commanded him. 6 And Joseph became king over Egypt, for he superintended over all Egypt, and all Egypt was under his care and under his counsel, for all Egypt inclined to Joseph after the death of Pharaoh, and they loved him exceedingly to reign over them.

7 But there were some people amongst them, who did not like him, saying, "No stranger shall reign over us;" still the whole government of Egypt devolved in those days upon Joseph, after the death of Pharaoh, he being the regulator, doing as he liked throughout the land without any one interfering.

8 And all Egypt was under the care of Joseph, and Joseph made war with all his surrounding enemies, and he subdued them; also all the land and all the Philistines, unto the borders of Canaan, did Joseph subdue, and they were all under his power and they gave a yearly tax unto Joseph.

9 And Pharaoh king of Egypt sat upon his throne in his father's stead, but he was under the control and counsel of Joseph, as he was at first under the control of his father. 10 Neither did he reign but in the land of Egypt only, under the counsel of Joseph, but Joseph reigned over the whole country at that time, from Egypt unto the great river Perath.

11 And Joseph was successful in all his ways, and the Lord was with him, and the Lord gave Joseph additional wisdom, and honor, and glory, and love toward him in the hearts of the Egyptians and throughout the land, and Joseph reigned over the whole country forty years.

12 And all the countries of the Philistines and Canaan and Zidon, and on the other side of Jordan, brought presents unto Joseph all his days, and the whole country was in the hand of Joseph, and they

brought unto him a yearly tribute as it was regulated, for Joseph had fought against all his surrounding enemies and subdued them, and the whole country was in the hand of Joseph, and Joseph sat securely upon his throne in Egypt.

13 And also all his brethren the sons of Jacob dwelt securely in the land, all the days of Joseph, and they were fruitful and multiplied exceedingly in the land, and they served the Lord all their days, as their father Jacob had commanded them.

14 And it came to pass at the end of many days and years, when the children of Esau were dwelling quietly in their land with Bela their king, that the children of Esau were fruitful and multiplied in the land, and they resolved to go and fight with the sons of Jacob and all Egypt, and to deliver their brother Zepho, the son of Eliphaz, and his men, for they were yet in those days slaves to Joseph.

15 And the children of Esau sent unto all the children of the east, and they made peace with them, and all the children of the east came unto them to go with the children of Esau to Egypt to
battle. 16 And there came also unto them of the
people of Angeas, king of Dinhabah, and they also sent unto the children of Ishmael and they also came unto them.

17 And all this people assembled and came unto Seir to assist the children of Esau in their battle, and this camp was very large and heavy with people, numerous as the sand of the sea, about eight hundred thousand men, infantry and cavalry, and all these troops went down to Egypt to fight with the sons of Jacob, and they encamped by Rameses.

18 And Joseph went forth with his brethren with the mighty men of Egypt, about six hundred men, and they fought with them in the land of Rameses; and the sons of Jacob at that time again fought with the children of Esau, in the fiftieth year of the sons of Jacob going down to Egypt, that is the thirtieth year of the reign of Bela over the children of Esau in Seir.

19 And the Lord gave all the mighty men of Esau and the children of the east into the hand of Joseph and his brethren, and the people of the children of Esau and the children of the east were smitten before Joseph.

20 And of the people of Esau and the children of the east that were slain, there fell before the sons of Jacob about two hundred thousand men, and their king Bela the son of Beor fell with them in the battle, and when the children of Esau saw that their king had fallen in battle and was dead, their hands became weak in the combat.

21 And Joseph and his brethren and all Egypt were still smiting the people of the house of Esau, and all Esau's people were afraid of the sons of Jacob and fled from before them.

22 And Joseph and his brethren and all Egypt pursued them a day's journey, and they slew yet from them about three hundred men, continuing to smite them in the road; and they afterward turned back from them.

23 And Joseph and all his brethren returned to Egypt, not one man was missing from them, but of the Egyptians there fell twelve men.

24 And when Joseph returned to Egypt he ordered Zepho and his men to be additionally bound, and they bound them in irons and they increased their grief.

25 And all the people of the children of Esau, and the children of the east, returned in shame each unto his city, for all the mighty men that were with them had fallen in battle.

26 And when the children of Esau saw that their king had died in battle they hastened and took a man from the people of the children of the east; his name was Jobab the son of Zarach, from the land of Botzrah, and they caused him to reign over them instead of Bela their king.

27 And Jobab sat upon the throne of Bela as king in his stead, and Jobab reigned in Edom over all the children of Esau ten years, and the children of Esau went no more to fight with the sons of Jacob from that day forward, for the sons of Esau knew the valor of the sons of Jacob, and they were greatly afraid of them.

28 But from that day forward the children of Esau hated the sons of Jacob, and the hatred and enmity were very strong between them all the days, unto this day.

29 And it came to pass after this, at the end of ten years, Jobab, the son of Zarach, from Botzrah, died, and the children of Esau took a man whose name was Chusham, from the land of Teman, and they made him king over them instead of Jobab, and Chusham reigned in Edom over all the children of Esau for twenty years.

30 And Joseph, king of Egypt, and his brethren, and all the children of Israel dwelt securely in Egypt in those days, together with all the children of Joseph and his brethren, having no hindrance or evil accident and the land of Egypt was at that time at rest from war in the days of Joseph and his brethren.

Jasher 59

1 And these are the names of the sons of Israel who dwelt in Egypt, who had come with Jacob, all the sons of Jacob came unto Egypt, every man with his household.

2 The children of Leah were Reuben, Simeon, Levi, Judah, Issachar and Zebulun, and their sister Dinah.

3 And the sons of Rachel were Joseph and Benjamin.

4 And the sons of Zilpah, the handmaid of Leah, were Gad and Asher.

5 And the sons of Bilhah, the handmaid of Rachel, were Dan and Naphtali.

6 And these were their offspring that were born unto them in the land of Canaan, before they came unto Egypt with their father Jacob.

[Genesis 46:9 The sons of Reuben: Hanoch, Pallu, Hezron, and Carmi.]

7 The sons of Reuben were Chanoch, Pallu, Chetzron and Carmi.

[Genesis 46:10 The sons of Simeon: Jemuel, Jamin, Ohad, Jachin, Zohar, and Shaul the son of a Canaanite woman.]

8 And the sons of Simeon were Jemuel, Jamin, Ohad, Jachin, Zochar and Saul, the son of the Canaanitish woman.

[Genesis 46:11 The sons of Levi: Gershon, Kohath, and Merari.]

9 And the children of Levi were Gershon, Kehath and Merari, and their sister Jochebed, who was born unto them in their going down to Egypt.

[Genesis 46:12 The sons of Judah: Er, Onan, Shelah, Perez, and Zerah; but Er and Onan died in the land of Canaan. The sons of Perez were Hezron and Hamul.]

10 And the sons of Judah were Er, Onan, Shelah, Perez and Zarach. 11 And Er and Onan died in the land of Canaan; and the sons of Perez were Chezron and Chamul.

[Genesis 46:13 The sons of Issachar: Tola, Puvah, Iob, and Shimron. 46: 23 The son of Dan: Hushim.]

12 And the sons of Issachar were Tola, Puvah, Job and Shomron.

[Genesis 46:14 The sons of Zebulun: Sered, Elon, and Jahleel. Genesis 46: 23 The son of Dan: Hushim.]

13 And the sons of Zebulun were Sered, Elon and Jachleel, and the son of Dan was Chushim.

[Genesis 46:24 The sons of Naphtali: Jahzeel, Guni, Jezer, and Shillem.]

14 And the sons of Naphtali were Jachzeel, Guni, Jetzer and Shilam.

[Genesis 46:16 The sons of Gad: Ziphion, Haggi, Shuni, Ezbon, Eri, Arodi, and Areli.]

15 And the sons of Gad were Ziphion, Chaggi, Shuni, Ezbon, Eri, Arodi and Areli.

[Genesis 46:17 The sons of Asher: Imnah, Ishvah, Ishvi, Beriah, and Serah their sister. The sons of Beriah: Heber and Malchiel.]

16 And the children of Asher were Jimnah, Jishvah, Jishvi, Beriah and their sister Serach; and the sons of Beriah were Cheber and Malchiel.

[Genesis 46:21 The sons of Benjamin: Bela, Becher, Ashbel, Gera, Naaman, Ehi, Rosh, Muppim, Huppim, and Ard.]

17 And the sons of Benjamin were Bela, Becher, Ashbel, Gera, Naaman, Achi, Rosh, Mupim, Chupim and Ord.

[Genesis 46:20 To Joseph in the land of Egypt were born Manasseh and Ephraim, whom Asenath, the daughter of Potiphera, priest of On, bore to him.]

18 And the sons of Joseph, that were born unto him in Egypt, were Manasseh and Ephraim.

[Genesis 46:26 All the souls who came with Jacob into Egypt, who were his direct offspring, besides Jacob's sons' wives, all the souls were sixty-six. 27 The sons of Joseph, who were born to him in Egypt, were two souls. All the souls of the house of Jacob, who came into Egypt, were seventy.]

19 And all the souls that went forth from the loins of Jacob, were seventy souls; these are they who came with Jacob their father unto Egypt to dwell there: and Joseph and all his brethren dwelt securely in Egypt, and they ate of the best of Egypt all the days of the life of Joseph.

20 And Joseph lived in the land of Egypt ninety-three years, and Joseph reigned over all Egypt eighty years.

22 Joseph lived in Egypt, he, and his father's house. Joseph lived one hundred ten years. 23 Joseph saw Ephraim's children to the third generation. The children also of Machir, the son of Manasseh, were born on Joseph's knees.

21 And when the days of Joseph drew nigh that he should die, he sent and called for his brethren and all his father's household, and they all came together and sat before him.

24 Joseph said to his brothers, "I am dying, but God will surely visit you, and bring you up out of this land to the land which he swore to Abraham, to Isaac, and to Jacob."

22 And Joseph said unto his brethren and unto the whole of his father's household, "Behold I die, and God will surely visit you and bring you up from this land to the land which he swore to your fathers to give unto them. 23 And it shall be when God shall visit you to bring you up from here to the land of your fathers, then bring up my bones with you from here."

25 Joseph took an oath of the children of Israel, saying, "God will surely visit you, and you shall carry up my bones from here."

24 And Joseph made the sons of Israel to swear for their seed after them, saying, "God will surely visit you and you shall bring up my bones with you from here."

25 And it came to pass after this that Joseph died in that year, the seventy-first year of the Israelites going down to Egypt.

26 So Joseph died, being one hundred ten years old, and they embalmed him, and he was put in a coffin in Egypt.

26 And Joseph was one hundred and ten years old when he died in the land of Egypt, and all his brethren and all his servants rose up and they embalmed Joseph, as was their custom, and his brethren and all Egypt mourned over him for seventy days. 27 And they put Joseph in a coffin filled with spices and all sorts of perfume, and they buried him by the side of the river, that is Sihor, and his sons and all his brethren, and the whole of his father's household made a seven day's mourning for him.

28 And it came to pass after the death of Joseph, all the Egyptians began in those days to rule over the children of Israel, and Pharaoh, king of Egypt, who reigned in his father's stead, took all the laws of Egypt and conducted the whole government of Egypt under his counsel, and he reigned securely over his people.

Exodus 1

1 Now these are the names of the sons of Israel, who came into Egypt (every man and his household came with Jacob): 2 Reuben, Simeon, Levi, and Judah, 3 Issachar, Zebulun, and Benjamin, 4 Dan and Naphtali, Gad and Asher.

Jasher 60

1 And when the year came round, being the seventy-second year from the Israelites going down to Egypt, after the death of Joseph, Zepho, the son of Eliphaz, the son of Esau, fled from Egypt, he and his men, and they went away.

2 And he came to Africa, which is Dinhabah, to
Angeas king of Africa, and Angeas received them
with great honor, and he made Zepho the captain
of his host. 3 And Zepho found favor in the sight of
Angeas and in the sight of his people, and Zepho
was captain of the host to Angeas king of Africa for
many days. 4 And Zepho enticed Angeas king of
Africa to collect all his army to go and fight with the
Egyptians, and with the sons of Jacob, and to
avenge of them the cause of his brethren.

5 But Angeas would not listen to Zepho to do this
thing, for Angeas knew the strength of the sons of
Jacob, and what they had done to his army in their
warfare with the children of Esau. 6 And Zepho was
in those days very great in the sight of Angeas and
in the sight of all his people, and he continually
enticed them to make war against Egypt, but they
would not.

7 And it came to pass in those days there was in the
land of Chittim a man in the city of Puzimna, whose
name was Uzu, and he became degenerately
deified by the children of Chittim, and the man died
and had no son, only one daughter whose name
was Jania. 8 And the damsel was exceedingly
beautiful, comely and intelligent, there was none
seen like unto her for beauty and wisdom
throughout the land.

9 And the people of Angeas king of Africa saw her
and they came and praised her unto him, and
Angeas sent to the children of Chittim, and he
requested to take her unto himself for a wife, and
the people of Chittim consented to give her unto
him for a wife.

10 And when the messengers of Angeas were going
forth from the land of Chittim to take their journey,
behold the messengers of Turnus king of Bibentu
came unto Chittim, for Turnus king of Bibentu also
sent his messengers to request Jania for him, to
take unto himself for a wife, for all his men had also
praised her to him, therefore he sent all his
servants unto her. 11 And the servants of Turnus
came to Chittim, and they asked for Jania, to be
taken unto Turnus their king for a wife.

12 And the people of Chittim said unto them, "We
cannot give her, because Angeas king of Africa
desired her to take her unto him for a wife before
you came, and that we should give her unto him,
and now therefore we cannot do this thing to
deprive Angeas of the damsel in order to give her
unto Turnus. 13 For we are greatly afraid of Angeas
lest he come in battle against us and destroy us,
and Turnus your master will not be able to deliver
us from his hand."
14 And when the messengers of Turnus heard all
the words of the children of Chittim, they turned
back to their master and told him all the words of
the children of Chittim. 15 And the children of
Chittim sent a memorial to Angeas, saying, "Behold
Turnus has sent for Jania to take her unto him for a
wife, and thus have we answered him;" and we
heard that he has collected his whole army to go to
war against thee, and he intends to pass by the
road of Sardunia to fight against thy brother Lucus,
and after that he will come to fight against thee.

16 And Angeas heard the words of the children of
Chittim which they sent to him in the record, and
his anger was kindled and he rose up and
assembled his whole army and came through the
islands of the sea, the road to Sardunia, unto his
brother Lucus king of Sardunia.

17 And Niblos, the son of Lucus, heard that his
uncle Angeas was coming, and he went out to meet
him with a heavy army, and he kissed him and
embraced him, and Niblos said unto Angeas, "When
thou askest my father after his welfare, when I shall
go with thee to fight with Turnus, ask of him to
make me captain of his host, and Angeas did so,
and he came unto his brother and his brother came
to meet him, and he asked him after his welfare."

18 And Angeas asked his brother Lucus after his
welfare, and to make his son Niblos captain of his
host, and Lucus did so, and Angeas and his brother
Lucus rose up and they went toward Turnus to
battle, and there was with them a great army and a
heavy people. 19 And he came in ships, and they
came into the province of Ashtorash, and behold
Turnus came toward them, for he went forth to
Sardunia, and intended to destroy it and afterward
to pass on from there to Angeas to fight with him.

20 And Angeas and Lucus his brother met Turnus in
the valley of Canopia, and the battle was strong and
mighty between them in that place. 21 And the
battle was severe upon Lucus king of Sardunia, and
all his army fell, and Niblos his son fell also in that
battle.

22 And his uncle Angeas commanded his servants
and they made a golden coffin for Niblos and they
put him into it, and Angeas again waged battle
toward Turnus, and Angeas was stronger than he,
and he slew him, and he smote all his people with
the edge of the sword, and Angeas avenged the
cause of Niblos his brother's son and the cause of
the army of his brother Lucus.

23 And when Turnus died, the hands of those that
survived the battle became weak, and they fled
from before Angeas and Lucus his brother.

24 And Angeas and his brother Lucus pursued them
unto the highroad, which is between Alphanu and
Romah, and they slew the whole army of Turnus
with the edge of the sword.

25 And Lucus king of Sardunia commanded his
servants that they should make a coffin of brass,
and that they should place therein the body of his
son Niblos, and they buried him in that place. 26
And they built upon it a high tower there upon the
highroad, and they called its name after the name
of Niblos unto this day, and they also buried Turnus
king of Bibentu there in that place with Niblos. 27
And behold upon the highroad between Alphanu
and Romah the grave of Niblos is on one side and
the grave of Turnus on the other, and a pavement
between them unto this day.

28 And when Niblos was buried, Lucus his father
returned with his army to his land Sardunia, and
Angeas his brother king of Africa went with his
people unto the city of Bibentu, that is the city of
Turnus.

29 And the inhabitants of Bibentu heard of his fame
and they were greatly afraid of him, and they went
forth to meet him with weeping and supplication,
and the inhabitants of Bibentu entreated of Angeas
not to slay them nor destroy their city; and he did
so, for Bibentu was in those days reckoned as one
of the cities of the children of Chittim; therefore he
did not destroy the city. 30 But from that day
forward the troops of the king of Africa would go to
Chittim to spoil and plunder it, and whenever they
went, Zepho the captain of the host of Angeas
would go with them.

31 And it was after this that Angeas turned with his
army and they came to the city of Puzimna, and
Angeas took thence Jania the daughter of Uzu for a
wife and brought her unto his city unto Africa.

Jasher 61

1 And it came to pass at that time Pharaoh king of
Egypt commanded all his people to make for him a
strong palace in Egypt. 2 And he also commanded
the sons of Jacob to assist the Egyptians in the
building, and the Egyptians made a beautiful and
elegant palace for a royal habitation, and he dwelt
therein and he renewed his government and he
reigned securely.

3 And Zebulun the son of Jacob died in that year,
that is the seventy-second year of the going down
of the Israelites to Egypt, and Zebulun died a
hundred and fourteen years old, and was put into a
coffin and given into the hands of his children. 4
And in the seventy-fifth year died his brother
Simeon, he was a hundred and twenty years old at
his death, and he was also put into a coffin and
given into the hands of his children.

5 And Zepho the son of Eliphaz the son of Esau,
captain of the host to Angeas king of Dinhabah, was
still daily enticing Angeas to prepare for battle to
fight with the sons of Jacob in Egypt, and Angeas
was unwilling to do this thing, for his servants had
related to him all the might of the sons of Jacob,
what they had done unto them in their battle with
the children of Esau. 6 And Zepho was in those
days daily enticing Angeas to fight with the sons of
Jacob in those days.

7 And after some time Angeas hearkened to the words of Zepho and consented to him to fight with the sons of Jacob in Egypt, and Angeas got all his people in order, a people numerous as the sand which is upon the sea shore, and he formed his resolution to go to Egypt to battle.

8 And amongst the servants of Angeas was a youth fifteen years old, Balaam the son of Beor was his name and the youth was very wise and understood the art of witchcraft.

9 And Angeas said unto Balaam, "Conjure for us, I pray thee, with the witchcraft, that we may know who will prevail in this battle to which we are now proceeding."

10 And Balaam ordered that they should bring him wax, and he made thereof the likeness of chariots and horsemen representing the army of Angeas and the army of Egypt, and he put them in the cunningly prepared waters that he had for that purpose, and he took in his hand the boughs of myrtle trees, and he exercised his cunning, and he joined them over the water, and there appeared unto him in the water the resembling images of the hosts of Angeas falling before the resembling images of the Egyptians and the sons of Jacob.

11 And Balaam told this thing to Angeas, and Angeas despaired and did not arm himself to go down to Egypt to battle, and he remained in his city.

12 And when Zepho the son of Eliphaz saw that
Angeas despaired of going forth to battle with the
Egyptians, Zepho fled from Angeas from Africa, and
he went and came unto Chittim. 13 And all the
people of Chittim received him with great honor,
and they hired him to fight their battles all the days,
and Zepho became exceedingly rich in those days,
and the troops of the king of Africa still spread
themselves in those days, and the children of
Chittim assembled and went to Mount Cuptizia on
account of the troops of Angeas king of Africa, who
were advancing upon them.

14 And it was one day that Zepho lost a young heifer, and he went to seek it, and he heard it lowing round about the mountain.

15 And Zepho went and he saw and behold there was a large cave at the bottom of the mountain, and there was a great stone there at the entrance of the cave, and Zepho split the stone and he came into the cave and he looked and behold, a large animal was devouring the

ox; from the middle upward it resembled a man, and from the middle downward it resembled an animal, and Zepho rose up against the animal and slew it with his swords.

16 And the inhabitants of Chittim heard of this thing, and they rejoiced exceedingly, and they said, "What shall we do unto this man who has slain this
animal that devoured our cattle?" 17 And they all
assembled to consecrate one day in the year to him, and they called the name thereof Zepho after his name, and they brought unto him drink offerings year after year on that day, and they brought unto him gifts.

18 At that time Jania the daughter of Uzu wife of king Angeas became ill, and her illness was heavily felt by Angeas and his officers, and Angeas said unto his wise men, "What shall I do to Jania and how shall I heal her from her illness?" And his wise men said unto him, "Because the air of our country is not like the air of the land of Chittim, and our water is not like their water, therefore from this has
the queen become ill. 19 For through the change of
air and water she became ill, and also because in her country she drank only the water which came from Purmah, which her ancestors had brought up with bridges."

20 And Angeas commanded his servants, and they brought unto him in vessels of the waters of Purmah belonging to Chittim, and they weighed those waters with all the waters of the land of Africa, and they found those waters lighter than the waters of Africa.

21 And Angeas saw this thing, and he commanded all his officers to assemble the hewers of stone in thousands and tens of thousands, and they hewed stone without number, and the builders came and they built an exceedingly strong bridge, and they conveyed the spring of water from the land of Chittim unto Africa, and those waters were for Jania the queen and for all her concerns, to

drink from and to bake, wash and bathe therewith, and also to water therewith all seed from which food can be obtained, and all fruit of the ground.

22 And the king commanded that they should bring of the soil of Chittim in large ships, and they also brought stones to build therewith, and the builders built palaces for Jania the queen, and the queen became healed of her illness.

23 And at the revolution of the year the troops of Africa continued coming to the land of Chittim to plunder as usual, and Zepho son of Eliphaz heard their report, and he gave orders concerning them and he fought with them, and they fled before him,
and he delivered the land of Chittim from them. 24
And the children of Chittim saw the valor of Zepho, and the children of Chittim resolved and they made Zepho king over them, and he became king over them, and whilst he reigned they went to subdue the children of Tubal, and all the surrounding islands.

25 And their king Zepho went at their head and they made war with Tubal and the islands, and they subdued them, and when they returned from the battle they renewed his government for him, and they built for him a very large palace for his royal habitation and seat, and they made a large throne for him, and Zepho reigned over the whole land of Chittim and over the land of Italia fifty years.

5 All the souls who came out of Jacob's body were seventy souls, and Joseph was in Egypt already.

6 Joseph died, as did all his brothers, and all that generation.

Jasher 62

1 In that year, being the seventy-ninth year of the Israelites going down to Egypt, died Reuben the son of Jacob, in the land of Egypt; Reuben was a hundred and twenty-five years old when he died, and they put him into a coffin, and he was given into the hands of his children.

2 And in the eightieth year died his brother Dan; he was a hundred and twenty years at his death, and he was also put into a coffin and given into the hands of his children.

3 And in that year died Chusham king of Edom, and after him reigned Hadad the son of Bedad, for thirty-five years; and in the eighty-first year died Issachar the son of Jacob, in Egypt, and Issachar was a hundred and twenty-two years old at his death, and he was put into a coffin in Egypt, and given into the hands of his children.

4 And in the eighty-second year died Asher his brother, he was a hundred and twenty-three years old at his death, and he was placed in a coffin in Egypt, and given into the hands of his children.

5 And in the eighty-third year died Gad, he was a hundred and twenty-five years old at his death, and he was put into a coffin in Egypt, and given into the hands of his children.

6 And it came to pass in the eighty-fourth year, that is the fiftieth year of the reign of Hadad, son of Bedad, king of Edom, that Hadad assembled all the children of Esau, and he got his whole army in readiness, about four hundred thousand men, and he directed his way to the land of Moab, and he went to fight with Moab and to make them tributary to him.

7 And the children of Moab heard this thing, and
they were very much afraid, and they sent to the
children of Midian to assist them in fighting with
Hadad, son of Bedad, king of Edom. 8 And Hadad
came unto the land of Moab, and Moab and the
children of Midian went out to meet him, and they
placed themselves in battle array against him in the
field of Moab.

9 And Hadad fought with Moab, and there fell of the children of Moab and the children of Midian many slain ones, about two hundred thousand men.

10 And the battle was very severe upon Moab, and when the children of Moab saw that the battle was sore upon them, they weakened their hands and turned their backs, and left the children of Midian to carry on the battle.

11 And the children of Midian knew not the
intentions of Moab, but they strengthened
themselves in battle and fought with Hadad and all
his host, and all Midian fell before him. 12 And
Hadad smote all Midian with a heavy smiting, and
he slew them with the edge of the sword, he left
none remaining of those who came to assist Moab.

13 And when all the children of Midian had
perished in battle, and the children at Moab had
escaped, Hadad made all Moab at that time
tributary to him, and they became under his hand,
and they gave a yearly tax as it was ordered, and
Hadad turned and went back to his land.

14 And at the revolution of the year, when the rest
of the people of Midian that were in the land heard
that all their brethren had fallen in battle with
Hadad for the sake of Moab, because the children
of Moab had turned their backs in battle and left
Midian to fight, then five of the princes of Midian
resolved with the rest of their brethren who
remained in their land, to fight with Moab to
avenge the cause of their brethren. 15 And the
children of Midian sent to all their brethren the
children of the east, and all their brethren, all the
children of Keturah came to assist Midian to fight
with Moab.

16 And the children of Moab heard this thing, and
they were greatly afraid that all the children of the
east had assembled together against them for
battle, and they the children of Moab sent a
memorial to the land of Edom to Hadad the son of
Bedad, saying,

17 "Come now unto us and assist us and we will
smite Midian, for they all assembled together and
have come against us with all their brethren the
children of the east to battle, to avenge the cause
of Midian that fell in battle."

18 And Hadad, son of Bedad, king of Edom, went
forth with his whole army and went to the land of
Moab to fight with Midian, and Midian and the
children of the east fought with Moab in the field of
Moab, and the battle was very fierce between
them.

19 And Hadad smote all the children of Midian and the children of the east with the edge of the sword, and Hadad at that time delivered Moab from the hand of Midian, and those that remained of Midian and of the children of the east fled before Hadad and his army, and Hadad pursued them to their land, and smote them with a very heavy slaughter, and the slain fell in the road.

20 And Hadad delivered Moab from the hand of Midian, for all the children of Midian had fallen by the edge of the sword, and Hadad turned and went back to his land.

21 And from that day forth, the children of Midian hated the children of Moab, because they had fallen in battle for their sake, and there was a great and mighty enmity between them all the days.

22 And all that were found of Midian in the road of the land of Moab perished by the sword of Moab, and all that were found of Moab in the road of the land of Midian, perished by the sword of Midian; thus did Midian unto Moab and Moab unto Midian for many days.

23 And it came to pass at that time that Judah the son of Jacob died in Egypt, in the eighty-sixth year of Jacob's going down to Egypt, and Judah was a hundred and twenty-nine years old at his death, and they embalmed him and put him into a coffin, and he was given into the hands of his children.

24 And in the eighty-ninth year died Naphtali, he was a hundred and thirty-two years old, and he was put into a coffin and given into the hands of his children.

25 And it came to pass in the ninety-first year of the Israelites going down to Egypt, that is in the thirtieth year of the reign of Zepho the son of Eliphaz, the son of Esau, over the children of Chittim, the children of Africa came upon the children of Chittim to plunder them as usual, but they had not come upon them for these thirteen years.

26 And they came to them in that year, and Zepho
the son of Eliphaz went out to them with some of
his men and smote them desperately, and the
troops of Africa fled from before Zepho and the
slain fell before him, and Zepho and his men
pursued them, going on and smiting them until they
were near unto Africa. 27 And Angeas king of Africa
heard the thing which Zepho had done, and it vexed
him exceedingly, and Angeas was afraid of Zepho all
the days.

Jasher 63

1 And in the ninety-third year died Levi, the son of Jacob, in Egypt, and Levi was a hundred and thirty-seven years old when he died, and they put him into a coffin and he was given into the hands of his children.

2 And it came to pass after the death of Levi, when all Egypt saw that the sons of Jacob the brethren of Joseph were dead, all the Egyptians began to afflict the children of Jacob, and to embitter their lives from that day unto the day of their going forth from Egypt, and they took from their hands all the vineyards and fields which Joseph had given unto them, and all the elegant houses in which the people of Israel lived, and all the fat of Egypt, the Egyptians took all from the sons of Jacob in those days.

3 And the hand of all Egypt became more grievous in those days against the children of Israel, and the Egyptians injured the Israelites until the children of Israel were wearied of their lives on account of the Egyptians.

7 The children of Israel were fruitful, and increased abundantly, and multiplied, and grew exceedingly mighty; and the land was filled with them.

8 Now there arose a new king over Egypt, who didn’t know Joseph.

4 And it came to pass in those days, in the hundred
and second year of Israel's going down to Egypt,
that Pharaoh king of Egypt died, and Melol his son
reigned in his stead, and all the mighty men of
Egypt and all that generation which knew Joseph
and his brethren died in those days. 5 And another
generation rose up in their stead, which had not
known the sons of Jacob and all the good which
they had done to them, and all their might in Egypt.

6 Therefore all Egypt began from that day forth to embitter the lives of the sons of Jacob, and to afflict them with all manner of hard labor, because they had not known their ancestors who had delivered them in the days of the famine.

7 And this was also from the Lord, for the children of Israel, to benefit them in their latter days, in order that all the children of Israel might know the Lord their God. 8 And in order to know the signs and mighty wonders which the Lord would do in Egypt on account of his people Israel, in order that the children of Israel might fear the Lord God of their ancestors, and walk in all his ways, they and their seed after them all the days.

9 Melol was twenty years old when he began to reign, and he reigned ninety-four years, and all Egypt called his name Pharaoh after the name of his father, as it was their custom to do to every king who reigned over them in Egypt.

10 At that time all the troops of Angeas king of Africa went forth to spread along the land of Chittim as usual for plunder. 11 And Zepho the son of Eliphaz the son of Esau heard their report, and he went forth to meet them with his army, and he fought them there in the road. 12 And Zepho smote the troops of the king of Africa with the edge of the sword, and left none remaining of them, and not even one returned to his master in Africa.

13 And Angeas heard of this which Zepho the son of Eliphaz had done to all his troops, that he had destroyed them, and Angeas assembled all his troops, all the men of the land of Africa, a people numerous like the sand by the sea shore. 14 And Angeas sent to Lucus his brother, saying, "Come to me with all thy men and help me to smite Zepho and all the children of Chittim who have destroyed my men, and Lucus came with his whole army, a very great force, to assist Angeas his brother to fight with Zepho and the children of Chittim."

15 And Zepho and the children of Chittim heard this thing, and they were greatly afraid and a great terror fell upon their hearts. 16 And Zepho also sent a letter to the land of Edom to Hadad the son of Bedad king of Edom and to all the children of Esau, saying,

17 "I have heard that Angeas king of Africa is
coming to us with his brother for battle against us,
and we are greatly afraid of him, for his army is very
great, particularly as he comes against us with his
brother and his army likewise. 18 Now therefore
come you also up with me and help me, and we will
fight together against Angeas and his brother Lucus,
and you will save us out of their hands, but if not,
know ye that we shall all die."

19 And the children of Esau sent a letter to the
children of Chittim and to Zepho their king, saying,
"We cannot fight against Angeas and his people for
a covenant of peace has been between us these
many years, from the days of Bela the first king, and
from the days of Joseph the son of Jacob king of
Egypt, with whom we fought on the other side of
Jordan when he buried his father."

20 And when Zepho heard the words of his
brethren the children of Esau he refrained from
them, and Zepho was greatly afraid of Angeas.

21 And Angeas and Lucus his brother arrayed all
their forces, about eight hundred thousand men,
against the children of Chittim.

22 And all the children of Chittim said unto Zepho,
"Pray for us to the God of thy ancestors,
peradventure he may deliver us from the hand of
Angeas and his army, for we have heard that he is a
great God and that he delivers all who trust in him."

23 And Zepho heard their words, and Zepho sought
the Lord and he said, 24 "O Lord God of Abraham
and Isaac my ancestors, this day I know that thou
art a true God, and all the gods of the nations are
vain and useless. 25 Remember now this day unto
me thy covenant with Abraham our father, which
our ancestors related unto us, and do graciously
with me this day for the sake of Abraham and Isaac
our fathers, and save me and the children of
Chittim from the hand of the king of Africa who
comes against us for battle."

26 And the Lord hearkened to the voice of Zepho,
and he had regard for him on account of Abraham
and Isaac, and the Lord delivered Zepho and the
children of Chittim from the hand of Angeas and his
people.

27 And Zepho fought Angeas king of Africa and all
his people on that day, and the Lord gave all the
people of Angeas into the hands of the children of
Chittim. 28 And the battle was severe upon
Angeas, and Zepho smote all the men of Angeas
and Lucus his brother, with the edge of the sword,
and there fell from them unto the evening of that
day about four hundred thousand men.

29 And when Angeas saw that all his men perished,
he sent a letter to all the inhabitants of Africa to
come to him, to assist him in the battle, and he
wrote in the letter, saying, "All who are found in
Africa let them come unto me from ten years old
and upward; let them all come unto me, and behold
if he comes not he shall die, and all that he has,
with his whole household, the king will take."

30 And all the rest of the inhabitants of Africa were
terrified at the words of Angeas, and there went
out of the city about three hundred thousand men
and boys, from ten years upward, and they came to
Angeas.

31 And at the end of ten days Angeas renewed the
battle against Zepho and the children of Chittim,
and the battle was very great and strong between
them. 32 And from the army of Angeas and Lucus,
Zepho sent many of the wounded unto his hand,
about two thousand men, and Sosiphtar the captain
of the host of Angeas fell in that battle.

33 And when Sosiphtar had fallen, the African
troops turned their backs to flee, and they fled, and
Angeas and Lucus his brother were with them.

34 And Zepho and the children of Chittim pursued
them, and they smote them still heavily on the
road, about two hundred men, and they pursued
Azdrubal the son of Angeas who had fled with his
father, and they smote twenty of his men in the
road, and Azdrubal escaped from the children of
Chittim, and they did not slay him.

35 And Angeas and Lucus his brother fled with the
rest of their men, and they escaped and came into
Africa with terror and consternation, and Angeas
feared all the days lest Zepho the son of Eliphaz
should go to war with him.

Jasher 64

1 And Balaam the son of Beor was at that time with Angeas in the battle, and when he saw that Zepho prevailed over Angeas, he fled from there and came to Chittim. 2 And Zepho and the children of Chittim received him with great honor, for Zepho knew Balaam's wisdom, and Zepho gave unto Balaam many gifts and he remained with him.

3 And when Zepho had returned from the war, he commanded all the children of Chittim to be numbered who had gone into battle with him, and behold not one was missed. 4 And Zepho rejoiced at this thing, and he renewed his kingdom, and he made a feast to all his subjects.

5 But Zepho remembered not the Lord and considered not that the Lord had helped him in battle, and that he had delivered him and his people from the hand of the king of Africa, but still walked in the ways of the children of Chittim and the wicked children of Esau, to serve other gods which his brethren the children of Esau had taught him; it is therefore said, "From the wicked goes forth wickedness."

6 And Zepho reigned over all the children of Chittim securely, but knew not the Lord who had delivered him and all his people from the hand of the king of Africa; and the troops of Africa came no more to Chittim to plunder as usual, for they knew of the power of Zepho who had smitten them all at the edge of the sword, so Angeas was afraid of Zepho the son of Eliphaz, and of the children of Chittim all the days.

7 At that time when Zepho had returned from the war, and when Zepho had seen how he prevailed over all the people of Africa and had smitten them in battle at the edge of the sword, then Zepho advised with the children of Chittim, to go to Egypt to fight with the sons of Jacob and with Pharaoh king of Egypt. 8 For Zepho heard that the mighty men of Egypt were dead and that Joseph and his brethren the sons at Jacob were dead, and that all their children the children of Israel remained in Egypt.

9 And Zepho considered to go to fight against them and all Egypt, to avenge the cause of his brethren the children of Esau, whom Joseph with his brethren and all Egypt had smitten in the land of Canaan, when they went up to bury Jacob in Hebron.

10 And Zepho sent messengers to Hadad, son of
Bedad, king of Edom, and to all his brethren the
children of Esau, saying, 11 "Did you not say that
you would not fight against the king of Africa for he
is a member of your covenant? Behold I fought with
him and smote him and all his people.

12 "Now therefore I have resolved to fight against Egypt and the children of Jacob who are there, and I will be revenged of them for what Joseph, his brethren and ancestors did to us in the land of Canaan when they went up to bury their father in Hebron.

13 "Now then if you are willing to come to me to assist me in fighting against them and Egypt, then shall we avenge the cause of our brethren."

14 And the children of Esau hearkened to the words of Zepho, and the children of Esau gathered themselves together, a very great people, and they went to assist Zepho and the children of Chittim in battle.

15 And Zepho sent to all the children of the east
and to all the children of Ishmael with words like
unto these, and they gathered themselves and
came to the assistance of Zepho and the children of
Chittim in the war upon Egypt. 16 And all these
kings, the king of Edom and the children of the east,
and all the children of Ishmael, and Zepho the king
of Chittim went forth and arrayed all their hosts in
Hebron.

17 And the camp was very heavy, extending in
length a distance of three days' journey, a people
numerous as the sand upon the sea shore which
can not be counted. 18 And all these kings and
their hosts went down and came against all Egypt in
battle, and encamped together in the valley of
Pathros.

19 And all Egypt heard their report, and they also gathered themselves together, all the people of the land of Egypt, and of all the cities belonging to Egypt, about three hundred thousand men. 20 And the men of Egypt sent also to the children of Israel who were in those days in the land of Goshen, to come to them in order to go and fight with these kings. 21 And the men of Israel assembled and were about one hundred and fifty men, and they went into battle to assist the Egyptians.

22 And the men of Israel and of Egypt went forth, about three hundred thousand men and one hundred and fifty men, and they went toward these kings to battle, and they placed themselves from without the land of Goshen opposite Pathros. 23 And the Egyptians believed not in Israel to go with them in their camps together for battle, for all the Egyptians said, "Perhaps the children of Israel will deliver us into the hand of the children of Esau and Ishmael, for they are their brethren."

24 And all the Egyptians said unto the children of Israel, "Remain you here together in your stand and we will go and fight against the children of Esau and Ishmael, and if these kings should prevail over us, then come you altogether upon them and assist us," and the children of Israel did so.

25 And Zepho the son of Eliphaz the son of Esau king of Chittim, and Hadad the son of Bedad king of Edom, and all their camps, and all the children of the east, and children of Ishmael, a people numerous as sand, encamped together in the valley of Pathros opposite Tachpanches. 26 And Balaam the son of Beor the Syrian was there in the camp of Zepho, for he came with the children of Chittim to the battle, and Balaam was a man highly honored in the eyes of Zepho and his men.

27 And Zepho said unto Balaam, "Try by divination for us that we may know who will prevail in the battle, we or the Egyptians."

28 And Balaam rose up and tried the art of divination, and he was skillful in the knowledge of it, but he was confused and the work was destroyed in his hand.

29 And he tried it again but it did not succeed, and
Balaam despaired of it and left it and did not
complete it, for this was from the Lord, in order to
cause Zepho and his people to fall into the hand of
the children of Israel, who had trusted in the Lord,
the God of their ancestors, in their war.

30 And Zepho and Hadad put their forces in battle
array, and all the Egyptians went alone against
them, about three hundred thousand men, and not
one man of Israel was with them. 31 And all the
Egyptians fought with these kings opposite Pathros
and Tachpanches, and the battle was severe against
the Egyptians.

32 And the kings were stronger than the Egyptians
in that battle, and about one hundred and eighty
men of Egypt fell on that day, and about thirty men
of the forces of the kings, and all the men of Egypt
fled from before the kings, so the children of Esau
and Ishmael pursued the Egyptians, continuing to
smite them unto the place where was the camp of
the children of Israel.

33 And all the Egyptians cried unto the children of
Israel, saying, "Hasten to us and assist us and save
us from the hand of Esau, Ishmael and the children
of Chittim."

34 And the hundred and fifty men of the children of
Israel ran from their station to the camps of these
kings, and the children of Israel cried unto the Lord
their God to deliver them.

35 And the Lord hearkened to Israel, and the Lord
gave all the men of the kings into their hand, and
the children of Israel fought against these kings, and
the children of Israel smote about four thousand of
the kings' men. 36 And the Lord threw a great
consternation in the camp of the kings, so that the
fear of the children of Israel fell upon them.

37 And all the hosts of the kings fled from before
the children of Israel and the children of Israel
pursued them continuing to smite them unto the
borders of the land of Cush. 38 And the children of
Israel slew of them in the road yet two thousand
men, and of the children of Israel not one fell.

39 And when the Egyptians saw that the children of
Israel had fought with such few men with the kings,
and that the battle was so very severe against
them,

40 All the Egyptians were greatly afraid of their lives
on account of the strong battle, and all Egypt fled,
every man hiding himself from the arrayed forces,
and they hid themselves in the road, and they left
the Israelites to fight. 41 And the children of Israel
inflicted a terrible blow upon the kings' men, and
they returned from them after they had driven
them to the border of the land of Cush.

42 And all Israel knew the thing which the men of
Egypt had done to them, that they had fled from
them in battle, and had left them to fight alone. 43
So the children of Israel also acted with cunning,
and as the children of Israel returned from battle,
they found some of the Egyptians in the road and
smote them there.

44 And whilst they slew them, they said unto them
these words: 45 "Wherefore did you go from us
and leave us, being a few people, to fight against
these kings who had a great people to smite us,
that you might thereby deliver your own souls?"

46 And of some which the Israelites met on the
road, they the children of Israel spoke to each
other, saying, "Smite, smite, for he is an Ishmaelite,
or an Edomite, or from the children of Chittim," and
they stood over him and slew him, and they knew
that he was an Egyptian. 47 And the children of
Israel did these things cunningly against the
Egyptians, because they had deserted them in
battle and had fled from them.

48 And the children of Israel slew of the men of
Egypt in the road in this manner, about two
hundred men. 49 And all the men of Egypt saw the
evil which the children of Israel had done to them,
so all Egypt feared greatly the children of Israel, for
they had seen their great power, and that not one
man of them had fallen.

50 So all the children of Israel returned with joy on
their road to Goshen, and the rest of Egypt
returned each man to his place.

Jasher 65

1 And it came to pass after these things, that all the counsellors of Pharaoh, king of Egypt, and all the elders of Egypt assembled and came before the king and bowed down to the ground, and they sat before him.

9 He said to his people, "Behold, the people of the children of Israel are more and mightier than we.

2 And the counsellors and elders of Egypt spoke unto the king, saying, 3 "Behold the people of the children of Israel is greater and mightier than we are, and thou knowest all the evil which they did to us in the road when we returned from battle.

4 "And thou hast also seen their strong power, for this power is unto them from their fathers, for but a few men stood up against a people numerous as the sand, and smote them at the edge of the sword, and of themselves not one has fallen, so that if they had been numerous they would then have utterly destroyed them. 5 Now therefore give us counsel what to do with them, until we gradually destroy them from amongst us, lest they become too numerous for us in the land.

10 "Come, let us deal wisely with them, lest they multiply, and it happen that when any war breaks out, they also join themselves to our enemies, and fight against us, and escape out of the land."

6 "For if the children of Israel should increase in the land, they will become an obstacle to us, and if any war should happen to take place, they with their great strength will join our enemy against us, and fight against us, destroy us from the land and go away from it."

7 So the king answered the elders of Egypt and said unto them, "This is the plan advised against Israel, from which we will not depart, 8 Behold in the land are Pithom and Rameses, cities unfortified against battle, it behooves you and us to build them, and to fortify them. 9 Now therefore go you also and act cunningly toward them, and proclaim a voice in Egypt and in Goshen at the command of the king, saying,

11 Therefore they set taskmasters over them to afflict them with their burdens. They built storage cities for Pharaoh: Pithom and Raamses.

10 "'All ye men of Egypt, Goshen, Pathros and all their inhabitants! The king has commanded us to build Pithom and Rameses, and to fortify them for battle; who amongst you of all Egypt, of the children of Israel and of all the inhabitants of the cities, are willing to build with us, shall each have his wages given to him daily at the king's order;' so go you first and do cunningly, and gather yourselves and come to Pithom and Rameses to build.

11 "And whilst you are building, cause a proclamation of this kind to be made throughout
Egypt every day at the command of the king. 12
And when some of the children of Israel shall come to build with you, you shall give them their wages daily for a few days.

13 "And after they shall have built with you for their daily hire, drag yourselves away from them daily one by one in secret, and then you shall rise up and become their task-masters and officers, and you shall leave them afterward to build without wages, and should they refuse, then force them with all
your might to build. 14 And if you do this it will be
well with us to strengthen our land against the children of Israel, for on account of the fatigue of the building and the work, the children of Israel will decrease, because you will deprive them from their wives day by day."

15 And all the elders of Egypt heard the counsel of the king, and the counsel seemed good in their eyes and in the eyes of the servants of Pharaoh, and in the eyes of all Egypt, and they did according to the word of the king.

16 And all the servants went away from the king, and they caused a proclamation to be made in all Egypt, in Tachpanches and in Goshen, and in all the cities which surrounded Egypt, saying,

17 "You have seen what the children of Esau and Ishmael did to us, who came to war against us and wished to destroy us.

18 Now therefore the king commanded us to fortify the land, to build the cities Pithom and Rameses, and to fortify them for battle, if they should again come against us. 19 Whosoever of you from all Egypt and from the children of Israel will come to build with us, he shall have his daily wages given by the king, as his command is unto us."

20 And when Egypt and all the children of Israel heard all that the servants of Pharaoh had spoken, there came from the Egyptians, and the children of Israel to build with the servants of Pharaoh, Pithom and Rameses, but none of the children of Levi came with their brethren to build. 21 And all the servants of Pharaoh and his princes came at first with deceit to build with all Israel as daily hired laborers, and they gave to Israel their daily hire at the beginning.

22 And the servants of Pharaoh built with all Israel, and were employed in that work with Israel for a month. 23 And at the end of the month, all the servants of Pharaoh began to withdraw secretly from the people of Israel daily.

24 And Israel went on with the work at that time, but they then received their daily hire, because some of the men of Egypt were yet carrying on the work with Israel at that time; therefore the Egyptians gave Israel their hire in those days, in order that they, the Egyptians their fellow-workmen, might also take the pay for their labor.

25 And at the end of a year and four months all the Egyptians had withdrawn from the children of Israel, so that the children of Israel were left alone engaged in the work. 26 And after all the Egyptians had withdrawn from the children of Israel they returned and became oppressors and officers over them, and some of them stood over the children of Israel as task masters, to receive from them all that they gave them for the pay of their labor.

27 And the Egyptians did in this manner to the children of Israel day by day, in order to afflict in their work.

28 And all the children of Israel were alone engaged in the labor, and the Egyptians refrained from giving any pay to the children of Israel from that time forward.

29 And when some of the men of Israel refused to work on account of the wages not being given to them, then the exactors and the servants of Pharaoh oppressed them and smote them with heavy blows, and made them return by force, to labor with their brethren; thus did all the Egyptians unto the children of Israel all the days. 30 And all the children of Israel were greatly afraid of the Egyptians in this matter, and all the children of Israel returned and worked alone without pay.

31 And the children of Israel built Pithom and Rameses, and all the children of Israel did the work, some making bricks, and some building, and the children of Israel built and fortified all the land of Egypt and its walls, and the children of Israel were engaged in work for many years, until the time came when the Lord remembered them and brought them out of Egypt.

32 But the children of Levi were not employed in the work with their brethren of Israel, from the beginning unto the day of their going forth from Egypt. 33 For all the children of Levi knew that the Egyptians had spoken all these words with deceit to the Israelites, therefore the children of Levi refrained from approaching to the work with their brethren.

34 And the Egyptians did not direct their attention to make the children of Levi work afterward, since they had not been with their brethren at the beginning, therefore the Egyptians left them alone.

35 And the hands of the men of Egypt were directed with continued severity against the children of Israel in that work, and the Egyptians made the children of Israel work with rigor.

36 And the Egyptians embittered the lives of the children of Israel with hard work, in mortar and bricks, and also in all manner of work in the field. 37 And the children of Israel called Melol the king of Egypt "Meror, king of Egypt," because in his days the Egyptians had embittered their lives with all manner of work.

12 But the more they afflicted them, the more they multiplied and the more they spread out. They were grieved because of the children of Israel.

38 And all the work wherein the Egyptians made the children of Israel labor, they exacted with rigor, in order to afflict the children of Israel, but the more they afflicted them, the more they increased and grew, and the Egyptians were grieved because of the children of Israel.

13 The Egyptians ruthlessly made the children of Israel serve, 14 and they made their lives bitter with hard service, in mortar and in brick, and in all kinds of service in the field, all their service, in which they ruthlessly made them serve.

Jasher 66

1 At that time died Hadad the son of Bedad king of Edom, and Samlah from Mesrekah, from the country of the children of the east, reigned in his place.

2 In the thirteenth year of the reign of Pharaoh king of Egypt, which was the hundred and twenty-fifth year of the Israelites going down into Egypt, Samlah had reigned over Edom eighteen years. 3 And when he reigned, he drew forth his hosts to go and fight against Zepho the son of Eliphaz and the children of Chittim, because they had made war against Angeas king of Africa, and they destroyed his whole army.

4 But he did not engage with him, for the children of Esau prevented him, saying, "He was their brother," so Samlah listened to the voice of the children of Esau, and turned back with all his forces to the land of Edom, and did not proceed to fight against Zepho the son of Eliphaz. 5 And Pharaoh king of Egypt heard this thing, saying, "Samlah king of Edom has resolved to fight the children of Chittim, and afterward he will come to fight against Egypt."

6 And when the Egyptians heard this matter, they increased the labor upon the children of Israel, lest the Israelites should do unto them as they did unto them in their war with the children of Esau in the days of Hadad.

7 So the Egyptians said unto the children of Israel, "Hasten and do your work, and finish your task, and strengthen the land, lest the children of Esau your brethren should come to fight against us, for on
your account will they come against us." 8 And the
children of Israel did the work of the men of Egypt day by day, and the Egyptians afflicted the children of Israel in order to lessen them in the land.

9 But as the Egyptians increased the labor upon the children of Israel, so did the children of Israel increase and multiply, and all Egypt was filled with the children of Israel.

10 And in the hundred and twenty-fifth year of Israel's going down into Egypt, all the Egyptians saw that their counsel did not succeed against Israel, but that they increased and grew, and the land of Egypt and the land of Goshen were filled with the
children of Israel. 11 So all the elders of Egypt and
its wise men came before the king and bowed down to him and sat before him.

12 And all the elders of Egypt and the wise men thereof said unto the king, "May the king live forever; thou didst counsel us the counsel against the children of Israel, and we did unto them
according to the word of the king. 13 But in
proportion to the increase of the labor so do they increase and grow in the land, and behold the whole country is filled with them.

14 "Now therefore our lord and king, the eyes of all Egypt are upon thee to give them advice with thy wisdom, by which they may prevail over Israel to destroy them, or to diminish them from the land;" and the king answered them saying, "Give you counsel in this matter that we may know what to do unto them."

15 And an officer, one of the king's counsellors, whose name was Job, from Mesopotamia, in the
land of Uz, answered the king, saying, 16 "If it
please the king, let him hear the counsel of his servant;" and the king said unto him, "Speak."

17 And Job spoke before the king, the princes, and before all the elders of Egypt, saying, 18 "Behold the counsel of the king which he advised formerly respecting the labor of the children of Israel is very good, and you must not remove from them that labor forever. 19 But this is the advice counselled by which you may lessen them, if it seems good to the king to afflict them.

20 "Behold we have feared war for a long time, and we said, 'When Israel becomes fruitful in the land, they will drive us from the land if a war should take place.' 21 If it please the king, let a royal decree go forth, and let it be written in the laws of Egypt which shall not be revoked, that every male child born to the Israelites, his blood shall be spilled upon the ground.

22 "And by your doing this, when all the male children of Israel shall have died, the evil of their wars will cease; let the king do so and send for all the Hebrew midwives and order them in this matter to execute it;" so the thing pleased the king and the princes, and the king did according to the word of Job.

15 The king of Egypt spoke to the Hebrew midwives, of whom the name of the one was Shiphrah, and the name of the other Puah,

23 And the king sent for the Hebrew midwives to be called, of which the name of one was Shephrah, and the name of the other Puah.

24 And the midwives came before the king, and stood in his presence.

16 and he said, "When you perform the duty of a midwife to the Hebrew women, and see them on the birth stool; if it is a son, then you shall kill him; but if it is a daughter, then she shall live."

25 And the king said unto them, "When you do the office of a midwife to the Hebrew women, and see them upon the stools, if it be a son, then you shall kill him, but if it be a daughter, then she shall live.

26 "But if you will not do this thing, then will I burn you up and all your houses with fire."

17 But the midwives feared God, and didn't do what the king of Egypt commanded them, but saved the baby boys alive.

27 But the midwives feared God and did not hearken to the king of Egypt nor to his words, and when the Hebrew women brought forth to the midwife son or daughter, then did the midwife do all that was necessary to the child and let it live; thus did the midwives all the days.

18 The king of Egypt called for the midwives, and said to them, "Why have you done this thing, and have saved the boys alive?"

28 And this thing was told to the king, and he sent and called for the midwives and he said to them, "Why have you done this thing and have saved the children alive?"

19 The midwives said to Pharaoh, "Because the Hebrew women aren't like the Egyptian women; for they are vigorous, and give birth before the midwife comes to them."

29 And the midwives answered and spoke together before the king, saying, 30 "Let not the king think that the Hebrew women are as the Egyptian women, for all the children of Israel are hale, and before the midwife comes to them they are delivered, and as for us thy handmaids, for many days no Hebrew woman has brought forth upon us, for all the Hebrew women are their own midwives, because they are hale."

20 God dealt well with the midwives, and the people multiplied, and grew very mighty.

31 And Pharaoh heard their words and believed them in this matter, and the midwives went away from the king, and God dealt well with them, and the people multiplied and waxed exceedingly.

21 Because the midwives feared God, he gave them families.

[Exodus 2:1 A man of the house of Levi went and took a daughter of Levi as his wife.]

Jasher 67

1 There was a man in the land of Egypt of the seed of Levi, whose name was Amram, the son of Kehath, the son of Levi, the son of Israel. 2 And this man went and took a wife, namely Jochebed the daughter of Levi his father's sister, and she was one hundred and twenty-six years old, and he came unto her.

3 And the woman conceived and bare a daughter, and she called her name Miriam, because in those days the Egyptians had embittered the lives of the children of Israel. 4 And she conceived again and bare a son and she called his name Aaron, for in the days of her conception, Pharaoh began to spill the blood of the male children of Israel.

5 In those days died Zepho the son of Eliphaz, son of Esau, king of Chittim, and Janeas reigned in his stead. 6 And the time that Zepho reigned over the children of Chittim was fifty years, and he died and was buried in the city of Nabna in the land of Chittim.

7 And Janeas, one of the mighty men of the children of Chittim, reigned after him and he reigned fifty years. 8 And it was after the death of the king of Chittim that Balaam the son of Beor fled from the land of Chittim, and he went and came to Egypt to Pharaoh king of Egypt. 9 And Pharaoh received him with great honor, for he had heard of his wisdom, and he gave him presents and made him for a counsellor, and aggrandized him.

10 And Balaam dwelt in Egypt, in honor with all the
nobles of the king, and the nobles exalted him,
because they all coveted to learn his wisdom.

11 And in the hundred and thirtieth year of Israel's
going down to Egypt, Pharaoh dreamed that he was
sitting upon his kingly throne, and lifted up his eyes
and saw an old man standing before him, and there
were scales in the hands of the old man, such scales
as are used by merchants. 12 And the old man took
the scales and hung them before Pharaoh. 13 And
the old man took all the elders of Egypt and all its
nobles and great men, and he tied them together
and put them in one scale. 14 And he took a milk
kid and put it into the other scale, and the kid
preponderated over all.

15 And Pharaoh was astonished at this dreadful
vision, why the kid should preponderate over all,
and Pharaoh awoke and behold it was a dream.

16 And Pharaoh rose up early in the morning and
called all his servants and related to them the
dream, and the men were greatly afraid.

17 And the king said to all his wise men, "Interpret I
pray you the dream which I dreamed, that I may
know it."

18 And Balaam the son of Beor answered the king
and said unto him, "This means nothing else but a
great evil that will spring up against Egypt in the
latter days. 19 For a son will be born to Israel who
will destroy all Egypt and its inhabitants, and bring
forth the Israelites from Egypt with a mighty hand.
20 Now therefore, O king, take counsel upon this
matter, that you may destroy the hope of the
children of Israel and their expectation, before this
evil arise against Egypt."

21 And the king said unto Balaam, "And what shall
we do unto Israel? Surely after a certain manner did
we at first counsel against them and could not
prevail over them. 22 Now therefore give you also
advice against them by which we may prevail over
them."

23 And Balaam answered the king, saying, "Send now and call thy two counsellors, and we will see what their advice is upon this matter and afterward thy servant will speak." 24 And the king sent and called his two counsellors Reuel the Midianite and Job the Uzite, and they came and sat before the king.

25 And the king said to them, "Behold you have both heard the dream which I have dreamed, and the interpretation thereof; now therefore give counsel and know and see what is to be done to the children of Israel, whereby we may prevail over them, before their evil shall spring up against us."

26 And Reuel the Midianite answered the king and said, "May the king live, may the king live forever.

27 "If it seem good to the king, let him desist from the Hebrews and leave them, and let him not stretch forth his hand against them.

28 "For these are they whom the Lord chose in days of old, and took as the lot of his inheritance from amongst all the nations of the earth and the kings of the earth; and who is there that stretched his hand against them with impunity, of whom their God was not avenged?

29 "Surely thou knowest that when Abraham went down to Egypt, Pharaoh, the former king of Egypt, saw Sarah his wife, and took her for a wife, because Abraham said, 'She is my sister,' for he was afraid, lest the men of Egypt should slay him on account of his wife.

30 "And when the king of Egypt had taken Sarah then God smote him and his household with heavy plagues, until he restored unto Abraham his wife Sarah, then was he healed. 31 And Abimelech the Gerarite, king of the Philistines, God punished on account of Sarah wife of Abraham, in stopping up every womb from man to beast.

32 "When their God came to Abimelech in the dream of night and terrified him in order that he might restore to Abraham Sarah whom he had taken, and afterward all the people of Gerar were punished on account of Sarah, and Abraham prayed to his God for them, and he was entreated of him, and he healed them.

33 "And Abimelech feared all this evil that came upon him and his people, and he returned to Abraham his wife Sarah, and gave him with her
many gifts. 34 He did so also to Isaac when he had
driven him from Gerar, and God had done wonderful things to him, that all the water courses of Gerar were dried up, and their productive trees did not bring forth.

35 "Until Abimelech of Gerar, and Ahuzzath one of his friends, and Pichol the captain of his host, went to him and they bent and bowed down before him to the ground.

36 "And they requested of him to supplicate for them, and he prayed to the Lord for them, and the Lord was entreated of him and he healed them.

37 "Jacob also, the plain man, was delivered through his integrity from the hand of his brother Esau, and the hand of Laban the Syrian his mother's brother, who had sought his life; likewise from the hand of all the kings of Canaan who had come together against him and his children to destroy them, and the Lord delivered them out of their hands, that they turned upon them and smote them, for who had ever stretched forth his hand against them with impunity?

38 "Surely Pharaoh the former, thy father's father, raised Joseph the son of Jacob above all the princes of the land of Egypt, when he saw his wisdom, for through his wisdom he rescued all the inhabitants of the land from the famine.

39 After which he ordered Jacob and his children to come down to Egypt, in order that through their virtue, the land of Egypt and the land of Goshen might be delivered from the famine.

40 "Now therefore if it seem good in thine eyes,
cease from destroying the children of Israel, but if it
be not thy will that they shall dwell in Egypt, send
them forth from here, that they may go to the land
of Canaan, the land where their ancestors
sojourned."

41 And when Pharaoh heard the words of Jethro he
was very angry with him, so that he rose with
shame from the king's presence, and went to
Midian, his land, and took Joseph's stick with him.
42 And the king said to Job the Uzite, "What sayest
thou Job, and what is thy advice respecting the
Hebrews?" 43 So Job said to the king, "Behold all
the inhabitants of the land are in thy power, let the
king do as it seems good in his eyes."

44 And the king said unto Balaam, "What dost thou
say, Balaam, speak thy word that we may hear it."
45 And Balaam said to the king, "Of all that the king
has counselled against the Hebrews will they be
delivered, and the king will not be able to prevail
over them with any counsel.

46 "For if thou thinkest to lessen them by the
flaming fire, thou canst not prevail over them, for
surely their God delivered Abraham their father
from Ur of the Chaldeans; and if thou thinkest to
destroy them with a sword, surely Isaac their father
was delivered from it, and a ram was placed in his
stead. 47 And if with hard and rigorous labor thou
thinkest to lessen them, thou wilt not prevail even
in this, for their father Jacob served Laban in all
manner of hard work, and prospered.

48 "Now therefore, O King, hear my words, for this
is the counsel which is counselled against them, by
which thou wilt prevail over them, and from which
thou shouldst not depart. 49 If it please the king let
him order all their children which shall be born
from this day forward, to be thrown into the water,
for by this canst thou wipe away their name, for
none of them, nor of their fathers, were tried in this
manner."

50 And the king heard the words of Balaam, and the
thing pleased the king and the princes, and the king
did according to the word of Balaam.

22 Pharaoh commanded all his people, saying, “You shall cast every son who is born into the river, and every daughter you shall save alive.”

51 And the king ordered a proclamation to be issued and a law to be made throughout the land of Egypt, saying, "Every male child born to the Hebrews from this day forward shall be thrown into the water."

52 And Pharaoh called unto all his servants, saying, "Go now and seek throughout the land of Goshen where the children of Israel are, and see that every son born to the Hebrews shall be cast into the river,
but every daughter you shall let live." 53 And when
the children of Israel heard this thing which Pharaoh had commanded, to cast their male children into the river, some of the people separated from their wives and others adhered to them.

54 And from that day forward, when the time of delivery arrived to those women of Israel who had remained with their husbands, they went to the field to bring forth there, and they brought forth in the field, and left their children upon the field and returned home.

55 And the Lord who had sworn to their ancestors to multiply them, sent one of his ministering angels which are in heaven to wash each child in water, to anoint and swathe it and to put into its hands two smooth stones from one of which it sucked milk and from the other honey, and he caused its hair to grow to its

knees, by which it might cover itself; to comfort it and to cleave to it, through his compassion for it.

56 And when God had compassion over them and had desired to multiply them upon the face of the land, he ordered his earth to receive them to be preserved therein till the time of their growing up, after which the earth opened its mouth and vomited them forth and they sprouted forth from the city like the herb of the earth, and the grass of the forest, and they returned each to his family and
to his father's house, and they remained with them.
57 And the babes of the children of Israel were
upon the earth like the herb of the field, through God's grace to them.

58 And when all the Egyptians saw this thing, they went forth, each to his field with his yoke of oxen and his ploughshare, and they ploughed it up as one ploughs the earth at seed time. 59 And when they ploughed they were unable to hurt the infants of the children of Israel, so the people increased and waxed exceedingly.

60 And Pharaoh ordered his officers daily to go to Goshen to seek for the babes of the children of Israel. 61 And when they had sought and found one, they took it from its mother's bosom by force, and threw it into the river, but the female child they left with its mother; thus did the Egyptians do to the Israelites all the days.

Jasher 68

1 And it was at that time the spirit of God was upon Miriam the daughter of Amram the sister of Aaron, and she went forth and prophesied about the house, saying, "Behold a son will be born unto us from my father and mother this time, and he will save Israel from the hands of Egypt."

2 And when Amram heard the words of his daughter, he went and took his wife back to the house, after he had driven her away at the time when Pharaoh ordered every male child of the house of Jacob to be thrown into the water.

Exodus 2

1 A man of the house of Levi went and took a daughter of Levi as his wife. 2 The woman conceived, and bore a son. When she saw that he was a fine child, she hid him three months.

3 So Amram took Jochebed his wife, three years after he had driven her away, and he came to her and she conceived. 4 And at the end of seven months from her conception she brought forth a son, and the whole house was filled with great light as of the light of the sun and moon at the time of their shining. 5 And when the woman saw the child that it was good and pleasing to the sight, she hid it for three months in an inner room.

6 In those days the Egyptians conspired to destroy all the Hebrews there. 7 And the Egyptian women went to Goshen where the children of Israel were, and they carried their young ones upon their shoulders, their babes who could not yet speak.

8 And in those days, when the women of the
children of Israel brought forth, each woman had
hidden her son from before the Egyptians, that the
Egyptians might not know of their bringing forth,
and might not destroy them from the land. 9 And
the Egyptian women came to Goshen and their
children who could not speak were upon their
shoulders, and when an Egyptian woman came into
the house of a Hebrew woman her babe began to
cry.

10 And when it cried the child that was in the inner room answered it, so the Egyptian women went and told it at the house of Pharaoh.

11 And Pharaoh sent his officers to take the children and slay them; thus did the Egyptians to the Hebrew women all the days.

3 When she could no longer hide him, she took a papyrus basket for him, and coated it with tar and with pitch. She put the child in it, and laid it in the reeds by the river's bank.

12 And it was at that time, about three months
from Jochebed's concealment of her son, that the
thing was known in Pharaoh's house. 13 And the
woman hastened to take away her son before the
officers came, and she took for him an ark of
bulrushes, and daubed it with slime and with pitch,
and put the child therein, and she laid it in the flags
by the river's brink.

4 His sister stood far off, to see what would be done to him.

14 And his sister Miriam stood afar off to know what would be done to him, and what would become of her words.

15 And God sent forth at that time a terrible heat in
the land of Egypt, which burned up the flesh of man
like the sun in his circuit, and it greatly oppressed
the Egyptians. 16 And all the Egyptians went down
to bathe in the river, on account of the consuming
heat which burned up their flesh.

5 Pharaoh's daughter came down to bathe at the river. Her maidens walked along by the riverside. She saw the basket among the reeds, and sent her servant to get it.

17 And Bathia, the daughter of Pharaoh, went also
to bathe in the river, owing to the consuming heat,
and her maidens walked at the river side, and all
the women of Egypt as well. 18 And Bathia lifted
up her eyes to the river, and she saw the ark upon
the water, and sent her maid to fetch it.

6 She opened it, and saw the child, and behold, the baby cried. She had compassion on him, and said, "This is one of the Hebrews' children."

19 And she opened it and saw the child, and behold the babe wept, and she had compassion on him, and she said, "This is one of the Hebrew children."

7 Then his sister said to Pharaoh's daughter, "Should I go and call a nurse for you from the Hebrew women, that she may nurse the child for you?"

8 Pharaoh's daughter said to her, "Go." The maiden went and called the child's mother.

9 Pharaoh's daughter said to her, "Take this child away, and nurse him for me, and I will give you your wages." The woman took the child, and nursed it.

10 The child grew, and she brought him to Pharaoh's daughter, and he became her son. She named him Moses, and said, "Because I drew him out of the water."

20 And all the women of Egypt walking on the river side desired to give him suck, but he would not suck, for this thing was from the Lord, in order to restore him to his mother's breast.

21 And Miriam his sister was at that time amongst the Egyptian women at the river side, and she saw this thing and she said to Pharaoh's daughter, "Shall I go and fetch a nurse of the Hebrew women, that she may nurse the child for thee?"

22 And Pharaoh's daughter said to her, "Go," and the young woman went and called the child's mother.

23 And Pharaoh's daughter said to Jochebed, "Take this child away and suckle it for me, and I will pay thee thy wages, two bits of silver daily;" and the woman took the child and nursed it.

24 And at the end of two years, when the child grew up, she brought him to the daughter of Pharaoh, and he was unto her as a son, and she called his name Moses, for she said, "Because I drew him out of the water."

25 And Amram his father called his name Chabar, for he said, "It was for him that he associated with his wife whom he had turned away."

26 And Jochebed his mother called his name Jekuthiel, "Because," she said, "I have hoped for him to the Almighty, and God restored him unto me."

27 And Miriam his sister called him Jered, for she descended after him to the river to know what his end would be.

28 And Aaron his brother called his name Abi Zanuch, saying, "My father left my mother and returned to her on his account."

29 And Kehath the father of Amram called his name Abigdor, because on his account did God repair the breach of the house of Jacob, that they could no longer throw their male children into the water.

30 And their nurse called him Abi Socho, saying, "In his tabernacle was he hidden for three months, on account of the children of Ham."

31 And all Israel called his name Shemaiah, son of Nethanel, for they said, "In his days has God heard their cries and rescued them from their oppressors."

32 And Moses was in Pharaoh's house, and was unto Bathia, Pharaoh's daughter, as a son, and Moses grew up amongst the king's children.

Jasher 69

1 And the king of Edom died in those days, in the eighteenth year of his reign, and was buried in his temple which he had built for himself as his royal residence in the land of Edom.

2 And the children of Esau sent to Pethor, which is upon the river, and they fetched from there a young man of beautiful eyes and comely aspect, whose name was Saul, and they made him king
over them in the place of Samlah. 3 And Saul
reigned over all the children of Esau in the land of Edom for forty years.

4 And when Pharaoh king of Egypt saw that the counsel which Balaam had advised respecting the children of Israel did not succeed, but that still they were fruitful, multiplied and increased throughout the land of Egypt,

5 Then Pharaoh commanded in those days that a proclamation should be issued throughout Egypt to the children of Israel, saying, "No man shall
diminish any thing of his daily labor. 6 And the man
who shall be found deficient in his labor which he performs daily, whether in mortar or in bricks, then his youngest son shall be put in their place."

7 And the labor of Egypt strengthened upon the children of Israel in those days, and behold if one brick was deficient in any man's daily labor, the Egyptians took his youngest boy by force from his mother, and put him into the building in the place
of the brick which his father had left wanting. 8
And the men of Egypt did so to all the children of Israel day by day, all the days for a long period.

9 But the tribe of Levi did not at that time work with the Israelites their brethren, from the beginning, for the children of Levi knew the cunning of the Egyptians which they exercised at first toward the Israelites.

Jasher 70

1 And in the third year from the birth of Moses, Pharaoh was sitting at a banquet, when Alparanith the queen was sitting at his right and Bathia at his left, and the lad Moses was lying upon her bosom, and Balaam the son of Beor with his two sons, and all the princes of the kingdom were sitting at table in the king's presence.

2 And the lad stretched forth his hand upon the
king's head, and took the crown from the king's
head and placed it on his own head. 3 And when
the king and princes saw the work which the boy
had done, the king and princes were terrified, and
one man to his neighbor expressed astonishment.

4 And the king said unto the princes who were before him at table, "What speak you and what say you, O ye princes, in this matter, and what is to be the judgment against the boy on account of this act?"

5 And Balaam the son of Beor the magician
answered before the king and princes, and he said,
"Remember now, O my lord and king, the dream
which thou didst dream many days since, and that
which thy servant interpreted unto thee. 6 Now
therefore this is a child from the Hebrew children,
in whom is the spirit of God, and let not my lord the
king imagine that this youngster did this thing
without knowledge.

7 "For he is a Hebrew boy, and wisdom and
understanding are with him, although he is yet a
child, and with wisdom has he done this and chosen
unto himself the kingdom of Egypt. 8 For this is the
manner of all the Hebrews to deceive kings and
their nobles, to do all these things cunningly, in
order to make the kings of the earth and their men
tremble.

9 "Surely thou knowest that Abraham their father
acted thus, who deceived the army of Nimrod king
of Babel, and Abimelech king of Gerar, and that he
possessed himself of the land of the children of
Heth and all the kingdoms of Canaan. 10 And that
he descended into Egypt and said of Sarah his wife,
she is my sister, in order to mislead Egypt and her
king.

11 "His son Isaac also did so when he went to Gerar and dwelt there, and his strength prevailed over the army of Abimelech king of the Philistines.

12 "He also thought of making the kingdom of the Philistines stumble, in saying that Rebecca his wife was his sister.

13 "Jacob also dealt treacherously with his brother, and took from his hand his birthright and his blessing.

14 "He went then to Padan-aram to the house of Laban his mother's brother, and cunningly obtained from him his daughter, his cattle, and all belonging to him, and fled away and returned to the land of Canaan to his father.
15 His sons sold their brother Joseph, who went down into Egypt and became a slave, and was placed in the prison house for twelve years.

16 "Until the former Pharaoh dreamed dreams, and withdrew him from the prison house, and magnified him above all the princes in Egypt on account of his interpreting his dreams to him.
17 And when God caused a famine throughout the land he sent for and brought his father and all his brothers, and the whole of his father's household, and supported them without price or reward, and bought the Egyptians for slaves.

18 "Now therefore my lord king behold this child has risen up in their stead in Egypt, to do according to their deeds and to trifle with every king, prince and judge.

19 "If it please the king, let us now spill his blood upon the ground, lest he grow up and take away the government from thy hand, and the hope of Egypt perish after he shall have reigned."

20 And Balaam said to the king, "Let us moreover call for all the judges of Egypt and the wise men thereof, and let us know if the judgment of death is due to this boy as thou didst say, and then we will slay him."

21 And Pharaoh sent and called for all the wise men of Egypt and they came before the king, and an angel of the Lord came amongst them, and he was like one of the wise men of Egypt.

22 And the king said to the wise men, "Surely you
have heard what this Hebrew boy who is in the
house has done, and thus has Balaam judged in the
matter. 23 Now judge you also and see what is due
to the boy for the act he has committed."

24 And the angel, who seemed like one of the wise men of Pharaoh, answered and said as follows, before all the wise men of Egypt and before the king and the princes:

25 "If it please the king let the king send for men
who shall bring before him an onyx stone and a coal
of fire, and place them before the child, and if the
child shall stretch forth his hand and take the onyx
stone, then shall we know that with wisdom has the
youth done all that he has done, and we must slay
him. 26 But if he stretch forth his hand upon the
coal, then shall we know that it was not with
knowledge that he did this thing, and he shall live."

27 And the thing seemed good in the eyes of the king and the princes, so the king did according to the word of the angel of the Lord.

28 And the king ordered the onyx stone and coal to be brought and placed before Moses.

29 And they placed the boy before them, and the lad endeavored to stretch forth his hand to the onyx stone, but the angel of the Lord took his hand and placed it upon the coal, and the coal became extinguished in his hand, and he lifted it up and put it into his mouth, and burned part of his lips and part of his tongue, and he became heavy in mouth and tongue.

30 And when the king and princes saw this, they
knew that Moses had not acted with wisdom in
taking off the crown from the king's head. 31 So
the king and princes refrained from slaying the
child, so Moses remained in Pharaoh's house,
growing up, and the Lord was with him. 32 And
whilst the boy was in the king's house, he was
robed in purple and he grew amongst the children
of the king.

33 And when Moses grew up in the king's house, Bathia the daughter of Pharaoh considered him as a son, and all the household of Pharaoh honored him, and all the men of Egypt were afraid of him.

34 And he daily went forth and came into the land of Goshen, where his brethren the children of Israel were, and Moses saw them daily in shortness of breath and hard labor.
35 And Moses asked them, saying, "Wherefore is this labor meted out unto you day by day?"

36 And they told him all that had befallen them, and all the injunctions which Pharaoh had put upon them before his birth.
37 And they told him all the counsels which Balaam the son of Beor had counselled against them, and what he had also counselled against him in order to slay him when he had taken the king's crown from off his head.

38 And when Moses heard these things his anger was kindled against Balaam, and he sought to kill him, and he was in ambush for him day by day.

39 And Balaam was afraid of Moses, and he and his two sons rose up and went forth from Egypt, and they fled and delivered their souls and betook themselves to the land of Cush to Kikianus, king of Cush.

40 And Moses was in the king's house going out and coming in, the Lord gave him favor in the eyes of Pharaoh, and in the eyes of all his servants, and in the eyes of all the people of Egypt, and they loved Moses exceedingly.

41 And the day arrived when Moses went to Goshen to see his brethren, that he saw the children of Israel in their burdens and hard labor, and Moses was grieved on their account.
42 And Moses returned to Egypt and came to the house of Pharaoh, and came before the king, and Moses bowed down before the king.

43 And Moses said unto Pharaoh, "I pray thee my lord, I have come to seek a small request from thee, turn not away my face empty;" and Pharaoh said unto him, "Speak."

44 And Moses said unto Pharaoh, "Let there be given unto thy servants the children of Israel who are in Goshen, one day to rest therein from their labor."
45 And the king answered Moses and said, "Behold I have lifted up thy face in this thing to grant thy request."

46 And Pharaoh ordered a proclamation to be issued throughout Egypt and Goshen, saying, 47 "To you, all the children of Israel, thus says the king, for six days you shall do your work and labor, but on the seventh day you shall rest, and shall not preform any work, thus shall you do all the days, as the king and Moses the son of Bathia have commanded."

48 And Moses rejoiced at this thing which the king had granted to him, and all the children of Israel did as Moses ordered them. 49 For this thing was from the Lord to the children of Israel, for the Lord had begun to remember the children of Israel to save them for the sake of their fathers.

50 And the Lord was with Moses and his fame went throughout Egypt. 51 And Moses became great in the eyes of all the Egyptians, and in the eyes of all the children of Israel, seeking good for his people Israel and speaking words of peace regarding them to the king.

Jasher 71

[Exodus 2:11 In those days, when Moses had grown up, he went out to his brothers, and looked at their burdens. He saw an Egyptian striking a Hebrew, one of his brothers.]

1 And when Moses was eighteen years old, he desired to see his father and mother and he went to them to Goshen, and when Moses had come near Goshen, he came to the place where the children of Israel were engaged in work, and he observed their burdens, and he saw an Egyptian smiting one of his Hebrew brethren.

2 And when the man who was beaten saw Moses he ran to him for help, for the man Moses was greatly respected in the house of Pharaoh, and he said to him, "My lord attend to me, this Egyptian came to my house in the night, bound me, and came to my wife in my presence, and now he seeks to take my life away."

12 He looked this way and that way, and when he saw that there was no one, he killed the Egyptian, and hid him in the sand.

3 And when Moses heard this wicked thing, his anger was kindled against the Egyptian, and he turned this way and the other, and when he saw there was no man there he smote the Egyptian and hid him in the sand, and delivered the Hebrew from the hand of him that smote him.

4 And the Hebrew went to his house, and Moses returned to his home, and went forth and came back to the king's house.

5 And when the man had returned home, he
thought of repudiating his wife, for it was not right
in the house of Jacob, for any man to come to his
wife after she had been defiled. 6 And the woman
went and told her brothers, and the woman's
brothers sought to slay him, and he fled to his
house and escaped.

13 He went out the second day, and behold, two men of the Hebrews were fighting with each other. He said to him who did the wrong, "Why do you strike your fellow?"

7 And on the second day Moses went forth to his brethren, and saw, and behold two men were quarreling, and he said to the wicked one, "Why dost thou smite thy neighbor?"

14 He said, "Who made you a prince and a judge over us? Do you plan to kill me, as you killed the Egyptian?" Moses was afraid, and said, "Surely this thing is known."

8 And he answered him and said to him, "Who has set thee for a prince and judge over us? Dost thou think to slay me as thou didst slay the Egyptian?" and Moses was afraid and he said, "Surely the thing is known?"

15 Now when Pharaoh heard this thing, he sought to kill Moses.

9 And Pharaoh heard of this affair, and he ordered Moses to be slain,

so God sent his angel, and he appeared unto
Pharaoh in the likeness of a captain of the guard.
10 And the angel of the Lord took the sword from
the hand of the captain of the guard, and took his
head off with it, for the likeness of the captain of
the guard was turned into the likeness of Moses.

But Moses fled from the face of Pharaoh,

11 And the angel of the Lord took hold of the right hand of Moses, and brought him forth from Egypt, and placed him from without the borders of Egypt, a distance of forty days' journey.

12 And Aaron his brother alone remained in the land of Egypt, and he prophesied to the children of Israel, saying,

13 "Thus says the Lord God of your ancestors, 'Throw away, each man, the abominations of his eyes, and do not defile yourselves with the idols of Egypt.'"

14 And the children of Israel rebelled and would not
hearken to Aaron at that time. 15 And the Lord
thought to destroy them, were it not that the Lord
remembered the covenant which he had made with
Abraham, Isaac and Jacob.

16 In those days the hand of Pharaoh continued to be severe against the children of Israel, and he crushed and oppressed them until the time when God sent forth his word and took notice of them.

Jasher 72

1 And it was in those days that there was a great war between the children of Cush and the children of the east and Aram, and they rebelled against the king of Cush in whose hands they were.

2 So Kikianus king of Cush went forth with all the children of Cush, a people numerous as the sand, and he went to fight against Aram and the children of the east, to bring them under subjection. 3 And when Kikianus went out, he left Balaam the magician, with his two sons, to guard the city, and the lowest sort of the people of the land.

4 So Kikianus went forth to Aram and the children of the east, and he fought against them and smote them, and they all fell down wounded before Kikianus and his people. 5 And he took many of them captives and he brought them under subjection as at first, and he encamped upon their land to take tribute from them as usual.

6 And Balaam the son of Beor, when the king of Cush had left him to guard the city and the poor of the city, he rose up and advised with the people of the land to rebel against king Kikianus, not to let him enter the city when he should come home. 7 And the people of the land hearkened to him, and they swore to him and made him king over them, and his two sons for captains of the army.

8 So they rose up and raised the walls of the city at the two corners, and they built an exceeding strong building.

9 And at the third corner they dug ditches without number, between the city and the river which surrounded the whole land of Cush, and they made the waters of the river burst forth there. 10 At the fourth corner they collected numerous serpents by their incantations and enchantments, and they fortified the city and dwelt therein, and no one went out or in before them.

11 And Kikianus fought against Aram and the
children of the east and he subdued them as
before, and they gave him their usual tribute, and
he went and returned to his land.

12 And when Kikianus the king of Cush approached
his city and all the captains of the forces with him,
they lifted up their eyes and saw that the walls of
the city were built up and greatly elevated, so the
men were astonished at this. 13 And they said one
to the other, "It is because they saw that we were
delayed, in battle, and were greatly afraid of us,
therefore have they done this thing and raised the
city walls and fortified them so that the kings of
Canaan might not come in battle against them."

14 So the king and the troops approached the city
door and they looked up and behold, all the gates
of the city were closed, and they called out to the
sentinels, saying, "Open unto us, that we may enter
the city." 15 But the sentinels refused to open to
them by the order of Balaam the magician, their
king, they suffered them not to enter their city. 16
So they raised a battle with them opposite the city
gate, and one hundred and thirty men of the army
at Kikianus fell on that day.

17 And on the next day they continued to fight and
they fought at the side of the river; they
endeavored to pass but were not able, so some of
them sank in the pits and died.

18 So the king ordered them to cut down trees to
make rafts, upon which they might pass to them,
and they did so. 19 And when they came to the
place of the ditches, the waters revolved by mills,
and two hundred men upon ten rafts were
drowned.

20 And on the third day they came to fight at the
side where the serpents were, but they could not
approach there, for the serpents slew of them one
hundred and seventy men, and they ceased fighting
against Cush, and they besieged Cush for nine
years, no person came out or in.

21 At that time that the war and the siege were
against Cush, Moses fled from Egypt from Pharaoh
who sought to kill him for having slain the Egyptian.
22 And Moses was eighteen years old when he fled
from Egypt from the presence of Pharaoh, and he
fled and escaped to the camp of Kikianus, which at
that time was besieging Cush.

23 And Moses was nine years in the camp of
Kikianus king of Cush, all the time that they were
besieging Cush, and Moses went out and came in
with them. 24 And the king and princes and all the
fighting men loved Moses, for he was great and
worthy, his stature was like a noble lion, his face
was like the sun, and his strength was like that of a
lion, and he was counsellor to the king.

25 And at the end of nine years, Kikianus was seized
with a mortal disease, and his illness prevailed over
him, and he died on the seventh day. 26 So his
servants embalmed him and carried him and buried
him opposite the city gate to the north of the land
of Egypt. 27 And they built over him an elegant
strong and high building, and they placed great
stones below.

28 And the king's scribes engraved upon those
stones all the might of their king Kikianus, and all
his battles which he had fought, behold they are
written there at this day.

29 Now after the death of Kikianus king of Cush it
grieved his men and troops greatly on account of
the war.

30 So they said one to the other, "Give us counsel
what we are to do at this time, as we have resided
in the wilderness nine years away from our homes.
31 If we say we will fight against the city many of us
will fall wounded or killed, and if we remain here in
the siege we shall also die.

32 "For now all the kings of Aram and of the
children of the east will hear that our king is dead,
and they will attack us suddenly in a hostile
manner, and they will fight against us and leave no
remnant of us. 33 Now therefore let us go and
make a king over us, and let us remain in the siege
until the city is delivered up to us."

34 And they wished to choose on that day a man
for king from the army of Kikianus, and they found
no object of their choice like Moses to reign over
them. 35 And they hastened and stripped off each
man his garments and cast them upon the ground,
and they made a great heap and placed Moses
thereon. 36 And they rose up and blew with
trumpets and called out before him, and said, "May
the king live, may the king live!"

37 And all the people and nobles swore unto him to
give him for a wife Adoniah the queen, the Cushite,
wife of Kikianus, and they made Moses king over
them on that day.

38 And all the people of Cush issued a proclamation
on that day, saying, "Every man must give
something to Moses of what is in his possession."
39 And they spread out a sheet upon the heap, and
every man cast into it something of what he had,
one a gold earring and the other a coin. 40 Also of
onyx stones, bdellium, pearls and marble did the
children of Cush cast unto Moses upon the heap,
also silver and gold in great abundance.

41 And Moses took all the silver and gold, all the
vessels, and the bdellium and onyx stones, which all
the children of Cush had given to him, and he
placed them amongst his treasures. 42 And Moses
reigned over the children of Cush on that day, in the
place of Kikianus king of Cush.

Jasher 73

1 In the fifty-fifth year of the reign of Pharaoh king
of Egypt, that is in the hundred and fifty-seventh
year of the Israelites going down into Egypt, reigned
Moses in Cush.

2 Moses was twenty-seven years old when he
began to reign over Cush, and forty years did he
reign. 3 And the Lord granted Moses favor and
grace in the eyes of all the children of Cush, and the
children of Cush loved him exceedingly, so Moses
was favored by the Lord and by men.

4 And in the seventh day of his reign, all the
children of Cush assembled and came before Moses
and bowed down to him to the ground. 5 And all
the children spoke together in the presence of the
king, saying, "Give us counsel that we may see what
is to be done to this city. 6 For it is now nine years
that we have been besieging round about the city,
and have not seen our children and our wives."

7 So the king answered them, saying, "If you will
hearken to my voice in all that I shall command you,
then will the Lord give the city into our hands and
we shall subdue it. 8 For if we fight with them as in
the former battle which we had with them before
the death of Kikianus, many of us will fall down
wounded as before. 9 Now therefore behold here
is counsel for you in this matter; if you will hearken
to my voice, then will the city be delivered into our
hands."

10 So all the forces answered the king, saying, "All
that our lord shall command that will we do."

11 And Moses said unto them, "Pass through and
proclaim a voice in the whole camp unto all the
people, saying,

12 'Thus says the king, "Go into the forest and bring
with you of the young ones of the stork, each man a
young one in his hand."'

13 "And any person transgressing the word of the
king, who shall not bring his young one, he shall die,
and the king will take all belonging to him.

14 "And when you shall bring them they shall be in
your keeping, you shall rear them until they grow
up, and you shall teach them to dart upon, as is the
way of the young ones of the hawk."

15 So all the children of Cush heard the words of
Moses, and they rose up and caused a proclamation
to be issued throughout the camp, saying, 16 "Unto
you, all the children of Cush, the king's order is, that
you go all together to the forest, and catch there
the young storks each man his young one in his
hand, and you shall bring them home. 17 And any
person violating the order of the king shall die, and
the king will take all that belongs to him."

18 And all the people did so, and they went out to the wood and they climbed the fir trees and caught, each man a young one in his hand, all the young of the storks, and they brought them into the desert and reared them by order of the king, and they taught them to dart upon, similar to the young hawks.

19 And after the young storks were reared, the king ordered them to be hungered for three days, and all the people did so.

20 And on the third day, the king said unto them, "Strengthen yourselves and become valiant men, and put on each man his armor and gird on his sword upon him, and ride each man his horse and take each his young stork in his hand. 21 And we will rise up and fight against the city at the place where the serpents are;" and all the people did as the king had ordered.

22 And they took each man his young one in his hand, and they went away, and when they came to the place of the serpents the king said to them, "Send forth each man his young stork upon the serpents."

23 And they sent forth each man his young stork at the king's order, and the young storks ran upon the serpents and they devoured them all and destroyed them out of that place.

24 And when the king and people had seen that all the serpents were destroyed in that place, all the people set up a great shout.

25 And they approached and fought against the city and took it and subdued it, and they entered the city. 26 And there died on that day one thousand and one hundred men of the people of the city, all that inhabited the city, but of the people besieging not one died.

27 So all the children of Cush went each to his home, to his wife and children and to all belonging to him. 28 And Balaam the magician, when he saw that the city was taken, he opened the gate and he and his two sons and eight brothers fled and returned to Egypt to Pharaoh king of Egypt. 29 They are the sorcerers and magicians who are mentioned in the book of the law, standing against Moses when the Lord brought the plagues upon Egypt.

30 So Moses took the city by his wisdom, and the children of Cush placed him on the throne instead of Kikianus king of Cush. 31 And they placed the royal crown upon his head, and they gave him for a wife Adoniah the Cushite queen, wife of Kikianus.

32 And Moses feared the Lord God of his fathers, so that he came not to her, nor did he turn his eyes to her. 33 For Moses remembered how Abraham had made his servant Eliezer swear, saying unto him, "Thou shalt not take a woman from the daughters of Canaan for my son Isaac."

34 Also what Isaac did when Jacob had fled from his brother, when he commanded him, saying, "Thou shalt not take a wife from the daughters of Canaan, nor make alliance with any of the children of Ham. 35 For the Lord our God gave Ham the son of Noah, and his children and all his seed, as slaves to the children of Shem and to the children of Japheth, and unto their seed after them for slaves, forever." 36 Therefore Moses turned not his heart nor his eyes to the wife of Kikianus all the days that he reigned over Cush.

37 And Moses feared the Lord his God all his life, and Moses walked before the Lord in truth, with all his heart and soul, he turned not from the right way all the days of his life; he declined not from the way either to the right or to the left, in which Abraham, Isaac and Jacob had walked. 38 And Moses strengthened himself in the kingdom of the children of Cush, and he guided the children of Cush with his usual wisdom, and Moses prospered in his kingdom.

39 And at that time Aram and the children of the east heard that Kikianus king of Cush had died, so Aram and the children of the east rebelled against Cush in those days. 40 And Moses gathered all the children of Cush, a people very mighty, about thirty thousand men, and he went forth to fight with Aram and the children of the east. 41 And they went at first to the children of the east, and when the children of the east heard their report, they went to meet them, and engaged in battle with them.

42 And the war was severe against the children of the east, so the Lord gave all the children of the east into the hand of Moses, and about three hundred men fell down slain. 43 And all the children of the east turned back and retreated, so Moses and the children of Cush followed them and subdued them, and put a tax upon them, as was their custom.

44 So Moses and all the people with him passed from there to the land of Aram for battle. 45 And the people of Aram also went to meet them, and they fought against them, and the Lord delivered them into the hand of Moses, and many of the men of Aram fell down wounded. 46 And Aram also were subdued by Moses and the people of Cush, and also gave their usual tax.

47 And Moses brought Aram and the children of the east under subjection to the children of Cush, and Moses and all the people who were with him, turned to the land of Cush. 48 And Moses strengthened himself in the kingdom of the children of Cush, and the Lord was with him, and all the children of Cush were afraid of him.

Jasher 74

1 In the end of years died Saul king of Edom, and Baal Chanan the son of Achbor reigned in his place.

2 In the sixteenth year of the reign of Moses over Cush, Baal Chanan the son of Achbor reigned in the land of Edom over all the children of Edom for thirty-eight years. 3 In his days Moab rebelled against the power of Edom, having been under Edom since the days of Hadad the son of Bedad, who smote them and Midian, and brought Moab under subjection to Edom. 4 And when Baal Chanan the son of Achbor reigned over Edom, all the children of Moab withdrew their allegiance from Edom.

5 And Angeas king of Africa died in those days, and Azdrubal his son reigned in his stead.

6 And in those days died Janeas king of the children of Chittim, and they buried him in his temple which he had built for himself in the plain of Canopia for a residence, and Latinus reigned in his stead.

7 In the twenty-second year of the reign of Moses
over the children of Cush, Latinus reigned over the
children of Chittim forty-five years. 8 And he also
built for himself a great and mighty tower, and he
built therein an elegant temple for his residence, to
conduct his government, as was the custom.

9 In the third year of his reign he caused a
proclamation to be made to all his skilful men, who
made many ships for him. 10 And Latinus
assembled all his forces, and they came in ships,
and went therein to fight with Azdrubal son of
Angeas king of Africa, and they came to Africa and
engaged in battle with Azdrubal and his army.

11 And Latinus prevailed over Azdrubal, and Latinus
took from Azdrubal the aqueduct which his father
had brought from the children of Chittim, when he
took Janiah the daughter of Uzi for a wife, so
Latinus overthrew the bridge of the aqueduct, and
smote the whole army of Azdrubal a severe blow.

12 And the remaining strong men of Azdrubal
strengthened themselves, and their hearts were
filled with envy, and they courted death, and again
engaged in battle with Latinus king of Chittim.

13 And the battle was severe upon all the men of
Africa, and they all fell wounded before Latinus and
his people, and Azdrubal the king also fell in that
battle.

14 And the king Azdrubal had a very beautiful
daughter, whose name was Ushpezena, and all the
men of Africa embroidered her likeness on their
garments, on account of her great beauty and
comely appearance. 15 And the men of Latinus saw
Ushpezena, the daughter of Azdrubal, and praised
her unto Latinus their king.

16 And Latinus ordered her to be brought to him,
and Latinus took Ushpezena for a wife, and he
turned back on his way to Chittim.

17 And it was after the death of Azdrubal son of Angeas, when Latinus had turned back to his land from the battle, that all the inhabitants of Africa rose up and took Anibal the son of Angeas, the younger brother of Azdrubal, and made him king instead at his brother over the whole land at Africa.

18 And when he reigned, he resolved to go to Chittim to fight with the children of Chittim, to avenge the cause of Azdrubal his brother, and the
cause of the inhabitants of Africa, and he did so. 19
And he made many ships, and he came therein with his whole army, and he went to Chittim.

20 So Anibal fought with the children of Chittim, and the children of Chittim fell wounded before Anibal and his army, and Anibal avenged his
brother's cause. 21 And Anibal continued the war for eighteen years with the children of Chittim, and Anibal dwelt in the land of Chittim and encamped
there for a long time. 22 And Anibal smote the children of Chittim very severely, and he slew their great men and princes, and of the rest of the people he smote about eighty thousand men.

23 And at the end of days and years, Anibal returned to his land of Africa, and he reigned securely in the place of Azdrubal his brother.

Jasher 75

1 At that time, in the hundred and eightieth year of the Israelites going down into Egypt, there went forth from Egypt valiant men, thirty thousand on foot, from the children of Israel, who were all of the tribe of Joseph, of the children of Ephraim the son
of Joseph. 2 For they said the period was completed which the Lord had appointed to the children of Israel in the times of old, which he had spoken to Abraham.

3 And these men girded themselves, and they put each man his sword at his side, and every man his armor upon him, and they trusted to their strength, and they went out together from Egypt with a mighty hand.

4 But they brought no provision for the road, only
silver and gold, not even bread for that day did they
bring in their hands, for they thought of getting
their provision for pay from the Philistines, and if
not they would take it by force.

5 And these men were very mighty and valiant men,
one man could pursue a thousand and two could
rout ten thousand, so they trusted to their strength
and went together as they were. 6 And they
directed their course toward the land of Gath, and
they went down and found the shepherds of Gath
feeding the cattle of the children of Gath.

7 And they said to the shepherds, "Give us some of
the sheep for pay, that we may eat, for we are
hungry, for we have eaten no bread this day." 8
And the shepherds said, "Are they our sheep or
cattle that we should give them to you even for
pay?" so the children of Ephraim approached to
take them by force. 9 And the shepherds of Gath
shouted over them that their cry was heard at a
distance, so all the children of Gath went out to
them.

10 And when the children of Gath saw the evil
doings of the children of Ephraim, they returned
and assembled the men of Gath, and they put on
each man his armor, and came forth to the children
of Ephraim for battle. 11 And they engaged with
them in the valley of Gath, and the battle was
severe, and they smote from each other a great
many on that day.

12 And on the second day the children of Gath sent
to all the cities of the Philistines that they should
come to their help, saying, 13 "Come up unto us
and help us, that we may smite the children of
Ephraim who have come forth from Egypt to take
our cattle, and to fight against us without cause."

14 Now the souls of the children of Ephraim were
exhausted with hunger and thirst, for they had
eaten no bread for three days. And forty thousand
men went forth from the cities of the Philistines to
the assistance of the men of Gath. 15 And these
men were engaged in battle with the children of
Ephraim, and the Lord delivered the children of
Ephraim into the hands of the Philistines. 16 And
they smote all the children of Ephraim, all who had
gone forth from Egypt, none were remaining but
ten men who had run away from the engagement.

17 For this evil was from the Lord against the children of Ephraim, for they transgressed the word of the Lord in going forth from Egypt, before the period had arrived which the Lord in the days of old had appointed to Israel.

18 And of the Philistines also there fell a great
many, about twenty thousand men, and their
brethren carried them and buried them in their
cities. 19 And the slain of the children of Ephraim
remained forsaken in the valley of Gath for many
days and years, and were not brought to burial, and
the valley was filled with men's bones.

20 And the men who had escaped from the battle came to Egypt, and told all the children of Israel all that had befallen them.

21 And their father Ephraim mourned over them for many days, and his brethren came to console him.

22 And he came unto his wife and she bare a son, and he called his name Beriah, for she was unfortunate in his house.

Jasher 76

1 And Moses the son of Amram was still king in the
land of Cush in those days, and he prospered in his
kingdom, and he conducted the government of the
children of Cush in justice, in righteousness, and
integrity. 2 And all the children of Cush loved
Moses all the days that he reigned over them, and
all the inhabitants of the land of Cush were greatly
afraid of him.

3 And in the fortieth year of the reign of Moses over Cush, Moses was sitting on the royal throne whilst Adoniah the queen was before him, and all the nobles were sitting around him. 4 And Adoniah the queen said before the king and the princes, "What is this thing which you, the children of Cush, have done for this long time? 5 Surely you know that for forty years that this man has reigned over Cush he has not approached me, nor has he served the gods of the children of Cush.

6 "Now therefore hear, O ye children of Cush, and let this man no more reign over you as he is not of our flesh. 7 Behold Menacrus my son is grown up, let him reign over you, for it is better for you to serve the son of your lord, than to serve a stranger, slave of the king of Egypt."

8 And all the people and nobles of the children of Cush heard the words which Adoniah the queen had spoken in their ears. 9 And all the people were preparing until the evening, and in the morning they rose up early and made Menacrus, son of Kikianus, king over them.

10 And all the children of Cush were afraid to stretch forth their hand against Moses, for the Lord was with Moses, and the children of Cush remembered the oath which they swore unto Moses, therefore they did no harm to him.

11 But the children of Cush gave many presents to Moses, and sent him from them with great honor.

12 So Moses went forth from the land of Cush, and went home and ceased to reign over Cush, and Moses was sixty-six years old when he went out of the land of Cush, for the thing was from the Lord, for the period had arrived which he had appointed in the days of old, to bring forth Israel from the affliction of the children of Ham.

Exodus 2:15b and lived in the land of Midian, and he sat down by a well.

13 So Moses went to Midian, for he was afraid to return to Egypt on account of Pharaoh, and he went and sat at a well of water in Midian.

16 Now the priest of Midian had seven daughters. They came and drew water, and filled the troughs to water their father's flock.

14 And the seven daughters of Reuel the Midianite went out to feed their father's flock. 15 And they came to the well and drew water to water their father's flock.

17 The shepherds came and drove them away; but Moses stood up and helped them, and watered their flock.

18 When they came to Reuel, their father, he said, "How is it that you have returned so early today?"
19 They said, "An Egyptian delivered us out of the hand of the shepherds, and moreover he drew water for us, and watered the flock."

20 He said to his daughters, "Where is he? Why is it that you have left the man? Call him, that he may eat bread."

16 So the shepherds of Midian came and drove them away, and Moses rose up and helped them and watered the flock.

17 And they came home to their father Reuel, and told him what Moses did for them. 18 And they said, "An Egyptian man has delivered us from the hands of the shepherds, he drew up water for us and watered the flock."

19 And Reuel said to his daughters, "And where is he? wherefore have you left the man?"

20 And Reuel sent for him and fetched him and brought him home, and he ate bread with him. 21
And Moses related to Reuel that he had fled from Egypt and that he reigned forty years over Cush, and that they afterward had taken the government from him, and had sent him away in peace with honor and with presents.

22 And when Reuel had heard the words of Moses, Reuel said within himself, "I will put this man into the prison house, whereby I shall conciliate the children of Cush, for he has fled from them."

23 And they took and put him into the prison house, and Moses was in prison ten years, and whilst Moses was in the prison house, Zipporah the daughter of Reuel took pity over him, and supported him with bread and water all the time.

24 And all the children of Israel were yet in the land of Egypt serving the Egyptians in all manner of hard work, and the hand of Egypt continued in severity over the children of Israel in those days.

25 At that time the Lord smote Pharaoh king of Egypt, and he afflicted with the plague of leprosy from the sole of his foot to the crown of his head; owing to the cruel treatment of the children of Israel was this plague at that time from the Lord
upon Pharaoh king of Egypt. 26 For the Lord had hearkened to the prayer of his people the children of Israel, and their cry reached him on account of their hard work.

27 Still his anger did not turn from them, and the hand of Pharaoh was still stretched out against the children of Israel, and Pharaoh hardened his neck before the Lord, and he increased his yoke over the children of Israel, and embittered their lives with all manner of hard work.

28 And when the Lord had inflicted the plague upon Pharaoh king of Egypt, he asked his wise men and
sorcerers to cure him. 29 And his wise men and
sorcerers said unto him, "That if the blood of little children were put into the wounds he would be
healed." 30 And Pharaoh hearkened to them, and sent his ministers to Goshen to the children of Israel to take their little children.

31 And Pharaoh's ministers went and took the infants of the children of Israel from the bosoms of their mothers by force, and they brought them to Pharaoh daily, a child each day, and the physicians killed them and applied them to the plague; thus
did they all the days. 32 And the number of the
children which Pharaoh slew was three hundred and seventy-five.

33 But the Lord hearkened not to the physicians of the king of Egypt, and the plague went on
increasing mightily. 34 And Pharaoh was ten years
afflicted with that plague, still the heart of Pharaoh was more hardened against the children of Israel.

35 And at the end of ten years the Lord continued
to afflict Pharaoh with destructive plagues. 36 And
the Lord smote him with a bad tumor and sickness at the stomach, and that plague turned to a severe boil.

37 At that time the two ministers of Pharaoh came from the land of Goshen where all the children of Israel were, and went to the house of Pharaoh and said to him, "We have seen the children of Israel slacken in their work and negligent in their labor."

38 And when Pharaoh heard the words of his ministers, his anger was kindled against the children of Israel exceedingly, for he was greatly grieved at his bodily pain.

39 And he answered and said, "Now that the children of Israel know that I am ill, they turn and scoff at us, now therefore harness my chariot for me, and I will betake myself to Goshen and will see the scoff of the children of Israel with which they are deriding me; so his servants harnessed the chariot for him."

40 And they took and made him ride upon a horse,
for he was not able to ride of himself; 41 And he
took with him ten horsemen and ten footmen, and went to the children of Israel to Goshen.

42 And when they had come to the border of Egypt, the king's horse passed into a narrow place, elevated in the hollow part of the vineyard, fenced on both sides, the low, plain country being on the
other side. 43 And the horses ran rapidly in that
place and pressed each other, and the other horses pressed the king's horse.

44 And the king's horse fell into the low plain whilst the king was riding upon it, and when he fell the chariot turned over the king's face and the horse lay upon the king, and the king cried out, for his flesh was very sore.

45 And the flesh of the king was torn from him, and his bones were broken and he could not ride, for this thing was from the Lord to him, for the Lord had heard the cries of his people the children of Israel and their affliction.

46 And his servants carried him upon their shoulders, a little at a time, and they brought him back to Egypt, and the horsemen who were with
him came also back to Egypt. 47 And they placed
him in his bed, and the king knew that his end was come to die, so Aparanith the queen his wife came and cried before the king, and the king wept a great weeping with her.

48 And all his nobles and servants came on that day and saw the king in that affliction, and wept a great
weeping with him. 49 And the princes of the king
and all his counselors advised the king to cause one to reign in his stead in the land, whomsoever he should choose from his sons.

50 And the king had three sons and two daughters
which Aparanith the queen his wife had borne to
him, besides the king's children of concubines. 51
And these were their names, the firstborn Othri,
the second Adikam, and the third Morion, and their
sisters, the name of the elder Bathia and of the
other Acuzi.

52 And Othri the first born of the king was an idiot,
precipitate and hurried in his words. 53 But Adikam
was a cunning and wise man and knowing in all the
wisdom of Egypt, but of unseemly aspect, thick in
flesh, and very short in stature; his height was one
cubit. 54 And when the king saw Adikam his son
intelligent and wise in all things, the king resolved
that he should be king in his stead after his death.

55 And he took for him a wife Gedudah daughter of
Abilot, and he was ten years old, and she bare unto
him four sons. 56 And he afterward went and took
three wives and begat eight sons and three
daughters.

57 And the disorder greatly prevailed over the king,
and his flesh stank like the flesh of a carcass cast
upon the field in summer time, during the heat of
the sun. 58 And when the king saw that his sickness
had greatly strengthened itself over him, he
ordered his son Adikam to be brought to him, and
they made him king over the land in his place.

59 And at the end of three years, the king died, in
shame, disgrace, and disgust, and his servants
carried him and buried him in the sepulcher of the
kings of Egypt in Zoan Mizraim. 60 But they
embalmed him not as was usual with kings, for his
flesh was putrid, and they could not approach to
embalm him on account of the stench, so they
buried him in haste.

61 For this evil was from the Lord to him, for the
Lord had requited him evil for the evil which in his
days he had done to Israel. 62 And he died with
terror and with shame, and his son Adikam reigned
in his place.

[Exodus 2:23 In the course of those many days, the king of Egypt died, and the children of Israel sighed because of the bondage, and they cried, and their cry came up to God because of the bondage.]

Jasher 77

1 Adikam was twenty years old when he reigned over Egypt, he reigned four years. 2 In the two hundred and sixth year of Israel's going down to Egypt did Adikam reign over Egypt, but he continued not so long in his reign over Egypt as his fathers had continued their reigns. 3 For Melol his father reigned ninety-four years in Egypt, but he was ten years sick and died, for he had been wicked before the Lord.

4 And all the Egyptians called the name of Adikam Pharaoh like the name of his fathers, as was their custom to do in Egypt. 5 And all the wise men of Pharaoh called the name of Adikam Ahuz, for short is called Ahuz in the Egyptian language. 6 And Adikam was exceedingly ugly, and he was a cubit and a span and he had a great beard which reached to the soles of his feet.

7 And Pharaoh sat upon his father's throne to reign over Egypt, and he conducted the government of Egypt in his wisdom.

8 And whilst he reigned he exceeded his father and all the preceding kings in wickedness, and he increased his yoke over the children of Israel.

9 And he went with his servants to Goshen to the children of Israel, and he strengthened the labor over them and he said unto them, "Complete your work, each day's task, and let not your hands slacken from our work from this day forward as you did in the days of my father."

10 And he placed officers over them from amongst the children of Israel, and over these officers he placed taskmasters from amongst his servants. 11 And he placed over them a measure of bricks for them to do according to that number, day by day, and he turned back and went to Egypt.

12 At that time the task-masters of Pharaoh
ordered the officers of the children of Israel
according to the command of Pharaoh, saying, 13
"Thus says Pharaoh, 'Do your work each day, and
finish your task, and observe the daily measure of
bricks; diminish not anything. 14 And it shall come
to pass that if you are deficient in your daily bricks, I
will put your young children in their stead.'" 15 And
the task-masters of Egypt did so in those days as
Pharaoh had ordered them.

16 And whenever any deficiency was found in the
children of Israel's measure of their daily bricks, the
task-masters of Pharaoh would go to the wives of
the children of Israel and take infants of the
children of Israel to the number of bricks deficient,
they would take them by force from their mother's
laps, and put them in the building instead of the
bricks; 17 Whilst their fathers and mothers were
crying over them and weeping when they heard the
weeping voices of their infants in the wall of the
building.

18 And the task-masters prevailed over Israel, that
the Israelites should place their children in the
building, so that a man placed his son in the wall
and put mortar over him, whilst his eyes wept over
him, and his tears ran down upon his child.

19 And the task-masters of Egypt did so to the
babes of Israel for many days, and no one pitied or
had compassion over the babes of the children of
Israel.

20 And the number of all the children killed in the
building was two hundred and seventy, some whom
they had built upon instead of the bricks which had
been left deficient by their fathers, and some whom
they had drawn out dead from the building. 21 And
the labor imposed upon the children of Israel in the
days of Adikam exceeded in hardship that which
they performed in the days of his father.

22 And the children of Israel sighed every day on
account of their heavy work, for they had said to
themselves, "Behold when Pharaoh shall die, his
son will rise up and lighten our work!"

23 But they increased the latter work more than
the former, and the children of Israel sighed at this
and their cry ascended to God on account of their
labor.

[Exodus 2:24 God heard their groaning, and God remembered his covenant with Abraham, with Isaac, and with Jacob. 25 God saw the children of Israel, and God was concerned about them.]

24 And God heard the voice of the children of Israel
and their cry, in those days, and God remembered
to them his covenant which he had made with
Abraham, Isaac and Jacob. 25 And God saw the
burden of the children of Israel, and their heavy
work in those days, and he determined to deliver
them.

26 And Moses the son of Amram was still confined
in the dungeon in those days, in the house of Reuel
the Midianite, and Zipporah the daughter of Reuel
did support him with food secretly day by day. 27
And Moses was confined in the dungeon in the
house of Reuel for ten years.

28 And at the end of ten years which was the first
year of the reign of Pharaoh over Egypt, in the place
of his father, 29 Zipporah said to her father Reuel,
"No person inquires or seeks after the Hebrew man,
whom thou didst bind in prison now ten years. 30
Now therefore, if it seem good in thy sight, let us
send and see whether he is living or dead, but her
father knew not that she had supported him."

31 And Reuel her father answered and said to her,
"Has ever such a thing happened that a man should
be shut up in a prison without food for ten years,
and that he should live?"

32 And Zipporah answered her father, saying,
"Surely thou hast heard that the God of the
Hebrews is great and awful, and does wonders for
them at all times.

33 "He it was who delivered Abraham from Ur of
the Chaldeans, and Isaac from the sword of his
father, and Jacob from the angel of the Lord who
wrestled with him at the ford of Jabbuk.

34 "Also with this man has he done many things, he
delivered him from the river in Egypt and from the
sword of Pharaoh, and from the children of Cush, so
also can he deliver him from famine and make him
live."

35 And the thing seemed good in the sight of Reuel,
and he did according to the word of his daughter,
and sent to the dungeon to ascertain what became
of Moses. 36 And he saw, and behold the man
Moses was living in the dungeon, standing upon his
feet, praising and praying to the God of his
ancestors. 37 And Reuel commanded Moses to be
brought out of the dungeon, so they shaved him
and he changed his prison garments and ate bread.

38 And afterward Moses went into the garden of
Reuel which was behind the house, and he there
prayed to the Lord his God, who had done mighty
wonders for him. 39 And it was that whilst he
prayed he looked opposite to him, and behold a
sapphire stick was placed in the ground, which was
planted in the midst of the garden. 40 And he
approached the stick and he looked, and behold the
name of the Lord God of hosts was engraved
thereon, written and developed upon the stick.

41 And he read it and stretched forth his hand and
he plucked it like a forest tree from the thicket, and
the stick was in his hand. 42 And this is the stick
with which all the works of our God were
performed, after he had created heaven and earth,
and all the host of them, seas, rivers and all their
fishes.

43 And when God had driven Adam from the
garden of Eden, he took the stick in his hand and
went and tilled the ground from which he was
taken. 44 And the stick came down to Noah and
was given to Shem and his descendants, until it
came into the hand of Abraham the Hebrew. 45
And when Abraham had given all he had to his son
Isaac, he also gave to him this stick.

46 And when Jacob had fled to Padan-aram, he
took it into his hand, and when he returned to his
father he had not left it behind him. 47 Also when
he went down to Egypt he took it into his hand and
gave it to Joseph, one portion above his brethren,
for Jacob had taken it by force from his brother
Esau.

48 And after the death of Joseph, the nobles of Egypt came into the house of Joseph, and the stick came into the hand of Reuel the Midianite, and when he went out of Egypt, he took it in his hand and planted it in his garden. 49 And all the mighty men of the Kinites tried to pluck it when they endeavored to get Zipporah his daughter, but they were unsuccessful.

50 So that stick remained planted in the garden of Reuel, until he came who had a right to it and took it. 51 And when Reuel saw the stick in the hand of Moses, he wondered at it, and he gave him his daughter Zipporah for a wife.

Jasher 78

1 At that time died Baal Channan son of Achbor, king of Edom, and was buried in his house in the land of Edom.

2 And after his death the children of Esau sent to the land of Edom, and took from there a man who was in Edom, whose name was Hadad, and they made him king over them in the place of Baal Channan, their king.

3 And Hadad reigned over the children of Edom forty-eight years.

4 And when he reigned he resolved to fight against the children of Moab, to bring them under the power of the children of Esau as they were before, but he was not able, because the children of Moab heard this thing, and they rose up and hastened to elect a king over them from amongst their brethren.

5 And they afterward gathered together a great people, and sent to the children of Ammon their brethren for help to fight against Hadad king of Edom. 6 And Hadad heard the thing which the children of Moab had done, and was greatly afraid of them, and refrained from fighting against them.

Exodus 2:21 Moses was content to dwell with the man. He gave Moses Zipporah, his daughter.

7 In those days Moses, the son of Amram, in Midian, took Zipporah, the daughter of Reuel the Midianite, for a wife.

8 And Zipporah walked in the ways of the daughters of Jacob, she was nothing short of the righteousness of Sarah, Rebecca, Rachel and Leah.

22 She bore a son, and he named him Gershom, for he said, "I have lived as a foreigner in a foreign land."

9 And Zipporah conceived and bare a son and he called his name Gershom, for he said, "I was a stranger in a foreign land;" but he circumcised not his foreskin, at the command of Reuel his father-in-law.

10 And she conceived again and bare a son, but circumcised his foreskin, and called his name Eliezer, for Moses said, "Because the God of my fathers was my help, and delivered me from the sword of Pharaoh."

23 In the course of those many days, the king of Egypt died, and the children of Israel sighed because of the bondage, and they cried, and their cry came up to God because of the bondage.

11 And Pharaoh king of Egypt greatly increased the labor of the children of Israel in those days, and continued to make his yoke heavier upon the children of Israel.

12 And he ordered a proclamation to be made in Egypt, saying, "Give no more straw to the people to make bricks with, let them go and gather themselves straw as they can find it. 13 Also the tale of bricks which they shall make let them give each day, and diminish nothing from them, for they are idle in their work."

14 And the children of Israel heard this, and they mourned and sighed, and they cried unto the Lord on account of the bitterness of their souls.

24 God heard their groaning, and God remembered his covenant with Abraham, with Isaac, and with Jacob. 25 God saw the children of Israel, and God was concerned about them.

[77:24 And God heard the voice of the children of Israel and their cry, in those days, and God remembered to them his covenant which he had made with Abraham, Isaac and Jacob. 25 And God saw the burden of the children of Israel, and their heavy work in those days, and he determined to deliver them.]

15 And the Lord heard the cries of the children of Israel, and saw the oppression with which the Egyptians oppressed them. 16 And the Lord was jealous of his people and his inheritance, and heard their voice, and he resolved to take them out of the affliction of Egypt, to give them the land of Canaan for a possession.

Exodus 3

1 Now Moses was keeping the flock of Jethro, his father-in-law, the priest of Midian, and he led the flock to the back of the wilderness, and came to God's mountain, to Horeb.

Jasher 79

1 And in those days Moses was feeding the flock of Reuel the Midianite his father-in-law, beyond the wilderness of Sin, and the stick which he took from his father-in-law was in his hand. 2 And it came to pass one day that a kid of goats strayed from the flock, and Moses pursued it and it came to the mountain of God to Horeb.

2 Yahweh's angel appeared to him in a flame of fire out of the middle of a bush. He looked, and behold, the bush burned with fire, and the bush was not consumed.

3 Moses said, "I will turn aside now, and see this great sight, why the bush is not burned."

3 And when he came to Horeb, the Lord appeared there unto him in the bush, and he found the bush burning with fire, but the fire had no power over the bush to consume it.

4 And Moses was greatly astonished at this sight, wherefore the bush was not consumed, and he approached to see this mighty thing, and the Lord called unto Moses out of the fire and commanded him to go down to Egypt, to Pharaoh king of Egypt, to send the children of Israel from his service.

4 When Yahweh saw that he turned aside to see, God called to him out of the middle of the bush, and said, "Moses! Moses!" He said, "Here I am."

5 He said, "Don't come close. Take your sandals off of your feet, for the place you are standing on is holy ground."

6 Moreover he said, "I am the God of your father, the God of Abraham, the God of Isaac, and the God of Jacob." Moses hid his face; for he was afraid to look at God.

7 Yahweh said, "I have surely seen the affliction of
my people who are in Egypt, and have heard their
cry because of their taskmasters, for I know their
sorrows. 8 I have come down to deliver them out of
the hand of the Egyptians, and to bring them up out
of that land to a good and large land, to a land
flowing with milk and honey; to the place of the
Canaanite, the Hittite, the Amorite, the Perizzite,
the Hivite, and the Jebusite. 9 Now, behold, the cry
of the children of Israel has come to me. Moreover I
have seen the oppression with which the Egyptians
oppress them. 10 Come now therefore, and I will
send you to Pharaoh, that you may bring my
people, the children of Israel, out of Egypt."

5 And the Lord said unto Moses, "Go, return to Egypt, for all those men who sought thy life are dead, and thou shalt speak unto Pharaoh to send forth the children of Israel from his land."

11 Moses said to God, "Who am I, that I should go to Pharaoh, and that I should bring the children of Israel out of Egypt?"

12 He said, "Certainly I will be with you. This will be the token to you, that I have sent you: when you have brought the people out of Egypt, you shall serve God on this mountain."

13 Moses said to God, "Behold, when I come to the children of Israel, and tell them, 'The God of your fathers has sent me to you;' and they ask me, 'What is his name?' What should I tell them?"

14 God said to Moses, "I AM WHO I AM," and he said, "You shall tell the children of Israel this: 'I AM has sent me to you.'"

15 God said moreover to Moses, "You shall tell the children of Israel this, 'Yahweh, the God of your fathers, the God of Abraham, the God of Isaac, and the God of Jacob, has sent me to you.' This is my name forever, and this is my memorial to all generations.'

16 "'Go, and gather the elders of Israel together, and tell them, 'Yahweh, the God of your fathers, the God of Abraham, of Isaac, and of Jacob, has appeared to me, saying, "I have surely visited you, and seen that which is done to you in Egypt; 17 and
I have said, I will bring you up out of the affliction of Egypt to the land of the Canaanite, the Hittite, the Amorite, the Perizzite, the Hivite, and the Jebusite, to a land flowing with milk and honey.'"

18 "'They will listen to your voice, and you shall come, you and the elders of Israel, to the king of Egypt, and you shall tell him, 'Yahweh, the God of the Hebrews, has met with us. Now please let us go three days' journey into the wilderness, that we
may sacrifice to Yahweh, our God.' 19 I know that
the king of Egypt won't give you permission to go, no, not by a mighty hand.

20 "I will reach out my hand and strike Egypt with all my wonders which I will do among them, and
after that he will let you go. 21 I will give this people
favor in the sight of the Egyptians, and it will happen that when you go, you shall not go empty-handed.

22 "But every woman shall ask of her neighbor, and of her who visits her house, jewels of silver, jewels of gold, and clothing; and you shall put them on your sons, and on your daughters. You shall plunder the Egyptians."

Exodus 4

1 Moses answered, "But, behold, they will not believe me, nor listen to my voice; for they will say, 'Yahweh has not appeared to you.'"

6 And the Lord showed him to do signs and wonders in Egypt before the eyes of Pharaoh and the eyes of his subjects, in order that they might believe that the Lord had sent him.

2 Yahweh said to him, "What is that in your hand?"
He said, "A rod." 3 He said, "Throw it on the
ground." He threw it on the ground, and it became
a snake; and Moses ran away from it.

4 Yahweh said to Moses, "Stretch out your hand,
and take it by the tail." He stretched out his hand,
and took hold of it, and it became a rod in his hand.

5 "That they may believe that Yahweh, the God of
their fathers, the God of Abraham, the God of Isaac,
and the God of Jacob, has appeared to you." 6
Yahweh said furthermore to him, "Now put your
hand inside your cloak." He put his hand inside his
cloak, and when he took it out, behold, his hand
was leprous, as white as snow.

7 He said, "Put your hand inside your cloak again."
He put his hand inside his cloak again, and when he
took it out of his cloak, behold, it had turned again
as his other flesh.

8 "It will happen, if they will not believe you or
listen to the voice of the first sign, that they will
believe the voice of the latter sign. 9 It will happen,
if they will not believe even these two signs or
listen to your voice, that you shall take of the water
of the river, and pour it on the dry land. The water
which you take out of the river will become blood
on the dry land."

10 Moses said to Yahweh, "O Lord, I am not
eloquent, neither before now, nor since you have
spoken to your servant; for I am slow of speech,
and of a slow tongue."

11 Yahweh said to him, "Who made man's mouth?
Or who makes one mute, or deaf, or seeing, or
blind? Isn't it I, Yahweh? 12 Now therefore go, and I
will be with your mouth, and teach you what you
shall speak."

13 He said, "Oh, Lord, please send someone else."
14 Yahweh's anger burned against Moses, and he
said, "What about Aaron, your brother, the Levite? I
know that he can speak well. Also, behold, he
comes out to meet you. When he sees you, he will
be glad in his heart.

15 "You shall speak to him, and put the words in his
mouth. I will be with your mouth, and with his
mouth, and will teach you what you shall do. 16 He
will be your spokesman to the people; and it will
happen, that he will be to you a mouth, and you will
be to him as God. 17 You shall take this rod in your
hand, with which you shall do the signs."

18 Moses went and returned to Jethro his father-in-law, and said to him, "Please let me go and return to my brothers who are in Egypt, and see whether they are still alive." Jethro said to Moses, "Go in peace."

19 Yahweh said to Moses in Midian, "Go, return into Egypt; for all the men who sought your life are dead."

[79:5a And the Lord said unto Moses, "Go, return to Egypt, for all those men who sought thy life are dead]

7 And Moses hearkened to all that the Lord had commanded him, and he returned to his father-in-law and told him the thing, and Reuel said to him, "Go in peace."

20 Moses took his wife and his sons, and set them on a donkey, and he returned to the land of Egypt. Moses took God's rod in his hand.

8 And Moses rose up to go to Egypt, and he took his wife and sons with him,

21 Yahweh said to Moses, "When you go back into
Egypt, see that you do before Pharaoh all the
wonders which I have put in your hand, but I will
harden his heart and he will not let the people go.
22 You shall tell Pharaoh, 'Yahweh says, Israel is my
son, my firstborn, 23 and I have said to you, "Let my
son go, that he may serve me"; and you have
refused to let him go. Behold, I will kill your son,
your firstborn.'"

24 On the way at a lodging place, Yahweh met Moses and wanted to kill him.

and he was at an inn in the road, and an angel of
God came down, and sought an occasion against
him. 9 And he wished to kill him on account of his
first born son, because he had not circumcised him,
and had transgressed the covenant which the Lord
had made with Abraham. 10 For Moses had
hearkened to the words of his father-in-law which
he had spoken to him, not to circumcise his first
born son, therefore he circumcised him not.

25 Then Zipporah took a flint, and cut off the
foreskin of her son, and cast it at his feet; and she
said, “Surely you are a bridegroom of blood to me.”
26 So he let him alone. Then she said, “You are a
bridegroom of blood,” because of the circumcision.

11 And Zipporah saw the angel of the Lord seeking
an occasion against Moses, and she knew that this
thing was owing to his not having circumcised her
son Gershom. 12 And Zipporah hastened and took
of the sharp rock stones that were there, and she
circumcised her son, and delivered her husband and
her son from the hand of the angel of the Lord.

27 Yahweh said to Aaron, “Go into the wilderness
to meet Moses.” He went, and met him on God’s
mountain, and kissed him.

13 And Aaron the son of Amram, the brother of
Moses, was in Egypt walking at the river side on
that day. 14 And the Lord appeared to him in that
place, and he said to him, "Go now toward Moses in
the wilderness," and he went and met him in the
mountain of God, and he kissed him.

15 And Aaron lifted up his eyes, and saw Zipporah
the wife of Moses and her children, and he said
unto Moses, "Who are these unto thee?" 16 And
Moses said unto him, "They are my wife and sons,
which God gave to me in Midian;" and the thing
grieved Aaron on account of the woman and her
children.

17 And Aaron said to Moses, "Send away the
woman and her children that they may go to her
father's house," and Moses hearkened to the words
of Aaron, and did so. 18 And Zipporah returned
with her children, and they went to the house of
Reuel, and remained there until the time arrived
when the Lord had visited his people, and brought
them forth from Egypt from the hand at Pharaoh.

28 Moses told Aaron all Yahweh’s words with which
he had sent him, and all the signs with which he
had instructed him.

29 Moses and Aaron went and gathered together
all the elders of the children of Israel. 30 Aaron
spoke all the words which Yahweh had spoken to
Moses, and did the signs in the sight of the people.
31 The people believed, and when they heard that
Yahweh had visited the children of Israel, and that
he had seen their affliction, then they bowed their
heads and worshiped.

19 And Moses and Aaron came to Egypt to the
community of the children of Israel, and they spoke
to them all the words of the Lord, and the people
rejoiced an exceeding great rejoicing.

20 And Moses and Aaron rose up early on the next
day, and they went to the house of Pharaoh, and
they took in their hands the stick of God.

21 And when they came to the king's gate, two young lions were confined there with iron instruments, and no person went out or came in from before them, unless those whom the king ordered to come, when the conjurors came and withdrew the lions by their incantations, and this brought them to the king.

22 And Moses hastened and lifted up the stick upon the lions, and he loosed them, and Moses and Aaron came into the king's house. 23 The lions also came with them in joy, and they followed them and rejoiced as a dog rejoices over his master when he comes from the field.

24 And when Pharaoh saw this thing he was astonished at it, and he was greatly terrified at the report, for their appearance was like the appearance of the children of God.

Exodus 5

1 Afterward Moses and Aaron came, and said to Pharaoh, "This is what Yahweh, the God of Israel, says, 'Let my people go, that they may hold a feast to me in the wilderness.'"

25 And Pharaoh said to Moses, "What do you require?" and they answered him, saying, "The Lord God of the Hebrews has sent us to thee, to say, 'Send forth my people that they may serve me.'"

26 And when Pharaoh heard their words he was greatly terrified before them, and he said to them, "Go today and come back to me tomorrow," and they did according to the word of the king.

27 And when they had gone Pharaoh sent for Balaam the magician and to Jannes and Jambres his sons, and to all the magicians and conjurors and counsellors which belonged to the king, and they all came and sat before the king.

28 And the king told them all the words which Moses and his brother Aaron had spoken to him, and the magicians said to the king, "But how came the men to thee, on account of the lions which were confined at the gate?"

29 And the king said, "Because they lifted up their rod against the lions and loosed them, and came to me, and the lions also rejoiced at them as a dog rejoices to meet his master."

30 And Balaam the son of Beor the magician answered the king, saying, "These are none else than magicians like ourselves. 31 Now therefore send for them, and let them come and we will try them," and the king did so.

2 Pharaoh said, “Who is Yahweh, that I should listen to his voice to let Israel go? I don’t know Yahweh, and moreover I will not let Israel go.”

3 They said, “The God of the Hebrews has met with us. Please let us go three days’ journey into the wilderness, and sacrifice to Yahweh, our God, lest he fall on us with pestilence, or with the sword.”

4 The king of Egypt said to them, “Why do you, Moses and Aaron, take the people from their work? Get back to your burdens!”

5 Pharaoh said, “Behold, the people of the land are now many, and you make them rest from their burdens.”

6 The same day Pharaoh commanded the taskmasters of the people, and their officers, saying,

7 “You shall no longer give the people straw to
make brick, as before. Let them go and gather straw
for themselves. 8 The number of the bricks, which
they made before, you require from them. You shall
not diminish anything of it, for they are idle;
therefore they cry, saying, ‘Let us go and sacrifice to
our God.’

[78:12 And he ordered a proclamation to be made in Egypt, saying, "Give no more straw to the people to make bricks with, let them go and gather themselves straw as they can find it. 13 Also the tale of bricks which they shall make let them give each day, and diminish nothing from them, for they are idle in their work."]

9 "Let heavier work be laid on the men, that they may labor therein; and don’t let them pay any attention to lying words.”

10 The taskmasters of the people went out, and
their officers, and they spoke to the people, saying,
“This is what Pharaoh says: ‘I will not give you
straw. 11 Go yourselves, get straw where you can
find it, for nothing of your work shall be
diminished.’” 12 So the people were scattered
abroad throughout all the land of Egypt to gather
stubble for straw.

13 The taskmasters were urgent saying, “Fulfill your work quota daily, as when there was straw!”

14 The officers of the children of Israel, whom Pharaoh’s taskmasters had set over them, were beaten, and demanded, “Why haven’t you fulfilled your quota both yesterday and today, in making brick as before?”

15 Then the officers of the children of Israel came
and cried to Pharaoh, saying, “Why do you deal this
way with your servants? 16 No straw is given to
your servants, and they tell us, ‘Make brick!’ and
behold, your servants are beaten; but the fault is in
your own people.”

17 But he said, “You are idle! You are idle!
Therefore you say, ‘Let us go and sacrifice to
Yahweh.’ 18 Go therefore now, and work, for no
straw shall be given to you, yet you shall deliver the
same number of bricks!”

19 The officers of the children of Israel saw that
they were in trouble, when it was said, “You shall
not diminish anything from your daily quota of
bricks!” 20 They met Moses and Aaron, who stood
in the way, as they came out from Pharaoh: 21 and
they said to them, “May Yahweh look at you, and
judge, because you have made us a stench to be
abhorred in the eyes of Pharaoh, and in the eyes of
his servants, to put a sword in their hand to kill us.”

22 Moses returned to Yahweh, and said, “Lord, why
have you brought trouble on this people? Why is it
that you have sent me? 23 For since I came to
Pharaoh to speak in your name, he has brought
trouble on this people; and you have not rescued
your people at all."

Exodus 6

1 Yahweh said to Moses, “Now you shall see what I
will do to Pharaoh, for by a strong hand he shall let
them go, and by a strong hand he shall drive them
out of his land.”

2 God spoke to Moses, and said to him, “I am
Yahweh; 3 and I appeared to Abraham, to Isaac,
and to Jacob, as God Almighty; but by my name
Yahweh I was not known to them.

4 "I have also established my covenant with them,
to give them the land of Canaan, the land of their
travels, in which they lived as aliens. 5 Moreover I
have heard the groaning of the children of Israel,
whom the Egyptians keep in bondage, and I have
remembered my covenant

6 "Therefore tell the children of Israel, 'I am
Yahweh, and I will bring you out from under the
burdens of the Egyptians, and I will rid you out of
their bondage, and I will redeem you with an
outstretched arm, and with great judgments: 7 and
I will take you to me for a people, and I will be to
you a God; and you shall know that I am Yahweh
your God, who brings you out from under the
burdens of the Egyptians.

8 "I will bring you into the land which I swore to
give to Abraham, to Isaac, and to Jacob; and I will
give it to you for a heritage: I am Yahweh.'"

9 Moses spoke so to the children of Israel, but they
didn't listen to Moses for anguish of spirit, and for
cruel bondage.

10 Yahweh spoke to Moses, saying, 11 "Go in, speak
to Pharaoh king of Egypt, that he let the children of
Israel go out of his land."

12 Moses spoke before Yahweh, saying, "Behold,
the children of Israel haven't listened to me. How
then shall Pharaoh listen to me, who am of
uncircumcised lips?"

13 Yahweh spoke to Moses and to Aaron, and gave
them a command to the children of Israel, and to
Pharaoh king of Egypt, to bring the children of Israel
out of the land of Egypt.

14 These are the heads of their fathers' houses. The
sons of Reuben the firstborn of Israel: Hanoch, and
Pallu, Hezron, and Carmi; these are the families of
Reuben. 15 The sons of Simeon: Jemuel, and Jamin,
and Ohad, and Jachin, and Zohar, and Shaul the son
of a Canaanite woman; these are the families of
Simeon. 16 These are the names of the sons of Levi
according to their generations: Gershon, and
Kohath, and Merari; and the years of the life of Levi
were one hundred thirty-seven years.

17 The sons of Gershon: Libni and Shimei, according
to their families. 18 The sons of Kohath: Amram,
and Izhar, and Hebron, and Uzziel; and the years of
the life of Kohath were one hundred thirty-three
years. 19 The sons of Merari: Mahli and Mushi.
These are the families of the Levites according to
their generations. 20 Amram took Jochebed his
father's sister to himself as wife; and she bore him
Aaron and Moses: and the years of the life of
Amram were a hundred and thirty-seven years. 21
The sons of Izhar: Korah, and Nepheg, and Zichri.

22 The sons of Uzziel: Mishael, and Elzaphan, and
Sithri. 23 Aaron took Elisheba, the daughter of
Amminadab, the sister of Nahshon, as his wife; and
she bore him Nadab and Abihu, Eleazar and
Ithamar. 24 The sons of Korah: Assir, and Elkanah,
and Abiasaph; these are the families of the
Korahites. 25 Eleazar Aaron's son took one of the
daughters of Putiel as his wife; and she bore him
Phinehas. These are the heads of the fathers'
houses of the Levites according to their families.

26 These are that Aaron and Moses, to whom
Yahweh said, "Bring out the children of Israel from
the land of Egypt according to their armies." 27
These are those who spoke to Pharaoh king of
Egypt, to bring out the children of Israel from Egypt.
These are that Moses and Aaron.

28 On the day when Yahweh spoke to Moses in the
land of Egypt, 29 Yahweh spoke to Moses, saying, "I
am Yahweh. Speak to Pharaoh king of Egypt all that
I speak to you."

30 Moses said before Yahweh, "Behold, I am of
uncircumcised lips, and how shall Pharaoh listen to
me?"

Exodus 7

1 Yahweh said to Moses, "Behold, I have made you
as God to Pharaoh; and Aaron your brother shall be
your prophet.

2 "You shall speak all that I command you; and
Aaron your brother shall speak to Pharaoh, that he
let the children of Israel go out of his land. 3 I will
harden Pharaoh's heart, and multiply my signs and
my wonders in the land of Egypt.

4 "But Pharaoh will not listen to you, and I will lay my hand on Egypt, and bring out my armies, my people the children of Israel, out of the land of Egypt by great judgments. 5 The Egyptians shall know that I am Yahweh, when I stretch out my hand on Egypt, and bring out the children of Israel from among them."

6 Moses and Aaron did so. As Yahweh commanded them, so they did. 7 Moses was eighty years old, and Aaron eighty-three years old, when they spoke to Pharaoh.

32 And in the morning Pharaoh sent for Moses and Aaron to come before the king, and they took the rod of God, and came to the king and spoke to him, saying, 33 "Thus said the Lord God of the Hebrews, 'Send my people that they may serve me.'"

8 Yahweh spoke to Moses and to Aaron, saying, 9 "When Pharaoh speaks to you, saying, 'Perform a miracle!' then you shall tell Aaron, 'Take your rod, and cast it down before Pharaoh, that it become a serpent.'"

34 And the king said to them, "But who will believe you that you are the messengers of God and that you come to me by his order? 35 Now therefore give a wonder or sign in this matter, and then the words which you speak will be believed."

10 Moses and Aaron went in to Pharaoh, and they did so, as Yahweh had commanded: and Aaron cast down his rod before Pharaoh and before his servants, and it became a serpent.

11 Then Pharaoh also called for the wise men and the sorcerers. They also, the magicians of Egypt, did the same thing with their enchantments. 12 For they each cast down their rods, and they became serpents: but Aaron's rod swallowed up their rods.

36 And Aaron hastened and threw the rod out of his hand before Pharaoh and before his servants, and the rod turned into a serpent.

37 And the sorcerers saw this and they cast each man his rod upon the ground and they became serpents. 38 And the serpent of Aaron's rod lifted up its head and opened its mouth to swallow the rods of the magicians.

39 And Balaam the magician answered and said, "This thing has been from the days of old, that a serpent should swallow its fellow, and that living things devour each other.

40 "Now therefore restore it to a rod as it was at first, and we will also restore our rods as they were at first, and if thy rod shall swallow our rods, then shall we know that the spirit of God is in thee, and if not, thou art only an artificer like unto ourselves."

41 And Aaron hastened and stretched forth his hand and caught hold of the serpent's tail and it became a rod in his hand, and the sorcerers did the like with their rods, and they got hold, each man of the tail of his serpent, and they became rods as at first.

42 And when they were restored to rods, the rod of Aaron swallowed up their rods.

43 And when the king saw this thing, he ordered the book of records that related to the kings of Egypt, to be brought, and they brought the book of records, the chronicles of the kings of Egypt, in which all the idols of Egypt were inscribed, for they thought of finding therein the name of Jehovah, but they found it not.

44 And Pharaoh said to Moses and Aaron, "Behold I have not found the name of your God written in this book, and his name I know not."

45 And the counsellors and wise men answered the king, "We have heard that the God of the Hebrews is a son of the wise, the son of ancient kings."

13 Pharaoh's heart was hardened, and he didn't listen to them; as Yahweh had spoken.

[Exodus 5:2 Pharaoh said, "Who is Yahweh, that I should listen to his voice to let Israel go? I don't know Yahweh, and moreover I will not let Israel go."]

46 And Pharaoh turned to Moses and Aaron and said to them, "I know not the Lord whom you have declared, neither will I send his people."

47 And they answered and said to the king, "The Lord God of Gods is his name, and he proclaimed his name over us from the days of our ancestors, and sent us, saying, 'Go to Pharaoh and say unto him, "Send my people that they may serve me."'

[Exodus 5:3 They said, "The God of the Hebrews has met with us. Please let us go three days' journey into the wilderness, and sacrifice to Yahweh, our God, lest he fall on us with pestilence, or with the sword."]

48 Now therefore send us, that we may take a journey for three days in the wilderness, and there may sacrifice to him, for from the days of our going down to Egypt, he has not taken from our hands either burnt offering, oblation or sacrifice, and if thou wilt not send us, his anger will be kindled against thee, and he will smite Egypt either with the plague or with the sword."

49 And Pharaoh said to them, "Tell me now his power and his might;" and they said to him, "'He created the heaven and the earth, the seas and all their fishes, he formed the light, created the darkness, caused rain upon the earth and watered it, and made the herbage and grass to sprout, he created man and beast and the animals of the forest, the birds of the air and the fish of the sea, and by his mouth they live and die.

50 "Surely he created thee in thy mother's womb, and put into thee the breath of life, and reared thee and placed thee upon the royal throne of Egypt, and he will take thy breath and soul from thee, and return thee to the ground whence thou wast taken."

51 And the anger of the king was kindled at their words, and he said to them, "But who amongst all the Gods of nations can do this? My river is mine own, and I have made it for myself."

[Exodus 5:6-9]

52 And he drove them from him, and he ordered the labor upon Israel to be more severe than it was yesterday and before.

53 And Moses and Aaron went out from the king's presence, and they saw the children of Israel in an evil condition for the task-masters had made their labor exceedingly heavy.

54 And Moses returned to the Lord and said, "Why hast thou ill treated thy people? For since I came to speak to Pharaoh what thou didst send me for, he has exceedingly ill used the children of Israel."

55 And the Lord said to Moses, "Behold thou wilt see that with an outstretched hand and heavy plagues, Pharaoh will send the children of Israel from his land.

56 And Moses and Aaron dwelt amongst their
brethren the children of Israel in Egypt. 57 And as
for the children of Israel the Egyptians embittered their lives, with the heavy work which they imposed upon them.

Jasher 80

14 Yahweh said to Moses, "Pharaoh's heart is
stubborn. He refuses to let the people go. 15 Go to
Pharaoh in the morning. Behold, he goes out to the water; and you shall stand by the river's bank to meet him; and the rod which was turned to a serpent you shall take in your hand.

1 And at the end of two years, the Lord again sent Moses to Pharaoh to bring forth the children of Israel, and to send them out of the land of Egypt.

16 You shall tell him, 'Yahweh, the God of the Hebrews, has sent me to you, saying, "Let my people go, that they may serve me in the wilderness:" and behold, until now you haven't listened. 17 Yahweh says, "In this you shall know that I am Yahweh. Behold, I will strike with the rod that is in my hand on the waters which are in the river, and they shall be turned to blood. 18 The fish that are in the river shall die, and the river shall become foul; and the Egyptians shall loathe to drink water from the river."'"

2 And Moses went and came to the house of Pharaoh, and he spoke to him the words of the Lord who had sent him, but Pharaoh would not hearken to the voice of the Lord, and God roused his might in Egypt upon Pharaoh and his subjects, and God smote Pharaoh and his people with very great and sore plagues.

19 Yahweh said to Moses, "Tell Aaron, 'Take your rod, and stretch out your hand over the waters of Egypt, over their rivers, over their streams, and over their pools, and over all their ponds of water, that they may become blood; and there shall be blood throughout all the land of Egypt, both in vessels of wood and in vessels of stone.'"

20 Moses and Aaron did so, as Yahweh commanded; and he lifted up the rod, and struck the waters that were in the river, in the sight of Pharaoh, and in the sight of his servants; and all the waters that were in the river were turned to blood. 21 The fish that were in the river died; and the river became foul, and the Egyptians couldn't drink water from the river; and the blood was throughout all the land of Egypt.

3 And the Lord sent by the hand of Aaron and turned all the waters of Egypt into blood, with all their streams and rivers. 4 And when an Egyptian came to drink and draw water, he looked into his pitcher, and behold all the water was turned into blood; and when he came to drink from his cup the water in the cup became blood. 5 And when a woman kneaded her dough and cooked her victuals, their appearance was turned to that of blood.

22 The magicians of Egypt did the same thing with their enchantments; and Pharaoh's heart was hardened, and he didn't listen to them; as Yahweh had spoken. 23 Pharaoh turned and went into his house, and he didn't even take this to heart. 24 All the Egyptians dug around the river for water to drink; for they couldn't drink the river water. 25 Seven days were fulfilled, after Yahweh had struck the river.

Exodus 8

1 Yahweh spoke to Moses, "Go in to Pharaoh, and tell him, 'This is what Yahweh says, "Let my people go, that they may serve me. 2 If you refuse to let them go, behold, I will plague all your borders with frogs: 3 and the river shall swarm with frogs, which shall go up and come into your house, and into your bedroom, and on your bed, and into the house of your servants, and on your people, and into your ovens, and into your kneading troughs: 4 and the frogs shall come up both on you, and on your people, and on all your servants."'"

5 Yahweh said to Moses, "Tell Aaron, 'Stretch out your hand with your rod over the rivers, over the streams, and over the pools, and cause frogs to come up on the land of Egypt.'"

6 Aaron stretched out his hand over the waters of Egypt; and the frogs came up, and covered the land of Egypt.

6 And the Lord sent again and caused all their waters to bring forth frogs, and all the frogs came into the houses of the Egyptians.

7 And when the Egyptians drank, their bellies were filled with frogs and they danced in their bellies as they dance when in the river. 8 And all their drinking water and cooking water turned to frogs, also when they lay in their beds their perspiration bred frogs.

7 The magicians did the same thing with their enchantments, and brought up frogs on the land of Egypt.

8 Then Pharaoh called for Moses and Aaron, and said, "Entreat Yahweh, that he take away the frogs from me, and from my people; and I will let the people go, that they may sacrifice to Yahweh."

9 Moses said to Pharaoh, "I give you the honor of setting the time that I should pray for you, and for your servants, and for your people, that the frogs be destroyed from you and your houses, and remain in the river only."

10 He said, "Tomorrow." He said, "Be it according to your word, that you may know that there is no one like Yahweh our God. 11 The frogs shall depart from you, and from your houses, and from your servants, and from your people. They shall remain in the river only."

Exodus 8

12 Moses and Aaron went out from Pharaoh, and
Moses cried to Yahweh concerning the frogs which
he had brought on Pharaoh. 13 Yahweh did
according to the word of Moses, and the frogs died
out of the houses, out of the courts, and out of the
fields. 14 They gathered them together in heaps,
and the land stank.

15 But when Pharaoh saw that there was a respite,
he hardened his heart, and didn't listen to them, as
Yahweh had spoken.

16 Yahweh said to Moses, "Tell Aaron, 'Stretch out
your rod, and strike the dust of the earth, that it
may become lice throughout all the land of Egypt.'"
17 They did so; and Aaron stretched out his hand
with his rod, and struck the dust of the earth, and
there were lice on man, and on animal; all the dust
of the earth became lice throughout all the land of
Egypt.

18 The magicians tried with their enchantments to
produce lice, but they couldn't. There were lice on
man, and on animal. 19 Then the magicians said to
Pharaoh, "This is God's finger:" and Pharaoh's heart
was hardened, and he didn't listen to them; as
Yahweh had spoken.

20 Yahweh said to Moses, "Rise up early in the
morning, and stand before Pharaoh; behold, he
comes out to the water; and tell him, 'This is what
Yahweh says, "Let my people go, that they may
serve me.

21 "Else, if you will not let my people go, behold, I
will send swarms of flies on you, and on your
servants, and on your people, and into your houses:
and the houses of the Egyptians shall be full of
swarms of flies, and also the ground whereon they
are.

22 "I will set apart in that day the land of Goshen, in
which my people dwell, that no swarms of flies shall
be there; to the end you may know that I am
Yahweh on the earth. 23 I will put a division
between my people and your people: by tomorrow
shall this sign be."'"

Jasher 80

9 Notwithstanding all this the anger of the Lord did
not turn from them, and his hand was stretched out
against all the Egyptians to smite them with every
heavy plague.

10 And he sent and smote their dust to lice, and the
lice became in Egypt to the height of two cubits
upon the earth. 11 The lice were also very
numerous, in the flesh of man and beast, in all the
inhabitants of Egypt, also upon the king and queen
the Lord sent the lice, and it grieved Egypt
exceedingly on account of the lice.

12 Notwithstanding this, the anger of the Lord did
not turn away, and his hand was still stretched out
over Egypt.

24 Yahweh did so; and there came grievous swarms of flies into the house of Pharaoh, and into his servants' houses: and in all the land of Egypt the land was corrupted by reason of the swarms of flies.

13 And the Lord sent all kinds of beasts of the field into Egypt, and they came and destroyed all Egypt, man and beast, and trees, and all things that were in Egypt.

25 Pharaoh called for Moses and for Aaron, and said, "Go, sacrifice to your God in the land!"

26 Moses said, "It isn't appropriate to do so; for we shall sacrifice the abomination of the Egyptians to Yahweh our God. Behold, shall we sacrifice the abomination of the Egyptians before their eyes, and
won't they stone us? 27 We will go three days'
journey into the wilderness, and sacrifice to Yahweh our God, as he shall command us."

28 Pharaoh said, "I will let you go, that you may sacrifice to Yahweh your God in the wilderness, only you shall not go very far away. Pray for me."

29 Moses said, "Behold, I go out from you, and I will pray to Yahweh that the swarms of flies may depart from Pharaoh, from his servants, and from his people, tomorrow; only don't let Pharaoh deal deceitfully any more in not letting the people go to
sacrifice to Yahweh." 30 Moses went out from
Pharaoh, and prayed to Yahweh.

31 Yahweh did according to the word of Moses, and he removed the swarms of flies from Pharaoh, from his servants, and from his people. There remained
not one. 32 Pharaoh hardened his heart this time
also, and he didn't let the people go.

14 And the Lord sent fiery serpents, scorpions, mice, weasels, toads, together with others creeping
in dust. 15 Flies, hornets, fleas, bugs and gnats,
each swarm according to its kind.

16 And all reptiles and winged animals according to their kind came to Egypt and grieved the Egyptians
exceedingly. 17 And the fleas and flies came into
the eyes and ears of the Egyptians. 18 And the
hornet came upon them and drove them away, and they removed from it into their inner rooms, and it pursued them.

19 And when the Egyptians hid themselves on account of the swarm of animals, they locked their doors after them, and God ordered the Sulanuth which was in the sea, to come up and go into Egypt.

20 And she had long arms, ten cubits in length of the cubit of a man.

21 And she went upon the roofs and uncovered the raftering and flooring and cut them, and stretched forth her arm into the house and removed the lock and the bolt, and opened the houses of Egypt.

22 Afterward came the swarm of animals into the houses of Egypt, and the swarm of animals destroyed the Egyptians, and it grieved them exceedingly. 23 Notwithstanding this the anger of the Lord did not turn away from the Egyptians, and his hand was yet stretched forth against them.

Exodus 9

1 Then Yahweh said to Moses, "Go in to Pharaoh, and tell him, 'This is what Yahweh, the God of the Hebrews, says: "Let my people go, that they may serve me.

2 "For if you refuse to let them go, and hold them still, 3 behold, Yahweh's hand is on your livestock which are in the field, on the horses, on the donkeys, on the camels, on the herds, and on the flocks with a very grievous pestilence. 4 Yahweh will make a distinction between the livestock of Israel and the livestock of Egypt; and nothing shall die of all that belongs to the children of Israel."'"

5 Yahweh appointed a set time, saying, "Tomorrow Yahweh shall do this thing in the land." 6 Yahweh did that thing on the next day; and all the livestock of Egypt died, but of the livestock of the children of Israel, not one died. 7 Pharaoh sent, and, behold, there was not so much as one of the livestock of the Israelites dead. But the heart of Pharaoh was stubborn, and he didn't let the people go.

24 And God sent the pestilence, and the pestilence pervaded Egypt, in the horses and asses, and in the camels, in herds of oxen and sheep and in man. 25 And when the Egyptians rose up early in the morning to take their cattle to pasture they found all their cattle dead. 26 And there remained of the cattle of the Egyptians only one in ten, and of the cattle belonging to Israel in Goshen not one died.

8 Yahweh said to Moses and to Aaron, "Take to you handfuls of ashes of the furnace, and let Moses sprinkle it toward the sky in the sight of Pharaoh.

9 "It shall become small dust over all the land of Egypt, and shall be a boil breaking out with boils on man and on animal, throughout all the land of Egypt."

10 They took ashes of the furnace, and stood before Pharaoh; and Moses sprinkled it up toward the sky; and it became a boil breaking out with boils on man and on animal. 11 The magicians couldn't stand before Moses because of the boils; for the boils were on the magicians, and on all the Egyptians.

12 Yahweh hardened the heart of Pharaoh, and he didn't listen to them, as Yahweh had spoken to Moses.

13 Yahweh said to Moses, "Rise up early in the morning, and stand before Pharaoh, and tell him, 'This is what Yahweh, the God of the Hebrews, says: "Let my people go, that they may serve me.

14 "For this time I will send all my plagues against your heart, against your officials, and against your people; that you may know that there is no one like me in all the earth. 15 For now I would have stretched out my hand, and struck you and your people with pestilence, and you would have been cut off from the earth;

16 "but indeed for this cause I have made you stand: to show you my power, and that my name may be declared throughout all the earth; 17 as you still exalt yourself against my people, that you won't let them go. 18 Behold, tomorrow about this time I will cause it to rain a very grievous hail, such as has not been in Egypt since the day it was founded even until now. 19 Now therefore command that all of your livestock and all that you have in the field be brought into shelter. Every man and animal that is found in the field, and isn't brought home, the hail shall come down on them, and they shall die."'"

20 Those who feared Yahweh's word among the servants of Pharaoh made their servants and their livestock flee into the houses. 21 Whoever didn't respect Yahweh's word left his servants and his livestock in the field.

27 And God sent a burning inflammation in the flesh of the Egyptians, which burst their skins, and it became a severe itch in all the Egyptians from the soles of their feet to the crowns of their heads. 28 And many boils were in their flesh, that their flesh wasted away until they became rotten and putrid.

29 Notwithstanding this the anger of the Lord did not turn away, and his hand was still stretched out over all Egypt.

22 Yahweh said to Moses, "Stretch out your hand toward the sky, that there may be hail in all the land of Egypt, on man, and on animal, and on every herb of the field, throughout the land of Egypt."

23 Moses stretched out his rod toward the heavens, and Yahweh sent thunder, hail, and lightning flashed down to the earth. Yahweh rained hail on the land of Egypt. 24 So there was very severe hail, and lightning mixed with the hail, such as had not been in all the land of Egypt since it became a nation.

30 And the Lord sent a very heavy hail, which smote their vines and broke their fruit trees and dried them up that they fell upon them.

25 The hail struck throughout all the land of Egypt all that was in the field, both man and animal; and the hail struck every herb of the field, and broke every tree of the field.

31 Also every green herb became dry and perished, for a mingling fire descended amidst the hail, therefore the hail and the fire consumed all things. 32 Also men and beasts that were found abroad perished of the flames of fire and of the hail, and all the young lions were exhausted.

26 Only in the land of Goshen, where the children of Israel were, there was no hail.

27 Pharaoh sent, and called for Moses and Aaron, and said to them, "I have sinned this time. Yahweh is righteous, and I and my people are wicked. 28 Pray to Yahweh; for there has been enough of mighty thunderings and hail. I will let you go, and you shall stay no longer."

29 Moses said to him, "As soon as I have gone out of the city, I will spread abroad my hands to Yahweh. The thunders shall cease, and there will not be any more hail; that you may know that the earth is Yahweh's. 30 But as for you and your servants, I know that you don't yet fear Yahweh God."

31 The flax and the barley were struck, for the barley was in the ear, and the flax was in bloom.

32 But the wheat and the spelt were not struck, for they had not grown up.

33 Moses went out of the city from Pharaoh, and spread abroad his hands to Yahweh; and the thunders and hail ceased, and the rain was not poured on the earth.

34 When Pharaoh saw that the rain and the hail and the thunders were ceased, he sinned yet more, and hardened his heart, he and his servants.

35 The heart of Pharaoh was hardened, and he didn't let the children of Israel go, just as Yahweh had spoken through Moses.

Exodus 10

1 Yahweh said to Moses, "Go in to Pharaoh, for I have hardened his heart, and the heart of his servants, that I may show these my signs among
them, 2 and that you may tell in the hearing of your son, and of your son's son, what things I have done to Egypt, and my signs which I have done among them; that you may know that I am Yahweh."

3 Moses and Aaron went in to Pharaoh, and said to him, "This is what Yahweh, the God of the Hebrews, says: 'How long will you refuse to humble yourself before me? Let my people go, that they may serve
me. 4 Or else, if you refuse to let my people go, behold, tomorrow I will bring locusts into your
country, 5 and they shall cover the surface of the earth, so that one won't be able to see the earth. They shall eat the residue of that which has escaped, which remains to you from the hail, and shall eat every tree which grows for you out of the field.

6 "Your houses shall be filled, and the houses of all your servants, and the houses of all the Egyptians; as neither your fathers nor your fathers' fathers have seen, since the day that they were on the earth to this day.'" He turned, and went out from Pharaoh.

7 Pharaoh's servants said to him, "How long will this man be a snare to us? Let the men go, that they may serve Yahweh, their God. Don't you yet know that Egypt is destroyed?"

8 Moses and Aaron were brought again to Pharaoh, and he said to them, "Go, serve Yahweh your God; but who are those who will go?"

9 Moses said, "We will go with our young and with our old; with our sons and with our daughters, with our flocks and with our herds will we go; for we must hold a feast to Yahweh."

10 He said to them, "Yahweh be with you if I will let you go with your little ones! See, evil is clearly before your faces. 11 Not so! Go now you who are men, and serve Yahweh; for that is what you desire!" They were driven out from Pharaoh's presence.

12 Yahweh said to Moses, "Stretch out your hand over the land of Egypt for the locusts, that they may come up on the land of Egypt, and eat every herb of the land, even all that the hail has left." 13 Moses stretched out his rod over the land of Egypt, and Yahweh brought an east wind on the land all that day, and all night; and when it was morning, the east wind brought the locusts.

14 The locusts went up over all the land of Egypt, and rested in all the borders of Egypt. They were very grievous. Before them there were no such locusts as they, nor will there ever be again. 15 For they covered the surface of the whole earth, so that the land was darkened, and they ate every herb of the land, and all the fruit of the trees which the hail had left. There remained nothing green, either tree or herb of the field, through all the land of Egypt.

33 And the Lord sent and brought numerous locusts into Egypt, the Chasel, Salom, Chargol, and Chagole, locusts each of its kind, which devoured all that the hail had left remaining.

34 Then the Egyptians rejoiced at the locusts, although they consumed the produce of the field, and they caught them in abundance and salted them for food.

16 Then Pharaoh called for Moses and Aaron in haste, and he said, "I have sinned against Yahweh your God, and against you. 17 Now therefore please forgive my sin again, and pray to Yahweh your God, that he may also take away from me this death."

18 He went out from Pharaoh, and prayed to Yahweh. 19 Yahweh turned an exceeding strong west wind, which took up the locusts, and drove them into the Red Sea. There remained not one locust in all the borders of Egypt.

35 And the Lord turned a mighty wind of the sea which took away all the locusts, even those that were salted, and thrust them into the Red Sea; not one locust remained within the boundaries of Egypt.

20 But Yahweh hardened Pharaoh's heart, and he didn't let the children of Israel go.

21 Yahweh said to Moses, "Stretch out your hand toward the sky, that there may be darkness over the land of Egypt, even darkness which may be felt."

22 Moses stretched out his hand toward the sky, and there was a thick darkness in all the land of Egypt for three days. 23 They didn't see one another, and nobody rose from his place for three days; but all the children of Israel had light in their dwellings.

36 And God sent darkness upon Egypt, that the whole land of Egypt and Pathros became dark for three days, so that a man could not see his hand when he lifted it to his mouth.

37 At that time died many of the people of Israel who had rebelled against the Lord and who would not hearken to Moses and Aaron, and believed not in them that God had sent them. 38 And who had said, "We will not go forth from Egypt lest we perish with hunger in a desolate wilderness, and who would not hearken to the voice of Moses."

39 And the Lord plagued them in the three days of darkness, and the Israelites buried them in those days, without the Egyptians knowing of them or rejoicing over them.

40 And the darkness was very great in Egypt for three days, and any person who was standing when the darkness came, remained standing in his place, and he that was sitting remained sitting, and he that was lying continued lying in the same state, and he that was walking remained sitting upon the ground in the same spot; and this thing happened to all the Egyptians, until the darkness had passed away.

24 Pharaoh called to Moses, and said, "Go, serve Yahweh. Only let your flocks and your herds stay behind. Let your little ones also go with you."

25 Moses said, "You must also give into our hand sacrifices and burnt offerings, that we may sacrifice to Yahweh our God.

26 "Our livestock also shall go with us. Not a hoof shall be left behind, for of it we must take to serve Yahweh our God; and we don't know with what we must serve Yahweh, until we come there."

27 But Yahweh hardened Pharaoh's heart, and he wouldn't let them go.

28 Pharaoh said to him, "Get away from me! Be careful to see my face no more; for in the day you see my face you shall die!" 29 Moses said, "You have spoken well. I will see your face again no more."

Exodus 11
1 Yahweh said to Moses, "Yet one plague more will
I bring on Pharaoh, and on Egypt; afterwards he will
let you go. When he lets you go, he will surely
thrust you out altogether. 2 Speak now in the ears
of the people, and let every man ask of his
neighbor, and every woman of her neighbor, jewels
of silver, and jewels of gold." 3 Yahweh gave the
people favor in the sight of the Egyptians. Moreover
the man Moses was very great in the land of Egypt,
in the sight of Pharaoh's servants, and in the sight
of the people.

4 Moses said, "This is what Yahweh says: 'About
midnight I will go out into the middle of Egypt, 5
and all the firstborn in the land of Egypt shall die,
from the firstborn of Pharaoh who sits on his
throne, even to the firstborn of the female servant
who is behind the mill; and all the firstborn of
livestock. 6 There shall be a great cry throughout all
the land of Egypt, such as there has not been, nor
shall be any more. 7 But against any of the children
of Israel a dog won't even bark or move its tongue,
against man or animal; that you may know that
Yahweh makes a distinction between the Egyptians
and Israel.

8 "All these servants of yours will come down to
me, and bow down themselves to me, saying, "Get
out, with all the people who follow you"; and after
that I will go out.'" He went out from Pharaoh in
hot anger.

9 Yahweh said to Moses, "Pharaoh won't listen to
you, that my wonders may be multiplied in the land
of Egypt." 10 Moses and Aaron did all these
wonders before Pharaoh, and Yahweh hardened
Pharaoh's heart, and he didn't let the children of
Israel go out of his land.

41 And the days of darkness passed away, and the
Lord sent Moses and Aaron to the children of Israel,
saying, "Celebrate your feast and make your
Passover, for behold I come in the midst of the
night amongst all the Egyptians, and I will smite all
their first born, from the first born of a man to the
first born of a beast, and when I see your Passover,
I will pass over you."

Exodus 12

1 Yahweh spoke to Moses and Aaron in the land of
Egypt, saying, 2 “This month shall be to you the
beginning of months. It shall be the first month of
the year to you. 3 Speak to all the congregation of
Israel, saying, ‘On the tenth day of this month, they
shall take to them every man a lamb, according to
their fathers’ houses, a lamb for a household; 4 and
if the household is too little for a lamb, then he and
his neighbor next to his house shall take one
according to the number of the souls; according to
what everyone can eat you shall make your count
for the lamb.

5 "Your lamb shall be without defect, a male a year
old. You shall take it from the sheep, or from the
goats: 6 and you shall keep it until the fourteenth
day of the same month; and the whole assembly of
the congregation of Israel shall kill it at evening. 7
They shall take some of the blood, and put it on the
two door posts and on the lintel, on the houses in
which they shall eat it. 8 They shall eat the flesh in
that night, roasted with fire, and unleavened bread.
They shall eat it with bitter herbs.

9 "Don’t eat it raw, nor boiled at all with water, but
roasted with fire; with its head, its legs and its inner
parts. 10 You shall let nothing of it remain until the
morning; but that which remains of it until the
morning you shall burn with fire.

11 "This is how you shall eat it: with your belt on
your waist, your shoes on your feet, and your staff
in your hand; and you shall eat it in haste: it is
Yahweh’s Passover.

12 "For I will go through the land of Egypt in that
night, and will strike all the firstborn in the land of
Egypt, both man and animal. Against all the gods of
Egypt I will execute judgments: I am Yahweh.

13 "The blood shall be to you for a token on the
houses where you are: and when I see the blood, I
will pass over you, and there shall no plague be on
you to destroy you, when I strike the land of Egypt.

14 "This day shall be to you for a memorial, and you shall keep it a feast to Yahweh: throughout your generations you shall keep it a feast by an ordinance forever.

15 "'Seven days you shall eat unleavened bread; even the first day you shall put away yeast out of your houses, for whoever eats leavened bread from the first day until the seventh day, that soul shall be cut off from Israel. 16 In the first day there shall be to you a holy convocation, and in the seventh day a holy convocation; no kind of work shall be done in them, except that which every man must eat, that only may be done by you.

17 "You shall observe the feast of unleavened bread; for in this same day have I brought your armies out of the land of Egypt: therefore you shall observe this day throughout your generations by an ordinance forever. 18 In the first month, on the fourteenth day of the month at evening, you shall eat unleavened bread, until the twenty first day of the month at evening.

19 "There shall be no yeast found in your houses for seven days, for whoever eats that which is leavened, that soul shall be cut off from the congregation of Israel, whether he be a foreigner, or one who is born in the land. 20 You shall eat nothing leavened. In all your habitations you shall eat unleavened bread.'"

21 Then Moses called for all the elders of Israel, and said to them, "Draw out, and take lambs according to your families, and kill the Passover. 22 You shall take a bunch of hyssop, and dip it in the blood that is in the basin, and strike the lintel and the two door posts with the blood that is in the basin; and none of you shall go out of the door of his house until the morning. 23 For Yahweh will pass through to strike the Egyptians; and when he sees the blood on the lintel, and on the two door posts, Yahweh will pass over the door, and will not allow the destroyer to come in to your houses to strike you.

24 "You shall observe this thing for an ordinance to
you and to your sons forever. 25 It shall happen
when you have come to the land which Yahweh will
give you, according as he has promised, that you
shall keep this service. 26 It will happen, when your
children ask you, 'What do you mean by this
service?' 27 that you shall say, 'It is the sacrifice of
Yahweh's Passover, who passed over the houses of
the children of Israel in Egypt, when he struck the
Egyptians, and spared our houses.'" The people
bowed their heads and worshiped.

28 The children of Israel went and did so; as Yahweh had commanded Moses and Aaron, so they did.

42 And the children of Israel did according to all that the Lord had commanded Moses and Aaron, thus did they in that night.

29 At midnight, Yahweh struck all the firstborn in the land of Egypt, from the firstborn of Pharaoh who sat on his throne to the firstborn of the captive who was in the dungeon; and all the firstborn of livestock.

43 And it came to pass in the middle of the night, that the Lord went forth in the midst of Egypt, and smote all the first born of the Egyptians, from the first born of man to the first born of beast.

30 Pharaoh rose up in the night, he, and all his servants, and all the Egyptians; and there was a great cry in Egypt, for there was not a house where there was not one dead.

44 And Pharaoh rose up in the night, he and all his servants and all the Egyptians, and there was a great cry throughout Egypt in that night, for there was not a house in which there was not a corpse.

45 Also the likenesses of the first born of Egypt,
which were carved in the walls at their houses,
were destroyed and fell to the ground. 46 Even the
bones of their first born who had died before this
and whom they had buried in their houses, were
raked up by the dogs of Egypt on that night and
dragged before the Egyptians and cast before them.

47 And all the Egyptians saw this evil which had
suddenly come upon them, and all the Egyptians
cried out with a loud voice. 48 And all the families
of Egypt wept upon that night, each man for his son
and each man for his daughter, being the first born,
and the tumult of Egypt was heard at a distance on
that night.

49 And Bathia the daughter of Pharaoh went forth with the king on that night to seek Moses and Aaron in their houses, and they found them in their houses, eating and drinking and rejoicing with all Israel.

50 And Bathia said to Moses, "Is this the reward for the good which I have done to thee, who have reared thee and stretched thee out, and thou hast brought this evil upon me and my father's house?"

51 And Moses said to her, "Surely ten plagues did the Lord bring upon Egypt; did any evil accrue to thee from any of them? Did one of them affect thee?" and she said, "No."

52 And Moses said to her, "Although thou art the first bor"n to thy mother, thou shalt not die, and no evil shall reach thee in the midst of Egypt.

53 And she said, "What advantage is it to me, when I see the king, my brother, and all his household and subjects in this evil, whose first born perish with all the first born of Egypt?"

54 And Moses said to her, "Surely thy brother and his household, and subjects, the families of Egypt, would not hearken to the words of the Lord, therefore did this evil come upon them."

31 He called for Moses and Aaron by night, and said, "Rise up, get out from among my people, both you and the children of Israel; and go, serve Yahweh, as you have said! 32 Take both your flocks and your herds, as you have said, and be gone; and bless me also!"

55 And Pharaoh king of Egypt approached Moses and Aaron, and some of the children of Israel who were with them in that place, and he prayed to them, saying, 56 "Rise up and take your brethren, all the children of Israel who are in the land, with their sheep and oxen, and all belonging to them, they shall leave nothing remaining, only pray for me to the Lord your God."

57 And Moses said to Pharaoh, "Behold though thou art thy mother's first born, yet fear not, for thou wilt not die, for the Lord has commanded that thou shalt live, in order to show thee his great might and strong stretched out arm."

33 The Egyptians were urgent with the people, to send them out of the land in haste, for they said, "We are all dead men."

58 And Pharaoh ordered the children of Israel to be sent away, and all the Egyptians strengthened themselves to send them, for they said, "We are all perishing."

34 The people took their dough before it was leavened, their kneading troughs being bound up in their clothes on their shoulders.

59 And all the Egyptians sent the Israelites forth, with great riches, sheep and oxen and precious things, according to the oath of the Lord between him and our Father Abraham.

60 And the children of Israel delayed going forth at night, and when the Egyptians came to them to bring them out, they said to them, "Are we thieves, that we should go forth at night?"

35 The children of Israel did according to the word of Moses; and they asked of the Egyptians jewels of silver, and jewels of gold, and clothing. 36 Yahweh gave the people favor in the sight of the Egyptians, so that they let them have what they asked. They plundered the Egyptians.

61 And the children of Israel asked of the Egyptians, vessels of silver, and vessels of gold, and garments, and the children of Israel stripped the Egyptians.

62 And Moses hastened and rose up and went to the river of Egypt, and brought up from thence the coffin of Joseph and took it with him. 63 The children of Israel also brought up, each man his father's coffin with him, and each man the coffins of his tribe.

Jasher 81

37 The children of Israel traveled from Rameses to Succoth, about six hundred thousand on foot who were men, besides children.

1 And the children of Israel journeyed from Rameses to Succoth, about six hundred thousand men on foot, besides the little ones and their wives.

38 A mixed multitude went up also with them, with flocks, herds, and even very much livestock.

2 Also a mixed multitude went up with them, and flocks and herds, even much cattle.

3 And the sojourning of the children of Israel, who dwelt in the land of Egypt in hard labor, was two hundred and ten years. 4 And at the end of two hundred and ten years, the Lord brought forth the children of Israel from Egypt with a strong hand.

[37 The children of Israel traveled from Rameses to Succoth, about six hundred thousand on foot who were men, besides children.]

5 And the children of Israel traveled from Egypt and from Goshen and from Rameses, and encamped in Succoth on the fifteenth day of the first month.

39 They baked unleavened cakes of the dough which they brought out of Egypt; for it wasn't leavened, because they were thrust out of Egypt, and couldn't wait, and they had not prepared any food for themselves.

40 Now the time that the children of Israel lived in Egypt was four hundred thirty years. 41 At the end of four hundred thirty years, to the day, all of Yahweh's armies went out from the land of Egypt. 42 It is a night to be much observed to Yahweh for bringing them out from the land of Egypt. This is that night of Yahweh, to be much observed of all the children of Israel throughout their generations.

43 Yahweh said to Moses and Aaron, “This is the
ordinance of the Passover. No foreigner shall eat of
it, 44 but every man’s servant who is bought for
money, when you have circumcised him, then shall
he eat of it. 45 A foreigner and a hired servant shall
not eat of it. 46 It must be eaten In one house. You
shall not carry any of the meat outside of the
house. Do not break any of its bones. 47 All the
congregation of Israel shall keep it.

48 "When a stranger shall live as a foreigner with
you, and will keep the Passover to Yahweh, let all
his males be circumcised, and then let him come
near and keep it; and he shall be as one who is born
in the land: but no uncircumcised person shall eat
of it. 49 One law shall be to him who is born at
home, and to the stranger who lives as a foreigner
among you.”

50 All the children of Israel did so. As Yahweh
commanded Moses and Aaron, so they did. 51 That
same day, Yahweh brought the children of Israel
out of the land of Egypt by their armies.

Exodus 13

1 Yahweh spoke to Moses, saying, 2 “Sanctify to me
all the firstborn, whatever opens the womb among
the children of Israel, both of man and of animal. It
is mine.”

3 Moses said to the people, “Remember this day, in
which you came out of Egypt, out of the house of
bondage; for by strength of hand Yahweh brought
you out from this place. No leavened bread shall be
eaten. 4 Today you go out in the month Abib.

5 "It shall be, when Yahweh shall bring you into the
land of the Canaanite, and the Hittite, and the
Amorite, and the Hivite, and the Jebusite, which he
swore to your fathers to give you, a land flowing
with milk and honey, that you shall keep this service
in this month.

6 "Seven days you shall eat unleavened bread, and
in the seventh day shall be a feast to Yahweh. 7
Unleavened bread shall be eaten throughout the
seven days; and no leavened bread shall be seen
with you. No yeast shall be seen with you, within all
your borders. 8 You shall tell your son in that day,
saying, 'It is because of that which Yahweh did for
me when I came out of Egypt.'

9 "It shall be for a sign to you on your hand, and for
a memorial between your eyes, that Yahweh's law
may be in your mouth; for with a strong hand
Yahweh has brought you out of Egypt. 10 You shall
therefore keep this ordinance in its season from
year to year.

11 "It shall be, when Yahweh shall bring you into
the land of the Canaanite, as he swore to you and
to your fathers, and shall give it you, 12 that you
shall set apart to Yahweh all that opens the womb,
and every firstborn which you have that comes
from an animal. The males shall be Yahweh's. 13
Every firstborn of a donkey you shall redeem with a
lamb; and if you will not redeem it, then you shall
break its neck; and you shall redeem all the
firstborn of man among your sons.

14 "It shall be, when your son asks you in time to
come, saying, 'What is this?' that you shall tell him,
'By strength of hand Yahweh brought us out from
Egypt, from the house of bondage. 15 When
Pharaoh stubbornly refused to let us go, Yahweh
killed all the firstborn in the land of Egypt, both the
firstborn of man, and the firstborn of animal.
Therefore I sacrifice to Yahweh all that opens the
womb, being males; but all the firstborn of my sons
I redeem.'

16 "It shall be for a sign on your hand, and for
symbols between your eyes: for by strength of hand
Yahweh brought us out of Egypt."

17 When Pharaoh had let the people go, God didn't
lead them by the way of the land of the Philistines,
although that was near; for God said, "Lest perhaps
the people change their minds when they see war,
and they return to Egypt"; 18 but God led the
people around by the way of the wilderness by the
Red Sea; and the children of Israel went up armed
out of the land of Egypt.

19 Moses took the bones of Joseph with him, for he had made the children of Israel swear, saying, "God will surely visit you, and you shall carry up my bones away from here with you."

6 And the Egyptians buried all their first born whom the Lord had smitten, and all the Egyptians buried their slain for three days.

20 They took their journey from Succoth, and encamped in Etham, in the edge of the wilderness.

7 And the children of Israel traveled from Succoth and encamped in Ethom, at the end of the wilderness.

21 Yahweh went before them by day in a pillar of cloud, to lead them on their way, and by night in a pillar of fire, to give them light, that they might go by day and by night: 22 the pillar of cloud by day, and the pillar of fire by night, didn't depart from before the people.

Exodus 14

1 Yahweh spoke to Moses, saying, 2 "Speak to the children of Israel, that they turn back and encamp before Pihahiroth, between Migdol and the sea, before Baal Zephon. You shall encamp opposite it by the sea.

3 Pharaoh will say of the children of Israel, 'They are entangled in the land. The wilderness has shut them in.' 4 I will harden Pharaoh's heart, and he will follow after them; and I will get honor over Pharaoh, and over all his armies; and the Egyptians shall know that I am Yahweh." They did so.

8 And on the third day after the Egyptians had buried their first born, many men rose up from Egypt and went after Israel to make them return to Egypt, for they repented that they had sent the Israelites away from their servitude.

9 And one man said to his neighbor, "Surely Moses and Aaron spoke to Pharaoh, saying, 'We will go a three days journey in the wilderness and sacrifice to the Lord our God.' 10 Now therefore let us rise up early in the morning and cause them to return, and it shall be that if they return with us to Egypt to their masters, then shall we know that there is faith in them, but if they will not return, then will we fight with them, and make them come back with great power and a strong hand."

5 The king of Egypt was told that the people had fled;

and the heart of Pharaoh and of his servants was changed towards the people, and they said, “What is this we have done, that we have let Israel go from serving us?”

11 And all the nobles of Pharaoh rose up in the morning, and with them about seven hundred thousand men, and they went forth from Egypt on that day, and came to the place where the children of Israel were.

12 And all the Egyptians saw and behold Moses and
Aaron and all the children of Israel were sitting
before Pi-hahiroth, eating and drinking and
celebrating the feast of the Lord. 13 And all the
Egyptians said to the children of Israel, "Surely you
said, 'We will go a journey for three days in the
wilderness and sacrifice to our God and return.' 14
Now therefore this day makes five days since you
went, why do you not return to your masters?"

15 And Moses and Aaron answered them, saying, "Because the Lord our God has testified in us, saying, 'You shall no more return to Egypt, but we will betake ourselves to a land flowing with milk and honey,' as the Lord our God had sworn to our ancestors to give to us."

16 And when the nobles of Egypt saw that the children of Israel did not hearken to them, to return to Egypt, they girded themselves to fight with Israel.

17 And the Lord strengthened the hearts of the children of Israel over the Egyptians, that they gave them a severe beating, and the battle was sore upon the Egyptians, and all the Egyptians fled from before the children of Israel, for many of them perished by the hand of Israel.

18 And the nobles of Pharaoh went to Egypt and told Pharaoh, saying, "The children of Israel have fled, and will no more return to Egypt, and in this manner did Moses and Aaron speak to us."

19 And Pharaoh heard this thing, and his heart and
the hearts of all his subjects were turned against
Israel, and they repented that they had sent Israel;
and all the Egyptians advised Pharaoh to pursue the
children of Israel to make them come back to their
burdens. 20 And they said each man to his brother,
"What is this which we have done, that we have
sent Israel from our servitude?"

21 And the Lord strengthened the hearts of all the Egyptians to pursue the Israelites, for the Lord desired to overthrow the Egyptians in the Red Sea.

6 He prepared his chariot, and took his army with him; 7 and he took six hundred chosen chariots, and all the chariots of Egypt, and captains over all them.

22 And Pharaoh rose up and harnessed his chariot, and he ordered all the Egyptians to assemble, not one man was left excepting the little ones and the women. 23 And all the Egyptians went forth with Pharaoh to pursue the children of Israel, and the camp of Egypt was an exceedingly large and heavy camp, about ten hundred thousand men.

8 Yahweh hardened the heart of Pharaoh king of Egypt, and he pursued the children of Israel; for the children of Israel went out with a high hand.

9 The Egyptians pursued them. All the horses and chariots of Pharaoh, his horsemen, and his army overtook them encamping by the sea, beside Pihahiroth, before Baal Zephon.

24 And the whole of this camp went and pursued the children of Israel to bring them back to Egypt, and they reached them encamping by the Red Sea.

10 When Pharaoh came near, the children of Israel lifted up their eyes, and behold, the Egyptians were marching after them; and they were very afraid. The children of Israel cried out to Yahweh.

25 And the children of Israel lifted up their eyes, and beheld all the Egyptians pursuing them, and the children of Israel were greatly terrified at them, and the children of Israel cried to the Lord.

11 They said to Moses, “Because there were no graves in Egypt, have you taken us away to die in the wilderness? Why have you treated us this way, to bring us out of Egypt? 12 Isn’t this the word that we spoke to you in Egypt, saying, ‘Leave us alone, that we may serve the Egyptians?’ For it were better for us to serve the Egyptians, than that we should die in the wilderness.”

13 Moses said to the people, “Don’t be afraid. Stand still, and see the salvation of Yahweh, which he will work for you today: for the Egyptians whom you have seen today, you shall never see them again. 14 Yahweh will fight for you, and you shall be still.”

26 And on account of the Egyptians, the children of Israel divided themselves into four divisions, and they were divided in their opinions, for they were afraid of the Egyptians, and Moses spoke to each of them.

15 Yahweh said to Moses, “Why do you cry to me?
Speak to the children of Israel, that they go
forward. 16 Lift up your rod, and stretch out your
hand over the sea, and divide it: and the children of
Israel shall go into the middle of the sea on dry
ground.

17 "Behold, I myself will harden the hearts of the
Egyptians, and they shall go in after them: and I will
get myself honor over Pharaoh, and over all his
armies, over his chariots, and over his horsemen. 18
The Egyptians shall know that I am Yahweh, when I
have gotten myself honor over Pharaoh, over his
chariots, and over his horsemen.”

27 The first division was of the children of Reuben,
Simeon, and Issachar, and they resolved to cast
themselves into the sea, for they were exceedingly
afraid of the Egyptians. 28 And Moses said to them,
"Fear not, stand still and see the salvation of the
Lord which He will effect this day for you."

29 The second division was of the children of
Zebulun, Benjamin and Naphtali, and they resolved
to go back to Egypt with the Egyptians. 30 And
Moses said to them, "Fear not, for as you have seen
the Egyptians this day, so shall you see them no
more for ever."

31 The third division was of the children of Judah
and Joseph, and they resolved to go to meet the
Egyptians to fight with them. 32 And Moses said to
them, "Stand in your places, for the Lord will fight
for you, and you shall remain silent."

33 And the fourth division was of the children of
Levi, Gad, and Asher, and they resolved to go into
the midst of the Egyptians to confound them, and
Moses said to them, "Remain in your stations and
fear not, only call unto the Lord that he may save
you out of their hands."

34 After this Moses rose up from amidst the
people, and he prayed to the Lord and said, 35 "O
Lord God of the whole earth, save now thy people
whom thou didst bring forth from Egypt, and let not
the Egyptians boast that power and might are
theirs."

36 So the Lord said to Moses, "Why dost thou cry
unto me? Speak to the children of Israel that they
shall proceed, and do thou stretch out thy rod upon
the sea and divide it, and the children of Israel shall
pass through it."

19 The angel of God, who went before the camp of Israel, moved and went behind them; and the pillar of cloud moved from before them, and stood behind them. 20 It came between the camp of Egypt and the camp of Israel; and there was the cloud and the darkness, yet gave it light by night: and one didn't come near the other all night.

21 Moses stretched out his hand over the sea, and Yahweh caused the sea to go back by a strong east wind all night, and made the sea dry land, and the waters were divided.

22 The children of Israel went into the middle of the sea on the dry ground, and the waters were a wall to them on their right hand, and on their left.

23 The Egyptians pursued, and went in after them into the middle of the sea: all of Pharaoh's horses, his chariots, and his horsemen.

24 In the morning watch, Yahweh looked out on the Egyptian army through the pillar of fire and of cloud, and confused the Egyptian army.

25 He took off their chariot wheels, and they drove them heavily; so that the Egyptians said, "Let's flee from the face of Israel, for Yahweh fights for them against the Egyptians!"

26 Yahweh said to Moses, "Stretch out your hand over the sea, that the waters may come again on the Egyptians, on their chariots, and on their horsemen." 27 Moses stretched out his hand over the sea, and the sea returned to its strength when the morning appeared; and the Egyptians fled against it. Yahweh overthrew the Egyptians in the middle of the sea.

28 The waters returned, and covered the chariots and the horsemen, even all Pharaoh's army that went in after them into the sea. There remained not so much as one of them.

37 And Moses did so, and he lifted up his rod upon the sea and divided it. 38 And the waters of the sea were divided into twelve parts,

and the children of Israel passed through on foot, with shoes, as a man would pass through a prepared road.

39 And the Lord manifested to the children of Israel his wonders in Egypt and in the sea by the hand of Moses and Aaron.

40 And when the children of Israel had entered the sea, the Egyptians came after them,

40b and the waters of the sea resumed upon them, and they all sank in the water, and not one man was left excepting Pharaoh, who gave thanks to the Lord and believed in him, therefore the Lord did not cause him to perish at that time with the Egyptians.

41 And the Lord ordered an angel to take him from amongst the Egyptians, who cast him upon the land of Ninevah and he reigned over it for a long time.

29 But the children of Israel walked on dry land in the middle of the sea, and the waters were a wall to them on their right hand, and on their left.

30 Thus Yahweh saved Israel that day out of the hand of the Egyptians; and Israel saw the Egyptians dead on the seashore. 31 Israel saw the great work which Yahweh did to the Egyptians, and the people feared Yahweh; and they believed in Yahweh, and in his servant Moses.

42 And on that day the Lord saved Israel from the hand of Egypt, and all the children of Israel saw that the Egyptians had perished, and they beheld the great hand of the Lord, in what he had performed in Egypt and in the sea.

Exodus 15

1 Then Moses and the children of Israel sang this song to Yahweh, and said,

43 Then sang Moses and the children of Israel this song unto the Lord, on the day when the Lord caused the Egyptians to fall before them.

"I will sing to Yahweh, for he has triumphed gloriously. / The horse and his rider he has thrown into the sea."

44 And all Israel sang in concert, saying, "I will sing to the Lord for He is greatly exalted, the horse and his rider has he cast into the sea;"

[Exodus 15:2-21]

behold it is written in the book of the law of God.

2 "Yahweh is my strength and song. / He has become my salvation. / This is my God, and I will praise him; / my father's God, and I will exalt him.

3 "Yahweh is a man of war. / Yahweh is his name. / 4 He has cast Pharaoh's chariots and his army into the sea. / His chosen captains are sunk in the Red Sea.

5 "The deeps cover them. / They went down into the depths like a stone. / 6 Your right hand, Yahweh, is glorious in power. / Your right hand, Yahweh, dashes the enemy in pieces.

7 "In the greatness of your excellency, you overthrow those who rise up against you. / You send out your wrath. It consumes them as stubble. / 8 With the blast of your nostrils, the waters were piled up. / The floods stood upright as a heap. / The deeps were congealed in the heart of the sea.

9 "The enemy said, 'I will pursue. I will overtake. I will divide the plunder. / My desire shall be satisfied on them. / I will draw my sword, my hand shall destroy them.' / 10 You blew with your wind. / The sea covered them. / They sank like lead in the mighty waters.

11 "Who is like you, Yahweh, among the gods? / Who is like you, glorious in holiness, / fearful in praises, doing wonders? / 12 You stretched out your right hand. / The earth swallowed them.

13 “You, in your loving kindness, have led the
people that you have redeemed. / You have guided
them in your strength to your holy habitation. / 14
The peoples have heard. / They tremble. / Pangs
have taken hold on the inhabitants of Philistia.

15 "Then the chiefs of Edom were dismayed. /
Trembling takes hold of the mighty men of Moab. /
All the inhabitants of Canaan have melted away. /
16 Terror and dread falls on them. / By the
greatness of your arm they are as still as a stone— /
until your people pass over, Yahweh, /until the
people pass over who you have purchased.

17 "You shall bring them in, and plant them in the
mountain of your inheritance, / the place, Yahweh,
which you have made for yourself to dwell in; / the
sanctuary, Lord, which your hands have established.
/ 18 Yahweh shall reign forever and ever.”

19 For the horses of Pharaoh went in with his chariots and with his horsemen into the sea, and Yahweh brought back the waters of the sea on them; but the children of Israel walked on dry land in the middle of the sea.

20 Miriam the prophetess, the sister of Aaron, took
a tambourine in her hand; and all the women went
out after her with tambourines and with dances. 21
Miriam answered them, “Sing to Yahweh, for he has
triumphed gloriously. / The horse and his rider he
has thrown into the sea.”

22 Moses led Israel onward from the Red Sea, and they went out into the wilderness of Shur; and they went three days in the wilderness, and found no water.

23 When they came to Marah, they couldn’t drink
from the waters of Marah, for they were bitter.
Therefore its name was called Marah. 24 The
people murmured against Moses, saying, “What
shall we drink?” 25 Then he cried to Yahweh.
Yahweh showed him a tree, and he threw it into the
waters, and the waters were made sweet.

There he made a statute and an ordinance for them, and there he tested them; 26 and he said, "If you will diligently listen to Yahweh your God's voice, and will do that which is right in his eyes, and will pay attention to his commandments, and keep all his statutes, I will put none of the diseases on you, which I have put on the Egyptians; for I am Yahweh who heals you."

45 After this the children of Israel proceeded on their journey, and encamped in Marah, and the Lord gave to the children of Israel statutes and judgments in that place in Marah, and the Lord commanded the children of Israel to walk in all his ways and to serve him.

27 They came to Elim, where there were twelve springs of water, and seventy palm trees: and they encamped there by the waters.

46 And they journeyed from Marah and came to Elim, and in Elim were twelve springs of water and seventy date trees, and the children encamped there by the waters.

Exodus 16

1 They took their journey from Elim, and all the congregation of the children of Israel came to the wilderness of Sin, which is between Elim and Sinai, on the fifteenth day of the second month after their departing out of the land of Egypt.

47 And they journeyed from Elim and came to the wilderness of Sin, on the fifteenth day of the second month after their departure from Egypt.

2 The whole congregation of the children of Israel murmured against Moses and against Aaron in the wilderness; 3 and the children of Israel said to them, "We wish that we had died by Yahweh's hand in the land of Egypt, when we sat by the meat pots, when we ate our fill of bread, for you have brought us out into this wilderness, to kill this whole assembly with hunger."

4 Then Yahweh said to Moses, "Behold, I will rain bread from the sky for you, and the people shall go out and gather a day's portion every day, that I may test them, whether they will walk in my law, or not. 5 It shall come to pass on the sixth day, that they shall prepare that which they bring in, and it shall be twice as much as they gather daily."

48 At that time the Lord gave the manna to the children of Israel to eat, and the Lord caused food to rain from heaven for the children of Israel day by day.

6 Moses and Aaron said to all the children of Israel, "At evening, then you shall know that Yahweh has brought you out from the land of Egypt; 7 and in the morning, then you shall see Yahweh's glory; because he hears your murmurings against Yahweh. Who are we, that you murmur against us?"

8 Moses said, "Now Yahweh shall give you meat to eat in the evening, and in the morning bread to satisfy you; because Yahweh hears your murmurings which you murmur against him. And who are we? Your murmurings are not against us, but against Yahweh."

9 Moses said to Aaron, "Tell all the congregation of
the children of Israel, 'Come near before Yahweh,
for he has heard your murmurings.'" 10 As Aaron
spoke to the whole congregation of the children of
Israel, they looked toward the wilderness, and
behold, Yahweh's glory appeared in the cloud.

11 Yahweh spoke to Moses, saying, 12 "I have
heard the murmurings of the children of Israel.
Speak to them, saying, 'At evening you shall eat
meat, and in the morning you shall be filled with
bread: and you shall know that I am Yahweh your
God.'"

13 In the evening, quail came up and covered the
camp; and in the morning the dew lay around the
camp.

14 When the dew that lay had gone, behold, on the
surface of the wilderness was a small round thing,
small as the frost on the ground. 15 When the
children of Israel saw it, they said to one another,
"What is it?" For they didn't know what it was.
Moses said to them, "It is the bread which Yahweh
has given you to eat."

16 This is the thing which Yahweh has commanded:
"Gather of it everyone according to his eating; an
omer a head, according to the number of your
persons, you shall take it, every man for those who
are in his tent." 17 The children of Israel did so, and
gathered some more, some less. 18 When they
measured it with an omer, he who gathered much
had nothing over, and he who gathered little had
no lack. They gathered every man according to his
eating.

19 Moses said to them, "Let no one leave of it until
the morning." 20 Notwithstanding they didn't listen
to Moses, but some of them left of it until the
morning, and it bred worms, and became foul: and
Moses was angry with them. 21 They gathered it
morning by morning, everyone according to his
eating. When the sun grew hot, it melted. 22 On
the sixth day, they gathered twice as much bread,
two omers for each one, and all the rulers of the
congregation came and told Moses.

23 He said to them, “This is that which Yahweh has spoken, ‘Tomorrow is a solemn rest, a holy Sabbath to Yahweh. Bake that which you want to bake, and boil that which you want to boil; and all that remains over lay up for yourselves to be kept until the morning.’”

24 They laid it up until the morning, as Moses asked, and it didn’t become foul, and there were no worms in it.

25 Moses said, “Eat that today, for today is a Sabbath to Yahweh. Today you shall not find it in
the field. 26 Six days you shall gather it, but on the
seventh day is the Sabbath. In it there shall be none.”

27 On the seventh day, some of the people went
out to gather, and they found none. 28 Yahweh said
to Moses, “How long do you refuse to keep my
commandments and my laws? 29 Behold, because
Yahweh has given you the Sabbath, therefore he gives you on the sixth day the bread of two days. Everyone stay in his place. Let no one go out of his
place on the seventh day.” 30 So the people rested
on the seventh day.

31 The house of Israel called its name Manna, and it was like coriander seed, white; and its taste was like
wafers with honey. 32 Moses said, “This is the thing
which Yahweh has commanded, ‘Let an omer-full of it be kept throughout your generations, that they may see the bread with which I fed you in the wilderness, when I brought you out of the land of
Egypt.’” 33 Moses said to Aaron, “Take a pot, and put an omer-full of manna in it, and lay it up before Yahweh, to be kept throughout your generations.”
34 As Yahweh commanded Moses, so Aaron laid it up before the Testimony, to be kept.

35 The children of Israel ate the manna forty years, until they came to an inhabited land. They ate the manna until they came to the borders of the land of
Canaan. 36 Now an omer is one tenth of an ephah.

49 And the children of Israel ate the manna for forty years, all the days that they were in the wilderness, until they came to the land of Canaan to possess it.

Exodus 17

1 All the congregation of the children of Israel traveled from the wilderness of Sin, by their journeys, according to Yahweh's commandment, and encamped in Rephidim; but there was no water for the people to drink.

50 And they proceeded from the wilderness of Sin and encamped in Alush.

2 Therefore the people quarreled with Moses, and said, "Give us water to drink." Moses said to them, "Why do you quarrel with me? Why do you test Yahweh?"

3 The people were thirsty for water there; and the
people murmured against Moses, and said, "Why
have you brought us up out of Egypt, to kill us, our
children, and our livestock with thirst?" 4 Moses
cried to Yahweh, saying, "What shall I do with these
people? They are almost ready to stone me."

5 Yahweh said to Moses, "Walk on before the
people, and take the elders of Israel with you, and
take the rod in your hand with which you struck the
Nile, and go. 6 Behold, I will stand before you there
on the rock in Horeb. You shall strike the rock, and
water will come out of it, that the people may
drink." Moses did so in the sight of the elders of
Israel. 7 He called the name of the place Massah,
and Meribah, because the children of Israel
quarreled, and because they tested Yahweh, saying,
"Is Yahweh among us, or not?"

51 And they proceeded from Alush and encamped in Rephidim.

8 Then Amalek came and fought with Israel in Rephidim.

52 And when the children of Israel were in Rephidim, Amalek the son of Eliphaz, the son of Esau, the brother of Zepho, came to fight with Israel.

53 And he brought with him eight hundred and one
thousand men, magicians and conjurers, and he
prepared for battle with Israel in Rephidim. 54 And
they carried on a great and severe battle against
Israel, and the Lord delivered Amalek and his
people into the hands of Moses and the children of
Israel, and into the hand of Joshua, the son of Nun,
the Ephrathite, the servant of Moses.

9 Moses said to Joshua, "Choose men for us, and go out, fight with Amalek. Tomorrow I will stand on the top of the hill with God's rod in my hand."

10 So Joshua did as Moses had told him, and fought with Amalek; and Moses, Aaron, and Hur went up to the top of the hill.

11 When Moses held up his hand, Israel prevailed. When he let down his hand, Amalek prevailed.

12 But Moses' hands were heavy; and they took a stone, and put it under him, and he sat on it. Aaron and Hur held up his hands, the one on the one side, and the other on the other side. His hands were steady until sunset.

13 Joshua defeated Amalek and his people with the edge of the sword.

55 And the children of Israel smote Amalek and his people at the edge of the sword, but the battle was very sore upon the children of Israel.

14 Yahweh said to Moses, "Write this for a memorial in a book, and rehearse it in the ears of Joshua: that I will utterly blot out the memory of Amalek from under the sky."

56 And the Lord said to Moses, "Write this thing as a memorial for thee in a book, and place it in the hand of Joshua, the son of Nun, thy servant, and thou shalt command the children of Israel, saying, 'When thou shalt come to the land of Canaan, thou shalt utterly efface the remembrance of Amalek from under heaven.'"

57 And Moses did so, and he took the book and
wrote upon it these words, saying, 58 "Remember
what Amalek has done to thee in the road when
thou wentest forth from Egypt. 59 Who met thee
in the road and smote thy rear, even those that were feeble behind thee when thou wast faint and weary.

60 "Therefore it shall be when the Lord thy God shall have given thee rest from all thine enemies round about in the land which the Lord thy God giveth thee for an inheritance, to possess it, that thou shalt blot out the remembrance of Amalek
from under heaven, thou shalt not forget it. 61 And
the king who shall have pity on Amalek, or upon his memory or upon his seed, behold I will require it of him, and I will cut him off from amongst his people."

62 And Moses wrote all these things in a book, and he enjoined the children of Israel respecting all these matters.

15 Moses built an altar, and called its name Yahweh
our Banner. 16 He said, "Yah has sworn: 'Yahweh
will have war with Amalek from generation to generation.'"

Jasher 82

1 And the children of Israel proceeded from Rephidim and they encamped in the wilderness of Sinai, in the third month from their going forth from Egypt.

Exodus 18

1 Now Jethro, the priest of Midian, Moses' father-in-law, heard of all that God had done for Moses, and for Israel his people, how that Yahweh had brought Israel out of Egypt.

2 At that time came Reuel the Midianite, the father-in-law of Moses, with Zipporah his daughter and her two sons, for he had heard of the wonders of the Lord which he had done to Israel, that he had delivered them from the hand of Egypt.

2 Jethro, Moses' father-in-law, received Zipporah,
Moses' wife, after he had sent her away, 3 and her
two sons. The name of one son was Gershom, for
Moses said, "I have lived as a foreigner in a foreign
land". 4 The name of the other was Eliezer, for he
said, "My father's God was my help and delivered
me from Pharaoh's sword."

5 Jethro, Moses' father-in-law, came with his sons and his wife to Moses into the wilderness where he was encamped, at the Mountain of God.

3 And Reuel came to Moses to the wilderness where he was encamped, where was the mountain of God.

6 He said to Moses, "I, your father-in-law Jethro, have come to you with your wife, and her two sons with her."

7 Moses went out to meet his father-in-law, and bowed and kissed him. They asked each other of their welfare, and they came into the tent.

4 And Moses went forth to meet his father-in-law with great honor, and all Israel was with him.

8 Moses told his father-in-law all that Yahweh had
done to Pharaoh and to the Egyptians for Israel's
sake, all the hardships that had come on them on
the way, and how Yahweh delivered them. 9 Jethro
rejoiced for all the goodness which Yahweh had
done to Israel, in that he had delivered them out of
the hand of the Egyptians.

5 And Reuel and his children remained amongst the Israelites for many days, and Reuel knew the Lord from that day forward.

10 Jethro said, "Blessed be Yahweh, who has
delivered you out of the hand of the Egyptians, and
out of the hand of Pharaoh; who has delivered the
people from under the hand of the Egyptians. 11
Now I know that Yahweh is greater than all gods
because of the thing in which they dealt arrogantly
against them."

12 Jethro, Moses' father-in-law, took a burnt offering and sacrifices for God. Aaron came with all the elders of Israel, to eat bread with Moses' father-in-law before God.

[Exodus 18:13 - 24:14]

15 Moses went up on the mountain, and the cloud covered the mountain.

[82:8 And the glory of the Lord rested upon Mount Sinai, and he called to Moses, and Moses came in the midst of a cloud and ascended the mountain.]

16 Yahweh's glory settled on Mount Sinai, and the cloud covered it six days. The seventh day he called to Moses out of the middle of the cloud.

6 And in the third month from the children of Israel's departure from Egypt, on the sixth day thereof, the Lord gave to Israel the ten commandments on Mount Sinai.

7 And all Israel heard all these commandments, and all Israel rejoiced exceedingly in the Lord on that day.

[Exodus 24:15 Moses went up on the mountain, and the cloud covered the mountain.]

8 And the glory of the Lord rested upon Mount Sinai, and he called to Moses, and Moses came in the midst of a cloud and ascended the mountain.

17 The appearance of Yahweh's glory was like devouring fire on the top of the mountain in the eyes of the children of Israel.

18 Moses entered into the middle of the cloud, and went up on the mountain; and Moses was on the mountain forty days and forty nights.

9 And Moses was upon the mount forty days and forty nights; he ate no bread and drank no water, and the Lord instructed him in the statutes and judgments in order to teach the children of Israel.

[Exodus 25:1 - 31:17]

10 And the Lord wrote the ten commandments which he had commanded the children of Israel upon two tablets of stone, which he gave to Moses to command the children of Israel.

Exodus 31:18 He gave to Moses, when he finished speaking with him on Mount Sinai, the two tablets of the testimony, stone tablets, written with God's finger.

11 And at the end of forty days and forty nights, when the Lord had finished speaking to Moses on Mount Sinai, then the Lord gave to Moses the tablets of stone, written with the finger of God.

Exodus 32

1 When the people saw that Moses delayed to come down from the mountain, the people gathered themselves together to Aaron, and said to him, "Come, make us gods, which shall go before us; for as for this Moses, the man who brought us up out of the land of Egypt, we don't know what has become of him."

12 And when the children of Israel saw that Moses tarried to come down from the mount, they gathered round Aaron, and said, "As for this man Moses we know not what has become of him. 13 Now therefore rise up, make unto us a god who shall go before us, so that thou shalt not die."

2 Aaron said to them, "Take off the golden rings, which are in the ears of your wives, of your sons, and of your daughters, and bring them to me."

14 And Aaron was greatly afraid of the people, and he ordered them to bring him gold

3 All the people took off the golden rings which were in their ears, and brought them to Aaron. 4 He received what they handed him, and fashioned it with an engraving tool, and made it a molten calf; and they said, "These are your gods, Israel, which brought you up out of the land of Egypt."

and he made it into a molten calf for the people.

5 When Aaron saw this, he built an altar before it; and Aaron made a proclamation, and said, "Tomorrow shall be a feast to Yahweh."

6 They rose up early on the next day, and offered burnt offerings, and brought peace offerings; and the people sat down to eat and to drink, and rose up to play.

7 Yahweh spoke to Moses, "Go, get down; for your people, who you brought up out of the land of Egypt, have corrupted themselves! 8 They have turned aside quickly out of the way which I commanded them. They have made themselves a molten calf, and have worshiped it, and have sacrificed to it, and said, 'These are your gods, Israel, which brought you up out of the land of Egypt.'"

15 And the Lord said to Moses, before he had come down from the mount, "Get thee down, for thy people whom thou didst bring forth from Egypt have corrupted themselves. 16 They have made to themselves a molten calf, and have bowed down to it,

9 Yahweh said to Moses, "I have seen these people, and behold, they are a stiff-necked people. 10 Now therefore leave me alone, that my wrath may burn hot against them, and that I may consume them; and I will make of you a great nation."

now therefore leave me, that I may consume them from off the earth, for they are a stiffnecked people.

11 Moses begged Yahweh his God, and said, "Yahweh, why does your wrath burn hot against your people, that you have brought out of the land of Egypt with great power and with a mighty hand? 12 Why should the Egyptians speak, saying, 'He brought them out for evil, to kill them in the mountains, and to consume them from the surface of the earth?' Turn from your fierce wrath, and repent of this evil against your people.

17 And Moses besought the countenance of the Lord, and he prayed to the Lord for the people on account of the calf which they had made,

13 "Remember Abraham, Isaac, and Israel, your servants, to whom you swore by your own self, and said to them, 'I will multiply your offspring as the stars of the sky, and all this land that I have spoken of I will give to your offspring, and they shall inherit it forever.'"

14 Yahweh repented of the evil which he said he would do to his people.

15 Moses turned, and went down from the mountain, with the two tablets of the testimony in his hand; tablets that were written on both their sides; on the one side and on the other they were written.

16 The tablets were the work of God, and the writing was the writing of God, engraved on the tables.

17 When Joshua heard the noise of the people as they shouted, he said to Moses, "There is the noise of war in the camp."

18 He said, "It isn't the voice of those who shout for victory. It is not the voice of those who cry for being overcome; but the noise of those who sing that I hear."

19 As soon as he came near to the camp, he saw the calf and the dancing. Then Moses' anger grew hot, and he threw the tablets out of his hands, and broke them beneath the mountain.

20 He took the calf which they had made, and burned it with fire, ground it to powder, and scattered it on the water, and made the children of Israel drink of it.

21 Moses said to Aaron, "What did these people do to you, that you have brought a great sin on them?"

22 Aaron said, "Don't let the anger of my lord grow
hot. You know the people, that they are set on evil.
23 For they said to me, 'Make us gods, which shall
go before us; for as for this Moses, the man who
brought us up out of the land of Egypt, we don't
know what has become of him.' 24 I said to them,
'Whoever has any gold, let them take it off:' so they
gave it to me; and I threw it into the fire, and out
came this calf."

25 When Moses saw that the people had broken
loose, (for Aaron had let them loose for a derision
among their enemies), 26 then Moses stood in the
gate of the camp, and said, "Whoever is on
Yahweh's side, come to me!" All the sons of Levi
gathered themselves together to him. 27 He said to
them, "Yahweh says, the God of Israel, 'Every man
put his sword on his thigh, and go back and forth
from gate to gate throughout the camp, and every
man kill his brother, and every man his companion,
and every man his neighbor.'"

and he afterward descended from the mount and in his hands were the two tablets of stone, which God had given him to command the Israelites.

18 And when Moses approached the camp and saw the calf which the people had made, the anger of Moses was kindled and he broke the tablets under the mount.

19 And Moses came to the camp and he took the calf and burned it with fire, and ground it till it became fine dust, and strewed it upon the water and gave it to the Israelites to drink.

28 The sons of Levi did according to the word of Moses: and there fell of the people that day about three thousand men.

29 Moses said, "Consecrate yourselves today to Yahweh, yes, every man against his son, and against his brother; that he may give you a blessing today."

20 And there died of the people by the swords of each other about three thousand men who had made the calf.

30 On the next day, Moses said to the people, "You have sinned a great sin. Now I will go up to Yahweh. Perhaps I shall make atonement for your sin."

21 And on the morrow Moses said to the people, "I will go up to the Lord, peradventure I may make atonement for your sins which you have sinned to the Lord."

31 Moses returned to Yahweh,
[Exodus 34:28 He was there with Yahweh forty days and forty nights;]
and said, "Oh, this people have sinned a great sin,
and have made themselves gods of gold. 32 Yet
now, if you will, forgive their sin—and if not, please blot me out of your book which you have written."

22 And Moses again went up to the Lord,
and he remained with the Lord forty days and forty nights.

23 And during the forty days did Moses entreat the Lord in behalf of the children of Israel, and the Lord hearkened to the prayer of Moses, and the Lord was entreated of him in behalf of Israel.

33 Yahweh said to Moses, "Whoever has sinned against me, him will I blot out of my book.

34 "Now go, lead the people to the place of which I have spoken to you. Behold, my angel shall go before you. Nevertheless in the day when I punish, I
will punish them for their sin." 35 Yahweh struck
the people, because they made the calf, which Aaron made.

[Exodus 33]

Exodus 34

1 Yahweh said to Moses, "Chisel two stone tablets like the first: and I will write on the tablets the words that were on the first tablets, which you broke.

2 "Be ready by the morning, and come up in the morning to Mount Sinai, and present yourself there
to me on the top of the mountain. 3 No one shall
come up with you or be seen anywhere on the mountain. Do not let the flocks or herds graze in front of that mountain."

24 Then spake the Lord to Moses to hew two stone tablets and to bring them up to the Lord, who would write upon them the ten commandments.

4 He chiseled two tablets of stone like the first; and Moses rose up early in the morning, and went up to Mount Sinai, as Yahweh had commanded him, and took in his hand two stone tablets.

25 Now Moses did so, and he came down and hewed the two tablets and went up to Mount Sinai to the Lord,

and the Lord wrote the ten commandments upon the tablets.

5 Yahweh descended in the cloud, and stood with him there, and proclaimed Yahweh's name.

6 Yahweh passed by before him, and proclaimed, "Yahweh! Yahweh, a merciful and gracious God, slow to anger, and abundant in loving kindness and
truth, 7 keeping loving kindness for thousands, forgiving iniquity and disobedience and sin; and that will by no means clear the guilty, visiting the iniquity of the fathers on the children, and on the children's children, on the third and on the fourth generation."

8 Moses hurried and bowed his head toward the earth, and worshiped. 9 He said, "If now I have found favor in your sight, Lord, please let the Lord go among us; although this is a stiff-necked people; pardon our iniquity and our sin, and take us for your inheritance."

10 He said, "Behold, I make a covenant: before all your people I will do marvels, such as have not been worked in all the earth, nor in any nation; and all the people among which you are shall see the work of Yahweh; for it is an awesome thing that I do with you.

11 "Observe that which I command you today. Behold, I drive out before you the Amorite, the Canaanite, the Hittite, the Perizzite, the Hivite, and the Jebusite.

12 "Be careful, lest you make a covenant with the inhabitants of the land where you are going, lest it
be for a snare in the middle of you: 13 but you shall
break down their altars, and dash in pieces their pillars, and you shall cut down their Asherah poles;
14 for you shall worship no other god: for Yahweh, whose name is Jealous, is a jealous God.

15 "Don't make a covenant with the inhabitants of the land, lest they play the prostitute after their gods, and sacrifice to their gods, and one call you
and you eat of his sacrifice; 16 and you take of their
daughters to your sons, and their daughters play the prostitute after their gods, and make your sons play the prostitute after their gods.

17 "You shall make no cast idols for yourselves. 18
"You shall keep the feast of unleavened bread.
Seven days you shall eat unleavened bread, as I
commanded you, at the time appointed in the
month Abib; for in the month Abib you came out of
Egypt.

19 "All that opens the womb is mine; and all your
livestock that is male, the firstborn of cow and
sheep. 20 You shall redeem the firstborn of a
donkey with a lamb. If you will not redeem it, then
you shall break its neck. You shall redeem all the
firstborn of your sons. No one shall appear before
me empty.

21 "Six days you shall work, but on the seventh day
you shall rest: in plowing time and in harvest you
shall rest.

22 "You shall observe the feast of weeks with the
first fruits of wheat harvest, and the feast of harvest
at the year's end. 23 Three times in the year all your
males shall appear before the Lord Yahweh, the
God of Israel. 24 For I will drive out nations before
you and enlarge your borders; neither shall any
man desire your land when you go up to appear
before Yahweh, your God, three times in the year.

25 "You shall not offer the blood of my sacrifice
with leavened bread. The sacrifice of the feast of
the Passover shall not be left to the morning.

26 "You shall bring the first of the first fruits of your
ground to the house of Yahweh your God. "You
shall not boil a young goat in its mother's milk."

27 Yahweh said to Moses, "Write you these words:
for in accordance with these words I have made a
covenant with you and with Israel."

28 He was there with Yahweh forty days and forty
nights;

he neither ate bread, nor drank water.
He wrote on the tablets the words of the covenant,
the ten commandments.

[Exodus 25:1 - 31:17]

26 And Moses remained yet with the Lord forty
days and forty nights, and the Lord instructed him
in statutes and judgments to impart to Israel.

*[82:25b and the Lord wrote the ten commandments
upon the tablets.]*

27 And the Lord commanded him respecting the
children of Israel that they should make a sanctuary
for the Lord, that his name might rest therein, and
the Lord showed him the likeness of the sanctuary
and the likeness of all its vessels.

29 When Moses came down from Mount Sinai with the two tablets of the testimony in Moses' hand,

28 And at the end of the forty days, Moses came down from the mount and the two tablets were in his hand.

when he came down from the mountain, Moses didn't know that the skin of his face shone by reason of his speaking with him.

30 When Aaron and all the children of Israel saw Moses, behold, the skin of his face shone; and they were afraid to come near him.

31 Moses called to them, and Aaron and all the rulers of the congregation returned to him; and Moses spoke to them.

32 Afterward all the children of Israel came near, and he gave them all the commandments that Yahweh had spoken with him on Mount Sinai.

33 When Moses was done speaking with them, he put a veil on his face.

34 But when Moses went in before Yahweh to speak with him, he took the veil off, until he came out; and he came out, and spoke to the children of Israel that which he was commanded.

35 The children of Israel saw Moses' face, that the skin of Moses' face shone: and Moses put the veil on his face again, until he went in to speak with him.

Exodus 35

1 Moses assembled all the congregation of the children of Israel, and said to them, "These are the words which Yahweh has commanded, that you
should do them. 2 'Six days shall work be done, but on the seventh day there shall be a holy day for you, a Sabbath of solemn rest to Yahweh: whoever
does any work in it shall be put to death. 3 You shall
kindle no fire throughout your habitations on the Sabbath day.'"

29 And Moses came to the children of Israel and spoke to them all the words of the Lord, and he taught them laws, statutes and judgments which the Lord had taught him.

30 And Moses told the children of Israel the word of the Lord, that a sanctuary should be made for him, to dwell amongst the children of Israel.

4 Moses spoke to all the congregation of the
children of Israel, saying, “This is the thing which
Yahweh commanded, saying, 5 ‘Take from among
you an offering to Yahweh. Whoever is of a willing
heart, let him bring it, Yahweh’s offering: gold,
silver, brass, 6 blue, purple, scarlet, fine linen,
goats’ hair, 7 rams’ skins dyed red, sea cow hides,
acacia wood, 8 oil for the light, spices for the
anointing oil and for the sweet incense, 9 onyx
stones, and stones to be set for the ephod and for
the breastplate.

10 “‘Let every wise-hearted man among you come,
and make all that Yahweh has commanded: 11 the
tabernacle, its outer covering, its roof, its clasps, its
boards, its bars, its pillars, and its sockets;

12 "the ark, and its poles, the mercy seat, the veil of
the screen; 13 the table with its poles and all its
vessels, and the show bread; 14 the lamp stand also
for the light, with its vessels, its lamps, and the oil
for the light;

15 "and the altar of incense with its poles, the
anointing oil, the sweet incense, the screen for the
door, at the door of the tabernacle;

16 "the altar of burnt offering, with its grating of
brass, it poles, and all its vessels, the basin and its
base; 17 the hangings of the court, its pillars, their
sockets, and the screen for the gate of the court; 18
the pins of the tabernacle, the pins of the court,
and their cords; 19 the finely worked garments, for
ministering in the holy place, the holy garments for
Aaron the priest, and the garments of his sons, to
minister in the priest’s office.’”

20 All the congregation of the children of Israel
departed from the presence of Moses. 21 They
came, everyone whose heart stirred him up, and
everyone whom his spirit made willing, and brought
Yahweh’s offering, for the work of the Tent of
Meeting, and for all of its service, and for the holy
garments.

31 And the people rejoiced greatly at all the good
which the Lord had spoken to them, through
Moses, and they said, "We will do all that the Lord
has spoken to thee."

32 And the people rose up like one man and they
made generous offerings to the sanctuary of the
Lord, and each man brought the offering of the
Lord for the work of the sanctuary, and for all its
service. 33 And all the children of Israel brought
each man of all that was found in his possession for
the work of the sanctuary of the Lord, gold, silver
and brass, and every thing that was serviceable for
the sanctuary.

22 They came, both men and women, as many as were willing-hearted, and brought brooches, earrings, signet rings, and armlets, all jewels of gold; even every man who offered an offering of gold to Yahweh.

23 Everyone, with whom was found blue, purple, scarlet, fine linen, goats' hair, rams' skins dyed red, and sea cow hides, brought them.

24 Everyone who offered an offering of silver and brass brought Yahweh's offering; and everyone, with whom was found acacia wood for any work of the service, brought it.

25 All the women who were wise-hearted spun with their hands, and brought that which they had spun, the blue, the purple, the scarlet, and the fine linen.

26 All the women whose heart stirred them up in
wisdom spun the goats' hair. 27 The rulers brought
the onyx stones, and the stones to be set, for the
ephod and for the breastplate; 28 and the spice,
and the oil for the light, for the anointing oil, and
for the sweet incense.

29 The children of Israel brought a freewill offering to Yahweh; every man and woman, whose heart made them willing to bring for all the work, which Yahweh had commanded to be made by Moses.

34 And all the wise men who were practiced in work came and made the sanctuary of the Lord, according to all that the Lord had commanded, every man in the work in which he had been practiced; and all the wise men in heart made the sanctuary, and its furniture and all the vessels for the holy service, as the Lord had commanded Moses.

30 Moses said to the children of Israel, "Behold, Yahweh has called by name Bezalel the son of Uri, the son of Hur, of the tribe of Judah. 31 He has filled him with the Spirit of God, in wisdom, in understanding, in knowledge, and in all kinds of workmanship; 32 and to make skillful works, to work in gold, in silver, in brass, 33 in cutting of stones for setting, and in carving of wood, to work in all kinds of skillful workmanship.

34 He has put in his heart that he may teach, both he, and Oholiab, the son of Ahisamach, of the tribe of Dan. 35 He has filled them with wisdom of heart, to work all kinds of workmanship, of the engraver, of the skillful workman, and of the embroiderer, in blue, in purple, in scarlet, and in fine linen, and of the weaver, even of those who do any workmanship, and of those who make skillful works.

[Exodus 36-39]

Exodus 40

1 Yahweh spoke to Moses, saying, 2 "On the first day of the first month you shall raise up the tabernacle of the Tent of Meeting. 3 You shall put the ark of the testimony in it, and you shall screen the ark with the veil. 4 You shall bring in the table, and set in order the things that are on it. You shall bring in the lamp stand, and light its lamps. 5 You shall set the golden altar for incense before the ark of the testimony, and put the screen of the door to the tabernacle.

6 "You shall set the altar of burnt offering before the door of the tabernacle of the Tent of Meeting. 7 You shall set the basin between the Tent of Meeting and the altar, and shall put water therein. 8 You shall set up the court around it, and hang up the screen of the gate of the court.

9 "You shall take the anointing oil, and anoint the tabernacle, and all that is in it, and shall make it holy, and all its furniture: and it will be holy. 10 You shall anoint the altar of burnt offering, with all its vessels, and sanctify the altar: and the altar will be most holy. 11 You shall anoint the basin and its base, and sanctify it.

35 And the work of the sanctuary of the tabernacle was completed at the end of five months, and the children of Israel did all that the Lord had commanded Moses.

36 And they brought the sanctuary and all its furniture to Moses; like unto the representation which the Lord had shown to Moses, so did the children of Israel.

37 And Moses saw the work, and behold they did it as the Lord had commanded him, so Moses blessed them.

12 "You shall bring Aaron and his sons to the door of the Tent of Meeting, and shall wash them with water. 13 You shall put on Aaron the holy garments; and you shall anoint him, and sanctify him, that he may minister to me in the priest's office. 14 You shall bring his sons, and put coats on them. 15 You shall anoint them, as you anointed their father, that they may minister to me in the priest's office. Their anointing shall be to them for an everlasting priesthood throughout their generations." 16 Moses did so. According to all that Yahweh commanded him, so he did.

Jasher 83

1 And in the twelfth month, in the twenty-third day of the month, Moses took Aaron and his sons, and he dressed them in their garments, and anointed them and did unto them as the Lord had commanded him, and Moses brought up all the offerings which the Lord had on that day commanded him.

[Leviticus 8:35 You shall stay at the door of the Tent of Meeting day and night seven days, and keep Yahweh's command, that you don't die: for so I am commanded." 36 Aaron and his sons did all the things which Yahweh commanded by Moses.]

2 Moses afterward took Aaron and his sons and said to them, "For seven days shall you remain at the door of the tabernacle, for thus am I commanded." 3 And Aaron and his sons did all that the Lord had commanded them through Moses, and they remained for seven days at the door of the tabernacle.

17 In the first month in the second year, on the first day of the month, the tabernacle was raised up. 18 Moses raised up the tabernacle, and laid its sockets, and set up its boards, and put in its bars, and raised up its pillars. 19 He spread the covering over the tent, and put the roof of the tabernacle above on it, as Yahweh commanded Moses. 20 He took and put the testimony into the ark, and set the poles on the ark, and put the mercy seat above on the ark.

4 And on the eighth day, being the first day of the first month, in the second year from the Israelites' departure from Egypt, Moses erected the sanctuary, and Moses put up all the furniture of the tabernacle and all the furniture of the sanctuary, and he did all that the Lord had commanded him.

21 He brought the ark into the tabernacle, and set
up the veil of the screen, and screened the ark of
the testimony, as Yahweh commanded Moses. 22
He put the table in the Tent of Meeting, on the side
of the tabernacle northward, outside of the veil. 23
He set the bread in order on it before Yahweh, as
Yahweh commanded Moses.

24 He put the lamp stand in the Tent of Meeting,
opposite the table, on the side of the tabernacle
southward. 25 He lit the lamps before Yahweh, as
Yahweh commanded Moses.

26 He put the golden altar in the Tent of Meeting
before the veil; 27 and he burned incense of sweet
spices on it, as Yahweh commanded Moses. 28 He
put up the screen of the door to the tabernacle. 29
He set the altar of burnt offering at the door of the
tabernacle of the Tent of Meeting, and offered on it
the burnt offering and the meal offering, as Yahweh
commanded Moses. 30 He set the basin between
the Tent of Meeting and the altar, and put water
therein, with which to wash. 31 Moses, Aaron, and
his sons washed their hands and their feet there.

32 When they went into the Tent of Meeting, and
when they came near to the altar, they washed, as
Yahweh commanded Moses. 33 He raised up the
court around the tabernacle and the altar, and set
up the screen of the gate of the court. So Moses
finished the work.

34 Then the cloud covered the Tent of Meeting, and
Yahweh's glory filled the tabernacle. 35 Moses
wasn't able to enter into the Tent of Meeting,
because the cloud stayed on it, and Yahweh's glory
filled the tabernacle. 36 When the cloud was taken
up from over the tabernacle, the children of Israel
went onward, throughout all their journeys;

37 but if the cloud wasn't taken up, then they didn't
travel until the day that it was taken up. 38 For the
cloud of Yahweh was on the tabernacle by day, and
there was fire in the cloud by night, in the sight of
all the house of Israel, throughout all their journeys.

[Leviticus 1-7]

[Leviticus 8-9]

5 And Moses called to Aaron and his sons, and they brought the burnt offering and the sin offering for themselves and the children of Israel, as the Lord had commanded Moses.

[Leviticus 10:1 Nadab and Abihu, the sons of Aaron, each took his censer, and put fire in it, and laid incense on it, and offered strange fire before Yahweh, which he had not commanded them. 2 Fire came out from before Yahweh, and devoured them, and they died before Yahweh.]

6 On that day the two sons of Aaron, Nadab and Abihu, took strange fire and brought it before the Lord who had not commanded them, and a fire went forth from before the Lord, and consumed them, and they died before the Lord on that day.

Numbers 7

1 On the day that Moses had finished setting up the tabernacle, and had anointed it and sanctified it, with all its furniture, and the altar with all its vessels, and had anointed and sanctified them;

7 Then on the day when Moses had completed to erect the sanctuary, the princes of the children of Israel began to bring their offerings before the Lord for the dedication of the altar.

2 the princes of Israel, the heads of their fathers' houses, offered. These were the princes of the tribes. These are they who were over those who were numbered:

8 And they brought up their offerings each prince for one day, a prince each day for twelve days.

3 and they brought their offering before Yahweh, six covered wagons, and twelve oxen; a wagon for every two of the princes, and for each one an ox: and they presented them before the tabernacle. 4
Yahweh spoke to Moses, saying, 5 "Accept these from them, that they may be used in doing the service of the Tent of Meeting; and you shall give them to the Levites, to every man according to his service."

6 Moses took the wagons and the oxen, and gave them to the Levites. 7 He gave two wagons and four oxen to the sons of Gershon, according to their service: 8 and he gave four wagons and eight oxen to the sons of Merari, according to their service, under the direction of Ithamar the son of Aaron the priest. 9 But to the sons of Kohath he gave none, because the service of the sanctuary belonged to them; they carried it on their shoulders.

10 The princes gave offerings for the dedication of the altar in the day that it was anointed, even the princes gave their offerings before the altar.

11 Yahweh said to Moses, "They shall offer their offering, each prince on his day, for the dedication of the altar."

12 He who offered his offering the first day was Nahshon the son of Amminadab, of the tribe of Judah,

13 and his offering was: one silver platter, the weight of which was one hundred thirty shekels, one silver bowl of seventy shekels, after the shekel of the sanctuary; both of them full of fine flour mixed with oil for a meal offering;

9 And all the offerings which they brought, each man in his day, one silver charger weighing one hundred and thirty shekels, one silver bowl of seventy shekels after the shekel of the sanctuary, both of them full of fine flour, mingled with oil for a meat offering.

14 one golden ladle of ten shekels, full of incense;

10 One spoon, weighing ten shekels of gold, full of incense.

15 one young bull, one ram, one male lamb a year old, for a burnt offering;

11 One young bullock, one ram, one lamb of the first year for a burnt offering.

16 one male goat for a sin offering;

12 And one kid of the goats for a sin offering.

17 and for the sacrifice of peace offerings, two head of cattle, five rams, five male goats, and five male lambs a year old. This was the offering of Nahshon the son of Amminadab.

13 And for a sacrifice of peace offering, two oxen, five rams, five he-goats, five lambs of a year old.

14 Thus did the twelve princes of Israel day by day, each man in his day.

Numbers 9

1 Yahweh spoke to Moses in the wilderness of Sinai,
in the first month of the second year after they had
come out of the land of Egypt, saying, 2 "Moreover
let the children of Israel keep the Passover in its
appointed season. 3 On the fourteenth day of this
month, at evening, you shall keep it in its appointed
season—according to all its statutes, and according
to all its ordinances, you shall keep it."

15 And it was after this, in the thirteenth day of the month, that Moses commanded the children of Israel to observe the Passover.

4 Moses spoke to the children of Israel, that they should keep the Passover.

5 They kept the Passover in the first month, on the fourteenth day of the month, at evening, in the wilderness of Sinai. According to all that Yahweh commanded Moses, so the children of Israel did.

16 And the children of Israel kept the Passover in its season in the fourteenth day of the month, as the Lord had commanded Moses, so did the children of Israel.

Numbers 1

1 Yahweh spoke to Moses in the wilderness of Sinai,
in the Tent of Meeting, on the first day of the
second month, in the second year after they had
come out of the land of Egypt, saying, 2 "Take a
census of all the congregation of the children of
Israel, by their families, by their fathers' houses,
according to the number of the names, every male,
one by one; 3 from twenty years old and upward,
all who are able to go out to war in Israel. You and
Aaron shall number them by their divisions.

4 "With you there shall be a man of every tribe;
everyone head of his fathers' house. 5 These are
the names of the men who shall stand with you: Of
Reuben: Elizur the son of Shedeur. 6 Of Simeon:
Shelumiel the son of Zurishaddai. 7 Of Judah:
Nahshon the son of Amminadab.

8 "Of Issachar: Nethanel the son of Zuar. 9 Of
Zebulun: Eliab the son of Helon.

10 "Of the children of Joseph: Of Ephraim: Elishama
the son of Ammihud. Of Manasseh: Gamaliel the
son of Pedahzur. 11 Of Benjamin: Abidan the son of
Gideoni. 12 Of Dan: Ahiezer the son of
Ammishaddai.

13 "Of Asher: Pagiel the son of Ochran. 14 Of Gad:
Eliasaph the son of Deuel. 15 Of Naphtali: Ahira the
son of Enan."

16 These are those who were called of the
congregation, the princes of the tribes of their
fathers; they were the heads of the thousands of
Israel. 17 Moses and Aaron took these men who are
mentioned by name. 18 They assembled all the
congregation together on the first day of the
second month; and they declared their ancestry by
their families, by their fathers' houses, according to
the number of the names, from twenty years old
and upward, one by one.

19 As Yahweh commanded Moses, so he numbered
them in the wilderness of Sinai.

17 And in the second month, on the first day
thereof, the Lord spoke unto Moses, saying, 18
"Number the heads of all the males of the children
of Israel from twenty years old and upward, thou
and thy brother Aaron and the twelve princes of
Israel."

19 And Moses did so, and Aaron came with the
twelve princes of Israel, and they numbered the
children of Israel in the wilderness of Sinai.

[Numbers 1:44 These are those who were numbered, whom Moses and Aaron numbered, and the princes of Israel, being twelve men: they were each one for his fathers' house. 45 So all those who were numbered of the children of Israel by their fathers' houses, from twenty years old and upward, all who were able to go out to war in Israel; 46 even all those who were numbered were six hundred three thousand five hundred fifty.]

20 And the numbers of the children of Israel by the houses of their fathers, from twenty years old and upward, were six hundred and three thousand, five hundred and fifty.

[Numbers 1:47 But the Levites after the tribe of their fathers were not numbered among them.]

21 But the children of Levi were not numbered amongst their brethren the children of Israel.

[Numbers 3:43 All the firstborn males according to the number of names, from a month old and upward, of those who were numbered of them, were twenty-two thousand two hundred seventy-three.]

22 And the number of all the males of the children of Israel from one month old and upward, was twenty-two thousand, two hundred and seventy-three.

[Numbers 3:39 All who were numbered of the Levites, whom Moses and Aaron numbered at the commandment of Yahweh, by their families, all the males from a month old and upward, were twenty-two thousand.]

23 And the number of the children of Levi from one month old and above, was twenty-two thousand.

24 And Moses placed the priests and the Levites each man to his service and to his burden to serve the sanctuary of the tabernacle, as the Lord had commanded Moses.

25 And on the twentieth day of the month, the cloud was taken away from the tabernacle of testimony.

[Numbers 10:33 They set forward from the Mount of Yahweh three days' journey.]

26 At that time the children of Israel continued their journey from the wilderness of Sinai, and they took a journey of three days, and the cloud rested upon the wilderness of Paran;

[Numbers 10:33b-11:17]

there the anger of the Lord was kindled against Israel, for they had provoked the Lord in asking him for meat, that they might eat.

[Numbers 11:18 "Say to the people, 'Sanctify yourselves against tomorrow, and you will eat flesh; for you have wept in the ears of Yahweh, saying, "Who will give us flesh to eat? For it was well with us in Egypt." Therefore Yahweh will give you flesh, and you will eat. 19 You will not eat one day, nor two days, nor five days, neither ten days, nor twenty days, 20 but a whole month, until it come out at your nostrils, and it is loathsome to you; because that you have rejected Yahweh who is among you, and have wept before him, saying, "Why did we come out of Egypt?"'"]

27 And the Lord hearkened to their voice, and gave them meat which they ate for one month.

[Numbers 11:33 While the flesh was yet between their teeth, before it was chewed, Yahweh's anger burned against the people, and Yahweh struck the people with a very great plague. 34 The name of that place was called Kibroth Hattaavah, because there they buried the people who lusted.]

28 But after this the anger of the Lord was kindled against them, and he smote them with a great slaughter, and they were buried there in that place. 29 And the children of Israel called that place Kebroth Hattaavah, because there they buried the people that lusted flesh.

[Numbers 11:35 From Kibroth Hattaavah the people traveled to Hazeroth; and they stayed at Hazeroth.]

30 And they departed from Kebroth Hattaavah and pitched in Hazeroth, which is in the wilderness of Paran.

Numbers 12

1 Miriam and Aaron spoke against Moses because of the Cushite woman whom he had married; for he had married a Cushite woman. 2 They said, "Has Yahweh indeed spoken only with Moses? Hasn't he spoken also with us?" And Yahweh heard it.

3 Now the man Moses was very humble, more than all the men who were on the surface of the earth. 4 Yahweh spoke suddenly to Moses, to Aaron, and to Miriam, "You three come out to the Tent of Meeting!" The three of them came out.

5 Yahweh came down in a pillar of cloud, and stood at the door of the Tent, and called Aaron and Miriam; and they both came forward.

6 He said, "Now hear my words. If there is a prophet among you, I, Yahweh, will make myself known to him in a vision. I will speak with him in a dream. 7 My servant Moses is not so. He is faithful in all my house. 8 With him, I will speak mouth to mouth, even plainly, and not in riddles; and he shall see Yahweh's form. Why then were you not afraid to speak against my servant, against Moses?" 9 Yahweh's anger burned against them; and he departed.

31 And whilst the children of Israel were in Hazeroth, the anger of the Lord was kindled against Miriam on account of Moses,

10 The cloud departed from over the Tent; and behold, Miriam was leprous, as white as snow. Aaron looked at Miriam, and behold, she was leprous.

and she became leprous, white as snow.

11 Aaron said to Moses, "Oh, my lord, please don't count this sin against us, in which we have done foolishly, and in which we have sinned.
12 Let her not, I pray, be as one dead, of whom the flesh is half consumed when he comes out of his mother's womb."

13 Moses cried to Yahweh, saying, "Heal her, God, I beg you!"

14 Yahweh said to Moses, "If her father had but spit in her face, shouldn't she be ashamed seven days? Let her be shut up outside of the camp seven days, and after that she shall be brought in again."

15 Miriam was shut up outside of the camp seven days, and the people didn't travel until Miriam was brought in again.

32 And she was confined without the camp for seven days, until she had been received again after her leprosy.

16 Afterward the people traveled from Hazeroth, and encamped in the wilderness of Paran.

33 The children of Israel afterward departed from Hazeroth, and pitched in the end of the wilderness of Paran.

Numbers 13

1 Yahweh spoke to Moses, saying,
2 "Send men, that they may spy out the land of Canaan, which I give to the children of Israel. Of every tribe of their fathers, you shall send a man, every one a prince among them."

34 At that time, the Lord spoke to Moses to send twelve men from the children of Israel, one man to a tribe, to go and explore the land of Canaan.

[Numbers 13:3-16]

35 And Moses sent the twelve men, and they came to the land of Canaan to search and examine it, and they explored the whole land from the wilderness of Sin to Rechob as thou comest to Chamoth.

17 Moses sent them to spy out the land of Canaan, and said to them, "Go up this way by the South, and go up into the hill country.
18 See the land, what it is; and the people who dwell therein, whether they are strong or weak, whether they are few or many;
19 and what the land is that they dwell in, whether it is good or bad; and what cities they are that they dwell in, whether in camps, or in strongholds;
20 and what the land is, whether it is fat or lean, whether there is wood therein, or not. Be courageous, and bring some of the fruit of the land." Now the time was the time of the first-ripe grapes.

21 So they went up, and spied out the land from
the wilderness of Zin to Rehob, to the entrance of
Hamath. 22 They went up by the South, and came
to Hebron; and Ahiman, Sheshai, and Talmai, the
children of Anak, were there. (Now Hebron was
built seven years before Zoan in Egypt.) 23 They
came to the valley of Eshcol, and cut down from
there a branch with one cluster of grapes, and they
bore it on a staff between two. They also brought
some of the pomegranates and figs. 24 That place
was called the valley of Eshcol, because of the
cluster which the children of Israel cut down from
there.

25 They returned from spying out the land at the end of forty days.

36 And at the end of forty days they came to Moses and Aaron, and they brought him word as it was in their hearts,

26 They went and came to Moses, to Aaron, and to all the congregation of the children of Israel, to the wilderness of Paran, to Kadesh; and brought back word to them and to all the congregation. They showed them the fruit of the land.

27 They told him, and said, "We came to the land where you sent us. Surely it flows with milk and honey, and this is its fruit.

28 "However the people who dwell in the land are
strong, and the cities are fortified and very large.
Moreover, we saw the children of Anak there. 29
Amalek dwells in the land of the South. The Hittite,
the Jebusite, and the Amorite dwell in the hill
country. The Canaanite dwells by the sea, and along
the side of the Jordan."

30 Caleb stilled the people before Moses, and said, "Let us go up at once, and possess it; for we are well able to overcome it!"

31 But the men who went up with him said, "We aren't able to go up against the people; for they are stronger than we."

32 They brought up an evil report of the land which they had spied out to the children of Israel, saying, "The land, through which we have gone to spy it out, is a land that eats up its inhabitants;

and ten of the men brought up an evil report to the children of Israel, of the land which they had explored,

and all the people who we saw in it are men of great stature. 33 There we saw the Nephilim, the sons of Anak, who come from the Nephilim. We were in our own sight as grasshoppers, and so we were in their sight."

Numbers 14

1 All the congregation lifted up their voice, and cried; and the people wept that night. 2 All the children of Israel murmured against Moses and against Aaron. The whole congregation said to them, "We wish that we had died in the land of Egypt, or that we had died in this wilderness! 3 Why does Yahweh bring us to this land, to fall by the sword? Our wives and our little ones will be captured or killed! Wouldn't it be better for us to return into Egypt?"

saying, "It is better for us to return to Egypt than to go to this land, a land that consumes its inhabitants."

4 They said to one another, "Let us make a captain, and let us return into Egypt."

5 Then Moses and Aaron fell on their faces before all the assembly of the congregation of the children of Israel.

6 Joshua the son of Nun and Caleb the son of Jephunneh, who were of those who spied out the land, tore their clothes. 7 They spoke to all the congregation of the children of Israel, saying, "The land, which we passed through to spy it out, is an exceeding good land.

37 But Joshua the son of Nun, and Caleb the son of Jephuneh, who were of those that explored the land, said, "The land is exceedingly good.

8 "If Yahweh delights in us, then he will bring us into this land, and give it to us; a land which flows with milk and honey.

38 "If the Lord delight in us, then he will bring us to this land and give it to us, for it is a land flowing with milk and honey."

9 "Only don't rebel against Yahweh, neither fear the people of the land; for they are bread for us. Their defense is removed from over them, and Yahweh is with us. Don't fear them."

10 But all the congregation threatened to stone them with stones.

39 But the children of Israel would not hearken to them, and they hearkened to the words of the ten men who had brought up an evil report of the land.

Yahweh's glory appeared in the Tent of Meeting to all the children of Israel. 11 Yahweh said to Moses, "How long will this people despise me? and how long will they not believe in me, for all the signs which I have worked among them? 12 I will strike them with the pestilence, and disinherit them, and will make of you a nation greater and mightier than they."

13 Moses said to Yahweh, “Then the Egyptians will
hear it; for you brought up this people in your might
from among them. 14 They will tell it to the
inhabitants of this land. They have heard that you
Yahweh are in the middle of this people; for you
Yahweh are seen face to face, and your cloud
stands over them, and you go before them, in a
pillar of cloud by day, and in a pillar of fire by night.

15 "Now if you killed this people as one man, then
the nations which have heard the fame of you will
speak, saying, 16 ‘Because Yahweh was not able to
bring this people into the land which he swore to
them, therefore he has slain them in the
wilderness.’ 17 Now please let the power of the
Lord be great, according as you have spoken,
saying,

18 "‘Yahweh is slow to anger, and abundant in
loving kindness, forgiving iniquity and disobedience;
and that will by no means clear the guilty, visiting
the iniquity of the fathers on the children, on the
third and on the fourth generation.’

19 Please pardon the iniquity of this people
according to the greatness of your loving kindness,
and according as you have forgiven this people,
from Egypt even until now.”

20 Yahweh said, “I have pardoned according to your
word: 21 but in very deed, as I live, and as all the
earth shall be filled with Yahweh’s glory; 22
because all those men who have seen my glory, and
my signs, which I worked in Egypt and in the
wilderness, yet have tempted me these ten times,
and have not listened to my voice;

23 "surely they shall not see the land which I swore
to their fathers, neither shall any of those who
despised me see it. 24 But my servant Caleb,
because he had another spirit with him, and has
followed me fully, him I will bring into the land into
which he went. His offspring shall possess it.

25 "Since the Amalekite and the Canaanite dwell in
the valley, tomorrow turn, and go into the
wilderness by the way to the Red Sea.”

[83:43 And the people dwelt in the wilderness of Paran a long time, and they afterward proceeded to the wilderness by the way of the Red Sea.]

26 Yahweh spoke to Moses and to Aaron, saying, 27 "How long shall I bear with this evil congregation, that murmur against me? I have heard the murmurings of the children of Israel, which they murmur against me.

40 And the Lord heard the murmurings of the children of Israel and he was angry and swore, saying,

[Numbers 14:30 "surely you shall not come into the land, concerning which I swore that I would make you dwell therein, except Caleb the son of Jephunneh, and Joshua the son of Nun.]

41 "Surely not one man of this wicked generation shall see the land from twenty years old and upward excepting Caleb the son of Jephuneh and Joshua the son of Nun.

28 "Tell them, 'As I live, says Yahweh, surely as you have spoken in my ears, so will I do to you. 29 Your dead bodies shall fall in this wilderness; and all who were numbered of you, according to your whole number, from twenty years old and upward, who have murmured against me,

42 "But surely this wicked generation shall perish in this wilderness, and their children shall come to the land and they shall possess it;"

30 "surely you shall not come into the land, concerning which I swore that I would make you dwell therein, except Caleb the son of Jephunneh, and Joshua the son of Nun.

[83:41 "Surely not one man of this wicked generation shall see the land from twenty years old and upward excepting Caleb the son of Jephuneh and Joshua the son of Nun.]

31 But your little ones, that you said should be captured or killed, them I will bring in, and they shall know the land which you have rejected. 32 But as for you, your dead bodies shall fall in this wilderness.

33 Your children shall be wanderers in the wilderness forty years, and shall bear your prostitution, until your dead bodies are consumed in the wilderness.

so the anger of the Lord was kindled against Israel, and he made them wander in the wilderness for forty years until the end of that wicked generation, because they did not follow the Lord.

[Numbers 14:25 "Since the Amalekite and the Canaanite dwell in the valley, tomorrow turn, and go into the wilderness by the way to the Red Sea."]

43 And the people dwelt in the wilderness of Paran a long time, and they afterward proceeded to the wilderness by the way of the Red Sea.

34 "After the number of the days in which you spied out the land, even forty days, for every day a year, you will bear your iniquities, even forty years, and you will know my alienation.' 35 I, Yahweh, have spoken. I will surely do this to all this evil congregation, who are gathered together against me. In this wilderness they shall be consumed, and there they shall die."

36 The men, whom Moses sent to spy out the land, who returned, and made all the congregation to murmur against him, by bringing up an evil report against the land, 37 even those men who brought up an evil report of the land, died by the plague before Yahweh.

38 But Joshua the son of Nun, and Caleb the son of Jephunneh, remained alive of those men who went to spy out the land.

39 Moses told these words to all the children of Israel, and the people mourned greatly. 40 They rose up early in the morning, and went up to the top of the mountain, saying, "Behold, we are here, and will go up to the place which Yahweh has promised: for we have sinned."

41 Moses said, "Why now do you disobey the commandment of Yahweh, since it shall not prosper? 42 Don't go up, for Yahweh isn't among you; that you not be struck down before your enemies. 43 For there the Amalekite and the Canaanite are before you, and you shall fall by the sword, because you turned back from following Yahweh, therefore Yahweh will not be with you."

44 But they presumed to go up to the top of the mountain. Nevertheless, the ark of Yahweh's covenant and Moses didn't depart out of the camp. 45 Then the Amalekites came down, and the Canaanites who lived in that mountain, and struck them and beat them down, even to Hormah.

[Numbers 15]

Numbers 16

1 Now Korah, the son of Izhar, the son of Kohath, the son of Levi, with Dathan and Abiram, the sons of Eliab, and On, the son of Peleth, sons of Reuben, took some men. 2 They rose up before Moses, with some of the children of Israel, two hundred fifty princes of the congregation, called to the assembly, men of renown. 3 They assembled themselves together against Moses and against Aaron, and said to them, "You take too much on yourself, since all the congregation are holy, everyone of them, and Yahweh is among them! Why do you lift yourselves up above Yahweh's assembly?"

4 When Moses heard it, he fell on his face. 5 He said to Korah and to all his company, "In the morning, Yahweh will show who are his, and who is holy, and will cause him to come near to him. Even him whom he shall choose, he will cause to come near to him.

Jasher 84

1 At that time Korah the son of Jetzer the son of Kehath the son of Levi, took many men of the children of Israel, and they rose up and quarreled with Moses and Aaron and the whole congregation.

6 "Do this: take censers, Korah, and all his company;
7 and put fire in them, and put incense on them
before Yahweh tomorrow. It shall be that the man
whom Yahweh chooses, he shall be holy. You have
gone too far, you sons of Levi!"

8 Moses said to Korah, "Hear now, you sons of Levi!

9 "Is it a small thing to you, that the God of Israel has separated you from the congregation of Israel, to bring you near to himself, to do the service of Yahweh's tabernacle, and to stand before the congregation to minister to them;

10 "and that he has brought you near, and all your
brothers the sons of Levi with you? Do you seek the
priesthood also? 11 Therefore you and all your
company have gathered together against Yahweh!
What is Aaron that you murmur against him?"

12 Moses sent to call Dathan and Abiram, the sons
of Eliab; and they said, "We won't come up! 13 Is it
a small thing that you have brought us up out of a
land flowing with milk and honey, to kill us in the
wilderness, but you must also make yourself a
prince over us?

14 "Moreover you haven't brought us into a land flowing with milk and honey, nor given us inheritance of fields and vineyards. Will you put out the eyes of these men? We won't come up."

15 Moses was very angry, and said to Yahweh, "Don't respect their offering. I have not taken one donkey from them, neither have I hurt one of them."

16 Moses said to Korah, "You and all your company
go before Yahweh, you, and they, and Aaron,
tomorrow. 17 Each man take his censer, and put
incense on them, and each man bring before
Yahweh his censer, two hundred fifty censers; you
also, and Aaron, each his censer."

18 They each took his censer, and put fire in them,
and laid incense on it, and stood at the door of the
Tent of Meeting with Moses and Aaron. 19 Korah
assembled all the congregation opposite them to
the door of the Tent of Meeting.

Yahweh's glory appeared to all the congregation. 20
Yahweh spoke to Moses and to Aaron, saying, 21
"Separate yourselves from among this
congregation, that I may consume them in a
moment!"

22 They fell on their faces, and said, "God, the God
of the spirits of all flesh, shall one man sin, and will
you be angry with all the congregation?"

23 Yahweh spoke to Moses, saying, 24 "Speak to
the congregation, saying, 'Get away from around
the tent of Korah, Dathan, and Abiram!'"

25 Moses rose up and went to Dathan and Abiram;
and the elders of Israel followed him. 26 He spoke
to the congregation, saying, "Depart, please, from
the tents of these wicked men, and touch nothing
of theirs, lest you be consumed in all their sins!"

27 So they went away from the tent of Korah,
Dathan, and Abiram, on every side. Dathan and
Abiram came out, and stood at the door of their
tents, with their wives, their sons, and their little
ones.

28 Moses said, "Hereby you shall know that
Yahweh has sent me to do all these works; for they
are not from my own mind. 29 If these men die the
common death of all men, or if they experience
what all men experience, then Yahweh hasn't sent
me.

30 "But if Yahweh makes a new thing, and the
ground opens its mouth, and swallows them up,
with all that belong to them, and they go down
alive into Sheol; then you shall understand that
these men have despised Yahweh."

31 As he finished speaking all these words, the
ground that was under them split apart. 32 The
earth opened its mouth and swallowed them up,
with their households, all of Korah's men, and all
their goods. 33 So they, and all that belonged to
them went down alive into Sheol. The earth closed
on them, and they perished from among the
assembly.

2 And the Lord was angry with them, and the earth opened its mouth, and swallowed them up, with their houses and all belonging to them, and all the men belonging to Korah.

34 All Israel that were around them fled at their cry;
for they said, "Lest the earth swallow us up!" 35
Fire came out from Yahweh, and devoured the two
hundred fifty men who offered the incense.

36 Yahweh spoke to Moses, saying, 37 "Speak to
Eleazar the son of Aaron the priest, that he take up
the censers out of the burning, and scatter the fire
away from the camp; for they are holy,

38 even the censers of these sinners against their
own lives. Let them be made beaten plates for a
covering of the altar, for they offered them before
Yahweh. Therefore they are holy. They shall be a
sign to the children of Israel."

39 Eleazar the priest took the bronze censers, which
those who were burned had offered; and they beat
them out for a covering of the altar, 40 to be a
memorial to the children of Israel, to the end that
no stranger, who isn't of the offspring of Aaron,
would come near to burn incense before Yahweh,
that he not be as Korah, and as his company; as
Yahweh spoke to him by Moses.

[Numbers 16:41-19:22]

3 And after this God made the people go round by
the way of Mount Seir for a long time.
4 At that time the Lord said unto Moses, "Provoke
not a war against the children of Esau, for I will not
give to you of any thing belonging to them, as much
as the sole of the foot could tread upon, for I have
given Mount Seir for an inheritance to Esau."

5 Therefore did the children of Esau fight against
the children of Seir in former times, and the Lord
had delivered the children of Seir into the hands of
the children of Esau, and destroyed them from
before them, and the children of Esau dwelt in their
stead unto this day.

6 Therefore the Lord said to the children of Israel,
"Fight not against the children of Esau your
brethren, for nothing in their land belongs to you,
but you may buy food of them for money and eat it,
and you may buy water of them for money and
drink it. 7 And the children of Israel did according
to the word of the Lord.

8 And the children of Israel went about the
wilderness, going round by the way of Mount Sinai
for a long time, and touched not the children of
Esau, and they continued in that district for
nineteen years.

9 At that time died Latinus king of the children of Chittim, in the forty-fifth year of his reign, which is the fourteenth year of the children of Israel's departure from Egypt. 10 And they buried him in his place which he had built for himself in the land of Chittim, and Abimnas reigned in his place for thirty-eight years.

11 And the children of Israel passed the boundary of the children of Esau in those days, at the end of nineteen years, and they came and passed the road of the wilderness of Moab. 12 And the Lord said to Moses, "Besiege not Moab, and do not fight against them, for I will give you nothing of their land." 13 And the children of Israel passed the road of the wilderness of Moab for nineteen years, and they did not fight against them.

14 And in the thirty-sixth year of the children of Israel's departing from Egypt the Lord smote the heart of Sihon, king of the Amorites, and he waged war, and went forth to fight against the children of Moab. 15 And Sihon sent messengers to Beor the son of Janeas, the son of Balaam, counsellor to the king of Egypt, and to Balaam his son, to curse Moab, in order that it might be delivered into the hand of Sihon.

16 And the messengers went and brought Beor the son of Janeas, and Balaam his son, from Pethor in Mesopotamia, so Beor and Balaam his son came to the city of Sihon and they cursed Moab and their king in the presence of Sihon king of the Amorites. 17 So Sihon went out with his whole army, and he went to Moab and fought against them, and he subdued them, and the Lord delivered them into his hands, and Sihon slew the king of Moab.

18 And Sihon took all the cities of Moab in the battle; he also took Heshbon from them, for Heshbon was one of the cities of Moab, and Sihon placed his princes and his nobles in Heshbon, and Heshbon belonged to Sihon in those days.

19 Therefore the parable speakers Beor and Balaam his son uttered these words, saying, "Come unto Heshbon, the city of Sihon will be built and established. 20 Woe unto thee Moab! Thou art lost, O people of Kemosh! Behold it is written upon the book of the law of God."

21 And when Sihon had conquered Moab, he placed guards in the cities which he had taken from Moab, and a considerable number of the children of Moab fell in battle into the hand of Sihon, and he made a great capture of them, sons and daughters, and he slew their king; so Sihon turned back to his own land. 22 And Sihon gave numerous presents of silver and gold to Beor and Balaam his son, and he dismissed them, and they went to Mesopotamia to their home and country.

23 At that time all the children of Israel passed from the road of the wilderness of Moab, and returned and surrounded the wilderness of Edom.

Numbers 20

1 The children of Israel, even the whole congregation, came into the wilderness of Zin in the first month. The people stayed in Kadesh. Miriam died there, and was buried there.

24 So the whole congregation came to the wilderness of Sin in the first month of the fortieth year from their departure from Egypt, and the children of Israel dwelt there in Kadesh, of the wilderness of Sin, and Miriam died there and she was buried there.

2 There was no water for the congregation; and they assembled themselves together against Moses and against Aaron. 3 The people quarreled with Moses, and spoke, saying, "We wish that we had died when our brothers died before Yahweh!

4 "Why have you brought Yahweh's assembly into this wilderness, that we should die there, we and our animals? 5 Why have you made us to come up out of Egypt, to bring us in to this evil place? It is no place of seed, or of figs, or of vines, or of pomegranates; neither is there any water to drink."

6 Moses and Aaron went from the presence of the assembly to the door of the Tent of Meeting, and fell on their faces. Yahweh's glory appeared to them.

7 Yahweh spoke to Moses, saying, 8 "Take the rod, and assemble the congregation, you, and Aaron your brother, and speak to the rock before their eyes, that it pour out its water. You shall bring water to them out of the rock; so you shall give the congregation and their livestock drink."

9 Moses took the rod from before Yahweh, as he
commanded him. 10 Moses and Aaron gathered the
assembly together before the rock, and he said to
them, “Hear now, you rebels! Shall we bring water
out of this rock for you?”

11 Moses lifted up his hand, and struck the rock
with his rod twice, and water came out abundantly.
The congregation and their livestock drank.

12 Yahweh said to Moses and Aaron, “Because you
didn’t believe in me, to sanctify me in the eyes of
the children of Israel, therefore you shall not bring
this assembly into the land which I have given
them.”

13 These are the waters of Meribah; because the
children of Israel strove with Yahweh, and he was
sanctified in them.

14 Moses sent messengers from Kadesh to the king
of Edom, saying: “Thus says your brother Israel:
You know all the travail that has happened to us; 15
how our fathers went down into Egypt, and we
lived in Egypt a long time. The Egyptians mistreated
us and our fathers. 16 When we cried to Yahweh,
he heard our voice, sent an angel, and brought us
out of Egypt. Behold, we are in Kadesh, a city in the
edge of your border.

25 At that time Moses sent messengers to Hadad
king of Edom, saying, "Thus says thy brother Israel,

17 “Please let us pass through your land. We will
not pass through field or through vineyard, neither
will we drink from the water of the wells. We will go
along the king’s highway. We will not turn aside to
the right hand nor to the left, until we have passed
your border.”

'Let me pass I pray thee through thy land, we will
not pass through field or vineyard, we will not drink
the water of the well; We will walk in the king's
road.'"

18 Edom said to him, “You shall not pass through
me, lest I come out with the sword against you.”

19 The children of Israel said to him, “We will go up
by the highway; and if we drink your water, I and
my livestock, then I will give its price. Only let me,
without doing anything else, pass through on my
feet.”

20 He said, “You shall not pass through.” Edom
came out against him with many people, and with a
strong hand. 21 Thus Edom refused to give Israel
passage through his border, so Israel turned away
from him.

26 And Edom said to him, "Thou shalt not pass
through my country," and Edom went forth to meet
the children of Israel with a mighty people.

27 And the children of Esau refused to let the children of Israel pass through their land, so the Israelites removed from them and fought not against them.

28 For before this the Lord had commanded the children of Israel, saying, "You shall not fight against the children of Esau," therefore the Israelites removed from them and did not fight against them.

22 They traveled from Kadesh: and the children of Israel, even the whole congregation, came to Mount Hor.

29 So the children of Israel departed from Kadesh, and all the people came to Mount Hor.

23 Yahweh spoke to Moses and Aaron in Mount Hor, by the border of the land of Edom, saying, 24 "Aaron shall be gathered to his people; for he shall not enter into the land which I have given to the children of Israel, because you rebelled against my word at the waters of Meribah.

30 At that time the Lord said to Moses, "Tell thy brother Aaron that he shall die there, for he shall not come to the land which I have given to the children of Israel."

25 "Take Aaron and Eleazar his son, and bring them up to Mount Hor; 26 and strip Aaron of his garments, and put them on Eleazar his son. Aaron shall be taken, and shall die there."

27 Moses did as Yahweh commanded. They went up into Mount Hor in the sight of all the congregation. 28 Moses stripped Aaron of his garments, and put them on Eleazar his son. Aaron died there on the top of the mountain, and Moses and Eleazar came down from the mountain.

31 And Aaron went up, at the command of the Lord, to Mount Hor, in the fortieth year, in the fifth month, in the first day of the month.

29 When all the congregation saw that Aaron was dead, they wept for Aaron thirty days, even all the house of Israel.

32 And Aaron was one hundred and twenty-three years old when he died in Mount Hor

Jasher 85

1 And king Arad the Canaanite, who dwelt in the south, heard that the Israelites had come by the way of the spies, and he arranged his forces to fight against the Israelites.

2 And the children of Israel were greatly afraid of him, for he had a great and heavy army, so the children of Israel resolved to return to Egypt. 3 And the children of Israel turned back about the distance of three days' journey unto Maserath Beni Jaakon, for they were greatly afraid on account of the king Arad.

4 And the children of Israel would not get back to
their places, so they remained in Beni Jaakon for
thirty days. 5 And when the children of Levi saw
that the children of Israel would not turn back, they
were jealous for the sake of the Lord, and they rose
up and fought against the Israelites their brethren,
and slew of them a great body, and forced them to
turn back to their place, Mount Hor.

Numbers 21

1 The Canaanite, the king of Arad, who lived in the
South, heard that Israel came by the way of
Atharim. He fought against Israel, and took some of
them captive.

6 And when they returned, king Arad was still
arranging his host for battle against the Israelites.

2 Israel vowed a vow to Yahweh, and said, “If you
will indeed deliver this people into my hand, then I
will utterly destroy their cities.”

7 And Israel vowed a vow, saying, "If thou wilt
deliver this people into my hand, then I will utterly
destroy their cities."

3 Yahweh listened to the voice of Israel, and
delivered up the Canaanites; and they utterly
destroyed them and their cities. The name of the
place was called Hormah.

8 And the Lord hearkened to the voice of Israel, and
he delivered the Canaanites into their hand, and he
utterly destroyed them and their cities, and he
called the name of the place Hormah.

4 They traveled from Mount Hor by the way to the
Red Sea, to go around the land of Edom. The soul
of the people was very discouraged because of the
journey.

9 And the children of Israel journeyed from Mount
Hor

5 The people spoke against God, and against
Moses, “Why have you brought us up out of Egypt
to die in the wilderness? For there is no bread, and
there is no water; and our soul loathes this light
bread.”

6 Yahweh sent fiery serpents among the people,
and they bit the people. Many people of Israel died.
7 The people came to Moses, and said, “We have
sinned, because we have spoken against Yahweh,
and against you. Pray to Yahweh, that he take away
the serpents from us.” Moses prayed for the
people.

8 Yahweh said to Moses, “Make a fiery serpent, and
set it on a pole. It shall happen, that everyone who
is bitten, when he sees it, shall live.” 9 Moses made
a serpent of brass, and set it on the pole. If a
serpent had bitten any man, when he looked at the
serpent of brass, he lived.

10 The children of Israel traveled, and encamped in
Oboth.

and pitched in Oboth, and they journeyed from
Oboth and they pitched at Ije-abarim, in the border
of Moab.

10 And the children of Israel sent to Moab, saying, "Let us pass now through thy land into our place," but the children of Moab would not suffer the children of Israel to pass through their land, for the children of Moab were greatly afraid lest the children of Israel should do unto them as Sihon king of the Amorites had done to them, who had taken their land and had slain many of them.

11 Therefore Moab would not suffer the Israelites to pass through his land, and the Lord commanded the children of Israel, saying, "That they should not fight against Moab," so the Israelites removed from Moab.

11 They traveled from Oboth, and encamped at Iyeabarim, in the wilderness which is before Moab, toward the sunrise. 12 From there they traveled, and encamped in the valley of Zered. 13 From there they traveled, and encamped on the other side of the Arnon, which is in the wilderness, that comes out of the border of the Amorites: for the Arnon is the border of Moab, between Moab and the Amorites.

12 And the children of Israel journeyed from the border of Moab, and they came to the other side of Arnon, the border of Moab, between Moab and the Amorites, and they pitched in the border of Sihon, king of the Amorites, in the wilderness of Kedemoth.

14 Therefore it is said in the book of the Wars of Yahweh, "Vaheb in Suphah, the valleys of the Arnon, 15 the slope of the valleys that incline toward the dwelling of Ar, leans on the border of Moab."

16 From there they traveled to Beer; that is the well of which Yahweh said to Moses, "Gather the people together, and I will give them water."

17 Then Israel sang this song: "Spring up, well! Sing to it, / 18 the well, which the princes dug, / which the nobles of the people dug, / with the scepter, and with their poles."

From the wilderness they traveled to Mattanah; 19 and from Mattanah to Nahaliel; and from Nahaliel to Bamoth; 20 and from Bamoth to the valley that is in the field of Moab, to the top of Pisgah, which looks down on the desert.

21 Israel sent messengers to Sihon king of the Amorites, saying, 22 "Let me pass through your land. We will not turn aside into field, or into vineyard. We will not drink of the water of the wells. We will go by the king's highway, until we have passed your border."

13 And the children of Israel sent messengers to Sihon, king of the Amorites, saying, 14 "Let us pass through thy land, we will not turn into the fields or into the vineyards, we will go along by the king's highway until we shall have passed thy border,"

23 Sihon would not allow Israel to pass through his border, but Sihon gathered all his people together, and went out against Israel into the wilderness, and came to Jahaz. He fought against Israel.

but Sihon would not suffer the Israelites to pass. 15
So Sihon collected all the people of the Amorites and went forth into the wilderness to meet the children of Israel, and he fought against Israel in Jahaz.

24 Israel struck him with the edge of the sword, and possessed his land from the Arnon to the Jabbok, even to the children of Ammon; for the border of the children of Ammon was strong.

16 And the Lord delivered Sihon king of the Amorites into the hand of the children of Israel, and Israel smote all the people of Sihon with the edge of the sword and avenged the cause of Moab.

25 Israel took all these cities. Israel lived in all the cities of the Amorites, in Heshbon, and in all its towns.

17 And the children of Israel took possession of the land of Sihon from Aram unto Jabuk, unto the children of Ammon, and they took all the spoil of
the cities. 18 And Israel took all these cities, and
Israel dwelt in all the cities of the Amorites.

26 For Heshbon was the city of Sihon the king of the Amorites, who had fought against the former king of Moab, and taken all his land out of his hand,
even to the Arnon. 27 Therefore those who speak in
proverbs say, "Come to Heshbon. / Let the city of Sihon be built and established;

28 "for a fire has gone out of Heshbon, / a flame from the city of Sihon. / It has devoured Ar of Moab, / The lords of the high places of the Arnon. /
29 Woe to you, Moab! / You are undone, people of
Chemosh! / He has given his sons as fugitives, / and his daughters into captivity, / to Sihon king of the Amorites.

30 "We have shot at them. / Heshbon has perished even to Dibon. / We have laid waste even to Nophah, / Which reaches to Medeba."

19 And all the children of Israel resolved to fight against the children of Ammon, to take their land also.

20 So the Lord said to the children of Israel, "Do not besiege the children of Ammon, neither stir up battle against them, for I will give nothing to you of their land, and the children of Israel hearkened to the word of the Lord, and did not fight against the children of Ammon."

31 Thus Israel lived in the land of the Amorites. 32
Moses sent to spy out Jazer. They took its towns, and drove out the Amorites who were there.

[85:29 Moses afterward sent some of the children of Israel to spy out Jaazer, for Jaazer was a very famous city.]

33 They turned and went up by the way of Bashan. Og the king of Bashan went out against them, he and all his people, to battle at Edrei.

21 And the children of Israel turned and went up by the way of Bashan to the land of Og, king of Bashan, and Og the king of Bashan went out to meet the Israelites in battle, and he had with him many valiant men, and a very strong force from the people of the Amorites.

22 And Og king of Bashan was a very powerful man,
but Naaron his son was exceedingly powerful, even
stronger than he was. 23 And Og said in his heart,
"Behold now the whole camp of Israel takes up a
space of three parsa, now will I smite them at once
without sword or spear."

24 And Og went up Mount Jahaz, and took therefrom one large stone, the length of which was three parsa, and he placed it on his head, and resolved to throw it upon the camp of the children of Israel, to smite all the Israelites with that stone.

25 And the angel of the Lord came and pierced the stone upon the head of Og, and the stone fell upon the neck of Og that Og fell to the earth on account of the weight of the stone upon his neck.

34 Yahweh said to Moses, “Don’t fear him, for I have delivered him into your hand, with all his people, and his land. You shall do to him as you did to Sihon king of the Amorites, who lived at Heshbon.”

26 At that time the Lord said to the children of Israel, "Be not afraid of him, for I have given him and all his people and all his land into your hand, and you shall do to him as you did to Sihon."

35 So they struck him, with his sons and all his people, until there were no survivors; and they possessed his land.

27 And Moses went down to him with a small
number of the children of Israel, and Moses smote
Og with a stick at the ankles of his feet and slew
him. 28 The children of Israel afterward pursued
the children of Og and all his people, and they beat
and destroyed them till there was no remnant left
of them.

[Numbers 21:32 Moses sent to spy out Jazer. They took its towns, and drove out the Amorites who were there.]

29 Moses afterward sent some of the children of
Israel to spy out Jaazer, for Jaazer was a very
famous city. 30 And the spies went to Jaazer and
explored it, and the spies trusted in the Lord, and
they fought against the men of Jaazer.

31 And these men took Jaazer and its villages, and
the Lord delivered them into their hand, and they
drove out the Amorites who had been there. 32
And the children of Israel took the land of the two
kings of the Amorites, sixty cities which were on the
other side of Jordan, from the brook of Arnon unto
Mount Herman.

33 And the children of Israel journeyed and came into the plain of Moab which is on this side of Jordan, by Jericho.

34 And the children of Moab heard all the evil which the children of Israel had done to the two kings of the Amorites, to Sihon and Og, so all the men of Moab were greatly afraid of the Israelites.

Numbers 22

1 The children of Israel traveled, and encamped in the plains of Moab beyond the Jordan at Jericho.

2 Balak the son of Zippor saw all that Israel had
done to the Amorites. 3 Moab was very afraid of
the people, because they were many. Moab was distressed because of the children of Israel.

35 And the elders of Moab said, "Behold the two kings of the Amorites, Sihon and Og, who were more powerful than all the kings of the earth, could not stand against the children of Israel, how then
can we stand before them? 36 Surely they sent us a
message before now to pass through our land on their way, and we would not suffer them, now they will turn upon us with their heavy swords and destroy us;" and Moab was distressed on account of the children of Israel, and they were greatly afraid of them, and they counselled together what was to be done to the children of Israel.

37 And the elders of Moab resolved and took one of their men, Balak the son of Zippor the Moabite, and made him king over them at that time, and Balak
was a very wise man. 38 And the elders of Moab
rose up and sent to the children of Midian to make peace with them, for a great battle and enmity had been in those days between Moab and Midian, from the days of Hadad the son of Bedad king of Edom, who smote Midian in the field of Moab, unto these days.

39 And the children of Moab sent to the children of Midian, and they made peace with them, and the elders of Midian came to the land of Moab to make
peace in behalf of the children of Midian. 40 And
the elders of Moab counselled with the elders of Midian what to do in order to save their lives from Israel.

4 Moab said to the elders of Midian, "Now this multitude will lick up all that is around us, as the ox licks up the grass of the field." Balak the son of Zippor was king of Moab at that time.

41 And all the children of Moab said to the elders of Midian, "Now therefore the children of Israel lick up all that are round about us, as the ox licks up the grass of the field, for thus did they do to the two kings of the Amorites who are stronger than we are."

5 He sent messengers to Balaam the son of Beor, to
Pethor, which is by the River, to the land of the
children of his people, to call him, saying, “Behold,
there is a people who came out of Egypt. Behold,
they cover the surface of the earth, and they are
staying opposite me. 6 Please come now therefore
curse me this people; for they are too mighty for
me. Perhaps I shall prevail, that we may strike
them, and that I may drive them out of the land; for
I know that he whom you bless is blessed, and he
whom you curse is cursed.”

7 The elders of Moab and the elders of Midian departed with the rewards of divination in their hand. They came to Balaam, and spoke to him the words of Balak.

8 He said to them, “Lodge here this night, and I will bring you word again, as Yahweh shall speak to me.” The princes of Moab stayed with Balaam.

9 God came to Balaam, and said, “Who are these men with you?”

10 Balaam said to God, “Balak the son of Zippor,
king of Moab, has said to me, 11 ‘Behold, the
people that has come out of Egypt covers the
surface of the earth. Now, come curse me them.
Perhaps I shall be able to fight against them, and
shall drive them out.’”

42 And the elders of Midian said to Moab, "We have heard that at the time when Sihon king of the Amorites fought against you, when he prevailed over you and took your land, he had sent to Beor the son of Janeas and to Balaam his son from Mesopotamia,

"and they came and cursed you; therefore did the hand of Sihon prevail over you, that he took your land.

43 "Now therefore send you also to Balaam his son, for he still remains in his land, and give him his hire, that he may come and curse all the people of whom you are afraid;" so the elders of Moab heard this thing, and it pleased them to send to Balaam the son of Beor.

44 So Balak the son of Zippor king of Moab sent
messengers to Balaam, saying, 45 "Behold there is
a people come out from Egypt, behold they cover
the face of the earth, and they abide over against
me. 46 Now therefore come and curse this people
for me, for they are too mighty for me,
peradventure I shall prevail to fight against them,
and drive them out, for I heard that he whom thou
blessest is blessed, and whom thou cursest is
cursed."

47 So the messengers of Balak went to Balaam and brought Balaam to curse the people to fight against Moab.

12 God said to Balaam, “You shall not go with them.
You shall not curse the people; for they are
blessed.” 13 Balaam rose up in the morning, and
said to the princes of Balak, “Go to your land; for
Yahweh refuses to permit me to go with you.”

48 And Balaam came to Balak to curse Israel, and
the Lord said to Balaam, "Curse not this people for
it is blessed."

14 The princes of Moab rose up, and they went to
Balak, and said, “Balaam refuses to come with us.”

15 Balak again sent princes, more, and more
honorable than they. 16 They came to Balaam, and
said to him, “Thus says Balak the son of Zippor,
‘Please let nothing hinder you from coming to me,
17 for I will promote you to very great honor, and
whatever you say to me I will do. Please come
therefore, and curse this people for me.’”

49 And Balak urged Balaam day by day to curse
Israel, but Balaam hearkened not to Balak on
account of the word of the Lord which he had
spoken to Balaam.

18 Balaam answered the servants of Balak, “If Balak
would give me his house full of silver and gold, I
can’t go beyond the word of Yahweh my God, to do
less or more. 19 Now therefore, please wait also
here this night, that I may know what Yahweh will
speak to me more.”

20 God came to Balaam at night, and said to him, “If
the men have come to call you, rise up, go with
them; but only the word which I speak to you, that
you shall do.”

21 Balaam rose up in the morning, and saddled his
donkey, and went with the princes of Moab. 22
God’s anger burned because he went; and
Yahweh’s angel placed himself in the way for an
adversary against him. Now he was riding on his
donkey, and his two servants were with him.

23 The donkey saw Yahweh’s angel standing in the
way, with his sword drawn in his hand; and the
donkey turned aside out of the way, and went into
the field. Balaam struck the donkey, to turn her into
the way.

24 Then Yahweh’s angel stood in a narrow path
between the vineyards, a wall being on this side,
and a wall on that side. 25 The donkey saw
Yahweh’s angel, and she thrust herself to the wall,
and crushed Balaam’s foot against the wall. He
struck her again.

26 Yahweh's angel went further, and stood in a
narrow place, where there was no way to turn
either to the right hand or to the left. 27 The
donkey saw Yahweh's angel, and she lay down
under Balaam. Balaam's anger burned, and he
struck the donkey with his staff.

28 Yahweh opened the mouth of the donkey, and
she said to Balaam, "What have I done to you, that
you have struck me these three times?" 29 Balaam
said to the donkey, "Because you have mocked me,
I wish there were a sword in my hand, for now I
would have killed you."

30 The donkey said to Balaam, "Am I not your
donkey, on which you have ridden all your life long
until today? Was I ever in the habit of doing so to
you?"

He said, "No."

31 Then Yahweh opened the eyes of Balaam, and
he saw Yahweh's angel standing in the way, with his
sword drawn in his hand; and he bowed his head,
and fell on his face. 32 Yahweh's angel said to him,
"Why have you struck your donkey these three
times? Behold, I have come out as an adversary,
because your way is perverse before me. 33 The
donkey saw me, and turned aside before me these
three times. Unless she had turned aside from me,
surely now I would have killed you, and saved her
alive."

34 Balaam said to Yahweh's angel, "I have sinned;
for I didn't know that you stood in the way against
me. Now therefore, if it displeases you, I will go
back again."

35 Yahweh's angel said to Balaam, "Go with the
men; but only the word that I shall speak to you,
that you shall speak." So Balaam went with the
princes of Balak.

36 When Balak heard that Balaam had come, he
went out to meet him to the City of Moab, which is
on the border of the Arnon, which is in the utmost
part of the border. 37 Balak said to Balaam, "Didn't
I earnestly send to you to call you? Why didn't you
come to me? Am I not able indeed to promote you
to honor?"

38 Balaam said to Balak, "Behold, I have come to you. Have I now any power at all to speak anything? The word that God puts in my mouth, that shall I speak."

39 Balaam went with Balak, and they came to
Kiriath Huzoth. 40 Balak sacrificed cattle and sheep,
and sent to Balaam, and to the princes who were
with him. 41 In the morning, Balak took Balaam,
and brought him up into the high places of Baal;
and he saw from there part of the people.

[Numbers 23:1 - Numbers 24:24]

Numbers 24:25 Balaam rose up, and went and returned to his place; and Balak also went his way.

50 And when Balak saw that Balaam would not accede to his wish, he rose up and went home, and Balaam also returned to his land and he went from there to Midian.

51 And the children of Israel journeyed from the plain of Moab, and pitched by Jordan from Beth-jesimoth even unto Abel-shittim, at the end of the plains of Moab.

Numbers 25

1 Israel stayed in Shittim; and the people began to play the prostitute with the daughters of Moab;

52 And when the children of Israel abode in the plain of Shittim, they began to commit whoredom with the daughters of Moab.

53 And the children of Israel approached Moab, and the children of Moab pitched their tents opposite to the camp of the children of Israel.

54 And the children of Moab were afraid of the
children of Israel, and the children of Moab took all
their daughters and their wives of beautiful aspect
and comely appearance, and dressed them in gold
and silver and costly garments. 55 And the children
of Moab seated those women at the door of their
tents, in order that the children of Israel might see
them and turn to them, and not fight against Moab.

56 And all the children of Moab did this thing to the children of Israel, and every man placed his wife and daughter at the door of his tent, and all the children of Israel saw the act of the children of Moab, and the children of Israel turned to the daughters of Moab and coveted them, and they went to them.

57 And it came to pass that when a Hebrew came to the door of the tent of Moab, and saw a daughter of Moab and desired her in his heart, and spoke with her at the door of the tent that which he desired,

whilst they were speaking together the men of the tent would come out and speak to the Hebrew like unto these words:

58 "Surely you know that we are brethren, we are all the descendants of Lot and the descendants of Abraham his brother, wherefore then will you not remain with us, and wherefore will you not eat our bread and our sacrifice?"

2 for they called the people to the sacrifices of their gods. The people ate and bowed down to their gods.

59 And when the children of Moab had thus overwhelmed him with their speeches, and enticed him by their flattering words, they seated him in the tent and cooked and sacrificed for him, and he ate of their sacrifice and of their bread.

60 They then gave him wine and he drank and became intoxicated, and they placed before him a beautiful damsel, and he did with her as he liked, for he knew not what he was doing, as he had drunk plentifully of wine.

3 Israel joined himself to Baal Peor. Yahweh's anger burned against Israel.

61 Thus did the children of Moab to Israel in that place, in the plain of Shittim, and the anger of the Lord was kindled against Israel on account of this matter,

[Numbers 25:9 Those who died by the plague were twenty-four thousand.]

and he sent a pestilence amongst them, and there died of the Israelites twenty-four thousand men.

4 Yahweh said to Moses, "Take all the chiefs of the people, and hang them up to Yahweh before the sun, that the fierce anger of Yahweh may turn away from Israel." 5 Moses said to the judges of Israel, "Everyone kill his men who have joined themselves to Baal Peor."

6 Behold, one of the children of Israel came and brought to his brothers a Midianite woman in the sight of Moses, and in the sight of all the congregation of the children of Israel, while they were weeping at the door of the Tent of Meeting.

62 Now there was a man of the children of Simeon whose name was Zimri, the son of Salu, who connected himself with the Midianite Cosbi, the daughter of Zur, king of Midian, in the sight of all the children of Israel.

7 When Phinehas, the son of Eleazar, the son of Aaron the priest, saw it, he rose up from the middle of the congregation, and took a spear in his hand. 8
He went after the man of Israel into the pavilion, and thrust both of them through, the man of Israel, and the woman through her body. So the plague was stayed from the children of Israel.

63 And Phineas the son of Elazer, the son of Aaron the priest, saw this wicked thing which Zimri had done, and he took a spear and rose up and went after them, and pierced them both and slew them, and the pestilence ceased from the children of Israel.

9 Those who died by the plague were twenty-four thousand.

[85:61b and he sent a pestilence amongst them, and there died of the Israelites twenty-four thousand men.]

10 Yahweh spoke to Moses, saying, 11 "Phinehas,
the son of Eleazar, the son of Aaron the priest, has turned my wrath away from the children of Israel, in that he was jealous with my jealousy among them, so that I didn't consume the children of Israel in my jealousy. 12 Therefore say, 'Behold, I give to
him my covenant of peace. 13 It shall be to him,
and to his offspring after him, the covenant of an everlasting priesthood, because he was jealous for his God, and made atonement for the children of Israel.'"

14 Now the name of the man of Israel that was slain, who was slain with the Midianite woman, was Zimri, the son of Salu, a prince of a fathers' house among the Simeonites. 15 The name of the
Midianite woman who was slain was Cozbi, the daughter of Zur. He was head of the people of a fathers' house in Midian.

16 Yahweh spoke to Moses, saying, 17 "Harass the
Midianites, and strike them, 18 for they harassed
you with their wiles, with which they have deceived you in the matter of Peor, and in the matter of Cozbi, the daughter of the prince of Midian, their sister, who was slain on the day of the plague in the matter of Peor."

Numbers 26

1 After the plague, Yahweh spoke to Moses and to
Eleazar the son of Aaron the priest, saying, 2 "Take
a census of all the congregation of the children of Israel, from twenty years old and upward, by their fathers' houses, all who are able to go out to war in Israel."

Jasher 86

1 At that time after the pestilence, the Lord said to
Moses, and to Elazer the son of Aaron the priest,
saying, 2 "Number the heads of the whole
community of the children of Israel, from twenty years old and upward, all that went forth in the army."

3 Moses and Eleazar the priest spoke with them in
the plains of Moab by the Jordan at Jericho, saying,
4 "Take a census, from twenty years old and
upward; as Yahweh commanded Moses and the
children of Israel." These are those that came out
of the land of Egypt.

[Numbers 26:5-50]

51 These are those who were numbered of the children of Israel, six hundred one thousand seven hundred thirty.

3 And Moses and Elazer numbered the children of Israel after their families, and the number of all Israel was seven hundred thousand, seven hundred and thirty.

52 Yahweh spoke to Moses, saying, 53 "To these
the land shall be divided for an inheritance
according to the number of names. 54 To the more
you shall give the more inheritance, and to the
fewer you shall give the less inheritance. To
everyone according to those who were numbered
of him shall his inheritance be given.

55 "Notwithstanding, the land shall be divided by
lot. According to the names of the tribes of their
fathers they shall inherit. 56 According to the lot
shall their inheritance be divided between the more
and the fewer."

57 These are those who were numbered of the
Levites after their families: of Gershon, the family of
the Gershonites; of Kohath, the family of the
Kohathites; of Merari, the family of the Merarites.
58 These are the families of Levi: the family of the
Libnites, the family of the Hebronites, the family of
the Mahlites, the family of the Mushites, the family
of the Korahites. Kohath became the father of
Amram.

59 The name of Amram's wife was Jochebed, the
daughter of Levi, who was born to Levi in Egypt. She
bore to Amram Aaron and Moses, and Miriam their
sister. 60 To Aaron were born Nadab and Abihu,
Eleazar and Ithamar. 61 Nadab and Abihu died
when they offered strange fire before Yahweh.

62 Those who were numbered of them were twenty-three thousand, every male from a month old and upward; for they were not numbered among the children of Israel, because there was no inheritance given them among the children of Israel.

4 And the number of the children of Levi, from one month old and upward, was twenty-three thousand,

63 These are those who were numbered by Moses and Eleazar the priest, who numbered the children of Israel in the plains of Moab by the Jordan at Jericho.

64 But among these there was not a man of them who were numbered by Moses and Aaron the priest, who numbered the children of Israel in the wilderness of Sinai. 65 For Yahweh had said of them, "They shall surely die in the wilderness." There was not a man left of them, except Caleb the son of Jephunneh, and Joshua the son of Nun.

and amongst these there was not a man of those numbered by Moses and Aaron in the wilderness of Sinai. 5 For the Lord had told them that they would die in the wilderness, so they all died, and not one had been left of them excepting Caleb the son of Jephuneh, and Joshua the son of Nun.

[Numbers 27-30]

Numbers 31

1 Yahweh spoke to Moses, saying, 2 "Avenge the children of Israel for the Midianites. Afterward you shall be gathered to your people."

6 And it was after this that the Lord said to Moses, "Say unto the children of Israel to avenge upon Midian the cause of their brethren the children of Israel."

3 Moses spoke to the people, saying, "Arm men from among you for the war, that they may go against Midian, to execute Yahweh's vengeance on Midian. 4 Of every tribe one thousand, throughout all the tribes of Israel, you shall send to the war."

5 So there were delivered, out of the thousands of Israel, a thousand of every tribe, twelve thousand armed for war. 6 Moses sent them, one thousand of every tribe, to the war, them and Phinehas the son of Eleazar the priest, to the war, with the vessels of the sanctuary and the trumpets for the alarm in his hand. 7 They fought against Midian, as Yahweh commanded Moses. They killed every male.

7 And Moses did so, and the children of Israel chose from amongst them twelve thousand men, being one thousand to a tribe, and they went to Midian. 8 And the children of Israel warred against Midian, and they slew every male,

8 They killed the kings of Midian with the rest of their slain: Evi, Rekem, Zur, Hur, and Reba, the five kings of Midian. They also killed Balaam the son of Beor with the sword.

also the five princes of Midian, and Balaam the son of Beor did they slay with the sword.

9 The children of Israel took the women of Midian captive with their little ones; and all their livestock, all their flocks, and all their goods, they took as plunder.

9 And the children of Israel took the wives of Midian captive, with their little ones and their cattle, and all belonging to them.

10 All their cities in the places in which they lived, and all their encampments, they burnt with fire. 11 They took all the captives, and all the plunder, both of man and of animal.

12 They brought the captives, and the prey, and the plunder, to Moses, and to Eleazar the priest, and to the congregation of the children of Israel, to the camp at the plains of Moab, which are by the Jordan at Jericho.

13 Moses, and Eleazar the priest, and all the princes of the congregation, went out to meet them outside of the camp.

14 Moses was angry with the officers of the army, the captains of thousands and the captains of hundreds, who came from the service of the war.
15 Moses said to them, "Have you saved all the women alive? 16 Behold, these caused the children of Israel, through the counsel of Balaam, to commit trespass against Yahweh in the matter of Peor, and so the plague was among the congregation of Yahweh.

17 "Now therefore kill every male among the little ones, and kill every woman who has known man by lying with him. 18 But all the girls, who have not known man by lying with him, keep alive for yourselves.

19 "Encamp outside of the camp seven days. Whoever has killed any person, and whoever has touched any slain, purify yourselves on the third day and on the seventh day, you and your captives.
20 As to every garment, and all that is made of skin, and all work of goats' hair, and all things made of wood, you shall purify yourselves."

21 Eleazar the priest said to the men of war who went to the battle, "This is the statute of the law which Yahweh has commanded Moses: 22 however the gold, and the silver, the brass, the iron, the tin, and the lead,

23 "everything that may withstand the fire, you shall make to go through the fire, and it shall be clean; nevertheless it shall be purified with the water for impurity. All that doesn't withstand the fire you shall make to go through the water. 24 You shall wash your clothes on the seventh day, and you shall be clean. Afterward you shall come into the camp."

10 And they took all the spoil and all the prey, and they brought it to Moses and to Elazer to the plains of Moab.

11 And Moses and Elazer and all the princes of the congregation went forth to meet them with joy.

25 Yahweh spoke to Moses, saying, 26 “Count the
plunder that was taken, both of man and of animal,
you, and Eleazar the priest, and the heads of the
fathers’ households of the congregation;

27 "and divide the plunder into two parts: between
the men skilled in war, who went out to battle, and
all the congregation. 28 Levy a tribute to Yahweh of
the men of war who went out to battle: one soul of
five hundred; of the persons, of the cattle, of the
donkeys, and of the flocks.

29 "Take it from their half, and give it to Eleazar the
priest, for Yahweh’s wave offering. 30 Of the
children of Israel’s half, you shall take one drawn
out of every fifty, of the persons, of the cattle, of
the donkeys, and of the flocks, of all the livestock,
and give them to the Levites, who perform the duty
of Yahweh’s tabernacle.”

31 Moses and Eleazar the priest did as Yahweh
commanded Moses.

12 And they divided all the spoil of Midian, and the
children of Israel had been revenged upon Midian
for the cause of their brethren the children of
Israel.

32 Now the plunder, over and above the booty
which the men of war took, was six hundred
seventy-five thousand sheep, 33 and seventy-two
thousand head of cattle, 34 and sixty-one thousand
donkeys, 35 and thirty-two thousand persons in all,
of the women who had not known man by lying
with him. 36 The half, which was the portion of
those who went out to war, was in number three
hundred thirty-seven thousand five hundred sheep:
37 and Yahweh’s tribute of the sheep was six
hundred seventy-five.

38 The cattle were thirty-six thousand; of which
Yahweh’s tribute was seventy-two. 39 The donkeys
were thirty thousand five hundred; of which
Yahweh’s tribute was sixty-one. 40 The persons
were sixteen thousand; of whom Yahweh’s tribute
was thirty-two persons.

41 Moses gave the tribute, which was Yahweh’s
wave offering, to Eleazar the priest, as Yahweh
commanded Moses.

42 Of the children of Israel’s half, which Moses
divided off from the men who fought 43 (now the
congregation’s half was three hundred thirty-seven
thousand five hundred sheep,

44 and thirty-six thousand head of cattle, 45 and thirty thousand five hundred donkeys, 46 and sixteen thousand persons), 47 even of the children of Israel's half, Moses took one drawn out of every fifty, both of man and of animal, and gave them to the Levites, who performed the duty of Yahweh's tabernacle; as Yahweh commanded Moses.

48 The officers who were over the thousands of the army, the captains of thousands, and the captains of hundreds, came near to Moses. 49 They said to Moses, "Your servants have taken the sum of the men of war who are under our command, and there lacks not one man of us.

50 "We have brought Yahweh's offering, what every man has gotten, of jewels of gold, armlets, and bracelets, signet rings, earrings, and necklaces, to make atonement for our souls before Yahweh."

51 Moses and Eleazar the priest took their gold, even all worked jewels. 52 All the gold of the wave offering that they offered up to Yahweh, of the captains of thousands, and of the captains of hundreds, was sixteen thousand seven hundred fifty shekels. 53 The men of war had taken booty, every man for himself.

54 Moses and Eleazar the priest took the gold of the captains of thousands and of hundreds, and brought it into the Tent of Meeting, for a memorial for the children of Israel before Yahweh.

[Numbers 32 - 36]

Jasher 87
1 At that time the Lord said to Moses, "Behold thy days are approaching to an end,

[Numbers 27:14 because in the strife of the congregation, you rebelled against my word in the wilderness of Zin, to honor me as holy at the waters before their eyes." (These are the waters of Meribah of Kadesh in the wilderness of Zin.)]

Numbers 27:15 Moses spoke to Yahweh, saying, 16 “Let Yahweh, the God of the spirits of all flesh, appoint a man over the congregation, 17 who may go out before them, and who may come in before them, and who may lead them out, and who may bring them in; that the congregation of Yahweh not be as sheep which have no shepherd.”

[Numbers 27:18 Yahweh said to Moses, “Take Joshua the son of Nun, a man in whom is the Spirit, and lay your hand on him. 19 Set him before Eleazar the priest, and before all the congregation; and commission him in their sight.]

take now Joshua the son of Nun thy servant and place him in the tabernacle, and I will command him," and Moses did so.

2 And the Lord appeared in the tabernacle in a pillar of cloud, and the pillar of cloud stood at the entrance of the tabernacle.

3 And the Lord commanded Joshua the son of Nun and said unto him, "Be strong and courageous, for thou shalt bring the children of Israel to the land which I swore to give them, and I will be with thee."

[Numbers 27:20 “You shall give authority to him, that all the congregation of the children of Israel may obey.”]

4 And Moses said to Joshua, "Be strong and courageous, for thou wilt make the children of Israel inherit the land, and the Lord will be with thee, he will not leave thee nor forsake thee, be not afraid nor disheartened."

[Numbers 27:21 “He shall stand before Eleazar the priest, who shall inquire for him by the judgment of the Urim before Yahweh. At his word they shall go out, and at his word they shall come in, both he, and all the children of Israel with him, even all the congregation.”]

[Numbers 27:22 Moses did as Yahweh commanded him. He took Joshua, and set him before Eleazar the priest, and before all the congregation. 23 He laid his hands on him, and commissioned him, as Yahweh spoke by Moses.]

5 And Moses called to all the children of Israel and said to them, "You have seen all the good which the Lord your God has done for you in the wilderness.
6 Now therefore observe all the words of this law, and walk in the way of the Lord your God, turn not from the way which the Lord has commanded you, either to the right or to the left."

7 And Moses taught the children of Israel statutes and judgments and laws to do in the land as the Lord had commanded him.

8 And he taught them the way of the Lord and his laws; behold they are written upon the book of the law of God which he gave to the children of Israel by the hand of Moses.

[Numbers 27:12 Yahweh said to Moses, "Go up into this mountain of Abarim, and see the land which I have given to the children of Israel. 13 When you have seen it, you also shall be gathered to your people, as Aaron your brother was gathered;]

9 And Moses finished commanding the children of Israel, and the Lord said to him, saying, "Go up to the Mount Abarim and die there, and be gathered unto thy people as Aaron thy brother was gathered."

[Deuteronomy 34:5 So Moses the servant of Yahweh died there in the land of Moab, according to Yahweh's word.]

10 And Moses went up as the Lord had commanded him, and he died there in the land of Moab by the order of the Lord, in the fortieth year from the Israelites going forth from the land of Egypt.

[Deuteronomy 34:8 The children of Israel wept for Moses in the plains of Moab thirty days, until the days of weeping in the mourning for Moses were ended.]

11 And the children of Israel wept for Moses in the plains of Moab for thirty days, and the days of weeping and mourning for Moses were completed.

Joshua 1

1 Now after the death of Moses the servant of Yahweh, Yahweh spoke to Joshua the son of Nun, Moses' servant, saying,

2 "Moses my servant is dead. Now therefore arise, go across this Jordan, you, and all these people, to the land which I am giving to them, even to the children of Israel.

3 "I have given you every place that the sole of your foot will tread on, as I told Moses. 4 From the wilderness, and this Lebanon, even to the great river, the river Euphrates, all the land of the Hittites, and to the great sea toward the going down of the sun, shall be your border.

5 "No man will be able to stand before you all the days of your life. As I was with Moses, so I will be with you. I will not fail you nor forsake you.

6 "Be strong and courageous; for you shall cause this people to inherit the land which I swore to their fathers to give them.

Jasher 88

1 And it was after the death of Moses that the Lord said to Joshua the son of Nun, saying,

2 "Rise up and pass the Jordan to the land which I have given to the children of Israel, and thou shalt make the children of Israel inherit the land.

3 "Every place upon which the sole of your feet shall tread shall belong to you, from the wilderness of Lebanon unto the great river the river of Perath shall be your boundary.

4 "No man shall stand up against thee all the days of thy life; as I was with Moses, so will I be with thee,

7 "Only be strong and very courageous. Be careful to observe to do according to all the law, which Moses my servant commanded you. Don't turn from it to the right hand or to the left, that you may have good success wherever you go.

"only be strong and of good courage to observe all the law which Moses commanded thee, turn not from the way either to the right or to the left, in order that thou mayest prosper in all that thou doest."

8 "This book of the law shall not depart from your mouth, but you shall meditate on it day and night, that you may observe to do according to all that is written in it; for then you shall make your way prosperous, and then you shall have good success.
9 Haven't I commanded you? Be strong and courageous. Don't be afraid. Don't be dismayed, for Yahweh your God is with you wherever you go."

10 Then Joshua commanded the officers of the people, saying, 11 "Pass through the middle of the camp, and command the people, saying, 'Prepare food; for within three days you are to pass over this Jordan, to go in to possess the land, which Yahweh your God gives you to possess it.'"

5 And Joshua commanded the officers of Israel, saying, "Pass through the camp and command the people, saying, 'Prepare for yourselves provisions, for in three days more you will pass the Jordan to possess the land.'"

6 And the officers of the children of Israel did so, and they commanded the people and they did all that Joshua had commanded.

12 Joshua spoke to the Reubenites, and to the Gadites, and to the half-tribe of Manasseh, saying,
13 "Remember the word which Moses the servant of Yahweh commanded you, saying, 'Yahweh your God gives you rest, and will give you this land.

14 "Your wives, your little ones, and your livestock, shall live in the land which Moses gave you beyond the Jordan; but you shall pass over before your brothers armed, all the mighty men of valor, and shall help them 15 until Yahweh has given your brothers rest, as he has given you, and they have also possessed the land which Yahweh your God gives them. Then you shall return to the land of your possession, and possess it, which Moses the servant of Yahweh gave you beyond the Jordan toward the sunrise.'"

16 They answered Joshua, saying, "All that you have commanded us we will do, and wherever you send us we will go. 17 Just as we listened to Moses in all things, so will we listen to you. Only may Yahweh your God be with you, as he was with Moses. 18 Whoever rebels against your commandment, and doesn't listen to your words in all that you command him shall himself be put to death. Only be strong and courageous."

Joshua 2

1 Joshua the son of Nun secretly sent two men out of Shittim as spies, saying, "Go, view the land, including Jericho." They went and came into the house of a prostitute whose name was Rahab, and slept there.

7 And Joshua sent two men to spy out the land of Jericho, and the men went and spied out Jericho.

2 The king of Jericho was told, "Behold, men of the children of Israel came in here tonight to spy out the land."

3 Jericho's king sent to Rahab, saying, "Bring out the men who have come to you, who have entered into your house; for they have come to spy out all the land."

4 The woman took the two men and hid them. Then she said, "Yes, the men came to me, but I didn't know where they came from.

5 About the time of the shutting of the gate, when it was dark, the men went out. Where the men went, I don't know. Pursue them quickly. You may catch up with them." 6 But she had brought them up to the roof, and hidden them under the stalks of flax which she had laid in order on the roof. 7 The men pursued them along the way to the fords of the Jordan River. As soon as those who pursued them had gone out, they shut the gate.

8 Before they had lain down, she came up to them on the roof. 9 She said to the men, "I know that Yahweh has given you the land, and that the fear of you has fallen upon us, and that all the inhabitants of the land melt away before you. 10 For we have heard how Yahweh dried up the water of the Red Sea before you, when you came out of Egypt; and what you did to the two kings of the Amorites, who were beyond the Jordan, to Sihon and to Og, whom you utterly destroyed.

11 "As soon as we had heard it, our hearts melted, and there wasn't any more spirit in any man, because of you: for Yahweh your God, he is God in heaven above, and on earth beneath. 12 Now therefore, please swear to me by Yahweh, since I have dealt kindly with you, that you also will deal kindly with my father's house, and give me a true sign; 13 and that you will save alive my father, my mother, my brothers, and my sisters, and all that they have, and will deliver our lives from death."

14 The men said to her, "Our life for yours, if you don't talk about this business of ours; and it shall be, when Yahweh gives us the land, that we will deal kindly and truly with you."

15 Then she let them down by a cord through the window; for her house was on the side of the wall, and she lived on the wall.

16 She said to them, "Go to the mountain, lest the pursuers find you. Hide yourselves there three days, until the pursuers have returned. Afterward, you may go your way."

17 The men said to her, "We will be guiltless of this your oath which you've made us to swear. 18 Behold, when we come into the land, tie this line of scarlet thread in the window which you used to let us down. Gather to yourself into the house your father, your mother, your brothers, and all your father's household.

19 "It shall be that whoever goes out of the doors of your house into the street, his blood will be on his head, and we will be guiltless. Whoever is with you in the house, his blood shall be on our head, if any hand is on him. 20 But if you talk about this business of ours, then we shall be guiltless of your oath which you've made us to swear."

21 She said, "Let it be as you have said." She sent them away, and they departed. Then she tied the scarlet line in the window.

22 They went, and came to the mountain, and stayed there three days, until the pursuers had returned. The pursuers sought them all along the way, but didn't find them.

23 Then the two men returned, descended from the mountain, crossed the river, and came to Joshua the son of Nun. They told him all that had happened to them. 24 They said to Joshua, "Truly Yahweh has delivered all the land into our hands. Moreover, all the inhabitants of the land melt away before us."

8 And at the end of seven days they came to Joshua in the camp and said to him, "The Lord has delivered the whole land into our hand, and the inhabitants thereof are melted with fear because of us."

Joshua 3

1 Joshua got up early in the morning; and they moved from Shittim, and came to the Jordan, he and all the children of Israel. They camped there before they crossed over.

9 And it came to pass after that, that Joshua rose up in the morning and all Israel with him, and they journeyed from Shittim,

2 After three days, the officers went through the middle of the camp; 3 and they commanded the people, saying, "When you see the ark of Yahweh your God's covenant, and the priests the Levites bearing it, then leave your place, and follow it. 4 Yet there shall be a space between you and it, about two thousand cubits by measure. Don't come near it, that you may know the way by which you must go; for you have not passed this way before."

5 Joshua said to the people, "Sanctify yourselves; for tomorrow Yahweh will do wonders among you."

6 Joshua spoke to the priests, saying, "Take up the ark of the covenant, and cross over before the people." They took up the ark of the covenant, and went before the people.

7 Yahweh said to Joshua, "Today I will begin to magnify you in the sight of all Israel, that they may know that as I was with Moses, so I will be with you. 8 You shall command the priests who bear the ark of the covenant, saying, 'When you come to the brink of the waters of the Jordan, you shall stand still in the Jordan.'"

9 Joshua said to the children of Israel, "Come here, and hear the words of Yahweh your God." 10 Joshua said, "By this you shall know that the living God is among you, and that he will without fail drive the Canaanite, and the Hittite, and the Hivite, and the Perizzite, and the Girgashite, and the Amorite, and the Jebusite out from before you.

11 "Behold, the ark of the covenant of the Lord of
all the earth passes over before you into the Jordan.
12 Now therefore take twelve men out of the tribes
of Israel, for every tribe a man. 13 It shall be that
when the soles of the feet of the priests who bear
the ark of Yahweh, the Lord of all the earth, rest in
the waters of the Jordan, that the waters of the
Jordan will be cut off. The waters that come down
from above shall stand in one heap."

14 When the people moved from their tents to pass
over the Jordan, the priests who bore the ark of the
covenant being before the people, 15 and when
those who bore the ark had come to the Jordan,
and the feet of the priests who bore the ark had
dipped in the edge of the water (for the Jordan
overflows all its banks all the time of harvest),

16 the waters which came down from above stood,
and rose up in one heap, a great way off, at Adam,
the city that is beside Zarethan; and those that
went down toward the sea of the Arabah, even the
Salt Sea, were wholly cut off. Then the people
passed over near Jericho. 17 The priests who bore
the ark of Yahweh's covenant stood firm on dry
ground in the middle of the Jordan; and all Israel
crossed over on dry ground, until all the nation had
passed completely over the Jordan.

and Joshua and all Israel with him passed the Jordan; and Joshua was eighty-two years old when he passed the Jordan with Israel.

Joshua 4

1 When all the nation had completely crossed over
the Jordan, Yahweh spoke to Joshua, saying,

2 "Take twelve men out of the people, a man out of
every tribe, 3 and command them, saying, 'Take
from out of the middle of the Jordan, out of the
place where the priests' feet stood firm, twelve
stones, and carry them over with you, and lay them
down in the place where you'll camp tonight.'"

4 Then Joshua called the twelve men, whom he had
prepared of the children of Israel, a man out of
every tribe. 5 Joshua said to them, “Cross before
the ark of Yahweh your God into the middle of the
Jordan, and each of you pick up a stone and put it
on your shoulder, according to the number of the
tribes of the children of Israel; 6 that this may be a
sign among you, that when your children ask in the
future, saying, ‘What do you mean by these
stones?’

7 "then you shall tell them, ‘Because the waters of
the Jordan were cut off before the ark of Yahweh’s
covenant. When it crossed over the Jordan, the
waters of the Jordan were cut off. These stones
shall be for a memorial to the children of Israel
forever.’”

8 The children of Israel did as Joshua commanded,
and took up twelve stones out of the middle of the
Jordan, as Yahweh spoke to Joshua, according to
the number of the tribes of the children of Israel.
They carried them over with them to the place
where they camped, and laid them down there. 9
Joshua set up twelve stones in the middle of the
Jordan, in the place where the feet of the priests
who bore the ark of the covenant stood; and they
are there to this day.

10 For the priests who bore the ark stood in the
middle of the Jordan, until everything was finished
that Yahweh commanded Joshua to speak to the
people, according to all that Moses commanded
Joshua; and the people hurried and passed over.

11 When all the people had completely crossed
over, Yahweh’s ark crossed over, with the priests, in
the presence of the people.

12 The children of Reuben, and the children of Gad,
and the half-tribe of Manasseh, crossed over armed
before the children of Israel, as Moses spoke to
them. 13 About forty thousand men, ready and
armed for war passed over before Yahweh to
battle, to the plains of Jericho. 14 On that day,
Yahweh magnified Joshua in the sight of all Israel;
and they feared him, as they feared Moses, all the
days of his life.

15 Yahweh spoke to Joshua, saying, 16 "Command
the priests who bear the ark of the testimony, that
they come up out of the Jordan."

17 Joshua therefore commanded the priests,
saying, "Come up out of the Jordan!" 18 When the
priests who bore the ark of Yahweh's covenant had
come up out of the middle of the Jordan, and the
soles of the priests' feet had been lifted up to the
dry ground, the waters of the Jordan returned to
their place, and went over all its banks, as before.

19 The people came up out of the Jordan on the
tenth day of the first month, and encamped in
Gilgal, on the east border of Jericho.

10 And the people went up from Jordan on the
tenth day of the first month, and they encamped in
Gilgal at the eastern corner of Jericho.

20 Joshua set up those twelve stones, which they
took out of the Jordan, in Gilgal. 21 He spoke to the
children of Israel, saying, "When your children ask
their fathers in time to come, saying, 'What do
these stones mean?' 22 Then you shall let your
children know, saying, 'Israel came over this Jordan
on dry land.

23 "For Yahweh your God dried up the waters of
the Jordan from before you, until you had crossed
over, as Yahweh your God did to the Red Sea, which
he dried up from before us, until we had crossed
over;

24 "that all the peoples of the earth may know that
Yahweh's hand is mighty; that you may fear
Yahweh your God forever.'"

Joshua 5

1 When all the kings of the Amorites, who were
beyond the Jordan westward, and all the kings of
the Canaanites, who were by the sea, heard how
Yahweh had dried up the waters of the Jordan from
before the children of Israel, until we had crossed
over, their heart melted, and there was no more
spirit in them, because of the children of Israel. 2 At
that time, Yahweh said to Joshua, "Make flint
knives, and circumcise again the sons of Israel the
second time."

3 Joshua made himself flint knives, and circumcised the sons of Israel at the hill of the foreskins. 4 This is the reason Joshua circumcised them: all the people who came out of Egypt, who were males, even all the men of war, died in the wilderness along the way, after they came out of Egypt.

5 For all the people who came out were circumcised; but all the people who were born in the wilderness along the way as they came out of Egypt had not been circumcised.

6 For the children of Israel walked forty years in the wilderness, until all the nation, even the men of war who came out of Egypt, were consumed, because they didn't listen to Yahweh's voice. Yahweh swore to them that he wouldn't let them see the land which Yahweh swore to their fathers that he would give us, a land flowing with milk and honey.

7 Their children, whom he raised up in their place, were circumcised by Joshua; for they were uncircumcised, because they had not circumcised them on the way. 8 When they were done circumcising the whole nation, they stayed in their places in the camp until they were healed.

9 Yahweh said to Joshua, "Today I have rolled away the reproach of Egypt off of you." Therefore the name of that place was called Gilgal, to this day.

10 The children of Israel encamped in Gilgal. They kept the Passover on the fourteenth day of the month at evening in the plains of Jericho.

11 And the children of Israel kept the Passover in Gilgal, in the plains of Jericho, on the fourteenth day at the month, as it is written in the law of Moses.

11 They ate unleavened cakes and parched grain of the produce of the land on the next day after the Passover, in the same day.

12 The manna ceased on the next day, after they had eaten of the produce of the land. The children of Israel didn't have manna any more; but they ate of the fruit of the land of Canaan that year.

12 And the manna ceased at that time on the morrow of the Passover, and there was no more manna for the children of Israel, and they ate of the produce of the land of Canaan.

13 When Joshua was by Jericho, he lifted up his eyes and looked, and behold, a man stood in front of him with his sword drawn in his hand. Joshua went to him and said to him, "Are you for us, or for our enemies?"

14 He said, "No; but I have come now as commander of Yahweh's army." Joshua fell on his face to the earth, and worshiped, and asked him, "What does my lord say to his servant?"

15 The prince of Yahweh's army said to Joshua, "Take your shoes off of your feet; for the place on which you stand is holy." Joshua did so.

Joshua 6

1 Now Jericho was tightly shut up because of the children of Israel. No one went out, and no one came in.

13 And Jericho was entirely closed against the children of Israel, no one came out or went in.

2 Yahweh said to Joshua, "Behold, I have given
Jericho into your hand, with its king and the mighty
men of valor. 3 All of your men of war shall march
around the city, going around the city once. You
shall do this six days.

14 And it was in the second month, on the first day of the month, that the Lord said to Joshua, "Rise up, behold I have given Jericho into thy hand with all the people thereof; and all your fighting men shall go round the city, once each day, thus shall you do for six days.

4 "Seven priests shall bear seven trumpets of rams'
horns before the ark. On the seventh day, you shall
march around the city seven times, and the priests
shall blow the trumpets. 5 It shall be that when they
make a long blast with the ram's horn, and when
you hear the sound of the trumpet, all the people
shall shout with a great shout; and the city wall
shall fall down flat, and the people shall go up,
every man straight in front of him."

15 "And the priests shall blow upon trumpets, and when you shall hear the sound of the trumpet, all the people shall give a great shouting, that the walls of the city shall fall down; all the people shall go up every man against his opponent."

6 Joshua the son of Nun called the priests, and said to them, "Take up the ark of the covenant, and let seven priests bear seven trumpets of rams' horns before Yahweh's ark."

7 They said to the people, "Advance! March around the city, and let the armed men pass on before Yahweh's ark."

8 It was so, that when Joshua had spoken to the
people, the seven priests bearing the seven
trumpets of rams' horns before Yahweh advanced
and blew the trumpets, and the ark of Yahweh's
covenant followed them. 9 The armed men went
before the priests who blew the trumpets, and the
ark went after them. The trumpets sounded as they
went.

16 And Joshua did so according to all that the Lord had commanded him.

10 Joshua commanded the people, saying, "You shall not shout, nor let your voice be heard, neither shall any word proceed out of your mouth, until the day I tell you to shout. Then you shall shout." 11 So he caused Yahweh's ark to go around the city, going about it once. Then they came into the camp, and stayed in the camp.

12 Joshua rose early in the morning, and the priests took up Yahweh's ark. 13 The seven priests bearing the seven trumpets of rams' horns in front of Yahweh's ark went on continually, and blew the trumpets. The armed men went in front of them. The rear guard came after Yahweh's ark. The trumpets sounded as they went. 14 The second day they marched around the city once, and returned into the camp. They did this six days.

15 On the seventh day, they rose early at the dawning of the day, and marched around the city in the same way seven times. Only on this day they marched around the city seven times. 16 At the seventh time, when the priests blew the trumpets,

17 And on the seventh day they went round the city seven times, and the priests blew upon trumpets.

Joshua said to the people, "Shout, for Yahweh has given you the city! 17 The city shall be devoted, even it and all that is in it, to Yahweh. Only Rahab the prostitute shall live, she and all who are with her in the house, because she hid the messengers that we sent. 18 But as for you, only keep yourselves from what is devoted to destruction, lest when you have devoted it, you take of the devoted thing; so you would make the camp of Israel accursed, and trouble it. 19 But all the silver, gold, and vessels of brass and iron, are holy to Yahweh. They shall come into Yahweh's treasury."

18 And at the seventh round, Joshua said to the people, "Shout, for the Lord has delivered the whole city into our hands. 19 Only the city and all that it contains shall be accursed to the Lord, and keep yourselves from the accursed thing, lest you make the camp of Israel accursed and trouble it. 20 But all the silver and gold and brass and iron shall be consecrated to the Lord, they shall come into the treasury of the Lord."

20 So the people shouted and the priests blew the trumpets. When the people heard the sound of the trumpet, the people shouted with a great shout, and the wall fell down flat, so that the people went up into the city, every man straight in front of him, and they took the city. 21 They utterly destroyed all that was in the city, both man and woman, both young and old, and ox, sheep, and donkey, with the edge of the sword.

21 And the people blew upon trumpets and made a great shouting, and the walls of Jericho fell down, and all the people went up, every man straight before him, and they took the city and utterly destroyed all that was in it, both man and woman, young and old, ox and sheep and ass, with the edge of the sword.

22 Joshua said to the two men who had spied out the land, “Go into the prostitute’s house, and bring the woman and all that she has out from there, as you swore to her.”

23 The young men who were spies went in, and brought out Rahab with her father, her mother, her brothers, and all that she had. They also brought out all of her relatives, and they set them outside of the camp of Israel.

24 They burned the city with fire, and all that was in it. Only they put the silver, the gold, and the vessels of brass and of iron into the treasury of Yahweh’s house.

22 And they burned the whole city with fire; only the vessels of silver and gold, and brass and iron, they put into the treasury of the Lord.

25 But Rahab the prostitute, her father’s household, and all that she had, Joshua saved alive. She lives in the middle of Israel to this day, because she hid the messengers, whom Joshua sent to spy out Jericho.

26 Joshua commanded them with an oath at that time, saying, “Cursed is the man before Yahweh, who rises up and builds this city Jericho. With the loss of his firstborn he will lay its foundation, and with the loss of his youngest son he will set up its
gates.” 27 So Yahweh was with Joshua; and his
fame was in all the land.

23 And Joshua swore at that time, saying, "Cursed be the man who builds Jericho; he shall lay the foundation thereof in his first-born, and in his youngest son shall he set up the gates thereof."

Joshua 7

1 But the children of Israel committed a trespass in the devoted things; for Achan, the son of Carmi, the son of Zabdi, the son of Zerah, of the tribe of Judah, took some of the devoted things. Therefore Yahweh’s anger burned against the children of Israel.

24 And Achan the son of Carmi, the son of Zabdi, the son of Zerah, son of Judah, dealt treacherously in the accursed thing, and he took of the accursed thing and hid it in the tent, and the anger of the Lord was kindled against Israel.

2 Joshua sent men from Jericho to Ai, which is beside Beth Aven, on the east side of Bethel, and spoke to them, saying, “Go up and spy out the land.”

25 And it was after this when the children of Israel had returned from burning Jericho, Joshua sent men to spy out also Ai, and to fight against it.

The men went up and spied out Ai. 3 They returned
to Joshua, and said to him, “Don’t let all the people go up; but let about two or three thousand men go up and strike Ai. Don’t make all the people to toil there, for there are only a few of them.”

26 And the men went up and spied out Ai, and they returned and said, "Let not all the people go up with thee to Ai, only let about three thousand men go up and smite the city, for the men thereof are but few."

4 So about three thousand men of the people went up there, and they fled before the men of Ai.

27 And Joshua did so, and there went up with him of the children of Israel about three thousand men, and they fought against the men of Ai.

5 The men of Ai struck about thirty-six men of them, and they chased them from before the gate even to Shebarim, and struck them at the descent. The hearts of the people melted, and became like water.

28 And the battle was severe against Israel, and the men of Ai smote thirty-six men of Israel, and the children of Israel fled from before the men of Ai.

6 Joshua tore his clothes, and fell to the earth on his face before Yahweh's ark until the evening, he and the elders of Israel; and they put dust on their heads.

29 And when Joshua saw this thing, he tore his garments and fell upon his face to the ground before the Lord, he, with the elders of Israel, and they put dust upon their heads.

7 Joshua said, "Alas, Lord Yahweh, why have you brought this people over the Jordan at all, to deliver us into the hand of the Amorites, to cause us to perish? I wish that we had been content and lived beyond the Jordan! 8 Oh, Lord, what shall I say, after Israel has turned their backs before their enemies! 9 For the Canaanites and all the inhabitants of the land will hear of it, and will surround us, and cut off our name from the earth. What will you do for your great name?"

30 And Joshua said, "Why O Lord didst thou bring this people over the Jordan? What shall I say after the Israelites have turned their backs against their enemies? 31 Now therefore all the Canaanites, inhabitants of the land, will hear this thing, and surround us and cut off our name."

10 Yahweh said to Joshua, "Get up! Why have you fallen on your face like that? 11 Israel has sinned. Yes, they have even transgressed my covenant which I commanded them. Yes, they have even taken some of the devoted things, and have also stolen, and also deceived. They have even put it among their own stuff. 12 Therefore the children of Israel can't stand before their enemies. They turn their backs before their enemies, because they have become devoted for destruction. I will not be with you any more, unless you destroy the devoted things from among you.

32 And the Lord said to Joshua, "Why dost thou fall upon thy face? rise, get thee off, for the Israelites have sinned, and taken of the accursed thing;

13 "Get up! Sanctify the people, and say, 'Sanctify yourselves for tomorrow, for Yahweh, the God of Israel, says, "There is a devoted thing among you, Israel. You cannot stand before your enemies until you take away the devoted thing from among you."

I will no more be with them unless they destroy the accursed thing from amongst them."

14 "'In the morning therefore you shall be brought near by your tribes. It shall be that the tribe which Yahweh selects shall come near by families. The family which Yahweh selects shall come near by households. The household which Yahweh selects shall come near man by man.

15 "It shall be, that he who is taken with the
devoted thing shall be burned with fire, he and all
that he has, because he has transgressed Yahweh's
covenant, and because he has done a disgraceful
thing in Israel.'"

16 So Joshua rose up early in the morning and
brought Israel near by their tribes. The tribe of
Judah was selected. 17 He brought near the family
of Judah; and he selected the family of the
Zerahites. He brought near the family of the
Zerahites man by man, and Zabdi was selected. 18
He brought near his household man by man, and
Achan, the son of Carmi, the son of Zabdi, the son
of Zerah, of the tribe of Judah, was selected.

33 And Joshua rose up and assembled the people, and brought the Urim by the order of the Lord, and the tribe of Judah was taken, and Achan the son of Carmi was taken.

19 Joshua said to Achan, "My son, please give glory
to Yahweh, the God of Israel, and make confession
to him. Tell me now what you have done! Don't
hide it from me!"

34 And Joshua said to Achan, "Tell me my son, what hast thou done,"

20 Achan answered Joshua, and said, "I have truly
sinned against Yahweh, the God of Israel, and this is
what I have done. 21 When I saw among the
plunder a beautiful Babylonian robe, two hundred
shekels of silver, and a wedge of gold weighing fifty
shekels, then I coveted them and took them.
Behold, they are hidden in the ground in the middle
of my tent, with the silver under it."

and Achan said, "I saw amongst the spoil a goodly garment of Shinar and two hundred shekels of silver, and a wedge of gold of fifty shekels weight; I coveted them and took them, and behold they are all hid in the earth in the midst of the tent."

22 So Joshua sent messengers, and they ran to the
tent. Behold, it was hidden in his tent, with the
silver under it. 23 They took them from the middle
of the tent, and brought them to Joshua and to all
the children of Israel. They laid them down before
Yahweh.

35 And Joshua sent men who went and took them from the tent of Achan, and they brought them to Joshua.

24 Joshua, and all Israel with him, took Achan the son of Zerah, the silver, the robe, the wedge of gold, his sons, his daughters, his cattle, his donkeys, his sheep, his tent, and all that he had; and they brought them up to the valley of Achor.

36 And Joshua took Achan and these utensils, and his sons and daughters and all belonging to him, and they brought them into the valley of Achor.

25 Joshua said, "Why have you troubled us?
Yahweh will trouble you today." All Israel stoned
him with stones, and they burned them with fire
and stoned them with stones. 26 They raised over
him a great heap of stones that remains to this day.
Yahweh turned from the fierceness of his anger.
Therefore the name of that place was called "The
valley of Achor" to this day.

37 And Joshua burned them there with fire, and all the Israelites stoned Achan with stones, and they raised over him a heap of stones, therefore did he call that place the valley of Achor, so the Lord's anger was appeased, and Joshua afterward came to the city and fought against it.

Joshua 8
1 Yahweh said to Joshua, "Don't be afraid, and
don't be dismayed. Take all the warriors with you,
and arise, go up to Ai. Behold, I have given into your
hand the king of Ai, with his people, his city, and his
land. 2 You shall do to Ai and her king as you did to
Jericho and her king, except you shall take its goods
and its livestock for yourselves. Set an ambush for
the city behind it."

3 So Joshua arose, with all the warriors, to go up to
Ai. Joshua chose thirty thousand men, the mighty
men of valor, and sent them out by night.

4 He commanded them, saying, "Behold, you shall
lie in ambush against the city, behind the city. Don't
go very far from the city, but all of you be ready. 5 I
and all the people who are with me will approach to
the city. It shall happen, when they come out
against us, as at the first, that we will flee before
them. 6 They will come out after us, until we have
drawn them away from the city; for they will say,
'They flee before us, like the first time.' So we will
flee before them, 7 and you shall rise up from the
ambush, and take possession of the city; for
Yahweh your God will deliver it into your hand. 8 It
shall be, when you have seized the city, that you
shall set the city on fire. You shall do this according
to Yahweh's word. Behold, I have commanded
you."

9 Joshua sent them out; and they went to set up
the ambush, and stayed between Bethel and Ai, on
the west side of Ai; but Joshua stayed among the
people that night.

10 Joshua rose up early in the morning, mustered
the people, and went up, he and the elders of
Israel, before the people to Ai. 11 All the people,
even the men of war who were with him, went up,
and came near, and came before the city, and
encamped on the north side of Ai. Now there was a
valley between him and Ai. 12 He took about five
thousand men, and set them in ambush between
Bethel and Ai, on the west side of the city. 13 So
they set the people, even all the army who was on
the north of the city, and their ambush on the west
of the city; and Joshua went that night into the
middle of the valley.

38 And the Lord said to Joshua, "Fear not, neither be thou dismayed, behold I have given into thy hand Ai, her king and her people, and thou shalt do unto them as thou didst to Jericho and her king, only the spoil thereof and the cattle thereof shall you take for a prey for yourselves; lay an ambush for the city behind it."

39 So Joshua did according to the word of the Lord, and he chose from amongst the sons of war thirty thousand valiant men, and he sent them, and they lay in ambush for the city.
40 And he commanded them, saying, "When you shall see us we will flee before them with cunning, and they will pursue us, you shall then rise out of the ambush and take the city," and they did so.

14 When the king of Ai saw it, they hurried and rose
up early, and the men of the city went out against
Israel to battle, he and all his people, at the time
appointed, before the Arabah; but he didn't know
that there was an ambush against him behind the
city.

41 And Joshua fought, and the men of the city went
out toward Israel, not knowing that they were lying
in ambush for them behind the city.

15 Joshua and all Israel made as if they were beaten
before them, and fled by the way of the wilderness.

42 And Joshua and all the Israelites feigned
themselves wearied out before them, and they fled
by the way of the wilderness with cunning.

16 All the people who were in the city were called
together to pursue after them. They pursued
Joshua, and were drawn away from the city. 17
There was not a man left in Ai or Beth El who didn't
go out after Israel. They left the city open, and
pursued Israel.

43 And the men of Ai gathered all the people who
were in the city to pursue the Israelites, and they
went out and were drawn away from the city, not
one remained, and they left the city open and
pursued the Israelites.

18 Yahweh said to Joshua, "Stretch out the javelin
that is in your hand toward Ai, for I will give it into
your hand." Joshua stretched out the javelin that
was in his hand toward the city.

19 The ambush arose quickly out of their place, and
they ran as soon as he had stretched out his hand,
and entered into the city, and took it. They hurried
and set the city on fire. 20 When the men of Ai
looked behind them, they saw, and behold, the
smoke of the city ascended up to heaven, and they
had no power to flee this way or that way. The
people who fled to the wilderness turned back on
the pursuers.

44 And those who were lying in ambush rose up out
of their places, and hastened to come to the city
and took it and set it on fire, and the men of Ai
turned back, and behold the smoke of the city
ascended to the skies, and they had no means of
retreating either one way or the other.

21 When Joshua and all Israel saw that the ambush
had taken the city, and that the smoke of the city
ascended, then they turned again, and killed the
men of Ai. 22 The others came out of the city
against them, so they were in the middle of Israel,
some on this side, and some on that side. They
struck them, so that they let none of them remain
or escape. 23 They captured the king of Ai alive, and
brought him to Joshua.

45 And all the men of Ai were in the midst of Israel,
some on this side and some on that side, and they
smote them so that not one of them remained.

24 When Israel had finished killing all the
inhabitants of Ai in the field, in the wilderness in
which they pursued them, and they had all fallen by
the edge of the sword, until they were consumed,
all Israel returned to Ai, and struck it with the edge
of the sword. 25 All that fell that day, both of men
and women, were twelve thousand, even all the
men of Ai. 26 For Joshua didn't draw back his hand,
with which he stretched out the javelin, until he
had utterly destroyed all the inhabitants of Ai.

*[88:47 And the children of Israel returned to the city
after having burned it, and they smote all those that
were in it with the edge of the sword. 48 And the
number of those that had fallen of the men of Ai,
both man and woman, was twelve thousand; only
the cattle and the spoil of the city they took to
themselves, according to the word of the Lord to
Joshua.]*

27 Israel took for themselves only the livestock and
the goods of that city , according to Yahweh's word
which he commanded Joshua. 28 So Joshua burned
Ai, and made it a heap forever, even a desolation,
to this day.

29 He hanged the king of Ai on a tree until the evening, and at sundown Joshua commanded, and they took his body down from the tree, and threw it at the entrance of the gate of the city, and raised a great heap of stones on it that remains to this day.

46 And the children of Israel took Melosh king of Ai alive, and they brought him to Joshua, and Joshua hanged him on a tree and he died.

47 And the children of Israel returned to the city
after having burned it, and they smote all those
that were in it with the edge of the sword. 48 And
the number of those that had fallen of the men of
Ai, both man and woman, was twelve thousand;
only the cattle and the spoil of the city they took to
themselves, according to the word of the Lord to
Joshua.

30 Then Joshua built an altar to Yahweh, the God of
Israel, on Mount Ebal, 31 as Moses the servant of
Yahweh commanded the children of Israel, as it is
written in the book of the law of Moses, an altar of
uncut stones, on which no one had lifted up any
iron. They offered burnt offerings on it to Yahweh
and sacrificed peace offerings.

32 He wrote there on the stones a copy of Moses'
law, which he wrote in the presence of the children
of Israel. 33 All Israel, their elders and officers, and
their judges, stood on both sides of the ark before
the priests the Levites, who carried the ark of
Yahweh's covenant, the foreigner as well as the
native; half of them in front of Mount Gerizim, and
half of them in front of Mount Ebal, as Moses the
servant of Yahweh had commanded at the first,
that they should bless the people of Israel.

34 Afterward he read all the words of the law, the
blessing and the curse, according to all that is
written in the book of the law. 35 There was not a
word of all that Moses commanded, which Joshua
didn't read before all the assembly of Israel, with
the women, the little ones, and the foreigners who
were among them.

Joshua 9

1 When all the kings who were beyond the Jordan,
in the hill country, and in the lowland, and on all
the shore of the great sea in front of Lebanon, the
Hittite, the Amorite, the Canaanite, the Perizzite,
the Hivite, and the Jebusite, heard of it 2 they
gathered themselves together to fight with Joshua
and with Israel, with one accord.

49 And all the kings on this side Jordan, all the kings of Canaan, heard of the evil which the children of Israel had done to Jericho and to Ai, and they gathered themselves together to fight against Israel.

3 But when the inhabitants of Gibeon heard what
Joshua had done to Jericho and to Ai, 4 they also
resorted to a ruse, and went and made as if they
had been ambassadors, and took old sacks on their
donkeys, and old, torn-up and bound up wine skins,
5 and old and patched shoes on their feet, and
wore old garments. All the bread of their food
supply was dry and moldy. 6 They went to Joshua at
the camp at Gilgal, and said to him and to the men
of Israel, “We have come from a far country. Now
therefore make a covenant with us.”

50 Only the inhabitants of Gibeon were greatly afraid of fighting against the Israelites lest they should perish, so they acted cunningly, and they came to Joshua and to all Israel, and said unto them, "We have come from a distant land, now therefore make a covenant with us."

7 The men of Israel said to the Hivites, “What if you live among us. How could we make a covenant with you?”

8 They said to Joshua, “We are your servants.” Joshua said to them, “Who are you? Where do you come from?”

9 They said to him, “Your servants have come from
a very far country because of the name of Yahweh
your God; for we have heard of his fame, all that he
did in Egypt, 10 and all that he did to the two kings
of the Amorites who were beyond the Jordan, to
Sihon king of Heshbon and to Og king of Bashan,
who was at Ashtaroth. 11 Our elders and all the
inhabitants of our country spoke to us, saying, ‘Take
supplies in your hand for the journey, and go to
meet them. Tell them, “We are your servants. Now
make a covenant with us.”’

12 "This our bread we took hot for our supplies out of our houses on the day we went out to go to you; but now, behold, it is dry, and has become moldy.

13 "These wine skins, which we filled, were new; and behold, they are torn. These our garments and our shoes have become old because of the very long journey."

14 The men sampled their provisions, and didn't ask counsel from Yahweh's mouth. 15 Joshua made peace with them, and made a covenant with them, to let them live. The princes of the congregation swore to them. 16 At the end of three days after they had made a covenant with them, they heard that they were their neighbors, and that they lived among them.

51 And the inhabitants of Gibeon over-reached the children of Israel, and the children of Israel made a covenant with them, and they made peace with them, and the princes of the congregation swore unto them, but afterward the children of Israel knew that they were neighbors to them and were dwelling amongst them.

52 But the children of Israel slew them not; for they had sworn to them by the Lord, and they became hewers of wood and drawers of water.

17 The children of Israel traveled and came to their cities on the third day. Now their cities were Gibeon, Chephirah, Beeroth, and Kiriath Jearim. 18 The children of Israel didn't strike them, because the princes of the congregation had sworn to them by Yahweh, the God of Israel. All the congregation murmured against the princes.

19 But all the princes said to all the congregation, "We have sworn to them by Yahweh, the God of Israel. Now therefore we may not touch them. 20 We will do this to them, and let them live; lest wrath be on us, because of the oath which we swore to them." 21 The princes said to them, "Let them live, so they became wood cutters and drawers of water for all the congregation, as the princes had spoken to them."

22 Joshua called for them, and he spoke to them, saying, "Why have you deceived us, saying, 'We are very far from you,' when you live among us? 23 Now therefore you are cursed, and some of you will never fail to be slaves, both wood cutters and drawers of water for the house of my God."

53 And Joshua said to them, "Why did you deceive me, to do this thing to us?"

24 They answered Joshua, and said, "Because your servants were certainly told how Yahweh your God commanded his servant Moses to give you all the land, and to destroy all the inhabitants of the land from before you. Therefore we were very afraid for our lives because of you, and have done this thing. 25 Now, behold, we are in your hand. Do to us as it seems good and right to you to do."

and they answered him, saying, "Because it was told to thy servants all that you had done to all the kings of the Amorites, and we were greatly afraid of our lives, and we did this thing."

26 He did so to them, and delivered them out of the hand of the children of Israel, so that they didn't kill them.

[88:52 But the children of Israel slew them not; for they had sworn to them by the Lord, and they became hewers of wood and drawers of water.]

27 That day Joshua made them wood cutters and drawers of water for the congregation and for Yahweh's altar to this day, in the place which he should choose.

54 And Joshua appointed them on that day to hew wood and to draw water, and he divided them for slaves to all the tribes of Israel.

Joshua 10

1 Now when Adoni-Zedek king of Jerusalem heard how Joshua had taken Ai and had utterly destroyed it; as he had done to Jericho and her king, so he had done to Ai and her king; and how the inhabitants of Gibeon had made peace with Israel, and were among them. 2 They were very afraid, because Gibeon was a great city, as one of the royal cities, and because it was greater than Ai, and all its men were mighty. 3 Therefore Adoni-Zedek king of Jerusalem sent to Hoham king of Hebron, Piram king of Jarmuth, Japhia king of Lachish, and Debir king of Eglon, saying, 4 "Come up to me and help me. Let us strike Gibeon; for they have made peace with Joshua and with the children of Israel."

55 And when Adonizedek king of Jerusalem heard all that the children of Israel had done to Jericho and to Ai, he sent to Hoham king of Hebron and to Piram king at Jarmuth, and to Japhia king of Lachish and to Deber king of Eglon, saying, 56 "Come up to me and help me, that we may smite the children of Israel and the inhabitants of Gibeon who have made peace with the children of Israel."

5 Therefore the five kings of the Amorites, the king of Jerusalem, the king of Hebron, the king of Jarmuth, the king of Lachish, and the king of Eglon, gathered themselves together and went up, they and all their armies, and encamped against Gibeon, and made war against it.

57 And they gathered themselves together and the five kings of the Amorites went up with all their camps, a mighty people numerous as the sand of the sea shore. 58 And all these kings came and encamped before Gibeon, and they began to fight against the inhabitants of Gibeon, and all the men of Gibeon sent to Joshua, saying, "Come up quickly to us and help us, for all the kings of the Amorites have gathered together to fight against us."

6 The men of Gibeon sent to Joshua at the camp at Gilgal, saying, "Don't abandon your servants! Come up to us quickly and save us! Help us; for all the kings of the Amorites that dwell in the hill country have gathered together against us."

7 So Joshua went up from Gilgal, he, and the whole army with him, including all the mighty men of valor. 8 Yahweh said to Joshua, "Don't fear them, for I have delivered them into your hands. Not a man of them will stand before you." 9 Joshua therefore came to them suddenly. He marched from Gilgal all night.

59 And Joshua and all the fighting people went up from Gilgal, and Joshua came suddenly to them, and smote these five kings with a great slaughter.

10 Yahweh confused them before Israel. He killed them with a great slaughter at Gibeon, and chased them by the way of the ascent of Beth Horon, and struck them to Azekah and to Makkedah.

60 And the Lord confounded them before the children at Israel, who smote them with a terrible slaughter in Gibeon, and pursued them along the way that goes up to Beth Horon unto Makkedah, and they fled from before the children of Israel.

11 As they fled from before Israel, while they were at the descent of Beth Horon, Yahweh hurled down great stones from the sky on them to Azekah, and they died. There were more who died from the hailstones than those whom the children of Israel killed with the sword.

61 And whilst they were fleeing, the Lord sent upon them hailstones from heaven, and more of them died by the hailstones, than by the slaughter of the children of Israel.

62 And the children of Israel pursued them, and they still smote them in the road, going on and smiting them.

12 Then Joshua spoke to Yahweh in the day when Yahweh delivered up the Amorites before the children of Israel. He said in the sight of Israel, "Sun, stand still on Gibeon! You, moon, stop in the valley of Aijalon!"

63 And when they were smiting, the day was declining toward evening, and Joshua said in the sight of all the people, "Sun, stand thou still upon Gibeon, and thou moon in the valley of Ajalon, until the nation shall have revenged itself upon its enemies."

13 The sun stood still, and the moon stayed, until the nation had avenged themselves of their enemies. Isn't this written in the book of Jashar? The sun stayed in the middle of the sky, and didn't hurry to go down about a whole day.

64 And the Lord hearkened to the voice of Joshua, and the sun stood still in the midst of the heavens, and it stood still six and thirty moments, and the moon also stood still and hastened not to go down a whole day.

14 There was no day like that before it or after it, that Yahweh listened to the voice of a man; for Yahweh fought for Israel.

65 And there was no day like that, before it or after it, that the Lord hearkened to the voice of a man, for the Lord fought for Israel.

Jasher 89

1 Then spoke Joshua this song, on the day that the Lord had given the Amorites into the hand of Joshua and the children of Israel, and he said in the sight of all Israel,

2 "Thou hast done mighty things, O Lord, thou hast performed great deeds; who is like unto thee? my lips shall sing to thy name.

3 "My goodness and my fortress, my high tower, I will sing a new song unto thee, with thanksgiving will I sing to thee, thou art the strength of my salvation.

4 "All the kings of the earth shall praise thee, the princes of the world shall sing to thee, the children of Israel shall rejoice in thy salvation, they shall sing and praise thy power.

5 "To thee, O Lord, did we confide; we said thou art our God, for thou wast our shelter and strong tower against our enemies.

6 "To thee we cried and were not ashamed, in thee we trusted and were delivered; when we cried unto thee, thou didst hear our voice, thou didst deliver our souls from the sword, thou didst show unto us thy grace, thou didst give unto us thy salvation, thou didst rejoice our hearts with thy strength.

7 "Thou didst go forth for our salvation, with thine arm thou didst redeem thy people; thou didst answer us from the heavens of thy holiness, thou didst save us from ten thousands of people.

8 "The sun and moon stood still in heaven, and thou didst stand in thy wrath against our oppressors and didst command thy judgments over them.

9 "All the princes of the earth stood up, the kings of the nations had gathered themselves together, they were not moved at thy presence, they desired thy battles.

10 "Thou didst rise against them in thine anger, and didst bring down thy wrath upon them; thou didst destroy them in thine anger, and cut them off in thine heart.

11 "Nations have been consumed with thy fury, kingdoms have declined because of thy wrath, thou didst wound kings in the day of thine anger.

12 "Thou didst pour out thy fury upon them, thy wrathful anger took hold of them; thou didst turn their iniquity upon them, and didst cut them off in their wickedness.

13 "They did spread a trap, they fell therein, in the net they hid, their foot was caught.

14 "Thine hand was ready for all thine enemies who said, Through their sword they possessed the land, through their arm they dwelt in the city; thou didst fill their faces with shame, thou didst bring their horns down to the ground, thou didst terrify them in thy wrath, and didst destroy them in thine anger.

15 "The earth trembled and shook at the sound of thy storm over them, thou didst not withhold their souls from death, and didst bring down their lives to the grave.

16 "Thou didst pursue them in thy storm, thou didst consume them in thy whirlwind, thou didst turn their rain into hail, they fell in deep pits so that they could not rise.

17 "Their carcasses were like rubbish cast out in the middle of the streets.

18 "They were consumed and destroyed in thine anger, thou didst save thy people with thy might.

19 "Therefore our hearts rejoice in thee, our souls exalt in thy salvation.

20 "Our tongues shall relate thy might, we will sing and praise thy wondrous works.

21 "For thou didst save us from our enemies, thou didst deliver us from those who rose up against us, thou didst destroy them from before us and depress them beneath our feet.

22 "Thus shall all thine enemies perish O Lord, and the wicked shall be like chaff driven by the wind, and thy beloved shall be like trees planted by the waters."

15 Joshua returned, and all Israel with him, to the camp to Gilgal.

23 So Joshua and all Israel with him returned to the camp in Gilgal, after having smitten all the kings, so that not a remnant was left of them.

16 These five kings fled, and hid themselves in the cave at Makkedah.

24 And the five kings fled alone on foot from battle, and hid themselves in a cave, and Joshua sought for them in the field of battle, and did not find them.

17 Joshua was told, saying, "The five kings have been found, hidden in the cave at Makkedah."

25 And it was afterward told to Joshua, saying, "The kings are found and behold they are hidden in a cave."

18 Joshua said, "Roll large stones to cover the cave's entrance, and set men by it to guard them;
19 but don't stay there. Pursue your enemies, and attack them from the rear. Don't allow them to enter into their cities; for Yahweh your God has delivered them into your hand."

26 And Joshua said, "Appoint men to be at the mouth of the cave, to guard them, lest they take themselves away;" and the children of Israel did so.

20 When Joshua and the children of Israel had finished killing them with a very great slaughter until they were consumed, and the remnant which remained of them had entered into the fortified cities,

21 all the people returned to the camp to Joshua at Makkedah in peace. None moved his tongue
against any of the children of Israel. 22 Then Joshua
said, "Open the cave entrance, and bring those five kings out of the cave to me."

23 They did so, and brought those five kings out of the cave to him: the king of Jerusalem, the king of Hebron, the king of Jarmuth, the king of Lachish, and the king of Eglon.

24 When they brought those kings out to Joshua, Joshua called for all the men of Israel, and said to the chiefs of the men of war who went with him, “Come near. Put your feet on the necks of these kings.” They came near, and put their feet on their necks.

27 And Joshua called to all Israel and said to the officers of battle, "Place your feet upon the necks of these kings," and Joshua said, "So shall the Lord do to all your enemies."

25 Joshua said to them, “Don’t be afraid, nor be dismayed. Be strong and courageous, for Yahweh will do this to all your enemies against whom you fight.”

26 Afterward Joshua struck them, put them to death, and hanged them on five trees. They were hanging on the trees until the evening.

27 At the time of the going down of the sun, Joshua commanded, and they took them down off the trees, and threw them into the cave in which they had hidden themselves, and laid great stones on the mouth of the cave, which remain to this very day.

28 And Joshua commanded afterward that they should slay the kings and cast them into the cave, and to put great stones at the mouth of the cave.

28 Joshua took Makkedah on that day, and struck it with the edge of the sword, with its king. He utterly destroyed it and all the souls who were in it. He left no one remaining. He did to the king of Makkedah as he had done to the king of Jericho.

29 And Joshua went afterward with all the people that were with him on that day to Makkedah, and he smote it with the edge of the sword. 30 And he utterly destroyed the souls and all belonging to the city, and he did to the king and people thereof as he had done to Jericho.

29 Joshua passed from Makkedah, and all Israel with him, to Libnah, and fought against Libnah. 30 Yahweh delivered it also, with its king, into the hand of Israel. He struck it with the edge of the sword, and all the souls who were in it. He left no one remaining in it. He did to its king as he had done to the king of Jericho.

31 And he passed from there to Libnah and he fought against it, and the Lord delivered it into his hand, and Joshua smote it with the edge of the sword, and all the souls thereof, and he did to it and to the king thereof as he had done to Jericho.

31 Joshua passed from Libnah, and all Israel with
him, to Lachish, and encamped against it, and
fought against it. 32 Yahweh delivered Lachish into
the hand of Israel. He took it on the second day,
and struck it with the edge of the sword, with all
the souls who were in it, according to all that he
had done to Libnah. 33 Then Horam king of Gezer
came up to help Lachish; and Joshua struck him and
his people, until he had left him no one remaining.

32 And from there he passed on to Lachish to fight
against it, and Horam king of Gaza went up to assist
the men of Lachish, and Joshua smote him and his
people until there was none left to him. 33 And
Joshua took Lachish and all the people thereof, and
he did to it as he had done to Libnah.

34 Joshua passed from Lachish, and all Israel with
him, to Eglon; and they encamped against it fought
against it. 35 They took it on that day, and struck it
with the edge of the sword. He utterly destroyed all
the souls who were in it that day, according to all
that he had done to Lachish.

34 And Joshua passed from there to Eglon, and he took that also, and he smote it and all the people thereof with the edge of the sword.

36 Joshua went up from Eglon, and all Israel with
him, to Hebron; and they fought against it. 37 They
took it, and struck it with the edge of the sword,
with its king and all its cities, and all the souls who
were in it. He left no one remaining, according to all
that he had done to Eglon; but he utterly destroyed
it, and all the souls who were in it.

35 And from there he passed to Hebron and fought
against it and took it and utterly destroyed it, and
he returned from there with all Israel to Debir and
fought against it and smote it with the edge of the
sword. 36 And he destroyed every soul in it, he left
none remaining, and he did to it and the king
thereof as he had done to Jericho.

38 Joshua returned, and all Israel with him, to
Debir, and fought against it. 39 He took it, with its
king and all its cities. They struck them with the
edge of the sword, and utterly destroyed all the
souls who were in it. He left no one remaining. As
he had done to Hebron, so he did to Debir, and to
its king; as he had done also to Libnah, and to its
king.

40 So Joshua struck all the land, the hill country, the South, the lowland, the slopes, and all their kings. He left no one remaining, but he utterly destroyed all that breathed, as Yahweh, the God of Israel, commanded.

41 Joshua struck them from Kadesh Barnea even to
Gaza, and all the country of Goshen, even to
Gibeon. 42 Joshua took all these kings and their
land at one time, because Yahweh, the God of
Israel, fought for Israel.

37 And Joshua smote all the kings of the Amorites from Kadesh-barnea to Azah, and he took their country at once, for the Lord had fought for Israel.

43 Joshua returned, and all Israel with him, to the camp to Gilgal.

38 And Joshua with all Israel came to the camp to Gilgal.

Joshua 11

1 When Jabin king of Hazor heard of it, he sent to Jobab king of Madon, to the king of Shimron, to the king of Achshaph, 2 and to the kings who were on the north, in the hill country, in the Arabah south of Chinneroth, in the lowland, and in the heights of Dor on the west, 3 to the Canaanite on the east and on the west, the Amorite, the Hittite, the Perizzite, the Jebusite in the hill country, and the Hivite under Hermon in the land of Mizpah.

39 When at that time Jabin king of Chazor heard all that Joshua had done to the kings of the Amorites, Jabin sent to Jobat king of Midian, and to Laban king of Shimron, to Jephal king of Achshaph, and to all the kings of the Amorites, saying, 40 "Come quickly to us and help us, that we may smite the children of Israel, before they come upon us and do unto us as they have done to the other kings of the Amorites."

4 They went out, they and all their armies with them, many people, even as the sand that is on the seashore in multitude, with very many horses and chariots. 5 All these kings met together; and they came and encamped together at the waters of Merom, to fight with Israel.

41 And all these kings hearkened to the words of Jabin, king of Chazor, and they went forth with all their camps, seventeen kings, and their people were as numerous as the sand on the sea shore, together with horses and chariots innumerable, and they came and pitched together at the waters of Merom, and they were met together to fight against Israel.

6 Yahweh said to Joshua, "Don't be afraid because of them; for tomorrow at this time, I will deliver them up all slain before Israel. You shall hamstring their horses and burn their chariots with fire."

42 And the Lord said to Joshua, "Fear them not, for tomorrow about this time I will deliver them up all slain before you, thou shalt hough their horses and burn their chariots with fire."

7 So Joshua came suddenly, with all the warriors, against them by the waters of Merom, and attacked them. 8 Yahweh delivered them into the hand of Israel, and they struck them, and chased them to great Sidon, and to Misrephoth Maim, and to the valley of Mizpah eastward. They struck them until they left them no one remaining.

43 And Joshua with all the men of war came suddenly upon them and smote them, and they fell into their hands, for the Lord had delivered them into the hands of the children of Israel. 44 So the children of Israel pursued all these kings with their camps, and smote them until there was none left of them, and Joshua did to them as the Lord had spoken to him.

9 Joshua did to them as Yahweh told him. He hamstrung their horses and burned their chariots with fire.

10 Joshua turned back at that time, and took Hazor, and struck its king with the sword: for Hazor used to be the head of all those kingdoms. 11 They struck all the souls who were in it with the edge of the sword, utterly destroying them. There was no one left who breathed. He burned Hazor with fire.

45 And Joshua returned at that time to Chazor and smote it with the sword and destroyed every soul in it and burned it with fire, and from Chazor, Joshua passed to Shimron and smote it and utterly destroyed it.

12 Joshua captured all the cities of those kings, with their kings, and he struck them with the edge of the sword, and utterly destroyed them; as Moses the servant of Yahweh commanded.

46 From there he passed to Achshaph and he did to it as he had done to Shimron. 47 From there he passed to Adulam and he smote all the people in it, and he did to Adulam as he had done to Achshaph and to Shimron. 48 And he passed from them to all the cities of the kings which he had smitten, and he smote all the people that were left of them and he utterly destroyed them.

13 But as for the cities that stood on their mounds, Israel burned none of them, except Hazor only. Joshua burned that.

14 The children of Israel took all the plunder of these cities, with the livestock, as plunder for themselves; but every man they struck with the edge of the sword, until they had destroyed them. They didn't leave any who breathed.

49 Only their booty and cattle the Israelites took to themselves as a prey, but every human being they smote, they suffered not a soul to live.

15 As Yahweh commanded Moses his servant, so Moses commanded Joshua. Joshua did so. He left nothing undone of all that Yahweh commanded Moses.

50 As the Lord had commanded Moses so did Joshua and all Israel, they failed not in anything.

16 So Joshua captured all that land, the hill country, all the South, all the land of Goshen, the lowland, the Arabah, the hill country of Israel, and the lowland of the same; 17 from Mount Halak, that goes up to Seir, even to Baal Gad in the valley of Lebanon under Mount Hermon. He took all their kings, struck them, and put them to death.

51 So Joshua and all the children of Israel smote the whole land of Canaan as the Lord had commanded them, and smote all their kings, being thirty and one kings, and the children of Israel took their whole country.

52 Besides the kingdoms of Sihon and Og which are on the other side Jordan, of which Moses had smitten many cities, and Moses gave them to the Reubenites and the Gadites and to half the tribe of Manasseh.

53 And Joshua smote all the kings that were on this side Jordan to the west, and gave them for an inheritance to the nine tribes and to the half tribe of Israel.

18 Joshua made war a long time with all those kings.

54 For five years did Joshua carry on the war with these kings, and he gave their cities to the Israelites, and the land became tranquil from battle throughout the cities of the Amorites and the Canaanites.

19 There was not a city that made peace with the children of Israel, except the Hivites, the inhabitants of Gibeon. They took all in battle.

20 For it was of Yahweh to harden their hearts, to
come against Israel in battle, that he might utterly
destroy them, that they might have no favor, but
that he might destroy them, as Yahweh
commanded Moses. 21 Joshua came at that time,
and cut off the Anakim from the hill country, from
Hebron, from Debir, from Anab, and from all the hill
country of Judah, and from all the hill country of
Israel: Joshua utterly destroyed them with their
cities.

22 There were none of the Anakim left in the land
of the children of Israel. Only in Gaza, in Gath, and
in Ashdod, did some remain.

23 So Joshua took the whole land, according to all
that Yahweh spoke to Moses; and Joshua gave it for
an inheritance to Israel according to their divisions
by their tribes. The land had rest from war.

Joshua 12

1 Now these are the kings of the land, whom the
children of Israel struck, and possessed their land
beyond the Jordan toward the sunrise, from the
valley of the Arnon to Mount Hermon, and all the
Arabah eastward: 2 Sihon king of the Amorites, who
lived in Heshbon, and ruled from Aroer, which is on
the edge of the valley of the Arnon, and the middle
of the valley, and half Gilead, even to the river
Jabbok, the border of the children of Ammon;

3 and the Arabah to the sea of Chinneroth,
eastward, and to the sea of the Arabah, even the
Salt Sea, eastward, the way to Beth Jeshimoth; and
on the south, under the slopes of Pisgah: 4 and the
border of Og king of Bashan, of the remnant of the
Rephaim, who lived at Ashtaroth and at Edrei, 5 and
ruled in Mount Hermon, and in Salecah, and in all
Bashan, to the border of the Geshurites and the
Maacathites, and half Gilead, the border of Sihon
king of Heshbon.

6 Moses the servant of Yahweh and the children of
Israel struck them. Moses the servant of Yahweh
gave it for a possession to the Reubenites, and the
Gadites, and the half-tribe of Manasseh.

7 These are the kings of the land whom Joshua and the children of Israel struck beyond the Jordan westward, from Baal Gad in the valley of Lebanon even to Mount Halak, that goes up to Seir. Joshua gave it to the tribes of Israel for a possession according to their divisions; 8 in the hill country, and in the lowland, and in the Arabah, and in the slopes, and in the wilderness, and in the South; the Hittite, the Amorite, and the Canaanite, the Perizzite, the Hivite, and the Jebusite:

9 the king of Jericho, one; the king of Ai, which is beside Bethel, one; 10 the king of Jerusalem, one; the king of Hebron, one;

11 the king of Jarmuth, one; the king of Lachish, one; 12 the king of Eglon, one; the king of Gezer, one;

13 the king of Debir, one; the king of Geder, one; 14 the king of Hormah, one; the king of Arad, one;

15 the king of Libnah, one; the king of Adullam, one; 16 the king of Makkedah, one; the king of Bethel, one;

17 the king of Tappuah, one; the king of Hepher, one; 18 the king of Aphek, one; the king of Lassharon, one;

19 the king of Madon, one; the king of Hazor, one; 20 the king of Shimron Meron, one; the king of Achshaph, one;

21 the king of Taanach, one; the king of Megiddo, one; 22 the king of Kedesh, one; the king of Jokneam in Carmel, one;

23 the king of Dor in the height of Dor, one; the king of Goiim in Gilgal, one;

24 the king of Tirzah, one: all the kings thirty-one.

[89:51 So Joshua and all the children of Israel smote the whole land of Canaan as the Lord had commanded them, and smote all their kings, being thirty and one kings, and the children of Israel took their whole country.]

Jasher 90

1 At that time in the fifth year after the children of Israel had passed over Jordan, after the children of Israel had rested from their war with the Canaanites, at that time great and severe battles arose between Edom and the children of Chittim, and the children of Chittim fought against Edom.

2 And Abianus king of Chittim went forth in that year, that is in the thirty-first year of his reign, and a great force with him of the mighty men of the children of Chittim, and he went to Seir to fight against the children of Esau.

3 And Hadad the king of Edom heard of his report, and he went forth to meet him with a heavy people and strong force, and engaged in battle with him in the field of Edom. 4 And the hand of Chittim prevailed over the children of Esau, and the children of Chittim slew of the children of Esau, two and twenty thousand men, and all the children of Esau fled from before them.

5 And the children of Chittim pursued them and they reached Hadad king of Edom, who was running before them and they caught him alive, and brought him to Abianus king of Chittim. 6 And Abianus ordered him to be slain, and Hadad king of Edom died in the forty-eighth year of his reign.

7 And the children of Chittim continued their pursuit of Edom, and they smote them with a great slaughter and Edom became subject to the children of Chittim. 8 And the children of Chittim ruled over Edom, and Edom became under the hand of the children of Chittim and became one kingdom from that day.

9 And from that time they could no more lift up their heads, and their kingdom became one with the children of Chittim. 10 And Abianus placed officers in Edom and all the children of Edom became subject and tributary to Abianus, and Abianus turned back to his own land, Chittim.

11 And when he returned he renewed his government and built for himself a spacious and fortified palace for a royal residence, and reigned securely over the children of Chittim and over Edom.

Joshua 13

1 Now Joshua was old and well advanced in years. Yahweh said to him, “You are old and advanced in years, and there remains yet very much land to be possessed.

12 In those days, after the children of Israel had driven away all the Canaanites and the Amorites, Joshua was old and advanced in years. 13 And the Lord said to Joshua, "Thou art old, advanced in life, and a great part of the land remains to be possessed."

2 "This is the land that still remains: all the regions
of the Philistines, and all the Geshurites; 3 from the
Shihor, which is before Egypt, even to the border of
Ekron northward, which is counted as Canaanite;
the five lords of the Philistines; the Gazites, and the
Ashdodites, the Ashkelonites, the Gittites, and the
Ekronites; also the Avvim, 4 on the south; all the
land of the Canaanites, and Mearah that belongs to
the Sidonians, to Aphek, to the border of the
Amorites;

5 "and the land of the Gebalites, and all Lebanon,
toward the sunrise, from Baal Gad under Mount
Hermon to the entrance of Hamath; 6 all the
inhabitants of the hill country from Lebanon to
Misrephoth Maim, even all the Sidonians. I will
drive them out from before the children of Israel.
Just allocate it to Israel for an inheritance, as I have
commanded you.

7 "Now therefore divide this land for an inheritance
to the nine tribes and the half-tribe of Manasseh."

14 "Now therefore divide this land for an
inheritance to the nine tribes and to the half tribe
of Manasseh," and Joshua rose up and did as the
Lord had spoken to him.

15 And he divided the whole land to the tribes of
Israel as an inheritance according to their divisions.

8 With him the Reubenites and the Gadites
received their inheritance, which Moses gave them,
beyond the Jordan eastward, even as Moses the
servant of Yahweh gave them: 9 from Aroer, that is
on the edge of the valley of the Arnon, and the city
that is in the middle of the valley, and all the plain
of Medeba to Dibon;

10 and all the cities of Sihon king of the Amorites,
who reigned in Heshbon, to the border of the
children of Ammon; 11 and Gilead, and the border
of the Geshurites and Maacathites, and all Mount
Hermon, and all Bashan to Salecah;

12 all the kingdom of Og in Bashan, who reigned in
Ashtaroth and in Edrei (the same was left of the
remnant of the Rephaim); for Moses attacked
these, and drove them out.

13 Nevertheless the children of Israel didn't drive
out the Geshurites, nor the Maacathites: but
Geshur and Maacath live within Israel to this day.

14 Only he gave no inheritance to the tribe of Levi. The offerings of Yahweh, the God of Israel, made by fire are his inheritance, as he spoke to him.

15 Moses gave to the tribe of the children of Reuben according to their families.

16 Their border was from Aroer, that is on the edge of the valley of the Arnon, and the city that is in the middle of the valley, and all the plain by Medeba;
17 Heshbon, and all its cities that are in the plain; Dibon, Bamoth Baal, Beth Baal Meon,

18 Jahaz, Kedemoth, Mephaath, 19 Kiriathaim,
Sibmah, Zereth Shahar in the mount of the valley,
20 Beth Peor, the slopes of Pisgah, Beth Jeshimoth,
21 all the cities of the plain, and all the kingdom of Sihon king of the Amorites, who reigned in Heshbon, whom Moses struck with the chiefs of Midian, Evi, Rekem, Zur, Hur, and Reba, the princes of Sihon, who lived in the land.

22 The children of Israel also killed Balaam the son of Beor, the soothsayer, with the sword, among the rest of their slain.

23 The border of the children of Reuben was the bank of the Jordan. This was the inheritance of the children of Reuben according to their families, the cities and its villages.

24 Moses gave to the tribe of Gad, to the children
of Gad, according to their families. 25 Their border
was Jazer, and all the cities of Gilead, and half the land of the children of Ammon, to Aroer that is near Rabbah;

26 and from Heshbon to Ramath Mizpeh, and Betonim; and from Mahanaim to the border of Debir;

27 and in the valley, Beth Haram, Beth Nimrah, Succoth, and Zaphon, the rest of the kingdom of Sihon king of Heshbon, the Jordan's bank, to the uttermost part of the sea of Chinnereth beyond the
Jordan eastward. 28 This is the inheritance of the
children of Gad according to their families, the cities and its villages.

29 Moses gave an inheritance to the half-tribe of Manasseh. It was for the half-tribe of the children of Manasseh according to their families.

30 Their border was from Mahanaim, all Bashan, all the kingdom of Og king of Bashan, and all the villages of Jair, which are in Bashan, sixty cities.

31 Half Gilead, Ashtaroth, and Edrei, the cities of the kingdom of Og in Bashan, were for the children of Machir the son of Manasseh, even for the half of the children of Machir according to their families.

32 These are the inheritances which Moses distributed in the plains of Moab, beyond the Jordan at Jericho, eastward.

33 But Moses gave no inheritance to the tribe of Levi . Yahweh, the God of Israel, is their inheritance, as he spoke to them.

16 But to the tribe at Levi he gave no inheritance, the offerings of the Lord are their inheritance as the Lord had spoken of them by the hand of Moses.

Joshua 14

1 These are the inheritances which the children of Israel took in the land of Canaan, which Eleazar the priest, Joshua the son of Nun, and the heads of the fathers' houses of the tribes of the children of Israel, distributed to them, 2 by the lot of their inheritance, as Yahweh commanded by Moses, for the nine tribes, and for the half-tribe.

3 For Moses had given the inheritance of the two tribes and the half-tribe beyond the Jordan; but to the Levites he gave no inheritance among them. 4 For the children of Joseph were two tribes, Manasseh and Ephraim. They gave no portion to the Levites in the land, except cities to dwell in, with their suburbs for their livestock and for their property. 5 The children of Israel did as Yahweh commanded Moses, and they divided the land.

6 Then the children of Judah came near to Joshua in Gilgal. Caleb the son of Jephunneh the Kenizzite said to him, "You know the thing that Yahweh spoke to Moses the man of God concerning me and concerning you in Kadesh Barnea.

7 "I was forty years old when Moses the servant of Yahweh sent me from Kadesh Barnea to spy out the land. I brought him word again as it was in my heart. 8 Nevertheless, my brothers who went up with me made the heart of the people melt; but I wholly followed Yahweh my God.

9 Moses swore on that day, saying, 'Surely the land where you walked shall be an inheritance to you and to your children forever, because you have wholly followed Yahweh my God.'

10 "Now, behold, Yahweh has kept me alive, as he spoke, these forty-five years, from the time that Yahweh spoke this word to Moses, while Israel walked in the wilderness. Now, behold, I am eighty-five years old, today. 11 As yet I am as strong today as I was in the day that Moses sent me. As my strength was then, even so is my strength now for war, to go out and to come in.

12 "Now therefore give me this hill country, of which Yahweh spoke in that day; for you heard in that day how the Anakim were there, and great and fortified cities. It may be that Yahweh will be with me, and I shall drive them out, as Yahweh said."

13 Joshua blessed him; and he gave Hebron to Caleb the son of Jephunneh for an inheritance. 14 Therefore Hebron became the inheritance of Caleb the son of Jephunneh the Kenizzite to this day, because he followed Yahweh, the God of Israel wholeheartedly.

15 Now the name of Hebron before was Kiriath Arba, after the greatest man among the Anakim. Then the land had rest from war.

17 And Joshua gave Mount Hebron to Caleb the son of Jephuneh, one portion above his brethren, as the Lord had spoken through Moses. 18 Therefore Hebron became an inheritance to Caleb and his children unto this day.

[Joshua 15-19]

19 And Joshua divided the whole land by lots to all Israel for an inheritance, as the Lord had commanded him.

Joshua 20

1 Yahweh spoke to Joshua, saying, 2 "Speak to the children of Israel, saying, 'Assign the cities of refuge, of which I spoke to you by Moses, 3 that the man slayer who kills any person accidentally or unintentionally may flee there. They shall be to you for a refuge from the avenger of blood. 4 He shall flee to one of those cities, and shall stand at the entrance of the gate of the city, and declare his case in the ears of the elders of that city. They shall take him into the city with them, and give him a place, that he may live among them.

5 "If the avenger of blood pursues him, then they
shall not deliver up the man slayer into his hand;
because he struck his neighbor unintentionally, and
didn't hate him before. 6 He shall dwell in that city
until he stands before the congregation for
judgment, until the death of the high priest that
shall be in those days. Then the man slayer shall
return, and come to his own city, and to his own
house, to the city he fled from.'"

7 They set apart Kedesh in Galilee in the hill country of Naphtali, Shechem in the hill country of Ephraim, and Kiriath Arba (also called Hebron) in the hill country of Judah.

8 Beyond the Jordan at Jericho eastward, they assigned Bezer in the wilderness in the plain out of the tribe of Reuben, Ramoth in Gilead out of the tribe of Gad, and Golan in Bashan out of the tribe of Manasseh.

9 These were the appointed cities for all the children of Israel, and for the alien who lives among them, that whoever kills any person unintentionally might flee there, and not die by the hand of the avenger of blood, until he stands trial before the congregation.

Joshua 21

1 Then the heads of fathers' houses of the Levites
came near to Eleazar the priest, and to Joshua the
son of Nun, and to the heads of fathers' houses of
the tribes of the children of Israel. 2 They spoke to
them at Shiloh in the land of Canaan, saying,
"Yahweh commanded through Moses to give us
cities to dwell in, with their suburbs for our
livestock."

3 The children of Israel gave to the Levites out of their inheritance, according to the commandment of Yahweh, these cities with their suburbs.

20 And the children of Israel gave cities to the Levites from their own inheritance, and suburbs for their cattle, and property, as the Lord had commanded Moses so did the children of Israel, and they divided the land by lot whether great or small.

21 And they went to inherit the land according to their boundaries, and the children of Israel gave to Joshua the son of Nun an inheritance amongst them.

22 By the word of the Lord did they give to him the city which he required, Timnath-serach in Mount Ephraim, and he built the city and dwelt therein.

[Joshua 21:4-22:34]

23 These are the inheritances which Elazer the priest and Joshua the son of Nun and the heads of the fathers of the tribes portioned out to the children of Israel by lot in Shiloh, before the Lord, at the door of the tabernacle, and they left off dividing the land.

24 And the Lord gave the land to the Israelites, and they possessed it as the Lord had spoken to them, and as the Lord had sworn to their ancestors.

Joshua 23

1 After many days, when Yahweh had given rest to Israel from their enemies all around, and Joshua was old and well advanced in years,

25 And the Lord gave to the Israelites rest from all their enemies around them, and no man stood up against them, and the Lord delivered all their enemies into their hands, and not one thing failed of all the good which the Lord had spoken to the children of Israel, yea the Lord performed every thing.

[Joshua 24:28 So Joshua sent the people away, each to his own inheritance.]

26 And Joshua called to all the children of Israel and he blessed them, and commanded them to serve the Lord, and he afterward sent them away, and they went each man to his city, and each man to his inheritance.

27 And the children of Israel served the Lord all the days of Joshua, and the Lord gave them rest from all around them, and they dwelt securely in their cities.

28 And it came to pass in those days, that Abianus king of Chittim died, in the thirty-eighth year of his reign, that is the seventh year of his reign over Edom, and they buried him in his place which he had built for himself, and Latinus reigned in his stead fifty years.

29 And during his reign he brought forth an army, and he went and fought against the inhabitants of Britannia and Kernania, the children of Elisha son of Javan, and he prevailed over them and made them tributary.

30 He then heard that Edom had revolted from
under the hand of Chittim, and Latinus went to
them and smote them and subdued them, and
placed them under the hand of the children of
Chittim, and Edom became one kingdom with the
children of Chittim all the days. 31 And for many
years there was no king in Edom, and their
government was with the children of Chittim and
their king.

32 And it was in the twenty-sixth year after the
children of Israel had passed the Jordan, that is the
sixty-sixth year after the children of Israel had
departed from Egypt, that Joshua was old,
advanced in years, being one hundred and eight
years old in those days.

2 Joshua called for all Israel, for their elders and for
their heads, and for their judges and for their
officers, and said to them, “I am old and well
advanced in years. 3 You have seen all that Yahweh
your God has done to all these nations because of
you; for it is Yahweh your God who has fought for
you.

33 And Joshua called to all Israel, to their elders,
their judges and officers, after the Lord had given to
all the Israelites rest from all their enemies round
about, and Joshua said to the elders of Israel, and
to their judges, "Behold I am old, advanced in years,
and you have seen what the Lord has done to all
the nations whom he has driven away from before
you, for it is the Lord who has fought for you.

4 "Behold, I have allotted to you these nations that
remain, to be an inheritance for your tribes, from
the Jordan, with all the nations that I have cut off,
even to the great sea toward the going down of the
sun. 5 Yahweh your God will thrust them out from
before you, and drive them from out of your sight.
You shall possess their land, as Yahweh your God
spoke to you.

6 “Therefore be very courageous to keep and to do
all that is written in the book of the law of Moses,
that you not turn aside from it to the right hand or
to the left; 7 that you not come among these
nations, these that remain among you; neither
make mention of the name of their gods, nor cause
to swear by them, neither serve them, nor bow
down yourselves to them; 8 but hold fast to
Yahweh your God, as you have done to this day.

34 "Now therefore strengthen yourselves to keep
and to do all the words of the law of Moses, not to
deviate from it to the right or to the left, and not to
come amongst those nations who are left in the
land; neither shall you make mention of the name
of their gods, but you shall cleave to the Lord your
God, as you have done to this day."

9 “For Yahweh has driven great and strong nations
out from before you. But as for you, no man has
stood before you to this day. 10 One man of you
shall chase a thousand; for it is Yahweh your God
who fights for you, as he spoke to you. 11 Take
good heed therefore to yourselves, that you love
Yahweh your God.

12 “But if you do at all go back, and hold fast to the remnant of these nations, even these who remain among you, and make marriages with them, and go in to them, and they to you;

13 "know for a certainty that Yahweh your God will no longer drive these nations from out of your sight; but they shall be a snare and a trap to you, a scourge in your sides, and thorns in your eyes, until you perish from off this good land which Yahweh your God has given you.

14 “Behold, today I am going the way of all the
earth. You know in all your hearts and in all your
souls that not one thing has failed of all the good
things which Yahweh your God spoke concerning
you. All have happened to you. Not one thing has
failed of it. 15 It shall happen that as all the good
things have come on you of which Yahweh your
God spoke to you, so Yahweh will bring on you all
the evil things, until he has destroyed you from off
this good land which Yahweh your God has given
you,

16 "when you disobey the covenant of Yahweh your God, which he commanded you, and go and serve other gods, and bow down yourselves to them. Then Yahweh’s anger will be kindled against you, and you will perish quickly from off the good land which he has given to you.”

Joshua 24

1 Joshua gathered all the tribes of Israel to Shechem, and called for the elders of Israel, for their heads, for their judges, and for their officers; and they presented themselves before God.

2 Joshua said to all the people, “Yahweh says, the God of Israel, ‘Your fathers lived of old time beyond the River, even Terah, the father of Abraham, and the father of Nahor: and they served other gods.

35 And Joshua greatly exhorted the children of Israel to serve the Lord all their days.

3 "I took your father Abraham from beyond the
River, and led him throughout all the land of
Canaan, and multiplied his offspring, and gave him
Isaac. 4 I gave to Isaac Jacob and Esau: and I gave to
Esau Mount Seir, to possess it. Jacob and his
children went down into Egypt.

5 "'I sent Moses and Aaron, and I plagued Egypt,
according to that which I did among them: and
afterward I brought you out. 6 I brought your
fathers out of Egypt: and you came to the sea. The
Egyptians pursued your fathers with chariots and
with horsemen to the Red Sea. 7 When they cried
out to Yahweh, he put darkness between you and
the Egyptians, and brought the sea on them, and
covered them; and your eyes saw what I did in
Egypt. You lived in the wilderness many days.

8 "'I brought you into the land of the Amorites, that
lived beyond the Jordan. They fought with you, and
I gave them into your hand. You possessed their
land, and I destroyed them from before you. 9 Then
Balak the son of Zippor, king of Moab, arose and
fought against Israel. He sent and called Balaam the
son of Beor to curse you, 10 but I would not listen
to Balaam; therefore he blessed you still. So I
delivered you out of his hand.

11 "'You went over the Jordan, and came to Jericho.
The men of Jericho fought against you, the Amorite,
the Perizzite, the Canaanite, the Hittite, the
Girgashite, the Hivite, and the Jebusite; and I
delivered them into your hand. 12 I sent the hornet
before you, which drove them out from before you,
even the two kings of the Amorites; not with your
sword, nor with your bow. 13 I gave you a land
whereon you had not labored, and cities which you
didn't build, and you live in them. You eat of
vineyards and olive groves which you didn't plant.'

14 "Now therefore fear Yahweh, and serve him in
sincerity and in truth. Put away the gods which your
fathers served beyond the River, in Egypt; and serve
Yahweh. 15 If it seems evil to you to serve Yahweh,
choose today whom you will serve; whether the
gods which your fathers served that were beyond
the River, or the gods of the Amorites, in whose
land you dwell; but as for me and my house, we will
serve Yahweh."

16 The people answered, “Far be it from us that we should forsake Yahweh, to serve other gods; 17 for it is Yahweh our God who brought us and our fathers up out of the land of Egypt, from the house of bondage, and who did those great signs in our sight, and preserved us in all the way in which we went, and among all the peoples through the middle of whom we passed. 18 Yahweh drove out from before us all the peoples, even the Amorites who lived in the land. Therefore we also will serve Yahweh; for he is our God.”

19 Joshua said to the people, “You can’t serve Yahweh, for he is a holy God. He is a jealous God. He will not forgive your disobedience nor your sins. 20 If you forsake Yahweh, and serve foreign gods, then he will turn and do you evil, and consume you, after he has done you good.”

21 The people said to Joshua, “No, but we will serve Yahweh.” 22 Joshua said to the people, “You are witnesses against yourselves that you have chosen Yahweh yourselves, to serve him.” They said, “We are witnesses.”

23 “Now therefore put away the foreign gods which are among you, and incline your heart to Yahweh, the God of Israel.”

24 The people said to Joshua, “We will serve Yahweh our God, and we will listen to his voice.”

36 And all the Israelites said, "We will serve the Lord our God all our days, we and our children, and our children's children, and our seed for ever."

25 So Joshua made a covenant with the people that day, and made for them a statute and an ordinance in Shechem. 26 Joshua wrote these words in the book of the law of God; and he took a great stone, and set it up there under the oak that was by the sanctuary of Yahweh. 27 Joshua said to all the people, “Behold, this stone shall be a witness against us, for it has heard all Yahweh’s words which he spoke to us. It shall be therefore a witness against you, lest you deny your God.”

37 And Joshua made a covenant with the people on that day, and he sent away the children of Israel, and they went each man to his inheritance and to his city.

28 So Joshua sent the people away, each to his own inheritance.

[90:26c and he afterward sent them away, and they went each man to his city, and each man to his inheritance.]

38 And it was in those days, when the children of Israel were dwelling securely in their cities, that they buried the coffins of the tribes of their ancestors, which they had brought up from Egypt, each man in the inheritance of his children, the twelve sons of Jacob did the children of Israel bury, each man in the possession of his children.

39 And these are the names of the cities wherein they buried the twelve sons of Jacob, whom the children of Israel had brought up from Egypt.

40 And they buried Reuben and Gad on this side Jordan, in Romia, which Moses had given to their
children. 41 And Simeon and Levi they buried in the city Mauda, which he had given to the children of Simeon, and the suburb of the city was for the children of Levi.

42 And Judah they buried in the city of Benjamin
opposite Bethlehem. 43 And the bones of Issachar and Zebulun they buried in Zidon, in the portion which fell to their children.

44 And Dan was buried in the city of his children in Eshtael, and Naphtali and Asher they buried in Kadesh-naphtali, each man in his place which he had given to his children.

[Joshua 24:32 They buried the bones of Joseph, which the children of Israel brought up out of Egypt, in Shechem, in the parcel of ground which Jacob bought from the sons of Hamor the father of Shechem for a hundred pieces of silver. They became the inheritance of the children of Joseph.]

45 And the bones of Joseph they buried in Shechem, in the part of the field which Jacob had purchased from Hamor, and which became to Joseph for an inheritance.

46 And they buried Benjamin in Jerusalem opposite the Jebusite, which was given to the children of Benjamin; the children of Israel buried their fathers each man in the city of his children.

29 After these things, Joshua the son of Nun, the servant of Yahweh, died, being one hundred ten years old.

47 And at the end of two years, Joshua the son of Nun died, one hundred and ten years old, and the time which Joshua judged Israel was twenty-eight years, and Israel served the Lord all the days of his life.

48 And the other affairs of Joshua and his battles and his reproofs with which he reproved Israel, and all which he had commanded them, and the names of the cities which the children of Israel possessed in his days, behold they are written in the book of the words of Joshua to the children of Israel, and in the book of the wars of the Lord, which Moses and Joshua and the children of Israel had written.

30 They buried him in the border of his inheritance in Timnathserah, which is in the hill country of Ephraim, on the north of the mountain of Gaash.

49 And the children of Israel buried Joshua in the border of his inheritance, in Timnath-serach, which was given to him in Mount Ephraim.

31 Israel served Yahweh all the days of Joshua, and all the days of the elders who outlived Joshua, and had known all the work of Yahweh, that he had worked for Israel.

32 They buried the bones of Joseph, which the children of Israel brought up out of Egypt, in Shechem, in the parcel of ground which Jacob bought from the sons of Hamor the father of Shechem for a hundred pieces of silver. They became the inheritance of the children of Joseph.

[90:45 And the bones of Joseph they buried in Shechem, in the part of the field which Jacob had purchased from Hamor, and which became to Joseph for an inheritance.]

33 Eleazar the son of Aaron died. They buried him in the hill of Phinehas his son, which was given him in the hill country of Ephraim.

50 And Elazer the son of Aaron died in those days, and they buried him in a hill belonging to Phineas his son, which was given him in Mount Ephraim.

Jasher 91

1 At that time, after the death of Joshua, the children of the Canaanites were still in the land, and the Israelites resolved to drive them out.

Judges 1

1 After the death of Joshua, the children of Israel asked of Yahweh, saying, “Who should go up for us first against the Canaanites, to fight against them?”

2 And the children of Israel asked of the Lord, saying, "Who shall first go up for us to the Canaanites to fight against them? and the Lord said, Judah shall go up."

2 Yahweh said, “Judah shall go up. Behold, I have delivered the land into his hand.”

3 Judah said to Simeon his brother, “Come up with
me into my lot, that we may fight against the
Canaanites; and I likewise will go with you into your
lot.” So Simeon went with him. 4 Judah went up,
and Yahweh delivered the Canaanites and the
Perizzites into their hand. They struck ten thousand
men in Bezek.

3 And the children of Judah said to Simeon, "Go up
with us into our lot, and we will fight against the
Canaanites and we likewise will go up with you, in
your lot, so the children of Simeon went with the
children of Judah." 4 And the children of Judah
went up and fought against the Canaanites, so the
Lord delivered the Canaanites into the hands of the
children of Judah, and they smote them in Bezek,
ten thousand men.

Judges 1

5 They found Adoni-Bezek in Bezek, and they fought
against him. They struck the Canaanites and the
Perizzites. 6 But Adoni-Bezek fled. They pursued
him, caught him, and cut off his thumbs and his big
toes.

7 Adoni-Bezek said, “Seventy kings, having their
thumbs and their big toes cut off, scavenged under
my table. As I have done, so God has done to me.”
They brought him to Jerusalem, and he died there.

8 The children of Judah fought against Jerusalem,
took it, struck it with the edge of the sword, and set
the city on fire.

9 After that, the children of Judah went down to
fight against the Canaanites who lived in the hill
country, and in the South, and in the lowland. 10
Judah went against the Canaanites who lived in
Hebron. (The name of Hebron before that was
Kiriath Arba.) They struck Sheshai, Ahiman, and
Talmai.

11 From there he went against the inhabitants of
Debir. (The name of Debir before that was Kiriath
Sepher.) 12 Caleb said, “I will give Achsah my
daughter as wife to the man who strikes Kiriath
Sepher, and takes it.” 13 Othniel the son of Kenaz,
Caleb’s younger brother, took it, so he gave him
Achsah his daughter as his wife.

14 When she came, she got him to ask her father
for a field. She dismounted from off of her donkey;
and Caleb said to her, “What would you like?”

15 She said to him, “Give me a blessing; because
you have set me in the land of the South, give me
also springs of water.” Then Caleb gave her the
upper springs and the lower springs. 16 The
children of the Kenite, Moses’ brother-in-law, went
up out of the city of palm trees with the children of
Judah into the wilderness of Judah, which is in the
south of Arad; and they went and lived with the
people.

Jasher 91

5 And they fought with Adonibezek in Bezek, and he fled from before them, and they pursued him and caught him, and they took hold of him and cut off his thumbs and great toes.

6 And Adonibezek said, "Three score and ten kings having their thumbs and great toes cut off, gathered their meat under my table, as I have done, so God has requited me," and they brought him to Jerusalem and he died there.

7 And the children of Simeon went with the children of Judah, and they smote the Canaanites with the edge of the sword.

17 Judah went with Simeon his brother, and they
struck the Canaanites who inhabited Zephath, and
utterly destroyed it. The name of the city was called
Hormah. 18 Also Judah took Gaza with its border,
and Ashkelon with its border, and Ekron with its
border. 19 Yahweh was with Judah; and drove out
the inhabitants of the hill country; for he could not
drive out the inhabitants of the valley, because they
had chariots of iron.

20 They gave Hebron to Caleb, as Moses had said,
and he drove the three sons of Anak out of there.
21 The children of Benjamin did not drive out the
Jebusites who inhabited Jerusalem, but the
Jebusites dwell with the children of Benjamin in
Jerusalem to this day.

22 The house of Joseph also went up against Bethel,
and Yahweh was with them.

8 And the Lord was with the children of Judah, and they possessed the mountain, and the children of Joseph went up to Bethel, the same is Luz, and the Lord was with them.

23 The house of Joseph sent to spy out Bethel. (The
name of the city before that was Luz.) 24 The
watchers saw a man come out of the city, and they
said to him, "Please show us the entrance into the
city, and we will deal kindly with you."

9 And the children of Joseph spied out Bethel, and the watchmen saw a man going forth from the city, and they caught him and said unto him, "Show us now the entrance of the city and we will show kindness to thee."

25 He showed them the entrance into the city, and
they struck the city with the edge of the sword; but
they let the man and all his family go. 26 The man
went into the land of the Hittites, built a city, and
called its name Luz, which is its name to this day.

10 And that man showed them the entrance of the
city, and the children of Joseph came and smote the
City with the edge of the sword. 11 And the man
with his family they sent away, and he went to the Hittites and he built a city, and he called the name thereof Luz, so all the Israelites dwelt in their cities, and the children at Israel dwelt in their cities, and the children of Israel served the Lord all the days of Joshua, and all the days of the elders, who had lengthened their days after Joshua, and saw the great work of the Lord, which he had performed for Israel.

12 And the elders judged Israel after the death of Joshua for seventeen years.

13 And all the elders also fought the battles of Israel against the Canaanites and the Lord drove the Canaanites from before the children of Israel, in order to place the Israelites in their land.

14 And he accomplished all the words which he had spoken to Abraham, Isaac, and Jacob, and the oath which he had sworn, to give to them and to their children, the land of the Canaanites.

15 And the Lord gave to the children of Israel the
whole land of Canaan, as he had sworn to their
ancestors, and the Lord gave them rest from those
around them, and the children of Israel dwelt
securely in their cities.

16 Blessed be the Lord for ever, amen, and amen.
17 Strengthen yourselves, and let the hearts of all
you that trust in the Lord be of good courage.

www.ingramcontent.com/pod-product-compliance
Lightning Source LLC
Chambersburg PA
CBHW080932300426
44115CB00017B/2792

* 9 7 8 1 9 3 6 5 3 3 3 4 3 *